P9-EKE-311

ALSO BY TED MORGAN

• • •

My Battle of Algiers

VALLEY OF DEATH

VALLEY OF DEATH

The Tragedy at Dien Bien Phu
That Led America into the Vietnam War

. . .

TED MORGAN

RANDOM HOUSE NEW YORK

Published in the United States by Random House, an imprint of
The Random House Publishing Group, a division of
Random House, Inc., New York.

RANDOM HOUSE and colophon are registered trademarks of
Random House, Inc.

Library of Congress Cataloging-in-Publication Data
Morgan, Ted.
Valley of death : the tragedy at Dien Bien Phu that led America
into the Vietnam War / Ted Morgan.
p.   cm.
Includes bibliographical references.
ISBN 978-1-4000-6664-3
eBook ISBN 978-1-588-36980-2
1. Dien Bien Phu, Battle of, Ðiên Biên Phu, Vietnam, 1954.
2. Indochinese War, 1946–1954—Causes.   3. United States—
Foreign relations—1945–1953.   4. United States—Foreign
relations—Vietnam.   5. Vietnam—Foreign relations—United States.
I. Title.
DS553.3.D5M665 2010
959.704'142—dc22   2009019714

Printed in the United States of America on acid-free paper

www.atrandom.com

2 4 6 8 9 7 5 3 1

First Edition

Book design by Liz Cosgrove

This book is for the soldiers who were sent to die in battle by politicians who have never seen combat.

Preface

...

In January 2008, my wife, Eileen, and I took a Vietnam Airlines flight from Hanoi to Dien Bien Phu, the site of the 1954 battle that ended French rule in Indochina. Our two-engine turboprop, made by Aérospatiale to land on short runways, was reminiscent of the U.S.–built Dakotas that the French had used to supply the base more than half a century ago, so that we had a sense of traveling backward in time as well as forward in space. The 187-mile flight took an hour (as against an hour and a half by the Dakotas), over a thick layer of cumulus clouds, until the altitude dropped to reveal rough-hewn mountains, bare-topped and covered with trails leading to hamlets buried in deep ravines.

Swerving to the right, the plane descended over a long valley of rice paddies as smooth and even as golf greens, surrounded by low mountains on three sides and broken up by clusters of dwellings. The spacious valley seemed anomalous in such a craggy landscape, only twenty miles from the Laotian border. At first sight it was understandable that the French had built an air-ground base there, for if the Vietminh had attacked en masse over the plain, ten miles long and five wide, they would have been massacred.

Our plane landed on what had been the French airstrip, now enlarged and made of concrete instead of perforated steel strips, which some inhabitants had recovered to use as fencing for their gardens. At the unassuming, whitewashed airport, clusters of relatives were waiting for arriving passengers. The twice-daily flights seemed to be something of an event in this isolated outpost, which took sixteen hours to reach by road. A young woman we struck up a conversation with told us she wanted to practice her English because she was studying to be an air traffic controller, which seemed a likely profession in this remote locale, still heavily dependent, as it had been during the battle, on transportation and supply by air.

In 1954, the civilian population of Dien Bien Phu was negligible. Today the town itself has a population of nine thousand, while the valley accommodates six times that number. Rows of women wearing conical straw hats can be seen bent over in the paddies, ankle-deep in water, picking rice shoots by hand as they have for centuries. If there is such a thing as military archaeology, Dien Bien Phu is an example of it, for some of the battle sites have been maintained as memorials, while others were obliterated to make way for housing and planting.

Our decrepit hotel was on May 7 Avenue (the date of the French surrender), a four-lane thoroughfare with a well-lit median, though there is little traffic after dark. The avenue was crowded with open-fronted, narrow shops that spilled out onto the teeming life of the sidewalks, so that the pedestrian had to thread his way past the parked motorbikes, spare tires, cases of soft drinks, piles of burlap bags, people eating on the ground from their rice bowls, and dogs rummaging through rubble. Side by side in their cramped spaces, the stores were like a horizontal but decaying department store, selling hardware, construction materials, furniture, cell phones, jackets of imitation leather, and on one block nothing but wedding dresses. Another block was reserved for barbers, who had set their chairs under shade trees and affixed large mirrors to a grated wall. Once they had placed their scissors and combs on low tables, they were in business—unless it rained. One block was lined with lottery ladies, seated behind folding tables, where the tickets were gathered in neat piles by denomination, or spread out like a fan. They recorded every transaction by hand in their account books.

Farther along the avenue a vast outdoor market unfolded, where Meo tribeswomen came down from the mountains, wearing their black costumes and multicolored cummerbunds, their thick black hair in topknots, to sell products ranging from the mundane to the exotic—oranges and tiny apples, indigenous roots, scrawny live turkeys in cages, elixirs in large jars containing snakes and lizards, or filled with dead bees floating in a murky liquid.

History creates its own geological layers, entombing the carnage of warfare under a bustling town. The scenery of battle—the man with a bandaged head being dragged under the arms by two others, the exploding shells forming craters, the staccato crackle of automatic fire drowning out shouts of command, the attacks and counterattacks barely visible through smoke-saturated air, and the knowledge that human life is incidental to both victory and defeat—is all submerged, along with the decayed bodies of the fallen. Now the civilian population attends to its daily needs, so that it never occurs to the children playing hopscotch, or to the mothers haggling over the price of an orange, or to the peasants carrying improbable loads at both ends of a bamboo pole balanced on their shoulders, that with every step they are treading on the fallen who have fertilized the soil.

The panoply of normalcy, with its tidy pleasures and habits, its twin concerns of health and wealth, has superseded the determination and spirit of sacrifice of the combatants who fought and died for a cause they believed in: for the Vietminh, independence from colonial rule; for the French, the pride of the career soldiers doing their job well enough to maintain that rule. The men who survived the battle, which lasted fifty-six days and nights, and the captivity that followed defeat lived through a time of such unimaginable suffering, when every day they saw their comrades killed and wounded, their grief mitigated by the adrenaline rush of remaining alive, that everything they returned to seemed pointless and insipid. One of the outstanding paratroop officers who fought there, Major Pierre Tourret, left the army in disgust after Dien Bien Phu, and found it hard to adjust to civilian life. "Peace is hell" became his catchword, which did not stop him from living into his eighties, preserved in vinegar.

. . .

The point of our visit was to study what was left of the French base, in order to form a clearer idea of how this great airborne battle was fought. When the first troops were dropped in on November 20, 1953, the rationale for the base was threefold: to block the advance of Vietminh troops heading toward Laos; to draw their troops away from the Tonkin (or Red River) Delta, where they seemed to be preparing an offensive; and by providing the base with artillery, tanks, and fighter-bombers, to draw the Vietminh into attacking where they were likely to suffer severe losses.

Eight centers of resistance (CRs) were built in the entrenched camp, all with women's names, on both sides of the Nam Yum River, which provided drinking water. The river was spanned by a Bailey bridge that is still in use. The airstrip was close by, as were the pits for the 155mm cannon and the tanks. By December 17, the base was operational.

Our guide to what remained of the base was Nguyen Tien Manh (known as Mike), a slight but athletic forty-one-year-old native of Dien Bien Phu. Round-eyed with a pencil mustache and an easy smile that revealed gaps in his teeth, he was familiar with the base's layout, for his uncle had fought at Dien Bien Phu and had told him that Vietminh losses were far greater than those admitted to. Mike had learned his English during four years in the Vietnamese army, but since his teacher was a fellow soldier, I found his accent hard to decipher, though Eileen did much better. Mike recruited a four-wheel-drive Toyota and a driver to reach the strongpoints, on many of which only a marker remained. We explored them over a period of four days, starting with Eliane 2. Preserved as a memorial, it was not the highest, but it was the most massive and elaborate, looming like a mastodon over the center of town, behind May 7 Avenue. It was three-sided, with two steep sides and one gentle slope known as the Champs-Elysées, where Vietminh assaults had been mowed down by French machine guns. In some places, the four rows of barbed wire that had surrounded it were preserved, which reminded me of James Dickey's comment: "All that is needed to understand World War I in its philosophical and historical meaning is to examine the barbed wire—a single strand will do—and to meditate on who made it, what it is for, why it is like it is." The similarities between World War I and Dien Bien Phu were obvious: trench warfare and barbed wire.

Eliane 2 was the site of the residence built by the former French provincial governor, and his fortified masonry cellar, used by the defenders as their command post, had been maintained, as had the French gun emplacements and trenches, cemented to prevent erosion. At the summit, a damaged French tank presided as a forlorn symbol of Vietminh victory, near a marble monument giving the names of the units that finally took the strongpoint. As Eileen photographed the tank, a group of Vietnamese army officers happened by. When she asked them to pose in front of the tank, they cheerfully complied.

Of the other Elianes, two had been cut back for housing, and only Eliane 1 and 4 were still intact, though they were now overgrown with high bushes, and were so steep that I wondered how the Vietminh could have climbed them while firing and cutting through the barbed wire. At the top, there were markers, again giving the dates of their downfall and the units that took them.

North of the Elianes rose Dominique 2, the highest of the strongpoints at 1,650 feet, with a flat top and a good view of the entire battlefield and the mountains beyond, where General Vo Nguyen Giap's divisions were hidden. This was another essential hill that had to be held, and again it was so steep that one wondered how Giap had managed, although Mike sprinted up it like a cross-country runner.

From the Dominiques, on a winding, muddy road, it was about half a mile to the northernmost CR, Béatrice, with its four positions on three hills separated by gullies. Located between a marshy loop of the Nam Yum and RP41, a twisting mountain road, which followed the river eastward, Béatrice guarded access to the valley from the northeast, between the river and the road. Positioned midway from the right flank of Gabrielle and the left flank of Dominique, it was supposed to protect both and was manned by a unit of elite Legionnaires.

The hills, cleared of undergrowth during the battle, were now once again mantled with thick bushes and trees. A concrete stairway had recently been built up the steepest hill, at the top of which the deep concrete bunkers of the Legionnaires remained intact, and there was a carved pink stone memorial showing the heroic Vietminh fighters. It was on Béatrice that one of Giap's men was killed when he blocked the aperture of a machine-gun emplacement with his body, or so Mike told us.

The northernmost CR of Gabrielle was reached after a steep five-hundred-yard hike from the road. The sandbag fortifications still piled there were a reminder that the strongpoint held by Algerian fusiliers had been carelessly built.

Directly across from Gabrielle there was a meticulously tended Vietminh cemetery. The long rows of tombstones were unmarked, but families who arrive with bouquets are shown a registry of names and the corresponding locations of the graves. Fifty-four years after the battle, the six hundred graves were freshly flowered.

Having covered the eastern and northern perimeters, we explored those to the west. Of the four connected hills forming Anne-Marie, one remained. The others had been razed to build an elementary school with a walled courtyard. The remaining hill was a reddish sandstone, with deep gullies and little vegetation. Several sides were nearly vertical, but one of the slopes was gentle enough to climb. From the top you could see the forest to the west from which the Vietminh had attacked.

As we descended from Anne-Marie, schoolchildren ran out of the courtyard and surrounded us, smiling and saying hello. They were neatly dressed and healthy-looking (one rarely sees an overweight Vietnamese), and eager to be photographed. To see a schoolyard filled with bright, contented children where a bloody battle had once been fought was a pleasant surprise.

To reach the five strongpoints of Huguette, built to protect the airstrip, we had to drive around the extended runway along a back road lined with wrecks of French guns and armored vehicles, the debris of battle, in front of which a small but busy outdoor market drew crowds of shoppers. Off the road we came to rice paddies where the Huguettes had been. There was nothing left but a damaged tank, its 75mm cannon disconsolately drooping, and the customary marker.

To get to the tank we had to cross several paddies over one-foot-wide glutinous berms separating one paddy from the other. The man working the paddies, who wore a pith helmet, showed us the way. Eileen stayed on terra firma while Mike sped along in the lead, and I fell behind, lurching like a tightrope walker. The man with the pith helmet helped me keep my equilibrium. At one point he took my hand and studied it palm-down. When he saw the liver spots, he asked how old I was. I said seventy-five. "This old, old man," the paddy farmer exclaimed. We reached the mangled tank and the marker explaining when and how it had been hit. We had a good view of the airstrip and the lawn that bordered it, where water buffalo grazed. Mike explained that they served the purpose of lawn mowers.

Heading south toward the last outpost, Isabelle, the valley broadened into green acres of rice shoots. This was flat land where the tanks of Isabelle could best maneuver. On the way, we passed a carved stone monument to the inhabitants of Noong Nhai, a hamlet where on April 25, 1954, French bombers killed 444 civilians, most of them women and children. The French said it was a mistake. The Vietnamese say it was in reprisal because the male inhabitants were fighting in the Vietminh ranks. The monument depicted the contorted faces of the victims.

Of the important outpost of Isabelle, the last to surrender, nothing remained but a marker. With a garrison of two thousand men defending five strongpoints, Isabelle was built on flat ground, but it was well constructed and well armed with one third of Dien Bien Phu's artillery and tanks.

. . .

Having covered all of Dien Bien Phu's strongpoints, there were two final but essential battle sites to examine: the bunkers where the generals who commanded the rival armies had planned the strategies that led to the French surrender.

Giap's had been dug into a mountain twenty-five miles northwest of Dien Bien Phu, Castries' was a deep fortified trench at the center of the headquarters post. Both had been maintained by the Vietnamese as they were during the battle.

Castries' bunker, a short distance from the Bailey bridge, was all that remained of the crowded Claudine center of resistance, except for wrecked tanks and artillery, and shell craters filled with garbage. One of the destroyed 105mm howitzers had a marking that said USA 1943.

Rising a few feet aboveground was a sixty-foot-long and twenty-four-foot-wide roof, a semicircle of corrugated steel, able to withstand mortar and 105mm shells. The roof was surrounded by a ten-foot-deep trench. Near the bunker stood a bas-relief of Castries, bareheaded and bowed, with his hands clasped in front of him, surrendering on May 7, 1954.

Steep steps led down to a narrow entrance. The seven-foot-high ceiling was made from perforated steel strips used for the runway. A series of rooms opened on both sides of the central aisle. The walls were made of heavy lumber covered with bamboo. In one room Castries slept and kept a bathtub. There was no toilet or running water, but water was brought in from outside. In another room stood a folding table where Castries ate and in the evening played bridge with his staff officers. Here he also kept his wine cellar, for which the bunker was the right temperature.

Other rooms were used for his office and for staff meetings. Some of the maps drawn up during the battle were still on the walls. Aside from positional maps, there was a "Map of Losses," with separate columns for the killed, the wounded, and the unaccounted for. The troops were divided by "Races: European, North African, African, Autochtone [Vietnamese], and Legionnaires," as if the Foreign Legion were a race apart; the majority were in fact German.

In the "First Period," from November 21, 1953, to March 12, 1954, a time of skirmishes before the real battle began, there were 151 killed, 797 wounded, and 89 unaccounted for, a total of 1,037.

In the "Second Period," from March 13 to May 5, two days before the surrender, there were 1,142 killed, 4,436 wounded, and 1,605 unaccounted for, a total of 7,183. Many of the latter were deserters known as the "Rats of Nam Yum," who improvised shantytowns on the high banks of the river and survived by scavenging supplies dropped by parachute and stripping neglected corpses.

Our visit to Giap's bunker was particularly evocative. The road, RP41, was being widened, and construction was well under way, though we drove through rain-rutted stretches of dirt to pavement and back again, bumping over mounds of asphalt used for resurfacing. In the valley below, houses on stilts bordered the river and white birds flew over cassava fields. Rice paddies had been dug into the sides of mountains in terraces, defying gravity. Mike pointed out a narrow path on the other side of the valley, dug by hand into the mountain, where hundreds of coolies had pulled heavy weapons to their emplacements in 1954.

As we reached Giap's headquarters, the road improved and we entered a forest where cutting down a tree could lead to arrest, for it was a designated ecological and historical zone. At the base of the hill stood a guardhouse, where a steep pebble-cemented path rose to the bunker, across a series of three-log bridges with no railings over gurgling streams. Mike thought the climb would be too much for Eileen, and she stayed behind against her better instincts.

At the top of the hill stood a modest house with a thatched roof and walls, and windows that closed with wooden panels. On entering, there was a cot on the left for a sentry and another on the right for Giap. In the main room stood a long bamboo table for briefings with a bench on each side made of split bamboo trunks. Farther on, near a thin torrent, were houses on stilts, where the headquarters staff and the Chinese advisers were barracked. A sixty-foot-long dormitory was fitted with bunk beds for soldiers.

The heart of the headquarters was a three-hundred-yard-long tunnel cut into the side of the mountain. Not unlike Castries' bunker, it had offices and rooms for staff meetings, with electricity, and a transmission center that had a direct link to China. In the kitchen, two clay stoves were equipped with exhausts that blew out smoke horizontally so it could not be seen from above.

French planes were unable to locate Giap's well-hidden headquarters, and it was never bombed. The meeting rooms in the tunnel had maps on the walls showing the locations of Vietminh units, artillery, and antiaircraft emplacements, as well as detailed maps of the French strongpoints. But there was no summary of Vietminh losses, like the precise accounting in Castries' bunker. Giap was secretive regarding casualties, which the French estimated at twenty thousand.

In the meantime, Eileen, still at the foot of the hill, noticed two couples in their sixties coming down followed by four young local girls. She asked one of the women if the climb was difficult. "My husband has bad knees and here he is. The girls helped and we gave them a fifty-dollar Indonesian note." Bad knees maybe, Eileen thought, but the husband looked like a wrestler, bald and thick through the chest. The other man was slighter, an aging preppy in his blue button-down oxford shirt and khakis. He asked Eileen where she was from. New York, she said. "You've come halfway around the world to see this," the man said, "and we're the victors here." The bald man said, as if apologizing for his friend: "It's all over. We have peace now."

The bald man's wife said, "Take the kids. They'll get you there." The oldest girl, about twelve, whose name was Fong, told Eileen, "You come to Giap's, you come," and they started up the hill, holding her hands and laughing, then gripping them as they helped her across the five bothersome log bridges. They were so young, Eileen thought, but their hands were already calloused. And they were so guileless and cheerful that she trusted them to keep her out of the mountain streams. And soon she joined Mike and me in Giap's tunnel. More for fun than profit, the girls operated an informal ferry service up the hill.

The button-down man was right, when he said, "We're the victors here." A people's army of Vietnamese peasants had crushed renowned battalions of combat-tested professional soldiers. Our reason for touring the base was to get a clearer idea of how a contained battle in a remote valley on the Laotian border ended French colonial rule in Indochina. A clearer idea of this ancient land of jungles and mountains, whose tectonic shocks were caused not by the earth's drift but by repeated invasion, and whose people were put into peonage not by natural disasters but by the whim of the colonizer. Dien Bien Phu, however, was but the final act in a long chain of events, the culmination of a protracted war that began in June 1940 with the fall of France.

On the day we left, we were waiting for the afternoon plane from Hanoi at the crowded airport when it started to rain. They announced a delay in the incoming flight that would take us out. Deep apprehension seized us. We did not want to stay one minute longer than we had to. No one wants to be stuck in a place where they don't belong. We sweated out the two-hour delay. But in those two hours we began to feel what every French soldier there had felt once the base was encircled and could only be reached by parachute drops—the insurmountable dread of entrapment.

Contents

...

Author's Note

...

My interest in the Indochina war goes back to 1956, when I was serving in the French army. I was a conscript named Sanche de Gramont, a second lieutenant. The two sergeants in my colonial infantry platoon outside the Algerian town of Medea had fought in northern Vietnam and were fond of reminiscing. In 1957 I was transferred to Algiers, where I served on the staff of the paratroop commander General Jacques Massu, another Indochina veteran. I met Marcel Bigeard, one of the major figures of Dien Bien Phu, and Yves Godard, a battalion commander in northern Vietnam. They both said, "We lost Indochina, we're not going to lose this one." But they were going against the tide of history.

In 1963 I was sent to Saigon by the *New York Herald Tribune* to cover the fall of Ngo Dinh Diem. Arriving cold, I was befriended by two outstanding reporters: David Halberstam, with whom I had covered the Katanga war in 1961, and Robert Shaplen, a Southeast Asia veteran who wrote for *The New Yorker*. It happened that Shaplen was in love with my cousin, Marguerite de Gramont, who shuttled in and out of Saigon bringing medical supplies to the Vietnamese. In 1966 I was living in Paris and ran into Halberstam, whom I invited to dinner. He brought along Bernard Fall, who had just published *Hell in a Very Small Place* and was generous with his insights. Fall was off to Saigon the next day, to cover the American war. Not long after, he was killed on a patrol with U.S. troops.

In 1967 and 1968, when I was writing for *The New York Times Maga-*

zine, I met two of the top figures at the Geneva Conference that followed the defeat at Dien Bien Phu: Pierre Mendès France and Georges Bidault. Mendès France had become prime minister after the defeat at Dien Bien Phu and ended the deadlock at Geneva. In 1967, after many ups and downs, he was running for a parliamentary seat in the mountainous Isère Department, where it's subzero in the winter. It's thanks to Mendès France that I'm deaf in one ear. Every profession has its occupational hazards, and I caught otitis following him around stumping in the mountains.

As for Bidault, he had been foreign minister during the battle, and head of the French delegation at Geneva, until Mendès France became premier in June 1954. When de Gaulle came to power in 1958, Bidault turned against him and was charged with conspiracy. When I interviewed him in 1968, he was living in Belgium, still fiery and unrepentant.

When Rob Cowley, the military historian and editor, asked me to write a book on the battle, I started looking at sources. I found that in France there was a vast literature of regimental memoirs, collections of letters home, and personal reminiscences that had been published in the last ten years. In Hanoi, I found many volumes by Vietminh participants, available in French. In Dien Bien Phu, photographs of the battle from the Vietminh side were on sale at the Military History Museum. Much new information has also come out in the United States on America's involvement in the battle, and on China's support of the Vietminh; the message traffic of the Chinese and Soviet delegations at Geneva has also been released. I felt that this wealth of fresh material justified a new account of the battle.

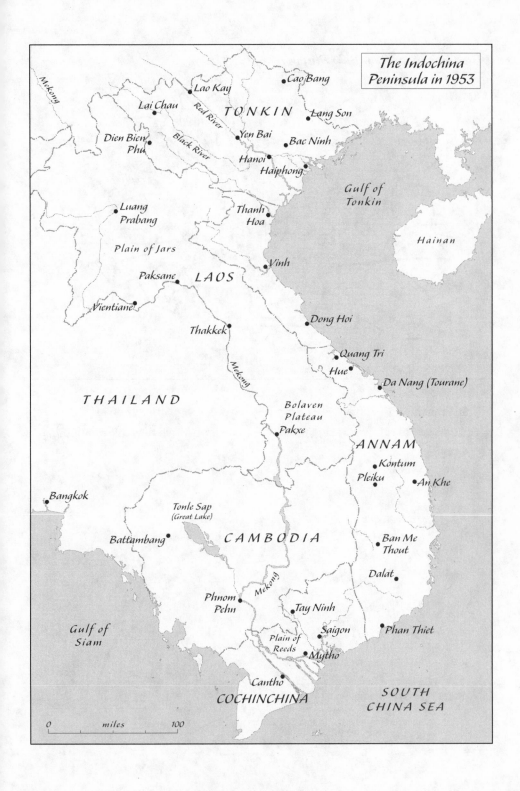

The Indochina
Peninsula in 1953

Mekong

Lao Kay

Cao Bang

Lai Chau

Red River

T O N K I N

Lang Son

Dien Bien
Phu

Black River

Yen Bai

Bac Ninh

Hanoi

Haiphong

Gulf of
Tonkin

Luang
Prabang

Thanh
Hoa

Hainan

Plain of Jars

Vinh

Paksane

L A O S

Vientiane

Dong Hoi

Thakkek

Quang Tri

Hue

Mekong

Da Nang (Tourane)

T H A I L A N D

Bolaven
Plateau
Pakxe

A N N A M

Kontum

Pleiku

An Khe

Bangkok

Tonle Sap
(Great Lake)

C A M B O D I A

Battambang

Ban Me
Thout

Dalat

Mekong

Phnom
Pehn

Tay Ninh

Gulf of
Siam

Plain of
Reeds

Saigon

Mytho

Phan Thiet

Cantho

C O C H I N C H I N A

S O U T H
C H I N A   S E A

0   miles   100

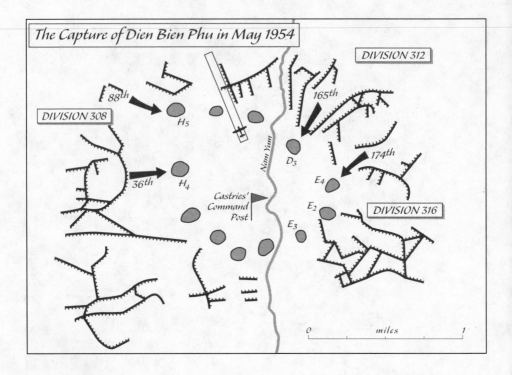

The Capture of Dien Bien Phu in May 1954

DIVISION 312

88th

DIVISION 308

165th

36th

174th

H5

H4

D3

E4

Nam Yum

Castries'
Command
Post

E2

E3

DIVISION 316

0   miles   1

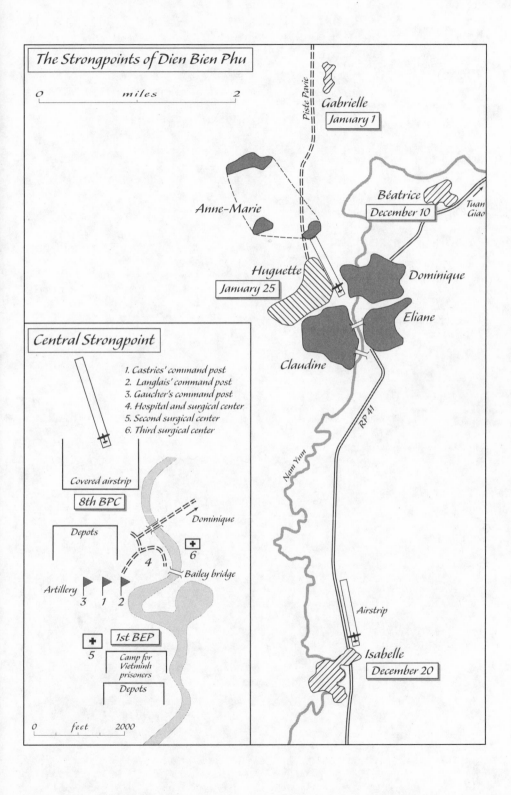

The Strongpoints of Dien Bien Phu

0   miles   2

Piste Pavie

Gabrielle
January 1

Anne-Marie

Béatrice
December 10

Tuan
Giao

Huguette
January 25

Dominique

Eliane

Claudine

RP 41

Nam Yum

Central Strongpoint

1. Castries' command post
2. Langlais' command post
3. Gaucher's command post
4. Hospital and surgical center
5. Second surgical center
6. Third surgical center

Covered airstrip

8th BPC

Depots

Dominique

4

6

Bailey bridge

Artillery
3   1   2

5

1st BEP

Camp for
Vietminh
prisoners

Depots

Airstrip

Isabelle
December 20

0   feet   2000

VALLEY OF DEATH

ACT I

The First Partition of Vietnam

. . .

Sometime or other, before the day is over, just as a matter of fact in straightening myself out, I'd like to try and find out just what it was, and why it was, that Indochina seemed to move from an idea which President Roosevelt had when he was alive that the French were not going to end up back in Indochina, and then sometime or other in 1945 they ended up. I don't know how they got there or what happened or what was done.

DEAN ACHESON, May 15, 1954, at the Princeton seminar
he conducted after leaving the State Department

· · ·

THIS ALL BEGAN when President Franklin Delano Roosevelt initially decided not to run for a third term in 1940. On May 8, Assistant Secretary of State Adolf Berle wrote in his diary: "It is understood that Roosevelt, unless the situation changes, will wait until the last minute and then issue a statement in favor of Mr. Hull." FDR was planning to endorse Secretary of State Cordell Hull for the nomination in July at the Democratic Convention in Chicago, before retiring to the life of a country gentleman in Hyde Park.

He had a compelling reason not to run, as he told the Nebraska senator George Norris: "I am tied down to this chair day after day and month after month. I can't stand it any longer. I can't go on with it." He was only fifty-eight, but he was exhausted, imprisoned in his wheelchair, his withered legs the size of the crutches he used to get in and out of cars, and he smoked too many cigarettes. He spoke with enthusiasm about moving his papers to Hyde Park, where he would write twenty-six articles for *Collier's* at $75,000 a year. He told his visitors that he'd had enough and Hull was the man.

By mid-May, however, the panzers had crossed the Meuse, demolishing the fortifications that extended the Maginot Line. On May 16, Berle revised his appraisal: "I really think the question of whether Mr. Roosevelt will run or not is being settled somewhere on the banks of the Meuse River. . . . He does not want to run unless circumstances are so grave that he considers it essential for the country's safety. . . . My private opinion is that circumstances are drafting him. . . . They are very likely to give us another four years for the President," breaking with the two-term tradition.

In early June, FDR's outspoken secretary of the interior, Harold Ickes, told him that Hull would make a poor candidate and a poor president. FDR said that Hull would be a different kind of president: It should not be forgotten that Woodrow Wilson had known nothing about government prior to his election. Others told FDR that Hull was inept and that his wife, Frances, was Jewish. But at a White House banquet, the president sat next to her and told her to get used to such affairs.

The unexpectedly swift fall of France changed Roosevelt's mind. By mid-June, Marshal Henri Philippe Pétain formed a government and asked Hitler for an armistice. If the French had stopped the Huns, the war might have ended, but England was next, which meant the continuation of American involvement. The issue now was democracy against fascism.

As late as June 20, however, FDR assured Hull that he backed him. Finally, on July 3, after the Republican Convention, which nominated Wendell Willkie, FDR told Hull he was running. Hull said he understood. On July 16, at the Democratic Convention, Senator Alben Barkley of Kentucky read a letter from the president saying he wanted to retire. Cries of "We want Roosevelt" arose, and on July 17, FDR was overwhelmingly nominated. He developed a pronounced animus against France, which he thought did not deserve to keep her colonial empire.

The Commissary Line

Among the war's unforeseen chain of events, who could have imagined that the fall of France in June 1940 would be one of the decisive factors in the Japanese bombing of Pearl Harbor in December 1941. By 1938, in its war with China, the Japanese had taken Canton, the major port and trading center of South China, while Chiang Kai-shek had retreated westward to Chungking. Canton was up the Pearl River from Hong Kong, with the Indochina port of Haiphong five hundred miles to the west. It was at Haiphong that the bulk of Chiang's military supplies arrived. From the port, they were loaded onto the French-built Haiphong railroad, which lumbered northward across the Chinese border to the old walled city of Kunming, the capital of Yunnan Province. It was vital for the Japanese to choke off Chiang's supply line.

Japan cast an angry eye toward Indochina, which allowed unfettered transit. The French colony was but a minor appendage to the south of the immense Chinese landmass, with a five-hundred-mile border with China and a thousand-mile coastline, seemingly glued as an afterthought to the Southeast Asian subcontinent of Burma and Thailand. To this barbell-shaped tail of China now known as Vietnam (the bells being Tonkin and Cochinchina, with the bar of Annam at one point only thirty-one miles wide), were added Laos and Cambodia: in all, an area about the size of Italy, mostly mountains and jungle, except for two fertile deltas, the Red River in the north and the Mekong in the south. These rice-rich floodplains provided the staple for twenty million natives, known as Annamites, while fifty thousand French *colons* skimmed the cream off an economy based on rubber, coal, tin, and tungsten.

There is a Japanese saying that crisis and opportunity are a couple. In September 1939, when Hitler invaded Poland, Japan saw an opportunity. The Japanese complained to the French about the shipment of war matériel from Haiphong to Kunming to support the Chiang regime. The French replied that since war had not been declared between Japan and China, shipments would not be halted. To show their displeasure, the Japanese bombed the railway line.

By June 1940, when panzer divisions were advancing on Paris, about 10,000 tons of war supplies were being shipped monthly from Haiphong to Kunming, and a backlog of 125,000 tons were piled up in the port's warehouses. As France collapsed, Marshal Pétain asked for an armistice on June 16. Three days later, the Japanese government presented the French ambassador in Tokyo with a demand that all shipments of war matériel from Haiphong cease and that a Japanese control commission be allowed into the port to ensure compliance.

The governor-general of Indochina, who had to respond to the Japanese demand, was General Georges Catroux, a distinguished officer who had fought in World War I. In 1940, Catroux was anti-German and pro-British, but when he asked for help from the British, the silence was deaf-

ening. He had no choice but to submit to the Japanese. Vichy's puppet government dismissed him in July, not because he had given in but because he
was considered disloyal.

Pétain replaced Catroux with an obedient sailor, Admiral Jean Decoux,
anti-British with fascist tendencies, who considered the Annamites a subject people. Just as Pétain collaborated with the Nazis in France, Decoux
gave in to Japanese demands on Indochina. The Japanese occupation was
incremental. On August 1, 1940, they demanded the right of transit for
their troops throughout Indochina, the use of airfields, and an economic
agreement that turned out to be somewhat one-sided. Each time Vichy
submitted to Japanese demands, new ones were made, much like a kidnap-
and-ransom scheme. On September 22, 1940, a revised agreement provided for more Japanese airfields in Tonkin; permission to station 6,000
troops; and the right of transit of up to 25,000 troops through Tonkin to
China. On September 27, Japan signed the Tripartite Pact with Germany
and Italy, which tied its operations in the Pacific with theirs in Europe to
form the Axis.

Indochina was the first of many colonies occupied by the Japanese in
Southeast Asia, as part of a secret program adopted in October 1940
called the Greater East Asia Co-prosperity Sphere. *Co-prosperity* meant
that the Japanese plundered the raw materials of the lands they invaded,
among them Malaya, Singapore, British Borneo, the Dutch East Indies,
the Philippines, Siam, and Indochina. But since Indochina was ruled by the
Vichy regime, while the other colonies were governed by the British, the
Dutch, or the Americans, the Japanese allowed the French administration
to remain in place. France was tractable and saved Japan from employing
their already stretched manpower in occupation duties.

The Japanese army called Indochina a "commissary line," which
meant that its troops in China could be supplied from there, and also that
the rice from Indochina would be used to feed them, while Japanese vehicles would roll on Indochinese rubber. Thus, in late 1940, the Japanese
confiscated facilities necessary for the pursuit of war, from coal mines to
rubber plantations to lumber factories. Vichy did not protest, for its aim
was to maintain the colonial status quo until the war was over.

We Mustn't Push Japan Too Much

In Washington, FDR's cabinet was divided over the president's Japan policy. His secretaries of war, the interior, and the treasury—respectively Henry Stimson, Harold Ickes, and Henry Morgenthau—were opposed to letting Japan buy U.S. oil, scrap iron, and steel. His secretary of state, Cordell Hull, as well as Hull's number two, Sumner Welles, were involved in delicate negotiations with the Japanese, which could be disrupted by bans on exports. The other three felt that the president was "coddling the Japs."

In July 1940, Ickes noted in his diary that the "glacially lofty Sumner Welles objected strenuously to putting petroleum products and scrap iron on the list for licenses." Ickes was irate. This was a time when oil for Spain was being transshipped to German U-boats right at the Spanish docks, while Japan had contracted for all the airplane gasoline on the Pacific coast for immediate delivery. Stimson warned FDR that the Japanese were trying to corner the aviation-fuel market.

On August 16, FDR told Morgenthau that "we mustn't push Japan too much or she'll take the Dutch East Indies," which had plenty of oil. But Ickes pointed out that if the Japanese came in, the Dutch would blow up their wells and refineries. Morgenthau kept himself informed on Indochina, where the French had caved in by signing a pact on September 22 that allowed Japanese troops to move in. Morgenthau noted in his diary: "Hull is out on a limb. He has twice scolded Japan if she goes into Indochina."

When the Japanese signed the Tripartite Pact with Germany and Italy on September 27, calling it a defensive alliance, Hull said: "That's like Jesse James and Cole Younger going into an alliance for self-defense." He seemed to be firming up.

But Hull still held back on interdicting scrap iron to Japan. He said the situation was delicate and the Japanese might take over Indochina at any time. Ickes felt that by selling them oil and scrap "we have made it possible to continue their career of aggression."

Finally, on September 29, 1940, FDR embargoed shipments of steel and scrap iron. But oil was still flowing. Morgenthau thought it was too little, too late. Ickes was convinced that Hull wouldn't do anything about oil until his hand was forced. Hull was "useless," Ickes wrote in his diary.

After FDR's election to a third term, Ickes was named petroleum coordinator for national defense. He was increasingly incensed that the United States was shipping oil and gasoline to Japan while rationing "our own people." On June 8, 1941, he told the president that the press was raising hell. FDR said, "Give Cordell a few more days." Ickes felt that Hull was being gulled by the Japanese.

On June 22, Ickes learned that more than two thousand barrels of lubricating oil were being sent to Japan aboard one of their tankers, which was docked in Philadelphia, at a time when U.S. plants could not meet their own needs. Ickes boiled over, and had the shipment held up. FDR "pinned my ears back," he wrote in his diary, for not consulting with the State Department. The president told Ickes that the United States and Japan were engaged in delicate negotiations. Furthermore, he saw oil as an integral part of foreign policy, not to be messed with by Ickes.

By this time, Hitler had invaded Russia, forcing Japan to make a difficult decision. Should they also attack Russia, from the Siberian side, or should they prepare to invade the colonies of Southeast Asia, using Indochina as an advance base, so they could assure their supply of raw materials in case of war with Britain and the United States? In his ongoing talks FDR was aware of the disconnect between the Japanese government, still working through diplomacy, and the Imperial Army, which was preparing for war. On July 1, 1941, he informed Ickes that "the Japs are having a real drag-down and knock-out fight among themselves . . . trying to decide which way they are going to jump—attack Russia, attack the South Seas . . . or whether they will sit on the fence and be more friendly with us. . . . It is terribly important for the control of the Atlantic for us to help keep the peace in the Pacific. I simply have not got enough Navy to go around—and every little episode in the Pacific means fewer ships in the Atlantic." At this point, FDR was still trying to avoid war with Japan. But in July the situation changed dramatically.

Those Two Fellows Looked Like a
Pair of Sheep-Killing Dogs

On July 20, 1941, FDR received some alarming information, thanks to the MAGIC intercepts, and told Ickes: "I would not be surprised if Japan should invade Indochina tomorrow. From Indochina, Japan could strike either at the Dutch East Indies or at Singapore or Burma. If they should strike successfully at Burma, it would mean the closing of the Burma Road, which is the last means of getting war supplies into China."

"Once again I raised the question of shipping oil to Japan," Ickes noted. "The president indicated that if Japan went overboard, we would ship no more oil. . . . We have gallantly pursued our appeasement toward Japan to the furthest possible point."

But FDR knew what Ickes did not—that on July 12, the Japanese ambassador to Vichy had presented new demands: the permission to dispatch land, sea, and air forces to southern Indochina; the occupation of eight air and two naval bases there; and the withdrawal of some French garrisons, their bases be occupied by the Japanese. Hull told the British ambassador to the United States, Lord Halifax: "They are now in possession of the whole of France's strategic province, pointing like a pudgy thumb towards the Philippines, Malaya, and the Dutch East Indies." FDR made one final stab at keeping the Japanese out of the south. On July 23, Sumner Welles told Japan's ambassador to the United States, Kichisaburo Nomura, that Japanese oil would be embargoed, since there was no basis for further talks. Nomura replied that an embargo of oil would "inflame Japanese public opinion." On July 24, FDR asked Nomura to withdraw Japanese troops from Indochina, which would then be regarded as neutral. The State Department denounced the Japanese invasion of the south as a move to establish bases for further conquests.

The president, who had been assistant secretary of the navy during World War I, loved to look at maps, and when he looked at a map of Southeast Asia he saw at once that Japanese bases in southern Vietnam were launching pads to attack Singapore, Sumatra, and Borneo, and threaten the Philippines.

On July 26, FDR froze all Japanese funds, to take effect August 1. Between July 1940 and July 1941, the United States had exported (to Japan and others) four million barrels of high-octane gasoline and ten million barrels of oil. In a single week in Los Angeles, Japanese tankers loaded four hundred thousand barrels. As of August 1, 1941, they would be unable to pay for more imports.

On July 27, Ickes noted in his diary: "Apparently France has been bluffed into letting Japan in effect take over Indochina. The reason given publicly was that Indochina required defense from the rapacious English, and since she was not in a position herself to defend Indochina, Japan was requested to go in to perform that Christian and charitable task."

Ickes wondered if FDR would fully enforce the freeze. "The president still unwilling to draw the noose tight," he wrote. "He thought it might be better to slip the noose around Japan's neck and give it a jerk now and then." On August 3, he received a call from Assistant Secretary of State Dean Acheson, who told him that FDR had signed the order barring the sale of high-octane aviation gasoline to the Japanese. Ickes was gratified that Hull was now taking a tougher line. Hull was saying that "nothing would stop them except force."

On December 3, FDR told Morgenthau that "he had the Japanese running around like a lot of wet hens, after he had asked them why they were sending so many military, naval, and air forces into Indochina." The wet hens, however, had decided in September that if their demands were not met in Washington, they would go to war. In mid-October, the warmongering Hideki Tojo was named prime minister.

On Sunday, December 7, 1941, Ickes attended the 2 P.M. cabinet meeting, where FDR said he had queried the Japanese regarding troops in Siam and along the Burma Road. "We are asked to believe," Ickes noted, "that Japan has troops in Indochina with the consent of the Vichy government and is anxious to guard against an attack by China. . . . It is suspected that Japan has many more troops in Indochina than the Vichy government agreed to be sent there. I believe the number agreed upon was 25,000."

Later that day the news came that the Japanese still had enough aviation gasoline to bomb Pearl Harbor, killing 2,344 Americans and sinking or damaging at anchor all those battleships named after states—among them the *Arizona*, the *Nevada*, the *Pennsylvania*, the *Tennessee*, the *West Virginia*. Fortunately they missed the carrier fleet, which was out to sea.

In 1941, Cordell Hull was seventy and not a well man. He suffered from diabetes and tuberculosis, and was often absent in times of crisis. On November 27 and 28, and again from December 1 to 3, he was bedridden. But on December 7 at 2 P.M., he was sitting in his office, awaiting the arrival of two Japanese envoys. For months he had been engaged in hollow negotiations with the special envoy Saburo Kurusu and Ambassador Nomura, patiently listening to their lies, as they lavished upon him assurances of good faith. They were sitting in his office when FDR phoned with news of the attack. Finally Hull's anger exploded and he called them "scoundrels and pissants." He told them: "In all my 50 years of public service I have never seen such infamous falsehoods and distortion." He told Lord Halifax the next day: "Those two fellows looked like a pair of sheep-killing dogs."

I Never Received a Greater Shock

There was no attempt by the Japanese to occupy any part of Hawaii, which was twice the distance from Japan as it was from San Francisco. The objective was to destroy the U.S. fleet, giving Japan a freer hand to establish a defense perimeter in the Pacific that stretched south from Burma and Malaya, across the four-thousand-mile-long barrier of the Dutch East Indies, and northward to the Philippines.

The answer to the president's question of why the Japanese were sending so many forces to Indochina was, in the words of a Japanese general, that it was "the pivot point of a folding fan" to attack Southeast Asia. Their aim was to expel the British, the Dutch, and the United States from their colonies and protectorates. Faced with the prospect of economic isolation, not only would they control the raw materials in these oil-and-rubber-rich possessions but they would launch an "Asia for the Asians" movement. Only the French would be allowed to remain, governed by the collaborationist Vichy regime.

The lightning offensive that followed Pearl Harbor threw the Allies into confusion. It was no spur-of-the-moment operation. The Japanese had been training and preparing for six months. They seemed suddenly to be all over the Pacific, with a mighty array of battle-ready troops, ships, and planes. Their principal advance base was Indochina, where they had massed their troops, docked their ships, and parked their bombers, within range of Malaya and Burma.

A few days after Pearl Harbor, from bases on nearby Taiwan, the Japanese invaded the northernmost major island in the Philippines, Luzon. General Douglas MacArthur held out in the southernmost island of Mindanao until March, and then left for Australia. The Japanese aim was to expel the Americans from the South Pacific and protect their eastern flank.

Next came the assault on the British. On December 6, a large Japanese naval force steamed out of Saigon into the South China Sea toward Malaya's eastern coast and the troops came ashore in landing craft at the undefended town of Singora. In the meantime, the 22nd Air Flotilla, based near Saigon, took off with eighty-eight bombers on December 9 and found a British fleet off Singapore. They sank the *Repulse* and the *Prince of Wales*, the fleet's prize battleships. A thousand crew members were lost. When he got the news, Churchill later wrote, "in all the war I never received a greater shock."

On December 18, three Japanese divisions, based on nearby Formosa, attacked the island of Hong Kong, off the coast of China. The British and Canadian garrison held out for a week but ran out of water and surrendered on Christmas Day.

In early 1942, the Japanese landed three divisions and proceeded down the long Malayan neck toward Singapore at the tip, beating the outgunned and outmaneuvered British and Australians back with a mixture of tank attacks and jungle fighting. The British fortress was on an island separated by a narrow strait. The British, expecting seaborne attacks, were not prepared for an assault on the land side. The big guns were pointed at the sea in fixed emplacements, and there were no fortifications or cannons landward. "I saw before me," Churchill later wrote, "the hideous spectacle of an almost naked island." Only a moat half a mile wide separated the British defenders from the Japanese.

In February the Japanese came out of the jungle before the fortress, which was crowded with an army of eighty-five thousand, the garrison plus the troops that had been beaten back. Their long retreat and the shocking conditions inside the fortress and the city behind it led to low morale. They were running out of food and water, disease was spreading, and the city streets were piled with unburied dead. On February 14, the tragic devoir of demolition began. The big guns and antiaircraft guns were destroyed, and the aviation-gasoline dumps were blown up. On February 15, Singapore surrendered. This was called the greatest disaster in British history since Yorktown.

The domino theory applied to the Japanese offensive. It was only a few miles across the Strait of Malacca from Singapore to Sumatra. Once Singapore fell, the Dutch East Indies were next.

With every advance, the Japanese consolidated their gains by establishing air bases from which they could hit the next target. Then the troops were leapfrogged to the next beachhead. Never did these troops go beyond the range of their air cover. This was the strategy that had been refined for months, while the British were entrenched in their meager garrisons.

At the same time that the battle for Singapore was raging, the Japanese were invading Siam via Indochina and moving toward the border with Burma. They bombed the capital, Rangoon, in late December. The British, after blowing up the oil refineries, retreated in good order in early March. By April, Japan found itself the conqueror of a vast Pacific domain, from which it had expelled all the colonial powers but the French.

During the time they occupied these newly conquered territories, the Japanese kindled nationalist feelings and encouraged independence movements. The Philippines, under benign U.S. tutelage since 1898, was granted independence in 1946. Burma became a republic in 1948. The Dutch East Indies became Indonesia in 1949. Malaya and the British slice of Borneo became a federation in 1948.

The only territory to remain under colonial rule was French Indochina, where the Japanese had allowed the helpful Vichy French to remain. Their occupation strategy went through three stages. First, in June 1940, they cut off the supplies transiting from the port of Haiphong to the Chinese city of Kunming. A year later, they turned Indochina into a "commissary line," to provide rice, rubber, and other commodities for their troops. Finally, when the United States shut the oil spigot in July 1941 and froze their assets, the Japanese implemented their plan to oust the Allies from Southeast Asia. This gave them access to the oil they needed to pur-

sue the war. It was the invasion of Japanese troops into southern Indochina that led FDR to act, which created a chain reaction. Aggression
led to sanctions, and sanctions led to further aggression. Deprived of U.S.
oil, the Japanese, while pretending to negotiate, had decided that their
only alternative was to invade Southeast Asia and bomb Pearl Harbor.
They gambled that the "weak American democracy" would not wage war.

The success of Japanese operations in Southeast Asia was made possible by the complicity of the Vichy regime in Hanoi, which allowed Japan to
turn the colony into a military base. At the same time, the arrangement
with the Japanese allowed the French to hang on in Indochina. The United
States, which had two major theaters to contend with, did not for the moment concern itself with Indochina.

Asia for the Asians

Vietnam was a land of villages, whose fields, irrigated by the nourishing
silt of the deltas, produced two rice crops a year, after labor-intensive
planting and harvesting. The iconic scene: a peasant wearing his conical hat, bent over a wooden plough pulled by a water buffalo. Each village, surrounded by a bamboo wall, was a self-contained entity, with its
mutual-aid society for matters such as funerals, as well as craft guilds and
clubs.

The colonial system created two unequal societies with a chronic inability to understand each other. The fifty thousand French saw all that
they had done for the locals—the number of educated Annamites, the
roads and harbors that brought them so many fine French products. The
twenty-three million Vietnamese saw what colonization had done to
them—the high rate of illiteracy and the forced labor, known as *corvées*,
to build and repair the roads "for their own good." The government mo-
nopoly that taxed salt, one of the few staples the villages could not produce, made it ten times as expensive as it would have been on the free
market. The rise of moneylenders and middlemen in rice sales led to fore-
closures and a decline in status when landowners became tenant farmers.
According to a century-old Vietnamese fable, the Frenchman was a blood-
sucking leech.

The French did educate a small number of the most promising Vietnamese, some of whom became leaders of the independence movement. The restricted class of graduates from Hanoi lycées found jobs in colonial offices but soon hit the bamboo ceiling. Paid less than the French, banned from their clubs, and promoted at a snail's pace, their resentment was channeled into political outlets. The *colon*, alluding to the time-honored practice of changing a child's name when he became a man, said: "What can you do with a people who, every time a child is sick, to make him well, they change his name?" When Hanoi radio compared Marshal Pétain to Joan of Arc, the Vietnamese who had been to French schools said: "Joan of Arc was a saint who saved France by defeating the British. Pétain surrendered to the Germans and the Japanese."

Collaboration became as easy as listening to the lies on Vichy radio. Japanese troops could not be everywhere in Indochina's eighty-five provinces. They spoke neither French nor Vietnamese. It was far better for the Japanese to let the French handle local government. At first, the Japanese were busy invading Southeast Asia. By February 1942, when that was done, the occupation settled into a period of entente cordiale. The Japanese presence was felt in the cities, but in the countryside it was hardly noticed.

Of course, both the French and the Vietnamese paid a price. Tons of rice were set aside for the Japanese army, which had an insatiable appetite. At the same time, the peasants were ordered to grow corn (which could be distilled into alcohol to make up for gas shortages), peanuts (needed for lubricating oil), and jute and hemp (for sacking and cordage). As a result, the Vietnamese harvested less rice, while turning over part of their remaining crop, which led to shortages.

Indochina was crucial to the Japanese war effort, which eventually took over much of the economy. The Japanese brought in their technicians to reorganize mining and forestry. Needing lumber for their ships and barracks, they deforested entire regions. In addition, Vichy agreed to pay for the cost of occupation, just as it paid the Nazis.

For the French *colon*, however, it was life almost as usual. The rubber planter and the tin-mine owner rarely saw a son of Nippon, and the bankers filled their pockets. In the cities, the French pursued their normal lives, attended by houseboys in their fine homes with tapestried dens for smoking opium, meeting at outdoor cafés for the afternoon apéritif, and driving to the resorts of Dalat on weekends for the horse races. As for the Annamites, they could live on rice and bananas. The *colons* deplored being cut off from France, for their wine cellars were depleted. But they survived on beer and anisette.

Admiral Decoux ruled like a Persian satrap, in complete charge of his province. Of course he had to pay tribute to the occupier. Of course he agreed to "recognize the supreme interests of Japan," while the Japanese promised to "respect the rights and interests of France." The protocols were observed, but the French did the bowing, with a correct collaborationist attitude. French troops roamed free in their efforts to suppress such Vietnamese resistance as there was. Decoux argued that France remained neutral, but was it neutral to enforce Vichy's anti-Jewish laws and purge his administration of Jews, even though the Japanese did not require it? Was it neutral to form a Milice-like legion to hunt down Jews, Gaullists, and Vietnamese rebels? By March 1945 there were ten thousand political prisoners in Decoux's jails. The alternative, according to Vichy, was a suicidal war against the Japanese.

The Japanese and the Vichy French competed to win the hearts and minds of the Vietnamese masses. Making a stab at benevolence, Admiral Decoux banned public whippings and the condescending *"tu"* form of address. To pull more Vietnamese into the French orbit, he increased enrollment in the schools from 450,000 in 1939 to 700,000 in 1944. Most of this augmentation was at the primary school level, but a passel of vocational schools were also launched. The University of Hanoi built a new wing and enrolled those students now unable to attend faculties in France.

An emphasis on sports was part of the plan to encourage French values. The situation was peaceful enough to organize an annual Tour d'Indochine, which sent hundreds of cyclists huffing up mountain and down dale over twenty-five hundred miles through the country's five states. More than a thousand sports trainers were hired to start clubs at the village level, such as the "Girl Guides" and "Young Buddhists." Decoux wanted to show that in spite of caving in to the Japanese occupiers he could still run a model colony. But the movement for sports and gymnastics, which grew to a million members, had the unintended result of becoming a training ground for Vietnamese nationalism. Decoux also hired thousands of Vietnamese employees, raising their salaries and breaking though the bamboo ceiling. Many of them later served Ho Chi Minh. Such were the papier-mâché reforms of Vichy.

The Japanese struck back with an "Asia for the Asians" campaign. The Vietnamese were swamped with Tokyo movies and magazines, judo classes, and radio lectures: "Do you want your country to be enslaved by Anglo-Americans? No, your mind is better than that of an animal, so you must help Japan fight the enemy." The Vietnamese soon saw through the ballyhoo, since the Japanese were responsible for maintaining the French colonial system and the ravenous "commissary line" that made their lives miserable. More effective were the Japanese promises that they could bring independence to Vietnam, and the many Japanese soldiers and officers who fraternized with anti-French Vietnamese.

He Is a Little Touched Here

Meanwhile, the war was being fought on two fronts, and the Allied leaders ran the show with conferences, inside which there were whims and affinities, likes and dislikes, as well as secret deals and a tendency to avoid direct confrontation through procrastination. But there was one issue that caused a serious rift in the alliance—colonialism, and particularly Indochina.

FDR felt strongly that colonialism had no place in the postwar world and that trusteeships should be established under the proposed United Nations, leading eventually to independence. Churchill, who in his youth had fought in India, the Sudan, and South Africa, was the stout defender of empire.

The president's genuine anticolonial principles did not exclude self-interest. Trusteeship under U.N. control would entail access to markets and raw materials when the United States emerged from World War II as a global power. Free markets would undercut French and British colonial monopolies. At the same time, FDR wanted "the brown people of the east," as he called them, to be self-governing.

When he spoke with complete candor, FDR blamed the war with Japan on colonialism, telling his son Elliott: "Don't think for a minute that Americans would be dying in the Pacific tonight if it hadn't been for the short-sighted greed of the French and the British and the Dutch."

He held a special grudge against the French for their abject surrender and the Vichy collaboration with Germany and Japan. Thanks to Vichy, the Japanese had obtained a strategic base without the wasteful investment of an occupation army. When FDR sent Admiral William D. Leahy to Vichy as ambassador, in the spring of 1941, his instructions were to remind "all and sundry that an Axis victory would mean the dismemberment of the French empire." At that very moment, Marshal Pétain was handing over to the Japanese the French military bases that would allow them to invade Southeast Asia.

Nor did FDR approve of General Charles de Gaulle, whom he met for the first time at the Casablanca Conference in January 1943. He thought the overbearing general's grandiloquence was delusional, and told his friend Felix Frankfurter, the Supreme Court justice, "he is a little touched here," as he tapped his head. Why should Pétain be rewarded for his collaboration and de Gaulle for his megalomania?

The president's anticolonial fixation surfaced at Placentia Bay, off the eastern tip of Newfoundland, on August 9, 1941, where he had his first face-to-face meeting with Churchill. FDR was aboard the heavy cruiser *Augusta,* while Churchill steamed in on the pride of his fleet, the battleship *Prince of Wales* (later sunk off Singapore). Churchill came as a pleader, hoping to get the American navy across the Atlantic and into a clash with Germany. He wanted to turn the meeting into a display of Anglo-American unity. That was why on August 11 he agreed to the vaporous declaration of principles solemnly called the Atlantic Charter. The third of its eight principles expressed "the right of all peoples to choose the form of government under which they will live; and they wish to see sovereign right and self-government restored to those who have forcibly been deprived of them."

If carried out, the charter would mean the end of Empire. But Churchill, still in his courtship phase, signed it, although he had to explain to the House of Commons that the clause only applied to European states like Poland. In a gem of sophistry, he said that those who had not been deprived of their rights in the first place because they did not have them did not count. For FDR, however, the Atlantic Charter applied all over the world.

Although half American, Churchill never grasped the deep hostility of many Americans toward their former colonizer, their race memory of imperial taxation. The polls in 1941 showed that 74 percent wanted to stay out of the war.

But as Churchill told his chiefs of staff two days after Pearl Harbor, when one of them advised a cautious approach to America: "That is the way we talked to her when we were wooing her; now she is in the harem, we talk to her quite differently." And so the two leaders cultivated each other's friendship, while often pursuing opposite aims.

In their correspondence and conferences, Churchill maintained a benign and nonconfrontational façade. Behind the scenes at the Foreign Office, there were deep misgivings concerning American policy on the colonial issue. On January 1, 1942, twenty-six nations signed a declaration calling for a postwar United Nations, which the British saw as a threat to their empire. Lord Halifax, the British ambassador to the United States, raised the issue directly with FDR, expressing his concern that the president might wish to place Malaya or Indonesia under trusteeship. The president replied that "the cases were quite different," since the British and the Dutch "had done a good job but the French were hopeless."

This was the crowning irony: that it was the Japanese who dismantled the colonial empires of Asia, taking Hong Kong and Malaya from the British, Indonesia from the Dutch, and Indochina from the French. The European colonies of Asia were falling like dominoes. The little yellow men were evicting the rapacious colonials and nurturing Asian nationalism.

Lord Halifax made what was perhaps the most astute remark regarding FDR's habit of sending up trial balloons, reporting that "the president . . . uses conversation as others use the first draft on paper . . . a method of trying out an idea. . . . But if you do it in conversation people say that you have changed your mind, that 'you never know when you have him,' and so on."

There was in the president much of this elusive quality, but on the issue of colonialism he remained for the moment resolute. At the Casablanca Conference in January 1943, he first raised with Churchill the issue of the British giving up India.

On March 28, 1943, Halifax stopped by the Oval Office and was astonished to find the president at his desk drawing on a map of Africa and actually scratching out parts of the French Empire that would be used as Allied bases, such as Dakar in Senegal and Bizerte in Tunisia. FDR had adopted the concept of "four policemen," the four permanent members of the U.N. Security Council (the United States, the Soviet Union, Britain, and China; France was to be excluded, though French bases would be used), who would police the world when the war was over. Later, of course, he had to give in to demands for a fifth Security Council seat for France. But Halifax at the time was rendered speechless.

That August, at the first Quebec Conference, a decision was made that would later ensure the return of Indochina to the French. On August 5, 1943, Churchill left on the *Queen Mary* with a staff of two hundred. He had long been mulling over the matter of the British high command being run from India. There had to be a separate command of operations in Southeast Asia, to be coordinated with the American China theater.

FDR arrived at the Citadelle of Quebec on August 17. He seemed tired and told Churchill: "You must know that I am not what I was." The day after the first plenary session on August 19, Churchill proposed Admiral Lord Mountbatten, "a man of great energy and daring," to head the proposed South East Asia Command, which would help the Americans "crush Japan's island empire." Setting up SEAC would have major political ramifications, since the British would later reestablish their colonial influence in Burma and Malaya and help the French reestablish theirs. For the moment, however, it was left undecided whether Indochina would be part of SEAC or the American China theater. FDR told Churchill that he wanted "a sheer anchor against the machinations of de Gaulle." By having a detachment in SEAC, the Free French were hoping to take part in Indochina operations. FDR was intent on stopping them.

Mountbatten, who wanted Indochina in his theater, called on Chiang Kai-shek in October 1943. Chiang told him that if he were to relinquish Indochina he would suffer a serious loss of face. Mountbatten proposed a "gentleman's agreement" under which both theaters could operate in Indochina.

France Has Milked It for One Hundred Years

In November 1943, two momentous conferences were held, one on the heels of the other, in Cairo and Tehran. Cairo was the only conference that Chiang Kai-shek was able to attend, and in Tehran FDR met Joseph Stalin for the first time. The president used both conferences to win the support of those two Allied leaders for his anticolonial views, particularly regarding Indochina. The State Department, as part of its postwar preparations, had suggested that Chinese troops might be used to liberate Indochina. The French objected strenuously, but FDR said it was a military matter, to be left to the discretion of the Joint Chiefs of Staff. He didn't want French troops used and if British troops were used they would bring the French in. When he went to Cairo and Tehran the matter of Indochina was still undecided.

FDR left Washington on November 11, boarded the battleship *Iowa*, crossed the Atlantic, steamed through the Strait of Gibraltar, and flew the last leg from Tunis to Cairo, arriving on November 22 at the spacious villa of his ambassador, Alexander C. Kirk. Chiang, a small man with a bald pate and an unlined face, called on his American ally the next day dressed in a freshly pressed khaki uniform. It was their first face-to-face meeting. Despite his disappointment with Chiang's armies, FDR turned on the charm and offered him a leading role in the occupation of Japan, which Chiang declined. Looking for another way to gratify Chiang, the president asked him if he had any interest in Indochina after the war. Chiang said he did not, for the Vietnamese people would be impossible to assimilate. He agreed, however, that Indochina should be independent, though its people were not prepared to be. On November 23, FDR told Churchill that Chiang had no designs on Indochina. "Nonsense!" Churchill grunted. "Winston," FDR replied, "you have 400 years of acquisition in your blood and you just don't understand how a country might not want to acquire land somewhere if they can get it."

On November 27, the president flew to Tehran, which sits atop a four-thousand-foot-high plateau. The Iranian capital was occupied by Soviet troops and FDR stayed on the Russian compound rather than at the U.S. legation, for security reasons. At their first face-to-face meeting on November 28, Stalin arrived buttoned to the neck in his military tunic with gold epaulets. FDR finally found an Allied leader who disliked the French as much as he did. Stalin said that France under Pétain was providing the Germans with ports and military equipment and should be punished. Nor did Stalin approve of de Gaulle, who acted like the head of a great state but had little power. FDR agreed with enthusiasm, and said there was an urgent need to prepare a trusteeship for Indochina. Stalin saw no reason "to shed blood to restore Indochina to the old colonial system." FDR agreed 100 percent. Trusteeship would give the Vietnamese twenty to thirty years to prepare for self-government.

At dinner that night, hosted by FDR, Stalin, perhaps unaccustomed to the president's martinis, grew violent on the subject of France, saying that its entire ruling class was rotten to the core and it had no right to retain its empire. Churchill listened in dismay, and upon his return to the British legation told his aides: "Stupendous issues are unfolding before our eyes and we are only specks of dust that have settled in the night on the map of the world." He had been kept out of FDR's meeting with Stalin for obvious reasons.

Having secured the assent of Chiang Kai-shek and Stalin, FDR returned to the United States in December, resolute in his purpose to keep the French out of Indochina. On January 24, 1944, he told Lord Halifax that the only reason the British opposed trusteeship was "that they fear the effect it would have on their own possessions and those of the Dutch." In a memo to Cordell Hull on the same day he said: "France has milked it for one hundred years. The people of Indochina are entitled to something better than that."

The British, however, had different plans. In February 1944, their Post-Hostilities Planning Committee stated that "to deprive France of her economic stake in Indochina would weaken her severely. . . . France would be encouraged to form a bloc, possibly with the Russians, opposed to an Anglo-American bloc." The postwar role of France in rebuilding Western Europe was now seen as a factor in the return of Indochina to French control. On April 4, a French military mission was attached to Mountbatten's headquarters in India. The United States and Britain were on different paths.

In the meantime, on March 3, with an election coming up in the fall, FDR was particularly jovial at a cabinet meeting, passing around the table a snapshot of a diapered baby captioned "The Fourth Term. Oh, God damn it!" After the meeting he discussed foreign policy with Vice President Henry Wallace and launched into a reminiscence: "Did I ever tell you the story of French Indochina? A year or so ago, when Churchill came over here, I called attention to the fact that the French had renounced their claims on Indochina in favor of the Japs six months before the United States was attacked. I believe that after the Japs are driven out, the French have no longer any claim to French Indochina and I am sure the Chinese will not want French Indochina." At Tehran, FDR continued, he had mentioned the trusteeship to Stalin, who came around the table and shook his hand to show how strongly he backed the idea. Then FDR said to Churchill, "Well, we are two to one against you on this. You'd better come across and we will make it unanimous." Churchill said, "Well, I will have to consult my cabinet."

There were still too many overriding considerations in the conduct of the war, such as the OVERLORD landing in June, so Churchill had no desire to antagonize FDR. In July 1944, Churchill asked his foreign secretary, Anthony Eden, to go slow on Indochina: "Roosevelt has been more outspoken to me on that subject than any other colonial matter, and I imagine it is one of his principal war aims to liberate Indochina from France. . . . Do you really want to go and stir all this up at such a time as this?" In August, however, he softened and allowed a French Corps Léger of five hundred men to join Mountbatten's command.

A Spirit of Ruthless Go-Getting

No decision had yet been made as to whether Indochina belonged in the British or American Pacific theater of operations. Mountbatten warned the Foreign Office on August 4, 1944, that the tempo of the war was quickening and that if Indochina was part of the American theater, it would have "a disastrous effect . . . on the British position in the Far East."

At the second Quebec Conference, from September 11 to 16, 1944, FDR and Churchill met as victors in Europe. The Germans were falling back to the Rhine and the Russians were about to invade Hungary. In Asia, the American plan was to regain the Philippines. As Churchill put it, "everything we have touched has turned to gold." And yet amid these brilliant victories, the colonial question still festered. At Quebec, Churchill was given an unequivocal Foreign Office memo, which stated: "It cannot legitimately be said that France has misruled Indochina. . . . French rule has given peace and political cohesion for a territory which has not geographical or ethnographical unity. . . . Any attempt to interfere with French sovereignty in Indochina . . . would put into question the future of all other Far Eastern colonial possessions that have been overrun by Japan" (read Singapore, Hong Kong, Malaya, and Burma). Churchill still felt, however, that he could not let Indochina dampen "the blaze of friendship."

In the last six months of his life, however, FDR became more adamant in his resolve to keep the French out of their former colony, where the Gaullists had begun minor resistance operations with the help of the British. In October 1944, he told Hull to "do nothing . . . [to help] resistance groups or in any other way in relation to Indochina."

In France, meanwhile, General de Gaulle had taken Paris in August and had formed his provisional government in September. For him, the issue of Indochina was not debatable. He planned to send two divisions there as soon as he could find the ships. Mountbatten approved of the French mission, but on November 18, FDR stated flatly that French troop movements did not have U.S. approval. In addition, he did not recognize the French mission at SEAC. A fuming Mountbatten warned the Foreign Office on December 9 that "American imperialists in the armed forces [are] determined to do what they please in the Far East. . . . On our side there is a sense of frustration and resentment, and on the American side there is a spirit of ruthless go-getting."

Mountbatten was probably referring to Joseph "Vinegar Joe" Stilwell, the commander of the China theater, who said the British were "bastardly hypocrites [who] do their best to cut our throats on all occasions, the pig fuckers." He viewed Mountbatten, a cousin of the royal family, as a "Glamour Boy . . . Enormous staff, endless walla walla, but damned little fighting," and he blocked most of his requests concerning the Free French.

But by December 1944, Stilwell had been recalled, since he was not shy about expressing his disdain for Chiang Kai-shek, whom he called "Peanut." According to his assistant, Frank Dorn, Stilwell had returned to China after a trip to Washington in August 1944 and delivered to Dorn "a top-secret verbal order which he said came from Roosevelt. Allegedly, the order was to prepare a plan to assassinate Chiang Kai-shek." Stilwell told Dorn that FDR was "fed up with Chiang and his tantrums," and told him, "in that Olympian manner of his, 'if you can't get along with Chiang, and can't replace him, get rid of him once and for all.' " Dorn devised a plan to sabotage Chiang's plane, but the final okay never came.

In February 1945, Stilwell was replaced by General Albert C. Wedemeyer. Mountbatten found Wedermeyer even more difficult than Stilwell. He claimed Indochina for his command and opined that "there would not be a British Empire after the war." Finally, an understanding was reached to divide Indochina into two commands.

By this time, FDR realized that Chiang Kai-shek, the centerpiece of his postwar Asian policy, was an unreliable ally who had divided his armies to fight the Chinese Communists in addition to Japan. It looked more and more as though postwar China was headed for civil war. Wise men with experience in the Far East, such as former ambassador to Tokyo Joseph Grew and James Clement Dunn of the State Department, advised the president that U.S. interests would be better served by a stable Indochina under French rule than by a China torn by civil war. France was also a crucial ally in Western Europe, where Soviet expansion was feared.

Thus it seemed that at the start of 1945, in the final months of his life, FDR began to feel ambivalent about Indochina. On January 1, he told his newly named secretary of state, Edward Stettinius, who had replaced the ailing Hull, that "I still don't want to get mixed up in a military effort toward the liberation of Indochina." But a few days later, when Halifax informed FDR that Mountbatten wanted to send French saboteurs into Indochina, he agreed to the plan if it was "absolutely necessary," but insisted that it should be kept secret so as not "to prejudice political decisions about Indochina in a sense favorable to restoration of the French status quo ante." FDR made a distinction between military needs and political outcomes. In reality, one followed the other. If the French were able to get boots on the ground, they just might keep Indochina.

I Give Him Only a Few Months to Live

Then came Yalta, FDR's final conference. On January 22, 1945, two days after his fourth-term inauguration, FDR left Washington for the Norfolk Navy Yard to board the cruiser *Quincy*. On January 30, he celebrated his sixty-third birthday aboard ship. Reaching Malta on February 2, he joined Churchill and they flew the rest of the way on the *Sacred Cow*, FDR's plane, landing on an icy runway ninety miles from Yalta. They drove to the Black Sea resort, where Stalin would soon arrive, and where the czars had built the white granite palace Livadia, which boasted fifty bedrooms but few bathrooms.

On February 4, Stalin came to call and FDR commented on de Gaulle's "effrontery" in expecting to be invited. He expressed his annoyance that "for two years the British have been artificially building up France."

On February 5, the discussion turned to the occupation of Germany. Should France be an occupying power? Churchill made the case for France, but Stalin said the French zone should be carved out of the British zone. However, full French participation was granted.

FDR discussed Indochina in a private meeting with Stalin on February 7. According to the minutes, "the President then said he had in mind for Korea a trusteeship, and also had in mind a trusteeship for Indochina . . . the President said the Indochinese people were of small stature, like the Javanese and Burmese, and were not warlike. He added that the French had done nothing to improve the natives since they had the colony." He also told Stalin that de Gaulle had asked for ships to carry French troops to Indochina. Stalin asked where de Gaulle was going to get the troops. FDR (with a wink) replied that de Gaulle would find troops as soon as he, Roosevelt, had found ships, but that so far he had been unable to find them.

The next day, however, there was an incident that accidentally killed the trusteeship plan. Secretary of State Stettinius used the word *trustee-ship* in a harmless aside. Churchill, who had been storing up his anger over American attempts to meddle with the Asian colonies of the British and the French, exploded: "I will not have one scrap of British territory flung into that area [of trusteeship]," he bellowed. "If every bit of land over which the British flag flies is to be brought into the dock, I shall object as long as I live." Stettinius explained that all he had in mind was taking the mandated islands given to the Japanese in the Pacific by the League of Nations.

Thus, the final communiqué on February 11 stated that trusteeships would be restricted to three categories: 1) existing mandates of the League of Nations from before the war; 2) territories detached from the enemy as a result of the present war; and 3) any other territory that might voluntarily be placed under trusteeship. Discussions of actual territories would be left for a later date.

Those conditions seemed to rule out a trusteeship for Indochina. But FDR may have felt that the second category applied to Indochina as it did to Korea, which had been a Japanese colony. That is why he lumped them together in his talk with Stalin. It could be argued that the French had lost Indochina to Japan in 1940. Apparently, FDR felt there was some wiggle room in determining Indochina's status, and that trusteeship remained a viable option. Talking to reporters on the way home, he mentioned Churchill's "mid-Victorian" outlook on colonial matters, adding: "Better to keep quiet just now." It should be added that in the words of Churchill's doctor, Charles Wilson (Lord Moran), FDR was "a very sick man" at Yalta, which may have affected his judgment and strength of will. Wilson continued: "He has all the symptoms of hardening of the arteries of the brain in an advanced state, so that I give him only a few months to live." The six-thousand-mile trip from the coast of Virginia to the coast of the Crimea did not help his health.

What Are You Americans Driving At?

On March 9, 1945, the Japanese in Indochina overthrew the Vichy regime and jailed the French officials and troops. At that time, the United States had an army of translators deciphering MAGIC intercepts, summaries of which were forwarded to the president, who followed policy developments in Japan blow by blow. By January 12, Japanese fears of a U.S. invasion of Indochina had grown when Admiral William F. Halsey shelled the coast. An intercepted Japanese navy message on January 17 warned that "landings in Indochina by Allied forces are imminent." On February 1, the Supreme War Leadership Conference in Tokyo decided on military action. The U.S. code services were aware of the details of the coup. The MAGIC summary for March 9 was headed: SHOWDOWN IN INDOCHINA EXPECTED TODAY.

The day before the coup, March 8, FDR saw General Wedemeyer, who was in Washington, and asked him not to help the French in his theater. Independence was the wave of the future, FDR said, not empires. On March 13, an angry de Gaulle blew up at U.S. ambassador Jefferson Caffery: "What are you Americans driving at? Do you want us to become one of the federated states under the Russian aegis? . . . The Russians are advancing apace. When Germany falls they will be upon us. If you are against us in Indochina there will be terrific disappointment here and nobody knows to what that will lead. We do not want to be Communist; we do not want to fall into the Russian orbit, but we hope you will not push us into it." This was the first time the French played the Communist card, which they would continue to play con brio. Perhaps impressed by Caffery's report, FDR allowed General Claire Chennault to give the French token support, but made it clear that assistance did not mean a change in policy. At another meeting on March 23, he told Wedemeyer that he must "watch carefully to prevent British and French political activities in the area" and should limit his support "as would be required in direct operations against the Japanese." Thus, while not wanting to hinder the war effort, FDR was still intent on preventing the French from returning to Indochina three weeks before his death.

In what may have been the president's final comment on the issue, on March 15 he told Charles Taussig of the State Department that he still felt Indochina should be placed under trusteeship, unless France pledged to assume the obligations of a trustee. "Then I would agree to France retaining these colonies with the provision that independence was the ultimate goal."

FDR died on April 12 and trusteeship died with him. The priorities by then were defeating Japan and saving Europe from the Russian Bear, and in both cases France was too important an ally to challenge her rights in Indochina. Why single out the French when the United States had no objections to the British or Dutch colonies? In the "what if" department, a thirty-year trusteeship under U.N. auspices might have avoided the war that ended with defeat at Dien Bien Phu, as well as a second war.

A Voice in the Wilderness

There was one political party that saw the Japanese occupation of Indochina not as a tragedy but as an opportunity, and that was the Communist Party of Indochina (CPI), led by Ho Chi Minh. When World War II broke out in September 1939, Ho was in China doing liaison work with the Chinese Communists. It was a bad time for the CPI. France had banned its Communist party following the Nazi-Soviet pact in June, and in Vietnam thousands of CPI members were jailed and many fled to South China. The leadership was decimated, the party was in disarray, and in September it went underground. In Kunming, about two hundred miles north of the Vietnamese border, Ho gathered the party remnants and built a network of Chinese contacts.

In May 1940, his two closest associates, Vo Nguyen Giap and Pham Van Dong, joined him in Kunming. When the French surrendered to Germany on June 22, 1940, Ho told his companions: "The French defeat represents every favorable opportunity for the Vietnamese revolution. We must seek every means to return home to take advantage of it." Return they did, starting the movement again practically from scratch. It was Ho's first stay in his homeland in thirty years after a peripatetic and hazardous career as a professional revolutionary. He was fifty years old. During those years he used a bewildering array of pseudonyms, but the one that stuck was Ho Chi Minh (Ho the Enlightened).

The classic moment of conversion from docility to resistance for many Vietnamese was their first experience of French brutality. Ho, who was born in 1890, was going to school in Hue at the age of seventeen while working as a translator for French officials when he was caught in a peasant demonstration. French troops opened fire on the unarmed demonstrators, and Ho changed sides. He was expelled from school and his name appeared on a police blacklist, so he went south to Saigon in 1911. There, wanderlust seized him and he found a job with one of the steamship companies that hired Vietnamese as waiters and kitchen help. He spent two years as a galley hand, stopping at ports of call in Asia and Africa, and becoming familiar with the wretched population of dockworkers and rickshaw men from Singapore to Calcutta. In Dakar, Senegalese laborers were ordered to swim out to his ship. When several drowned in rough waters, the French sailors on deck laughed at their comical efforts to stay afloat. The repeated lesson of his travels was: "Colonialism breeds cruelty."

In 1913, Ho jumped ship in New York, beginning an odyssey that lasted almost thirty years. In Paris in 1920, he joined the Communist Party, for Lenin's text on colonialism seemed to offer a solution to the Vietnamese dilemma: the Communist parties of the industrialized West would become allied with nationalist movements in the colonies against Western imperialism. In 1923, he went to Russia and enrolled in the University of the Toilers of the East. A year later, he was in China as a Comintern agent. Then to Hong Kong, where in 1930 he founded the Vietnamese Communist Party, which had about three hundred members. Then back to Moscow, from 1934 to 1938, then on assignment in China.

In 1940, Ho realized that the Japanese would invade Indochina with the complicity of the Vichy regime. The new strategy would mean becoming an ally of the Allies, since he foresaw that the Japanese would use Indochina to invade Southeast Asia, and that this would lead to world war. He had been receiving news on conditions in the interior and he realized that the time was right for return.

His aides, hunting for a safe location to use as a base, came upon the limestone caves of Pac Bo, in Cao Bang Province. They were less than a mile from the Chinese border (perfect if Ho and his aides had to leave in a hurry), hidden in cliffs surrounded by jungle. The area was peopled by Nung tribesmen, who had always been hostile to the French.

On January 28, 1941, Ho left with his aides for the forty-mile trek on jungle trails and over mountain streams, reaching the village of Pac Bo in early February. He was entering his country for the first time in thirty years. He set up headquarters in a cave on the side of a cliff, and slept on a bed of branches. A fire was kept lit to ward off the damp. Those days would be remembered as the dawn of the long battle for independence, Ho's first fragile foothold inside his homeland.

Starting from the caves of Pac Bo with a handful of loyal aides, this was a staggering organizational effort: to build more guerrilla bases, until the Vietnamese communists had a network throughout Indochina, and to cement his leadership, after having been so long out of the country. He began by training guerrillas, fifty at a time, the classrooms in jungle clearings. They were, he said, like the pilings in a riverbed. "It is they who will maintain the soil at low tide." By August he had moved from the village level to the county to the province.

After December 7, 1941, Ho realized that his prediction had been correct and that regional wars had become a world war. He had to return to China to inform the government of Chiang Kai-shek that he had forces ready to fight the Japanese, but needed weapons and financing. He also wanted to obtain Chinese recognition of the Vietminh, as his followers were now called. As Ho was walking down Perfect Glory Street in a Chinese village on August 27, 1942, he was arrested on suspicion of being a Japanese spy. For more than a year, he was shuttled through thirteen districts and eighteen jails. One of his teeth fell out and his hair turned gray. His body was covered with sores. Eventually, in late August 1944, he was allowed to return to Indochina.

The Man Who Looks Always Angry

In Ho's absence, Giap and Pham were busy. The military situation outside Indochina had changed dramatically. The German defeats in Russia and the June 1944 landing in Normandy announced the defeat of Hitler. In the Pacific, the Japanese were losing carriers and planes as the Americans took island after island. In Burma, the fighting raged. In the Philippines, the Americans attacked in mid-September. The Japanese were losing the war on multiple fronts, although in Indochina the cozy arrangement with the French persisted, even after Pétain had been ousted. De Gaulle had formed a provisional government in September and was desperately looking for ships to carry troops to Indochina. In Hanoi, the government of

Admiral Decoux still functioned, although some of the French civilian and military officials had begun leaning toward de Gaulle.

Vo Nguyen Giap in 1944 was thirty-three, twenty years younger than Ho, and, as every great military leader must be, he was a man of action with a chess player's mind. One of his sayings was: "A pawn can bring victory; a bad move can lose two knights." He had studied Napoleon's campaigns, which he knew down to the battalion level, and modeled his thinking on Clausewitz.

Some called Giap "the man who looks always angry." Round-faced and high-browed, with thick eyebrows over hooded eyes, his short, squat wrestler's body seemed always to be circling an opponent. He came from a family of anti-French militants. His Mandarin father died in prison in 1919. One of his sisters, also arrested, died a few weeks after being released. By the age of ten, Giap had two good reasons to hate the French.

His obvious intelligence brought him to the lycée in Hue, on the banks of the Perfume River, spanned by an iron bridge that Eiffel had built. He came to the notice of the Sûreté in his teens, and was expelled from the lycée for taking part in a strike. He studied for his exams in jail and went on to law school. In 1937, he joined the Communist Party of Indochina and married a fellow party member. A daughter was born in 1939. Caught up in party activities, he flunked his bar exam and taught history at a school in Hanoi, while writing articles for banned newspapers. His sister-in-law went to Russia to train for the party. Upon her return to Saigon, she was arrested, tried, sentenced to death, and shot. In 1940, Giap fled to China, and his wife went to her family in Vinh, about three hundred miles south of Hanoi. She was arrested, sentenced to fifteen years, and sent to Hanoi Central Prison.

It was in China that Giap first met Ho, who taught him that political action must precede any military offensive, "as the dawn precedes the day." Giap studied Maoist tactics at a guerrilla warfare school and learned to speak and write Chinese. In 1942, he returned to the caves of Pac Bo with forty men and their families, having been taught that every man, woman, and child was a soldier. In Ho's absence, he began forming small cadres that could fan out and train others. Didn't all religious groups begin with apostles? They had to be able to communicate with the peasants, whom they taught in lean-to bamboo huts with roofs of leaves, in jungle villages.

By the summer of 1944, Giap had a force of three hundred poorly armed men. It was then that he learned that his wife had died in prison, which only strengthened his resolve. He led shock troops south of Pac Bo into the area of Cao Bang, advancing, as he put it, "like a snowball," creating new bases as he went, to the edge of the Red River Delta.

When Ho returned in September 1944, he found Giap thinking in terms of wholesale insurrection. "The phase of peaceful revolution has passed," he told Giap, "but the hour of general insurrection has not yet come." Why risk a huge setback? Ho did agree to form armed propaganda teams, which would mobilize the masses and at the same time attack isolated French posts.

By December 22, 1944, the first team of thirty-one men and women was ready. They had among them seventeen rifles and a machine gun. Giap wanted a modest victory so that the news would spread through the villages. They attacked a small post whose French officer was off horseback riding. When the officer returned he was killed, and the native Vietnamese troops were released. The Vietminh collected a number of weapons. With each post captured, Giap's brigades increased their armory.

On November 11, 1944, Ho Chi Minh received a gift from the heavens. Lieutenant Rudolph Shaw, the American pilot of a reconnaissance plane, had engine trouble while flying over the mountainous Sino-Indochinese border and parachuted into the Tonkin jungle. A Vietminh unit found him and took him to Pac Bo, forty miles away, where Ho greeted him in English with the question, "Where are you from?"

Shaw's arrival was providential. Ever since June 18, 1919, when Ho had rented a tuxedo and a bowler and gone to Versailles with a petition on behalf of a "Group of Annamite Patriots," he had believed that the United States, as a result of its own history, had an understanding of the colonial problem. He knew that the United States had promised independence to the Philippines. When Shaw asked for help in getting to the Chinese border, Ho offered to escort him to his base in Kunming. Shaw was Ho's entrée to the American command, to whom he could offer his services. They left in December. Once they had crossed the border, however, the Chinese flew Shaw to Kunming and left Ho to shift for himself.

Ho proceeded to Kunming on foot. By the time he reached his destination in January 1945, Shaw had been repatriated to the United States. Despite the departure of his calling card, Ho decided to stay in Kunming with the local Vietminh representative, who ran a coffee shop near the headquarters of the Office of Strategic Services. He was hoping that his retrieval of a downed U.S. airman would earn him a meeting with General Claire Chennault, commander of the U.S. Fourteenth Air Force, in Kunming.

The French Had Lost Face

There was a time when Admiral Jean Decoux, the governor-general of Indochina, had liked to travel around the country, taking part in ceremonies. But since the death of his wife in a car accident, he was morose and deskbound. Aside from his personal problems, the political situation was disastrous. He was a governor-general without a government to answer to, for the men of Vichy had fled to Germany as de Gaulle took Paris. He could not trust his own subordinates, among whom the Free French had made incursions. He knew that General Eugene Mordant, the commander of the French Indochina army, had secretly joined de Gaulle. The admiral hounded the Gaullists in his government with courts-martial and one-way tickets to France.

Decoux was still opposed to any action against the Japanese. Why should Indochina be "liberated" when it was not "occupied"? Despite the demise of Vichy, he remained a good sailor who kept his hand on the tiller. He advised the Gaullists in Paris on August 31, 1944, that Indochina's "neutrality" in the Pacific should be maintained so that "we can survive the end of the fighting without loss." The Free French radio, however, had already announced that Indochina's fate would be settled on the battlefield between France and Japan.

Decoux left Hanoi in February 1945 for his annual trip to Saigon, where he liked to look out the windows of his palatial office at the tricolor floating on the breeze, a symbol of the French sovereignty he had been able to maintain since 1940. In the late afternoon of March 9, he was waiting for the arrival of the Japanese ambassador, Matsumoto Shunichi, whom he thought of as a crude martinet, completely lacking in finesse.

The reason for Matsumoto's visit, Decoux believed, was to discuss the annual rice quota and the French payment for the Japanese occupation, now that fresh troops had been brought in out of fear of an Allied invasion. When Matsumoto arrived at 6:30 P.M., Decoux recalled in his memoirs, he seemed "preoccupied and a bit nervous." As it happened, he was not there for the rice quota, but to present an ultimatum: Decoux was given two hours to place all French forces under Japanese command, as well as the entire government apparatus. An astounded Decoux realized that this "abominable act," in which the Japanese had shown "their consummate Machiavellanism," meant the end of French sovereignty. It was a coup, pure and simple. The Japanese were taking over, completely erasing fifty-five years of French rule.

Some of the slippage in Decoux's government had alarmed the Japanese. He had begun to delay and bicker on the cost of occupation. In September 1944, he had lifted the press ban on articles mentioning de Gaulle. In many government offices, the portraits of Pétain and the Vichy slogans were removed.

The Japanese occupation had been unique in that the sixty thousand French troops had been allowed to remain in their forts and keep their weapons. But in early 1945, the Japanese got wind of Free French activities among *attentiste* elements. French Gaullists were transmitting information on troop movements to help the Americans in their air raids and coastal attacks, and hiding downed American airmen.

More than that, however, the coup was the result of the fortunes of war. The battle of Leyte Gulf, from October 23 to 26, 1944, had crippled the Japanese fleet. The Americans had liberated Manila in early 1945. Admiral William Halsey, commander of the Third Fleet carrier task force, was collecting intelligence on targets along the Indochina coast from French officials, lighthouse keepers, and customs men. When he had enough to "cover the waterfront," as he put it, he sent a task force under Rear Admiral Gerald Bogan on January 9, 1945. It consisted of four carriers, two battleships, six cruisers, and twenty destroyers. As the ships headed for the Indochina coast, Halsey wired: "Give 'em hell." On January 12, half an hour before sunrise, the task force struck Japanese shipping along the coast. U.S. naval aircraft sank forty-four ships, including fifteen warships and twelve oil tankers. Halsey said it was "one of the heaviest blows to Japanese shipping of any day of the war." The attack practically eliminated sea traffic along the Indochina coast. Since U.S. forces were advancing in the Pacific with amphibious landings, the Japanese feared Indochina would be next. Japanese units were moved from Burma and South China as reinforcements under the command of Yuichi Tsuchihashi, the booted, sabered, and tonsured veteran of Java and the Philippines. The order went out "to dispose of French influence in Indochina."

When Decoux was presented with the ultimatum, he realized that if he accepted it he would be branded a traitor to France. He said he had to consult with his military commanders and quickly left his office. By 9 P.M. Decoux was considered to have rejected the ultimatum. He was tracked down, arrested, and detained in a village eighty miles north of Saigon, Loc Ninh.

General Tsuchihashi immediately issued the takeover order to the sixty-seven thousand Japanese troops in Indochina. They attacked French garrisons and police stations, arrested French citizens, and took possession of government buildings, factories, banks, radio stations, and post offices. They seized the weapon stocks in French armories. They released the more than five thousand Vietnamese political prisoners who were locked up in infamous jails such as Poulo Condor, with its tiger cages.

In Hanoi, an hour before the coup, Paul Mus was at the home of General Mordant, who had secretly been named commander of Free French forces in Indochina. Mordant's instructions from de Gaulle were to take part in the liberation of Indochina to ward off any Allied attempts at trusteeship. But now he was facing arrest by the Japanese, and gave himself up the next morning. With the coup, Free French efforts collapsed. Many were captured, some were killed, and others fled toward the Chinese border.

Paul Mus was an unlikely undercover agent to have parachuted into Indochina, being overweight and myopic. He was a distinguished teacher and historian who had grown up in Vietnam and spoke the language fluently. He had seen the Hanoi lycées turn into breeding grounds for revolutionaries. Giap was in his geography class. In January, he had been dropped near Hanoi, and landed in a swamp. After being rescued by villagers, he made his way to General Mordant.

When a phone call alerted the general that the Japanese were storming the Vauban-style fortress known as the Citadelle, he loaned Mus a car to see what was happening. Mus drove into central Hanoi, and when he turned down a side street he saw Japanese soldiers running toward the walls encircling the Citadelle. They carried bamboo ladders to scale the walls over one shoulder while firing with their free hands. Around the main gate lay bodies of the fallen, as the French garrison inside put up a fight. Mus saw Vietnamese scampering out of a side exit, carrying metal plates from the mess hall—they were the waiters, fleeing. Inside the courtyard, flames leaped up as the French burned their archives.

Mus ran into a Free French colleague, Captain Bouvaret, and they decided to flee Hanoi at dawn and try to reach the French post of Son La, two hundred fifty miles to the west. In the next eleven days, without maps, compasses, or provisions, they covered ground on foot, on horseback, and by sampan, guided by Vietnamese made friendly by a Frenchman speaking Annamite. During the trip each man lost forty pounds. Bouvaret caught malaria and Mus's feet were worn down to the bone, but on March 21 they reached Son La.

As Mus later recounted, the Japanese takeover was a cataclysmic experience. In a single night, French sovereignty was shattered. Or rather, the appearance of sovereignty, since the Japanese maintained sixty-seven thousand troops in Indochina and used it as the linchpin of their expansion. "When I left Hanoi," Mus recalled, "thousands of Vietnamese were also fleeing, back to their villages. I saw in their faces a mixture of apprehension and resolution. This was the Annamite nation at last prepared to do what had to be done. The French had 'lost face,' they had been eclipsed and humiliated on March 9, and Indochina would never been the same."

In his *Memoires de guerre,* de Gaulle wrote rather cold-bloodedly that "French blood shed on Indochinese soil would give us an important voice [in later negotiations]. . . . I desired that our troops should fight, no matter how desperate their situation."

In the March 9 coup, an estimated two thousand French officers and men were killed, and twelve thousand were interned. The detention centers were breeding grounds for epidemics, and nearly all of the captives came down with typhoid, cholera, or malaria, although their wives and Vietnamese mistresses (*congai*) were allowed to improve their rations. It was a humbling experience for the French, who were treated the same way they had treated the Vietnamese. The entire colonial scaffolding was dismantled before their eyes.

Suddenly We Were Able to Come Out of the Trees

The Vietnamese took note with deep satisfaction that French power was ephemeral. They became convinced that the colonial power would never return. The French had not been swept out by the hatred of the Vietnamese but by the broom of history. The Vietnamese silently applauded when the tricolor came down and the rising sun went up. Many French officials were replaced by Vietnamese who were experiencing their first taste of power.

For the Vietminh, the March 9 coup was decisive. As Giap recalled: "After so many years of clandestine operations, surviving deep in the forests, slipping past villages in the dark, repressing a cough, placing each foot gingerly one after the other, suddenly we were able to come out of the trees, walk easily along roads amidst the fields, and be received warmly by our countrymen."

Vietminh instructions issued on March 12 pointed out that the Japanese would find it difficult to govern as an Allied invasion loomed. A campaign of strikes and guerrilla attacks had to be organized. French troops were interned and Japanese troops were stretched thin. The guerrilla units could move more freely in the interior. It was an unparalleled opportunity.

The Japanese had allowed the French puppet Bao Dai to remain in place as emperor. He spent much of his time gambling and hunting in the mountains outside the imperial capital of Hue. In April he named a retired history teacher, Tran Trong Kim, prime minister. To mark the end of colonial rule, all French place-names were abolished. Gone were the streets named after heroes of colonialism such as Jules Ferry and Joseph Gallieni. Vietnamese was now the official language for government documents. Court proceedings were conducted in Vietnamese, which effectively blackballed most French lawyers. In Hanoi that May, the Japanese opened a training school for public officials, the first step toward self-rule. In July, they left the administration of Hanoi, Haiphong, and other cities to the Vietnamese. Censorship was relaxed and the Vietnamese press was allowed to denounce colonial practices and discuss the outlines of a free Vietnam. Street parades were permitted, and a rally in Saigon on March 18 drew fifty thousand.

The Japanese had evacuated most of their jungle posts, moving troops to the coastal areas in anticipation of an invasion and giving free rein to the Vietminh, which declared a liberated zone of six border provinces in June. That month the provincial chief of Thai Nguyen Province, forty miles north of Hanoi, warned the Japanese consul general Nishimura Kumao that "Vietminh rebels and pirates [are] forming large bands in the interior to sow disorder. They are abducting district chiefs, pillaging rice warehouses, and abducting tax collectors. In every town, crowds march behind the red flag with the yellow star."

The Vietminh were able to present themselves as the rescuers of a population that was then suffering the scourge of famine. Japanese demands that the peasants plant crops other than rice had led to a 20 percent drop in the rice acreage in Tonkin. This could still have been enough for the north's nine million inhabitants, had not the Japanese and the French stockpiled tons of rice for their own needs. Cochinchina, with its thriving Mekong Delta, had a rice surplus, but deliveries to the north had become increasingly problematic. The railway line north from Saigon was chopped into sections by Allied bombing, as was Route 1, the main road. Trucks could not get through because the bridges had been blown. Reaching Tonkin was hazardous and time-consuming, requiring portages by wagon and coolie.

By December 1944, villagers in the north were eating grass and bark. By February 1945, thousands were dying. The streets of Hanoi were strewn with corpses lying curled in the fetal position. In the countryside, roads were lined with rotting, fly-covered bodies, and beggars roamed the villages eating the scraps left outside doors in bowls for dogs. Ignoring the famine, the Japanese continued to warehouse tons of rice, while issuing ration cards to the Vietnamese. Mortality statistics from Tonkin provinces in May 1945 added up to 380,000 dead, though some areas did not report. Later estimates raised the figure to one million, and the Vietminh claimed two million. In five months, 10 percent of the Tonkin population died of starvation.

In hundreds of villages, the Vietminh elected "liberation councils" to organize the harassment of the enemy. They closed down markets, destroyed roads, cut telephone wires, and attacked isolated patrols. But their main activity was famine relief. At first they issued leaflets warning village officials of "severe punishment" if they helped the collectors of rice quotas. Then they began to form bands of villagers to break into rice depots. On country roads, they ambushed rice-filled carts. Break-ins became common in the Red River Delta. Vietminh leaders reported that in the province of Hung Yen, forty thousand villagers received six hundred tons of "liberated" rice. One granary alone was stocked with one hundred tons. Storage rooms on rice plantations were also "liberated." On the Luoc River, an armed Vietminh band forced two rice-filled sampans to give up their cargo, which villagers carried home in heavy sacks. These exploits made the Vietminh seem heroic, for they were the only ones who were alleviating the famine, the worst disaster in the recent history of Vietnam. The death toll due to Japanese priorities was greater than that of the two nuclear bombs dropped on Japan.

Would You Like to Work for the Americans?

Charles Fenn was a London-born soldier of fortune who, while still in his teens, shipped out on the liner *Aquitania* as a bellboy. He made his way to America, became a citizen, and moved from job to job. When the war broke out, he went to China as a news photographer, and in 1942 he joined the Marines. A year later, when the Office of Strategic Services was formed by "Wild Bill" Donovan, Fenn was detached to the fledgling intelligence agency with the rank of lieutenant. He became known as "Troublesome Fenn," because he went his own way and always knew best. Fenn felt the OSS was overly bureaucratic, and bent on taking over smaller, independent intelligence groups. His comment on the jurisdictional disputes that gummed up the works was, "Let Rome in Tiber melt, and the wide arch of the rang'd Empire fall! Here is my space. Kingdoms are clay."

Fenn was loaned to the Air-Ground Air Service (AGAS), which rescued downed fliers. He was stationed in Kunming, General Chennault's headquarters. AGAS was more to his liking. He handled a net of agents inside Indochina who sent in reports on the radio. Kunming was also to his liking. It had become a cosmopolitan metropolis of three hundred thousand people and was the reception point for supplies that came over the Hump—the Himalayas—from Burma. In the streets with thousand-year-old paving stones as big as chessboards, carts that seemed as old as the streets, pulled by small horses, navigated among the jeeps, the soldiers of many nations, and the swarms of girls. The Chinese girls, Fenn felt, were not on a par with the belles in the polo photographs of American magazines, but they were serviceable. Fenn had a room in the Commerce Hotel where he received his lady friends. The nights were enlivened by dance parties with cases of whiskey and women dressed up "like whores at a wedding." A 10 P.M. curfew had to be established in the city to dampen the exuberance. As Fenn explained it, although U.S. personnel were not involved in combat, there was a constant battle between the GIs chasing tail and the MPs trying to stop them from getting it.

In 1945, at the age of thirty-eight, with his resemblance to Douglas Fairbanks and his leisurely duties at AGAS, Fenn was living the good life. But in March, after the Japanese coup, his agents were shut down and stopped sending reports. It was then that Fenn remembered hearing about a pilot named Shaw, brought in by an Annamite named Ho, who had refused a pile of cash but wanted to meet Chennault. Fenn made inquiries and was told that Ho was still in Kunming and spent his time at the Office of War Information library reading magazines.

Fenn arranged a meeting on March 17 at the Dragon's Gate Café. A frail-looking Annamite showed up, wearing a white cotton suit, with a younger man named Pham. Ho "had the brightest eyes I ever saw," Fenn recalled. Having heard that he was a Communist, Fenn asked if that was the case.

"Some of our members are Communists and some are not," Ho said. "The Chinese and the French call all of us Communists who don't fit into their pattern."

"Would you like to work for the Americans?" Fenn asked.

He explained that Ho and his men could rescue pilots and collect intelligence.

"We could try," Ho said.

"And what would you want in return?"

"American recognition for our League of Independence. Medicine and arms."

"How big is your league?"

"Several hundred at our base. But many thousands scattered over Annam."

Fenn knew that dissidents always exaggerate their manpower, but was nonetheless impressed by Ho's calm and levelheaded manner. "I felt the wing of genius touch mine," he later recalled.

Responding to Ho's request, Fenn took him to meet Chennault. In his faded cotton tunic and sandals, Ho faced the general in his tropical worsted uniform, complete with Sam Browne belt and two rows of medals. Both men knew how to turn on the charm. Chennault told Ho how grateful he was about the rescued pilot. Ho told Chennault how glad he was to help Americans and particularly Chennault, whose exploits with the Flying Tigers he greatly admired. Ho then asked Chennault for his photograph. "There's nothing Chennault liked more than giving his photograph," Fenn recalled. The general rang a bell and a secretary came out with some eight-by-ten glossies. Ho took his pick and Chennault picked up his Parker Golden Arrow pen and wrote in his bold script, "Yours Sincerely, Claire L. Chennault."

The plan was that Ho should return to his camp with two of Fenn's agents and the necessary equipment. The Americans' most urgent need was weather reports, without which Chennault's planes could not fly. One of the agents was a Chinese radio operator, Mac Shin, who spoke some English, had gone to parachute school, and was trained to use a tommy gun. He had the kind of confidence that made him assume everyone liked him. The other was Frank Tan, a Chinese American who had grown up in Boston. But his father, a doctor, felt that he was discriminated against and took the family back to China. Tan was a resourceful and reliable agent who got along well with Ho.

Ho's last request prior to their departure in April was for six Colt .45s in their original wrappings, which Fenn provided. Their equipment included a generator, a transmitter, and a variety of small arms. They needed two L-5s, small planes used for short hops, to reach the Chinese border town of Jingxi. Pham Van Dong was left behind in Kunming. In Jingxi they collected porters for the two-hundred-mile hike through Japanese territory. Then they set out, walking at night for two weeks, reaching Ho's headquarters at the caves of Pac Bo in the last week of April 1945.

Back in Kunming, the OSS, which had lost its French agents in the March coup, told Fenn to pass along the reports he was getting from Ho's headquarters. Then Fenn was told that the Ho operation was coming under OSS control. He felt that he was being pushed around, but had to acquiesce.

The head of OSS special intelligence in China, Colonel Paul E. Helliwell, had been asking General Wedemeyer's headquarters for a green light to work with anti-Japanese Vietnamese. On March 1, in a memo to Wedemeyer, the colonel wrote: "There are a number of revolutionary native groups . . . anti-French as well as anti-Japanese." They were willing to help "in return for monetary advances, or, in some cases, arms and ammunition. . . . I feel it is quite important that we get to work on straight OSS activities in that country." Eight days later the coup gave his request a greater urgency.

The mind-set of a number of OSS officers in China was anticolonial, in line with the views of FDR. OSS officer Austin Glass had lived in Indochina for twenty-five years while working for Standard Oil, and was married to a Vietnamese woman. He wrote in his final report in July 1945: "I do not believe the French have ever understood the Annamite mentality. . . . The liberty they claim for themselves they deny for others. . . . The semi-slavery of the plantation coolies, the corralling of peasants for forced labor on dikes, roads, etc., all are cases in point . . . that is what they have been doing for one hundred years."

Another OSS officer, Archimedes Patti, had run the Indochina desk in Washington in 1944. When he asked Donovan about using Indochinese as agents, the OSS chief told him: "Use anyone who will work with us against the Japanese, but do not become involved in French-Indochinese politics."

On April 13, 1945, Patti arrived in Kunming to take over the Indochina desk of the OSS. He questioned Glass on the situation in Vietnam and learned that AGAS had struck a deal with Ho via Fenn. Patti first thought of using as agents some of the French who had crossed the border into China after the coup, but found "an unattractive picture of indifference, vengefulness, and selfish interests. . . . With their overriding desire for an early recognition of their colony, they withheld critical political and military intelligence. . . . They obstructed American attempts to function within Indochina."

For Patti, the Vietminh were worth a try. He set up a meeting with Ho in the Chinese border town of Jingxi on April 27, while Ho was still in Pac Bo. Ho listed his grievances against the French and explained that he was already working with AGAS to rescue downed airmen. He made it clear, however, that he was open to further collaboration. Patti recalled that "Ho's sincerity, pragmatism, and eloquence made an indelible impression on me." Patti saw no conflict with American policy in Ho's ultimate goal of a free Vietnam, since he was being pressed to obtain results. "They wanted everything and they wanted it right away," Patti said. Ho and the Vietminh seemed to be the answer.

In early May, Ho's group left Pac Bo for a new forward base, a tiny village in the jungle called Tan Trao, not far from the provincial capital of Thai Nguyen. Having been joined by Giap, they arrived at Tan Trao on May 21. They were now only sixty miles from Hanoi. Other groups joined them, some armed guerrillas and some students. Frank Tan reported to Fenn that Mac Shin was teaching the students radio techniques "and they all love him." Every day the guerrillas drilled with the new weapons, though one had a 1904 Remington rifle and another had a flintlock. The air drops were coming in with additional radio transmitters and Ho set up stations in various locations to collect weather data. Ho distributed the six Colts to the leaders of the groups that joined him, to ensure their loyalty. "The American general wanted to send each one of you a token of his regard," he said.

Back in Kunming, Patti was trying to convince his superior, Colonel Helliwell, that it was time to drop OSS teams into Ho's forward base. Even though they were "Marxists," Patti said, their "immediate concern was to fight the Japanese." In the first week of June, Ho informed Patti that he had one thousand well-trained guerrillas ready. Helliwell agreed to send in a small unit dubbed the Deer Team, led by Major Allison Thomas, who admitted that he knew nothing about Indochina, except "that it was a

French colony and the missionaries came over first." However, Thomas, who was in his mid-twenties, had proved himself working behind the lines in France after D-day.

On July 16, 1945, Major Thomas dropped into Tan Trao with five others: a radioman, a weapons man, and three French envoys who were not OSS. They were welcomed by two hundred Vietminh. Thomas was "flabbergasted" when the Vietminh returned a wad of dollars that had fallen out of his pocket when he landed in a banyan tree. A bamboo archway said WELCOME TO OUR AMERICAN FRIENDS, and they celebrated with a case of Hanoi beer captured from the Japanese in a raid on a small hill station the previous day.

The three Frenchmen, two of whom were actually Annamites from the colonial troops, were soon spotted by Giap and sent back to Kunming as untrustworthy. Major Thomas, like other Americans who came into contact with Ho, immediately liked him. In his initial report to Kunming, on July 17, he said: "Forget the Communist Bogy. VML [Viet Minh League] is not Communist. Stands for freedom and reform from French harshness." He also asked for more men, including a medic, and miscellaneous equipment, ranging from maps and mosquito nets to ten M3s with silencers, "good for Jap sentries." His instructions were to work with the guerrillas and find targets of opportunity for the air force.

The rest of the Deer Team landed in the drop zone on July 29, and included the medic Paul Hoagland and René Defourneaux, a Frenchman who had come to the United States at the age of eighteen in 1939 and joined the army in 1942. Detached to the OSS, he was sent to Kunming. In the Vietminh camp he called himself Raymond Douglass. Giap was there to greet them, and apologized for Ho's absence. Upon being told that Ho was ill, Hoagland and Defourneaux went to the village where he was staying. "On a mat in the darkest corner of the room lay a pile of bones covered with yellow, dry skin," Defourneaux recalled. "A pair of glassy eyes stared at us. The man was shaking like a leaf and obviously running a high fever."

"This man doesn't have long for this world," Hoagland said. He had trained as a nurse and served aboard a Swedish liner as a medic. He diagnosed Ho's high fever as a result of malaria, dengue, or dysentery. He ad-

ministered quinine, sulfa, and other medication, and within ten days Ho
was up and about. It is entirely possible that the life of the future president
of North Vietnam was saved by an American medic.

In early August, the Deer Team and the Vietminh guerrillas built a
training camp with barracks for soldiers, a rifle range, and an infirmary.
The OSS men chose forty recruits to train in the use of M1 carbines,
Thompson submachine guns, Brens, bazookas, mortars, flamethrowers,
and hand grenades. They, in turn, would train others. Giap marveled at
seeing his company standing in tidy rows with American rifles and shining bayonets.

Elsewhere, on August 6, a bomb was dropped. Thomas wrote in his
diary for August 16: "Wild hilarity today. At 9 A.M. we heard by our radio
that negotiations for final surrender were almost finished." Giap's troops
marched on Hanoi, and the Deer Team marched with them. After a four-
day slog in the rain, picking off green leeches, Giap's miniature army attacked the provincial capital of Thai Nguyen. The Japanese were dug in
behind the concrete ramparts of an old French fort and firing broke out at
6 A.M. on August 20. Even though the war was over, the OSS team fought
side by side with the Vietminh. Major Thomas, acting against orders,
could not resist this last chance to see the troops the Deer Team had
trained in action. He helped plan the attack and took part in the surrender
negotiations. Defourneaux thought he had "gone nuts." Why take the
chance of getting bumped off now? Six Japanese and three Vietnamese
were in fact killed.

Ho and Giap now saw an opportunity to take over Vietnam, since the
Japanese had surrendered and the French troops were still locked up. In a
single month, the Deer Team had trained a core of two hundred guerrillas
that formed the cadre of Giap's army, allowing Ho to call for "a general insurrection to seize power throughout the country." On August 16, a People's Congress had convened in Tan Trao to approve the flag of an
independent Vietnam—a gold star upon a field of red.

For the Deer Team, the war was over. Thai Nguyen was their last battle,
and the first for Ho and Giap in their war of independence. On August 26,
Thai Nguyen celebrated its freedom with a parade. Then it was on to Hanoi
for the Vietminh and back to Kunming for the Deer Team. Vietminh guer-

rillas invested Hanoi unopposed and by the end of August were in control of the city. They occupied the major public buildings. But they were not in control of the south, which was alive with armed groups of various persuasions. In Hanoi, however, Ho Chi Minh proclaimed Vietnam's independence on September 2, 1945.

The United States Recognizes French Sovereignty over Indochina

Nineteen forty-five was one of those years in which too much was going on in rapid sequence, as if, in geological terms, the planet was being hit by a succession of earthquakes, tsunamis, and hurricanes. The death of FDR in April, followed by the founding of the United Nations in San Francisco; the German surrender in May, the Potsdam Conference in July, the surrender of Japan in August. And the proclamation of Indochina's independence in September.

Harry S. Truman took the oath of office on April 12 and became the thirty-third president of the United States. He was thrown into the bubbling international cauldron with little experience in foreign affairs, at a time when the Grand Alliance was breaking up and the Soviets were using their elbows. In Truman's lap lay all the issues that FDR had deferred, his high-flown Wilsonian rhetoric masking his sphere-of-influence arrangements.

Truman inherited the loose ends. "Shall we invade Japan proper or shall we bomb and blockade?" he asked himself in his diary. The firebombing had begun in March, but still Japan did not admit defeat. The policy of unconditional surrender, announced at Casablanca in 1943, now seemed to be prolonging the war. Why not let the Japanese keep their emperor, whose rule was symbolic? General George C. Marshall argued that an invasion would be necessary to end the war. But the island-hopping strategy was causing huge losses.

One day after FDR's death, Undersecretary of the Army Robert A. Lovett told the State-War-Navy Coordinating Committee that Roosevelt's ban on helping the French in Indochina was "a source of serious embarrassment to the military." The State Department member of the committee said that in his bailiwick there was "a divergence of views." The Sub-committee for the Far East expressed support for FDR's anticolonial line, while in the European subcommitee, there was no wish to antagonize France, which was needed to rebuild Europe and check Soviet expansion.

Trusteeship had never been more than a gleam in FDR's eye, and now that gleam had faded. After his triumphant entry into Paris in August 1944, de Gaulle formed a provisional government, which was duly recognized by Britain and the United States. De Gaulle wanted to take part in the operations against Japan to reaffirm France's sovereignty over Indochina. But FDR was against incorporating French troop contingents into Mountbatten's South East Asia Command. An OSS report on August 9, 1944, said that if French forces were used to oust Japan, "U.S. chances for directly influencing Indochinese policy" might be reduced.

France, after all, was a stricken nation, whose contribution to the Allied cause had been marginal. Thus, France was relegated to a minor position, and was not invited to either Yalta or Potsdam. De Gaulle had to fight for his seat at the diplomatic table. As the influential Texas senator Tom Connally put it: "The U.S., England, Russia, and China are the four nations that have shed their blood for the rest of the world, whereas France's part in the war has only been that of a small nation."

In 1945, however, the United States began moving in the direction of restoring France's colonial possessions. On April 21, the U.N. conference opened in San Francisco, with plenary sessions at the War Memorial Opera House. It labored on until June 23, mainly due to Soviet intransigence and obstructionism, a forecast of the Cold War. But for France the conference ended with a victory, since it began with the Big Four and concluded with the Big Five—the permanent members of the Security Council.

The French delegate was de Gaulle's foreign minister, Georges Bidault, an antiappeasement journalist of the thirties turned Resistance leader during the war. The skeptical, caustic Bidault was attending his first international conference, which he found to be "run exactly like an American political convention." It was also his first encounter with John Foster Dulles, who was there as an adviser to Senator Arthur Hendrick Vandenberg. Bidault found Dulles to be "naïve and clumsily sly," with a "notorious lack of subtlety and insight."

He had better luck with Harold Stassen, elected governor of Minnesota at the age of thirty-two (the youngest ever) but now serving as a naval officer. Detached to the U.N. delegation to handle trustee matters, Stassen was against breaking up colonial empires and told Bidault they were like "the American federal system." Bidault had even better luck with the novice Secretary of State Stettinius, who told him on May 8 that "the record is entirely innocent of any official statement of the United States government questioning, even by implication, French sovereignty over Indochina." This was a clever way of announcing a change in policy, without seeming to depart from Roosevelt's wishes, which had been off the cuff, never formally declared. Then in June came a statement from the State-War-Navy Coordinating Committee that "the United States recognize French sovereignty over Indochina." Truman was on board, even though he had hoped to carry out his predecessor's wishes.

In June 1945, de Gaulle named General Jacques-Philippe Leclerc commander of an expeditionary corps for Indochina. It was Leclerc who had led the French 2nd Armored Division into Paris and accepted the German surrender.

At his headquarters in the mountain resort of Kandy, Ceylon, which boasted a temple housing one of Buddha's teeth, Mountbatten was an unhappy admiral. Born Battenberg, he was the great-grandson of Queen Victoria and a favorite of Churchill's, who in 1943 named him supreme Allied commander in Southeast Asia. In October 1943 he had made a "gentlemen's agreement" with Chiang Kai-shek that their commands could share Indochina. But in February 1945, General Wedemeyer, Chiang Kai-shek's chief of staff, told the British that he was "diametrically opposed to [Mountbatten's] agreement with Gismo [Chiang Kai-shek]." Mountbatten protested to the Foreign Office on February 8 that it was "militarily indefensible that this command be hampered by American obstruction which we know to be based on purely political considerations." Mountbatten was head of South East Asia Command, and Wedemeyer was supposed to be his subordinate.

Mountbatten had in fact been dropping Gaullist agents into Indochina from an airport near Calcutta. On January 23, 1945, three U.S. planes shot down three British bombers on a mission over Indochina, mistaking them for Japanese planes. Could this be called friendly fire? Mountbatten had his doubts. Yet he was not deterred, and informed General Wedemeyer in May that he planned to conduct twenty-six more sorties over Indochina. Wedemeyer was furious. He was convinced the British were trying to sway political developments. They could drop weapons the French might use against the Vietminh, who were fighting the Japs. He complained to General Marshall on May 28 that the British intrusion in his theater pointed to the existence of a "British and French plan to re-establish their pre-war political and economic positions in Southeast Asia."

But Wedemeyer was behind the curve, and General Marshall informed him on June 4 that the new State Department position "eliminates the political necessity of curtailing Lord Mountbatten's operations in Indochina." When Patrick Hurley, the U.S. ambassador to China, warned President Truman that the British were "trying to reestablish French imperialism," Secretary of State Stettinius on June 7 brought him up to speed: "The United States welcomes French participation in the Pacific war to the extent practical, and U.S. forces in China are free to cooperate with French Resistance groups in Indochina." But Wedemeyer continued to insist that Indochina was entirely within the China theater.

Wedemeyer was on target regarding the intentions of the British, who feared that if the United States opposed a French return to Indochina their colonies would be next. As the British ambassador in Chungking put it in February 1944, "any attempt to abrogate French rule in Indochina cannot fail to react on the position of other nations holding possessions in the Far East, e.g. the Dutch and ourselves." Britain also needed France as a strong partner in Europe, the key to postwar stability. An unfriendly power within 250 miles of London was out of the question. And what would France be without its empire? France needed Indochina to reassert herself as a great power.

The Dreadful Division at Potsdam

On July 16, 1945, Averell Harriman, the U.S. ambassador to the Soviet Union, was driving through the wasteland of Berlin on the way to the suburb of Potsdam, where the Big Three conference was about to begin. Entire blocks of apartment houses had toppled into the streets as if pushed by a giant hand, giving him a keen sense of what defeat had wrought. The Russians had already stripped the factories, according to their interpretation of "surplus tools" agreed to at Yalta.

Potsdam was in the Russian zone, and everywhere he saw green-capped Soviet troops, even in trees. The conference was to take place in the Cicilienhof Palace, a two-story country estate of ivy-covered stone overlooking a lake. In the courtyard, the Soviets had planted a red star of geraniums. Untouched by the war, Potsdam was a serene location, with many stately homes where the delegations stayed.

The Americans were occupying a lakeside villa dubbed the "Little White House." President Truman had worked hard while crossing the Atlantic aboard the heavy cruiser *Augusta,* and had brought with him Henry Stimson, who was still secretary of war. Still, Truman felt at a disadvantage, for he had never met the other principals, Churchill and Stalin, who were bound to compare him to his predecessor. He wrote his mother: "I wish this trip was over. I hate it, but it has to be done."

The French were excluded from Potsdam, not being counted among the victorious nations. It was as if there was a sign that said FRENCH NOT ALLOWED, recalled the historian Paul Mus. What a disastrous impression that made on the Vietnamese, who saw France treated as a second-rate, expendable nation.

Momentous decisions were on the agenda, such as German reparations, elections in Eastern Europe, and the surrender of Japan. Meanwhile, in the desert near Alamogordo, New Mexico, at 5:30 A.M. on July 16, a nuclear implosion bomb was successfully tested. When Truman heard the news that evening, he said it took a great load off his mind.

On July 17, Stalin dropped by the Little White House for an impromptu lunch of liver and bacon and announced that he would be ready to declare war on Japan on August 15, a pledge he had made at Yalta. An elated Truman wrote in his diary: "Fini Japs." By July 21, Stimson had the first full report on the enormous energy generated by the bomb, the first of which would be ready between August 1 and August 6. Truman was "tremendously pepped up by it," Stimson wrote in his diary. "He said it gave him a totally new feeling of confidence." At the same time, Truman began to wonder if Russia was still needed against Japan. But the U.S. Joint Chiefs, who were at the conference, wanted the Russians to come in to save American troops from conducting a land war in Asia. No one yet knew what the effect of the bomb would be.

On July 24, Truman told Stalin that the United States had a weapon "of unusual destructive force." Stalin nodded and said nothing, according to his translator, V. N. Pavlov. He didn't have to say anything, since he already knew about the bomb from his spies and had launched his own nuclear program. Churchill was also told in more specific detail.

In the meantime, the conference dragged on. The camaraderie of past conferences was lacking. Stalin was an ally in Manchuria but a foe in Eastern Europe. The postwar landgrab had begun. Stalin was bent on annexing the areas where he had boots on the ground. Churchill had to return to London after the unexpected Labour landslide replaced him with the mousy Clement Attlee, who had been brought to Potsdam just in case.

The only one left of the original Big Three was Stalin, who lorded over the others. Truman wondered why, even though he was taller than both Stalin and Churchill, the press described him as short. It occurred to Harriman that while TERMINAL was the U.S. code word for Potsdam, there was nothing terminal about it, for it raised more problems than it solved. The news about the bomb made it clear that Japan could be defeated without Soviet help. But it was too late to tell Stalin he was neither needed nor wanted. George Marshall believed that the bomb, which rendered the island-hopping strategy obsolete, would save half a million American lives.

On the large questions, Potsdam got nowhere, but other decisions were made that would have vast international repercussions. Surrender planning, an often overlooked aspect of war, is in fact as crucial as combat. In a world war, allied armies must be mobilized in multiple theaters to disarm and repatriate the enemy.

At the Pentagon, by May 1945, staff papers on surrender tactics were circulating in the multilayered War Plans bureaucracy. The planners were focused on the invasion of the Japanese home islands. This meant not diverting U.S. troops in surrender operations to the many other locations where the Japanese were entrenched. But because Japanese surrender did not seem imminent, many specific issues were not addressed. The feeling was that it would take time to rest and reequip the troops who would move into all the places in Southeast Asia and the Pacific that the Japanese held. Also, surrender had to be coordinated with the Allies, who would provide those troops outside Japan. The Soviets were expected to occupy Manchuria and northern Korea, while the Americans would occupy the Japanese home islands. General MacArthur had asked for twenty-two divisions for Japan alone.

At the Potsdam Conference, the surrender arrangements were made at a meeting of the Combined Chiefs of Staff of the participating powers, on July 24. (The U.S. Joint Chiefs were General George Marshall, General Henry H. "Hap" Arnold, and Admiral Ernest King.) Churchill asked Mountbatten to be there, and told him about the bomb, but specified that he should keep it to himself. Mountbatten attended the meeting at a time when he was deeply impressed by the battle of Okinawa, which had just ended. It had taken eighty-two days and cost twelve thousand American lives. The Japanese simply would not surrender. The kamikaze (divine wind) flew nineteen hundred suicide sorties and sank twenty-six ships. In the ground fighting, there were few wounded Japanese. They either died of their wounds, returned to the front lines to be killed, or committed suicide. The men held hand grenades to their stomachs and blew themselves up, while the generals committed ceremonial hara-kiri. If this was the way they defended outlying islands, Mountbatten thought, what would they do in their homeland? Thus, when he was told about the bomb, he felt that it was the only way to proceed. At the same time, he was concerned that he had to tell his staff to prepare for a quick Japanese surrender without giving them a reason why. His South East Asia Command had a vast surrender area extending from Burma to Malaya to the Dutch East Indies. He had expected to occupy these areas in stages, one at a time, but if the bomb was used he would have to occupy them all at once. In Burma there were still 60,000 Japanese, in Malaya 116,000, half a million in the Dutch East Indies, and 110,000 in Indochina.

His worst headache was Indochina, where his command was in dispute with Wedemeyer's China theater. He hoped to be in charge of surrender for all Indochina, since he was also responsible for adjacent Siam. But the Combined Chiefs decided otherwise. Since the French were not ready with troops and ships to reoccupy their colony, the surrender of Indochina was divided between the Chinese in the north and the British in the south. The boundary was set at the 16th parallel, south of Tourane (Da Nang). It was a purely military decision, made to release American commanders from mopping up Japanese troops in the former colonies of the British, the Dutch, and the French. That way they could concentrate on the main effort of occupying the home islands. It had, however, political implications. In the north, the Chinese occupation gave Ho Chi Minh a window of opportunity to establish a Democratic Republic of Vietnam. In the south, the British helped the French gain a foothold that would extend into reconquest and war. According to the minutes of the July 24 meeting, Mountbatten agreed to the partition, while expressing concern that "the French might find the proposition a little less agreeable." But in time he came to feel that "the dreadful division at Potsdam" prevented any unified settlement for Indochina and proved to be the origin of the long and bitter wars to follow. Partition was a disaster, he felt, for which the entire world suffered for years.

That was the point of view of an imperialist, but for the anticolonialist Paul Mus, the fact that the French had no part in the surrender arrangements made their return illegitimate. They would arrive on the heels of the British. It would seem as if they were sneaking back, in a kind of second-story break-in, doomed from the start. But at the time, no one imagined that this small corner of Asia had much significance in the context of ending the war. On August 1, 1945, the last day of Potsdam, Truman wrote Chiang Kai-shek that the north of Indochina would be included in the China theater. Chiang replied that he was pleased to comply. A few days earlier, on July 26, the Potsdam Proclamation called for Japan's unconditional surrender and warned that refusal would mean Japan's "prompt and utter destruction." The Japanese reply was *mokusatsu* (to kill with silence). Truman approved the use of the bomb; its assembly and delivery were under way. The first bomb was dropped on Hiroshima on August 6. Still the Japanese did not surrender. The Soviets declared war on Japan on August 9 and stormed into Manchuria, just as *Bock's Car* was flying to Nagasaki, carrying the "Fat Man" bomb. On August 10, Emperor Hirohito ordered an end to the war. Truman announced the surrender on August 14 (retaining the emperor). He had to make some far-reaching decisions that are still being debated. Was the A-bomb necessary? Was Soviet help against Japan necessary? The partition of Vietnam was a minor item of the surrender strategy, except to the French, who protested in vain.

At the Pentagon's Office of Planning and Defense, Colonel Robert Wood observed: "When the Japanese surrendered, it caught the whole goddamn administrative machinery with their pants down." Forces in the Pacific were dispersed. Troops earmarked for combat were now needed for occupation. There were two million Japanese troops in China. Who was going to disarm them? The Joint Chiefs of Staff were faced with over-whelming surrender problems: to assemble the shipping, which would tie up the entire U.S. Navy; to land a division in South Korea, to prevent the Soviets from swallowing up the entire country; to prepare a surrender document, giving each theater commander his orders. After the first bomb exploded, it was a race against the clock. General Order No. 1 was drafted by Colonel Charles Bonesteel and Colonel Dean Rusk, working from a wall map. It called for the occupation of the Japanese home islands and south-ern Korea by U.S. forces. The dividing line in Korea was pushed far enough north so that Seoul was in the U.S. zone. Northern Korea went to the Sovi-ets and the rest of Southeast Asia went to the British, with the exception of northern Vietnam, where Chinese troops moved in. The lines Bonesteel and Rusk drew facing a deadline rearranged the postwar world.

The surrender documents had to be approved by the British, the Chi-nese, and the Soviets. For the latter, surrender arrangements were but a continuation of the wartime game of grab. On August 16, Stalin asked to occupy the northern half of the home island of Hokkaido. In a show of firmness, Truman informed him that the Japanese home islands would surrender only to U.S. troops. It was clear that the United States had de-feated Japan almost single-handedly. But in other ways, the results of the surrender policy were ruinous. Korea was partitioned, which led to a war. China was on the verge of civil war. How could Truman foresee that invit-ing Stalin to declare war on Japan would help Mao Tse-tung defeat Chiang Kai-shek four years later?

On September 2, 1945, the surrender documents were signed aboard the USS *Missouri* in Tokyo Bay. Winning the war was simple—a matter of two bombs—compared to winning the surrender. Events took on a momentum of their own, with U.S. troops in Japan, China, and Korea, Soviet troops in Korea and Manchuria, and British and Chinese troops in Indochina. Truman described postwar Asia as a "land grab stampede."

France Means to Recover Its Sovereignty over Indochina

In his base camp of Tan Trao, Ho Chi Minh was following the news on the radio. The first bomb. The second bomb. The surrender. But for Ho, as well as for the Allies, the surrender came too soon. He was not ready for a full-scale war against the French. In addition, Chinese and British occupation forces would arrive in Vietnam within a month. However, with the French still locked up and the Japanese out of the picture, there was a tempting vacuum. Ho decided to occupy Hanoi, declare the independence of Vietnam, and form a government before the Chinese poured over the border. It was mid-August, and he had roughly until mid-September. On August 16, 1945, he summoned sixty delegates to a National People's Congress in Tan Trao and called for a general insurrection.

Hundreds of Vietminh militants in Hanoi were enrolled in units formed to occupy government buildings. August 19 was a Sunday. The stores were shuttered. Red flags hung from every lamppost. At noon, from a balcony of the Municipal Theater, a Vietminh officer told a crowd of twenty thousand that the insurrection was under way. The crowd formed columns, each marching on a strategic building—city hall, police headquarters, the main post office, water and electricity facilities. Japanese soldiers looked on, while the fifteen thousand French civilians barricaded themselves in their homes. By sundown Hanoi was in the hands of the Vietminh, which named a People's Committee to run things.

In Hanoi and other cities, the Vietminh seized power in a bloodless coup, taking advantage of the interregnum after the Japanese had laid down their arms, the French were still detained, and the occupiers had not yet arrived. From the Delta to the mountains, the corrupt incumbency of mandarins and notables was evicted, prison doors were opened, French taxes were abolished, land rents reduced, communal rice fields distributed, and equality proclaimed.

One August morning at dawn, an American warship docked at

Haiphong. The naval lieutenant and later senator Mark Hatfield saw the colored tiles of the gambling casino at the top of the hill lit by the sun. Behind the harbor, he saw the squalid huts at the base of the hill. The casino, he reflected, was symbolic of colonial power, in contrast to the absolute deprivation, the rags and the poverty of an exploited people.

Meanwhile, in Washington on August 22, General de Gaulle met President Truman, who pledged not to hinder the return of the French. Encouraged by the change of direction since the death of FDR, de Gaulle gave a press conference on August 24, stating that "the position of France in Indochina is very simple. France means to recover its sovereignty over Indochina." He was told in Washington that U.S. Lend-Lease supplies could be used by Leclerc's forces as long as the insignia were removed, so that the United States could not be accused of assisting a colonial power.

De Gaulle had named a commissioner for Indochina. He was Jean Sainteny, an insurance broker in civilian life, who was stranded in Kunming trying to catch an OSS flight to Hanoi. But in Kunming it was raining biblical torrents. The streets were navigable only by boat, and no planes were taking off. Finally, on August 22, he left with the OSS agent Archimedes Patti, who was heading a thirteen-man "Mercy Team" to arrange for the liberation of twenty thousand Allied prisoners of war and fifteen thousand civilians.

Flying into Hanoi, Sainteny saw what he thought at first were fields of poppies, which turned out to be Vietminh flags. As he drove into the city, huge crowds were gathered on the Avenue Carnot, but hardly a white face. Somehow Sainteny coaxed the Japanese into letting him occupy the governor-general's palace. He found the silver, the china, and the linen to be in good order, but the houseboys had fled. Sainteny was the odd man out, even though he represented, for the moment, the French presence in Indochina. The Japanese ignored him, and the old-time *colons* still loyal to Vichy avoided him. He was not allowed out of the building he occupied, which was guarded by one ring of Japanese and another of Vietminh. His first wire to Kunming said: "Situation in Hanoi worse than anything we could have imagined." His second wire on August 24 said that the Japanese had furnished weapons and a patrol boat to the Vietminh. A few days later the French presence grew to eleven when he was joined by some navy men who came in via Haiphong. When Patti paid them a visit, Sainteny was fuming over a headline in a local paper that said: VIET MINH FIGHTING WITH U.S. TROOPS IN TONKIN WILL SOON BE HERE TO OUST THE FRENCH OPPRESSORS WHO LAST YEAR STARVED TWO MILLION PEOPLE.

Patti saw Hanoi as "a boiling caldron of conflicting interests," with an unstable population of 150,000. Armed Japanese out of uniform plundered French homes and set fire to Vietnamese shops and warehouses. Five thousand French troops were still imprisoned in the Citadelle, a garrison complex of buildings sandwiched between the botanical garden and the sports stadium. French schools were closed and French doctors were evicted from the Institut Pasteur. On August 24, the formation of a "Provisional People's Government" was announced. There followed a blizzard of edicts ranging from repealed taxes to an order that all armed groups disband and join the Vietnam Liberation Army.

Provisional Government Groping in the Dark

On August 25, Ho Chi Minh, the president of the provisional government, crossed the Doumer Bridge and entered Hanoi, soon to be followed by Giap and his men. They were unopposed by the thirty thousand Japanese still in and around the city. In all his fifty-five years, Ho had never been to Hanoi. He and Giap stayed with sympathizers, in a badly lit two-story house on an ancient street. "Uncle," as Giap called him, wearing brown shorts and a crumpled hat, kept his beat-up typewriter on a small table covered by green felt. He slept on a cot that was folded into a corner during the day. He was changing the history of his country, but his hosts did not even know his name.

Standing on a balcony, Giap saw the Chinese advance troops struggle in. "Their faces were puffy and jaundiced," he recalled. "Their yellow uniforms, the shade of turmeric, were ragged and filthy. They lugged baskets full of junky items on poles. Some even brought women and children. Many had legs swollen by beriberi." They did not look like a victorious army.

Ho was facing a perilous situation. There was no money in the state treasury and no rice in the warehouses. Ninety percent of the population was illiterate. Few had any government experience. Foreign troops were due from all directions. But for every problem there was a solution. "We will make mistakes but we will correct them," Ho said. Giap could not help but remember Lenin's words: "It is difficult to seize power, but it is even more difficult to keep it."

On August 26, acting as a middleman, Patti arranged a meeting between Giap and Sainteny. It did not go well. Sainteny was unable to avoid the patronizing tone of the colonial overseer. Why had the Vietminh, he asked, recklessly chosen to let the world know that the French presence in Indochina was no longer welcome? In excellent French, Giap replied that he was not there to be lectured. Sainteny realized that the old order was doomed and expressed in vague terms a desire for change. Giap asked him to be specific. Sainteny said he hoped for a Franco-Annamite alliance. Once Giap left, Sainteny told Patti that he felt he had convinced the Vietminh leader that getting along without the French was an "infantile presumption."

At the first cabinet meeting on August 27, September 2 was fixed as Independence Day. Chinese troops had begun to stream across the border in large numbers. Giap told Patti he was concerned that the Chinese might overthrow the provisional government and replace it with Vietnamese "renegades" they were bringing with them.

On August 29, Patti met with Ho Chi Minh, who seemed to want American help without openly asking for it. Ho told Patti that Emperor Bao Dai had abdicated in Hue, passing power to the Vietminh. Like Giap, Ho was worried that the Chinese would bring their own Vietnamese, whom he called "pseudo-nationalists" and "lackeys of the Kuomintang." The Chinese might try to force these opportunists on him to form a puppet government.

After his meeting with Ho, Patti reported to the OSS in Kunming: "Provisional government groping in the dark . . . I am convinced that they are not politically mature. . . . They call 'nationalization' . . . essential to the livelihood of the new government. . . . Whole business has misguided Soviet tinge." On September 1, he cabled: "Provisional Government . . . is composed of left-wing elements." In his memoirs, however, Patti was less critical of the infant regime. He kept shuttling from Ho's humble residence to Sainteny's governor-general's palace, he wrote, and though the distance was short, the transition took him from feeling the elation of launching a free nation to sensing the anxieties of maintaining an unwanted and dying empire.

On Sunday, September 2, 1945, crowds began converging in the morning on Hanoi's Ba Dinh Square, where a platform had been erected for the occasion. All vehicular traffic was blocked by the human wave of mottled groups typical of the Vietnamese population: gnarled and barefoot mountain people, villagers led by their elders, Buddhist monks and Catholic priests, peasant women in yellow turbans with layered skirts, city women wearing long four-paneled skirts, workers in open-collared white shirts and blue pants. Downtown Hanoi was a rippling red sea of flags, and banners strung across streets. DOWN WITH FRENCH COLONIALISM. INDEPENDENCE OR DEATH. A poster showed a Vietnamese being decapitated, with the caption: HERE IS FRENCH DOMINATION.

An autumn sun bathed the square as the dignitaries arrived on the platform. Below them stood a guard of honor in pith helmets and khaki uniforms. Bands played and militias marched, carrying an array of weapons that ranged from spears to submachine guns. A contingent of female soldiers astonished the Vietnamese who filled the square.

A little after 2 P.M., a gaunt man approached the microphone. Having roamed the globe for thirty years, he was back among his people, most of whom were seeing him for the first time, when he was introduced as "the liberator and savior of the nation." The crowd was hushed as he spoke. His opening sentences sounded familiar to the OSS men in the crowd: "We hold these truths to be self-evident. That all men are created equal, that they are endowed by their creator with certain inalienable rights, and that among these are Life, Liberty, and the Pursuit of Happiness." Ho had borrowed from the American Declaration of Independence to underscore that September 2 was the Vietnamese Fourth of July.

He stopped and asked: "My fellow citizens, can you hear what I'm saying?" A mighty roar assured him that they could. Ho went on to describe French depredations as "counter to the ideals of humanity and justice," and concluded that "we have won back our independence from Japanese hands and not from the French." It was a mesmerizing performance. As

Giap listened, he felt that Ho had revived the nation, offering freedom to each citizen. Whatever difficulties lay ahead, the colonial power would have to fight to regain its lost paradise.

Ho Chi Minh Is Riding a Wild Horse Bareback and Holding Only One Rein

The jubilation of September 2, however, soon turned to anxiety, as the population of Vietnam nervously awaited the arrival of the Chinese in the north and the British in the south. Caught up in his meetings with Ho and Sainteny, Archimedes Patti began to realize that he had no inkling of what the Truman policy might be toward the takeover of Vietnam by the Communists. On September 4, he flew to Chungking to seek advice from the U.S. embassy and military brass. There he met with Brigadier General George Olmsted, standing in for Wedemeyer, OSS colonel Paul Helliwell, and John Hall Paxton, the second secretary at the embassy.

Olmsted said that Indochina had been neglected in light of more pressing issues, but that it was time to address the problems there. Apparently the trusteeship issue had been abandoned. But where did that leave them?

Helliwell asked, "What is the policy? Do we help the French take control? Do we help Ho set up a quote democratic unquote regime? Or do we bug out?"

Paxton said, "Ho Chi Minh is in place but riding a wild horse bareback and holding only one rein." The United States had not recognized his government but could perhaps give him moral support.

It occurred to Patti: You ask for policy guidance and you draw a blank.

On September 9, Patti returned to Hanoi, flying south at about a thousand feet. Below, he could see what looked like a giant earthworm crawling along Route Coloniale 2. Dropping lower to get a closer look, he saw a mix of bicycles, animal-drawn wagons, and military vehicles. Men on foot with bundles over their shoulders prodded flocks of chickens and geese, herds of pigs and water buffalo. This armed menagerie was Chiang Kai-shek's 93rd Yunnan Division.

The next day, back in Hanoi, Patti heard shouted instructions and the racing of engines. The bulk of the 180,000 occupation troops were entering the city. There seemed to be two distinct armies, one of disciplined men in blue uniforms, carrying American weapons, who quickly fanned out beyond Hanoi, and a rear echelon of derelicts who sat in private court-yards brewing tea and doing their laundry.

For Jean Sainteny, the Chinese occupation was like one of the seven plagues. "We plunged into an incredible chaos," he recalled. The Chinese ignored him. His authority existed only on paper. Every day he encountered open hostility. The occupiers threw French families out of their homes and did nothing when civilians were mugged in the street by overexcited Vietnamese youths.

When General Lu Han, the commander of this ragtag army, arrived in Hanoi on September 14, he evicted Sainteny from the governor-general's palace. The humbled commissioner moved to a small villa near the Bank of Indochina. Lu Han asked the French, who still ran the bank, for 150 million piastres for urgent military needs, plus 96 million piastres a month for occupation expenses. He arbitrarily raised the exchange rate between the Chinese yuan and the Vietnamese piastre from 1 to 1.5, increasing the purchasing power of the occupation troops by 50 percent. Every flight from Kunming brought in millions of Chinese yuan, which the troops could exchange at the inflated rate.

As it turned out, the Chinese occupation was focused on profiteering. Disarming the Japanese was secondary to looting; buying and selling to governing; and confiscation to the maintenance of security. The Chinese requisitioned private homes and sold the furniture and fixtures and even the tiles off the roofs. Through front men, Chinese officers bought hotels and shops, factories and plantations.

As Sainteny put it, "the Chinese practiced every form of looting and chicanery." Chinese gendarmes at the airport searched luggage and "con-fiscated" what they wanted. Vehicles belonging to French civilians were also confiscated and sold to dealers. In Haiphong Harbor, small craft were seized and sent to China. Lu Han generously donated to the Kunming li-brary two hundred rare volumes stolen from the Hanoi library. Sainteny saw a grand piano loaded aboard a Kunming-bound plane.

For Ho Chi Minh, the plunder of his country, added to the shaky econ-omy and the famine, was one more burden. And yet he tried to avoid clashes. He had to walk a tightrope to keep from giving the Chinese an excuse to replace his provisional government with the Vietnamese puppets they had brought along.

It also became clear that the Chinese intended to prolong the occupation as long as they could, not only to fill their pockets but to extract concessions from the French in return for leaving. The Chinese wanted the French to give up ownership of the part of the Haiphong–Kunming railroad in Chinese territory. They also wanted a customs-free port for Chinese imports and exports in Haiphong, and the return of prewar French territorial concessions in half a dozen Chinese cities.

When Lu Han met Ho Chi Minh on September 16, the general gave tacit recognition to the Vietminh regime by addressing him as "President Ho." They struck an informal deal: Ho agreed to the bloated exchange rate and Lu Han accepted the provisional government. When Lu Han demanded to know the troop strength of the Liberation Army, Ho disingenuously told him that there was no such army, but only a national guard. For Ho, Lu Han's most annoying demand was to set back the clocks one hour to conform to Chinese time, which he saw as a typical example of Chinese arrogance. However, Ho kept his complaints to himself and tried to meet Lu Han's demands, whether for sugar, lightbulbs, or opium.

Ho needed weapons. The Chinese let him know that guns taken from the Japanese could be had for a price—cash only. This led to Gold Week, from September 16 to 22, when the Vietnamese were asked to donate their coins and jewelry at long tables covered with white cloth in front of the governor-general's building. Speeches were interspersed with music as well-to-do Vietnamese in long silken mandarin coats deposited their belongings alongside peasants offering humble wedding bands. After a personal appeal from Ho, the Vietminh collected 815 pounds of gold worth twenty million piastres, two thirds of which was used to buy arms.

Gold Week was also a popularity poll, giving Ho a mandate for change. He enacted measures such as land reform and exemption from the head tax. He outlawed the hated state monopolies on salt, alcohol, and opium, banning use of the latter two, as well as prostitution and gambling. Forced labor was abolished and an eight-hour workday was decreed. Workers were encouraged to form unions. A nationwide literacy program was launched.

In the meantime, Archimedes Patti's days of glory as go-between were

numbered. On September 16, General Philip E. Gallagher, the chief of the
U.S. Military Advisory and Assistance Group (MAAG), arrived in Hanoi attached to General Lu Han's staff. Gallagher took an immediate dislike to
Patti, whom he said "talks too much . . . he loves to appear mysterious and
is an alarmist. . . . When I enter a room I expect him to come out from
under the rug." Although temperamental opposites, Gallagher and Patti
both favored the Vietminh over the French. In a letter to a friend on September 20, Gallagher reported that "Ho Chi Minh . . . is definitely in the sad-
dle. . . . He is a product of Moscow, a Communist. . . . They now claim their
independence. . . . They are armed, well supplied, and will resist all French
efforts to take over Indochina. . . . Ho looks upon America as the savior of
all nations. . . . Confidentially, I wish the Annamites could be given their
independence, but of course, we have no voice in the matter." This was a
personal opinion in the absence of discernible American policy. Many of
the Americans who met Ho Chi Minh preferred him and his followers to
the French colonists, even though they could not resolve the paradox of a
Moscow-trained Communist who claimed to be pro-American.

On September 28, 1945, the official surrender ceremony was held at
the governor-general's palace, beneath the flags of the Big Four—America, Britain, China, and the Soviet Union. No French flag flew, nor did the
Vietminh flag, for neither was recognized by the Chinese as a participant
in the war. General Tsuchihashi signed the official document. On September 29, Patti left Hanoi. On October 1, the OSS was disbanded, as were
many other temporary wartime agencies. One of "Wild Bill" Donovan's
last memos to Truman, on September 27, asserted that General Lu Han
was an open advocate of an end to colonial rule and was "satisfied to support the Vietminh."

Americans Will Be Regarded with Suspicion

Thanks to family connections and a will to strive, Colonel A. Peter Dewey
had compiled, by the age of twenty-eight, an impressive résumé. He was
the son of an isolationist congressman from Illinois who was also an international banker, and the nephew of Thomas E. Dewey, the governor of
New York who ran twice for president. After majoring in French history at

Yale, Dewey found a slot in the Paris office of *The Chicago Daily News.* When war broke out, he managed to attach himself to the Polish Military Ambulance Corps, from which he emerged with ribbons on his chest—the Croix de Guerre, the Croix du Combattant, and the Order of Polonia Restituta. Back in America, he wrote a book on the fall of France. In 1942, he joined the army as a second lieutenant and a year later he was attached to the OSS. On August 10, 1944, he was parachuted from a Flying Fortress into southern France, leading a team of ten men. In the next six weeks, he sent intelligence on German troop movements that contributed to the destruction of the First and the Eighth German armies. The Resistance group he joined up with captured 184 Germans. In April 1945, General Donovan personally awarded him the Legion of Merit, while the French gave him the Legion of Honor and a second Croix de Guerre. In September 1945, he was sent to Saigon as the head of a seven-man team.

As in Hanoi, where the OSS preceded the Chinese, Dewey arrived on September 4, nine days prior to the arrival of the British general. His instructions warned that Americans "will be regarded with suspicion," since U.S. colonial policy "did not endorse the subjugation of Indochina to France." His mission was to "represent American interests" and collect intelligence. He and his team set up shop in a fine villa on the edge of a Saigon golf course previously occupied by a Japanese admiral.

As in Hanoi, the Vietminh in Saigon had taken control of government buildings after the Japanese surrender. But in the streets, the situation was chaotic. Two days before Dewey's arrival, the independence ceremony on the Rue Catinat had turned violent. Shots were fired near the cathedral at one end of the street, and Father Tricoeur, a bearded prison chaplain friendly to the Vietnamese, was killed on the presbytery steps. The ensuing rampage against French civilians left four dead and one hundred injured. Ho Chi Minh's influence was not as solid in the south, with its jumble of parties and religious sects. Saigon was alive with armed groups of various allegiances, among them the "anti-white" Cao Dai and the Trotskyite Struggle Group. The Vietminh attempted to form a united front and operate an orderly government, as they had in Hanoi, but their success was limited. Dewey's team tried to make sense of the political maneuvering, but it seemed like total anarchy, with the Vietnamese looting and molesting the French civilian population of twenty thousand, which tried to stay out of sight.

Dewey reported that the Vietminh had obtained some weapons from the Japanese and were hiding them in caskets and graves belowground. He was busy with the repatriation of American POWs, and his team was beginning to connect with the Vietminh. Dewey found 4,549 Allied POWs in two camps outside Saigon, including 240 Americans, whom he had flown out. He reported on September 7 that the Gaullist commissioner Jean Cédile had been in Saigon since August 23 and was insisting on restoring French authority. The Vietminh were calling their government "bourgeois-democratic" to enhance their appeal, and blamed "provocateurs" for the incidents on Independence Day. Meanwhile the Trotskyites were inciting the population against the British occupiers.

The advance unit of the 20th Indian Division (Gurkhas) arrived on September 12, followed by General Douglas D. Gracey a day later. The differences between the Chinese and British occupations were that the former had an army of 180,000 blanketing all of Tonkin, prepared to remain for a year, while the British only had 8,000 troops stationed in Saigon, hoping for a quick exit after turning their zone over to the French.

Douglas Gracey, a slim, mustached postcard general, had spent his entire career in various outposts of the British Empire. He was known for his bravery and fairness, but he was also a *pukka sahib* who tolerated no nonsense from the natives. He demonstrated his attitude upon landing at the Saigon airport. Two delegations were on hand to meet him—the Japanese, bowing and saluting, and a small group of Vietminh. Gracey greeted the Japanese and ignored the Vietminh, who tried to arrange a meeting. Gracey refused to see them. "The Vietnamese came to see me," he recalled, "and said, 'welcome' and all that sort of thing. It was an unpleasant situation and I promptly kicked them out." An early report from Gracey described the Vietminh as having "a very large hooligan element out to make mischief, many of whom are criminals of the worst type."

In the meantime, Colonel Dewey was collecting political intelligence and obtaining information from his sources in the Vietminh. Gracey found Dewey's conduct "blatantly subversive," and asked him on September 13 to suspend his activities. When Dewey tried to protest, Gracey refused to see him. Gracey reported that Dewey was "in and out of obscure alleys in his dealings with the Vietminh."

When it became all too obvious that Gracey's mission was to restore the French, the Vietminh called for a general strike on September 19. They tried to shut down the electricity and the water. Gracey responded on September 21 by imposing martial law and a strict curfew. All demonstrations, public meetings, and weapons, including bamboo spears, were banned. Looters and vandals were to be summarily shot.

From his headquarters in Kandy, Mountbatten worried that Gracey's proclamation had exceeded his instructions. Labour was in power at home, and there was bound to be a fracas in the House of Commons. When Gracey stated that he was acting "with strict impartiality," Dewey thought, "What gall!" since his measures targeted only the Vietnamese. To help carry out his martial-law order, Gracey recruited the four thousand Japanese still in Saigon, whom he was supposed to disarm. He was too short of troops to do the job on his own.

Cédile, the French commissioner, told Gracey that the Vietminh were planning a massive attack. Cédile pointed out that 1,400 French troops of the 11th Colonial Infantry Regiment had been detained outside Saigon since the March 9 coup. Why not free them and arm them to make up for the shortfall of British troops? Early on September 22, the French were released and the next day they took back the public buildings in Saigon. Those Vietnamese who resisted were beaten or shot. By the morning of September 23, French troops stood guard at city hall, the police stations, and other key buildings. When Dewey complained that Vietnamese were being attacked in the street, Gracey declared him persona non grata.

The cycle of violence and reprisal had begun. On September 24, armed bands of Vietnamese descended on the fashionable French neighborhood of Cité Hérault and murdered more than 150 men, women, and children in the streets and in their homes. As an intelligence memo in Washington to Secretary of State James Byrnes put it: "When French former prisoners of war were armed and put to guarding bridges, the anti-white trend exploded . . . [the Annamites] took up their slogan 'Death to all Europeans.' "

On September 24, Dewey sent his final wire: "Cochinchina is burning. The French and British are finished here, and we ought to clear out of

Southeast Asia." By this time, the Vietminh had fled the city and re-grouped in the countryside. The outskirts were unsafe, with armed bands on the move. Saigon was in effect blockaded by the Vietminh.

Dewey went to the airport to catch his flight on the twenty-sixth, but it was delayed. So he and the other team member in his jeep, Captain Herbert Bluechel, decided to go back to the OSS villa for lunch. Dewey was driving, and a hundred yards from the villa, they came to a roadblock, two big logs that Dewey had to maneuver an *S* around. He slowed down. A burst from a hidden machine gun ten feet away struck Dewey in the head and killed him. The jeep veered off the road and turned over, shielding Bluechel, who was able to make it back to the villa, pursued by armed Vietnamese. But after sporadic firing the Vietnamese vanished. Later, the Vietminh said the incident was a mistake. Had they known Americans were in the jeep, they would not have fired. Gracey had ordered Dewey not to fly the U.S. flag from his jeep, saying he was not "flag rank." Dewey's body was never found. It seems to have been removed by his attackers and buried elsewhere. Dewey has the dubious honor of being the first American serviceman killed in postwar Vietnam. It was later learned that the roadblock had been manned by members of the Vietminh's Advance Guard Youth, who set fire to the jeep and dumped Dewey's body in a well.

In his last letter to his wife, Dewey wrote: "The country is incredibly lovely and I bought thee a green Buddha carved from a tusk, thin and svelte and covered in waxen flowers and filled with serenity. . . . These last two weeks have been incredibly exhausting, but I hope soon, oh, my dearest one, that I shall be home again."

Dewey was eulogized in Congress. Rep. Harold Knutson, a Minnesota Republican, said the shot that killed him "may be in a sense another shot 'heard round the world' in awakening the American people to the necessity of deciding how far we as a nation are going to support with military forces the colonial policies of other nations."

On September 28, Mountbatten summoned Colonel Jean Cédile and General Gracey for a meeting in Singapore. Concerned about reactions in the House of Commons, he urged the two men to negotiate with the Vietminh. However, the British secretary of state for war, J. J. Lawson, who happened to be in Singapore visiting the troops, told Mountbatten that

British policy was not to interfere with the internal affairs of French Indochina. The Labour reaction soon came. Tom Driberg, a prominent Labour MP, said on September 30 that Gracey had acted with "maximum ineptitude and considerable cruelty." A few days later, another eminent MP, Harold Laski, said: "It is a matter of regret and bitter shame that British and Indian troops should be sent to restore tyranny in Pacific areas." From India, Jawaharlal Nehru, then negotiating his own country's independence from Britain, said, "We have watched the British intervention there with growing anger, shame, and helplessness that Indian troops should be used for Britain's dirty work."

Nonetheless, in early October, Gracey used Spitfires against the roadblocks outside Saigon. Mountbatten ordered Gracey to restrict his troops to the Saigon area, which he had been obliged to do in any case. But a swift evacuation of British troops depended on the arrival of the French, who were lagging. Two brigades of British reinforcements arrived in transports. Both ships triggered mines that had been laid by U.S. forces off Cape Saint Jacques during World War II. One was able to reach Saigon Harbor; the other had to be towed to Singapore for repairs. On October 3, one thousand French troops in two British steamers from Ceylon landed in Saigon. Two days later, General Leclerc, the commander of the expeditionary force, arrived with his staff. By early December, 21,500 French troops had landed thanks to British support. The British began evacuating on December 19, but did not close down their mission until January 20, 1946. At his farewell ceremony, General Gracey declined to accept any French decorations, in order to make it clear that his mission was not to help French interests but to disarm Japanese troops.

It Was Like Wiping Your Ass with a Hoop

In 1945, France was on its knees, bled white by the Germans of its manpower and finances. Two thirds of its merchant navy was destroyed and the railroads were mangled by sabotage and bombardment. Two and a half million POWs, conscripted workers, and deportees were on their way home. The purge of Vichy collaborators resulted in ten thousand executions and forty thousand prison terms. The economy had to be rebuilt from the ground up. Wartime rationing was still enforced—one third of a pound of meat per week—though there was a thriving black market.

The world had changed. France was easy to ignore. In Paris, the government was unwilling to antagonize the United States with a massive reconquest of Indochina. All this, added to the transportation problem, led to the policy of "small packets" for the war about to begin. The French defeat of 1940 had created in public opinion a distaste for military campaigns, and, in any case, Indochina was far, far away. In 1945, there was a longing for peace.

Such was the situation at home that General Leclerc had to contend with. His solution was to muster, aside from his own 2nd Armored Division, colonial regiments made up of the huge reservoir of men in North and West Africa. In Morocco and Algeria, many of the men demobilized after World War II wanted to reenlist. Army service was preferable to the misery of their lives as civilians. In Rabat, Moroccans slept in front of the recruitment office so they could be first in line in the morning. Half of the regiments serving in Indochina were colonial. The Foreign Legion's twenty thousand men, most of them German, made up another 20 percent. They never complained, and when they were killed, no one claimed their corpses.

Leclerc also tried to make up the shortfall with a massive recruitment of Vietnamese troops. It was cheaper than bringing troops from France, and there was also a political factor, to show that many Vietnamese were ready to fight the Vietminh at the side of the French. They knew the country, spoke the language, and many of them came from ethnic minorities that sided with the French.

Leclerc flew to Saigon on October 5, 1945, and the first 2,000 men of his 2nd Armored Division arrived from Marseilles four days later, led by Colonel Jacques Massu and his tanks. Massu's men joked that he was a descendant of Cyrano de Bergerac, with "the king of noses." Then the destroyer *Triomphant* unloaded 1,500 men from the 5th Colonial Infantry. Another 1,000 troops landed in Saigon aboard the *Richelieu*, and by November 1, Leclerc had 4,500 men. Then the 9th Colonial Infantry Division arrived aboard eight American troopships. They had been stationed in Germany and knew nothing about fighting in the jungle against guerrilla units, but during the long crossing they were given the usual lectures on the ravages of VD and drinking bad water.

Soon, the *Émile Bertin* steamed up the Saigon River, carrying the 5th Colonial Infantry. One of its officers, Captain Roger Trinquier, saw columns of black smoke in the distance, darkening the sky. A naval officer told him: "The Viets are setting fire to our rubber warehouses. We don't have the men to protect them, and once lit, they're hard to put out." The river smelled of war. Armed men on deck fired at the shore, just in case. Trinquier saw the smokestacks of sunken patrol boats labeled with anti-French slogans.

Leclerc said he needed two hundred thousand men. By the end of the year he had twenty-eight thousand and 3,235 vehicles. On October 25, he launched his mopping-up operations in Cochinchina, declaring: "We are fighting for the reestablishment of French greatness." Once Saigon was "pacified," Massu and his tanks headed south to My Tho, a Vietminh stronghold on the Mekong River. They realized they were no longer advancing on Strasbourg. This was a new kind of war. The Vietminh dug up the roads, destroyed bridges, and attacked from the rear. In the countryside, they crouched low in rice paddies, breathing through bamboo sticks until an isolated Frenchman came by.

As the French advanced, the Vietminh practiced scorched-earth tactics—villages burned, crops destroyed, the villagers vanished. If the Viets took French prisoners, they killed or maimed them. Wounded men were found with their arms cut off at the elbow. Vietminh atrocities hardened the new arrivals. The French continued to "pacify" the south, using the "oil spot" technique of taking a town and moving into the surrounding area. By the end of 1945, the front was stabilized in a twelve-mile area around Saigon.

Leclerc headed north toward Tonkin, knowing, however, that he could not enter Hanoi prior to an agreement with the Chinese occupiers. His campaign had to be carefully timed with that agreement, but the Chinese stubbornly refused to leave. The arrival of General Raoul Salan in Saigon on October 23 brought him the man he needed. Salan had spent so many years in Indochina that he was known as "the Mandarin." He had a son by a Vietnamese "wife." He was known as a diplomatic general. Leclerc sent him to Hanoi as his envoy to reach an agreement with the Chinese. When Salan arrived on October 31, the Metropole Hotel was full of frightened French refugees. The Chinese were still looting. In the Citadelle, four thousand French troops were still locked up. The Vietminh took a belligerent position: "If peaceful methods fail, we must take up arms." Salan estimated that Giap had thirty-five thousand men in the Tonkin Delta.

Getting nowhere in Hanoi, Salan left for Chungking on January 7, 1946. He thought he could strike a deal there because Chiang Kai-shek needed the occupation troops back in China to reoccupy Manchuria after the departure of the Soviets. But the Chinese hedged and procrastinated. "It was like wiping your ass with a hoop," Salan said. One Chinese diplomat told him: "We don't really want to give you back Indochina. It's one of our satellites, like Mongolia and Tibet."

One of the Finest Twelfth-Century Minds

On January 20, 1946, an event took place that shocked the French nation: General de Gaulle left office. He didn't resign, he simply left, out of disgust with the squabbling of the political parties. In October 1945, the French had voted for a National Assembly that would draft a new constitution. France's first postwar parliament was made up of 160 Communists, 152 MRPs (Mouvement Républicain Populaire, or Christian Democrats), 142 Socialists, and about 100 members of other smaller parties.

De Gaulle was hoping that a new constitution would confer strong executive powers upon the presidency. But parliamentary bodies are not in the habit of reforming themselves. Having got wind that the Assembly's constitutional committee was planning to strip the presidency of power and make it subordinate to the Assembly, de Gaulle quit after two months in office. "It's as bad as it was in 1940," he told his son Philippe. "I'm not a magician. I'm not an oracle, I've had enough."

De Gaulle's abrupt departure had repercussions in Indochina, for he had set up a dual command that he could no longer control. Along with Leclerc as military chief, he had named a high commissioner in charge of political matters, Admiral Thierry d'Argenlieu, to whom Leclerc was subordinate. As de Gaulle later told his son, the two got along "like a cat and dog in the same sack."

In the thirties, d'Argenlieu had left the navy to enter a Carmelite monastery, where he was known as Father Louis de la Trinité. Politically, he was on the right, and sided with the Action Française for the return of the monarchy. When de Gaulle left for London in 1940, d'Argenlieu was one of the few naval officers to join him, for he hated the Germans worse than the British. Short in stature but long on arrogance, he was said to have "one of the finest 12th century minds." His one lasting achievement was to propose the cross of Lorraine as the emblem of the Free French.

The tragic devolution into full-scale war that took place in Indochina in 1946 was largely due to de Gaulle's hapless two-headed command. In the vacuum of authority created by the revolving governments in France, each man pursued his own policy. D'Argenlieu, convinced that de Gaulle would soon return to power, sabotaged all efforts for a negotiated peace. Leclerc was a realist who knew that a long war would lead to disaster. When he asked for reinforcements, he was given excuses. He had two somewhat conflicting aims: to restore the lost prestige of the French army and to give the Vietnamese some degree of freedom. Leclerc believed that the movement toward autonomy was irreversible in Asia. It was folly to try to maintain the old system. His mission, however, was to regain military control in the north. He was prepared to negotiate, but only from a position of strength.

They Are Strong on Parades

In the meantime, faced with a French invasion from the south, as well as the inroads made by the puppets of the Chinese, Ho Chi Minh worked at shoring up his government. He established a farm credit bureau for loans to peasants, to broaden his base of support. The Japanese had relinquished all police powers, and handed over public facilities and the railroad, which flew the Vietnamese flag. The Hanoi Central Prison was packed with "enemies of the people," collaborators, traitors, and other unsavory types. Ho discreetly beefed up the army, so as not to draw the attention of the Chinese, forming base camps with arms depots and training schools.

On November 11, 1945, Ho abolished the Indochinese Communist Party (in name only), a tactical move to reduce the antagonism of possible non-Communist allies. For he had decided on a united-front approach, rallying the nationalists instead of having to fight them. To those in his entourage who objected, he said: "Isn't manure filthy? But if it is good fertilizer of the rice, won't you use it?"

In mid-December, he formed a coalition government and called for a general election on January 6, 1946, to vote for a National Assembly of 250 seats, 70 of which were reserved for non-Communists. He wanted to avoid hostilities with the French, whom he knew would arrive as soon as the Chinese left.

By January 1946, General Philip Gallagher, who had followed developments in Indochina while serving on General Wedemeyer's staff, was back in Washington. He reported to the State Department that the Ho Chi Minh regime was "remarkably effective," and popular with "all the enthusiastic and the young, but there were too few of them . . . trained people are lacking." He didn't think they were ready for self-government, though the demand for independence was widespread. "The deep-seated hatred for the French has been fanned by exceedingly clever Vietminh propaganda," he went on. In military terms, "they are strong on parades," and show a willingness "to fight to the last man," but in a war with the French "they would be slaughtered."

On February 20, 1946, Paris announced that the Chinese had agreed to let the French replace them in March. Ho Chi Minh knew he didn't have much time. In Chungking, Salan had finally been making headway, and an agreement was reached on February 28. The French gave in to Chinese demands: the loss of their enclaves in a half dozen Chinese cities; the sale of part of the Haiphong–Kunming railroad; and a free port for Chinese goods in Haiphong.

This was the signal Leclerc had been waiting for to embark his troops for Haiphong. He wanted to get them there before the rainy season, and he had only a few days around March 5 to reach Haiphong Harbor at high tide.

In February 1946, the fleet in Saigon, the most formidable French amphibious force since the Dardanelles, prepared for the trip to Haiphong. Leclerc led his flotilla of fifteen warships aboard the cruiser *Émile Bertin*. The 21,000 men of the colonial regiments and the 2nd Armored Division were carried on the aircraft carrier *Béarn*, which had been turned into a troop transport, complete with landing craft. Loading the ships took three weeks, and they steamed into the South China Sea on February 28, arriving outside Haiphong Harbor on March 5.

Leclerc thought the landing of his troops had been cleared with the Chinese, who still had units manning the harbor. At 8:30 A.M. on March 6, he sent the first landing craft into the narrow channel marked by buoys on the Cua Cam River, escorted by the torpedo boat *Triomphant.* But General Wang, the Chinese commander in Haiphong, claimed he had no orders to let the French land. At 9:30 he opened fire. The French held their fire for half an hour, which cost twenty dead and forty wounded. Finally, Leclerc gave the order to respond. The *Triomphant* hit a Chinese ammunition dump, setting off a chain of explosions, and the big guns of French warships pounded the docks. Leclerc and his fleet marked time outside the harbor, waiting for the diplomatic mix-up to be ironed out. According to Giap, the Chinese generals sometimes ignored orders from Chungking, and General Wang wanted to prolong his stay until after the opium harvest.

On March 2, Ho Chi Minh convened the National Assembly for the first time, in the Municipal Theater. The 250 representatives (all but 70 were Vietminh) elected him president of a coalition government. At a secret meeting of party leaders on March 5, there were calls to take up arms. Ho argued against it. As he later told the historian Paul Mus: "It is better to sniff French shit for a while than to eat Chinese shit for the rest of our lives."

Ho had been talking on and off to Jean Sainteny, the commissioner for Tonkin. Both were willing to compromise, but the sticking point for Sainteny was the word *independence.* Leclerc knew that without a prior agreement with Ho, there would be trouble when his troops came in. If fighting broke out, the Chinese would have an excuse to prolong their stay. He let Sainteny and Ho know there had to be a Vietminh government in place to welcome them when they landed. With the French closing in, Ho became more flexible. On March 6, an agreement was signed calling for French recognition of the Democratic Republic of Vietnam, as a "free state within the French Union." Ho had complained that he did not know what the French Union was—"Is it round or is it square?"—but he gave in. The DRV would have "its own government, parliament, army and finances," again "within the French Union." The French agreed to hold a referendum in southern Vietnam on joining the DRV. Ho agreed to let fifteen thousand French troops replace the Chinese, to be gradually withdrawn over five years. Ho later told Paul Mus: "A free state within the French Union was a little bit like saying, 'You will be locked up in a cell with invisible bars.' " Some of Ho's followers were stunned by the agreement, but, as Giap put it, "the fate of the nation hung by a thread."

On March 18, twelve hundred French troops aboard 220 trucks crossed the Doumer Bridge into Hanoi. One of them was the ambulance driver Jean Baud. He griped that the sixty-two mile drive from Haiphong had taken six hours, because of huge potholes in the road and a long wait at the narrow, six-thousand-foot-long Doumer Bridge, built as a railroad bridge but now used for vehicles. In Hanoi, he saw Vietnamese lying face up in the streets, their mouths open, their arms spread out, dying of hunger, ignored by passersby. The troops mingled with the people, bargained in the markets, ate the soup flavored with *nuoc mam*. The men of three armies rubbed shoulders: the Chinese about to depart; the Vietminh there to stay; the French, who knew for how long? French civilians carrying flags hailed Leclerc as he drove his jeep through Hanoi, which reminded him of his triumphant entry into Paris in 1944. Young women climbed onto the tanks to kiss the men in the open turrets. The next day Leclerc went to the Citadelle to free the troops interned there, and on the twenty-second, at a military parade, both the French and DRV anthems were played.

It was a splendid welcome. Leclerc hoped the truce with the Vietminh would hold, for he didn't have the troops for a prolonged war. Losses are the language of war and he already had six hundred dead and sixteen hundred wounded in the mopping-up operation. The terrain was favorable to the Viets. He would rather negotiate than have to conquer Tonkin. France would be spared a costly war in a faraway place.

He Is a Vile Cad

From Saigon, High Commissioner d'Argenlieu announced that he wanted a meeting with Ho. On March 24, 1946, Ho and several of his ministers were flown to Ha Long Bay, known for its limestone cliffs, east of Haiphong. The admiral was waiting with Leclerc aboard his flagship, the *Émile Bertin*, making the point that Ho was coming to see him on French soil. He gave Ho a twenty-one-gun salute, recognizing him as a chief of state. After reviewing the French fleet that steamed by (was it intended to intimidate him?), the former monk and onetime Comintern agent got down to business. Ho said he wanted to go to Paris to finalize the March 6 agreement. D'Argenlieu replied, "You don't go to Paris just like that," and proposed a preparatory conference in the mountain resort of Dalat prior to formal talks later. Ho, who wanted to bypass the admiral, insisted on final talks in France. D'Argenlieu cabled Paris that "Ho has all the techniques of a revolutionary leader. . . . His policy will be to evade all provisions of the March 6 accords." Ho's aim in going to Paris was to get media attention and the support of left-wing parties.

Leclerc was omitted from the discussions in d'Argenlieu's cabin. Furious, he blew up at the admiral. Later, when d'Argenlieu saw General Salan, he said: "General Leclerc has been rude to me. I don't want to run the risk of a Munich in Indochina. No more concessions." Salan noted that the admiral's hat added three inches to his height.

In the meantime, back in Hanoi, Leclerc asked Paul Mus, who knew Ho Chi Minh well, to see him. Ho asked, "What is this French Union, is it round or is it square?" Mus was one of the few Frenchmen who understood what Ho meant. He was referring to the Vietnamese expression, "The sky is round, the earth is square." Mus replied that the French Union was not prefabricated and would be assembled by both sides. But that was not to be.

Salan and Leclerc went to Calcutta on April 13 to see Marshal Alphonse Juin, the French chief of staff, who was passing through. Juin showed them a letter he had received from d'Argenlieu, which said: "Generals Leclerc and Salan refuse to submit to my authority. I would like to have them removed from my command and sent back to France."

Leclerc told Juin: "I cannot remain under orders from this man. He lacks intellectual honesty. He is a vile cad, too cowardly to tell me face to face."

Juin asked Leclerc to stay in Indochina for the time being, but Leclerc's days were numbered. Leclerc left on July 19, 1946, to be inspector of the army in North Africa. On November 28, 1947, his plane crashed over the Sahara during a sandstorm and he was killed.

The conference in Dalat opened in mid-April. D'Argenlieu refused to discuss the referendum on Cochinchina, a vital part of the March 6 agreement. He also argued that being within the French Union meant close supervision by France. After more than a month of fruitless talks, the Vietminh delegation gave up. Ho would try his chances in Paris.

When Ho and his delegation left on May 31, 1946, he had as a traveling companion General Salan, who had been fired by d'Argenlieu, and the two got to know each other. Travel by air was then a series of arduous hops. Stranded in Rangoon due to weather, they shared a mosquito net in an airplane hangar. Then on to Calcutta, Baghdad, and Cairo.

It was in Cairo in early June that Ho learned he had been betrayed. In his absence, d'Argenlieu announced an Autonomous Republic of Cochinchina, in violation of the March 6 agreement. Ho wanted to return to Hanoi at once, telling Salan: "Don't make Cochinchina our Alsace-Lorraine."

"In Paris, you can settle your problems with more important officials than those in Saigon," Salan insisted. Together they visited the pyramids and the Sphinx.

In France there was yet another government crisis. One had fallen, the next had not yet been named. Ho was sent to Biarritz to take the waters. He was stuck in the summer resort while d'Argenlieu was engineering the partition of Vietnam. Ho visited Lourdes, fished for tuna, and attended a bullfight.

A government was formed under Georges Bidault, who came to Le Bourget airport to greet Ho on June 22. The conference opened at Fontainebleau on July 6. Ho soon realized that it was a sham. Many of the delegates didn't even attend. The French refused to set a firm date for the referendum in Cochinchina. The pointless negotiations lumbered on until

September 10, when Ho and his delegation threw in the towel. It was obvious that the French were negotiating in bad faith.

On September 14, 1946, shortly before his departure, Ho signed a meaningless "Modus Vivendi" with the French, agreeing to a cease-fire in Cochinchina. He later said he was afraid he'd be arrested if he didn't sign. On September 19, he embarked from Toulon, arriving in Haiphong Harbor on October 20. He had been away for almost four months at a time of crisis, and had returned on a slow boat. Why? Ho said that as a onetime galley hand, it was a pleasant change to travel on a ship as a passenger. Years later, he admitted that he feared he might be murdered if he returned by air.

By November, d'Argenlieu was playing a game of "flinch," provoking the Vietminh and hoping they would respond so that he could crack down. The admiral went to Paris on November 13 for consultations, leaving the hawkish General Valluy in charge in Saigon. At that time, there was a dispute over who should run the customs office in Haiphong Harbor, "the lungs of Tonkin," vitally important to both the French and the Vietminh. The real argument was over who would control the economy. For the French, Haiphong was the tapered end of the wedge.

A modus vivendi had established mixed commissions for customs and foreign trade. But in September, General Louis Morlière, commander of Tonkin, unilaterally set up an agency in Haiphong to monitor fuel imports. By carrying out seaborne inspections, the French hoped to curtail the smuggling of oil and weapons brought in by Chinese junks for the Vietminh. The commander of Haiphong, Colonel Debès, gave orders at the end of October for the use of tanks and artillery, in case the French had to use force. Thus the stage was set for a clash.

The Moment Has Arrived to Teach a Hard Lesson

On November 20, 1946, the French seized a Chinese junk smuggling oil to Haiphong. As the flat-bottomed vessel was towed into port, Vietminh militia fired from the shore. The French fired back, and by evening had taken strategic points in the city. The toll for the day was 250 Vietnamese and 7 French killed. By all accounts, the French had been trigger-happy.

At this point, on November 22, two cables reached Colonel Debès on the course of action to take. One from General Morlière in Hanoi called for a peaceful solution. The other, from General Valluy, who was standing in for d'Argenlieu in Saigon, said: "The moment has arrived to teach a hard lesson to those who have so treacherously attacked us. By every possible means you must take complete control of Haiphong and force the government and the army into submission." Later, Valluy would explain that his wire "was the expression, perhaps a bit emphatic, of a long-contained indignation."

Debès, obeying Valluy, sent the Haiphong Administrative Committee an ultimatum on the same day. It was intended to provide a pretext for his planned offensive. He demanded that all Vietnamese military or semimilitary personnel evacuate the Chinese quarters of Haiphong by November 23, at 9 A.M. When they failed to do so, he launched his attack at 10 A.M. on November 24. He had at his disposal field artillery and the cruisers *Suffren* and *Savorgnan de Brazza* in the harbor, with their 152mm guns. The bombardment flattened the densely populated and flimsily built Vietnamese neighborhoods. Civilians fleeing their homes were strafed by French Spitfires. Estimates of the number of Vietnamese killed ranged from one thousand to six thousand.

France, now under a new constitution, had been without a government since early November. The caretaker government in Paris received a copy of Valluy's order, but by the time it was decoded on November 23, the damage was done. Thus, Paris did not react to the massacre, and failed to conduct an inquiry as to why the military had acted on its own. Upon his return to Saigon in December, d'Argenlieu reproved Morlière for "his extremely conciliatory methods." Morlière was dismissed in January 1947 and replaced by Colonel Debès, who was promoted and awarded the Legion of Honor.

Haiphong was the match that lit the fuse of the war, an incident that resonated like the assassination of an archduke or the bombing of a naval facility. The question was, who would control Hanoi? In December, Giap chafed at French provocations. Red-capped Legionnaires vandalized Vietminh publications in the kiosks on Trang Tien Street. Motorcycle patrols harassed the Vietminh traffic police. The two armies coexisted uneasily. Ho asked how long Hanoi could hold out if the French widened the war. A month, Giap said. Ho decided to pull out his government and his troops, leaving the militias under his command to defend Hanoi, and giving Giap time to reposition in the jungle.

Sainteny, "the man of March 6," was back in Hanoi and saw Ho in early December. Ho said he wanted to avoid a complete break with the French. Sainteny thought Ho was stalling for time, perhaps waiting for a more amenable government in Paris. From Saigon, Valluy blamed the "hatred and bad faith" of the Ho government and warned Paris that "their present military dispositions are provocative in nature."

In Paris on December 12, 1946, a government was finally formed under the seventy-four-year-old Léon Blum, the old Socialist who had in the past been anticolonialist. More than a month had passed with no government, conferring autonomy at a critical time on the hawks in Indochina. But Blum the pacifist Socialist was unable to restore order. Ho Chi Minh, who had fond memories of the Popular Front in the thirties, sent Blum a wire on December 15, pleading for an entente. But the wire was mysteriously held up, and by the time Blum received it on December 26, it was too late. By mid-December in Hanoi, twenty-thousand people were enrolled in Vietminh militias, first-aid teams, and police patrols. The militias built barricades to block the streets in downtown Hanoi. Drivers and fare collectors overturned their trams. Stately trees along the avenues were drilled with holes into which dynamite was inserted to fell them. Earthen embankments rose on main thoroughfares, strengthened with wooden pillars. The road from Haiphong to Hanoi was cut. Children and the elderly left the city in rickshaws with their bundles and bedding. Factories were dismantled and removed. Government officials evacuated their offices.

On December 16 in Saigon, in a secret meeting among Valluy, Sainteny, Morlière, and Debès, war plans were discussed. The next day, Valluy ordered the removal of the Hanoi barricades, and armored cars crashed through them on Lo Duc Street. On the eighteenth, troop carriers escorted by tanks moved into downtown and occupied the ministries of Finance, Commerce, and Public Works. When General Morlière sent Ho an ultimatum demanding the disarmament of the Vietminh, Ho responded with an order to attack French installations. The attack was scheduled for December 19, which became known as "the Vespers of Hanoi."

At his office in Hanoi on that day, Jean Sainteny lamented that all the ground gained in March had now been lost due to indecision in France. Did they want to keep the empire or abandon it? He heard rumors that a general Vietminh assault was imminent. But when nothing had happened by 8 P.M., he told a colleague: "Apparently it's not for tonight. I'm going home."

General Morlière had given him the use of an armored car. It rumbled through a darkened downtown. He was surprised there were no streetlights. The Vietminh had knocked out the power station. Moments later, his vehicle struck a mine, which sent it crashing into the trees that lined the street and bouncing in front of a store, where it caught fire. Sainteny and the four crewmen, all wounded, managed to extricate themselves before the vehicle's munitions exploded. Crawling along the pavement, Sainteny was hit by shrapnel. His back was bleeding heavily and his right hip was broken. For two hours the crewmen lay on the sidewalk, waiting for help. Garland, the crew chief, was dying, his head in Sainteny's lap. Finally, a French patrol picked them up. Sainteny was operated on at the Lanessan Hospital and twenty pieces of shrapnel were removed from his back and arms. The hospital was under Vietminh attack and the orderlies picked up rifles to dislodge snipers in the trees and on rooftops. Sainteny was recalled to France to recover from his wounds.

On December 23 in Paris, Premier Blum announced, "We have been faced with the task of responding to violence," and declared the resolution of the government to take a hard line.

The Concern About Communist Expansion Led to a Fixation

Ho Chi Minh fled Hanoi on December 23 and announced over Radio Vietnam that the war was on. It was almost as if, sick of the haggling, both sides longed for the certainty of conflict. In a prophetic analysis on December 30, the London *Times* wrote: "Any colonial power which puts itself in the position of meeting terrorism with terrorism might as well wash its hands of the whole business and go home. . . . We are about to see a French army reconquer the greater part of Indochina, only to make it impossible for any French merchant or planter to live outside barbed wire perimeters thereafter."

Abbot Low Moffat, chief of the Division of Southeast Asian Affairs at the State Department, was in Hanoi in early December. His mission was to warn Ho Chi Minh not to use force. Ho received him in bed, with a black muffler around his neck. His voice was weak. He was obviously unwell. He spoke of his friendship with the young Americans of the OSS in the jungle and how they had treated the Vietnamese as equals. He knew the United States disliked Communism, he told Moffat, but independence, not Communism, was his only aim. "Perhaps 50 years from now the United States will be Communist, and then you will not object if Vietnam is also."

Moffat tended to be partial to Vietnamese independence, but he realized that his department's policy had made an abrupt turn when he received the following cable on December 6 from Undersecretary of State Dean Acheson: "Keep in mind Ho's clear record as agent international Communism absent evidence recantation Moscow affiliations, confused political situation France and support Ho receiving French Communist party. Least desirable eventuality would be establishment Communist-dominated Moscow-oriented state Indochina." As the civil war in China had exposed Chiang Kai-shek as an unreliable ally, Washington now had to rely on the French. It became an article of faith that the Communist character of the Ho Chi Minh regime made the French presence necessary.

After another trip to Southeast Asia, Moffat reported that "because of recent French action believe permanent political solution can now be based only on independent Vietnam (alternative is gigantic armed colonial camp)." Moffat realized, however, that in the State Department, "a concern about Communist expansion . . . led to a fixation . . . that affected our objective analysis of certain problems."

Émile Bollaert, a little-known but well-reputed Gaullist Resistance leader, was sent to Hanoi as high commissioner in March 1947. He brought what might be called "a breeze of change." Among those of his advisers who favored continued negotiations with the Vietminh was Paul Mus, who had a sympathetic understanding of the Vietnamese people he had grown up with. In a last-ditch effort to avert full-scale war, Mus agreed to secretly meet with Ho Chi Minh at his hideout in the provincial capital of Thai Nguyen.

Mus left on foot at dawn on May 11, 1947, trudging forty miles over dirt roads past French watchtowers, into a no-man's-land where their military presence ended. He knew that Ho would not accept the offer to lay down his arms, but perhaps a talk would be fruitful. He reached Ho's headquarters at 3 A.M. on May 12 and was led into a candlelit room. He saw the outline of a gaunt face behind a table. Ho dismissed Mus's proposal at once, telling him: "Within the French Union, there is no place for cowards. If I accepted your terms, I would be one." Ho told his men to send Mus back to Hanoi at dawn.

Mus knew that even if the French had half a million troops, Ho could count on the loyalty of millions of villagers. In the Red River Delta alone, there were seven thousand villages. The French were unable to rally the men and women working the flat, irrigable, tillable land. The peasants would tend their rice paddies by day and pick up their weapons at night. This was not a war for control of territory, but for control of the people.

In France, Mus reflected, the individual was more important than the community. In Vietnam, it was the reverse. Every individual was part of a unit—family, clan, village. The individual's duty was to know what was expected of him. In order to succeed, the Vietminh had to appeal to the peasants. They used the concept of virtue as a contrast to French oppression. They explained the redistribution of land as a way of maintaining communal values, making Marxism acceptable to the peasants. The villagers worked the fields with their hands: You couldn't pick rice with a bulldozer. Village society was close-knit, with all sorts of clubs, from wrestlers to whistling-bird breeders. There were even clubs for people born in the same year.

The Vietminh did not wish to disturb the social life of the village, but they believed that in a decent society, the money lenders and rice merchants would be replaced with a credit cooperative. This was not a façade to disguise their Marxism, but a recognition of conditions under the French. The Vietminh were able to mobilize the peasants with a system of land sharing and power sharing in most villages. In recalcitrant villages they used harsher methods, forcing young men to join militia units and indoctrinating them, or killing antagonists.

And now the French and the Vietminh were at each other's throats, but bound to interact and coexist in war as in peace. Paul Mus thought of the Montagnard tribesmen. Their punishment for adultery was to tie the guilty couple together, put them on a raft, and push the raft downstream. They ended up either drowned or smothered. The French and the Vietminh were now on that raft.

ACT II

The Colonial War Becomes a Proxy War

. . .

· · ·

I N 1947, THE GREAT POWERS were not paying close attention to the war in Indochina. Their focus was on Europe, where the Soviets were gobbling up Eastern Europe, and the Americans were trying to stop them from advancing farther west. The Chinese were in the midst of a civil war. Abbot Moffat explained the absence of U.S. involvement: "With French forces back in Indochina and all potential leverage gone, there was little that the U.S. could do to alter the course of events."

U.S. policy, as the Pentagon Papers put it, had "an undertone of indifference. . . . Indochina appeared to be one region in which the United States might enjoy the luxury of abstention." On January 8, 1947, the United States approved the sale of arms to France, "except in cases which appear to relate to Indochina."

A few voices in the State Department sounded the alarm. John Carter Vincent, the director of the Office of Far Eastern Affairs, warned in a memo on December 23, 1946: "The French themselves admit that they lack the military strength to reconquer the country. With inadequate forces, with public opinion sharply at odds, with a government rendered largely ineffective through internal divisions, the French have tried to accomplish in Indochina what a strong and united Britain has found it unwise to attempt in Burma. Given the present elements in the situation, guerrilla warfare may continue indefinitely." By and large, as full-scale hostilities began to erupt, the U.S. position was that the French and the Vietnamese must work it out.

This Whore of a Tropical Country

From the first months, French losses were unexpectedly high, due not only to combat but to the scourges of alcoholism, venereal diseases (known as "a kick from Venus"), and tropical maladies. Bad water made the troops drink more beer and wine. Pernod was a cheap favorite. Drinking led to accidents and fights. It got to the point where the military command punished drunks with fines and prison time.

In what one soldier called "this whore of a tropical country," the men were stricken with malaria, amoebic dysentery, bilharzia, and other unnamed parasites, not to mention typhoid, tuberculosis, cholera, and meningitis. In operations in the rice paddies, leeches attached themselves to men's bodies and had to be removed with lit cigarettes. During the monsoon season, it took only twenty-four hours for men's boots to be covered with green mushrooms. In many small posts, the rudimentary infirmaries were not up to the task.

Over the course of the war, from 1947 to 1954, 288,000 cases of syphilis, gonorrhea, and chancres were recorded. Many men were repeatedly infected. Upon landing in 1945, the French were given a million English condoms (the French word for condom means "English overcoat"), but they didn't seem to help. Saigon was alive with prostitutes. It was said that Ho Chi Minh had a corps of "Amazons," young women who agreed to contract venereal disease so they could pass it along to French soldiers. Penicillin was in short supply, and the high command decreed that those afflicted with the *mal d'amour* would have to pay for their own medication or face eight days in prison. Due to venereal scourges, it was not unusual for half a garrison to be hospitalized.

As it was, the army of 120,000 (only 50,000 of them French) didn't have the manpower to carry out their multiple missions: defend the strongpoints and depots; protect the roads and bridges; and conduct pacification operations in the villages. This left too few men to pursue the guerrillas. As the war progressed, the manpower crisis got worse. Companies that should have had one hundred men were down to eighty. Troops in fortified positions were reluctant to venture beyond their protected enclaves. The French were limited to countering Vietminh offensives, unable to conduct any of their own. The Indochina war was a manpower war, and it was lost because the French did not have enough boots on the ground. How futile their battles seemed to be. They killed three hundred Viets, and the next day six hundred were back.

The lack of manpower created layers of difficulty. There weren't enough officers. Captains were in command of battalions. The men, sent on leave every three months, were exhausted. The food was bad, hygiene was worse, and men on sick leave were not replaced. As a result, recruiters in France enlisted physical wrecks and the mentally defective. Men arrived with dossiers that said: "Unfit for marching." The age limit for recruits was extended in both directions, down to eighteen and up to forty-five. Many of these recruits were incapable of fighting the kind of jungle war dictated by the Vietminh. They were told the Viets were assassins and bandits, escapees from the cages of Poulo Condor, primitives armed with machetes. But after being in combat, the recruits came to respect their adversaries, who were crafty, meticulous, and resourceful. When the Viets laid mines on roads that French convoys used, they covered them with tire tracks to make the road seem safe. In the rice paddies, they wore fronds on their helmets so planes could not spot them. With time, some of the French troops began saying, "They're fighting for their independence just as we did against the Boches." There were atrocities on both sides, particularly in the execution of prisoners (though the French also used Viets to carry their wounded). The killing of French prisoners was attributed to the fanaticism of political commissars. Captured soldiers were impaled, sawed up, emasculated, drowned, buried alive. After an attack on a train in February 1948, the guards were thrown alive into the boiler of the locomotive. As a result of such atrocities, some men in combat kept their last bullet for themselves.

As the conflict wore on, there was a gradual deterioration in the quality of the men. In one regiment of colonial infantry, the reinforcements were Algerian illiterates. Even in the Foreign Legion, even in the elite paratroopers, the quality dropped. In principle, the time of service was twenty-four months, but it was raised to thirty months in 1948. Those who reenlisted (and there were some) received bonuses.

The instability of the Fourth Republic resulted in inadequate funding for the war. The successive coalitions in Paris were incapable of formulating a coherent policy, since each one had to compromise in order to obtain a majority.

At the time of full-scale war in 1947, the French air force was practically nonexistent. Not that a guerrilla war fought in the jungle could be won with airpower. But planes were needed to supply posts in areas hard to reach by road, and to evacuate the wounded. In 1947, the French had nine American C-47s, for which they had to get spare parts in the Philippines. From 1947 to 1949, there was a permanent spare-parts mission in Manila. Added to the C-47s were sixteen German Ju-52s, the slow mules that did the heavy lifting. Their crews used them as bombers, tossing bombs out by hand or building bomb racks under the fuselages. Of course, they never knew what they were hitting. Finally, they had twenty-four Spitfires built in 1943, fighter planes not intended to support troops on the ground, since they fired bursts of only fifteen seconds—inadequate for strafing. With this air force of planes of many nations, spare-parts problems abounded. In 1948, the 4th Fighter Squadron, based in Nha Trang, sent this plaintive message to Paris: "We have no more tires for our Spitfires. There are days when we don't have a Spitfire in the sky." In 1949, the Spitfires were retired. Too old to fly, they became accident-prone. The French had bought them in 1946 after the Americans had refused their request for P-47 Thunderbolts.

Maintenance became a huge problem. In the monsoon climate, some airfields turned into swamps during the rainy season. Most were made of dirt; only a few were cement. Only Tan Son Nhut, in Saigon, was open to large cargo planes all year round. In the high heat, the landing strips became too hot to walk on, and mechanics could only work in the early morning or at dusk. After five hundred hours of flight, a plane's engine had to be changed, but often there weren't replacements. The air force lost on average one plane a month for lack of spare parts.

And yet, in spite of these drawbacks, the French made headway in 1947, the first full year of the war. They seized the initiative, while the Vietminh retreated to their jungle and mountain strongholds and kept to defensive maneuvers. General Morlière cleaned up Hanoi street by street. At the end of January, James O'Sullivan, the U.S. consul in Saigon, reported that the Vietminh had fought "with unforeseen courage and stubborn-ness."

Faced with an enemy armed with heavy weapons and assisted by a navy and an air force, Ho Chi Minh returned to his old base of Tan Trao, in the mountainous area known as the Viet Bac. He avoided combat, and Giap broke up his regiments into guerrilla units and divided his army into three tiers—regular forces, regional units, and local militias.

The French extended their perimeter along the Red River Delta with four-towered blockhouses. They secured the Hanoi–Haiphong corridor and seized most of the provincial capitals in Tonkin and Annam. The Viet-minh responded by sabotaging the Haiphong–Hanoi railroad. To put an end to the mines, the French placed flatcars crowded with chained Viet prisoners in front of the locomotives. In Saigon, grenades were thrown into cafés and movie houses. At night, isolated soldiers were assassinated. An instructor in a para regiment told his men: "Always have a *camarade* along, even when you're fucking."

The French were superior in equipment and training, but the Vietminh knew the terrain and had much more potential manpower. Ho's recruit-ment efforts in the villages began paying off. The isolation of the villagers, who had little contact with the colonial government, favored the Viet-minh. An old proverb said: "The mountains are high and the emperor is far away." Believing in the justice of their cause strengthened Vietminh re-solve, as did fighting in the land of their ancestors against an occupying power. In the first year of the war the pattern emerged of the French hold-ing the cities and towns while the Vietminh held the countryside.

Get Up, You're Overdoing It

In Europe, the Soviets were in their *nyet* period and America was reaching a level of frustration that would spur a response. The temperature rise was visible at the Council of Foreign Ministers in Paris in April 1946. Premier Georges Bidault presided in the Luxembourg Palace, built by King Henri IV for his consort. Ernest Bevin and Vyacheslav Molotov were there, as was Secretary of State James Byrnes with his adviser Senator Arthur Vanden-berg. Molotov was "maddeningly obdurate," Vandenberg recorded in his diary, whatever the topic—German reparations, the Italian fleet, or the borders of Yugoslavia. "An entire afternoon throwing commas and colons at one another." His exasperation mounted as the meetings wore on until May 17. "Shadow-boxing," he called them, "Punch and Judy." He felt the United States was being "punched around by stubborn, contemptuous, irrational dictators from the Kremlin." They should be reminded that they "would not even be on earth if it were not for America."

At the official dinner before their departure, Vandenberg kept staring at a jovial, rosy-cheeked, well-fed Frenchman, and was told that he was Maurice Thorez, secretary-general of the French Communist Party. "How," he exclaimed, "can such a healthy-looking man be a Communist?"

The Communists were still the most popular party in France, which made American policy makers wonder whether France could be trusted as an ally. The Socialist premier, Paul Ramadier, who had replaced Léon Blum in January 1947, had to include Communist cabinet ministers in his government.

This matter was addressed by Undersecretary of State Dean Acheson, on February 22, 1947: "In France, with four Communists in the government controlling the most important unions and undermining the factories and the army, with nearly one third of the electorate voting Communist in the midst of constantly deteriorating economic conditions, the Russians can open the trapdoor at any moment of their choosing."

Premier Ramadier was trying to improve matters in Indochina. He fired Admiral d'Argenlieu, who returned to his cloister. The admiral had fallen into the habit of showing visitors photographs of French women and children slaughtered by the Vietminh. To take d'Argenlieu's place, Émile Bollaert left for Saigon on March 5.

On March 11, the debate on Indochina opened in the National Assembly. The minister of war, Paul Coste-Floret (of the prowar MRP Party), delivered a glowing picture of French victories. The Hanoi–Haiphong road was open. Hue was in French hands. An armored column had besieged Nam Dinh (in the Red River Delta, southwest of Haiphong). "The success of our armies is complete," he concluded.

Coste-Floret's exposé was met with turbulence on the benches. Cries of "Fascists" were countered with those of "Muscovites," and "Agents of American trusts" with "Agents of the Kremlin."

Coste-Floret had been on inspection in Indochina, where he saw General Salan, back from Paris. According to Salan, the minister's main concern was the Vinogel, the wine concentrate sent to the troops. "It's not something you drink," Coste-Floret explained, "it's something you eat. I'm going to send some decent wine. The Navy has promised me the ships." Salan told him: "You might send a few battalions as well."

On March 12, in Washington, before both houses of Congress, there came a sea change in U.S. foreign policy that signaled the end of isolationism and the birth of containment and global involvement. President Truman, alarmed at Soviet encroachments in Greece and Turkey, announced what became known as his doctrine: "I believe that it must be the policy of the United States to support free people who are resisting attempted subjugation by an armed minority or by outside pressure." Truman, however, did not limit the policy to Greece and Turkey, but made it applicable to the entire world. It was an open-ended doctrine of intervention that is still being used today. George Frost Kennan, the architect of containment, later regretted his influence, saying that it led to the belief that "all another country had to do was to demonstrate the existence of a Communist threat in order to qualify for American aid." The French became particularly adept at playing the Communist card in Indochina.

In Paris, at the National Assembly, the Indochina debate was continuing at full throttle. On March 18, 1947, the deputies rose to pay homage "to the brave soldiers in Indochina." François Billoux, the minister of defense and one of the four Communists mentioned by Acheson, refused to stand. The Socialist ex-premier Felix Gouin, who was sitting next to him, said: "Get up, you're overdoing it." Billoux stayed seated.

Ramadier was shocked that the man in charge of the armed forces had refused to join a tribute to French soldiers. To make matters worse, the Communist leader Jacques Duclos announced that his party was rejecting Ramadier's Indochina policy. Up until then, they had either voted for the military budget or abstained.

On April 25, Ramadier decided to expel the Communists from his cabinet. He had the support of Foreign Minister Georges Bidault, who had recently been to Moscow, where he came to the conclusion that no agreement with Stalin was possible. Bidault was an emotional man, and found the Soviet regime terrifying. In addition, Truman's speech had altered the international chessboard. The need to halt Soviet expansion had put the French Communists on the defensive. Leaders of the other parties realized that they could not play both sides, but must place themselves firmly in the Western camp.

May 4, 1947, was a decisive day in the history of the Fourth Republic. There was a vote of confidence over a bill on prices and salaries, which Premier Ramadier won by 360 to 186. The Communist bloc voted against the bill. That evening, Ramadier convened the Communist cabinet ministers and told them that since they were not in agreement with government policy they could not remain in the cabinet. This amounted to an anti-Communist coup d'état. The Communists were now a party of pariahs. Five ministers (not four as Acheson thought) were fired: Maurice Thorez, minister of state; François Billoux, minister of defense; Ambroise Croizat, minister of labor; Charles Tillon, minister of reconstruction; and Georges Maranne, minister of health.

A Dangerously Outmoded Colonial Outlook

When George Catlett Marshall resigned as Army Chief of Staff in November 1945, President Truman sent him on a mission to China to negotiate a settlement between Chiang Kai-shek and Mao Tse-tung. Marshall was there for a year, but the mission failed. Upon his return, Truman, who greatly admired him, named him secretary of state, on January 8, 1947, in the place of James Byrnes.

Marshall saw Indochina in the light of France's role in the restoration of Europe. In a wire to the U.S. ambassador to Paris, Jefferson Caffery, on February 3, he said that the United States wanted to help return France to her position as a world power. But "at same time we cannot shut our eyes to the fact that there are two sides [to] this [Indochina] problem and that our reports indicate both lack of French understanding of the other side and a . . . dangerously outmoded colonial outlook and methods. . . . Colonial empires in the 19th century are rapidly becoming things of the past. . . . On the other hand we do not lose sight of fact that Ho Chi Minh has direct Communist connections. . . . It is basically matter for two parties to work out for themselves."

On May 13, in another wire to Caffery, Marshall was still hopeful of some arrangement: "Key is our awareness that in respect developments affecting position Western democratic powers in South Asia, we essentially in same boat as French, also as British and Dutch. . . . We consider as best safeguards a continued close association between newly-autonomous peoples and powers long responsible for their welfare." He seemed to be willfully ignoring the reality that in Indochina, the "close association" had turned to war.

On June 14, 1947, Charles Reed, the U.S. consul in Saigon, reported that High Commissioner Bollaert "radiated optimism" and said he wanted to end the war, but were the French sincere? They were dickering with Emperor Bao Dai to return to power, when it was clear that a majority of Vietnamese backed Ho Chi Minh. "Something must be done to eradicate the distrust and almost contempt of the French for the natives. . . . Times have changed and the natives have a right to more than semblance of independence." Some of the spirit of the OSS men who had preferred Ho to the French was still alive in this interregnum between World War II and the Cold War.

At this point, Marshall had already delivered his June 5 address at Harvard calling for the reconstruction of sixteen European countries. Marshall had seen Stalin in April and realized that there was no chance of solving the German question. He reported to Truman that Stalin wanted the breakup of Europe into two blocs.

Ramadier's expulsion of the Communist ministers in May turned out to be prescient. It was not certain that Marshall Plan aid would be granted to countries where the Communists shared power. The promise of aid from April 2, 1948, until June 30, 1952, was a life preserver for a country on the edge of bankruptcy. France in the summer of 1947 could not pay for its vital imports of oil and coal. The war in Indochina was a bottomless drain. Bread was still rationed, at half a pound a day, less than during the war. The French grabbed the life preserver, throwing themselves into the American lifeboat. Accepting Marshall Plan aid led to Communist-inspired strikes and demonstrations. In November, the government feared a Communist insurrection, with three million workers out on strike and the sabotage of passenger trains. But in December the strikes abated, and soon the Marshall Plan millions began to flow. Directly or indirectly, the aid would help finance the war in Indochina.

General Salan returned in May 1947 to Hanoi, still in ruins from the fighting that had not stopped until mid-February. The regulars at the Metropole bar talked only of massacres. Luckily, the Chinese border provinces were still held by Chiang Kai-shek. On his inspection tour, however, Salan found unmotivated, exhausted troops. When he walked into the mess, the men rose and began shouting *"La quille!,"* the traditional term for being mustered out. At the time, there were still some conscripts in the Indochina army, though that was soon to end.

By the end of summer, Salan was in command of seventeen infantry and three paratroop battalions, supported by tanks and artillery, and a few planes. In September, General Valluy, the commander in chief, ordered a fall-winter offensive to follow the end of the rainy season. After the three-month offensive, the French were in control of the border with China on a one-hundred-mile strip from Lang Son to Cao Bang. Salan announced that the operation was a success, since the main road to China via Cao Bang could no longer be used by the Vietminh. "Only isolated bands" of Vietminh were left, he said. In fact, Giap's forces had dispersed into inaccessible areas, ending the prospect of a short war.

French troops were stationed in posts, the number of which grew exponentially, until by 1954 there were nine hundred of them, manned by 82,470 men, which immobilized two thirds of the army. There were posts of every description, some round, some square, some triangular; some in abandoned churches with machine guns in the belfry. Others were in pagodas, or abandoned factories, or built from scratch. Some had bamboo walls and towers. Others were made of concrete and barbed wire. Some isolated posts had no radio link. Others had artillery, but were allowed only forty-five shells a month. The war was fought on the cheap. The posts were usually short of ammunition or rations. One fort got a case of condoms instead of grenades.

Life in the posts consisted of waiting for attacks. The French knew when the *bo dois* (Vietminh soldiers) would strike. From 1948 on, the Vietminh often utilized light artillery preparation, followed by human-wave attacks, usually at night. The French knew they had to hold out until dawn, when reinforcements might arrive. As one soldier said after an attack, "it was the longest night of my life."

When the French forces landed in 1945, they thought the war would be a cakewalk. Morale was high. "We were farting flames," one lieutenant said. But by 1947, dejection had set in. One noncom wrote home: "There are days when we are so discouraged that we would like to give it all up. Convoys under attack, roads cut, firing in all directions every night, the indifference at home." And yet 1947 was probably the most successful year of the war. It was also the year with the highest number of French casualties: 3,185 killed and 2,696 wounded.

High Commissioner Bollaert was a liberal who wanted to confer a degree of independence upon Vietnam. But with whom could he negotiate? Bao Dai had been used as a puppet more times than he could remember. Blasé and cynical, his only true passion was hunting. He was, however, able to rally the Catholics and the non-Communist nationalists. The "emperor," who was living in well-upholstered exile in Hong Kong, did not seem interested in returning, and it took the French more than a year to bring him around.

On March 8, 1949, Bao Dai went to the Élysée Palace in Paris and signed an agreement with President Vincent Auriol, which incorporated the so-called Republic of Cochinchina into a single Vietnamese state. This agreement was subject to ratification by the National Assembly, which took its time.

There were two reasons behind the French courtship of Bao Dai. The first was that the war was a stalemate. The second was that the French, in order to obtain American aid, had to make a gesture toward Indochina's independence.

The Jungle Is Neutral

As Orde Wingate, whose Chindit guerrillas harassed Japanese forces in Burma, once put it, "The jungle is neutral. It does not take sides." After being driven from Viet Bac in the Salan offensive, Ho Chi Minh in 1948 moved into the heavily forested mountains close to the Chinese border, where the French did not pursue him. His troops, who had no vehicles and were lightly armed, could march all day, each man carrying a small bag of rice and some salt. The French, with their jeeps, trucks, and armored vehicles, stuck to the roads.

General Giap adopted the Maoist model of three stages of guerrilla warfare: defensive, equilibrium, and counteroffensive. In January 1948, the standing committee of the reconstituted Indochinese Communist Party decreed the end of the first stage. The equilibrium stage was described as: guerrilla units on the attack; hit the enemy where he is not; hit his belly and his back; destroy his roads; begin to form battalion-size units. Aside from fighting, the troops had to learn how to cut off the enemy's supply lines and launch diversionary attacks. They had to be told there was no point in beginning to shout when they were still a hundred yards from the enemy.

The Vietminh command, ensconced on the border, established a pattern of cooperation with the Chinese. Nationalist troops still controlled South China, but in some towns they could be bribed.

In 1948, General Salan followed a methodical policy of building fortified posts along the border and on high points above the jungle. Those that could not be reached by road were supplied by aging Ju-52s. This was the "medieval" side of the war, the posts with towers. The little Beau Geste forts manned by one or two companies were a logistical and tactical nightmare. The cost in casualties to keep them supplied was coupled with their inability to control the infiltration of Viets.

Road conditions slowed French columns to a crawl. Outside the main towns, single-track dirt lanes turned into rivers in the rainy season. The jungle encroached on roads that were not maintained. Jeep aerials caught on the arching bamboo. In 1948, instead of seeking open battles, the Vietminh began to ambush convoys and strangle small posts.

Each French column had its unit of engineers to repair the repeatedly sabotaged roads, which were opened by mine-clearing crews, with the help of village militias, who were often the same people that had laid the mines. Fallen trees were removed by bulldozers. The columns had to wait as the sappers and road openers did their work. When a column was stalled, it was ripe for ambush; when it suffered losses, more men were killed evacuating the wounded in jeeps.

In February 1948, General Valluy went back to France, and General Salan moved to Saigon to replace him as commander in chief. Salan was absorbed in defensive tactics, protecting the roads, building the posts, forming the convoys. He now realized it would be a long war, and complained of the inertia in Paris. Paris responded by replacing him with General Roger Blaizot, who had never been to Indochina. Changes in the high command led to changes in strategy as abrupt as the hairpin turns on RC4. Blaizot wanted to mount expansive operations, but was frustrated by a lack of troops.

It Seems Definitely That Indochina Will Go Communist

In 1948, from June 21 to 26, in Bangkok, a conference on Southeast Asia was held under the chairmanship of Edwin F. Stanton, U.S. ambassador to Thailand. It was attended by the U.S. chiefs of mission in the area, including George M. Abbott, the U.S. consul general in Saigon. The conference was a sign that the State Department, while still focused mainly on Europe, had begun to realize that Southeast Asia might become troublesome.

As Abbott put it, Chiang Kai-shek's control over South China was tenuous. "There would be little to prevent the establishment of a Communist corridor between South China and Indochina."

Abbott delivered some talking points that seemed to sum up State Department thinking at the time:

> Ho Chi Minh is a very interesting and much debated personality. Isaacson, a writer for *Newsweek*, saw Ho and afterwards was convinced that Ho is not a Stalinist. . . .
>
> In 1931, when Ho was in prison, the man who shared his cell for six weeks commented that Ho is a violent Moscow Communist and even is no longer Asiatic. . . .
>
> In early 1946 in New York, it is said that Thorez denounced Ho as a Trotskyite. . . .
>
> The only way to play this from our own interests is to reject the Isaacson theory. . . . Why can't we send someone in to find out just what the situation is? . . . In the first place we just couldn't do it be-

cause of our white skin. . . . An effective intelligence officer would have to have a little brown blood. Then we wouldn't be able to trust him. . . .

It seems definitely that Indochina will soon go Communist. . . . The feeling now may not be necessarily towards the Communists but against the French, and in their desire for independence, they first want to win the war, and then face Communism. . . .

Just how can the French win the war, except by dealing with Ho? That's the only way. And in dealing with Ho, he will gain prestige and save face. . . .

I don't think we can count on the French. . . . At this point they only want us to come in and help run the natives out. . . . I don't think Indochina is really worth worrying about, except from the standpoint of preventing the further spread of Communism. We don't need Indochina as a strategic location for bases.

In his closing remarks, Ambassador Stanton said: "It is abundantly clear that a great effort is being made to spread Communism in this part of the world."

Echoing Stanton's conclusion in a speech before the House of Representatives on March 15, 1948, Lyndon Johnson said airpower was the answer to any threat from Asia. "Without superior air power," he warned, "America is a bound and throttled giant, impotent and easy prey to any yellow dwarf with a pocket knife."

Indochina may not have been worth worrying about, but at least it was on the State Department radar screen. The first full-length policy paper on Indochina appeared on September 27, 1948. It was highly critical of the French:

"The French have employed about 115,000 troops in Indochina with little result. . . . The failure of French governments to deal successfully with the Indochinese question has been due, in large measure, to the overwhelming internal issues facing France."

Three years after the end of World War II, the French were "fighting a desperate and apparently losing struggle in Indochina."

As far as American policy went, there was a quandary. Since France was doing nothing to recognize the legitimate political aspirations of the Vietnamese, the United States did not wish to help them prosecute a colonial war. However, the United States needed a friendly France in pursuit of America's aims in Europe. Perhaps a compromise solution could be found somewhere between military reconquest and complete withdrawal. But for the moment the United States was not prepared to intervene.

The French conducted no major offensives in 1948, as they pursued a political solution with Bao Dai. In China, however, the civil war was in its final stages. Chiang's army had lost the will to fight, and Manchuria fell to the Communists, who captured 470,000 Nationalist troops.

Coincidentally, Vietminh armament improved. On July 25, 1948, an isolated earthwork fort held by one hundred Legionnaires at Phu Thong Hoa, near the Chinese border forty miles southwest of Cao Bang, was attacked by two Vietminh battalions. For the first time, they used artillery preparation with mortars and 75mm recoilless guns. The Legionnaires held out in hand-to-hand combat until a relief column arrived, but it was a signal that the Vietminh could attack at battalion strength with light artillery. If 1947 was the year of the French, 1948 was the year of the ambush and of reaching the second stage.

Was Ho Chi Minh an Asian Tito?

In January 1949, Dean Acheson replaced George C. Marshall as secretary of state. Despite his focus on Europe, he found himself trying to disentangle the knots in the Indochina tapestry. On February 15, before an executive session of the House Foreign Affairs Committee, he expressed a somewhat derisive view of the inhabitants of Southeast Asia. "These people," he said, "are about 95 or 96 percent illiterate. They do not have the simplest ideas of social organization. They do not know about starting schools. They do not know about dealing with the most primitive ideas of public health. They do not know how to organize to build roads. . . . Government is something of a mystery." What they needed were foreign advisers to show them "how you go about collecting taxes, and how to get teachers; how to teach the children, where you have desks or chairs and so forth." As it happened, at the time Acheson spoke the Vietminh were re-

ceiving their first advisers, Chinese Communists who were not there to
teach them about desks and chairs.

In the first week of April 1949, the French foreign minister, Robert
Schuman, came to Washington to sign the NATO defense pact. Monastic
in appearance, stooped, bald, and long-nosed, Schuman was a devout
Catholic bachelor who had grown up in Lorraine when it was under Ger-
man occupation. He served in the Kaiser's army in World War I, but
fought in the Resistance in World War II. Schuman gave Acheson the
French line on Indochina: France, at great expense, was fighting against
Communism on behalf of all democracies and should receive U.S. aid.

Acheson told him that France should do more to satisfy nationalist aspirations, and quoted Edmund Burke: "Not the least of the arts of diplomacy is to grant graciously what one no longer has the courage to
withhold."

The Élysée Agreement with Bao Dai, signed on March 8, was clearly
aimed at convincing the United States that France was moving toward Indochina's independence, but Acheson was not convinced. On May 10,
Acheson advised the U.S. consul in Saigon that he hoped for success of the
Bao Dai experiment, but that the United States would recognize his government "at the proper time," since the National Assembly had not ratified the agreement. The United States did not want to back a "puppet
regime." The French must make the Bao Dai regime attractive to the nationalists. They "must see urgent necessity in view possibly short time remaining before Commie successes in China are felt Indochina." This sense
of urgency was the result of Mao Tse-tung's victories in 1949. The civil
war was all but over. As Acheson had told the House committee on February 15: "The will to fight of the Chinese armies has disappeared." Chiang
Kai-shek fled to Formosa, taking China's gold reserves with him.

Chiang's defeat strengthened Acheson's resolve not to negotiate with
Ho Chi Minh. On May 20, Acheson advised the U.S. consul in Hanoi that
Ho was an "outright Commie." The question of his nationalism was "irrelevant. All Stalinists in colonial areas are nationalists." At the same time,
in keeping with the "on the one hand while on the other hand" style of
State Department communications, Acheson raised for the first time the
chance that Ho Chi Minh could become an Asian Tito. "It must of course

be conceded theoretical possibility exists estab National Communist state on pattern Yugoslavia in any area beyond reach Soviet army." However, Indochina "will doubtless be by no means out of reach Chi Comm hatchet men and armed forces." As for aid to the French, the China experience showed that no amount of U.S. military and economic aid could save a government when it loses its will to fight. U.S. policy was at an impasse.

The Asian Tito theory was buried with Mao Tse-tung's victories. The United States could not negotiate with a leader who followed the Maoist model in fighting the French and who could now count on massive aid from China. Ho Chi Minh had often said that Indochina could be the Switzerland of Asia, but that could be seen as Leninist casuistry. In his letters to Truman, Ho asked for the same status as the Philippines, but received no reply. The United States did not give Ho the opportunity to prove the sincerity of his remarks. The zeitgeist was against him. With Mao Tse-tung in power, Ho openly embraced Communism, needing China as an ally. Mao's policy of "leaning to one side" meant alliances with other Communist nations. The United States also began gradually "leaning to one side," the side of the French, as the issue of colonialism was shoved aside by the need for containment.

You'll Learn on the Job

In May 1949, the French army chief of staff, General Revers, went to Indochina to evaluate the military situation. He arrived in Hanoi on June 6 and spent two weeks visiting bases and talking to soldiers. The secret report he turned in on June 29 concluded that there could be no military solution to the conflict. But to obtain a political solution, France needed to be in a favorable military position. Revers proposed that French forces in Tonkin retrench to a fortified rectangle bounded by Hanoi and Haiphong to the south and the two border outposts of Lang Son and Mon Cai to the north. "No one knows what they're fighting for," Revers wrote. "The officers doubt our will to win. . . . Indochina needs a military leader with authority and prestige."

Only fifty numbered copies of Revers' report were printed, but in less than two weeks one of them was leaked, creating a political scandal that went on for months, though the source of the leak was never discovered. By August, extracts of the report were broadcast on Vietminh radio and Revers' career was over. His pessimism affected French public opinion. Paris papers, in particular the Communist press, began to run atrocity stories: in Dalat, French troops shot twenty imprisoned Vietminh in retaliation for the killing of a police inspector. In Paris, the Communists coined the slogan "Not one man, not one cent" for the war in Indochina. Longshoremen refused to load Indochina-bound supply ships. Troop convoys had to be escorted by gendarmes.

In August 1949, Premier Henri Queuille named General Marcel Carpentier to replace the ineffective Blaizot. In his meeting with Queuille, Carpentier, who had been stationed in Morocco, said: "I know nothing about Indochina."

"No matter," said Queuille, "you'll learn on the job."

Carpentier pleaded that he was not well, that he had hepatitis and a heart condition. He was sent to the Val-de-Grâce military hospital for a checkup and pronounced fit for duty. Arriving in Saigon on September 3, Carpentier was told that an ambush on Route Coloniale 4 had destroyed thirty GM trucks. It was a bad time. The French were taking heavy losses. On October 2, Dean Acheson was told that Léon Pignon, the new high commissioner and an old-guard colonialist, had called Carpentier's attitude "so passive and defensive . . . that his qualifications for supreme military leadership must be questioned."

In December, Carpentier flew back to Paris for consultations. President Vincent Auriol asked him what his solution was. "No military solution is possible," Carpentier said. "We must have a political solution."

"Never!" Auriol interjected. "We cannot be the ones who abandoned Indochina."

Carpentier was not the only pessimist. On July 1, 1949, the U.S. National Security Council had said in its NSC 51 report: "The Indochinese situation is in an advanced state of deterioration. . . . It has not been in the realm of practicability for France to crush the Vietminh by military means. . . . The French military effort has therefore dwindled to footling punitive campaigns. . . . As we do not contribute aid directly to Indochina the charges are passed on to us in Europe." In 1948, Marshall Plan aid had partially armed three French divisions in Germany "while about 100,000 French troops with American equipment were and still are being squandered in Indochina on a mission which can be justified only in terms of Gallic mystique." It seemed blindingly clear then that the war in Indochina was impeding the defense of Europe.

Only in the fall of 1949, when Mao's victory in China was complete, was there a slight nuance in the State Department position. In a September 17 memo on talks between Acheson and Robert Schuman, the secretary of state was described as backing away from his earlier position and agreeing to help out with Bao Dai once the Élysée Agreement was ratified. Schuman said it would "perhaps" be ratified in November.

On October 11, Acheson saw the prime minister of India, Jawaharlal Nehru, who said the Bao Dai experiment was "doomed." "The Emperor," Nehru said, "lacked the character, ability and prestige." Nehru said the argument that Ho Chi Minh was using a popular front government to liquidate his opposition was a wrong-headed application of Eastern European experience to Asian countries. In India and Burma, the Communists had failed to take over the nationalist movements. The same would happen in Indochina. This struck Acheson as specious, since taking power depended on the strength of the Communist faction, and Ho was already in control.

In the closing months of 1949, once Mao Tse-tung had announced the People's Republic of China, "the course of U.S. policy was set to block Communist expansion in Asia," as the Pentagon Papers put it. On December 30, the National Security Council put out NSC 48/2, the first U.S. document proposing a policy approved by the president. In Indochina, "action should be taken to bring home to the French the urgency of removing the barriers to the obtaining by Bao Dai or other non-Communist nationalist leaders of the support of a substantial proposition of the Vietnamese."

In its tortured prose, this was what Acheson had been recommending. He now felt that there was no alternative to Bao Dai. In Paris, Ambassador David Bruce warned that "no French cabinet would survive the running of the Parliamentary gauntlet if it suggested the withdrawal at present or in the near future of French troops from Indochina." Bruce also recommended direct financing of the war by the Marshall Plan. The stage was set for American involvement.

Getting Something Out of Stalin Is Like Taking Meat from the Mouth of a Tiger

In 1949, Vietminh units in Tonkin kept up their guerrilla operations while consolidating their radio communications and supply bases. The strategy of ambushes on convoys was kept up, as were the attacks on posts. Vietminh tactics were to take a post and then abandon it before French reinforcements arrived.

The Vietminh saw their war as a replica of the civil war in China on a smaller scale. They were surprised at how swiftly Chiang Kai-shek had collapsed. Between 1945 and 1949, Mao and Ho had been absorbed in their own struggles. Contacts between them were limited because Chiang's troops occupied South China. Ho was careful not to antagonize Chiang, who could attack him from the north. But now, having a friendly neighbor on the border meant an end to isolation, a change in the balance of power, the start of massive aid. One of Giap's priorities in the spring of 1949 was to open up the border. General Blaizot cooperated by abandoning the border posts west of Lang Son in order to concentrate his forces.

Mao Tse-tung proclaimed his government on October 1, 1949, but Ho Chi Minh waited with due deliberation until Mao was in control of the border provinces—Yunnan, Kwangsi, and Kwangtung—before sending his message of congratulations on November 26. In his offer of "brotherly relations," a centuries-old history of hostilities was erased. Mao Tse-tung left for Moscow in mid-December, but prior to his departure he sent Ho Chi Minh a message that a team was arriving to help him draft a list of his needs, and that the Vietminh should send a delegation to Peking. The Vietminh delegation crossed the border in late December. By that time the Maoists had raised the red flag on their side of the international bridge linking Mon Cai and Tung Hing.

In 1950, Chinese aid transformed the war. Giap's army approached the third stage in the armed struggle—counteroffensive. The border with China was a jagged length of jungle and mountains more than six hundred miles long that stretched from Laos in the west to the Gulf of Tonkin in the east. The eastern side of the border, which had serviceable roads to Nanning and other Chinese cities, was heavily guarded by the French, but most of the small posts on the western border were abandoned.

The French planned to recognize Communist China, as the British had done. They hoped that recognition, accompanied by fruitful commerical exchange, would dampen Mao Tse-tung's eagerness to recognize the Ho Chi Minh regime and to start supporting it militarily. But Mao beat them to it by recognizing the Democratic Republic of Vietnam on January 16, 1950, wiring his assent from Moscow. Angered, the French charged Mao with violating international law, in that Vietnam was part of the French Union, and the only legitimate government was Bao Dai's. Mao paid a price for his "proletarian internationalism," but knew where his priorities were.

In mid-January, the first Red mission arrived in Vietnam under Luo Guibo, a member of the Central Military Commission. He came to Ho Chi Minh's redoubt in Tuyen Quang Province with a telegraph operator, secretaries, and guards, to assess the Vietminh's needs. In the meantime, Ho Chi Minh had left for China on foot, and walked for fourteen days before reaching Nanning on January 18, where he learned that Mao had recognized his government. He went on to Peking, where it was arranged that he should travel to Moscow and meet Stalin. He left with Chinese foreign minister Chou En-lai on February 3.

Stalin had studiously ignored Indochina. He had doubts about Ho Chi Minh's orthodoxy. His suspicions had been aroused when Ho tried to cotton up to the OSS teams, and when he abolished the Indochinese Communist Party. Stalin treated Ho with open contempt, but did offer recognition, while warning that "because of the limits of natural conditions, it will be mainly China that helps you. What China lacks, we will provide." Mao and Ho left Moscow together, and on the long train ride through Siberia back to Peking, Mao confided that "getting something out of Stalin is like taking meat from the mouth of a tiger."

We Are Not Exactly Popular Among These Native Peoples

Soviet recognition on January 30, 1950, triggered an immediate American response. Acheson announced on February 1 that "the recognition by the Kremlin of Ho Chi Minh's Communist movement in Indochina comes as a surprise" and "should remove any illusions as to the 'nationalist' nature of Ho Chi Minh's aims, and reveals Ho in his true colors as the mortal enemy of native independence in Indochina." And yet the Stalin-defying nationalist Tito also recognized the Vietminh regime. But after the loss of China, American policy refused to countenance that Communism and nationalism could be in any way linked.

Another consequence of Peking's and Moscow's recognition of the movement was that the French National Assembly ratified the Élysée Agreement on February 1, and the United States recognized the Bao Dai regime on February 2. The French lost no time in asking the United States for aid. The Indochina war became a proxy war fought behind the scenes by China and the United States, with similar methods. As if acting in tandem, both countries sent aid missions to their respective proxies, followed by arms shipments and military missions, but no troops on the ground. In the wake of the Luo Guibo mission, the Chinese arms deliveries began arriving in February, at which point the French noticed that the Vietminh were fighting with 105mm howitzers. The Chinese could supply Ho with impunity over trails on the unguarded stretches of the border. South China became the Vietminh base area.

On March 6, 1950, U.S. secretary of defense Louis Johnson warned that "the choice confronting the United States is to support the legal government of Indochina or face the extension of Communism over the remainder of the continental area of Southeast Asia." Ten days later, the first U.S. mission was on its way to Saigon.

The mission was led by R. Allen Griffin, publisher of *The Monterey Peninsula Herald,* who had wartime experience in China and was a friend of Acheson's. Griffin and half a dozen civilian and military experts toured Southeast Asia for several weeks. Their goal was to assess military as well as economic needs in order to prevent "a repetition of the circumstances leading to the fall of China." The focus was on Vietnam and the mission concluded that U.S. aid should be sent directly to the Bao Dai government.

Upon his return, Griffin said at a State Department meeting on May 4 that the French "cannot afford a continued military cost of hundreds of millions of dollars a year in a campaign that has failed and that has no prospect in bringing about a military conclusion." He described a welcoming arch he had seen leading to a village that said COMMUNISM NO, COLONIALISM NEVER. "The arch undoubtedly represents the spirit of at least 90 percent of the Indochinese," he said. Griffin saw General Carpentier as an officer of "the highest caliber," who had been willing to arm native battalions with American small arms and who admired Griffin's friends, generals Alfred Gruenther and Mark Clark.

Later, in a talk at San Francisco State College, Griffin expressed his private views, giving vent to what may have been the first description of the "Ugly American": "We are not exactly popular among these native peoples. . . . We are rich, and too frequently, ostentatious in our spending. Even the American typists in our embassies receive more pay than their Prime Minister. We seldom exhibit the virtue of humility. We not infrequently show a complete lack of understanding of the ancient ways of life. . . . Sometimes our kindness appears somewhat condescending. Our record at home with the Negro is not unknown to them; and worse than that, many of their students who have come to this country have been the victims of slights and humiliation due to our rude and ignorant color-consciousness. There is a debit side to the ledger on the American."

In Congress, there were still a few skeptics who objected to backing France. On March 29, 1950, when Dean Acheson appeared before the Senate Foreign Relations Committee, Theodore Green, a Rhode Island Democrat, asked: "Are we not defending what is left of French policy there and supporting an unpopular king and a corrupt government?" Acheson agreed, but added: "We have to be careful . . . that we do not press the French to the point where they say, 'All right, take the damned country, we don't want it,' and put their soldiers on ships and send them back to France." On the basis of the Griffin recommendations, Acheson announced a program of "rapid economic aid" to Indochina.

Truman's War

On April 24, 1950, Truman approved NSC 64, which espoused the domino theory: "It is doubtful that the combined native Indochinese and French troops can successfully contain Ho Chi Minh's forces" now that the Chinese were on the border. "The neighboring countries of Thailand and Burma could be expected to fall under Communist domination. . . . The balance of Southeast Asia would then be in grave hazard." From Saigon, the U.S. chargé, Edmund A. Gullion, chimed in on May 6: If Indochina fell, "most of the colored races of the world would in time fall to the Communist sickle."

On May 1, 1950, Truman approved $10 million for Indochina. His decision was linked to the capture of the island of Hainan by the Chinese. Hainan, only a hundred miles from Haiphong, dominated the Gulf of Tonkin. From the island, the Chinese could easily ship supplies to Ho with small craft. In early May, the Griffin mission returned and recommended $60 million in economic aid and $75 million in military aid. On May 24, the United States announced that it was sending an aid mission to Indochina. At this point, the tragedy of Indochina became the shared responsibility of the French and the Americans.

U.S. aid began to trickle into Indochina in June. A few C-47 Dakotas landed in Saigon, with their white stars painted over. A Liberty ship steamed up the Saigon River, preceded by a minesweeper. The mangrove-covered banks were lined with French troops. Jeeps were unloaded, inaugurating the great flow that would cut the cost of the war for France.

Chinese aid was also pouring in. In the southern provinces of Kwangtung and Kwangsi, thousands of coolies built four roads to the border from scratch. Within a few months, hundreds of Molotova trucks drove from Canton, Kunming, and other Chinese cities over the newly built roads and on to distribution depots. Chinese armaments gave the Vietminh the same fire power as the French, with the exception of planes and heavy artillery.

In the last week of June, however, America's attention was diverted to Korea. On June 24, North Korean troops breached the 38th parallel. Truman, reflecting that this was how World War II had started, committed American troops under a U.N. Security Council resolution. Russia, boycotting the Security Council over the U.N. membership of Nationalist China, was not present to veto the resolution. Yugoslavia, sometimes mentioned as the analogue to Indochina in Europe, abstained. Truman went to war without congressional approval, on the advice of Senator Tom Connally. He met with congressional leaders, who approved his action. It was only after Chinese troops invaded en masse that Korea was called "Truman's War."

Indochina became the second front of the Korean War, since both countries had a border with China. On June 27, Truman announced an "acceleration in the furnishing of military assistance to the forces of France and the Associated states in Indochina." As for supplying aid directly to the Bao Dai government, Commander in Chief Marcel Carpentier was quoted in *The New York Times* as saying: "I will never agree to equipment being given directly to the Vietnamese. If this should be done I would resign within 24 hours. The Vietnamese have no generals, no colonels, no military organization. . . . The equipment would be wasted, and in China, the United States has had enough of that."

Do Not Show the Victor's Arrogance

While in China earlier that year, Ho Chi Minh had asked his new friend Mao Tse-tung for military experts at the divisional, regimental, and battalion levels. Mao said he would send advisers but not commanders. On April 17, 1950, a Chinese Military Advisory Group (CMAG) was formed. Officers with combat experience in the civil war were picked from three field armies. On June 27, Mao gave the advisers a pep talk, underlining the touchiness of the Vietnamese. "Do not look down on them," Mao said. "Do not show the victor's arrogance. Treat them as comrades." Since Vietnam had long been a Chinese satellite, ancient animosities might still rankle.

In July, CMAG set up headquarters in the city of Nanning, close to the border, with seventy-nine advisers. It was clear to the Chinese that Giap had serious command problems, since Ho had asked for help at all levels. Giap's troops had little combat experience above the company level. In the summer of 1950, twenty thousand Vietnamese crossed the border into China to be trained and armed, and then returned to Vietnam organized in field divisions.

With Chinese aid in the pipeline, Ho Chi Minh decided to plan a border campaign using four crack China-trained regiments. He wanted to concentrate on the important French post of Cao Bang on RC4, and asked for a senior adviser to coordinate the border operation.

The adviser was dispatched on July 7, 1950. Most Maoist generals came from peasant stock, but Chen Cheng had been born to a wealthy landowner, and began his Confucian education at the age of six. As soon as he could swing a saber, at fourteen, he joined the army of a Hunan warlord. Five years later, disgusted by the warlord's corruption, he joined the Communists and fought heroically in the civil war. He was known as "the scholar general."

After joining Giap's army, General Chen Cheng spent time with various units and recorded in his diary on July 22 that the Vietminh were neglecting the recruitment of women, who made up half the population. As a result, they were not ready to fight a "people's war." He reported to the Central Military Commission in Peking that Vietminh units trained in China showed "high morale," but the cadres above the battalion level "lack command experience in actual combat." He recommended that by winning some initial victories against small, isolated posts, before tackling the well-defended post of Cao Bang, they would gain the necessary experience.

On July 28, Chen visited Ho at his headquarters in Thai Nguyen. Ho threw open his arms and hugged him. Chen told Ho that the Vietminh were not ready to attack Cao Bang, but had to learn the tactics of surrounding a post, drawing in a rescue force, and wiping it out. They should attack the smaller post of Dong Khe, midway between Cao Bang and Lang Son on RC4, to lure French reinforcements out of those larger posts. Ho agreed. Chen continued to harbor reservations regarding the Vietminh commanders, writing in his diary on July 29 that they showed "impatience" and a "sole emphasis on weapons" rather than strategy.

By the fall of 1950, Giap had a regular army of 250,000, armed with artillery and mortars. The French, by listening to Radio Peking, knew that the Vietminh would launch a general offensive in the fall. Peking had become not only a supplier but the propaganda arm of the Vietminh.

We Found Vietnam More Confused and Irresolute Than Ever

The next step after Truman called for accelerated aid to Indochina was sending a combined mission of State Department, Defense Department, and Economic Cooperation Administration (ECA) experts to Southeast Asia. This mission arrived in Saigon on July 15, 1950, led by John F. Melby, a special assistant to Dean Rusk, the assistant secretary for the Far East.

Melby felt he'd drawn the assignment because no one who outranked him wanted it. He was a China hand and veteran foreign service officer, who lacked the reverence for his superiors that smoothes the way in a State Department career. He thought of Rusk as someone who avoided taking sides. It was rumored that Melby never voted. He played his cards close to his vest and never stood up for anyone. As for his direct superior, the flamboyant William S. B. Lacy, director of the Office of Philippine and Southeast Asian Affairs, Melby perceived the prevailing racist attitude of his time. Lacy told him after a trip to Korea: "I wanted a woman in the worst kind of way, but all those niggers out there, you just can't put your prick in one of those. I had to wait until I got to London so I could get me a proper whore." Lacy was a real Virginia gentleman, Melby thought.

The Melby mission arrived in Saigon with instructions to find ways to help the French. Melby saw the mission as "an almost knee-jerk reaction to the Communist victory in China." U.S. interest until then had been negligible. The State Department had few Asia experts. The main prerequisite was not to annoy the British, the principal colonial power in Asia.

In Saigon, they saw High Commissioner Pignon and Commander in Chief Carpentier, who received them uneasily, wary of American objections to colonialism. Carpentier insisted that the Vietnamese must not be involved in the aid program at any level. Melby and his team inspected French military dispositions. Melby realized that the problem was not the French posts but the mobility of the Vietminh forces. Since French intelligence on Vietminh intentions was practically nonexistent, their strategy was to build blockhouses and secure lines of communication in order to respond to enemy troop concentrations. But they only responded during the day. The night belonged to the Vietminh.

Graves B. Erskine, the Marine major general who headed the Defense Department wing of the mission, was clearly skeptical of the French approach. The French justified their Maginot Line attitude by claiming the Vietminh would fade away without Chinese help. They asserted the Chinese were massing troops on the border, but Melby flew over it with Erskine, who said, "You couldn't conceal a goat on that terrain, much less an army." Carpentier was furious when he found out the Americans had gone to look for themselves.

Carpentier was sure the blockhouse system would prevail. But the contrast was obvious between French immobility and the Vietminh hit-and-run tactics. Melby became aware of this when he turned the corner outside the Hotel Continental in Saigon and someone on a bicycle dropped a bomb at his heels. He had time to run for it before it exploded and the only damage was broken windows. Carpentier insisted thereafter on giving him an armed escort.

French hospitality was bountiful, with one dinner party after another: fine cuisine, great wines, multiple toasts to friendship and cooperation. One course consisted of a single spear of canned white asparagus on a gold plate. Nevertheless, Melby felt he could not condone the French position in his report. That would be a sellout. The French did not live up to their promises. Their colonial policy was as intransigent as ever.

Melby's report, cabled to Rusk on August 7, 1950, said: "Hatred and distrust of the French is so deep-rooted that no real basis for long-range cooperation exists or can exist on the present basis. The French military effort . . . has so far failed to break Vietminh military strength. . . . The French are entranced with the analogy of tapping on a jar which later shatters. . . . The French also fail to make proper use of Vietnamese troops, apparently on the hypothesis, as the commanding officer at Lang Son put it, if more use were made then greater concessions to Vietnam would be required. It is obvious that the French also fear that armed Vietnamese might turn on them." Melby proposed that the French undertake to give Vietnam its independence within a time period of from five to thirty years. "American identification with France," he concluded, "will further weaken American influence in Asia."

Back in Washington in mid-August, Melby was invited to attend a meeting of the State Department Policy Planning Staff under George F. Kennan. Melby read his report, a few desultory questions were asked, and that was that. He realized that he was swimming against the tide. His mission had been overshadowed by the invasion of Korea, which made the containment of Communism in Asia the priority. General Erskine, whose division might soon be sent to Korea, hammered away at containment, sweeping aside all objections to French tactics, in spite of what he'd seen.

On August 16, 1950, Truman received the State Department weekly review, which said a program of $31 million for the French army and Associated States had been approved. All the equipment provided in the initial $15 million would arrive in Indochina by October, including forty Hellcat fighter planes and forty-two landing craft.

Melby and Erskine made another tour of Southeast Asia in the fall, but they stayed in Saigon only one day, October 2, 1950. Cochinchina was stable, but the French had abandoned control of a sizable mountainous area along the Chinese border to the Vietminh. Pignon told Melby that the French did not have the troops to improve their position. He needed ten thousand more men. General Carpentier remained passive at a time that demanded offensive spirit. The caliber of Vietminh troops had improved to the point where they compared favorably to the French, due to training in China.

"I found Pignon depressed and discouraged," Melby reported. He said that in Paris there was "a willingness to make almost any political concession but no willingness to make any military or financial concessions. . . . We found Vietnam more confused and irresolute than ever. A kind of stalemate has been reached which bodes no good for anyone except the Vietminh."

Melby's days at the State Department were numbered. His troubles may have started with a letter on December 3 to the Virginia gentleman Bill Lacy on the failure of U.S. intelligence in Southeast Asia: "The situation is a disgrace. . . . For all practical purposes we know little or nothing of what goes on. . . . I found the best to be the CIA," but the armed services attachés "had no competence or business being there." In Hong Kong, he got "only the most nebulous kind of rumors" about Chinese troop movements on the Indochina border. In Bangkok, the service attachés assured him that a prominent Chinese general was in Burma or Formosa. But that same day Melby saw him in the street. These examples "could be multiplied endlessly," Melby said. His remarks did not go down well with the agencies he blamed. In the final analysis, however, he was a victim of the McCarthy follies. Joe McCarthy's claims in 1950 of Communists in the State Department led to a tightening of security that bordered on paranoia. In the spring of 1951, Melby came before the Loyalty Security Board. It soon became clear that the only plausible charge against him was that he'd had an affair with the author Lillian Hellman, an alleged

Communist. When he was questioned again in the fall, he was formally charged. The board decided that his continued employment was not in the national interest. On May 23, 1953, he was told: "Please clean out your office." At that time he was the highest-ranking Foreign Service officer to be fired. He ended up teaching in a Canadian university.

There were still those in the State Department who did not think the suppression of Asian nationalism was anything to fret over. An unnamed Foreign Service officer reportedly dismissed those concerns as a needless preoccupation with "the patter of naked brown feet."

Charton, We Will Cut Off Your Balls

By mid-August, 1950, General Chen Cheng had joined Giap in the border area. Giap entrusted him with the command of the forthcoming operation. It seemed that the French were deploying troops along RC4. The question was, when and where should Giap's army attack? Chen was invited to brief the Vietminh commanders above the regimental level. He spoke for four hours, pointing out "deficiencies." The plan was, as he had told Ho in July, to attack a smaller post first and then to attack Cao Bang.

In the events that led to this first turning point of the war, the two sides misjudged each other. The French did not believe the Vietminh had the strength to take border posts, whereas by September, Giap had thirty thousand well-armed men in the border area. The Vietminh thought the French were beefing up the border posts, which was not the case. General Revers in his 1949 report had first recommended the evacuation of Cao Bang, the most heavily fortified post on the northern border, which could resist, it was said, an assault from fifteen battalions. Cao Bang was commanded by the veteran Legionnaire Colonel Charton. General Carpentier kept putting off the evacuation, which was a huge problem in itself. Cao Bang was a thriving cosmopolitan zone, with three thousand civilians, and a polyglot population, besides the French, of German Legionnaires, Moroccan Tabors, Vietnamese partisans and their families, and Chinese merchants. Across the town were scattered food shops, a movie house, cafés, gambling dens, and whorehouses. Morale was high, even though at night Vietminh loudspeakers in the jungle blared in French: "Surrender!

Death to the mercenaries and traitors!" A Hungarian deserter named Domei had rallied the Vietminh and given the names of the officers in the post, and the loudspeakers added: "Charton, we will cut off your balls."

By July 1950, it became apparent that the posts on the 110-mile stretch of RC4 between Cao Bang and Lang Son were too spaced out to bar the Vietminh supply routes from China. In addition, the ambushes and sabotage had gotten so bad that Cao Bang was now supplied by air. It had become an isolated enclave in the Vietminh-liberated zone. Its upkeep and supply were not worth the cost.

By September 1950, when the convoys could no longer get through, Carpentier decided on evacuation. Cao Bang had a three-thousand-foot-long airstrip where Dakotas and Junkers could land. The civilians, as well as the sick and the wounded, could be evacuated by air. The troops, consisting of a Foreign Legion battalion, a Moroccan Tabor battalion, and about a thousand Vietnamese partisans, could then destroy their vehicles and artillery and quietly leave on foot. They would have the element of surprise and be on their way before the Vietminh could react.

Colonel Charton, who knew RC4 by heart, did not think the troops would last long on foot without heavy weapons. From Cao Bang, RC4 was a twelve-foot-wide dirt road that proceeded southeast through a chaotic landscape of rugged mountains covered with forest, steep grades with no shoulders, limestone cliffs, ravines, and torrents that washed across the road. As Charton said later: "We were surrounded by Viets. I felt seriously threatened." He asked for a relief column to come up from Lang Son, the regional headquarters 110 miles southeast of Cao Bang, and meet him at kilometer 22, at the hamlet of Nam Nang. That was as far as he could safely advance. The relief column would arrive, board his people onto trucks, and escort them back to Lang Son. It sounded as simple as a school bus picking up children in the morning.

General Alessandri, the crusty Indochina veteran who had led his troops to China in 1945, escaping from the Japanese, argued that Cao Bang must be held, since it was the strongest post on the northern frontier. General Carpentier replied, "I know all your arguments, but I'll breathe a sigh of relief when the last man leaves Cao Bang." "And I'll utter a cry of distress," Alessandri responded.

Carpentier agreed to send a relief column from Lang Son. It would be commanded by Colonel Le Page, a fifty-year-old artillery officer who had fought in World War I. He had not seen combat since then and was unaccustomed to infantry operations, but the French were shorthanded. The relief column consisted of two battalions of Moroccan Tabors and one battalion of Moroccan fusiliers, a total of 2,695 men. Carpentier had a fetish for secrecy, keeping to himself until the last moment the date of the evacuation and the time and place of the two columns' rendezvous.

On September 16, he informed the military command in Hanoi that he was evacuating Cao Bang, "the date to be fixed at the latest on Oct. 15. . . . Evacuation by air to Lang Son of women, children, and elderly. Male civilians to evacuate with the troops over RC4."

On the day that Carpentier's message to Hanoi went out, Generals Chen Cheng and Giap launched their attack on the small post of Dong Khe, on RC4, thirty-seven miles south of Cao Bang. Four Vietminh battalions armed with artillery and mortars quickly seized the post, manned by 250 Legionnaires. By September 17 there were 40 French killed and 7 wounded. At 6:30 P.M., General Houang Van Tai ordered a human-wave assault and there was heavy fighting until dawn, when the French saw for the first time Vietminh fighters wearing steel helmets. About 20 survivors made it to That Khe, the post twelve miles to the south. At 6:30 A.M. on September 18, a Morane observation plane spotted a Vietminh flag flying over the ruins of Dong Khe. The Legionnaires lost 193 men and 8 officers were killed or taken prisoner.

General Chen Cheng was not pleased with the performance of Giap's troops. He listed their mistakes in his September diary entries: They did not follow the attack plan punctually. The attack was supposed to begin at dusk on September 16, but the units were not ready until dawn on the next day. When the sun rose they had to withdraw in case of a French air strike, and they did not return until dusk. Vietminh commanders were afraid of going to the front and lost contact with their units. Some cadres concealed bad news in false combat reports.

What Chen did not realize was that he had spoiled the French plan for the evacuation of Cao Bang. The commander of the relief column, Colonel Le Page, would be blocked at Dong Khe.

General Carpentier could have decided that, with important Vietminh forces astride RC4 at Dong Khe, it would be better to postpone the evacuation of Cao Bang. Ignoring the possibility that one or both columns might come under attack, he persisted. And yet the Deuxième Bureau (French military intelligence) knew that at least twenty Vietminh battalions had massed in the strip between RC4 and the border, along with three artillery battalions. The August intelligence report warned that "the progress made by the rebels could transform the nature of the war in Tonkin." The anxieties of the Deuxième Bureau, however, did not penetrate the thick hides of the French high command. Carpentier was counting on secrecy and swiftness.

Now that Dong Khe had been lost, Carpentier gave Colonel Le Page an additional task. On his way to Cao Bang, Le Page would stop at Dong Khe and recapture the post. Carpentier made taking Dong Khe sound like an effortless chore. The plan was that Colonel Le Page should leave in late September and proceed to That Khe, the halfway point to Cao Bang. There, a battalion of Legion paratroopers had been dropped on September 18 to reinforce his column. Le Page should then proceed to Dong Khe and retake it on the morning of October 2. In the afternoon, he should continue up RC4 to kilometer 22 at Nam Nang, the point of juncture with Charton's column from Cao Bang. Le Page wondered why he was being asked to move through difficult terrain without artillery or reserves, and without a plan for the evacuation of the wounded.

In Cao Bang, Colonel Charton had his doubts. He thought the order to evacuate such a strong position was absurd. Because of Carpentier's obsession with secrecy, Charton had not yet been given his date of departure. He had been told not to make obvious preparations, such as blowing up his ammunition dump. Between September 21 and 27, an airlift took out 2,500 civilians, until a typhoon interrupted the flights. Charton sent an officer in reconnaissance up to kilometer 22 to inspect the road. The officer found no obstacles. The Vietminh battalions were massing farther south.

The airlift at Cao Bang did not go unobserved by the Vietminh. They were not sure whether it might presage an eventual evacuation. General Chen Cheng's strategy was still to take smaller posts first. After taking Dong Khe, he maintained some troops in the citadel, and placed machine-gun nests on high points, which could fire down on the post. He planned to take That Khe next.

Colonel Le Page left Lang Son on September 18 with his Moroccans and reached That Khe the next day. There, he joined up with the paratroopers who had been dropped in to reinforce his column. They sat in That Khe for ten days waiting for Captain Constans, who was coordinating the operation from Lang Son, to give the order to head north toward Cao Bang. Between the China border and That Khe, the Vietminh had massed thirty thousand troops, and a French force of thirty-five hundred was unknowingly heading right into their midst. No one had thought of an alternative route in case Le Page was unable to take Dong Khe. If anything went wrong, the French would have to improvise.

On September 29, Le Page was told to move on Dong Khe and use two of his four battalions to clear the area. The twelve miles from That Khe to Dong Khe involved a three-mile climb to the Luong Phai Pass, followed by a two-mile descent into the jungle. The Vietminh had blown the bridges, and the road was pitted with mine craters and blocked by landslides. Le Page explained to Captain Constans back in Lang Son that he was stalled, but Constans replied: "No delays can be allowed." So Le Page abandoned his trucks and continued on foot, taking twenty-eight hours to reach Dong Khe at 5 P.M. on October 1. Not a shot had been fired, but the Vietminh were watching and drawing him in. Machine-gun fire stopped the column as they approached the Dong Khe post. Le Page decided to wait until the next day for better weather so he could call in an air strike.

On October 2, with the *crachin* (drizzle) persisting, Le Page moved toward the post, but the attack failed. Vietminh forces massed on both sides of RC4 outnumbered his men ten to one. Le Page took heavy casualties. At noon, there was a change in plans. He was ordered to get off RC4 and take a trail northwest that would lead to kilometer 22. By outflanking the Vietminh at Dong Khe, he could still relieve Charton.

On October 2 in Cao Bang, Colonel Charton was given his date and time of departure—6 A.M. on October 3—and made the final preparations for evacuation. He destroyed his food supplies, hosing down the hills of rice in the warehouse with gasoline. His engineers prepared the timers to blow up 150 tons of munitions. Most of his cannons were thrown into the river, dismantled. The Chinese merchants held "going out of business" sales, disposing of their cognac and champagne at rock-bottom prices. The last Ju-52 evacuated the post archives and secretarial staff.

In the evening, Charton received a message that Le Page was held up at Dong Khe. Charton was told to proceed to kilometer 22 but then get off RC4 and take the trail that would lead him to the Le Page column. Charton decided to take trucks and artillery until he reached kilometer 22 at Nam Nang. He still had five hundred civilians who had not been evacuated, as well as soldiers wounded and unfit to march. He would destroy the trucks and guns before getting off RC4.

Charton's first elements started leaving in the early hours of October 3. The entire column—the Tabors, the Foreign Legion, and the Vietnamese partisans—as well as the civilians, was on RC4 by 6 A.M. Charton had knocked out the power plant and evacuated fifteen small posts around Cao Bang. He led the column in his jeep, followed by the engineers who had set the timers. As they left, the explosions threw up debris that rained on the departing garrison. A visitor to the site later saw a crater fifty yards wide. Charton had about 2,500 men—636 Legionnaires, 916 Moroccans, 1,000 Vietnamese partisans, and 44 engineers—mixed with six armored cars, thirteen trucks, eight jeeps, two 105mm howitzers, forty Bofors antiaircraft guns mounted on wheels, and two mortars. The civilians carried their belongings in bags. One couple lugged a sewing machine. The column proceeded cautiously, expecting ambushes. At 6 P.M. they stopped at kilometer 18, on a hill. Charton saw that farther on, RC4 was badly chopped up with alternating trenches in a herringbone pattern.

As Charton left Cao Bang, the Le Page column was marching through the jungle to outflank the Vietminh at Dong Khe. Le Page was ordered to divide his men, leaving two battalions as a rear guard. His objective was to reach a pass in the Na Keo mountain chain and drop down into the Cax Co Valley, where he would join up with Charton coming from the north. At 3 A.M., an advance unit of Tabors reached a peak in the chain and came face-to-face with Vietminh forces, losing seven killed and seventeen wounded. Le Page was trapped between hammer and anvil, the Viets in Dong Khe and the Viets who now blocked his advance in the jungle, where they had dug artillery and machine-gun emplacements. At 6 A.M., the

Tabors fought off another assault in close combat. Two Vietminh battalions relieved each other, but there was no relief for the French, who had to fight instead of sleep. At noon on October 3, Le Page had reached a pass that led into the valley. A message from Captain Constans said: "Charton group km 18. Have given orders to get off RC4 at Nam Nang in direction of Quang Liet [a hamlet six miles south of Nam Nang]. All the elements at your disposal must cover his movement." Engulfed by Vietminh units, Le Page was in no position to cover any movements but his own. But Captain Constans kept pelting him with messages. During the night of October 3, the men of Le Page's column buried their dead and made stretchers from bamboo poles for the wounded. The Legionnaire paratroopers, who were bringing up the rear, had been ambushed with severe losses. Their doctor, Pedoussant, halted the group so that he could change bandages and give the wounded water. An angry Legionnaire captain fell back and yelled: "Here's the one who's fucking us up." At the time of the ambush, the coolies carrying the wounded had run off. Moving the stretchers became a terrible ordeal when you had to fight at the same time. Some of the men fell asleep while marching and had to be shaken awake.

By the morning of October 4, Charton reached kilometer 22 and engineers destroyed the vehicles and the howitzers. He was told to take the Quang Liet trail and liaison with Le Page. Into the jungle Charton's column headed, with Legionnaires carrying the children of civilians on their shoulders. But they could not find the trail, long unused and covered with vegetation.

Charton decided to follow a stream south of Nam Nang through the thick jungle. His Vietnamese partisans led the way, cutting through the hanging creepers with their machetes, followed in single file by the Tabors and Legionnaires, overcome by heat, and trailed by distressed civilians, who were not expecting such an excursion, and stretcher-bearers. They advanced at the rate of three hundred yards an hour but at first did not encounter any Vietminh. The laggards began to collapse. At 4:30 P.M., a wire from Constans said: "Every hour counts. Get rid of all useless weight." Charton muttered: "If only we had a Morane [spotter plane] to guide us."

On October 4, the Le Page column was moving toward the Cax Co Valley in disarray. Some units were lost in the jungle. The Vietminh had moved in closer and the French were under constant fire. These were men who had not slept or eaten in forty-eight hours, encumbered by a growing number of wounded. Le Page rallied his troops and they spent the night in a hollow overlooking the valley.

On October 5, General Carpentier, who was in Saigon, and knew absolutely nothing about the difficulties of the two columns, wired Captain Constans in Lang Son: "Why is Charton advancing so slowly? Did he go against my orders and carry heavy equipment? I am extremely discontented with the way this operation has been conducted." Charton at the time was in jungle so dense that he could see only thirty feet ahead. Some units were lost. Many civilians refused to go farther. One elderly man slit his wrists. By evening, the column reached the crest of a mountain. They saw a parachute drop of supplies a mile away. They knew they were close to Le Page.

Le Page, having spent the night in a hollow, had advanced on October 5 to a narrow gap between piles of limestone boulders, the only passage off the cliff to the Cax Co Valley and the hamlet of Quang Liet, where Charton was supposed to show up. It was a steep thousand-yard descent over rocks and dense jungle. The remainder of Le Page's column was surrounded. Le Page could hear the Vietminh bugles, followed by battle cries. An advance group of thirty Legionnaires commanded by Lieutenant Tchiabrichvilli was attacked at the pass, with only three survivors. The lieutenant lay on his back, his vacant eyes staring at the sky, his jump boots and pistol gone. On this day of heavy combat, one hundred Legionnaires were killed or wounded.

On October 6, General Chen Cheng received a telegram from Mao Tsetung, who was closely monitoring the battle from Peking, and who gave him instructions on the final stage: "Plan first to concentrate your main forces on eliminating the enemy troops southwest of Dong Khe who have now been surrounded by us, and then surround and annihilate the enemy troops escaping south from Cao Bang. . . . We can defeat the enemies both in Cao Bang and Dong Khe and thus win two victories."

The final assault was carried out according to Mao's instructions. On October 6, mortar and machine-gun fire poured down on the Le Page column as it tried to break through the pass into the Cax Co Valley. Le Page's troops were dispersed in hills around the valley, trying to contain the Viets. At 5 A.M., the 350 remaining Legionnaires stormed through the boulders into the pass and were met by Vietminh mortars, machine guns, and grenades. In less than an hour the battalion was wiped out. All the company commanders and most of the section chiefs were killed. The Moroccan Tabors in the hills fled their positions when they came under fire. They galloped downhill through the boulders and the first to be killed were trampled by the next wave. Some went berserk and fired on their fellow soldiers. Two Moroccans pulled a wounded third, each grabbing a leg, so that his head banged on the boulders and killed him, in one of the scenes of despair and folly. When one Tabor asked the paratroop captain Jeanpierre, "What is the way out?" he replied: "Just follow the bodies of the Legionnaires." Le Page had to leave his wounded behind. One of the wounded, Dr. Rouvière, hit in the knee and wrist, out of bandages and medication, asked to keep his revolver.

Arriving above the Quang Liet Valley on the night of October 6, Charton saw hundreds of fireflylike lights flickering in the jungle below. A Vietminh regiment was marching toward him, carrying torches. Behind him, thousands more Vietminh were hidden, waiting until dawn. Le Page, who was supposed to rescue Charton, wired that he was in a desperate situation, with more than a hundred wounded. The tables were turned, and Charton would have to try to rescue Le Page, for his column, apart from the civilians, was virtually intact.

At 5 A.M., the mortar rounds started exploding, and Le Page's Tabors were surrounded. His Legionnaires tried to break through. Their commander, Major Forget, was killed. The Moroccans wandered around in a daze, without weapons. One of the captains had removed his stripes.

In the afternoon of October 7, Colonel Le Page and a group of Vietnamese partisans managed to reach Charton. The juncture was finally made between the two destroyed columns. Charton decided to take the remaining Legionnaires and break out to the post of That Khe, twelve miles south of the Viet-held Dong Khe. But they ran into an ambush, and Charton was hit by grenade fragments in the face and belly. A *bo doi* came at him with a bayonet, but a *can bo* (political commissar) said: "It's a colonel. Take him alive for questioning." Le Page was also captured. Four months into his captivity, Charton was forced to sign an article saying: "I am a captive. . . . For the first time in my life I have time to ponder. . . . Can France continue this war with some hope of winning it? No, for Asia wants her freedom and China, with her 475 million people, borders on Vietnam. . . . Vietnam, aided by China, can carry on an endless war. . . . The Vietnam people's uprising cannot be put down."

The Vietminh officers at the battle site were calm and deliberate, giving orders and taking notes, while orderlies with cotton masks sorted out the heaps of dead and wounded, piling up the former and taking away the latter, slung on bamboo poles carried by coolies.

Of the 5,807 men in both French columns, 1,338 made it out, usually in small groups. More than half of those taken prisoner died in captivity. Of the 479 Legionnaires parachuted into That Khe to join Le Page, 23 survived, led by Captain Jeanpierre, who had a map and a compass. They followed a track along a stream and when they heard Viets, they waded into the stream, in water up to their thighs, against the current. At night they slept on the bank. One dawn in mid-October they saw the first houses of That Khe. Entering the citadel they came upon a Vietminh officer who asked them: "Do you think this is an unjust war?" The Vietminh had taken That Khe.

Le Page and Charton, unable to defend themselves in captivity, took the burden of blame, Le Page for dispersing his battalions (even though he was ordered to) and for not articulating his forces properly. He was accused of exuding a sense of defeatism by saying, "I don't know how we're going to take Dong Khe if it's solidly held." In fact, he was right. It was impossible to take Dong Khe with the troops he had, and equally impossible to follow trails into the jungle that didn't exist. Charton was accused of disobeying orders.

The negligence of the high command was to blame. They had underestimated the size and armament of Vietminh forces, set up a rendezvous without a unified command, and kibitzed from a distance, with General Carpentier in Saigon, nine hundred miles away, and Captain Constans in Lang Son. Constans, a haughty and luxury-loving paratrooper captain, lived in the governor's mansion, with servants and a chauffeur, who took him on his rounds in a Mercedes. He kept a small Praetorian Guard of German Legionnaires, all six-footers. Tall himself but puffy-faced, Constans was often mocked by his men. In Saigon, Carpentier, who seemed to find the smell of battle distasteful, sat in his office looking at maps, far from the fray.

Cao Bang marked the first time in the history of the French Empire that a colonized people had beaten French troops in a pitched battle. The Vietminh destroyed seven battalions of France's regular army. It seemed inconceivable that Maoist tactics could triumph over the École de Guerre. The loss of 4,469 men killed or captured threw the entire expeditionary corps into deep gloom. In his stupor, General Carpentier decided to evacuate Lang Son, fearing encirclement and annihilation. In fact, the Vietminh had also suffered heavy losses and were not ready to advance on Lang Son, defended as it was by six infantry battalions, a tank squadron, and artillery. Lang Son was evacuated on October 18 by Captain Constans. In his haste, he left behind 1,300 tons of munitions and 4,000 rifles.

From October 27 to 30, 1950, the Vietminh assembled its commanders above the battalion level to analyze the battle. General Chen Cheng addressed them on all four days. They discussed issues ranging from the promotion of the valorous to the repair of captured artillery. As for prisoners of war, it was decided to recruit the Vietnamese partisans. Chen Cheng also listed the Vietminh officers' shortcomings—delays in carrying out orders, lax discipline, and indifference toward their men. He praised the courage of the soldiers but told the officers not to take too much pride in their victory. In November, Chen left Vietnam for a posting in Korea. He had demonstrated to Giap's army the effectiveness of Maoist tactics and inflicted on the French the worst defeat of the war. By the end of the year, the French had abandoned practically all of Tonkin north of the Red River Delta, clearing the border for the Vietminh supply lines.

The French in Indochina Are Not Fighting

One week after the French defeat at Cao Bang, President Truman went on a fourteen-thousand-mile round-trip flight to a pinprick island in the Pacific. It was Muhammad going to the mountain, a rendezvous between

Truman and General Douglas MacArthur, the commander of U.N. forces in Korea. Truman was willing to make the effort so that MacArthur would not be too long absent from his headquarters in Tokyo.

The presidential cortege consisted of three planes, the *Independence* for Truman and his staff, a second plane for the press, and a third for the bigwigs—who included Chairman of the Joint Chiefs of Staff Omar Bradley; ambassadors Averell Harriman and Philip Jessup; Admiral Arthur Radford, commander of the Pacific Fleet; and Dean Rusk, assistant secretary of state. Secretary of State Acheson declined to go along, seeing the trip as a stunt on the eve of midterm elections.

The president stopped in Honolulu and visited Tripler Army Medical Center, which was packed with wounded from Korea. As he walked through the wards, a young Marine with a patch over one eye called out: "Mr. President, you called this a police action—it's a real war."

At dawn on October 15, 1950, the three planes landed at Wake Island. The conference consisted of a single meeting, from 9 A.M. to 11 A.M. Truman sat at a long table in a civil aeronautics building, flanked by MacArthur and Harriman, with fifteen other advisers. Truman opened the talks by saying, "Now, General, suppose you start things off by telling us how things are going in Korea." MacArthur, who had boldly landed at Inchon in September, displayed an ardent belief in his own infallibility, announcing that "formal resistance would be over by Thanksgiving" and "Winter will whip those that we don't." As he spoke, U.S. forces were advancing into North Korea. Truman asked about the four hundred thousand Chinese troops in Manchuria, just across the North Korean border. "Do you think they might try to intervene to help the North Koreans?" he asked. "I believe that if they did I could take care of them," MacArthur said. The discussion turned to problems that would arise once the war was over, and then meandered to the fate of Indochina.

Ever since America's entry into Korea in June, the French had been insisting that Indochina was the same war as the war in Korea. America, no longer at war in Europe, was at war in Asia. The common enemies were Soviet and Chinese Communism. In the fall issue of *Foreign Affairs*, the Gaullist supporter Jacques Soustelle had written an essay entitled "Indochina and Korea: One Front." Since France and the United States were both tied down in Asia, it seemed obvious "that the entire strategy must be conceived as a whole."

At the Wake Island conference, however, it became clear that those present had deep apprehensions regarding the Indochina war. It seemed odd, said MacArthur, that "they have the flower of the French army in Indochina and yet they are not fighting. . . . They should have settled the issue in about four months." Admiral Radford thought this was because "they have no popular backing from the local Indochinese." Truman said the lack of French success was "the most discouraging thing we face."

"Should the French Prime Minister come to Washington," Truman said, "he is going to hear some very plain talk. I am going to talk cold turkey to him. If you don't want him to hear that kind of talk, keep him away from me." Radford said he had seen some French ships in Hawaii and had the impression that "they were not anxious to go to Indochina and were dragging their feet."

Truman referred to Philip Jessup's fourteen-country tour of Asia in March. Jessup had reported that the French were "failing to put over their viewpoint" and making "somewhat the same mistake that the British General Braddock had made in the French and Indian War." In 1754, Braddock was advancing on Fort Duquesne and fell into a French-Indian ambush. He lost nine hundred of his fourteen hundred men and died of his wounds.

Yellow Men Will Be Killed by Yellow Men Rather Than by White Men

In France, the Cao Bang defeat added to the climate of pessimism. On November 22 in the National Assembly, the mood was somber:

Edmond Michelet, of the Gaullist RPF Party: "The tragedy of Cao Bang cost France 3,400 men [the correct figure had not been compiled]. This is the first crack in a condemned building. . . . The insufficiency of our Air Force is dramatic."

Daniel Mayer, Socialist: "These methods cannot continue. The failure is obvious."

Pierre de Chevigné, of the MRP (Christian Democrat) Party: The truth is that we do not have the means to impose a military solution in Indochina."

The up-and-coming Radical Socialist deputy Pierre Mendès France pressed for immediate negotiations with the Vietminh "to get France out of the hornet's nest. . . . We cannot pursue this faraway ruinous war, materially and morally, that can have no solution."

But others on the right said that not pursuing the war would mean all those men had died for nothing. After all, France was defending the free world. It was her duty to persevere. The decisive National Assembly vote in support of the Pleven government's policy to continue the war was 337 to 187. It was in part an emotional reaction to the defeat at Cao Bang and in part an expression of hope for more U.S. aid.

Marshal Juin, who went to Indochina on an inspection trip in November 1950, summed the situation up pithily: "Is France ready to pay the cost in human lives and money, while compromising our security in Europe, to maintain Indochina in the French Union? If the nation does not think so, there are two solutions:

1. Negotiate with Ho Chi Minh.
2. Bring the matter before the United Nations.

It is up to France to choose."

In Washington as well as in Paris, as the year ended, the disappointment over lack of progress was keen, particularly with France's inability to build a Vietnamese army. A joint State-Defense report on December 6, 1950, bluntly said: "Much of the stigma of colonialism can be removed if, when necessary, yellow men will be killed by yellow men rather than by white men." On December 29, a CIA report called the French position "precarious" and warned that unless it improved, the French could be driven out of Tonkin in six to nine months.

My Presence Is Worth a Division

After the disaster of Cao Bang, France needed a savior. In Hanoi, the high command was sunk in near despair. There was talk of evacuating civilians. The army cried out for a magnetic leader who could galvanize the troops into action. The government in Paris was considering sending Jean de Lattre de Tassigny, who had led the French First Army from its landing in the south of France on August 16, 1944, into Germany, where he was a witness to the Nazi capitulation. President Auriol wanted him, but Premier Pleven warned that "half the officers will resign, for he has the reputation of being a butcher of men." De Lattre had his detractors, who saw him as a megalomaniac with a hair-trigger temper. He made huge scenes over minor matters. But even his detractors admitted that he was no armchair general and that he knew how to command.

In early January, Jules Moch, the minister of defense, made him a formal offer. De Lattre accepted, on condition that he exercise both military and civilian commands. He didn't want to be a mere general, but the emperor of Indochina. He told Moch: "I have nothing to gain and everything to lose, and that is why I accept." If his reply had a Delphic ring, coming from a sixty-one-year-old five-star general whose fourth war this would be, it can be better understood by seeing de Lattre as the sum of his wounds.

He was born in 1889 in a town in the Vendée, land of peasant uprisings, where his father was the mayor. The de Lattres were austere Catholics with military ancestors, and seven-year-old Jean showed both ambition and indecisiveness when he announced: "I will be a general or I will be pope." He chose the former. In September 1914, as a lieutenant in the 12th Dragoons, he was sent out on patrol on horseback in a fought-over area near Pont-à-Mousson. His colonel told him: "Don't try to be brave. Husband the lives of your men."

Ignoring this sound advice, de Lattre came upon twenty Bavarian cuirassiers. His unit galloped toward them, sabers drawn. He killed two before being pierced by a lance like a chicken on a spit. Hit in the shoulder and spitting blood, he fell from his horse with the lance still stuck in him. They were in enemy territory. His men could not remove him, but found a couple who were willing to hide him in their cellar. The lance was cut away and his shoulder was bandaged. De Lattre was one of the last French officers to be wounded in a cavalry charge. Once the front had stabilized into trench warfare, the cavalry officers were transferred to infantry regiments.

In 1915, he was hit by shrapnel and temporarily lost the use of his right arm. In July 1916, at Thiaumont, he was enveloped in a cloud of poison gas and had to be evacuated with damaged lungs. Combat takes its toll, and in the hospital he had his first nervous seizures.

In 1920, he was posted to Morocco and fought in the war against the rebel Abd el-Krim. While strolling through the souk in Fez on March 13, 1924, he was stabbed three times in the face by a Moroccan. The deep cut beneath his left eye required thirty-five stitches, and he suffered partial paralysis of his face. On August 25, 1925, while fighting in the Rif Mountains, he was shot in the knee and thereafter walked with a limp. He returned to France and married in 1927, his spirit intact inside a damaged body. In 1928, his son Bernard was born. He too went to officers' school and was sent to Indochina in 1949. De Lattre was close to his son. Bernard was his private reason for going to Vietnam.

Prior to his departure, de Lattre shopped around for a number two. He chose Raoul Salan, who was back in Paris, saying: "He's a defeatist, and he's not very intelligent, but he knows Indochina reed by reed and stream by stream." They landed in Saigon on December 17, 1950, and it was there that de Lattre had his first outburst. The plane taking them to Hanoi was General Carpentier's, and had four stars on the fuselage. But de Lattre was a five-star general. He threw a fit and would not depart until a fifth star had been added.

Upon his arrival in Hanoi, he modestly told his aides, "My presence is worth a division." He held a military parade with flags and bands as a way of announcing his presence, at a time when Vietminh radio trumpeted that its troops were massing to take the city. De Lattre's method was to make a series of swift decisions to wake up the somnolent bureaucracy. He cancelled plans for the evacuation of civilians. He purged the officers who had taken part in the Cao Bang defeat, from General Carpentier on down.

In the American press, the man with the "Napoleonic jaw and Roman nose" was applauded for having banished "defeatism" and infused a new spirit and energy in Saigon and Hanoi. De Lattre was one of the few French generals who courted the press, whose panegyrics helped validate the war to the American public. Tillman Durdin of *The New York Times* wrote that de Lattre had wrought "a miracle" and "within a week had visited by air all the major cities," proclaiming "the days of looseness are over! We shall not yield another inch of territory." On January 5, 1951, de Lattre announced, somewhat prematurely, that "the Communist drive for Hanoi has been smashed completely and the situation now rests in our hands."

In the profiles that appeared, his preference for orange juice countered the conventional image of the wine-swilling French. He was democratic, as shown by his willingness to bawl out anyone from a corporal to a general. His explosions of temper, however, were kept private. One of his aides, Captain Jean de Royer, said: "How can a great man be so odious?" His vanity was such that when he gave a dinner at the governor-general's palace, the ladies were instructed to rise when he entered the room.

One dissenting voice was that of *The New York Times'* respected military analyst Hanson Baldwin, who wrote on January 5, 1951, that de Lattre was a man of "much temperament and little tact," who "proved to be one of the most difficult French officers with whom Americans had to deal during the last war."

Now, however, as he shuttled between Hanoi and Saigon, de Lattre turned on the charm with the head of the U.S military mission, General Francis G. Brink. The mission, intended to monitor the "end use" of shipments, had arrived in August 1950 with a skeleton team of ten. In 1951, the number grew to 128. De Lattre's ability to turn the war around was in large part dependent on the opening of the aid spigot.

Already in 1950, the arrival of a dozen Bell P-63 Kingcobras had allowed the French to retire their ancient Spitfires. A cautionary note was sounded on November 20 by John Ohly, the deputy director of the Mutual Defense Assistance Program, when he expressed concern that "the demands on the United States for Indochina are increasing almost daily . . . and we are getting ourselves into a position where our responsibilities tend to supplant rather than complement those of the French and where failures are attributed to us as though we're at fault. . . . We may be on the road to being a scapegoat. . . . These situations unfortunately have a way of snowballing."

Alors! When Will This Incident Be Over?

In January 1951, de Lattre knew a Vietminh attack was coming. He asked General Brink for an emergency delivery, and the general prevailed on MacArthur to ship over from his stocks in Japan thirty Sherman tanks, as well as B-26 bombers and F8F Bearcats, the tubby fighter-bombers that carried the petroleum jelly known as napalm.

Inflated by his victory at Cao Bang, General Giap now planned to attack the Red River Delta. The French had made the worst mistake of the war by abandoning their posts on the northern border. The way was clear for the movement of supplies and advisers from China. Giap felt that the balance of power was shifting in his favor. In January, he had eighty battalions within twenty-five miles of Hanoi. It was time to move to the third and decisive stage, the counteroffensive. His plan was to send elements of two newly armed "iron" divisions, the 308th and the 312th, across the Red River and attack the provincial capital of Vinh Yen, twenty-five miles northwest of Hanoi.

Giap launched the third step prematurely, at the exact time when, thanks to de Lattre, the French had renewed their fighting spirit and firepower. On January 13, two Vietminh regiments crossed the Red River and inflicted heavy losses on a French mobile group (a motorized brigade with tanks and artillery). The Bearcats, which had arrived just in time, dropped napalm, allowing the French to pull back. Other Vietminh regiments moved on Vinh Yen from the north. At nightfall on January 14, they streamed down from the hills.

From Hanoi, de Lattre ordered all his combat planes to the battle. Short of transport, he commandeered civilian airliners in Saigon and flew reinforcements in. On January 16, he landed in Vinh Yen in a Morane spotter plane. Finding the commander of the garrison, Colonel Redon, de Lattre asked: "Alors! When will this incident be over?" The astonished colonel replied: "You're calling this an incident, General? We are facing eight Vietminh battalions." Officers in the field were not accustomed to seeing the commander in chief in person.

The battle ended on January 17, when the Vietminh troops attacking in human waves were splattered in open terrain with napalm. As Ngo Van

Chieu, one of the officers in the battle, later recalled: "The planes dive and hell opens before my eyes. . . . An intense flame which seems to spread for hundreds of meters, sows terror in the ranks. . . . Men flee and I can no longer restrain them. There is no way to live under that torrent of fire."

By noon on the seventeenth, Giap had ordered a withdrawal. He had sixteen hundred casualties, and another five hundred taken prisoner. As a Reuters dispatch put it: "Chanting 'there is no God but Allah,' fierce Moroccan mountaineers swept into Vietminh Communist rebels in the battle raging 20 miles from Hanoi. . . . Overhead, Kingcobra fighters strafed Vietminh troops in foxholes." The French suffered 43 dead and 160 wounded. De Lattre, who in the past had been criticized for wasting the lives of his men, was struck by the Vietminh's indifference to life. The *bo dois* were there to be slaughtered. The first wave was sent into the barbed wire with only a few grenades. But with his victory at Vinh Yen, de Lattre had saved Hanoi.

Wei Guoqing, the top Chinese adviser, wired Mao on January 27, 1951, that the Vietminh army needed reorganization. Mao replied on January 29, asking Wei "to adopt an attitude of patience and persuasion toward the Vietminh commanders so as to make them accept your ideas but not arouse their resentment. Their current shortcomings are the ones that the Chinese army also possessed when it was young. There is nothing strange about it." The Chinese too had been impatient to launch large-scale attacks.

Indochina Is a Key Area of Southeast Asia

On January 26, 1951, prior to French premier René Pleven's trip to Washington to see President Truman, Secretary of State Acheson briefed the Senate Committee on Foreign Relations, who seemed to draw a blank on Indochina. Senator Alexander Wiley, a Wisconsin Republican, asked: "Do I understand, Mr. Secretary, that we have air forces in Indochina?" Acheson replied that we did not, but we had made planes available. Senator Theodore Green, Democrat from Rhode Island, said he understood the United States had given the French some planes. "Those were the B-26s that I have just been talking about," Acheson said.

Senator J. William Fulbright, an Arkansas Democrat, asked if progress was being made. Acheson said: "General de Lattre has taken hold of the thing and some new vigor has been put into it."

René Pleven, the tall, robust Breton who had served in nine governments, saw Truman on January 29, 1951, but there was little plain talk. By that time, Chinese troops had routed MacArthur, and Truman was in a plaintive mood. "They have mistreated our people every time they had a chance." As a result, "we reached the same conclusions you did," to continue the fight. The communiqués said: "There exists a fundamental identity of views between our two countries." Pleven described "the great cost, both in lives and money" that France had paid "in resisting the Communist onslaught." Truman promised that U.S. aid would be expedited "in increased quantities."

On February 6, 1951, General Brink was in Washington and told his people at the Pentagon that American weapons were playing an important role in the war and "this is the first time I've seen people really fighting Communists in Asia." On February 25, the National Security Council considered Pleven's request and concluded that "Indochina is a key area of Southeast Asia and is under immediate threat." State and Defense should prepare a program of "practicable measures" including military assistance. Consequently, in 1951, military aid to Indochina rose to $170 million. Among the shipments, the aircraft carrier *Arromanches* arrived in the fall with more Kingcobras, which became the backbone of the French air force in Indochina, as well as more napalm-carrying Bearcats and twin-engine B-26 Invaders. To these were added F6F Hellcats, the flying trucks that carried a two-thousand-pound payload, and Helldivers, two-seat dive-bombers reputed for having destroyed Japanese ships.

The French Have a Knotty Problem on That One

For de Lattre, February was spent finding tons of concrete to build posts in the Red River Delta. Hundreds of these posts were erected in a sweeping semicircle, with an overlapping radius of fire, from pillboxes manned by ten men to elaborate emplacements with artillery and tanks. De Lattre's critics saw a new Maginot Line, but de Lattre argued that he had to secure the Red River Delta, which would bar the Vietminh's access to rice. He could then form more mobile groups to attack Giap's battalions. To carry out this plan, he needed reinforcements. But in Paris, the French Joint Chiefs were concerned that if they sent more troops, they would deplete French forces needed for the defense of Europe. De Lattre was told: "The duty of a general is to make the most of what he has."

De Lattre appealed to President Auriol, who urged him to come to Paris and make his case. At the end of February, de Lattre was in bed with a high fever. He didn't make it to Paris until March 14, and summed up the situation for Auriol at the Élysée Palace: The Vietminh had five divisions. Bao Dai was useless. De Lattre had to build a Vietnamese army.

On March 17, 1951, at 8:45 A.M., de Lattre saw General Dwight D. Eisenhower, who was then supreme commander of NATO. They discussed Indochina, and Ike recorded in his diary that "the French have a knotty problem on that one—the campaign out there is a draining sore in their side. Yet if they quit and Indochina falls to the Commies, it is easily possible that the entire Southeast Asia and Indonesia will go, soon to be followed by India." The logic of the domino theory had become accepted among American decision-makers.

Later that day, de Lattre appeared before the French Committee for National Defense to make his case: The Vietminh had 88 battalions, he had 59, 25 of them tied down in static posts. He had 68,000 troops, plus 18,000 Vietnamese. He needed 24,000 more men. They were found for de Lattre in North Africa—eleven battalions, three armored regiments, four artillery groups, and two battalions of engineers.

Forgive Me for Not Having Been Able to Protect Our Son

After the Vinh Yen defeat, Ho Chi Minh admitted at the Second Party Congress in February 1951 that the decision to advance to the third stage of warfare was controversial. Opinions were divided, but Giap decided on a second operation in March. This time, the 308th Division would march on the town of Mao Khe, nineteen miles north of Haiphong. Around a community intended to house the workers in a coal mine, de Lattre had built one of his posts. Since he was away in Paris, General Salan took command. Salan had reliable intelligence that Giap's troops were moving east, away from Hanoi. He stationed reserves armed with howitzers near Haiphong, prepared air support, and brought ships into the estuary of the Red River.

When Giap launched his human-wave attack on March 28, the French garrison fell back on the Mao Khe church. French firepower came into play from naval guns, howitzers, and air strikes. The Vietminh retreated with one thousand dead. De Lattre arrived in Haiphong on March 28, in time to congratulate Salan.

In April, de Lattre launched his Vietnamese army by embedding Vietnamese recruits within French regiments. One of the regiments chosen was the 1st Chasseurs, the only tank regiment in Tonkin, where de Lattre's twenty-three-year-old son, Bernard, was a lieutenant. Bernard spent April recruiting and training a Vietnamese battalion stationed in the town of Nam Dinh, forty-three miles southwest of Haiphong, at the end of one loop of the de Lattre line.

De Lattre had seen little of his son since arriving. Bernard insisted on being treated the same as his men, and refused to accept invitations to official dinners in Hanoi. His only goal was to be a worthy leader. But he did spend Sunday, May 27, with his father. He thanked God it wasn't an official dinner. He had de Lattre to himself, but his father looked tired; he'd had a bout of colitis.

After defeats north of Hanoi and north of Haiphong, Giap moved his regiments southward in May, through the Delta, in order to attack the more vulnerable posts of the de Lattre line on the Day River. He also wanted to break the resistance of the two Catholic communities there, at Nam Dinh and Ninh Binh. Slowed by monsoons, it took him weeks to slog through the paddy fields. Alerted to Giap's movements, de Lattre assembled eight motorized brigades, including his son's 1st Chasseurs.

On May 29, Bernard's battalion was back in Nam Dinh, resting after two days of operations. At 3 A.M., he was summoned to Ninh Binh on a rescue mission. A unit of eighty navy commandos was holed up in the church there, surrounded by Viets. The closest French unit was Bernard's. But finding the road cut, they had to leave their armor behind and take landing craft up the Song Van River, arriving at noon. They fought their way to the church, where they found twenty surviving commandos. By nightfall, they were outside the village in an exposed position. At 3 A.M. on May 30, a barrage of mortar shells poured down. Bernard de Lattre was killed as he was sending a message over the radio, as were most of the other officers in his battalion. His body, covered with twenty-eight shrapnel wounds, was shipped to Hanoi. De Lattre cabled his wife in Paris: "Forgive me for not having been able to protect our son." But Bernard had not wanted protection.

The battle on the Day River continued into June. Giap's troops were hit by air strikes and artillery. A Reuters dispatch on June 3 said: "French Union forces have beaten back three attacks by Indochina's Vietminh insurgents stabbing at the underbelly of the French-held Tonkin Delta in a seven-day battle for possession of the rice harvest." On June 10, Giap withdrew, leaving behind nine thousand dead and a thousand captives. Giap, experienced in hit-and-run attacks with small units, showed himself less capable in divisional warfare. Ho Chi Minh banned the slogan "Prepare for the shift to the general offensive." It was back to guerrilla tactics. Giap had to explain his errors to the Central Committee, one of whom said he should be replaced.

De Lattre struggled with his emotions: grief at the death of his son, satisfaction at the victory on the Day River, and growing fear that the only thing as bad as not receiving American aid was receiving it. As Donald Heath, the U.S. minister to Indochina, reported to Acheson on May 15, 1951, de Lattre was complaining that the aid made the French look "like a poor cousin in Vietnamese eyes." De Lattre told Heath: "Why don't you get rid of some of your ECA men and your missionaries? Then we could find housing for MAAG [the military mission]." Heath was convinced that tensions over economic aid were an obstacle to U.S. policy. De Lattre felt that Indochina was being swamped by American acronyms such as STEM (Special Technical and Economic Mission). Heath spoke to a French diplomat in Saigon who claimed that France had been compelled to accept economic aid in order to get military aid. When the United States dealt directly with the Bao Dai government, it undercut French prestige. The Americans, said this diplomat, seemed to think Indochina had been "discovered in 1950 . . . with the arrival of U.S. water pumps and tractors. . . . If a medical first aid station is opened, it is the inauguration of public health in Indochina." And yet this was what the French had been doing at "25 times the volume and with 1/25th the publicity." Worse than STEM's chest-thumping was the USIE (United States Information and Educational Exchange), whose English classes reminded the French diplomat of the time the Russians had opened a language course "in the blind belief that all that is good is Russian." It was outrageous that so many Vietnamese were learning English when so few of them knew French. Another source of annoyance was the translated books, since the first one to be distributed was a history of the United States. And why this invasion of Americans, Heath was asked, five times as many as all other foreigners combined? Was there a plan to turn Vietnam into a zone of American influence after the French had left?

Heath saw de Lattre at the end of May and found him looking "old and worn out . . . He spoke very low, almost in reverie, but very bitter." The main reason was the death of his son. "In a bona fide war," de Lattre told Heath, he would have had the consolation that Bernard had died a hero's death. Instead, he had been sacrificed on behalf of "an ungrateful people," the Vietnamese civilians who had failed to tell his battalion there were Viets in the area, and who hissed *"vendus"* (finks) to the Vietnamese recruits. Later, when Heath saw Bao Dai, the emperor expressed concern that de Lattre "might now conceive the war as one of revenge."

In spite of his disappointment at the "ungrateful" conduct of the Vietnamese in Ninh Binh, de Lattre threw himself into the recruitment of the Vietnamese army. On July 11, 1951, he was the commencement speaker at the Lycée Chasseloup-Laubat in Saigon. "I want you to be men," he told the graduating class. "If you're Communists, join the Vietminh. If you're patriots, fight for your country, for this is your war. France can't fight it for you. You've got to fight it for yourselves."

The Will and Genius of de Lattre Is Arrayed
Against the Stalinist Dynamic

In a way his address at the lycée was his farewell speech, for on July 29, exhausted and heavy-hearted, he left for France to recover at a spa, and to prepare for a September trip to Washington. That July, U.N. forces had recaptured most of South Korea, and cease-fire talks began. The U.S. government started paying closer attention to Indochina. Although Congress was still focused on Korea, Senator Hubert Humphrey said in August that "it should pay tribute to the valuable defense of freedom which the French troops are making in Indochina. If Indochina were lost, it would be as severe a blow as if we were to lose Korea."

In Saigon, the U.S. legation tirelessly promoted de Lattre. On August 18, with Heath in Washington for consultations, the chargé, Edmund Gullion, reported that de Lattre, who was not in Vietnam at the time, was "confronting the divided and listless Viets. . . . The will and genius of de Lattre is arrayed against the Stalinist dynamic."

In Washington, where saving Indochina from Communism had become a priority, de Lattre was intent on selling the war to his American ally. His willingness to raise a Vietnamese army would test his sincerity. When he arrived in New York in mid-September aboard the *Ile de France*, Humphrey Bogart and Lauren Bacall were among his fellow passengers, back from filming *The African Queen* on location. Bogie told the press: "Africa is a good place to stay away from." *Time* reported in a September 24 cover story that, not to be outdone by star power, "the French MacArthur, impeccable from kepi to pigskin gloves, and profile to the lens [of press photographers] pointed theatrically toward his country's copper gift to the U.S." At a press conference upon landing, de Lattre delivered what would be the main theme of his visit: "The war in Indochina is not a colonial war, it is a war against Red colonialism; as in Korea, it is a war against Communist dictatorship."

Time made de Lattre the personification of a winnable war. On the cover, against a background of flooded rice paddies and a fort flying the tricolor, his resolute likeness did not admit defeat. Heaping on the praise, *Time* effused that he had inspired the troops and shipped the slackers home. He understood the importance of napalm in jungle fighting. At the same time, behind the tough exterior there was a tender heart that mourned his son. A reporter who knew him told *Time*, "Sometimes a sudden memory will wring from him an uncontrollable sob." *Time*'s only caveat was an admission that "half the Indochinese would still vote for Ho rather than the French-supported Bao [Dai] in free elections."

In Washington, de Lattre kicked off his offensive with a September 16 appearance on the popular radio program *Meet the Press*, where he promised that victory would come within "months, perhaps one or two years." This type of wishful thinking was reminiscent of MacArthur. De Lattre said the war was costing "between two and three billions of dollars every year. . . . We have 38,000 killed in Indochina and more than 100,000 lost in all. . . . The citizens of Indochina are very desirous to join the national armies [this was more pie in the sky]. . . . The American Mission in Indochina helps me with equipment. . . . The Chief of that Mission, General Brink . . . is for me a great friend, a great supporter, a great help." Gone were the reservations de Lattre had expressed to Donald Heath regarding U.S. aid.

De Lattre had a chat with Truman and quoted the president as telling him the United States "would not let Indochina fall into enemy hands." On September 20, he met at the Pentagon with the Joint Chiefs and Secretary of Defense Robert Lovett, and gave his domino presentation. If Tonkin fell, so would Southeast Asia and India. The entire Muslim world would be engulfed. Lovett wasn't buying this doomsday scenario and told de Lattre that "the United States has a primary obligation in other theaters, whereas your primary obligation is in your own theater." De Lattre blustered that unless the United States delivered the goods he would tell his countrymen to proceed "without hope of victory." He complained that U.S. deliveries were late. He said he sometimes felt like "a beggar." He wanted to feel that "I am your man just as General Ridgway is your man. Your spirit should lead you to send me these things without my asking." Lovett promised to "do everything for [your] theater within our capabilities." "Do not say *my* theater," de Lattre retorted. "It is *our* theater." This exchange seemed to make an impression and deliveries were speeded up.

The flip side of U.S. aid, however, as de Lattre had already observed, was that the more the Americans got involved, the more they wanted to influence events. As the chargé, Edmund Gullion, put it on October 16, "We are justified in concerning ourselves with the political base of military success; the prospect for democratic institutions, forms of suffrage, administration of justice, economic and social improvement of the masses, progressive relaxation of police control. . . . These are also weapons in this war."

At his final appearance, a lunch at the National Press Club on September 30, de Lattre stayed on message, saying: "Once Tonkin is lost, there is really no barrier before Suez, and I will leave it to your imagination how defeatism and defeat would swell up as time passes, how Communist fifth columns would get into the game in every country as strong external Communist forces apply pressure on their frontiers." No one from the press questioned his assumptions, and he left for France convinced he had swayed American public opinion.

I'm Going to Join Bernard

It seemed inconceivable, in the light of his forceful Washington campaign, that de Lattre had less than four months to live. Back in Paris, he saw his doctor, Petchot-Bacqué, on October 4, 1951. That evening, his wife, Simone, came into the library where he was calmly working. De Lattre told her: "You know, in three months, I may not be here."

His wife thought he was talking about a new assignment.

"Petch tells me I have cancer of the hip."

De Lattre was nonetheless determined to return to Indochina, where General Giap was back on the offensive, after the rainy season. By October 19, he was in Saigon with his wife. He told Bao Dai he'd been away acting as "an itinerant missionary." On October 30, he flew to Ninh Binh to see where his son had been killed. There was nothing left of the hamlet, but he knelt in the rubble to pray. De Lattre was wasting away, always tired. He could hardly walk and was bathed in sweat. He wasn't up to conducting operations, and seemed absorbed in making sure the troops got Christmas presents. In Paris it was rumored that he had lost his aggressive spirit. The wires from the Committee for National Defense were written with vinegar.

In November, de Lattre decided to recapture Hoa Binh, the key post blocking the Vietminh's north–south line of communications, on RC6, thirty miles southwest of Hanoi. Three paratroop battalions took the post on November 15, joined by three mobile groups with tank support and naval units on the Black River. Giap pulled back into the hills and bided his time. De Lattre insisted on flying into Hoa Binh, passing the troops in review, and handing out decorations. It was his last hurrah.

One of de Lattre's final tasks before leaving Indochina was to welcome a visiting member of the House of Representatives, John F. Kennedy, who was in his anticolonialist period. When Kennedy was briefed by Heath, he asked why the Vietnamese should be expected to fight to keep their country part of France. When de Lattre met the young representative, he found him so annoying that he wrote a letter of complaint to the U.S. embassy. Upon his return to Washington, Kennedy declared: "In Indochina we have allied ourselves to the desperate effort of a French regime to hang on to the remnants of empire. . . . The task is rather to build a strong native non-Communist sentiment . . . and rely on that . . . rather than upon the legions of General de Tassigny." To do otherwise "spells fore-doomed failure."

De Lattre left Indochina in late November, just missing General J. Lawton Collins, the army chief of staff, who toured the area and said, "This is largely a General de Lattre show. If anything should happen to him, there could well be a collapse in Indochina."

Admiral Arthur Radford, commander of naval forces in the Pacific, came through in early December. When he landed at Tan Son Nhut, he wondered at the French love of protocol: Troops were stationed every ten yards on the road and a motorcycle escort was provided. At the governor-general's palace, he stayed in an enormous room with ceilings twenty feet high and overhead fans. He met with Bao Dai, a pleasant but unimpressive young man a little on the portly side. He flew over limestone chimneys to the Delta and saw the de Lattre line of forts in overlapping semicircles. But it bothered him that even though de Lattre had greatly improved the army, French officers constantly denigrated the capabilities of the enemy.

Back in Paris, de Lattre was hospitalized on December 20 in a private clinic in Neuilly. He underwent two operations, one on his bladder and one for the cancer on his hip. After the operations, he fell into a coma. In his waking moments, he said, "I'm going to join Bernard." On January 11, 1952, he died. He was given his *bâton de maréchal* posthumously.

The French Are Now in Good Shape

The departure of de Lattre from Indochina in November 1951 forced a rethinking of what was called in Washington "the policy circle." Intelligence was coming in that the Chinese Communists were preparing for massive intervention. A December 19 memo to Secretary of State Acheson warned that "action on a large scale may be expected on or about the 18th of December."

As the year ended, Acheson received a pessimistic cable from Ambassador David Bruce in Paris. "French policy in regard to Indochina war is rapidly moving toward a crisis," he reported. "Public sentiment for withdrawal . . . will gain steadily. . . . We may soon be presented with a definite either/or situation. . . . Either we increase our present aid to Indochina . . . or the French will be compelled to reexamine their policy."

The Military Assistance Program summary at the end of 1951 showed that since the start of the program in 1950, $163,600,000 worth of goods had been shipped to Indochina. Aside from weapons, the aid included materials for road construction and medical supplies. Many of the shipments were behind schedule. Korea still had first call.

On a final note for 1951, the year of de Lattre, let us summon John F. Melby, who headed the second U.S. mission to Indochina in July 1950, but was fired in May 1953 for consorting with Communists. The absurdity of the charges became obvious in the light of his lecture to the National War College in December 1951, after another trip to Southeast Asia. On Indochina he was more pro-French than his bosses at the State Department. In a sly reference to Melby's womanizing, which later got him in trouble, the officer who introduced him said, "I am sure you are going to be as fast on your feet with us as with the ballerinas in Moscow," where Melby had served.

"What has happened since the arrival of de Lattre," Melby said, "is almost beyond belief." The French were now "in good shape," and had recovered all the territory they had lost except for the border posts. Melby was alone among American officials in praising the national army. "A lot of people tend to scoff at these armies," he said. "Yet they have done not too badly. They look well. I had occasion a year and a half ago to go out on a couple of patrols with the Vietnamese troops in the Tonkin area, and I can assure you they were far more ruthless in the way they handled the Vietminh forces than any Frenchman would ever be. In fact, we had some difficulty getting them to leave at least one Vietminh, whom we captured on patrols, with his head still on his body so he could be brought back for questioning. Their idea was simply to bring back the heads and leave the bodies there—that should be evidence enough."

Melby was reminded of the Duke of Wellington's remarks during one of the Peninsular campaigns when his advisers scoffed at the Spanish guerrillas he was using. Wellington said: "I don't know what they do to the enemy, but they scare the hell out of me." Another encouraging sign, Melby said, was the pattern of defections among Vietminh forces. (In fact, there were far more defections in the nationalist army.) On balance, he concluded, "we can foresee a military solution to the military problem in Indochina within one to three years."

The Accumulation of French Government Neuroses

On January 5, 1952, Winston Churchill, once again prime minister, was dining on President Truman's yacht when the conversation turned to the prospects for a European army. The idea had come from René Pleven when he was French premier in 1950: a unified army as a counterweight to Soviet might, to be called the European Defense Community. Churchill, the Former Naval Person, expressed an unfavorable view of the EDC. As Dean Acheson recalled, "He pictured a bewildered French drill sergeant sweating over a platoon made up of a few Greeks, Italians, Germans, Turks and Dutchmen, all in utter confusion over the simplest orders." How could the rank and file work up any enthusiasm, Churchill wondered, "singing 'March, NATO, march on.' "

British foreign secretary Anthony Eden explained that the proposal did not contemplate any such mixing of nationalities; it would create units of twelve thousand men of a single nationality. The sticking point, Eden said, was that a strong West German army bothered the French, who had not yet decided whether to treat Germany as an ally or an enemy. Thus the treaty was in limbo.

Acheson spent much of his time that year pushing the EDC along, even though the British declined to be a member. The French wanted restrictions, so that the German force did not exceed the size of theirs. But they were hamstrung by the war in Indochina, which swallowed up so much of their military capacity. For the United States, the EDC became a foreign policy cornerstone. Thus, a linkage was established between the Indochina war and the French acceptance of the treaty. The United States would help with one to obtain the other.

Thanks to its obsession with the EDC, which carried over from Truman to Eisenhower, the United States became locked in an unstated equation that required paying for the Indochina war to obtain French support of the EDC. It was finally stated in December 1953 by Theodore Streibert, the director of the United States Information Agency, when he admitted that "our policy in helping France and Vietnamese win the war in Indochina is contingent on ratification by French of EDC." The French gave in to the temptation to procrastinate on the EDC in order to maintain the cash flow.

Acheson in early 1952 was frustrated by "the accumulation of French government neuroses"—fear of Germany and the outcome in Indochina, and, in spite of the massive aid, seeing America as the main source of its troubles. At an executive session of the Senate Foreign Relations Committee on January 14, Acheson raised the question of a possible invasion of Indochina. He said the Chinese should be warned that "if you fellows come in you will be pasted." Chairman Tom Connally of Texas asked whether the Indochina war had begun as "a colonial dispute."

Acheson's reply showed that the government had jettisoned all semblance of opposition to colonialism: "The Vietnamese have got all the liberty and opportunity they can possibly handle or want. The French are not only not getting anything out of Indochina, they are putting an awful lot in, and that burden is a very hard one." Unconvinced, Connally observed that "ultimately, I think France is going to have to get out . . . because they [the Vietnamese] are not going to put up with colonialism."

From Donald Heath, now raised to the rank of ambassador in Saigon,

Acheson heard another dissonant note on January 20. Heath had been talking to Emperor Bao Dai, who was exasperated with the French stalling on independence issues. It was all very well to claim that French pride and prestige were at stake, the emperor said, but they had to face reality. Perhaps it would not be "utterly tragic" if the Chinese did invade. At least then, he, Bao Dai, could lead the resistance against "the hated traditional enemy." Taken aback, Heath replied that with "Commie ruthlessness and efficiency," the Chinese could easily suppress any resistance, and that "at present time only Fr Union forces keep Vietnam from becoming Chi colony." Heath was a short, rotund man with "a disconcerting resemblance to Stan Laurel," as one member of his staff put it, and he was fond of using the phrase "fighting the good fight." After having been portrayed as a colonial conflict in the early years of the Truman administration, the war was now seen as vital to the security of the free world.

The Ship Has a Helmsman at the Rudder but No Captain at the Wheel

The year of de Lattre was followed by the year of Salan, who had neither the charisma nor the brilliance of his predecessor. At age fifty-four, he was a three-star general doing the job of a five-star. Standoffish with the press, he did not garner glowingly inflated profiles. He had no powerful backers in Paris, and it was open season for sniping. Admiral Radford, who made one of his periodical inspection tours in 1952, said "Salan was overcautious and defense-minded," and conducted the war with a World War I "barbed-wire" strategy. He waited for the enemy to attack his forts in the hope of inflicting more casualties than he suffered, giving the Vietminh the initiative. He must have been told by Paris to hold down losses, Radford guessed.

In Salan's favor, it was said that he knew Indochina. He was rumored to practice Buddhism and collect opium pipes, and he kept an elephant tusk in his office, as did the mandarins of ancient China. But where were the bold operations of de Lattre? To be fair, Salan didn't have the troops. When he asked for reinforcements, he was told there weren't any. His loyal aide, General Allard, noted in his diary: "The ship has a helmsman at the rudder, but no captain at the wheel." Thus the ship was going around in circles.

The way the French worked it, as Edmund Gullion of the U.S. embassy in Saigon later recalled, was that there was a rainy season and a campaign season. "In May or June, we usually get French estimates of success based on Vietminh losses in the preceding fall. . . . [Each set] of estimates soon proves equally disappointing. By October, French Union troops are found bottled up in mountain defiles far from their bases. . . . They are rumbling about late or lacking American aid and lack of American understanding. . . . There is widespread speculation that the French may pull out. We promise more aid. The French make a stand. They give us new estimates and the round begins once more."

In 1952, while Salan spent the monsoon months trying to clear the Vietminh out of the Red River Delta, Giap built up his main force and distributed the equipment from China. He now had a regular army of three hundred thousand and a militia of two million. On January 23, French intelligence in Saigon reported that in the previous four months, China had sent across the border 4,000 tons of weapons, including 100,000 hand grenades (soon exploding in the bars of Saigon), 75mm recoilless rifles of Russian and Chinese make with 10,000 shells, 10 million cases of cartridges, and thousands of Skoda rifles. With the opening of armistice talks in Panmunjom, Peking had doubled its aid, and added antiaircraft guns and howitzers.

Ho Chi Minh decreed "self-reliance," and factories sprang up in the jungle, arsenals in every province, and workshops in every district, producing mortars. His hold on the civilian population was based on the Maoist "three antis"—corruption, waste, and bureaucracy—as well as Maoist slogans such as "patriotic emulation." The ceaseless indoctrination was punctuated by a train of congresses and campaigns. On May Day, there was a "Congress of Emulation Combatants and Model Cadres," followed by a "Rectification" campaign, during which fifteen thousand cadres were subjected to a period of "thought reform" to raise their political consciousness.

Land reform copied the Maoist practice of reducing rents and redistributing acreage. Ho also borrowed the "three together" system, under which trained cadres lived with peasants in order to share their misery and hatred for landlords. The peasants then denounced their landlords, who were brought before kangaroo courts and sentenced on the spot, sometimes to death. These pilot projects led to an agrarian reform law providing for the confiscation of French-owned land and that of the "traitors" who worked with them.

Under an exchange agreement signed in Peking in July 1952, the Vietminh made partial payment for Chinese weapons with timber, rice, and opium. Goods moved freely since the French had abandoned their border posts. A Sino-Vietnamese control committee with twelve transportation teams supervised the shipments. The agreement also stipulated that the Vietminh could send their wounded to China for treatment. On November 6, 1952, a Sino-Vietnamese postal agreement was signed. It was the first time the Vietminh were able to exchange mail with another country. It was also a sign that much of Vietnam was "liberated" and had its own stamps and post offices.

Chinese troops did not, as in Korea, invade Tonkin. But battalions of advisers moved across the border, five thousand in 1951 and seven thousand in 1952, as well as one thousand medics in September 1952, and platoons of truck drivers, radio operators, and construction workers. General Giap later disingenuously denied the Chinese influence, saying in 1982 that "our military science does not owe anything to the Chinese military philosophy [which] refuses the possibility of an uprising in cities [as in the battle of Hanoi]."

In early 1952, Luo Guibo, the head of the Chinese Military Advisory Group in Vietnam, recommended an offensive in the northwest, which was dotted with thinly garrisoned French posts blocking the routes into Laos. In these so-called Thai highlands, the mountains and lack of passable roads gave the Vietminh a tactical advantage, making it hard for the French to bring up artillery, while their troops had to advance on foot. Far from their bases, the French would experience supply shortages. The northwest operations would create a second front, drawing French troops away from the Red River Delta. If successful, it would consolidate a liberated zone extending from the Laotian border to the Vietminh headquarters in Viet Bac.

On February 16, 1952, Luo Guibo outlined a plan before the Central Military Commission in Peking. In the first stage, Giap's troops would cross the Red River and attack the post of Nghia Lo, midway between the Red and Black rivers. They would then cross the Black River into the highlands, where two French posts—Son La and Na San—were lined up twelve miles from each other. The attack would be launched in mid-September in the hope of reaching the Laotian border by the end of the year. The Central Military Commission approved the plan on April 19 and Giap assembled his forces.

France Lacked the Will to Draft Its Own Men for Service in Indochina

In Washington, Dean Acheson was so concerned that the Chinese would invade Indochina that he considered evacuating Hanoi. As he explained it to the British ambassador, Sir Oliver Franks, on June 17: If the Chinese came in, "we would have to do something," but "none of [the choices] were pleasant." It was a mistake "to defend Indochina in Indochina . . . we could not have another Korea. . . . We could not put ground forces in Indochina" but "we could take air and naval action."

Acheson said the U.S. Navy was talking to the French "regarding port sizes, capacity of ships, etc., with regard to evacuation."

The next day, however, the secretary of state received a visit from the civilian boss in Indochina, Jean Letourneau, minister of the Associated States, who painted a rosy picture that inspired Acheson with "the feeling of encouragement and confidence." According to Letourneau, the military situation was developing favorably. Much had been accomplished toward the creation of a Vietnamese army. The Associated States were close to independence and were handling their political, financial, and economic affairs. The 150th U.S. ship bearing arms and munitions had recently arrived in Saigon. It was, as Candide put it, the best of all possible worlds.

Later that month, in London, Acheson was brought back to reality. Prior to talks with the French foreign minister, Robert Schuman, Acheson met Anthony Eden at the Foreign Office to plan their strategy. Eden anticipated that Schuman would take "the now familiar line that there was little prospect for victory in Indochina and that unless a general settlement were reached the best we could hope for would be a stalemate."

The French were talking out of both sides of their mouths, waxing optimistic in their quest for American aid and waning pessimistic in international conferences. In Saigon, General Salan got nowhere with his requests for more troops. He flew to Paris in July to lobby the ministers, but found them all vacillating about whether to stay or go. They adopted the eyedropper policy, Salan lamented. No one wanted to take a risk that might get him voted out of office, and it was out of the question to send French conscripts. As General Matthew Ridgway put it, "France lacked the will to draft its own young men for service in Indochina." Salan left Paris empty-handed, and returned to Saigon in early September, feeling like Sisyphus pushing a boulder uphill.

Letourneau's assertion that the Associated States were moving toward independence took a blow at the United Nations. On September 19, in a Security Council debate on their admission to the U.N., the application was vetoed by the Soviets, who said the Indochinese states were "Franco-American puppets." To admit the Bao Dai state would be "an insult to the people of Indochina."

In Our War, Where Is the Front?

In early September 1952, Ho Chi Minh secretly went to Peking to coordinate the fall strategy. In a wire to Giap on September 30, he confirmed that the initial stage of the campaign would be limited to Nghia Lo, which commanded tracks to the Laotian border. Ho went on to Moscow to attend the 19th Party Congress of the Communist Party of the Soviet Union, and was back in Vietnam in December, having missed the fall offensive.

Giap was at the front, west of the Black River, with three divisions. In mid-October, he threw an entire division at the battalion-size post of Nghia Lo. In ten days of fighting the base was taken. The French retreated forty miles to their second line of defense on Route Provinciale 41, the posts of Na San and Son La. Na San had an airstrip that could take C-47 Dakotas, and Salan wanted to test his theory that a well-defended garrison with artillery and air support could survive without road links. In his advocacy of the *base aéroterrestre*, Na San became the precursor of Dien Bien Phu.

Na San, defended by a dozen battalions, had an outer ring of positions on hilltops three miles across, dug in behind barbed wire and minefields, and an inner ring protecting the airstrip, where the rows of howitzers and mortars were stationed. On the night of November 23, a Vietminh battalion stormed a sandbag blockhouse held by 110 Legionnaires, whose machine-gun nests covered the barbed wire. The Vietminh left behind sixty-four corpses. Giap's infiltration tactics had failed and he stopped to take stock. The French could hear the Viets chopping down trees to get a clear field of fire. The intermission gave them time to fly in three hundred more tons of barbed wire, one hundred trucks and jeeps, timber for dugouts, and stocks of rations and ammunition.

In early 1952, Howard Simpson, a young World War II veteran from California, arrived in Saigon as a U.S. Information Agency officer. He was one of those meddlesome Americans de Lattre had complained about who monitored the use the French were making of American aid. It did not take Simpson long to experience the underlying condescension, resentment, and obstructionism of the French. When he was sent on the end-use missions in the field, they organized long lunches with beaucoup wine to fog the mind.

By hanging out with the press corps, Simpson kept reasonably well informed. In the fall, there were rumors of a Giap offensive in the northwest, which could force the French to move troops away from the Delta and extend their already strained lines of communication. French radio intercepts identified the 308th and 312th divisions on the Red River, with twenty thousand coolies in support. After the fall of Nghia Lo, General Salan ordered other posts to fall back on Na San, with its airstrip. The twelve battalions garrisoned there had built strong defenses. When Giap launched his attack on Na San, Simpson was sent to Hanoi with the mission of seeing how U.S. equipment was being used in combat. In Hanoi, he reflected, you knew you were close to a shooting war—the heavy military traffic, the mud-splattered vehicles, a tank park on the outskirts.

In early December, Simpson caught a ride to Na San aboard a Dakota bringing ammunition to a battle the French were hailing as a victory. The flight took a little less than an hour. The Dakota dipped through the cloud cover to the mountains below. The sun made the barbed wire glint, and Simpson could see the excavated positions in the hills and the communication trenches. The Dakota bumped along the airstrip, and he jumped through the open cargo doors as an empty truck backed up to take on the ammunition. The planes had to be unloaded quickly, since one landed every ten minutes.

Na San was humming with the activity of what the historian Martin Windrow called "a military goulash": Legionnaires unrolling barbed wire as they broke out in a German marching song, Moroccans in striped burnooses and turbans pulling mules burdened with cases of artillery shells up a steep hill. Simpson could smell *nuoc mam,* fish sauce, on the Vietnamese wounded being carried on stretchers into the surgical unit, which flew a Red Cross flag.

He found the cavelike, sandbagged command post, with earthen walls and a roof of logs, and introduced himself to the post commander, Colonel Jean Gilles. The one-eyed, strongly built para greeted him warily. Gilles wasn't used to American civilians dropping in. He sat with his staff officers at a trestle table covered with maps, telephones, and radios. Messages were sent and received, and radio static hung in the air, as outside the howitzers roared.

Simpson was told in a briefing that Vietminh sappers carrying bangalore torpedoes (metal tubes packed with explosives) threw themselves on the barbed wire so the men behind them could get through. So far in the battle, more than five hundred Viet corpses in padded jackets had been buried. Every day, the barbed wire, festooned with chunks of clinging flesh, had to be repaired.

That night, Simpson brought a fifth of Scotch to the officers' mess, and the mood progressed from stiffness to joviality. Even Père Gilles took a slug. The food wasn't out of cans. There was a *salade russe.* Leaving the mess, Simpson saw tracers from defensive positions piercing the darkness. An occasional flare dropped by a C-47 lit up the barbed wire. The fighting lasted until daylight, and blue skies meant a resumption of the airlift. Simpson borrowed a typewriter and managed to knock out a report on the

French performance. It was clear that Giap was pulling back his division. Colonel Gilles was in a foul mood, even though the battle would win him a general's star. His paras, who should have been in the jungle ambushing Viets, were in a static, defensive mode. Simpson decided it was time to get out. He gave the rest of his Scotch to the mess officer and hitched a ride on a Bristol transport. The French had held. Salan was vindicated.

Just as one American was observing the battle of Na San from the French side, another American was behind Vietminh lines with General Giap. Joseph Starobin, foreign editor of the Communist-connected magazine *New Masses*, had crossed the border from China in 1952 to report on the war from the Vietminh side. At Giap's unnamed headquarters, a bamboo shed with a roof of thatched palm leaves, Starobin sat across from the general at a large table covered by a green cloth. His aides handed Giap a large colored map, which he unrolled on the table. Over their heads hung the first lightbulb Starobin had seen in weeks; he could hear the whir of a generator.

Giap pointed to the dirt path outside. "Our boulevards," he said. He wore a khaki uniform without insignia, and smiled constantly, as if that was the correct expression to adopt with an American. "In our war," he said, "where is the front?" The front was fluid; the Vietminh were everywhere and nowhere. On Giap's map, most of the northwest was shaded in red, with thin green lines indicating French communication routes. Giap claimed that 120 French posts had been taken, though the French still held Na San. "We are leaving them there," he said. "Let them use their supplies to hold it." He did not mention that Na San had cost him three thousand casualties.

"This illustrates the French dilemma," Giap went on. "Either they try to extend their strong-points once again, with their depleted manpower, in which case they spread themselves thin, or else they move out of their strong-points, which frees territory and population to us." In addition, he said, the French were now fighting with a largely foreign army, consisting of many Moroccans and Germans, for example. He claimed to have captured "prisoners of no less than 24 nationalities."

The main advantage Giap's troops had was mobility. "In the battle for Na San," Giap said, "we had to move deep into the valleys. We had to cross

30 streams, some of them 250 yards wide, and make our way over high mountains. The French officers whom we captured told us later they did not see how we could have done it. They did not comprehend how our forces could appear at Na San hundreds of kilometers from our bases."

Giap looked at his watch and said, "Take care. Don't catch malaria." Then he was gone.

The French Should Stop Sitting in Their Beau Geste Forts on Champagne Cases

The presidential campaign of 1952 amounted to a changing of the guard. The Republicans, sidelined for twenty years, had a hugely popular war-hero candidate, who made the governor of Illinois seem irrelevant. Ike's teammate, Richard Nixon, doubled as attack dog, barking "Adlai the Appeaser" and "Ph.D. graduate of Dean Acheson's Cowardly College of Communist Containment."

Ike ran on ending the war in Korea and rolling back the Communist threat. He carried thirty-nine of forty-eight states, winning 55.1 percent of the vote to Stevenson's 44.4 percent. Republicans won both houses of Congress. Truman, who wanted continuity in foreign policy, arranged a meeting with Ike prior to the inauguration, at the White House on November 18. Truman was flanked by the apostles of containment, Averell Harriman and Dean Acheson, who raised the problem of Indochina. Despite a lack of "aggressive attitude from a military point of view," Acheson said, and of "fence-sitting by the population," which was "the central problem," it was vital to keep Indochina from the Communists. Acheson stressed that Chinese intervention in Indochina "is an urgent matter upon which the new administration must be prepared to act."

Ike sat there chewing the earpiece of his spectacles. He didn't like being lectured to by the departing Democrats. Truman later told Merle Miller that "nothing that was said was getting through to him. He got there mad and he stayed mad. . . . He was used to getting his ass kissed." The meeting lasted twenty minutes.

On November 20, Ike announced his choice of John Foster Dulles as secretary of state and Charles E. Wilson, president of General Motors, as secretary of defense. Ike planned to handle Defense himself, but he needed a strong secretary of state. Dulles had the pedigree. His maternal grandfather had been Benjamin Harrison's secretary of state, and his uncle Robert Lansing had been Woodrow Wilson's. Dulles himself was a member of the delegation at Versailles in 1919. The British, who feared that he wanted to bomb China, tried to block his nomination. Churchill called him a "stupid sermonizer."

Dulles told the House Foreign Relations Committee in January 1953 that Indochina "is, in some ways, more dangerous . . . than any other situation in the world." Pressure grew from the Joint Chiefs for more military involvement. One idea was to help the French develop their port and air facilities in the Red River Delta without antagonizing the Chinese. Another was to assist the French in training the Vietnamese army.

But just as the United States decided to get more involved, in France public opinion was increasingly antiwar. In Saigon, the dapper, mustached Robert McClintock had arrived as chargé while Donald Heath was on home leave. He added a qualifier to Heath's "the French are fighting a good fight": "but they could be doing a hell of a lot better." McClintock said the United States should cut off funds unless the French "stopped sitting in their Beau Geste forts on champagne cases." In Washington, Admiral Radford, soon to be named chairman of the Joint Chiefs of Staff, agreed, telling Assistant Secretary of State John M. Allison on February 4 that "unless the French radically change their outlook and adopt a much more aggressive spirit," they would never break the stalemate.

The two allies were at cross-purposes: the United States was determined that the French must hang on in Indochina, while doubting their ability to do so; the French government was leaning toward talks to end the war, but wanted increased American aid so that it could negotiate from a position of strength. Thus when René Mayer, the premier since January, came to Washington in late March 1953, his job was to convince the Americans that the French, who had long given up on total victory, leaving the Chinese border unguarded, still had the will to fight.

Prior to Mayer's arrival, Dulles cabled his ambassador in Paris, Douglas Dillon: "We envisage Indochina situation with real sense of urgency." He was hoping for "considerable increased effort having as its aim liquidation of principal regular enemy forces within period of say, twenty-four months."

Mayer arrived with his foreign minister, Georges Bidault, and Jean Letourneau, the minister for the Associated States. Their mission was to pretend to be pursuing the war aggressively. When they saw the president on March 20, Ike said he hesitated to grant more aid unless the French had a war plan. Letourneau improvised one on the spot: 80,000 more men for a total native army of 120,000 and an offensive north of the Delta. Letourneau estimated the Vietminh defeat would come in 1955, the exact time frame Dulles had suggested to Dillon.

When Ike raised the issue of "obtaining the confidence of the local people," he was rebuffed by Bidault, who, as Ike later recalled, "evaded and refused to commit himself to an out-and-out renunciation of any French colonial purposes."

Dulles, however, liked René Mayer, a pro-American businessman, and told Ike at a breakfast meeting on March 24 that "Mayer is a real friend." If an agreement couldn't be reached with him, "it was doubtful that it could be done at all."

The Joint Chiefs responded that Letourneau's presentation was a hope, not a plan, as long as the French had to rely on a national army that did not yet exist. They would have preferred that the French cut the supply lines with China, for a start. At an April 24 meeting of the Joint Chiefs and the State Department, General Hoyt S. Vandenberg, the air force chief of staff, said that "the French have not been taking the native people into their confidence. They don't seem to trust the native forces enough to want to use them in large units." The whole French defensive position was one of "not really wanting to fight the war to a conclusion. . . . If the French keep up in this manner, we will be pouring money down a rat hole."

Paul Nitze, the head of Policy Planning at State, said that even if the Letourneau plan could not achieve complete success, the alternative was complete defeat if the United States cut off aid. General Lawton Collins replied that the Joint Chiefs were willing to back the plan, "but we should first put the squeeze on the French to get off their fannies."

In France, Apathy Was Turning to Disenchantment

On March 5, 1953, Joseph Stalin died of a stroke at the age of seventy-four, just forty-four days after Ike had been sworn in. His pudgy successor, Georgy Malenkov, called for "peaceful coexistence" and made conciliatory gestures toward the West. Charles E. Bohlen, the American ambassador in Moscow, could see the signs of change. An article in *Pravda* denounced "the cult of personality." The Soviet press toned down its "Hate America" campaign. On April 16, Ike welcomed the Soviet initiatives. *Pravda* ran his speech in full, which Bohlen said would never have happened under Stalin.

Dulles, however, saw the reaching out as a sign of weakness in the Kremlin, and a time for the United States to get tough. In Paris in late April for a foreign ministers' meeting with the British and French, he repeated to Bidault the need to take the offensive and develop a local army with native officers. "We must demonstrate to Congress that the things the French are doing are important to the free world," Dulles said. But the French were not insensitive to Malenkov's entreaties and considered some form of entente with the Soviet Union.

In Saigon that spring, the 250th shipload of American equipment docked in the harbor, just as Giap launched an offensive into northern Laos and took the capital of Sam Neua Province. Vietminh radio trumpeted that Sam Neua was the first liberated province in Laos. The *bo doi*, carrying their little bags of four days' rations containing rice, salt, and *nuoc mam*, moved through jungles and mountains that the French considered impassable. They got to within twenty-five miles of the Laotian capital of Luang Prabang, where King Sisavang Vong was in residence. Giap's strategy was to attack a vulnerable point, diverting French troops from the Delta. When those troops moved to the west, the Vietminh returned to the Delta, easily bypassing the posts de Lattre had built. In May, however, the Vietminh divisions in Laos, exhausted and far from their bases, pulled out with the onset of the monsoon season.

On April 24, 1953, Premier René Mayer reprimanded General Salan for pulling his troops out of Sam Neua. "You have too many land-air bases to defend and we cannot satisfy your demands," Salan was told. "Your principal task is to constitute a powerful offensive mass."

The Giap offensive set off more alarm bells in Washington. The peace talks in Panmunjom were winding down. What would the end of the Korean War bring the Vietminh in terms of Chinese aid? French intelligence had already spotted Vietminh cadres being trained as pilots in China.

The French regime in Saigon suffered another blow when a parliamentary mission of inquiry came through in May 1953 and issued a scathing report accusing the top civilian, Jean Letourneau, of exercising a "veritable dictatorship without limitation or control." The "Norodom Palace clique" was "insensible to the daily tragedy of the war." In Saigon, "gambling, depravity, love of money and power corrupted the morale and destroyed the will." There were daily scandals in "the granting of licenses, the transfer of piastres, and commercial transactions. . . . Our representatives in Saigon have allowed themselves to get inveigled into the tempting game of power and intrigue."

In Paris, political leaders had lost all hope in Bao Dai, who, as President Auriol put it, "bought a villa in Morocco from the Comte de Paris [heir to the French throne], kept a private plane in case he needed to skip, and built tennis courts to amuse his girlfriends." A poll published in *Le Monde* in May 1953 showed that 35 percent of the French population wanted negotiations, 15 percent wanted to leave, and 15 percent wanted to stay. The remainder had no opinion. Apathy was turning to disenchantment, as the French realized that the war was a series of blunders without end, and that the befuddled coalition governments in Paris were not up to the task.

ACT III

Navarre Takes Command

· · ·

A hedgehog is a small mammal named for its pig-like snout and its fondness for hedges. It curls up into a ball when threatened, displaying dense erectile spines.

American Heritage Dictionary

• • •

WHEN PRESIDENT EISENHOWER discussed Indochina in the early months of 1953, he found himself trying to reconcile competing American concerns: the desire to give autonomy to the Associated States; the Cold War security need to assist the French; and their inability to win the war. At a National Security Council meeting on May 6, he said that "nothing could possibly save Indochina and that continued U.S. assistance would amount to pouring our money down a rat hole" unless "the French made it clear to the people of Indochina that they were serious about giving them independence, and at the same time appointed an effective military commander." On the same day, to push that last item along, he wired Ambassador Douglas Dillon in Paris that he wanted General Salan replaced with a "forceful and inspirational leader."

Two days later, René Mayer picked a new commander, the fifty-five-year-old Henri Navarre, who was at the time on an inspection tour in Germany. He was serving as chief of staff to Marshal Juin, head of NATO's Central European Command. Navarre returned to NATO headquarters in Fontainebleau, where Juin informed him that Salan was out of favor and that Mayer wanted him replaced. Since Navarre was a staff man and not a combat general, Mayer had met him over the years at various conferences and admired his finesse. Mayer called him "the intelligent general." Navarre told Juin he had never served in Asia and knew nothing about Indochina. Juin replied: "Someone has to do it."

Navarre, the son of a professor of Greek in Toulouse, had been an intelligence officer for most of his career. He developed the unflappable aloofness of a man whose mind stores secrets. His silver hair was brushed back, his eyes were hooded, and he was light on his feet, giving him a nimble, wary, catlike demeanor.

In Paris, René Mayer said that Navarre's ignorance regarding Indochina was an advantage. "You will see it with fresh eyes." Navarre's mission, Mayer informed him, was to find "an honorable way out." He should leave at once, study the situation for a month, and report back to Paris. "But don't ask for too many reinforcements."

What Are You Doing in This Shithouse?

Navarre flew to Saigon on May 19, 1953, taking along a young captain he trusted, Jean Pouget, as his aide-de-camp. On the plane, almost as if talking to himself, Navarre said, "I thought I was headed for command in Central Europe. I've always liked the Black Forest and the mist on the Rhine. I got along well with the Germans. And then they send me to Saigon. It's all the more stupid because I've got 99 chances out of 100 of losing whatever reputation I have."

"Well then," asked Pouget, "why did you accept?"

Navarre looked out the window at the cloud-streaked expanse and did not reply. Pouget realized that only a strict sense of duty kept Navarre from discouragement.

On May 21, two days after Navarre's departure, the René Mayer government was overthrown, by a vote of 328 to 244, after asking for emergency funds. For nearly a month, in what the French call *pagaille* ("mess" or "muddle"), there was no government. The situation reminded one writer of a famously absurd phrase uttered by Foreign Minister Georges Bidault: "I don't know where we're going, but we will get there without detours."

Left to his own devices, Navarre may well have benefited from the absence of a government. His reception in Saigon was somewhat strained. Salan, who had been hoping to stay on and earn an additional star, was barely polite. Navarre's number two, General Gonzalez de Linarès, known as "Uncle Li," had been Navarre's classmate at Saint-Cyr, the French military academy. His first words to Navarre were: "What are you doing in this shithouse?"

Since Linarès and the rest of Salan's team were leaving, Navarre had to find replacements in a hurry. In a meeting with Linarès and Jean Letourneau, the French high commissioner, Navarre said he had thought of General René Cogny as commander for Tonkin.

"Don't do it," Linarès said, "he's a bastard."

Letourneau said, "He may have faults, but he's a fine officer." The rotund and jovial Letourneau had a policy of never offending anyone.

René Cogny, whose grandfather had been an agricultural laborer in Normandy and whose father served as a customs clerk, was ambitious and hard-driving. A massive, chiseled forty-nine-year-old artillery officer, well over six feet tall, he also held degrees in law and political science. It was under de Lattre that he had risen, clearing entire areas of the Red River Delta until he became known as "the Man of the Delta." His method was to evacuate villages and then blow them to bits, as he stood in the midst of his batteries. Cogny was known as a self-promoter who liked to regale the press with his exploits. He was overfond of motorcycle escorts, whereas Navarre hated ostentation. Navarre had a genuine dislike of being talked about. Pouget had to cajole and argue to get him to talk to the press. Navarre and Cogny may have been opposites in temperament, but Cogny had an admirable combat record.

When Cogny arrived in Saigon to hear the news of his promotion, wearing his artillery officer's peaked cap and carrying a cane (the result of a prolonged stay in Buchenwald in 1943), he told Navarrre, "You will not regret this." Cogny now had three stars and a motorcycle escort, and could live up to his nickname, "Coco the Siren."

Salan left with sixty other officers on May 28 aboard an ocean liner, the *Marseilles*. Navarre had to reignite the machinery of war. After the rains, he would be face-to-face with Giap. He shuttled between Saigon and Hanoi, getting the hang of things. As a longtime intelligence officer, he was pleased to see that Colonel Guibaud, the head of the Deuxiéme Bureau, had broken the three Vietminh codes—for operations, planning, and supplies. The supply code was particularly revealing. Guibaud's code

breakers, working out of a villa in Dalat, had overheard in their radio intercepts an order for "special rations," which indicated the presence of Soviet advisers among the Vietminh, since the "comrades" did not eat rice.
Other messages acknowledged receipt of automatic weapons from China.
The locations of Vietminh arms depots were a guide for forthcoming operations.

In Hanoi, however, a wall map in Navarre's office showed the French-
controlled areas of Indochina in white, about 25 percent of the total surface; the contested areas, in pink, amounted to another 25 percent; the
rest, in red, were the Vietminh-controlled areas. It was known as the "leprosy map."

Once Salan and Letourneau had left, Navarre went on an inspection
tour from June 15 to early July, visiting the troops. The situation was much
worse than he had been led to believe. Orders were not obeyed, secrets
were not kept, units remained within their barbed-wire enclosures. It all
had to be shaken up. In the Tonkin Delta, where the French had five divisions and a thousand posts, the Vietminh had been able to infiltrate sixty
thousand men, who controlled five thousand of the seven thousand villages. With so many men pinned down in posts, the Delta was the nightmare of the high command.

In terms of the will to win, thought Navarre, the Vietminh were
united, while the French were divided, with the Communists and Gaullists
in the National Assembly opposed to the war. The Vietminh kept its secrets, while in Paris secrets were routinely leaked. Navarre didn't even
know where the Vietminh headquarters—a cluster of well-guarded bamboo huts, a few dozen aides, easily movable—was. The Vietminh led a
monastic life, while in Saigon, the glittering social scene was awash in
champagne dinners, women with low necklines, golf and tennis, and the
rumor mill. The Vietminh waged war. The French command deployed
troops from their air-conditioned offices.

What Makes Them So Tough?
What Is the Force That Makes Them Resist?

France was now demanding more American aid on the grounds that Indochina was a barrier to Communism. But as Admiral Radford, who would soon be named chairman of the Joint Chiefs of Staff, knew only too well, they couldn't handle the aid they had. They wanted more planes but had serious problems with maintenance, such as a lack of periodic inspection and the absence of modern stock-control records. The small air force section of MAAG in Saigon tried to correct French habits. Finally, in July 1953, fifty-five U.S. Air Force specialists were assigned to French units at the squadron level, providing instruction in such matters as corrosion control and depot organization. General Trapnell, the head of MAAG, concluded that the French were not amenable "to any change or modernization of their traditional methods."

On May 23, the French asked for an additional aircraft carrier for the Indochina theater. The United States handed it over in September, but the French crew did not arrive to man it until December. When the carrier left for Toulon in April 1954, to begin its first tour of Indochina, it was diverted to Bombay to deliver thirty-two French-built Ouragan jet fighters to the Indian air force. Why was France selling its jets to India when Washington was delivering U.S. jets to France to help build up its NATO forces? General C. H. Bonesteel, a member of the National Security Council, observed in a memo to Robert Cutler, the president's special assistant for national security affairs: "The French will have had the *Belleau Wood* a whole year without making use of her in the fight for Indochina. Moreover, she is currently being used as a delivery wagon rather than a combat vessel."

Equally alarming was the French inability to train a Vietnamese army. All U.S. efforts to help were rebuffed. Trapnell told the French that in Korea the United States had trained major generals in six months. The French said they didn't need any Vietnamese major generals. Then the French relented and sent a mission to Korea. The mission returned convinced, as one of their officers put it, that "the American sausage machine is simply too vast, and the Americans are . . . training men for set-piece battles on a continuous front."

However unhappy Washington was with the way the French fought the war, excessive criticism or withdrawal of aid would only further impede the French effort and topple the government of Premier Joseph Laniel, bringing about a return of the left and a withdrawal of the French from Indochina and NATO.

A June 4, 1953, National Intelligence Estimate warned of a buildup in Chinese deliveries to the Vietminh: "The Vietminh will continue to receive a steady flow of material assistance from the Chinese Communists, and the amount may increase at any time. The Vietminh do not have and probably cannot develop, within the time period of this estimate, the capability to make such effective use of heavy equipment—armor, artillery, and aircraft—from the Chinese Communists as to permit successful attacks against strong concentrations of regular French forces." This estimate proved to be off the mark in several respects: the Vietminh did not have any aircraft and they were less than a year from launching a successful attack.

Given the increase in Chinese aid, the United States had to step up its own aid. Encouraged by the appointment of Navarre, and despite his own misgivings, Eisenhower asked Congress in June to pass a mutual security bill that included $400 million for Indochina for 1953. Both houses passed the bill, though for the first time attempts were made to impose conditions. A June 16 report of the House Foreign Affairs Committee expressed the hope that the aid would go directly to the Associated States rather than to the French.

In the Senate, lively debate erupted when the Arizona Republican Barry M. Goldwater, who later became a self-described shoot-from-the-hip champion of U.S. victory in Vietnam, called for an amendment that no funds should be given to the French until they "set a target date for . . . complete independence. . . . The people of Indochina . . . have been fighting for the same thing for which 177 years ago the people of the American colonies fought." This was the man whom Lyndon Johnson called "trigger-happy" when he ran against him in 1964.

"By supporting France," Goldwater went on, "we are saying to the great men who penned the document and whose ghosts must haunt these walls, that we do not believe entirely in the Declaration of Independence."

Otherwise, as "surely as day follows night our boys will follow this $400 million."

Everett Dirksen, the Illinois Republican, had recently visited Indochina and said of the Vietminh: "What makes them so tough? What is the force that makes them resist? . . . They preach nationalism and freedom." Dirksen said that while in Vietnam he had asked the U.S. military men what would constitute a victory. They replied: "We cannot even get a definition of victory, because no one seems to know."

Despite Goldwater's eloquent plea for Vietnamese independence, other senators protested that Congress should not legislate foreign policy. Passing an amendment curtailing aid might make the French leave Indochina, which would mean a Communist victory. The amendment was defeated. The defense of Indochina won the day. However, the prolonged Senate debate, on June 29 and 30 and July 1, showed there was strong support for exerting pressure on the French.

With Navarre in place, a U.S. military mission arrived in Saigon on June 20 on its own inspection tour, led by Lieutenant General John W. "Iron Mike" O'Daniel, the army commander in chief in the Pacific. He was accompanied by a dozen advisers, including the counterinsurgency expert Edward Geary Lansdale, the model for the title character in Graham Greene's *The Quiet American*, who later wrote: "French paternalism was turning over the controls of self-rule too slowly and grudgingly. . . . I didn't see how Navarre was going to win unless he made radical changes to get the Vietnamese nationalists much more deeply involved."

O'Daniel told Navarre that French forces must take the initiative with "aggressive guerrilla warfare," deploy "more indigenous forces," and "enunciate the future position of the French in the country." Navarre offered a plan that seemed to mirror American concerns, and O'Daniel was impressed by his energy and confidence. In his report on July 14, 1953, however, O'Daniel noted that the plan "would require a complete change in French military psychology . . . and would entail some risk . . . which the French are unwilling to take." When O'Daniel briefed a Joint Chiefs–State Department meeting on July 17, he said the French had used the word *difficult* so many times that he made it a rule that anyone in the American group who used it would be fined a dollar.

Indochina Does Not Really Matter

In England, Churchill suffered a stroke on June 23, 1953, at the age of seventy-nine. "A disturbance of the cerebral circulation has developed," said the medical bulletin. His speech was slurred, he was unable to walk, but he kept smoking and drinking. "I am a hulk," he said, "only breathing and excreting." Bedridden, he received visitors; one of them, on July 5, was Field Marshal Bernard Montgomery, the victor of El Alamein. They discussed the state of the world.

"Korea does not really matter now," Churchill said. "I'd never heard of the bloody place till I was seventy-four. . . . And Indochina, too, does not really matter. We gave up India. Why shouldn't France give up In-dochina?"

"Indochina matters strategically," Monty replied. "If Indochina goes, Siam goes too. And then Malaya would be in danger."

By mid-July, Churchill felt better. He was looking forward to attending the tripartite conference in the fall in Bermuda—England, France, and the United States—which President Eisenhower would also attend. "Dulles is ambitious to be one of those big figures in the world," Churchill observed, "and I am not in a position to make a fuss. Bidault's only aim is to prevent the conference doing anything."

You Are Ending Your War in Korea;
We Cannot Ignore Our Obligation to End Our War.

Ever since Premier René Mayer had been dumped on May 21, 1953, Pres-ident Vincent Auriol and his tacticians were desperately trotting out Fourth Republic wheelhorses to form a government. As the weeks went by, they tried Antoine Pinay and Edgar Faure, and they tried Pierre Mendès France, who fell short of a majority by only thirteen votes. Auriol feared that if the crisis continued there would be a coup d'état. In the last week of June, he turned to Joseph Laniel, who benefited from the discontent in public opinion, which reduced the number of bench-sitters in the Na-tional Assembly. On June 26, Laniel was invested by a vote of 398 to 206. In his opening speech, he sounded decidedly unwarlike, in keeping with the mood of those who elected him. "Who in this assembly," he asked, "can say that he would not devote all his energy toward ending this sanguinary war if that were possible? We will work toward that possibility, whether in negotiations following the Korean armistice or other negotiations with the Associated States."

Laniel came from a family in the Calvados area of Normandy. His great-grandfather had run a laundry at the time of Napoleon. The family prospered, and Joseph Laniel owned a castle with dozens of servants and a game park where he took his friends hunting. He also owned an entire village, renting the church to the parish priest and the school to the prefecture. The rent was one franc a year. His source of pride, however, was that his father had served in the National Assembly for thirty-six years, and he had served for twenty-one years, a total family record of fifty-seven years unmatched by any other member. "I succeeded my father," he liked to say.

Was it a coincidence that on July 3, two days after the U.S. Senate debate on granting independence to Indochina as a condition for further aid, Laniel announced that the French wanted to *parfaire* ("complete" or "perfect") the independence of the Associated States and were ready to open talks? In Paris, Ambassador Dillon reported that the Laniel government realized the "wave of nationalism sweeping Asia could not be opposed and that independence was a question of all or nothing."

Now that France had a government, a foreign ministers' meeting was arranged in Washington on July 12, 1953. Two weeks before Panmunjom, Bidault, the perennial foreign minister, told Dulles: "You are ending your war in Korea in response to your public opinion, and we cannot ignore our obligation to end our war. When you finally sign the peace in Korea, it will be difficult to explain to the French people that we have to continue our war in Indochina."

It would make the position of the French government "absolutely impossible," Bidault said. Dulles proposed a separate conference to discuss Indochina. He said that a conference now from a "bankrupt" position "could only end in complete disaster." In Korea, the armistice talks were backed by the unstated U.S threat of "unpleasant measures." Dulles concluded: "If we can work out the Navarre plan and make progress demonstrating that we have the will and the capability to sustain that plan, there might then be the prospect of success in negotiation."

You've Got to Write Eisenhower
That It's Take It or Leave It

In early July, having finished his inspection tour and formulated his plan, Navarre left for Paris. On July 4, on the drive from Orly Airport, he heard on the radio that the Laniel government had recognized the Associated States. All three states—Cambodia, Laos, and Vietnam—would negotiate new agreements for membership in the French Union. These measures were merely old clothes cleaned and pressed in response to American pressure, but they complicated Navarre's task. In addition, two Fourth Republic stalwarts were given posts that would undermine Navarre's authority. Marc Jacquet was named secretary of state for the Associated States. Maurice Dejean, the ambassador to Tokyo, was named commissioner general in Indochina. Navarre saw himself hemmed in by pontificating politicians.

Navarre was ready to present his plan before the Committee for National Defense, presided over by President Vincent Auriol, and consisting of the top military brass, Premier Laniel, and cabinet ministers, but he had to wait until Foreign Minister Bidault returned from Washington. On July 24 at the Élysée Palace, the twenty or so members of the committee heard his top-secret reports, one on the conduct of operations, the other on the development of the Vietnamese army. Auriol specified that no notes should be taken.

Navarre projected an increase of personnel in Vietnamese units from 165,000 to 217,000 in 1954. The "Vietnamization" of garrisons in the Red River Delta alone would free up 82,000 French troops for offensive actions.

As for his operations, in a first phase, from the spring of 1953 to autumn 1954, Navarre planned to pacify southern Vietnam while maintaining a "defensive mentality" in the north and avoiding large-scale confrontations. In the second phase, from late 1954 to 1956, he would launch offensives against Vietminh strongholds in the north.

Navarre's goal was not to defeat the Vietminh, but "to create military conditions that would allow the government to negotiate a satisfactory, honorable solution to the Indochinese affair." He had to show the Vietminh it had no chance of winning by force of arms, in order to prod it toward the negotiating table.

The presentation of Navarre's report was followed by a long and rambling discussion, during which it came out that the French did not have the funds to finance the plan. Premier Laniel said, "The first thing to do is make a desperate effort to obtain more aid from the Americans." Laniel told the minister of finance, Edgar Faure, "Edgar, I'll handle it, I'll talk to Douglas." Faure replied, "You've got to write to Eisenhower that it's take it or leave it." Three days later, the armistice was signed at Panmunjom, which conferred a certain urgency to the French requests.

The Fourth Republic politicians prized cronyism above competence. Laniel had an old friend at the American embassy in Paris, Douglas MacArthur II, the nephew of the general. He had met MacArthur in Vichy in 1942, when he was working under Ambassador William D. Leahy, and Laniel was in the Resistance. Laniel gave MacArthur military information—a German battalion was garrisoned on an airstrip in the Jura, for instance—and forty-eight hours later it would be bombed. He often invited MacArthur to Normandy to hunt.

Navarre was distraught over the lack of seriousness of the politicians. On the question of independence for the Associated States, Bidault told him: "If you let the streetcar employees in Lille travel free, those in Perpignan will demand the same." "Perhaps," Navarre replied, "but is that a reason to give it?"

Navarre was even more distraught on July 30 when he saw in the weekly *France-Observateur* that the top-secret minutes of the Committee for National Defense meeting had been leaked to one of its reporters. Navarre was quoted as saying that during the time it took to launch his plan, he would be unable to defend Laos. Providing military secrets to the Vietminh, he felt, was like giving away the combination to the safe. And what would the reaction of the Americans be upon learning that he was ready to let Luang Prabang fall, since U.S. aid was based on defending all of Southeast Asia? Leaking the minutes of a meeting attended only by the top brass and cabinet ministers confirmed his conviction of the *pourriture* (rot) in the government. The source of the leak was never discovered. The reporter, Roger Stéphane, spent a month in jail but did not reveal his sources.

Upon his return to Saigon, Navarre was faced with another shocking article, this time in the American press. The August 3, 1953, issue of *Life* ran text and pictures by the noted photographer of the Korean War David Douglas Duncan, who had spent eight weeks roaming around Vietnam. At Lai Chau, a key post in the northwest, forty-five miles from the Chinese border, Duncan shot empty desks under a wall clock that said 3 P.M., to show that the siesta was the order of the day. Near the Haiphong airport, he shot long rows of U.S. bombs resting unused on carriers, and in Saigon he found a transport depot filled with inactive vehicles. In the text, he described a "languid" war fought on "banker's hours," where "many rear area officers have been joined by their wives and families." He concluded that "ineffective French tactics and the ebbing French will make it seem that Indochina is all but lost to the Communist world."

Navarre was appalled that a journalist who had been helped everywhere he went had "grossly insulted French troops." His ambivalent feelings toward U.S. aid, like de Lattre's before him—needing it but resenting it—were awakened. Of course he was happy to have the aid, which had transformed the conflict from a sinful colonial war to a saintly war against Communism. But he felt that while the Americans were helping him materially they were subverting him morally. They were part of the problem, with their anticolonial fixation, their imperturbable self-confidence, their almost total ignorance, and their "get out of the way so I can take your place" attitude. For that was the goal, was it not, to substitute U.S. influence for French? Not a week went by without some form of American pressure, visiting demagogues stating that "the war cannot be won by native troops" or "France must grant full independence."

Douglas MacArthur II, Laniel's friend, was now in Washington as counselor to Livingston Merchant, assistant secretary of state for European affairs. On September 4, at the regular State-JCS meeting, he articulated the State Department position: "For our part, we feel that there is no real alternative to giving the French the help which they are asking unless it is that of accepting gradual French withdrawal from Indochina."

When the NSC met on September 9, Secretary of State Dulles came out fighting for the aid program. Eisenhower was on vacation, but had told Dulles that Indochina was now "the first priority." While Korea "might be an insulated loss," Indochina "could not be insulated." Now, Dulles said, "for the first time . . . we have a French commanding general, Navarre, with a dynamic approach to the military problem." Dulles specified that if the aid program was approved, Eisenhower wanted appropriate congressional leaders to be notified, so that the decision would not take them by surprise, since the aid would go to France directly and be used partly to build an Indochinese army.

Defense Secretary "Engine Charlie" Wilson said he would go ahead with the aid regardless of the opinion of Congress.

Dulles agreed that Eisenhower had the right to distribute the aid without congressional approval, but it was preferable to have the goodwill of Congress and inform them in a timely way.

An aid package of $385 million for 1954 was approved. One condition was that Navarre would accept "close military advice."

Thruston B. Morton, a popular former House member from Kentucky, was now assistant secretary of state for congressional relations. Morton conferred with the ranking senators on the Senate Foreign Relations and Armed Services committees, Walter George and Richard Russell, both Georgia Democrats. Morton reported that George "just accepted it and never asked a question and was very gracious." But Russell said: "You are pouring money down a rat hole. The worst mess we ever got into, this Vietnam. The president has decided it. . . . I'll keep my mouth shut . . . but this is going to be one of the worst things this country ever got into." Russell later expressed regret that he had not taken a stronger stand.

When Laniel heard the news, he gloated: "The Americans gave me 385 million dollars, which they had refused to René Mayer. I obtained that thanks to my close friendship with Douglas MacArthur. . . . He had good connections with the Republicans and his wife is the daughter of Senator Barkley, the leader of the Democrats in Congress." Laniel didn't seem to realize that Barkley had been Truman's vice president from 1949 to 1953. Nor could he know what influence MacArthur had in formulating a policy that was adopted by Dulles and the Joint Chiefs, or whether MacArthur had puffed up his role a bit too forcefully.

This Plan Will Contribute to the Final Defeat
of Colonial Rule

By the time General Navarre arrived in Indochina in May 1953, General Giap had three hundred thousand well-armed and well-trained men, and more were arriving regularly from their training camps in China. The French had 250,000 men, but 150,000 were on the defensive in stationary posts. As for the Vietnamese army that Navarre was counting on, it numbered around 165,000, but many units were not ready for combat. Navarre divided Vietnam into northern and southern theaters along the 18th parallel. His plan was to clean out the guerrillas in central and southern Vietnam by the spring of 1954 and then attend to the Vietminh bases in Tonkin.

Prior to Navarre's arrival, the Fourth Plenum of the Vietminh Workers' Party was held in late January. Giap's forces were told to avoid open battle with French units and to search out the weak points in enemy positions. The main field of operations should be in the northwest, where the area from the Chinese border to the Laotian border was in the hands of the Vietminh, except for scattered French posts. Eventually, the Vietminh would move into Laos.

Following the plenum, the Chinese adviser Wei Guoqing left for Peking to outline the plan for Laos. He was back on March 5 to direct operations. The Chinese leadership told Wei to stick to the northwest and focus on the French post of Lai Chau, which was manned by Thai partisans and some French troops and sat in the middle of thick jungle, terrain favorable to the Vietminh. Giap, however, wanted to concentrate his troops in the Red River Delta to liberate Hanoi and Haiphong. The Chinese insisted on an invasion of Laos that would cause political problems for the French among the Associated States. The correct strategy was debated for months.

On August 22, 1953, the Vietminh politburo decided to shift the emphasis from the northwest to the Delta. The shift was reported to Peking by the Chinese adviser Luo Guibo. Mao opposed the change and urged that the Vietminh focus on the northwest. An August 29 cable from the Chinese Central Military Commission said: "We should first annihilate enemies in the Lai Chau area, liberating north and central Laos. . . . By

adopting this strategy, we will be able to limit the human and financial resources of the enemy troops. . . . This plan will contribute to the final defeat of colonial rule."

In September, the politburo met again to thrash out whether the main
thrust for the fall-winter campaign should be the Delta or the northwest.
Ho Chi Minh gave in to the Chinese plan, which would allow the Vietminh
to attack isolated French posts in terrain that made it difficult for the
French to bring in reinforcements. In this proxy war, it was the same with
the Chinese as with the Americans: Each backer wanted a say in the conduct of the war. But the Chinese were far more successful in getting their
way than the Americans.

On October 10, Peking informed Ho Chi Minh that Wei Guoqing had
been named chief military adviser while Luo Guibo was named political
adviser. Wei Guoqing left for Peking to consult with Mao. In late October,
he returned and worked out a plan with Giap for the fall-winter campaign.
Vietminh forces would focus on Lai Chau and try to seize the entire
province by the spring of 1954. Then lower Laos would become the target
of attacks from two directions. In mid-November, units of Giap's 316th Division headed for Lai Chau.

The War in Indochina Is Doomed. . . .
We Should Spend the Money on Schools

While Navarre was in Paris, General Cogny launched Operation HIRON-
DELLE (swallow), an airborne raid on Lang Son, a Vietminh base close to
the Chinese border, at the juncture of the east–west RC4 and the
north–south RC1. Hidden in caves was a network of depots for military
supplies from China.

On July 17, two thousand paratroopers of the 6th BPC, commanded by
Major Marcel Bigeard, and another thousand from Captain Pierre Tourret's 8th Choc were dropped near the caves. A Foreign Legion battalion
covered their retreat on RC1. Twenty-two paratroopers were hurt on landing. When the paratroopers reached the caves, they found teams of
guards, whom they killed in a brief firefight. They photographed the supplies with their Chinese and Soviet markings before the engineers set their

charges and blew up six Molotova trucks, one thousand Skoda submachine guns, twenty thousand pairs of shoes, and five hundred cartons of
Russian cigarettes. The paratroopers pulled out and reconnoitered with
the Legionnaires, who took them back to Hanoi in trucks. The results were
modest in terms of the number of troops employed, but HIRONDELLE was
nonetheless an example of a successful airborne operation. The paratroopers had borrowed from the Vietminh the element of surprise.

Even a modest success should have given Navarre a lift in the course of
his Paris meetings, but the July 24 talks with the Committee for National
Defense were so disappointing that he began to reflect on his statement
that Laos was not part of his plan. On July 26, he cabled a directive to his
staff for the fall campaign season. He had been worrying about Laos and
the committee's hesitation. Laos was a sparsely populated land with bad
roads where forty thousand Buddhist monks went from house to house,
wooden bowls in hand, preaching the sanctity of life, which extended to
the thousands of stray dogs who roamed the alleys of Luang Prabang at
night. The dogs kept the French commander there, General Gardet, from
sleeping, and he sent out three-man teams to shoot them. The Laotian
government lodged a strong protest with the French, and General Gardet
was relieved of his command. The Laotians were not warriors and Laos
was infested with Pathet Lao guerrillas. Laos had an ineffective army and
a few garrisons of French troops to prop them up.

Navarre felt he had to protect the Laotian border. His directive asked
his staff to study the possibility of Dien Bien Phu as a ground-air "hedgehog" base. He felt that the spacious valley on the Laotian border, which
was occupied by the Vietminh, had many advantages. He proposed to
"take by surprise the position of Dien Bien Phu," which had a long-
abandoned airstrip, and man it with five battalions. With the French
solidly implanted on the border, Navarre could counter the latent menace
to Luang Prabang and reestablish the situation in Laos.

Navarre returned to Saigon in early August 1953, a deeply troubled
man. The only policy of the government in Paris was to ask for more
American aid. In the prevailing political vacuum, he had to make crucial
decisions, knowing full well that if anything went wrong he would be
blamed. When he raised the question of defining French goals, the only

answer was wait and see. The French no longer knew why the war was being fought. For the Americans, it was a war against Communism, as in Korea. The Associated States wanted their independence. But the French? They said they too were fighting Communism, while in reality they wanted to maintain the French Union. The policy was one of trickery, to promise independence "within the French Union," and then to withhold it, while asking the Vietnamese to take part in the war in the name of non-existent independence. In Paris, Navarre had argued for a French Union that was more than a façade, so that the Vietnamese would participate wholeheartedly in the war, but he got nowhere. And that was his dilemma: the enemy had a clearly defined goal; the French were up to their ears in hypocrisy.

Navarre also deplored the lack of support for the war in public opinion. The Korean armistice in late July had been a turning point, making the French public hope for a similar solution. The politicians, instead of squelching those hopes, fanned them. All the influential groups, from the League of the Rights of Man to the Conference for Peace in Indochina, were antiwar. The politicians had lost faith in the war to the point where the minister of finance, Edgar Faure, said, "Whether we win or whether we lose, we will not remain in Indochina," while the Socialist deputy Marcel-Edmond Naegelen announced, "The war in Indochina is doomed. . . . We should spend the money on schools."

Well, Navarre had a war to fight, even though he had to fight it with troops that were an amalgam of races and nationalities, like the legions of decadent Rome, in contrast to the ethnic sameness of the enemy. He had a minority of French, with a majority of black, yellow, Arab, and German. Navarre reflected that the Vietminh kept their plans secret but seemed to know all about his. They had informants in every village, and conversations in the officers' messes were picked up by the Vietnamese waiters. What was a wall of silence for the Vietminh was a sieve for the French.

For the time being, he put the Dien Bien Phu hedgehog on the back burner until Giap's intentions became clearer. He did, despite his complaints about Vietminh secrecy, receive a stream of intelligence reports—radio intercepts, reports from agents, captured documents, and prisoner interrogations—that showed a conflicting pattern. This was because the

Vietminh had not yet fixed on a strategy. Navarre knew that Giap had four divisions on the edge of the Delta. Cogny was sure this would be the site of the Vietminh fall-winter campaign.

But Navarre's most urgent task was the evacuation of the hedgehog base in Na San, in the northwest highlands, whose nine battalions were at the mercy of their airborne supply lines. He felt that Na San served no purpose, being surrounded by Vietminh. On August 3, he flew to Hanoi to discuss the evacuation with Cogny. The airlift, lasting from August 7 to 12, with Dakotas landing on average every six minutes, increased Navarre's confidence in ground bases supplied by air. When Captain Pouget told him the evacuation was worth a press conference, he said: "If I succeed, they sing my praises, and if I fail they drag me though the mud."

In the meantime, in Washington, President Eisenhower, having allocated $385 million in additional aid for Indochina, tried to find reasons for optimism. General John W. "Iron Mike" O'Daniel had toured Indochina from June 20 to July 10, and sent a copy of the Navarre Plan to Washington. The plan was seen as a marked improvement in military thinking. On August 4, 1953, Eisenhower addressed the Governors' Conference in Seattle and said: "When the United States votes $400 million to help that war, we are not voting for a giveaway program. We are looking for the cheapest way we can to prevent the occurrence of something that would be of terrible significance for the United States of America—our security, our power and ability to get certain things we need." In October, Admiral Radford, the gung ho onetime navy pilot, now chairman of the Joint Chiefs, received encouraging reports from General Trapnell, the head of the MAAG mission.

Despite his profound resentment of all signs of American interference, Navarre professed to enjoy a "splendid spirit of cooperation" with Trapnell. Navarre's view of O'Daniel, who liked to recall that he had helped liberate Alsace, was that he had a bulldog mentality, investigating everything in sight, and interfering in war plans. What were suggestions under Trapnell took on a tone of intransigence under O'Daniel.

In early October 1953, Navarre was in his office in Hanoi studying the big wall map with Cogny, who was worried about the buildup of Vietminh divisions on the edge of the Delta. Intelligence reports said that four divisions—the 304th, 308th, 312th, and 320th—had sent elements inside the Delta. General Cogny felt proprietary about the Delta, where he had established his reputation. The Red River Delta and its one thousand posts were to him the heart of the war, as was the sixty-mile stretch of road between Hanoi and Haiphong. If the road was cut, they might have to evacuate Hanoi. Cogny wanted all available reserves sent to the Delta. In a heated exchange, Navarre refused. He didn't want his reserves tied up in the Delta waiting for Vietminh divisions that might or might not attack.

When Navarre received intelligence that the 320th Division was stockpiling food and munitions in hidden depots not far from the southern tip of the De Lattre line at Ninh Binh, he decided to retaliate with another operation named for a bird, MOUETTE (seagull). He sent out seven mobile groups, commanded by the paratroop general Jean Gilles, who had a slight limp and a glass eye, but who was adept at solving the tactical problems that each battle presents. One of his tank commanders was the dashing cavalry officer Christian de Castries.

On October 15, Gilles moved his small army south of Ninh Binh to the crossroads hamlet of Lai Cac, improvised a fortified camp, and waited for the enemy. Elements of the 320th Division crossed the Day River at night in light rattan barges and prepared to infiltrate the Delta. Gilles's brigades provided the necessary barrier. In the ensuing battle, which lasted three weeks, the French, with tanks, artillery, and air support, gave the Vietminh a mauling. The French claimed they had destroyed one third of the Vietminh division, killing 1,000 and wounding 2,500, while they lost 113 killed, 505 wounded, and 151 missing.

You Cannot Bar a Direction

On October 22, 1953, France signed a mutual defense pact with Laos, which obligated Navarre to improve his defense of the Laotian border against Vietminh incursions. In early November, as he studied intelligence reports in his air-conditioned Saigon office, it became apparent that Giap's 308th and 312th Divisions were moving toward the northwest, while the 316th Division was heading for the Laotian border. The Chinese had finally obtained the assent of Ho Chi Minh and General Giap for operations against Lai Chau. Vietminh patrols started moving toward Lai Chau, where Thai partisans were garrisoned with the French. They were no match for Giap's regulars.

Navarre had to act. Na San had been evacuated. Lai Chau was about to be overrun. There were no other French strongpoints between the Vietminh and the Laotian border. Navarre's thoughts returned to Dien Bien Phu, that oblong valley on the Laotian border, wedged among the mountain chains of the northwest highlands.

Dien Bien Phu was not a place-name, like Saigon or Hanoi, but an administrative designation: seat of the Border County Prefecture. As Gertrude Stein said of Oakland, there was no *there* there. The valley was about eleven miles long by six wide, about the length of 180 Manhattan city blocks, and from the East River to the Hudson in width. The main village, known as Muong Thanh to the Vietnamese, was on a rise. In front of its houses with steep-pitched roofs made of rice straw, chickens and black pigs rooted in the vegetable gardens.

Smaller hamlets lined both banks of the Nam Yum River, which traversed the valley from north to south. Its tributaries linked Dien Bien Phu by water to Lai Chau and Luang Prabang, carrying travelers in Thai canoes with swallow-tailed sterns.

The villagers, about thirteen thousand of them, harvested rice by hand with short sickles. Between March and August, five feet of rain irrigated the paddies and turned the valley into a swamp, making Dien Bien Phu the most important rice granary in the northwest. The Vietminh, which got its rice from many sources, including China, considered the rice there useful but not vital in feeding its troops. On the surrounding slopes, Meo tribesmen planted poppies, and sold opium to the Vietminh, who used it as currency in the markets of Bangkok to buy weapons of all nations.

With its network of roads and rivers, Dien Bien Phu was a strategic location commanding routes from northwestern Vietnam to the heart of Laos. The Pavie Trail, a mule track named after a nineteenth-century French explorer, connected Dien Bien Phu with Lai Chau, while RP41 ran northward toward the Vietminh depot of Tuan Giao. The valley was surrounded by mountain ranges with peaks reaching six thousand feet, one to the north covered with forest and limestone chimneys, and another to the east.

For centuries, Dien Bien Phu had been a place of transit for caravans of oxen carrying goods from Burma. It was a clearinghouse, where five currencies were legal tender. The first battle of Dien Bien Phu took place in 1814, when the king of Luang Prabang sent ten thousand men and ninety elephants to subdue the tribesmen, who beat them back. When the French first came in, they subdued the tribesmen, but since the valley was malaria-ridden and far from Hanoi, it remained a remote frontier outpost. The main duty of the French administrator was to collect taxes, which led to sporadic uprisings that were brutally repressed. The Meo tribesmen also took up arms, refusing to pay a percentage of the opium harvest as taxes. The French burned the crops and put a price on the heads of the uprisings' leaders, and "pacification" was achieved in 1921.

When Navarre studied the map of Dien Bien Phu, he saw that it was 185 miles from Hanoi and 310 miles from the Chinese border. It was a vastly different site for an army with planes that could fly in supplies and heavy armament than for troops supplied by foot through trackless mountains and impenetrable jungle. The French could bring in tanks and artillery, while it seemed improbable that the Vietminh could bring in anything heavier than 75mm recoilless rifles. In addition, the Vietminh would have to attack the French post over flat terrain, where they would be massacred by artillery and air strikes. The Vietminh presently occupied the valley but had only a battalion garrisoned there.

Since Dien Bien Phu had an airstrip, Navarre thought in terms of a ground-air base, or hedgehog, manned by half a dozen battalions, with artillery support, that would be versatile enough for both defense and offense. In Navarre's overall strategy, Dien Bien Phu was far from being the decisive battle it became. It was one of several operations to be conducted at the same time. MOUETTE was still being fought, and other operations were planned in central Vietnam and the Delta.

Navarre's reports in early November told him that the 316th Division would reach Dien Bien Phu between December 7 and 11. The French had to get there first, in time to establish the base, and organize their forces to stop the enemy assault. The airdrop had to take place between November 20 and 25.

On November 2, Navarre drafted Directive 852, calling for an airborne occupation of Dien Bien Phu within that time frame. His reasoning was that not only would he get there ahead of the Vietminh to build his base, he would seize the two thousand-ton rice harvest and the opium crop of the Meo tribesmen.

On November 3, Navarre sent his trusted aide Colonel Louis Berteil to Hanoi to deliver and explain the secret directive to General Cogny, the commander of Tonkin, whose focus was primarily on the Delta. On November 4, Berteil met with Cogny and his three top officers: Colonel Dominique Bastiani, his chief of staff; Lieutenant Colonel Denef, his chief of operations; and Lieutenant Colonel Multrier, head of logistics. All three objected that Dien Bien Phu was a sideshow that would drain troops away from the projected battle in the Delta. They were of course protecting their turf, since the French were stretched thin and had to rob Peter to pay Paul. Navarre had received only a small part of his hoped-for reinforcements.

In a written report, Bastiani gave a pessimistic analysis of the Dien Bien Phu operation. "Since the evacuation of Lai Chau is already planned," he said, "all that the occupation of Dien Bien Phu can be is a preparatory measure for the defense of Laos, which is not threatened for the moment. Another reason given is to bar the way to Luang Prabang. But in that kind of landscape, you cannot bar a direction. That is a European notion invalid here. The Viets pass around you, as you have seen in the Delta."

"I am convinced," he concluded, "that Dien Bien Phu will become, whether we like it or not, a drain on manpower, without any useful purpose, as soon as it is pinned down by a single regiment. . . . The consequences of such a decision may be very serious."

General Cogny was in a difficult position. He had been one of the first to propose Dien Bien Phu as a ground-air base. But he was also "the Man of the Delta." And yet he could not directly dispute an order from the commander in chief, who was responsible for the overall strategy in Indochina, while he was commander only for Tonkin. In a wire to Navarre on November 6, he said: "Operational zone Northwest remains secondary to the Delta theater. It is certain, however, that a base in Thai country would reap political and strategic advantages. It is up to you to decide." In essence, he was saying: Yes, of course we should protect the Laotian border, but the Delta is far more important. Whatever troops I am deprived of in my zone should be made up for.

With his knowledge of classical Greece, Navarre dubbed the operations CASTOR and POLLUX, after the twin deities who rescued shipwrecked sailors. The occupation of Dien Bien Phu was the Castor part, to be followed by Pollux, the evacuation of Lai Chau. He named General Jean Gilles, the veteran paratrooper who had commanded at Na San, as the leader of the CASTOR operation.

Gilles, ever conscious of losses among his elite paratroopers, had not forgotten the Vietminh's night attacks at Na San, and feared a repeat at Dien Bien Phu. At a meeting in Hanoi on November 11 with General Cogny and other officers, he asked whether it was worthwhile to risk his battalions in a drop over terrain where the Vietminh were implanted. General Jean Dechaux, head of the Northern Tactical Air Group, who was also present, said his concern was the safety of the landing strip. It had to be well defended so that his planes could land and take off. His fighters could not make it from Hanoi to Dien Bien Phu and back without belly tanks. Only the B-26 bombers carried enough fuel for the round-trip. Bad weather that could interrupt supply flights also had to be considered. The garrison would need eighty tons of supplies a day. Colonel Jean-Louis Nicot, in charge of air transport, said, "Since supplying the Dien Bien Phu garrison must be done entirely by air, our entire transport fleet will be absorbed in the task, to the detriment of all other needs."

On November 12, Cogny, again equivocating, wrote Navarre: "Berteil will tell you that he found here little enthusiasm, among my staff as well as among the paras and aviators, for this operation. However, these opinions do not interfere with our sense of discipline."

At another meeting on November 15, General Dechaux focused on the strain the operation would place on the air force. "Our pilots are exhausted," he said. "They're flying 120 to 150 hours a month. We've been told by the Health Service that it can't continue." After a great deal of back and forth, General Pierre Bodet, Navarre's deputy, put an end to the discussion by saying, "This operation will take place because the government considers it essential."

Thus, on November 15, General Cogny cabled to Navarre his halfhearted approval. Were it not for the political situation regarding Laos, he said, he would continue to object. But Navarre's command was at a higher level and he had to look at the larger canvas. Cogny's staff was not enthusiastic. Nor were the paratroopers or the air force chiefs. But their opinions were also based on a partial view.

No Unfavorable Opinion Was Expressed
Before the Battle

On the same day, November 15, 1953, the portly and energetic Marc Jacquet, newly named secretary of state for the Associated States, arrived in Saigon with some bad news for General Navarre. There was no question of weakening French forces in Europe to favor Indochina, which meant no more reinforcements beyond the eight battalions he had been sent. Jacquet did not show much respect for Premier Laniel, who had appointed him. "That imbecile won't last long," he told Navarre. "The next Premier will be Mendès France. I will be part of his team and I can assure you, *mon Général*, that I will actively support you." Jacquet had no experience of Indochina, and one high-ranking officer said of him: "He can't tell the paddy from the rice."

Navarre decided it was time to brief the civilian powers on Dien Bien Phu. He met again on November 18 with the newly arrived Jacquet. They were joined by Maurice Dejean, the commissioner general. "To counter the Vietminh plan," Navarre said, "I'm thinking of occupying the basin of Dien Bien Phu. The goal of this risky operation will be to defend Laos. What do you think?"

"Not to do it is unthinkable," Dejean exclaimed.

Jacquet, pulling on his pipe, said: "If we let the Vietminh take Luang Prabang, public opinion in France will collapse and our war to maintain the French Union will collapse."

Thus Navarre had the backing of the politicians, although the military continued to object. He flew to Hanoi to work out the final details with Cogny and his staff. Gilles and Dechaux were there, as were Bastiani and General René Masson, Cogny's deputy attached to the Vietnamese army.

"Do you have any objections to present regarding Operation Castor?" Navarre asked. According to Bastiani's notes, all were "unanimous in objecting." General Dechaux said the operation would take up the entire maintenance capacity of his air transport. Gilles again pointed out the dangers of dropping paratroopers over enemy-held terrain. "Even if there is only one Vietminh battalion," he said, "the paras, spread out over the drop, might have trouble regrouping and finding their matériel. If there were other Viets nearby the situation could turn bad." General Masson emphatically agreed, saying, "You're going to lose 50 percent of your paras."

In his memoir, *Agonie de l'Indochine,* Navarre made the astounding statement: "No unfavorable opinion was expressed before the battle." In his office, he moved little arrows over wall maps, not realizing that a map is to the territory as a name is to the person. When you're looking at a map, you don't sweat from the heat, or smell the jungle, or get mired in a swamp, or find yourself blinded by fog.

After listening to his generals, Navarre said, "Gentlemen, I've heard your deliberations and I've decided that Operation Castor will take place on November 20." He asked General Gilles to designate the units and work out the details of the drop. Closeted with his aides, Gilles had less than three days to plan the logistics of dropping five thousand paratroopers and their service units into an enemy-occupied valley. Once the valley was held, General Gilles, who had commanded the ground-air base at Na San, would be in charge of the post. Now resigned to the operation, he saw Dien Bien Phu as a base for forays into Laos that would distract the Vietminh from the Delta and as a way to seize the valley's rice harvest.

Returning to Saigon, Navarre attended to his normal business while waiting for the operation to unfold. On November 19, he received a trio of Americans led by Ambassador Donald Heath, shepherding Senator Alexander Smith, a New Jersey Republican, and Francis Wilcox, chief of staff for the Senate Foreign Relations Committee. The Americans questioned Navarre about his overall plan, and he deprecated having his name attached to it. Once again, he explained that circumstances required him to fight an essentially defensive war until the summer of 1954, but this would not preclude tactical offensives. When the Vietnamese army was built up, it would free up some French units from their present duties in stationary posts. He would then have a sufficient striking force to engage the Vietminh armies in the north in a decisive battle. He hoped to inflict a military defeat on the Vietminh by April or May 1955.

In his report, Senator Smith, chairman of the subcommittee on Southeast Asia, said: "I am convinced [the plan] is based on sound principle and holds considerable promise for the termination of hostilities." If the plan is carried out, "I believe the Communists can be defeated." In their talk, General Navarre did not mention the still secret Dien Bien Phu operation.

An important visitor from Paris also awaited him, Admiral Georges-Étienne Cabanier. Cabanier had a message confirming what Marc Jacquet had already told Navarre: no more reinforcements. The decision of the Committee for National Defense, of which Cabanier was a member, was: "Adjust your aims to the means you have at your disposal." This could have been an opportunity for Navarre to call off Dien Bien Phu, but the operation was so far advanced he could not bring himself to do it. Joseph Laniel later said that Cabanier's visit should have been seen by Navarre as "an invitation to be cautious." Navarre listened patiently as he was told that President Auriol and Premier Laniel wanted to know whether the time was ripe for negotiations. The French objective in Indochina, Laniel said, was "to make the enemy realize it is impossible for him to win a military victory." Navarre hoped that Dien Bien Phu was the answer to an improved military posture, but so did General Giap. Both commanders saw the battle as a way to gain an advantage in any eventual negotiations.

You Are Going Where Men Go to Die

In Hanoi, the final preparations were made. Colonel Jean-Louis Nicot, head of the transport command, put together crews for the sixty-five Douglas C-47 Dakotas. Thirty-three of them would take off from the military airport, Bac Mai, and thirty-two from Gia Lam, the civilian airport. Each plane could carry twenty-five paratroopers, and the flying time to Dien Bien Phu was estimated at seventy-six minutes.

At 6 P.M. on November 19, the commanders of the first two paratroop battalions to be dropped, Major Marcel Bigeard of the 6th Colonial Parachute Battalion (BPC), and Major Jean Bréchignac of the 2nd Light Infantry Parachute Battalion (BCP), were summoned by Navarre's deputy, the brisk General Bodet. "You're jumping tomorrow on Dien Bien Phu, assuming the weather permits," he said.

Thirty-seven-year-old Marcel Bigeard was a legendary officer with a hard-earned sense of his own worth, who habitually showed contempt for office-bound superiors. The son of a railway worker, he joined the Free French in World War II and was parachuted into France in 1944 to lead a Maquis resistance unit. A year later he was in Indochina, running commandos in Thai country, adopting the methods of the enemy in the jungle. Eight years of fighting had given him a fatalistic view of mortality. A studied indifference to danger became a strategy of survival. He never carried a weapon into battle, seeing his role as entirely tactical, needing only a radio and maps. One of his officers said, "He's like one of those famous country chefs who never use a recipe. It's all intuition." His battalion was employed for the most dangerous missions, to drop into besieged forts or rescue units trapped in the jungle. Ascetic, impatient, a despot for fitness, hardened in mind and body, he told his officers before each mission, "You are going where men go to die." Bigeard, known as "Bruno," was tall and lean, with eyes that had what the Spanish call *mirada fuerte* (the unblinking gaze). Major Jean Bréchignac, or "Brech," was a *baroudeur* (battle tested) in Bigeard's image, but more modest. Both men believed only in their units and their men, and their trust was reciprocated.

At 11 P.M., Bigeard briefed the company commanders of his battalion, which consisted of 651 men, 200 of them Vietnamese. One of the results of the shortfall in reinforcements was that even the elite battalions were mixed, in what the French called *jaunissement* (yellowing). They were to be at the Bac Mai airfield at 6 A.M. and they would dropped over Drop Zone (DZ) Natasha (meaning "north") along with a company of engineers, whose job it would be to repair the airstrip. Bréchignac's battalion, consisting of 827 men, including 420 Vietnamese, was to be dropped at the same time on DZ Simone (for "south"). In the afternoon, a third battalion would be dropped, Major Jean Souquet's 1st BPC, consisting of 911 men, including 423 Vietnamese.

Bigeard's officers studied the map and the aerial photographs of the drop zones. Lieutenant Francis de Wilde said, "This time we won't have to go home on foot. Hanoi is 300 kilometers away and Luang Prabang 180."

Lieutenant Hervé Trapp observed, "They don't seem too sure about the number of rebel forces in the area. I hope we don't have any unpleasant surprises."

Then it was the turn of company commanders to brief their section chiefs and noncoms. In Captain Trapp's company, two corporals from the surgical unit were talking about the weather. "It's cold out there," Cazeneuve told his pal, the tall and amusingly solemn Pingwarski. "Take some wool."

"I'll take the sweaters off the wounded," Pingwarski said.

"They'll be full of holes," Cazeneuve replied. They both had a good laugh. Among the paratroopers, gallows humor was de rigueur.

Lieutenant Lucien Le Boudec inspected his gear, the soles and laces of his jump boots, his submachine gun with the folding grip that was also the ammunition clip, his jump record book. He tried to cram four days of rations into his musette bag.

It was pitch-black when they got to Bac Mai airfield at six and were given their chutes. Le Boudec gathered his platoon and told the men, "As soon as you land, regroup." Loaded with their gear, they climbed into a Dakota and sat on canvas and tubing benches along the sides of the plane. They were hot and uncomfortable in their steel helmets and camouflage jumpsuits, upholstered on their backs and chests with parachute packs. "Let's get going, so we don't have to fight in the heat," one of the men said. But they had to wait more than an hour while weather conditions were vetted.

Let Us Be Proud of What We Have Accomplished

At 5 A.M., a C-47 equipped with a radio command post had taken off with three generals aboard—the paratrooper Gilles, Dechaux of Northern Tactical Air Group, and Navarre's deputy, Pierre Bodet, who would make the final decision on whether to launch Airborne Battle Group 1. The fate of three battalions of paratroopers depended on a clear day. When the generals reached the valley at around 6:15 A.M., they could not see it for the fog. They flew in circles, hoping the fog would burn off with the rising sun. At around seven the mist began to evaporate and they could see the shimmering meanders of the river and the checkerboard pattern of the rice paddies. At 7:15, Bodet gave Hanoi the green light.

The first wave of sixty-five Dakotas took off in groups of three, their wings ten yards apart. Lieutenant Le Boudec saw Hanoi vanish beneath him as his plane circled in the sky, waiting to fall into formation, and then headed due west at an altitude of 3,200 feet. As the plane approached the valley he saw the faces of the men tighten and felt a rumble in his stomach. A little after ten, the order was barked out: *"Debout! Accrochez!"* (Stand up! Hook up!) He swallowed and his ears hummed as he fixed his chute line to the guideline that ran along the roof of the fuselage. The Dakota dropped to six hundred feet. "Thirty seconds!" came the call. He was in jump position waiting for the buzzer, and then he jumped headfirst, and soon he saw the sky above him blossom with green-and-white chutes.

As it happened, the 910th Battalion of the 148th Vietminh Regiment, armed with mortars and 75mm recoilless cannons, was garrisoned in the village of Dien Bien Phu. That morning, at the exact location of Drop Zone Natasha, near the airstrip, two Vietminh companies were deployed for a training exercise with mortars.

DZ Natasha was covered with rice paddies separated by low dikes and fields of elephant grass that looked flat from the air but were six feet high. It took about two and a half minutes to land, and the Viets started firing while Bigeard's men were still in the air. The battalion doctor, Captain Jean Raymond, was killed by small-arms fire before he landed, becoming the first French fatality at Dien Bien Phu.

Luckily, as it turned out, the paratroopers landed over a strip of terrain about a mile long, too large for them to be encircled, and the ensuing battle turned into a lethal game of hide-and-seek in the elephant grass. Further complicating matters, the Vietminh wore camouflage uniforms like the paratroopers, many of whom were Vietnamese. Le Boudec landed in a clump of bushes and struggled free from his harness. He saw four men in a clearing with a smoke pot lit for regrouping. All around him he could hear calls and whistles, and, from the Viets, mortar fire, fortunately falling wide of the mark. He slogged through a rice paddy to join the others, one of whom was Captain Trapp, who had his ear on the radiophone. Trapp's radio operator, Peressin, lay at his feet, a bullet through the chest.

Bigeard had landed in the elephant grass with his guard and radioman. There was heavy firing all around. He gathered fifteen men and they crouched behind a dike at the edge of a rice paddy. But where were his mortars? Lieutenant Jacques Allaire had found three tubes but no shells.

Bréchignac and his 2nd BCP were no help; they had been dropped too far south. But they too landed in elephant grass and took heavy fire. Corporal Estor was carrying smoke grenades in a bag, which slipped from his hands as he landed and fell between the legs of a large water buffalo, who started chewing on it. Bullets were whistling by Estor's head and he abandoned the bag. He ran across a field lined with straw mannequins for the Viets' bayonet practice. On a hut he saw a red flag with a yellow hammer and sickle. He finally found Bréchignac's command team, and one of the officers said: "This is pure shit."

In the meantime, Bigeard had made radio contact with a Morane spotter plane, which could relay his message to the B-26 bombers circling above until they could tell the French from the enemy. He called for the planes to strafe outside the drop zone and bomb the village, adding: "We have a number of dead and wounded."

The air strike took the pressure off Bigeard, and the Viets began to pull back. By 1:30 P.M., Lieutenant Allaire had recovered some mortar shells and Bigeard attacked the village, which was fiercely defended by Viets covering the withdrawal of the regimental headquarters staff. Le Boudec, advancing on the village with Lieutenant Trapp and his men, could see small men hopping like jackrabbits from bush to bush. As Trapp's group approached, firing came from under a house on stilts. The Viet was hiding behind a dead horse. Bauer, a marksman with a telescopic sight, took him out.

At 3 P.M., a fleet of Dakotas dropped Major Jean Souquet's battalion over DZ Natasha, along with a light artillery unit. Lieutenant Trapp later wrote his wife, Simone, that the paras who jumped in the afternoon "were a bit surprised to find upon landing Viet cadavers all around them." The paras recovered a total of 90 uniformed Vietminh bodies. All but 4 of their wounded were carried away. The French had 15 dead and 53 wounded, and those seriously hurt were evacuated by helicopter. One of the first tasks within the Dien Bien Phu perimeter was to put together a small cemetery, later enlarged, with wooden crosses, circled by a rope handrail, where the French dead were buried wrapped in parachutes. The order of the day said: "Let us be modest, our comrades would have done as much. But let us also be proud of what we have accomplished."

A total of 2,343 men had been dropped, including special units such as engineers, light artillery, communications, and medical services, as well as forty tons of equipment. The engineers set up tents along the 4,600-foot airstrip and started repairing it. This was the first priority for a base that would receive all its supplies from the air. On their first night, the three battalions bivouacked around the ruined village, where Bigeard had set up his headquarters.

I'll Be Happier When You Have Found a Successor for Me

On the evening of November 20, General Navarre saw Ambassador Heath and told him he was much encouraged over the success of his three-battalion parachute drop over Dien Bien Phu. He said that his forces there "should be able to thwart Viet Minh operations against Lai Chau." Navarre was being disingenuous, for he had already, on November 13, sent a secret order for the evacuation of Lai Chau. In Hanoi, General Cogny gave a press conference describing the drop as "the beginning of an offensive." He gave away information that made General Giap realize the French had broken his codes. Giap changed them, except for the supply code. Navarre later reprimanded his number two.

At 8 A.M. on November 21, the drop continued with the 1st Foreign Legion Parachute Battalion (BEP), whose 653 men (336 of them Vietnamese), were sent to positions at the north of the perimeter. The forty-nine-year-old General Gilles, the camp commander, jumped with them, after tucking his glass eye in a pocket of his jumpsuit. Lieutenant Colonel Pierre Langlais, his deputy commander, also jumped. The forty-four-year-old bad-tempered Breton broke his ankle on landing and had to be flown back to Hanoi, cursing all the way.

In the afternoon, the 656-man 8th Paratroop Shock Battalion (Choc) was dropped. This was a unit with jungle-fighting experience, led by thirty-three-year-old Captain Pierre Tourret, who had fought with and learned from Bigeard, and who had the same ethic of risking what his men risked.

Until the airstrip was fixed, everything from canned cassoulet to barbed wire had to be dropped from the air, with or without parachutes. The bales of barbed wire, each weighing a ton, were dropped without, and when they hit the ground they bounced around like tumbleweed. Woe to the absentminded—more than one man was killed.

A bulldozer with its metal scoop was needed to clear and level the airstrip. But here, Major André Sudrat's engineers were faced with a catch-22. No plane carrying a bulldozer could land on the airstrip in its present condition, but it could not be upgraded without one. So, for the first time in the history of warfare, a six-ton bulldozer was dropped by parachute.

This was an involved operation in itself. On November 16, just in time for CASTOR, the French had received twelve of the aptly named Flying Boxcars, the twin-engine Fairchild C-119 Pacbets with their double tail and big cargo doors in the back, each of which could carry six tons. They arrived at the Cat Bi military airport near Haiphong with U.S. advisers from the 8081st Quartermaster Air Supply and Packaging Company, under Captain Donald Fraser, to train the French in transport techniques for heavy equipment.

The bulldozer was divided into two parts: the front shovel, which weighed two tons, and the cab, engine, and tracks, weighing four tons. Both parts were strapped to metal platforms. On November 21 at 2 P.M., two C-119s took off, each carrying a part of the bulldozer. When they reached the drop zone, marked with a big white canvas *T*, the heavier half with the engine went out the cargo doors attached to three large parachutes, each capable of carrying two tons. But the straps attaching one of the chutes to the platform broke, and the bulldozer plummeted earthward. One of the crew members told the pilot, "Don't fly any lower, it's going to bounce." The bulldozer vanished out of sight in a rice paddy, until all that could be seen was the exhaust pipe. The steel blade landed without mishap right on the *T*. The sappers continued their work with pick and shovel to fill the more than one hundred pits the Vietminh had dug in the runway. Two days later, the engineers tried again, with twice as many parachute straps tied to the platform. "It landed as gently as a butterfly on a flower," one of them said. Once the bulldozer had done its work, the 4,600-foot airstrip was covered with 22,800 perforated steel strips, anchored by 15,000 spikes, and a drainage system was installed to keep the ground dry. Gooseneck landing lights lined the runway. A movable control tower directed the traffic.

Major Sudrat also brought in a water purifier that took fifty gallons a minute from the Nam Yum River. Drinking the unpurified river water meant a sure case of amoebic dysentery. He posted signs asking the men not to piss upstream from the purifier, or dump their garbage, but in vain.

On Sunday morning, November 23, the last of the six paratroop battalions landed in Dien Bien Phu, the 5th Vietnamese Parachute Battalion (BPVN), with its 38 officers, mostly French, 109 noncoms, and 818 men. It was accompanied by a unit of light artillery, who were dropped along with eight 75mm recoilless rifles, each weighing 175 pounds, and one thousand shells that weighed 25 pounds each. The camp now had 4,466 paratroopers, all put to work as day laborers to make the camp habitable, as well as assorted other units.

In the afternoon, a Beaver, a Canadian bush plane, landed on a repaired section of the airstrip with a load of bicycles, plus one general, who unfolded himself from the tiny plane. The massive Cogny was in a jovial mood, basking in the limelight of Paris headlines (TONKIN PARATROOPERS RAIN DOWN ON DIEN BIEN PHU). General Gilles came to greet him at the airstrip on his folding motor scooter. Gilles had decided that he had had enough of ground-air bases. Speaking with the Catalan accent of the eastern Pyrenees, the land of his birth, Gilles said: "I'll feel happier when you've found a successor for me." Gilles was battle-weary. His face had begun to look like a boxer's, mangled in bouts. Cogny, who was a foot taller, looked down at Gilles and said: "We're thinking about it."

"At Na San I spent six months of my life like a rat in a hole. Use me in the open air," Gilles said. He did not mention the heart condition that eventually killed him.

Cogny's good mood got the better of him. "That's a promise," he said. "It will only be a matter of days."

As Gilles gave Cogny a guided tour, several Morane observation planes landed, nicknamed "Grasshoppers" for their spindly legs. Aboard one of them was Surgeon General Jeansotte, a veteran of both world wars. Jeansotte inspected the surgery unit, an underground warren with bamboo walls covered with six feet of earth and logs, and the morgue, where the planks of unassembled coffins were piled up. He took an inventory of the blood plasma, the antibiotics, the anesthetics. He saw the dentist's office, with the sign on the door showing a huge molar. The camp hummed with activity—men digging latrines, setting up field kitchens, filling sandbags, opening crates, shoveling, chopping, burning. But before departing, General Jeansotte expressed his concern that if the Vietminh were able to bring artillery to the surrounding crests, "it will be worse than anything we saw on the Somme."

We Decided to Wipe Out at All Costs the Whole Enemy Force at Dien Bien Phu

Dien Bien Phu was a heavily armed military base of around five thousand men, built from scratch and supplied and protected from air bases 185 miles away. But what was its purpose? General Navarre felt the need to explain it to his American allies, but he tended to obfuscate. Perhaps he was not quite sure himself. The paradox was that the base's purpose only became clear after the fact. On November 23, Navarre told General Harold Bull, the deputy chief of the Office of National Estimates, that the reason for the operation was that the Vietminh 316th Division was moving toward Lai Chau and Luang Prabang. In reality, however, CASTOR at its inception had been paired with POLLUX, the evacuation of Lai Chau, whose garrison was already being removed. Navarre apparently wanted to keep the difficult evacuation a secret until it was completed.

Navarre added that he could now deny the rice crop being harvested at Dien Bien Phu to the Vietminh. The French had gained the initiative, he said, and one of the enemy's greatest disadvantages was that it had to move heavy artillery with human labor. Each artillery piece required a minimum of 150 men for transport and servicing. Despite this shortcoming, Navarre said, the Vietminh should not be underestimated. Their planning was meticulous. Prior to an attack, a maquette of the target was built in a rear training area, and their attack force rehearsed its tactics as many as fifteen times, memorizing the terrain so that even in a night assault it would be familiar. General Bull was impressed by Navarre's dispassionate analysis of his enemy.

Another explanation for the CASTOR operation came from the London *Times* on November 23. Dien Bien Phu was "the center of a fertile opium-growing district which has been the Vietminh's most important source of revenue." The Vietminh paid for many of its expenses by selling opium, *The Times* asserted, collecting a million dollars a year from the area to pay its troops, buy medical supplies and U.S. weapons, and reimburse the Chinese for equipment.

As General Giap saw it, "Dien Bien Phu was a completely isolated position far away from all the enemy's bases. The only means of supply was by air. . . . On our side we had picked units which we could concentrate to achieve supremacy in power. The problem of supplying the front, though difficult, was not insoluble. . . . We decided to wipe out at all costs the whole enemy force at Dien Bien Phu."

Long after the events, when he no longer had to deal with Indochina on a day-to-day basis, President Eisenhower wrote in his memoirs: "Finally, they came along with this Dien Bien Phu plan. As a soldier, I was horror-stricken. I just said, 'My goodness, you don't pen up troops in a fortress, and all history shows that they are just going to be cut to pieces. . . . I don't think anything of this scheme.' " At the time, however, he had no other option but to help the French.

Ten days before General Navarre told General Bull that the purpose of the drop at Dien Bien Phu was to protect Lai Chau, the order for evacuation had gone out. Lai Chau was the capital of the Thai Federation, governed by an eighty-year-old feudal lord, Deo Van Long, who had a modest court made up of charming princesses, a corps de ballet, and a few thousand partisans. He collected taxes and improved his net worth with opium sales. He was, however, a faithful ally of France, who could not be allowed to fall into the hands of the Viets. Lai Chau had a French garrison and an airstrip, but it lay at the bottom of a narrow ravine and air traffic could be fired at from above. With the prospect of the 316th Division arriving in the area in December, it had become indefensible, and the secret order for evacuation reached the garrison commander, Lieutenant Colonel Trancart, on November 13.

The evacuation was to take place in three phases. An initial battalion of seven hundred Thais would leave Lai Chau on November 15 and march fifty-five miles south to Dien Bien Phu over the Pavie Trail. Then, from December 5 to 8, the family, court, and civilian government of Deo Van Long would be airlifted to Hanoi, along with the French garrison. The last to leave, in small groups between December 8 and 11, would be the remaining Thai partisans, around two thousand in number, some with families.

By the time the first battalion left on November 15, forward elements of the 316th Division had reached the area. The Vietminh moved fast, even in trackless jungle. Each man carried his weapon, his shovel, his rice and water and salt. They marched with sandals on their feet, and rested ten minutes every hour.

Harassed by Vietminh patrols, the partisans had to get off the Pavie Trail and make their way through the jungle. It took them eight days to advance fifty miles, still leaving them six miles from Dien Bien Phu. On November 23, General Gilles sent a unit of Bréchignac's paratroopers to meet up with the battered Thai unit. The next day, they all managed to make their entrance into Dien Bien Phu in good order, their officers riding mountain ponies, flying the Thai flag.

That's What They Call Inflation

Some compared Dien Bien Phu to a gypsy camp, others to a Depression-era Hooverville, with men gathered around fires, tin-roofed shacks, litter-strewn alleyways, and rows of tents and underground bunkers. "It's organized, sort of," observed Lieutenant Allaire. Some said it was like a return to World War I, with trenches and barbed wire.

Men began writing letters home. Lieutenant Samalens, of the 6th BPC, who didn't want to alarm his pregnant wife, Blanche, told her that Dien Bien Phu was a holiday camp like Club Med. "Everything is built of bamboo," he wrote. "The women bathe naked in the river and wear long black robes and colorful turbans with silver ornaments."

The Legionnaire captain Chevalier wrote his wife, Germaine: "To call it a *cuvette* (basin) gives a false impression. It's more like an immense stadium twenty kilometers long and eight wide. The stadium belongs to us, the bleachers in the mountains to the Viets."

After a few days, the villagers who had initially fled returned to their hamlets with their children. The women sat in front of their houses and husked rice by pounding it with mallets, while tending to their pigs and chickens. A brisk trade was carried on between Bigeard's men, who were bivouacked in the main village, and the locals. Cazeneuve told his pal Pingwarski, "The first day, I got a horse for a kilo of salt. Now I'm getting a chicken for two kilos."

"That's what they call inflation," Pingwarski said. The paras, who considered manual labor beneath them, were kept busy clearing brush and felling trees to establish the six-mile-square perimeter of the base. They threw the brush on smoking bonfires. And they had no time to spare for the captivating women with the swaying gait, in their embroidered dresses and scarves.

November 25 was a memorable day; the first C-47 Dakota landed with its cargo, making Dien Bien Phu an operational air-ground base. Heavy equipment no longer had to be dropped by parachute. Two 105mm howitzers in detached pieces were flown in on a British Bristol 170 Freighter. This twin-engine cargo plane, rented from a civilian company, could carry two jeeps or a truck, and had just enough flying time to cover the round-trip from Hanoi. Unlike the 75mm howitzers, which could fire only horizontally, the 105s could fire at any angle and were placed at the center of the compound.

Now that the big cargo planes could land, a coherent system of centers of resistance (CRs) covering all four sides of the camp perimeter was built. Above all, the airstrip had to be protected. Each CR was given a woman's name, in order of the letters of the alphabet, from Anne-Marie to Isabelle. Each consisted of a number of strongpoints—such as Isabelle 1, 2, and 3—with interlocking fields of fire. Each strongpoint had its own radio and medical services, artillery or mortars in open pits, and heavy machine guns installed in blockhouses. Each had fields of barbed wire strung from pickets at thigh height and studded with mines, extending eighty yards out to stop human-wave attacks. Communicating trenches linked the strongpoints, each of which was built by the troops that occupied them. They had the help and advice of Major André Sudrat's 31st Engineer Battalion (BMG), with its one hundred officers and three hundred sappers. But the engineers were overworked—preparing the airstrip, building a

Bailey bridge over the Nam Yum River, and designing the command post—
so the troops did most of the construction themselves.

It took well over a month for each CR to be built. First the ground had
to be prepared so the posts had a clear field of fire. Then trenches had to be
dug, not the capacious pits of World War I but narrow, shoulder-deep fur-
rows patterned in zigzags. Finally, dugouts and blockhouses were built.
Since World War I, the norm for stopping an artillery shell was overhead
protection of three feet of packed earth between two layers of logs six
inches thick, with a top layer of stone or sheet metal. But there was no
stone in the valley and Dien Bien Phu was short of lumber and sheets of
corrugated metal. Each CR had to improvise, and the results varied depending on the troops. The Legion posts, with their high component of
Wehrmacht veterans, did the best job, while the Thai posts were carelessly
built.

The command headquarters, named Claudine, was built where the village had stood, south of the airstrip. It extended from the Pavie Trail to the
Nam Yum River. Claudine became a crowded "downtown" of tents and
labyrinthine dugouts. The command post, buried under six feet of earth
and logs, had a central hall giving on both sides into offices with earthen
walls covered by rattan hangings. Here was the intelligence office, the
briefing room, and offices for the commander and his staff. Here was the
radio link with Hanoi. This was what Gilles had meant by living like a rat.
It was not for the claustrophobic.

The two paratroop battalions that had first jumped in provided a central reserve. On the west, the Legionnaires and Thai partisans of the
Huguette CR protected the airstrip. North of the airstrip was CR Anne-
Marie, also manned by the partisans. Anne-Marie 1 and 2 rose from rice
paddies, while 3 and 4 were at the northern end of the runway. Blocking
access to the Pavie Trail at the northeast was Gabrielle, the key northern
bastion rising like the prow of a ship from the soggy plain a mile from the
airstrip, and held by Algerian infantry. Astride the Pavie Trail, but closer to
the command post, were Dominique 3 and 4, while Dominique 1 and 2
were on hills, also manned by Algerians. To the west of the command post
were more rice paddies with no hills for strongpoints, except for Françoise,
a small post commanded by a sergeant. To the east, between the Nam Yum

River and RP41, was CR Béatrice, perilously close to the forest and held by a highly regarded unit of Legionnaires. Isolated at the southern end of the perimeter, and supposedly self-sufficient, was Isabelle, with its own airstrip and artillery, on a loop of the Nam Yum, manned by Legionnaires and Algerians. Each of these stations was within a mile or so of the center, like the houses in a medieval village clustered around a cathedral, but there was a dangerous distance between them.

It Is Impossible to Lay Down Arms Until Victory Is Completely Won

There was an unplanned synchronicity to the strategies of the two adversaries. By November, the Chinese had convinced the Vietminh that by moving divisions into the northwest, they could capture Lai Chau and advance into Laos. At the same time, General Navarre planned to use Dien Bien Phu to protect Laos and launch offensive operations. Each side was acting independently of the other, as in a game of blindman's bluff.

In mid-November, while knowing nothing about Operation CASTOR, Giap sent the 316th Division to Lai Chau, to be followed by elements of the 308th Division. At a senior officers' conference on November 19, Giap said, "The northwest is the main front. . . . Forces to be employed: two to three divisions." Some troops were already moving rapidly to Lai Chau "to annihilate part of the enemy's forces should he try to withdraw them."

The airborne landing at Dien Bien Phu played into the Vietminh strategy. As soon as it became known, the Chinese military adviser General Wei Guoqing proposed a campaign to surround Dien Bien Phu. Giap agreed to escalate the war from guerrilla hit-and-run tactics to a pitched battle in a clearly defined area, involving several divisions and heavy armament that would come from China. After Lai Chau, the Vietminh divisions would move southward to the mountains surrounding Dien Bien Phu.

These decisions took place at a time when proposals for a negotiated peace were coming from different directions. The Russians, on November 27, 1953, proposed a four-power conference on Germany that was expected to spill over into Indochina. The Chinese played both sides, hoping that negotiations would keep the Americans from direct involvement in the war, while continuing to arm and supply the Vietminh. In Paris, Premier Laniel also played both sides, telling the antiwar crowd in the National Assembly that he was all for "a just and honorable conclusion that would end the war," while asking the Americans for more funds to prosecute it. In France, however, the hostility to the war had reached such a pitch that wall posters in Paris said, DON'T GIVE BLOOD TO THE ARMY. X-ray machines and other medical supplies were sabotaged by longshoremen. Stretcher cases disembarking at Marseille were met by rock-throwing antiwar militants.

The United States, however, remained firm, and when Vice President Nixon visited Indochina in early November 1953, his words were a rebuttal to Laniel: The United States would never approve a peace that "would place people who want independence under foreign bondage. It is impossible to lay down arms until victory is completely won."

In Washington, the State Department was not quite sure what to make of the situation. On November 27, Philip Bonsal, the director of the Office of Philippine and Southeast Asian Affairs, sent a memo to Walter S. Robertson, assistant secretary of state for Far Eastern Affairs, titled "Westward Movement of Vietminh Units": "Army G-2 tell us that four of the six Vietminh infantry divisions in North and Central Vietnam are now moving westward. . . . Perhaps in anticipation of this movement, the French commander, General Cogny, dropped six parachute battalions at Dien Bien Phu on Nov. 20. This operation was the largest air force exercise so far executed in the war. Continued occupation of Dien Bien Phu will block Vietminh use of one of the two principal East-West roads leading into northern Laos. . . . The enemy movement may not take its final form for several weeks. Nevertheless, the Vietminh are moving some forty to fifty thousand troops away from the perimeter for a still undisclosed purpose."

General Navarre had the same intelligence, but his reaction was relief that Giap's divisions were moving away from the Delta. He didn't want to fight five divisions there, added to the eighty thousand Vietminh who had already infiltrated French lines. Everyone in Hanoi was relieved, he said, that the Delta had been spared. The battle had merely changed locations, and was now at Dien Bien Phu. But even if the Vietminh had forty thousand troops and thirty thousand coolies there, how could they keep that many men supplied 250 miles from their bases? Colonel Berteil, Navarre's number two, kept him informed. But Berteil was so heartily in favor of CAS-TOR that the initials *DBP* were said to mean *Du Berteil Pur* (Berteil all over). Berteil worked eighteen hours a day and knew the Vietminh's supply needs: for five divisions, thirty tons of rice a day, which meant three hundred trucks. Where would they get the rice and how would they move it? The same went for munitions, gasoline, medicine, and all the rest. In all, they needed two thousand trucks, with gasoline, drivers, and repair teams, for RP41 was bombed daily. He believed that the Vietminh would be unable to fight a sustained battle.

I'd Rather You Picked Somebody Else

On November 29, 1953, the Swedish newspaper *Expressen* published a rare interview with Ho Chi Minh. Its enterprising correspondent Svante Löfgren had sent Ho five questions three weeks prior via Peking. The questions were vetted by the Chinese and the Russians. Ho sent back his answers, playing into the international mood for negotiations. He said that "if the French government wish[es] to have an armistice and to resolve the question of Vietnam by negotiations, the people and government of the Democratic Republic of Vietnam are ready to examine the French proposals."

Ho Chi Minh, however, was being faithful to the old adage, "If you want peace, prepare for war," for as he wrote Giap a few days later: "This campaign is a very important one, not only militarily, but also politically, not only for domestic reasons, but for international ones as well. So all of our people, all of our armed forces, and the entire Party must be entirely united to get the job done."

In any case, as the result of all these peace rumblings, the involved Western powers—United States, France, and Britain—decided to meet in Bermuda in December, to make sure they were all on the same page, and to emphasize the "vital importance" of the French war effort "to the defense of the free world."

On November 29, Navarre and Cogny flew to Dien Bien Phu. On the plane, Cogny told his superior that he had promised to relieve Gilles.

"Who is our candidate?" Navarre asked.

"I'm thinking of Castries. A cavalryman would be ideal at Dien Bien Phu, where the situation will be mobile. We need someone who can harry and harass the Viets."

"He's my choice also," Navarre said. "You can appoint him whenever you like."

"I would rather you told him yourself," Cogny said.

They landed at Dien Bien Phu at 1:15 P.M., and Navarre pinned the Croix de Guerre on men who had shown valor in Operation CASTOR. Gilles then drove his two superiors around the valley over dusty tracks. Upon seeing the amount of open terrain, Navarre began to think this was indeed a job for a cavalryman. They could bring in tanks, who could flatten the Viets if they ever dared to approach the valley.

On November 30, Navarre and Cogny flew down to Thai Binh, at the mouth of the Red River, near the southern tip of the Delta, where Castries was stationed. The fifty-one-year-old Colonel Christian Marie Ferdinand de la Croix de Castries was unprepossessing in appearance, slight of build, narrow-shouldered, and stooped. His face had the end-of-the-line look that comes from a lack of crossbreeding in aristocratic families—hooded eyes, a nose made for brandy snifters, and a weak chin. But he tried to cut a dashing figure with his riding crop, red cavalry cap, and red foulard.

Castries came from a military family that went back to the Crusades. One of his ancestors had been named general at the age of twenty-five by Louis XIV, while another went to America with Lafayette. The young Castries was a playboy, whose number of mistresses almost balanced his gambling debts. He lived up to his family's motto: "To our horses, to our women, and those who ride them." One of his after-dinner pranks was to break a wine glass and chew on the pieces.

Instead of attending the elite cavalry school at Saumur, where many of his forebears had gone, he rose through the ranks. In his day, cavalry officers had to go through a decathlon to test their endurance. One of the pranklike events involved drinking a magnum of champagne and servicing a prostitute in less than half an hour. Castries was an outstanding rider, world champion in the high jump in 1933 and in the long jump two years later.

When the cavalry converted to armor, Castries became a tank commander. One of the reasons Navarre chose a mere colonel, for a command that required a general, was that Castries had been one of his officers in the Italian campaign of 1944. While racing ahead of his men, his jeep hit a mine and he broke both legs. In Indochina he was wounded again. There was no questioning his bravery and audacity in combat, which had earned him eighteen citations. His organizational skills were another matter. As an assiduous bridge and poker player, he believed in intuition.

When Castries was offered the job, he said: "If you're thinking of setting up an entrenched camp, this isn't my line. I'd rather you picked somebody else."

Navarre said: "Dien Bien Phu must become an offensive base. That's why I've picked you."

"We need a mountain cavalryman out there," Cogny chimed in. "You will be that cavalryman, and roam the wide-open spaces of the highlands."

Castries had his doubts regarding his ability to maneuver from a hedgehog camp, but he kept them to himself.

On December 1, General Trapnell, the head of the MAAG in Saigon, reported to the head of U.S. Pacific Command at Pearl Harbor that Navarre was still uncertain where the Vietminh main thrust would come— Annam, Laos, or Dien Bien Phu, where the French had massed six battalions. Navarre had told Trapnell that he wanted "to invite the enemy to attack the Dien Bien Phu area." Trapnell expressed a "reasonable doubt that the French have the will to seize initiative by operations threatening enemy supply lines from China. . . . It is apparent that the Vietminh will have the initiative."

In Washington, the National Intelligence Estimate for December 1, 1953, predicted that "gradual deterioration of French will to continue the Indochina War has been checked at least temporarily by the Laniel-Navarre plan and the greatly increased United States financial assistance. . . . The French are seeking to regain the military and political initiative. . . . The French. . . . probably aim at improving their position sufficiently to negotiate a settlement. . . . while preserving a position for France in the Far East."

Bidault Looks Like a Dying Man.
Laniel Is Actually Dying Upstairs.

In London on December 1, 1953, Evelyn Shuckburgh packed his bags for the conference in Bermuda, which he inaccurately called the first Big Three summit in eight years, since Potsdam. Shuckburgh, the private secretary to Foreign Secretary Anthony Eden, wasn't sure whether the main business would be Europe or the Far East. He privately believed that Churchill, who was back at the post of prime minister, had proposed Bermuda in order to reestablish rapport with his old friend Eisenhower now that he was president.

On the flight, in the Stratocruiser *Canopus*, Churchill said he was "anti-Frog." Eden said that "the French are pretty hopeless, but France is a geographical necessity." As for the Americans, "they mistake movement for action. As long as something is happening they are quite happy."

The British arrived in a downpour on December 2. The Royal Welch Fusiliers formed a guard of honor at the airport, and both black and white inhabitants braved the rain and stood waving on the road to the Mid Ocean Club, a few steps from the golf links. When Eden prepared Churchill for the meeting with Eisenhower and Dulles, Shuckburgh thought Winston looked "old, weary, and inconsequential." Eden, grouchy as always, said he was "confused and wrong on almost every issue," and "raring to be rude to the French." Premier Laniel, looking like a Normandy butter-and-eggs man, pink-cheeked and rotund, had arrived under the weather, with his foreign minister, Bidault, who strutted around like a Gallic bantam rooster.

Eisenhower arrived on December 4, and struck Shuckburgh as "more ceremonial, withdrawn, royal, than last year." At the first meeting that afternoon, Bidault suggested that since Stalin's death there was a Soviet "new look" that should be cultivated. This was heresy to Ike, who "came down like a ton of bricks" on Bidault, saying, "It is the same old woman of the streets, even if she has on a new hat." Shuckburgh thought the president was very rude and vulgar.

One of the factors complicating the conference was that the Soviets had proposed a meeting in Berlin to discuss Germany and Austria, but wanted to invite China. On December 5, the foreign ministers met to decide whether to attend the Berlin meeting. The French and the British were for it, but Secretary of State Dulles said the Russians only wanted to divide the West and delay the formation of the European Defense Community, which would allow the United States to reduce its ground forces in Europe. Dulles told Eden and Bidault that they were falling into a trap, which annoyed Eden, who resented Dulles's knee-jerk anti-Soviet reactions and disapproved of his garterless green socks.

Between meetings, the great men sunbathed and chatted on the pink coral beach of the Mid Ocean Club. In the afternoon there was another meeting, although Laniel was in bed with pneumonia and a fever of 104. Bidault filled in.

As Bidault rambled on, Eisenhower had a "wild and distraught look in his eyes," and chewed on his spectacles, Shuckburgh noticed, but when Ike spoke to back up Churchill, "it was in a forceful and rather domineering way, but with a quick broad smile." Bidault's refusal to budge on the EDC cast a pall on the conference.

Not until the final meeting, at 5 P.M. on December 7, did Indochina come up. Bidault asserted that the Vietminh were stagnating, and had formed special courts for the growing number of deserters. They had reached their ceiling in strength, even though the Chinese were increasing their supplies of guns and trucks. Reinforcements had been sent from France, which did not help the defense of Europe. The Vietnamese army continued to grow, though it needed more officers. At present, thirty of the targeted fifty-four battalions had been activated. By not trying to defend everything everywhere, Bidault said, Navarre had created a force of maneuver.

None of this would have been possible without American aid, Bidault allowed, and France was *grande dame* enough to say thank you. And to those who alleged that it was not the French who were fighting the war, he wanted to point out that every year, the equivalent of a graduating class of officers from Saint-Cyr was cut down. The war would be lost without the hundred thousand French troops serving in Indochina. Those troops had to be rotated, since they faced not only the enemy but the tropical climate, with its mosquitoes, fever, and dysentery. It was hard to conduct a war from eighteen thousand kilometers away. In his lengthy exposé, Bidault made no mention of Operation CASTOR.

Churchill then said he would like to pay his heartfelt compliments to France for her valiant effort to preserve her empire and the cause of freedom. Eisenhower asked to join Churchill in his tribute to the French for the "magnificent campaign waged for so long and at such a cost." He also wanted to say that he had heard "the finest reports" about General Navarre. On a more practical note, Ike was happy to announce that another aircraft carrier would be turned over to the French in a few days, along with twenty-five transport aircraft and some helicopters.

Then came the time to draft the communiqué. A conference that had begun in vagueness ended in farce. Laniel was still bedridden, in a room upstairs from the meetings, and every time a line was drafted or a word was changed, Bidault had to run up to get Laniel's agreement and then back down again. Shuckburgh observed, "Bidault looks like a dying man. Laniel is actually dying upstairs." Eisenhower, who thought the entire conference was a waste of time, left the table in a rage, then came back, and told Dulles, "Never again will I come to one of these unless it is all prepared and agreed on beforehand."

The only result of Bermuda was that Dulles grudgingly assented to talks in Berlin as long as they were held soon and did not last long. In Paris, Bidault told the press, "Need I underline that our language was not one of abdication, but expressed our desire for peace." Ike's reaction, spelled out in a December 10 memo, was that "it is clear that the French (perhaps correctly) consider that the situation is in better shape than it has been for a long time."

Shuckburgh stayed an extra day, buying silk scarves for his wife and a coral necklace for his daughter. He picked bouquets of oleander and poinsettia to take back to England.

As Marquis Childs later wrote in his 1958 book *Eisenhower: Captive Hero,* "The Bermuda Conference in . . . [one] respect proved to have been a sad deception." Those present "accepted from Georges Bidault a rosy picture of the war in Indochina that was almost entirely false. The United States was paying up to nearly a billion dollars annually of the cost of that conflict, and Bidault encouraged the hope that with a little more time and a little more money the war . . . would be brought to a successful conclusion. . . . Whether the president and Dulles preferred to accept the optimistic view, they seem to have put full credence in Bidault's wishful dream, which concealed such a fearful reality."

Paul Sturm, the U.S. consul in Hanoi, reported on December 5 that "it is too early to affirm basic change in Vietnam fall campaign plans, which have been generally assumed to hinge on a major effort against [the] Delta." By December 9, however, he was hearing "rumors . . . that elements of Vietminh Divisions 308 and 312 were turning toward the northwest to join Division 316 in Thai country."

In Washington, the need for good news had made the Pentagon and the State Department fasten on the O'Daniel report. "Iron Mike" had traveled around Indochina from November 6 to 15 and had written his report in Honolulu between November 17 and 19. Since he had not been told about Operation CASTOR, the report was outdated when he signed it. His overly optimistic view concluding that the Navarre Plan was sound and would bring a decisive victory was balm to the officials who read the report and may have influenced Eisenhower and Dulles in Bermuda. As the Pentagon Papers later put it, "The temptation to 'go along' with the French until the Vietminh were defeated was all the more attractive because of the *expectation* of victory which pervaded official Washington. Before Dien Bien Phu, Gen. O'Daniel consistently reported that victory was in reach if the United States continued its support. . . . Gen. O'Daniel submitted a progress report which . . . said French Union forces held the initiative and would begin offensives in mid-January in the Mekong Delta. . . . Meanwhile, a relatively small force would attempt to keep the Vietminh off balance in the Tonkin Delta until October 1954, when the French would begin a major offensive."

The O'Daniel memo became the foundation for official optimism. It was an example of bureaucratic lag, when outdated information supersedes more recent reports. General Matthew Ridgway waited until 1976 to give his opinion of "Iron Mike": "Personally, and this is not for attribution, I was not impressed with him. I thought he was inclined to be overoptimistic."

I Have Decided to Accept the Battle

Dien Bien Phu had settled into a waiting mode. Colonel André Lalande, commander of the 3rd Foreign Legion Infantry Regiment (REI), who had been twice wounded at El Alamein, wrote his wife, Marie-Françoise, on November 30: "Waiting for we know not what weighs on us. . . . There's always a slight sense of dread before a battle. Nothing has happened yet. We're waiting for the Viets." More armament arrived daily. The first artillery was flown in on November 25, in the form of two 105mm howitzers. More 105s kept arriving every other day until there were twenty-four, with a range of about seven miles.

In Saigon, Navarre also waited. The surprise occupation of Dien Bien Phu presented intriguing possibilities. Were the Vietminh prepared for a prolonged battle as opposed to guerrilla attacks? Navarre studied his options as he leafed through a pile of radio intercepts, with the skepticism that experienced intelligence officers develop.

By November 28, Navarre had on his desk the order of march of the Vietminh divisions heading toward Laos—the 316th in the vanguard, followed by the 308th, 312th, and then the 351st Heavy Division. That would mean a force of thirty-five thousand men, supported by twice as many coolies. It seemed clear that the bulk of Giap's army was advancing on Dien Bien Phu. But Navarre, whose reputation was based on the perceptive reading of intelligence reports, held to the belief that these forces could only be elements rather than entire divisions. On December 1, he complained to General Trapnell that the equipment coming in from China included 75s and 105s, as well as trucks and artillery tractors. He wondered why the Viets needed all this artillery. Dien Bien Phu was 310 miles from the Chinese border, and they would never get it through the mountains. There weren't any roads. Not even trails.

Navarre convinced himself that he could win a decisive battle at Dien Bien Phu. On December 3, he gave Cogny a "personal and secret instruction," saying: "I have decided to accept the battle" along the following lines:

• If Lai Chau is threatened, evacuate. (In fact, the evacuation had already begun.)

- The phases of the battle would last at most a month.
- The garrison at Dien Bien Phu would be reinforced.

Navarre's decision went against his own plan, which was to "try to avoid a general battle with the enemy battle corps" in the 1953–54 dry season. But he began to see Dien Bien Phu as an opportunity not to be missed, since it would draw off Vietminh forces and allow him to conduct other operations in the Delta and central Vietnam. This was the *abcès de fixation* (magnet for enemy forces) explanation that Navarre gave on December 4 to Ambassador Heath and a visiting congressman, Edward J. Thye, a Minnesota Republican on the Senate Appropriations Committee. There was no doubt, Navarre said, that the Vietminh had been planning a serious attack in the Delta and that the taking of Dien Bien Phu had spoiled their plan.

That same day, the U.S. Army attaché in Saigon, Colonel Leo W. H. Shaughnessy, reported that the information on Vietminh movements was "sparse and conflicting. VM counter-intelligence always tightens before major operations. This fact, coupled with usual problems of getting timely accurate info on moving troop units, results in temporary 'blind spot' in French intelligence."

The Tamers of Iron Horses

As suggested by his Chinese advisers, Giap was moving his divisions away from the Delta into the northwest, at a time when the Soviets and the Chinese had launched a peace offensive to bring about a negotiated settlement in Indochina. A victorious battle for either side would set the stage for a favorable agreement. Thus, while Ho Chi Minh proposed negotiation, he also told the party faithful in early December, "The enemy is trying to trick us by dropping bait in the water; if we rush in like a school of fish . . . they will easily defeat us."

The obstacle for both sides was logistics. For the French, the battle hinged on keeping the airstrip open, while the Vietminh had to figure out how to bring heavy weapons through the mountains and how to attack over flat terrain without being massacred. The French had an air force.

The Vietminh had home-field advantage and could count on the support of the rural population.

On December 6, over the Voice of Vietnam radio, Giap issued a mobilization order. An army of coolies responded, transforming the war. Thousands of coolies were assigned to encampments along the truck routes, where they tied treetops together over the roads and built bridges slightly underwater. On treeless stretches they brushed away tire treads as soon as convoys passed.

Supplies took a week to get from the Chinese border to the main Vietminh depot at Tuan Giao. New roads were built from the depot to Dien Bien Phu, thirty-seven miles to the southwest. Roads cut by rivers with no bridges were divided into sectors. Each sector had its Molotova trucks, which shuttled from one end of a sector to the other. At a portage, the cargo from one sector was unloaded and carried on boats or rafts to the next sector. The trucks drove at night and turned their headlights off at the sound of planes.

The hauling of artillery was the most agonizing part of the supply operations. Men died turning themselves into human wedges to keep big guns from slipping off mountain roads. On trails too narrow for trucks, one man carried a mortar baseplate and another the tube, two others a pole from which hung a wheel, four men a 105mm howitzer breechblock, and others the barrel of a 75mm recoilless rifle. In all, over the course of the battle, the Vietminh were able to bring in 144 artillery pieces, 36 anti-aircraft guns, and some twelve-tube Katyusha rocket launchers. They were able to outgun the French.

The French sent out sorties daily to bomb the roads. At the 1955 commission of inquiry, conducted by General Catroux and others, General Dechaux explained why his air force failed. Each time they bombed a road it was repaired. Entire villages were mobilized, and there was an incessant caravan from dusk to dawn of barefoot coolies carrying torches, wooden shovels, and straw baskets, filling the craters. "It wasn't just a matter of cutting a road," Dechaux said, "we had to keep the Viets from replacing it. They worked at night, they had ten hours, and eighteen in case of fog. We could fly at night, but our sorties were not up to par. We failed in our most demanding mission."

One of those who heard Giap's call on December 6 was Dinh Van Ty, a bicycle repairman in the hamlet of Pho Moi, nestled in the coastal hills of Thanh Hoa Province, 135 miles southwest of Hanoi. He attended a meeting at which a Vietminh cadre said, "The French have established an important garrison in Dien Bien Phu valley, which is surrounded by our troops. Our men there are in dire need of food. We in the rear must do everything to supply them." Volunteers jostled to add their names to the list. About a hundred were chosen to form a company, with Dinh as its leader.

The volunteers' bicycles had to be turned into pack bikes that could carry four hundred pounds of rice. The mudguards and chain covers were removed and frail aluminum wheel rims were replaced by stronger ones made of steel. The front and rear forks were replaced by iron rods and stronger brakes. Each bicycle was fitted with two hard bamboo sticks, one to elongate the handlebars and help the steering and the other to lengthen the seat shaft, as a support for pushing.

The company was divided into teams of five, each of which had its own food and plastic sheets to protect the rice in case of rain. Dinh, who had learned his trade as a child, brought his tool kit and a box of spare parts. They set out in the afternoon and picked up loads of rice at the nearby storehouse of Cam Thuy. It was 250 miles to Dien Bien Phu. Each man was given as much as he could carry, from two hundred to four hundred pounds. They traveled at night on a road that wound through a forest, and passed a "long-haired army" carrying rice to the front on foot in baskets hanging from bamboo poles. The women sang and laughed and one called out, "Why don't you get on your bikes? You'll soon get tired of pushing them." Her friend said, "Maybe they don't know how to ride them." "What," the first one replied, "those tamers of iron horses?"

Dinh was not worried about his men, whose morale was high. He worried about the bicycles. With loads up to four hundred pounds, they could advance without mishap only on flat ground. If there was a grade, one wheel would bear most of the weight, and the tire would burst. Dinh spent much of his time repairing inner tubes. He cut off the legs of his khaki pants, sliced them into strips, and wound the strips around the inner tubes before inflating them. The next day there were no forced stops for repairs.

Soon the entire company was wearing shorts, even though they were crossing an area infested with mosquitoes.

On flat ground, the bikes moved almost by themselves. It was possible to hold a bike with one hand and smoke a Cam Thuy cigarette with the other. Problems arose at the mountain passes. At the Ban Phe Pass, the slope was so steep it took six men to push a single bike. One man held the handlebars. Two men ahead of the bike pulled it by a rope. Three men pushed from behind. That day, after hauling fifteen bikes up to the pass, Dinh collapsed from exhaustion. The company rested at the top and someone produced sesame sweets. Five men were needed for each bike to go downhill, braking and holding on with ropes attached to the handlebars.

They reached a river with a swift current and no bridge. Dinh waded in waist-deep and was almost carried downstream. "Let's stretch a rope across the stream," Dinh said. "We'll cling to it while crossing. The bags of rice must be taken off the bikes and carried across one by one. Then the bikes must go."

One of the men asked, "But how do we get the rope across?"

One of the youngest members of the company took off his shirt and said, "I'll cross first. I used to work on a barge. I know what to do."

He fastened one end of the rope around his waist and started across, struggling not to be swept away. Pushing against the current, he reached the other side. First they brought the rice across. Each bag was wrapped in a plastic sheet so it wouldn't get soaked, attached to the rope, and pulled across. Then came the bicycles, which only the strongest could carry over without losing their footing.

Once across the stream, they reached RP41, which was paved. That part was a ramble, but many night marches lay ahead, sometimes on good roads, sometimes over hills covered with elephant grass. When they reached terrain with scorched vegetation and bomb craters, they knew they were not far from the front. Their common task brought the men closer. If a man ran a fever, he was given the last tablet of quinine. Thanks to this sense of unison, they got through without a serious mishap, and finally reached the hills around Dien Bien Phu with their supply of rice. Years later, after having moved to Hanoi, Dinh ran into one of the others in the company, and their conversation drifted back to the Brigade of Iron Horses.

If You Lose an Inch of Ground, You're Done For

On December 7, 1953, a day after Giap proclaimed mobilization, Colonel Castries arrived in Dien Bien Phu to take command of the Groupement Opérationnel du Nord-Ouest, or GONO, as the garrison was called. He had with him the acerbic forty-four-year-old Breton Colonel Langlais, still in a cast with his broken ankle; Colonel Charles Piroth, the artillery commander; and his secretary, twenty-eight-year-old Paule Bourgeade. As their Dakota landed, they could see plumes of smoke rising from the brush still being burned.

General Gilles, happy to be leaving, was on the airstrip to greet the new commander, who was wearing his trademark foulard and red forage cap, and hustled him into his jeep for a tour of the base. As they drove, raising clouds of dust, Gilles filled Castries in. The evacuation of Lai Chau had resumed, and some of the regular units were being airlifted into Dien Bien Phu. The Thai partisans would be arriving on foot. The evacuation was a disaster, leaving Dien Bien Phu exposed to the north, but there was one small benefit—the infirmary there had an X-ray machine, which was being flown over.

At the time of Castries' arrival, four of the six paratroop battalions who had jumped on November 20 were being sent back to Hanoi, to be replaced by Algerians and Foreign Legion. A total of 3,470 paras would be flown out, while 4,680 infantrymen would be flown in. Castries now had a total of twelve battalions.

Gilles and Castries toured the strongpoints, most of which were still under construction. It was all new to the commander, who hardly knew what questions to ask. They discussed the size of the perimeter. General Cogny had ordered that there must be freedom of movement out to six miles from the airstrip in all directions. That was a lot of ground to cover with the troops available. Castries was faced with a crucial decision on the size of the perimeter. If it was too small, the enemy could close in. If it was too spacious, it would be spread thin and the enemy could break through.

He had, however, asked for tanks, which he believed could maneuver in the valley with artillery support. Gilles' final words to the commander were: "Watch out. If you lose an inch of ground, you're done for."

On December 9, Ambassador Heath reported that General Navarre "felt quite certain that Vietminh would attack Dien Bien Phu, where they would meet, he was quite confident, a costly repulse."

You Were Sitting on My Stomach

As we have seen, Operation POLLUX, the evacuation of Lai Chau, had begun in mid-November, when the first column fought its way south to Dien Bien Phu. But it was not until December 5, acting on the intelligence that the Vietminh 316th Division was approaching Lai Chau, that General Cogny gave the following order: "The Lai Chau troops [Thai partisans] will pull out on foot toward Dien Bien Phu on the evening of December 7 to achieve the element of surprise." By this time, the evacuation of the civilians and the French garrisons by air had been completed.

Lieutenant Colonel André Trancart, who was in command of Lai Chau, had to hastily organize the removal of the partisans. There remained between two thousand and three thousand badly trained and poorly armed Thais, many of them with families. When they were told they were to proceed on foot fifty-five miles south over difficult and possibly Viet-infested terrain to Dien Bien Phu, massive desertions ensued. Those who stayed were divided into four groups commanded by three French lieutenants and a sergeant. Trancart staggered their departures between December 5 and 12, along different itineraries, not knowing that the first elements of the 316th Division had arrived south of Lai Chau in early December. On December 12, after destroying their vehicles, the last group of partisans pulled out, leaving behind them the stench of burning rubber. Lai Chau was a ghost town.

The result of this poorly planned exodus was catastrophic. Of the estimated two thousand partisans who left Lai Chau, only Lieutenant Wieme and his two hundred men were able to outflank the Vietminh and reach Dien Bien Phu on December 16. Lieutenant Guillermit and his seven companies were attacked on December 8 southeast of Lai Chau and wiped out after a forty-eight-hour battle. Lieutenant Ulpat's group of six companies was blocked by a Vietminh detachment on the Pavie Trail. A dozen men escaped and were picked up by choppers. The group led by Sergeant Blanc made it to the village of Muong Pon, a rallying point ten miles north of Dien Bien Phu, where it was surrounded and destroyed. As Colonel Langlais told the 1955 commission of inquiry: "The Thais were a bunch of scared peasants without the slightest military training, determined not to fight, and the unfortunate European officers were sacrificed."

Since it was Castries' intention to maneuver outside the base, he sent a couple of battalions to rescue the Thai units under Sergeant Blanc, surrounded at Muong Pon. He entrusted the mission to his two reserve battalions of paras under the command of Colonel Langlais—the 1st BEP (Legionnaires) and the 5th BPVN (Vietnamese). A third battalion, the 8th Choc, would later join up with them.

Before dawn on December 11, the two para units started out, with the Legionnaires in the lead. Shivering in the chill of the early-morning fog, the troops marched to the northernmost point of the basin into a narrow gorge that ran alongside RP41. Not wanting to fall into a trap, they sent recon units to the right, who came upon a recently abandoned Vietminh post, with sleeping bags still unrolled.

Langlais decided not to take the road and ordered the men into the jungle, where they had to march single file, with high elephant grass reducing the visibility to ten yards. Lieutenant Georges Roux was in the lead. When they had advanced three hundred yards, the Vietminh attacked, "all shouting and firing at once," Roux recalled. "They had as many automatic weapons as we did, and they fired non-stop." Roux and his men lay flat on their stomachs. Langlais called in artillery from Dien Bien Phu, and under the fire of the howitzers, the Vietminh melted away. Lieutenant Roux evacuated his wounded and the others pressed on, up ridge and down swale, cutting through the elephant grass with machetes. Exhausted point men, gasping for breath, had to be replaced every fifteen minutes.

By nightfall on December 11, the two units had advanced only a little more than two miles and were still about seven miles from Muong Pon. They stopped on high ground, and started moving again at 4 A.M. on December 12, again encountering elephant grass that was higher than they were. They were running out of water, so some was dropped in by parachute. Langlais, limping on his bad ankle, had his arms around two paras. He kept his men marching, with only brief stops, for thirty-six hours.

At dawn on December 13, they could hear firing from Muong Pon, and stepped up the pace, but then the firing stopped, and a Morane spotter plane reported that the village was in flames. Langlais gave his exhausted men a rest, and the 8th Choc battalion arrived at the scene. All they could do was return to Dien Bien Phu. The return would be perilous since the Vietminh knew where they were.

The three units started back on the afternoon of December 13, each taking a turn at the lead. Lieutenant Pierre Lalanne of the Vietnamese paratroop battalion recalled that he was in the rear guard on a fairly open trail, with high elephant grass barring visibility on both sides, when at 3 P.M. firing broke out. Hidden in the high grass, the Vietminh had let the first two battalions go by and attacked the third, first with mortars, then with grenades, then with automatic fire.

Another lieutenant, Lucien Béal, his face and torso covered with blood, ran toward Lalanne, who took him to the battalion surgeon. Dr. Pierre Rouault, flanked by four stretcher-bearers, found a clearing and lay Béal on his back. Blood was bubbling from his mouth and he was gasping for breath. Rouault opened his case of surgical instruments and took out a scalpel. He sat on Béal's stomach and made an incision in his throat to open the airway. Then he inserted a tube, taping it to Béal's neck. Soon Béal began to breathe again. Rouault had performed a tracheotomy without anesthetic in a clearing in the jungle, in the midst of a firefight. Béal was flown to Hanoi, where the bullets that hit him were removed at Lanessan Hospital. Later, Rouault asked him, "Why were you screaming like a pig while I operated?" Béal told him, "You were sitting on my stomach where I was shot." Béal ended up a three-star general and was posted to the Caribbean island of Martinique, where he liked to ride a bicycle to and from his office. One evening he was struck by a drunken driver and killed on the way home.

Pinned down on the trail by an unseen enemy, as the three units were, the jungle took on an almost human, malevolent quality, as menacing an antagonist as the Vietminh. Langlais called in Bearcats, four of which were parked on the Dien Bien Phu airstrip. These single-seat, single-engine fighter-bombers with four wing guns came in at such a low altitude that a wing clipped the top of a tree. They fired napalm and 20mm rockets, and took out a Vietminh machine-gun nest, allowing the Legionnaires in the lead to move on. But the two sides were at such close quarters that the napalm incinerated some French troops. Lieutenant Lalanne recalled "the horrible stink of burned bodies, blackened and twisted into grotesque shapes, with their metal belt buckles encrusted in their remains." The Legionnaires and Vietnamese paratroopers suffered forty-seven dead and missing and sixty-nine wounded. The dead were buried in a ditch planted with bamboo stakes, to which were attached planks from ammunition cases. The survivors were back in Dien Bien Phu on December 15, having achieved nothing. Contrary to General Cogny's December directive that Dien Bien Phu "must have a resolutely offensive character that will increase with the arrival of fresh troops and the improvement of the defensive perimeter," the concept of sorties was now permanently discredited.

If I Were Your Father, I'd Spank You

Two days later, on December 17, 1953, the brass descended on Dien Bien Phu—Navarre, Cogny, and Henri Lauzin, the air force commander. Their Dakota landed at 11:30 A.M. Castries greeted them on the airstrip wearing his "bananas," as the French call decorations. Behind him, a platoon of Moroccan Tabors wearing turbans and white spats presented arms.

Before the big wall map in his underground command post, Castries briefed Navarre on recent events. The Vietminh now barred the way between Lai Chau and Dien Bien Phu. The units he had tried to send through had been beaten back. Navarre wanted to try another sortie. He was still bent on showing that units from Dien Bien Phu could link up with other French troops. Navarre's intelligence told him that the routes southwest from Dien Bien Phu into Laos were open. At the same time, three battalions under Major Vaudrey had moved out of Luang Prabang and taken the Laotian post of Muong Khoua, which was about sixty miles southwest of Dien Bien Phu. Navarre told Castries to send some units into Laos, where they would link up with Vaudrey's battalions. They would meet at the halfway point between Dien Bien Phu and Muong Khoua, the Laotian hamlet of Sop Nao. Their linkup would prove that the French were still able to keep routes open between Dien Bien Phu and Laos.

It was then the turn of the artillery commander to brief Navarre on his field of fire. Colonel Charles Piroth was a lumbering, good-humored man of forty-eight with a face as round and rosy as a Bayonne ham. In December 1946, while commanding an artillery unit north of Saigon, he had been wounded in the left arm but refused to leave his battery. By the time he arrived at the Saigon hospital, his arm had to be amputated above the elbow. He formed the habit of tucking his left sleeve into his belt.

Piroth had his own staff under the designation *P.C. Feu* (Firing Command), to which all requests for artillery came. The command was divided into two groups, one of 105mm howitzers to defend the centers of resistance, and the other of 105s and 155s as counterbatteries against Vietminh artillery. The guns in the second group had to be able to fire in all directions and could not be placed in fortified enclosures. They were aligned in a series of open pits with a diameter of ten yards, each of which had a fortified bunker for the artillery officers, who were exposed only when firing. In battle, the officers jumped back and forth from the bunkers to the guns. In addition, thirty-two 120mm mortars were distributed among the CRs for their defense. Piroth had eight detachments of artillery observers spread among the centers of resistance.

Piroth told Navarre that he had twenty-four 105s and was expecting four 155s, the heaviest cannon the French had in Indochina. He had a stockpile of twenty-seven thousand artillery shells. He knew exactly the number of shells to be fired and the cadence of fire. He did not believe that the Vietminh were capable of getting their artillery through. Even if they did they would not have enough shells, and they would have to place their guns on the reverse slopes, hidden from the Dien Bien Phu basin by the crest line, and lob their shells in. If they built emplacements on the slopes facing the French camp, he would destroy them. This was a masterly exposé from a veteran artillery officer. If counterbattery artillery operations were an art, Piroth was an artist.

In the afternoon, in the lukewarm December sun, Navarre and the others inspected the centers of resistance. Navarre was concerned that some showed poor construction, in the timber framework, loose barbed wire, and insufficient communicating trenches. He knew that defensive lines can be breached, as Maginot himself admitted, and that any CR was only as good as the ones around it. But when he expressed his concern to Cogny, the reply was: "We must do nothing to keep them from attacking." Navarre called for another bastion, Huguette, to be built to the west of the airstrip.

At the northeastern CR Béatrice, manned by Legionnaires, Lieutenant Colonel Jules Gaucher told his distinguished guests that he had removed every bramble and thicket until Béatrice was "as clean-shaven as a Thai whore's cunt." At the age of forty-eight, Gaucher had been a Legionnaire for twenty-five years. He didn't mind taking the dirty jobs; he liked them, just as he liked fighting in the bars of Hanoi. Brawny and hard-drinking, he was what the French call an *armoire à glace* (wardrobe trunk). Having served in Indochina since 1940, he felt that he had earned the right to be obstreperous.

Navarre climbed up onto the roof of the Béatrice command post and looked down on RP41 and the jungle-covered hills. Turning to Piroth, he expressed concern that this isolated outpost might be a target for enemy artillery. Piroth replied: "No Viet cannon will fire more than three rounds before it is located and destroyed."

Later, when the petite and gutsy reporter Brigitte Friang, who had qualified for her paratroop certificate with six jumps, was dropped into Dien Bien Phu, she told Piroth: "My dear colonel, you must realize that the Viets are in the hills. They will fire straight at you."

"Poor little Brigitte," Piroth replied. "If I were your father, I'd spank you."

Is This What They Call Waging War?
It Is Utterly Pointless.

According to plan, Major Vaudrey marched his Moroccans and Legionnaires into Sop Nao and waited for the troops from Dien Bien Phu. Under the command of the indefatigable Langlais, the 8th Choc and the 1st BEP battalions started out on December 21 and reached Sop Nao two days later. Vaudrey and Langlais toasted each other with flasks of rum. The scene was captured by two reporters. One of them, Brigitte Friang, was embedded with Major Vaudrey. She worked for the magazine *Indochine Sud Est Asiatique* and called the linkup "a communiqué operation." Dixie Reed, an American photographer with the U.S. aid mission, arrived in a medevac helicopter, wearing a tie and wing-tip shoes.

Once the photographs were taken, both forces about-faced and went back to their bases. Captain Pierre Tourret of the 8th Choc persuaded Langlais that they should not take the trail back to Dien Bien Phu. Instead they returned through rapids and thick fog over high slopes. Each time they got to one peak they saw another, but they escaped ambush. Emerging onto a plateau on December 25, they saw the Nam Yum Valley below.

In a letter home, Lieutenant Nénert of the 1st BEP wrote: "We endured a forced march of twelve to thirteen hours a day in an unbelievable landscape, peaks, gorges, jungle. . . . Survival rations barely edible. It was hot as hell during the day and freezing cold at night. A thick fog until 11 A.M. We didn't see any Viets. This liaison was totally devoid of tactical interest. Both sides met, shook hands, and went home. Is this what they call waging war? It is utterly pointless."

At the 1955 commission of inquiry, General Catroux asked Langlais: "You conducted an operation with Laos. Was this a liaison operation or did it have tactical value?"

Langlais: "We wanted to be able to say that we had succeeded in realizing an operation from Dien Bien Phu to Laos. My goal was to shake hands with Major Vaudrey and return."

Catroux: "Did you engage the enemy?"

Langlais: "Fortunately not, or I would have lost a battalion. My goal was to play hide-and-seek with the enemy. . . . I took the most difficult trails on the way back."

Catroux: "Did you have guides?"

Langlais: "I had a single guide for twelve hundred men."

Catroux: "So it was a symbolic operation . . . which accomplished nothing to demonstrate how other units could come to the assistance of Dien Bien Phu."

Langlais: "What it showed was that we had to admit that no overland

liaison was possible between Dien Bien Phu and any other location."
(What he meant was that if you took one trail in you couldn't take it back
out.)

In the midst of these operations outside the perimeter, more equipment
was arriving to strengthen Dien Bien Phu. In early December, in a huge
hangar in Hanoi, a team of Legionnaire mechanics, most of whom had
worked on panzers, took apart ten M24 Chaffee tanks, each of which
weighed eighteen tons. The turret alone weighed four tons. The rest of the
tank was broken down into 180 elements. The Flying Boxcars, with their
huge loading doors at the rear, carried the turrets and the C-47 Dakotas
carried the rest. By December 18, the first tanks had been flown to Dien
Bien Phu and were reassembled on a makeshift assembly line next to the
airstrip. The Vietminh were watching, and within days the French picked
up radio intercepts that 90mm antitank guns had crossed the Chinese border. By December 29, the first assembled tanks took a spin in the valley to
test their engines and fire a few rounds from their 75mm cannons.

Between December 26 and 28, the four American-made 155mm guns
arrived, weighing five and a half tons each, with a twelve-mile range. They
too had to be taken apart and flown in, along with their shells and tools. If
they were that difficult to move, thought the French, how could the Viets
bring in any of their own?

A big problem for Piroth was the scale of the maps. Identifying enemy
artillery meant hours of studying maps with slide rules. But the scale of
the maps was 1/100,000, reducing one kilometer on the ground to one
centimeter on paper, inadequate for plotting targets. The French had to
rely on aerial photographs, even though they flattened out contour detail.
Artillery spotters with range-finding binoculars mounted on tripods spent
hours scanning hills. They went up in Moranes and dropped grenades that
released colored smoke if they saw a target. Piroth himself went up in December, squeezing his bulky frame behind the pilot and juggling his radio,
maps, and binoculars with his one arm. The pilot had to catch a thermal
in order to take off. They spotted a tiny clearing in the hills to the east, but
when his men fired at it, they could not confirm a direct hit.

À la Hussarde! You Know What That Means, Castries!

Back in Saigon, Navarre dreaded the social obligations of the season. He decided to spend Christmas with the 10,910 men now stationed at Dien Bien Phu. He could not reveal to them, however, the contents of the letter he had just sent Paris: "Given the new means of the enemy, one cannot guarantee a victory." His intelligence sources told him the Vietminh were bringing heavy weapons into Dien Bien Phu.

Castries did his best to provide a festive atmosphere. Under a tent outside his command post, a long table was covered with parachute silk, upon which bottles of champagne stood at attention next to plates of tinned foie gras. Outside, Legionnaires had hung a leafless tree with paper garlands and bits of cotton soaked in iodine. After the champagne banquet, the chaplain said midnight mass under the stars, raising his arms as if reaching out to the crests where the Vietminh waited. Young men on their knees asked for his benediction.

After mass, Castries held a *réveillon* (midnight supper) in his quarters for the higher-ranking officers. He served cold *boudin* (blood sausage), "a dish you don't forget," one of his guests remarked. Colonel Gaucher, his tongue loosened by champagne, proposed a toast: "*À la Hussarde!* You know what that means, Castries!" *À la Hussarde* meant "in the hussar manner of rape and plunder." "For some reason it's coming back to me like acid indigestion," Gaucher said. "*À la Hussarde* was the radio message announcing the Japanese attack on March 9, 1945. That was how the war started." Gaucher, then a battalion commander in Hanoi, had managed to get his men out and march them westward to Dien Bien Phu, beyond the reach of the Japanese. "In Dien Bien Phu, I got a radio message from General de Gaulle, saying, 'If you hold, Indochina is saved.' " Then he shouted: "Did you hear that, Castries?" With the Japanese closing in, Gaucher had managed to evacuate what remained of his troops across the border into China.

The garrison on that Christmas Eve was in high spirits. Navarre later told the commission of inquiry that "they were looking forward to a great victory," which some of the men confirmed in their letters home. Second Lieutenant Jean Fox wrote his sister on December 26, "If they attack, there'll be plenty of yellow meat in the barbed wire." But others were not so optimistic. Lieutenant Étienne Michel wrote his wife, Denise, on January 31, 1954: "The more time goes by, the less I think the Viets will attack. They'd take huge losses. . . . It would be useless butchery, and pointless to lose friends for such a stupid cause. . . . And what thanks do we get from France, which isn't worthy of its soldiers?"

Aside from Dien Bien Phu, Navarre had ordered a major operation on December 7 called ATLANTE. This was an attack on the narrow, necklike coastal strip that linked northern and southern Vietnam, 230 miles long and 45 miles wide. The Vietminh were holding the neck as a staging area to attack the south. Even though he knew that no more reinforcements were due, Navarre was planning multiple operations. ATLANTE involved forty thousand troops, and included landing craft to charge ashore in central Annam. By comparison, he still saw Dien Bien Phu as a sideshow. But when ATLANTE was launched on January 20, the Vietminh had vanished.

Navarre's misgivings regarding Dien Bien Phu increased when, on December 28, Castries' chief of staff, Colonel Louis Guth, was killed by a sniper within the perimeter. Guth had gone on reconnaissance with an escort from Anne-Marie, the westernmost center of resistance. He got out of his jeep in a clearing encircled by thick bushes to look at his map when a burst of automatic fire hit him, cutting him diagonally from the abdomen to the shoulder. Captain Compain ran toward him and was hit in the right leg. A jeep took Compain and Guth's body to the surgical team of Jean Thuries, who told Compain, "You're moaning, I'll give you a shot."

"It's not that," Compain said. "I was responsible for the colonel and he's dead." Guth was taken to the morgue, an open pit in front of which were assembled boards in kits, to be used as needed for coffins.

On December 31, Navarre sent a secret instruction to Cogny, asking him to prepare a plan for the evacuation of Dien Bien Phu. It was codenamed XENOPHON, after the author of the *Anabasis*, who led his Ten Thousand through hostile territory in Corduene in 400 B.C.

Navarre's instruction said:

> We must consider the possibility that the battle will not go in
> our favor:

- If our defenses are breached by powerful attacks conducted by weapons we have not seen before.
- If Dien Bien Phu is "smothered," that is, if the enemy is able to prevent the use of the airstrip with its artillery or antiaircraft guns.

In these two cases, Dien Bien Phu will be evacuated, but this is of course the worst scenario, which I am determined to carry out only in the last extremity.

Castries later told the commission of inquiry: "The Viets would not have let us leave just like that. The battalions that got out last would have been destroyed and we would have had to leave behind our equipment. The last day it might have worked would have been December 20."

Thus Navarre was requesting an evacuation plan that was no longer feasible. Of course, he could not know that at the time. And yet he was already hedging his bets, writing Marc Jacquet, the French secretary of state for the Associated States, on January 1, 1954: "Two weeks ago I was 100 percent sure of winning at Dien Bien Phu. . . . But given the new means that our intelligence is announcing—37mm antiaircraft guns and perhaps heavy artillery and motor vehicles—if they really exist in large numbers and the adversary can put them in action—I can no longer guarantee success."

Jacquet, who had contributed little at policy meetings other than puffing on his pipe to see which way the wind was blowing, thought Navarre was too pessimistic. Meanwhile, Commissioner General Maurice Dejean, better known for his champagne dinners in Saigon than his military knowledge, said in his message to the troops on January 3: "We cannot lose this war unless we refuse to do what has to be done to win it."

Navarre, however, was sending out the message that a defeat at Dien Bien Phu would not matter that much. Donald Heath, the pudgy American ambassador fond of wide-brimmed fedoras, who reported almost daily to Washington, cabled on January 3, 1954: "Navarre said loss of Dien Bien Phu would not prevent his moving on to eventual victory." Thus, instead of evacuating, Navarre reinforced the garrison with three more infantry battalions and the tank squadron.

Memorials erected at battle sites.
Photos by Eileen Morgan.

Castries' underground bunker. *Photo by Eileen Morgan.*

Huge billboard on main avenue warning against heroin and AIDS. *Photo by Eileen Morgan.*

The Bailey bridge today. *Photo by Eileen Morgan.*

A school now stands at the site of the Anne-Marie strongpoint. *Photo by Eileen Morgan.*

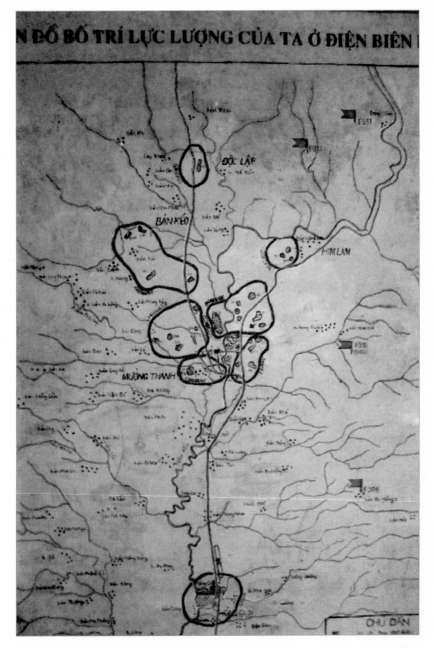

Plan of attack on a wall of Giap's bunker. *Photo by Eileen Morgan.*

The Big Three at Yalta. *Photo courtesy of FDR Library, Hyde Park.*

Roosevelt, on the arm of his son Elliott, and Churchill at their first wartime meeting, in August 1941, at which they signed the Atlantic Charter. *Photo courtesy of FDR Library, Hyde Park.*

Giap's troops enter Hanoi. *Photo courtesy of Vietnam Military History Museum.*

The civilian population conducts anti-French demonstrations. *Photo courtesy of Vietnam Military History Museum.*

Hauling the artillery to Dien Bien Phu. *Photo courtesy of Vietnam Military History Museum.*

Thousands of coolies carrying supplies.
*Photos courtesy of Vietnam Military
History Museum.*

Vietminh troops storm Béatrice, at the base of which lies a destroyed French plane. *Photos courtesy of Vietnam Military History Museum.*

Vietminh antiaircraft fire hits a French plane. *Photo courtesy of Vietnam Military History Museum.*

The underground infirmary. *Photo courtesy of Vietnam Military History Museum.*

The helmets of French dead. *Photo by Eileen Morgan.*

French paratroopers above Dien Bien Phu, November 20, 1953. *Photo courtesy of AP Images.*

The Chinese-made six-packs of 122mm rockets, reminiscent of the Russian "Stalin's Organs," were first used on May 6. *Photo courtesy of Vietnam Military History Museum.*

The red and gold Vietminh flag is raised over Castries' bunker. *Photo courtesy of Vietnam Military History Museum.*

The attack on the Bailey bridge, May 7. *Photo courtesy of Vietnam Military History Museum.*

Crossing the Bailey bridge. *Photo courtesy of Vietnam Military History Museum.*

Castries surrenders. *Photo courtesy of Vietnam Military History Museum.*

The memorial at the site. *Photo by Eileen Morgan.*

The Bombing Campaign Suffered from a
Lack of Leadership

By now, Dien Bien Phu was a coherent base manned by twelve battalions, with an airstrip and eight centers of resistance: Claudine (headquarters) at the center, below the airstrip; Huguette and Anne-Marie to the north-northwest; Gabrielle to the north; Béatrice, Dominique, and Eliane east of the airstrip; and Isabelle, three miles to the south, with its own surgical unit, tanks, artillery, and small airstrip, in splendid isolation. Equipment on the base included forty-four jeeps, seventy-three trucks, and two ambulances. Each CR consisted of several independent strongpoints, often occupying hills.

The air force, monitoring Viet movements and bombing roads and convoys, reported that, at night, large numbers of headlights were heading into the surrounding countryside. Only in mid-December did a lieutenant colonel on Navarre's staff ask to take the gun seat of a B-26 on a night flight to confirm the evidence. He was startled to see that the trucks did not even bother to douse their lights as he flew over. On December 30, Second Lieutenant Saint-Laux, a reconnaissance pilot, landed at Dien Bien Phu to take pictures at low altitude. As he flew north on January 1, 1954, toward the Vietminh depot of Tuan Giao, he swerved around a mountain and came face-to-face with a Vietminh unit of fifty men marching in good order. His right wing passed ten yards over their heads, sending them scurrying in all directions, as if he'd kicked over an anthill. He kept passing and repassing, firing bursts from his 12.7mm machine guns until he was out of ammunition. When he got back to the base, he was awarded extra champagne to celebrate New Year's Day.

Navarre ordered the air force to concentrate on Tuan Giao. From January 8 to 10, ninety-eight tons of bombs were dropped, but the Vietminh depots were hidden in the forest and dispersed in small lots. Only three bombers at a time were sent out, which had little effect. An air force report said: "There was no concentration on the targets. . . . The bombing campaign suffered from a lack of leadership. . . . The young squadron commanders had no experience of aerial bombardment. There were no massed formations, not even of six aircraft. The pilots, who came from transport units, lacked aggressiveness and were too accustomed to the safety of flying over our own lines." Giap's supply routes were now protected by anti-aircraft guns. Four fighter-bombers were hit and one was shot down. Planes had to be diverted to suppress the antiaircraft guns.

When two Algerian battalions were flown in on December 26 and 27, replacing the 5th BPVN, who had seen their share of the fighting, they brought with them two Mobile Field Bordellos (*Bordels Mobiles de Campagne*), one with eleven Algerians and the other with five Vietnamese, each with its own madam. The women were barracked in underground bunkers, the Algerians at Dominique and the Vietnamese at Claudine, and later served as nurses. General Castries' secretary, Paule Bourgeade, said she thought of herself as a soldier, but she was the only soldier who wore Dior perfume. Now she was no longer the only woman in the camp. A unit of gendarmes had also arrived to maintain order in this community of twelve thousand. While in Hanoi, they had looked for Legionnaires wanted for tearing apart a bistro or leaving without paying. Here on the base, they followed cases of theft and broke up quarrels.

Dien Bien Phu Is Surrounded on All Sides by Enemy Forces

As the new year opened, the base fell into a routine. Planes landing and departing, trucks loading and unloading. The mornings were cold and foggy. The sun came out at noon. Aside from patrols, the men carried out their daily tasks, fetching water from the river, or enduring endless visits from VIPs, generals of all nations for whom they had to put on their gear, stand at attention, and answer dumb questions. "Do you think it will hold? France is counting on you." Dien Bien Phu had become a tourist attraction, like the Catacombs of Paris.

Lieutenant Brudieu wrote his brother Jacques: "I received the visit of two English generals. They were very polite and told me everything was tip-top." Lieutenant Jacques Rastouil reported that a cabinet minister was wearing his Legion of Honor rosette twice, on his shirt and on his jacket. Dr. Sauveur Verdaguer was surprised by the visit of Graham Greene on January 7 and offered him an aperitif. Verdaguer joked about opening a nightclub for Anglo-Saxon tourists. The floor show would feature Vietminh raids. Then there were the weekend warriors who spent a few hours with the "heroes of Dien Bien Phu" so they could say they had tasted battle. They arrived in the morning and left in the afternoon.

In their leisure time, the men traded with the villagers for chickens or pigs, or watched the ladies of the evening taking the sun, or swam in the Nam Yum. They formed volleyball teams and played cards. Friendships sprang up among men who came from the same town or officers who had been in the same class at Saint-Cyr. In the evening over drinks, the Legionnaires supplied the music, an Italian with his guitar, the Germans with their marching songs. As for Castries, he spoke to Cogny in Hanoi every day on the radio telephone, and in the evening he looked for bridge partners.

The base now had its PIMs (*Prisonniers Interne Militaire*), Vietminh prisoners used as day laborers, who were kept under guard in a compound. Resigned to their fate, the PIMs did not try to escape. If a soldier mistreated one, he was punished.

As Colonel Langlais told the commission of inquiry in 1955, work on the base was still being done. "Gabrielle [the northernmost post] wasn't finished, a large part of the camp wasn't finished. On January 25, the last of twelve battalions, the 2nd Foreign Infantry Regiment (REI) arrived, and we were just starting Huguette," to the west of the airstrip. Three days later, Lieutenant Rastouil of the newly arrived Legionnaire battalion wrote his wife, Pierrette: "It's hard here, very hard. This morning I thought, I'd give the rest of my life for five minutes with my children."

Castries was told to continue the recon patrols despite the losses of men and ammunition. Each time the men left their forts the Viets fought them back. An entire platoon might be lost, and the only reason for the patrols was that the high command wanted to prove that the troops had freedom of action outside the camp. On January 12, Captain Bernard Cabiro took a unit of the 1st BEP (Legionnaires) to recon a village a couple of miles southwest of Isabelle. After passing some abandoned villages, they came to a patch of rice paddies. Lieutenant de Brandon was studying his compass when a bullet smashed through it and into his hand. Small-arms fire came from the paddy fields. Then the Viets started firing mortars from the hillside. Lieutenant Marc Nénert, who had called the march into Laos "utterly pointless," was killed by mortar fire. "This little promenade cost us four dead and thirty-five wounded," Cabiro said. Between November 20, 1953, and January 15, 1954, the French lost 853 men killed and wounded—about 8 percent of the garrison.

On January 15, 1954, the U.S. consul in Hanoi, Paul Sturm, saw General Cogny, who told him: "Patrols have proved Dien Bien Phu to be surrounded on all sides by enemy forces lying just outside artillery range. Reconnaissance in any direction now provokes strong enemy reaction." Sturm reported that "Cogny appeared less confident with regard to outcome of eventual attack on Dien Bien Phu, tending to qualify his statements with such remarks as 'at least I think so.' There is no doubt that if three enemy divisions, supported by artillery and anti-aircraft, are thrown against Dien Bien Phu, stronghold's position will be critical."

There was little rejoicing at the base on January 17, when René Coty replaced Vincent Auriol for a seven-year term as the second president of the Fourth Republic. When the National Assembly discussed the budget, Finance Minister Edgar Faure arranged that U.S. aid would not be itemized, so that those funds could be allocated to other expenses besides Indochina. Laniel remained premier, having won a vote of confidence by 319 to 249. "We desire peace," he said. "We would like to negotiate. . . . Ho Chi Minh has offered nothing concrete to open a dialogue. . . . But if we take Korea as a model, we must keep fighting until we come to an agreement." Although the Laniel government was notable for its longevity, France was rudderless, divided over the European Defense Community and drained by the Indochina war.

On January 21, David Heath cabled from Saigon that Marc Jacquet had told him: "It is absolutely necessary for Navarre to produce some victories within the next few months or opposition parties in French Parliament would force any government in power to initiate negotiations with Ho Chi Minh. . . . Jacquet insisted the best thing would be for the Vietminh to attack Dien Bien Phu as they are expected to do and have French inflict a bloody defeat on them. That could greatly diminish French opposition to war in Indochina." Jacquet said there could be no "decisive defeat of the Vietminh unless there were American participation . . . with American fliers, mechanics and technical warfare specialists."

Step by Step, We Are Moving into
This War in Indochina

In Washington, the topic of the day was what to do about Indochina. The White House was at odds with Congress, while government departments argued among themselves. When the National Security Council met on January 8, 1954, the State Department said the French position was so critical as to "force the United States to decide now to utilize U.S. forces in Southeast Asia." The Defense Department, however, was against committing troops, saying they should be used only "in extremity."

Admiral Radford, chairman of the Joint Chiefs of Staff, argued that the United States should do "everything possible" to forestall a French defeat at Dien Bien Phu" and "even send an aircraft carrier" (which Ike had promised at Bermuda). The French were asking Radford for twenty-two more B-26s and ground crews to keep them maintained. Eisenhower said, "We could certainly send planes and men to take over the maintenance."

Allen Dulles, Eisenhower's director of central intelligence and the brother of Secretary of State John Foster Dulles, reported that the garrison at Dien Bien Phu was surrounded by Vietminh. Though the French position was strong, he said, "they were locked in it." The loss of Dien Bien Phu would result in "psychological damage" that could cripple the French will to win, "while the Vietminh might feel it was worth the losses they would suffer."

President Eisenhower said "with great force" that "this seems to be another case where the French don't know what to do—whether to go it alone or to get assistance from other nations." He "simply could not imagine the United States putting ground forces anywhere in Southeast Asia, except possibly Malaya." If the United States replaced the French in Indochina, "the Vietnamese could be expected to transfer their hatred to us."

On January 16, Eisenhower set up a special committee on Indochina, headed by Undersecretary of State Walter Bedell Smith. Having been Ike's trusted chief of staff in World War II, Smith had hoped to be named secretary of state. He did not hold John Foster Dulles in high esteem. Allen Dulles; Roger Kyes, deputy secretary of defense; and C. D. Jackson, a White House aide, were also named to the committee. Eisenhower wanted them to come up with "an area plan."

The mood in Congress was "no troops for Indochina," even though anti-China feelings ran high. When John Foster Dulles appeared in executive session before the House Foreign Affairs Committee on January 19, the Georgia Democrat Henderson Lanham asked:

"Are we ready to go to war with China or are we simply going to slap them on the wrist with a blockade? . . . Are we going to run a colossal bluff, or do we really mean to back it up?"

Dulles said that only Congress could declare war.

Lanham: "That hasn't always been observed. Witness Korea."

Dulles said he doubted that Ike would go to war "to prevent the loss of Indochina, though other steps could be taken."

Those other steps were mentioned in Eisenhower's budget message on January 21, 1954, when he said more aid was required "to enable those gallant forces to sustain an offensive that will provide the opportunity for victory."

The special committee under Smith met on January 29 to assess a French request for twenty-two more B-26s and four hundred U.S. Air Force mechanics to be stationed in Indochina. Smith proposed sending two hundred. Roger Kyes questioned whether that might eventually lead to sending combat forces. This thorny question was bumped up to the president, with the proviso that the mechanics would not be exposed to combat and possible capture.

Later that day, Eisenhower approved sending the mechanics. A first installment of 9 officers and 136 men from the 8081st Quartermaster Air Supply and Packaging Company was sent to Da Nang with seven hundred tons of equipment, aboard a squadron of C-119s painted gray and flown by two dozen pilots under contract to the CIA-owned Civil Air Transport Company. The mechanics built their own headquarters, repair shops, and testing stands.

Congress had not been consulted, and when the export of mechanics was leaked to the press, there was an uproar. On January 29, the Mississippi Democrat John Stennis, a member of the Senate Armed Services Committee, wrote Secretary of Defense Charles Wilson: "As always, when we send one group we shall have to send another to protect the first and we shall be fully involved."

One reason the mechanics were needed was that on December 20, 1953, U.S. Air Force colonel Maurice Casey had led a flight of fifteen C-119s from Japan to Haiphong with crews from the 483rd Troop Carrier Wing. They covered 2,300 nautical miles in twenty hours. Major Thomas Yarborough, who had ten thousand hours of flying time on C-47s in World War II, remained in Indochina in charge of the crews.

It was unusual for Eisenhower to act without consulting Congress, but he didn't like to be second-guessed on military matters. He told Smith on February 3 that Congress should be briefed. Kyes and Radford met with the Senate Armed Services Committee and found the members miffed at having been ignored. The committee's chairman, Leverett Saltonstall (a Republican from Massachusetts), saw the president on February 8 with other Republican leaders. They voiced their objections to sending uniformed Americans to Indochina. Eisenhower said the deployment of mechanics was a small project that would serve a large purpose, "to prevent all of Southeast Asia from falling to the Communists." He promised that the mechanics would be withdrawn by June 15. The senators were mollified, except for Stennis, who said on the Senate floor on February 9 that "step by step, we are moving into this war in Indochina. . . . I am afraid we will move to a point from which there will be no return."

At a February 10 press conference, Eisenhower did his best to quell fears that another Korea was in the works: "No one could be more bitterly opposed to ever getting the United States involved in a hot war in that region than I am," he said. "Consequently, every move that I make is calculated, so far as a human can do it, to make certain that does not happen."

Our Men Died in Many Ways

In January 1954, General Giap's living quarters consisted of a one-room hut on the side of a hill, in a forested area near a sliver of a waterfall. The hut's only furnishings were a cot and a bamboo table big enough for maps. Near the hut his sappers had dug a three-hundred-yard-long underground gallery equipped with electricity and telephones, with offices where meetings were held. This was the most difficult time, the time of preparation, where a hundred matters had to be attended to daily, from the placement of artillery positions to the digging of approach trenches near the French base. But the overriding priority, the one that gave him insomnia and made him feel so debilitated that a troupe from the army theater came to sing him songs, was supplies. In his office there was a wall chart with red lines that rose and fell in zigs and zags, indicating the amount of rice or munitions that arrived daily. The first thing Giap did when he rose at dawn was to consult the graph, which was kept current for him.

One morning, one of the lines dropped straight down. Giap asked why. "Heavy rains yesterday," he was told. "Rain or no rain, our soldiers can't fight on empty stomachs," he said. Some of the troops were eating grass and leaves. If it wasn't rain that turned the trails into swamps, it was fallen rocks that barred the way, or French bombing and strafing. Giap's infantry divisions were not fully in place. The 316th Division, after taking Lai Chau, had moved southward to encircle Dien Bien Phu, while the 308th Division was in hidden encampments. The 312th Division and the 351st Heavy Division were still on the march, the infantry and artillery advancing together, the foot soldiers helping to push the cannons on wheels uphill, a hundred men on a single cannon, with a winch at the top the only piece of machinery, tightening the cables notch by notch.

To some extent, Giap was able to protect his supply lines with 37mm antiaircraft guns from China, placed at choke points such as river crossings. Bombing the supply routes became dangerous for the French, but the strikes nonetheless contributed to keeping Giap behind schedule.

The Chinese had trained four Vietminh antiaircraft battalions and sent them to the front. They also sent Korean veterans to instruct Giap's troops in sniping tactics, and a dozen army engineers to show them how to dig trenches that would allow them to move close to outlying French posts without exposure to their firepower. Equipment from China included two hundred trucks, one hundred cannons, and ten thousand artillery shells.

Building the artillery emplacements also turned out to be enormously time-consuming. Contrary to Colonel Piroth's artillery manual, which dictated that cannons must be placed on reverse slopes, with the shells lobbed mortar-style over the crests, Giap placed his big guns on the slopes facing Dien Bien Phu. His artillery officers, who despite their Chinese advisers were not as well trained as the French, could thus fire by direct observation at fixed targets.

It took a week to position a single howitzer from the point where the truck had unloaded it, pulling it by hand along the last miles of narrow track to the emplacements in the hills. These were caves dug into the slopes and reinforced with logs, from which the guns could be rolled out to fire and then back in. The entrances to the caves were camouflaged and the Vietminh artillery officers spent days making dummy emplacements, igniting small charges to simulate flashes.

The hazards of the supply routes were described by the twenty-seven-year-old battalion commander Bui Tin, who said: "Our men died in many ways. . . . They lost their way, they fell from high bridges, venomous snake bites meant instant death. Tree falls during typhoons crushed them in their hammocks. Flash floods were very dangerous. There were fevers, malaria, even tiger attacks. The small jungle leeches attached themselves during the night, so a man would awake weakened and covered with his own blood." To palliate these dangers, in addition to combat wounds, Giap's medical team consisted of a single surgeon, Dr. Ton That Tung, and six assistants.

Giap had to decide when to attack and whether to attack the entire base or pick off the strongpoints one by one. His military committee met on January 14 to discuss strategy. There was a political factor involved. The Big Four's Berlin Conference was opening on January 25, and launching the attack around that time might make the French more pliant. Lively debate took place on the date of the attack and the tactics to be used. This was, after all, the first time the Vietminh were attacking a fortified base with division-size units. China's contribution gave Giap firepower equal to the French. The committee decided to attack on January 26.

On January 24, General Wei Guoqing, the top Chinese adviser, received instructions from Peking: "While attacking Dien Bien Phu, you should avoid making assaults of equal strength from all directions; rather, you need to adopt a strategy of separating and encircling the enemy forces, and annihilate them bit by bit."

This seemed to rule out a massive attack. In any case, as the day neared, Giap did not feel he was ready. His approach trenches hadn't been dug. His gun emplacements were not yet well hidden and "would become the targets of enemy air strikes," as he later put it. The French had reinforced the base with tanks and Bearcat fighter-bombers. "We were not 100 percent sure of victory," Giap said. He called off the January 26 attack.

Eventually There Will Be Two Indochinas, as There Are Two Koreas

Navarre's intercepts told him that the Chinese had sent 37mm antiaircraft guns to Giap's army. On January 22, 1954, two American antiaircraft experts, Captains Robert F. Lloyd and Robert W. Mickey, toured Dien Bien Phu and warned that the placement of 37mm guns on the approaches would be successful against slow-moving transport planes. However, they said in their report, the guns would be difficult to hide. Soon after, the pilots of C-119s dropping their cargo from five hundred feet began to see flak coming at them from the hills surrounding Dien Bien Phu.

Navarre's intercepts also told him that Giap planned to attack on January 26. He knew that an influential Chinese mission was guiding the strategy at Dien Bien Phu. "I've been waiting for a chance to fight the Viets in a set battle," Navarre said. But then the intercepts told him the battle was put off.

Waiting tried the patience of the men at the base. Captain Pichelin wrote his sister-in-law Françoise: "The Viets don't dare attack. We wish they would so we could give them the worst licking of the war."

When it became apparent that Giap's attack had been cancelled, the frustration grew. Lieutenant Colonel Gaucher wrote his wife: "In the last forty-eight hours, we all expected an attack that never came. We now wonder whether the Viets will ever attack. Our defenses must be making them think twice."

On January 26, with no attack in sight, Dien Bien Phu received five distinguished visitors: Maurice Dejean, the commissioner general; Marc Jacquet, the secretary of state for the Associated States; General Navarre; General Cogny; and General Clément Blanc, the army chief of staff, a World War I veteran who had served at Verdun.

Castries was at the airstrip, leaning on his cane in front of an honor guard when they landed. Jacquet, a captain in the air force reserve, asked: "Well, Castries, where are we at?"

"Look around you at all the fortified strongpoints," Castries replied. "We've put our shoulder to the wheel."

"I congratulate you," Jacquet said. Then, looking around at a squadron of tanks: "How did you get these machines here?"

"We flew them in in parts," Cogny explained.

After lunch at the command post (ham, sautéed potatoes, a salad, canned peaches, and a respectable Bordeaux), Jacquet studied the big wall map and said, "Gabrielle and Béatrice seem to be far from the center. . . . May I ask what you consider to be the number of rebel forces?"

"Four divisions, at least," Cogny said.

Navarre explained, "What we're trying to do is draw the rebel forces to Dien Bien Phu, to keep them from invading Laos. We've had American generals, veterans of Korea, tell us how satisfied they were with our deployment. They invested a lot of money here and they don't want us to lose."

"My only desire is to believe you, General," Jacquet said.

After lunch, Jacquet and General Blanc visited Colonel Piroth in his command post. It was heartening to see this one-armed man, his sleeve neatly folded and pinned to his shoulder for this important occasion, gesticulate as he proudly showed off his guns.

Jacquet wondered what would happen if the Vietminh hit the airstrip with artillery. "Colonel," he said, "I know there are hundreds of guns lying idle in Hanoi. You ought to take advantage of a minister's visit to have a few sent to you on the side."

"Look at my plan of fire, *Monsieur le minister*," Piroth replied, "I've got more guns than I need."

General Blanc, himself an artillery officer, asked Piroth if he was sure. "If I have thirty minutes warning," Piroth said, "my counterbattery will be effective." General Blanc was left wondering, what if he doesn't have thirty minutes warning?

After the other dignitaries had returned to Hanoi, Castries asked Jacquet, "Are you planning to spend the night with us, *Monsieur le minister*?"

"It would be a pleasure," Jacquet said, "but I'm dining with Dejean tonight at the Metropole."

As Castries escorted the minister to his plane, Jacquet asked: "Colonel, forget the 'minister.' Man to man, what do you think of all this?"

Castries: "As long as we can keep the airstrip open, we've got a chance."

"And if not?"

"It would be complicated."

At the commission of inquiry in 1955, General Catroux asked Colonel André Lalande, commander of the 3rd REI: "Did it seem to you that these high personages wanted to know if you could hold?"

"They displayed the optimism of the official visitor," Lalande said. "The only one who had any doubts was General Blanc."

Catroux: "In what form?"

"He hoped that the Viets wouldn't attack. He felt that if they did we'd never get out."

Catroux: "But didn't General Blanc say that the fortifications of Gabrielle were as good as those of Verdun?"

"Yes, and he wasn't the only one."

The men of Dien Bien Phu had been half hoping for and half dreading the attack, and when it did not come, there was a drop in morale, a general lassitude. Captain Yves Hervouet, the tank commander, wrote his brother on February 2: "We've been fighting this war for eight years . . . but the mental laziness of the army is hard to take. . . . Why can't we adapt to the enemy's style of fighting. . . . In France, they're fed up with the war. . . . Eventually there will be two Indochinas, as there are two Koreas."

On January 27, Navarre was stunned to learn that Giap had removed the 308th Division from its bivouacs in the hills and sent it into Laos. Did this mean that Giap was giving up on Dien Bien Phu in favor of an invasion of Laos? In fact, it was a feint, a quick raid to fool the French regarding his intentions.

Langlais told the 1955 commission: "One entire division, the 308th, left without our knowing. It spread panic in Laos. All the airdrops over Dien Bien Phu stopped. [Planes were being diverted to Laos.] The division went through Muong Khoua [sixty-eight miles from Dien Bien Phu], and besieged Muong Sai, which was only eighty kilometers from Luang Prabang. We dropped in a battalion and saved the post. And then the division turned around and came back. The offensive proved that using Dien Bien Phu to keep the Viets out of Laos was a fantasy. This led Navarre to do some deep thinking. He was perplexed. What was the meaning of this diversion? It seemed like a sudden decision, as if they had thought, 'Let's send in this division and see what happens.' "

Molotov Showed Great Pallyness

On January 19, 1954, Evelyn Shuckburgh was skiing in Switzerland with his family when he was told he was wanted in Berlin for a conference of foreign ministers of the four occupying powers in Germany. All he knew was that it had to do with the reunification of Germany through free elections. Since Berlin was divided, the Russians insisted on alternate sessions in West Berlin and at the Soviet embassy in East Berlin, where the blue and red pencils for delegates were stamped MADE IN SACCO AND VANZETTI FACTORY.

Shuckburgh flew into Tempelhof with Anthony Eden on January 22. It was bitter cold. On the following day they were both invited to lunch by the French high commissioner, André François-Poncet. Shuckburgh congratulated François-Poncet on the food. "Yes, my chef is good when he isn't drunk," said François-Poncet. "Better at lunch than at dinner." Eden was in a bad mood, grumbling about Churchill, who had said he planned to resign in May. Eden said that if Winston didn't resign, he would. Shuckburgh compared Eden to "a sea anemone, covered with sensitive tentacles, recording currents of opinion around him," acutely vain and self-conscious, by turn irritated, charming, and petulant. A skillful negotiator.

While waiting for the conference to start, they went to see a horse-jumping event, won by a French officer. Eden complained that in the London papers, a story about the deaths of seventeen children falling though the ice had pushed him off the front page. How terribly vain and egocentric he was, thought Shuckburgh, only interested in himself, his politics, and his popularity. And yet it was such open schoolboy vanity that one couldn't find it detestable.

The conference opened on January 25, and Eden and Shuckburgh drove to the Allied Control Commission building through empty streets, except for the odd Berliner waving his hat. Vyacheslav Molotov, the Russian foreign minister, arrived with an entourage of twenty. Shuckburgh thought Molotov looked like a Mongol, with his yellow face and white mustache. Molotov greeted Eden very cheerfully. The square conference table seated five on each side. Shuckburgh thought it looked cozy.

The agenda was supposed to be the reunification of Germany and a peace treaty with Austria, but at the outset Molotov took an entirely different direction. He proposed another conference, to be held in Geneva in late April, to discuss Korea and Indochina, with the participation of the Big Four plus Communist China. In doing so, he split the Western allies.

John Foster Dulles, with his customary Cold War pugnacity, replied, "Who is this Chou En-lai whose addition to our circle would make possible all that so long seemed impossible? He is the leader of a regime which gained de facto power on the Chinese mainland through bloody war . . . which became an aggressor in Korea . . . which promoted the aggression in Indochina by training and equipping the aggressors."

As for the ostensible purpose of the conference, Germany and Austria, it got nowhere. On January 30, Eden delivered his speech on free German elections. Molotov rebutted it on February 4, saying, "There are two governments in Germany, each with its own police, currency, and administration. The interests of each must be taken into account. The differences between them are too great for unification."

Molotov also dismissed the treaty with Austria. By February 9, Eden felt it was pointless to continue talking. Nor had the matter of the Geneva Conference been settled. "News from Indochina [on the Vietminh incursion into Laos] is very bad," Shuckburgh noted in his diary, "and some think Molotov has been stalling on the Far East item until the Vietminh gain some great success. They are closing in on Luang Prabang."

On February 11, Shuckburgh noted that "Eden is annoyed with Dulles for . . . not wanting to give way over China. . . . American public opinion might easily turn on him for agreeing too readily to sit down with the Chinese Communists." He also felt that Eden was "keen to get a conference [at Geneva] so as to have some 'success' to go home with."

It was the French foreign minister, Georges Bidault, however, who bluffed Dulles into changing his mind. Bidault told Dulles that if China was not included at Geneva the Laniel government would fall and the government that replaced it would refuse to ratify the European Defense Treaty so central to U.S. policy in Europe. After all, Bidault argued, the United States had consented to meet with the Chinese when discussing the cease-fire in Korea. "The French wish to seize every opportunity to make peace in Indochina," Bidault said. "Every form of conversation which would allow real progress to be made in the restoration of peace would be welcome." Dulles became convinced that opposing French desires would split the Western alliance.

The British had no objection to China's presence, having already recognized the Maoist regime. Eden found a face-saving device for Dulles: China could attend, but would not be a "convening power."

Dulles explained his reversal to the National Security Council on February 26: "If we had vetoed the resolution regarding Indochina, it would have probably cost us French membership in the EDC as well as Indochina itself."

On the last day of the Berlin Conference, February 18, Shuckburgh noted that "Molotov came around to our seats and shook us all by the hand. . . . Great pallyness." It was not surprising that Molotov was in a good mood, since he had triumphed. No headway had been made on a united Germany, but he had managed to include China in a major international conference, ending its diplomatic ostracism. The Soviets were already calling China's presence "virtual recognition." The joint communiqué said that the signatories had "reached the following agreement. . . . That the problem of restoring peace in Indochina shall also be discussed at the conference [of the Big Four at Geneva in April] . . . to which the Chinese People's Republic and other interested states will be invited." With Geneva two months away, the U.S. role in Indochina evolved from pushing the French to win the war to helping them end it with dignity.

General Navarre saw Geneva as a political blunder that would intensify Chinese aid and prompt the Vietminh to launch a general offensive. Captured Vietminh documents explained the offensive as a way "to exercise pressure on the Geneva Conference." Like stepping-stones, Bermuda had led to Berlin and Berlin was leading to Geneva, which was a monumental mistake, thought Navarre, because it had agreed to China's presence, and because it had announced a forum where a military victory by either side would enhance its position. Geneva created a deadline for victory.

The Geneva Conference Sealed the Fate of Dien Bien Phu

In Saigon, General Navarre maintained a sanguine façade. On the day after Berlin ended, he said at a press conference: "The Vietminh offensive [in Laos] is slack, or about at its peak. . . . Giap's offensive is blocked." On the same day, February 19, Giap brought the 318th Division back from Laos, so that he could concentrate his forces at Dien Bien Phu. On February 21, Navarre told Ambassador Heath that "Dien Bien Phu is a veritable jungle Verdun which he hopes will be attacked as it will result in terrific casualties to the Vietminh and will not fall."

In his book, *Agonie de l'Indochine,* published in 1956, Navarre wrote: "The government, without asking for the advice of the military, fell into the fatal trap of the Geneva Conference. The mindless decision to hold this conference at the very moment when the conditions of battle could not be modified completely changed the problem. The Vietminh command threw in all its forces. China increased its aid, and our nationalist Vietnamese army fell apart. On the day the Geneva Conference was announced, the fate of Dien Bien Phu was sealed."

Before the 1955 commission of inquiry, Navarre went into greater detail. "Without the Berlin Conference, it's likely that the Viets wouldn't have attacked Dien Bien Phu. . . . They knew the war was going to go on for a long time, and they wouldn't have risked four out of seven divisions at Dien Bien Phu. It was only after the Berlin Conference when it was announced that Indochina would be discussed in Geneva."

Catroux: "In mid-February?"

Navarre: "That's right. Otherwise I would have had a small attack on a strongpoint so they could say, 'You see, we took a strongpoint.' "

In Washington, high-ranking briefers of Congress delivered mixed messages that reflected confused thinking regarding the outcome of Berlin. On February 16, Undersecretary of State Walter Bedell Smith told the Senate Foreign Relations Committee that there could be "a kind of walling off of an area, while supporting the native elements who are willing to be supported in the other part of the area." Thus was a U.S.-sponsored partition of Vietnam first broached.

Two days later, Admiral Radford chose to ignore the new realities when he briefed the House Foreign Affairs Committee and said there was "no danger" of the French being driven out of Dien Bien Phu. "The Vietminh," he said, "are not anxious to engage in a showdown fight because their ammunition supplies are not large and a great deal of it is homemade."

On February 24, an apologetic Dulles came before the Senate Foreign Relations Committee, which teemed with pro–Chiang Kai-shek China hands such as William F. Knowland, the influential California Republican. Dulles said that he could not prevent the inclusion of Red China in peace talks without causing the fall of the Laniel-Bidault government, "the best government we could have in France." He did not seem to grasp the implications of the conference he had just attended when he predicted that "there will probably not be any major or decisive engagements during the remaining two months of March and April of the fighting season." All the French had to do was "hold on for two months." This again was wishful thinking.

Two of the senators present did not buy his forecast. Hubert Humphrey said the testimony given by Smith, Radford, and Dulles was "inconsistent and conflicting," and that Geneva should not be looked at as a "great opportunity." Guy M. Gillette, the Iowa Democrat, said: "I think our position relative to Indochina is unsound, illogical, and untenable."

The mood in Washington was summed up in a February 12 letter from Philip W. Bonsal, now State Department director for Southeast Asia, to Ambassador Heath. He was searching for ways to stiffen the French, he said, "in an atmosphere of intense public and Congressional interest. There have been leaks galore: Leaks about planes; leaks about mechanics. . . . Most important, there has been a leaking of pessimism and a lack of confidence in French generalship and in French intentions." Many believed the war could not be won unless "American brains and will power" could compensate for "French inadequacies."

The Navarre Plan Is a Bust

Giap's headquarters were in the Muong Phang hills, about six miles north of Dien Bien Phu. With a telescope, he could see the planes on the airstrip, and tanks rumbling from post to post. February 3, 1954, was the Vietnamese New Year, and Giap celebrated by firing thirty or so rounds from his 75mm recoilless rifles at the airstrip. Colonel Piroth fired back with 105s, which wasted hundreds of shells hitting dummy emplacements. Giap congratulated his gun crews with a holiday feast of meatballs and sweets.

On February 22, as the 318th Division was returning from Laos, Giap met with his military committee and they agreed that Dien Bien Phu was now the crucial front. Since the French could not evacuate the base they had to reinforce it. Giap would maintain the initiative. The longer it took, the more the French would use up their supplies and munitions, and the more casualties they would suffer. The body count was vital to the French, who, unlike the Vietminh, found replacements hard to come by. For the first time, Giap's divisions would have artillery and antiaircraft guns. They would destroy Dien Bien Phu strongpoint by strongpoint. As for the weather, "if the battle continues into the rainy season, we are on the slopes and can dig drainage ditches while the enemy on the plain will be deep in mud."

In February 1954, the men on the plain felt the frustration of waiting, as well as a heightened respect for the enemy. Almost daily now, there were skirmishes when the French left the perimeter, and they did not get the best of them. On February 3, Colonel Guibaud of the Deuxième Bureau in Hanoi informed Navarre that Dien Bien Phu was surrounded by twenty-seven battalions armed with artillery. This information came from Captain Jacques Noël, the intelligence officer at Dien Bien Phu, who was getting his information from Vietminh POWs and a few deserters (known as *ralliés*), who might or might not have been plants. One of them said the divisions involved were the 304th, 308th, 312th, and 316th. Another mentioned Chinese and European advisers.

On February 7, Pierre de Chevigné, secretary of state at the War Ministry in Paris, flew to the base. When his plane was fired on by Vietminh antiaircraft guns, it made a dive for the airstrip, which was being pounded by mortar fire. There was no honor guard to greet him. Castries roared up in his jeep and told Chevigné to jump in, while Chevigné stood there in shock. He now knew why pilots called Dien Bien Phu the "chamber pot." Having commanded troops in the Free French forces during World War II, Chevigné felt at ease with the officers he spoke to. Although Castries told him he was prepared to crush four Vietminh divisions, the officers said that it had become too dangerous to go outside the perimeter.

On February 12, Colonel Gaucher wrote his wife: "The Navarre Plan is a bust. We're at a dead end. The Viets are on the offensive and all we can do is fight back. Everybody's fed up."

And yet, they were still being sent out. On February 15, in a typical operation, Captain Pichelin of the 8th Choc, attacked a hill the Vietminh had just occupied. They were halfway up when all hell broke loose. The Viets, waiting until the French got close, fired from dug-in positions. Pichelin sent in a flamethrower unit to force them out of their holes. The battle lasted seven hours and Pichelin never got to the top of the hill. An astonished Colonel Langlais said: "The Viets fought with amazing zeal." On February 23, Captain Pichelin wrote his father: "How much longer do we have to rot in this hole? The rainy season is coming in less than a month and will prevent any important operation. The river will overflow its banks and we'll have to take to the hills."

On February 17, Major Doctor Paul Grauwin arrived to head the Antenne Chirurgicale Mobile (Mobile Surgical Unit). His head was shaved and his eyes were blue behind rimless glasses. This nearsighted Flemish giant was known for the empathy he felt for his patients. His job was to triage the wounded and separate those to be evacuated to Hanoi from those who had to be operated on at once. The miniature hospital in Dien Bien Phu had only forty-two beds, but Grauwin surmised that most of the wounded would be flown out. The surgical unit was well dug in, and the walls of the operating theater, which measured thirteen feet by ten, were hung with parachute silk. But it opened out on a trench six feet deep with no roof. The triage center where the wounded arrived was a tent, also in the open.

On February 19, the minister of defense, René Pleven, flew into Dien

Bien Phu with General Paul Ely, head of the French Joint Chiefs of Staff and adviser to Pleven, and General Pierre Fay, the air force chief of staff. They had been sent to Indochina by the Laniel government to study the situation after Navarre's pessimistic comments and had landed in Saigon on February 9. As it happened, General Clément Blanc, the army chief of staff, was in Saigon finishing up his tour on the day they arrived. Pleven asked to see Blanc, who briefed him and the others for four hours on February 10. Blanc's bugaboo was the monsoon season. "After April 15," he said, "Dien Bien Phu will be a swamp and the trenches and shelters will collapse. . . . Castries in his command post will be swimming in forty centimeters of water. . . . If we don't act at once we will lose six thousand tons of equipment and without a doubt some units. We must pull out in the next two months at least six battalions and four thousand tons of equipment. . . . After April 15, it will be too late."

General Fay, who had commanded the French air force in Indochina from October 1945 to May 1946, knew what the weather was like and was concerned about the airstrip. The Pleven party decided to see for themselves and were given the standard tour. Tall but stooped, Pleven wore a panama hat and sunglasses as if summering on the Riviera. Fay felt that Dien Bien Phu should be evacuated, but Ely argued that despite the "tactical inconvenience of location," the base was a strong position that could withstand attack.

The Legionnaire captain Chevalier wrote his wife: "Today, Pleven came on his little visit to give himself a thrill, but no luck, the Viets absolutely refused to fire a single shot. They were content to observe from the heights around us."

Back in Saigon, Fay asked for a tête-à-tête with Navarre, who was an old friend. On February 26, Navarre told him that his meteorologists had established that the monsoon would not interrupt the airlift. All discussions on reducing the garrison were moot now that it became clear that the 308th Division had left Laos.

At a press conference, Pleven said: "It is impossible for the Vietminh to obtain a victory at Dien Bien Phu." Brigitte Friang, who was in attendance, told Pleven she didn't see how France could win. An annoyed Pleven said he wondered whether her news reports could be trusted. In his own report, he wrote: "Dien Bien Phu is a strongly fortified position. It would take an important army to attack it, with a high risk of failure. The problem that remains to be studied is the coming of the rainy season." "Official optimism" was the watchword.

On February 27, a Bearcat patrol led by Captain Claude Payen dropped some five-hundred-pound bombs on Vietminh positions two and a half miles northeast of Dien Bien Phu. Payen was surprised to see projectiles streaming past his plane. It was just like a war movie, he thought.

Twenty-five years later, at that point a general, Payen took part in a military conference in China. He got to talking with a Chinese general who told him in fluent French, "We really fooled you when we sent you a deserter who gave you the location for Giap's headquarters. The next morning, you bombed the wrong valley."

On February 28, a plane to evacuate the wounded landed at the base. Aboard the plane was a *convoyeuse*, a nurse to take care of the wounded during the flight. On that day, Geneviève de Galard, who later became known, somewhat extravagantly, as the "Angel of Dien Bien Phu," was on duty. On this first visit she witnessed a horrible accident. Two Bearcats collided on landing, and one was cut in half by the propeller of the other. One pilot was killed and the other, Paul Perfetti, literally scalped by the propeller, was in a coma with a fractured skull. Dr. Grauwin decided that he should be flown to Saigon at once for surgery. He was the only passenger in Geneviève's care. He died in the hospital ten days later.

The Vietminh were closing in. At night, they left leaflets near the airstrip that said: DIEN BIEN PHU WILL BE YOUR GRAVE. Another leaflet, for the German Legionnaires, said: GÜTE HEIMKEHR (Have a good trip home). Inside the base, among the officers, the feelings ranged from high hopes to distress. On March 5, Lieutenant Colonel Gaucher wrote to his wife, Arlette: "The Viets will want to try something spectacular before the Geneva Conference. If they try it here, they'll break their teeth." On March 9, Captain Pichelin wrote: "I've been here three months and it's getting harder and harder. We're living underground the way they did in 1914. We're breathing dust that penetrates everything, even the bread we eat. Our clothes are always filthy."

After a visit on March 8, a reporter for *Le Monde*, Robert Guillain, described a widespread desire for battle. "We'll show them," he wrote. "That is the phrase employed by all. They are itching for a fight. If Giap attacks, all of them, from the men to the high command, see a battlefield where, for the first time, they will have a chance to destroy his divisions." Guillain's editor in Paris added a cautionary footnote: "The visiting journalist allows himself to become a spokesman."

Back in Paris on March 11, Pleven appeared before a committee for national defense. The army was not beaten, he said, but it was tired. The Vietnamese army was slow to develop. Everything should be done at Geneva to end the conflict under acceptable conditions. Pleven proposed that General Ely go to Washington, where he had been invited by Admiral Radford, to coordinate the two countries' policies, since the Americans seemed to want a swift military solution.

Get the Fuck off My Base

In March, General Giap prepared for battle. He knew that the outcome would hinge on air support. His top priority was to destroy French planes on the ground. On the night of March 4, a commando of Vietminh regulars cut through the barbed-wire enclosure at Hanoi's Gia Lam airport, destroying three DC-3s and damaging five others and two smaller planes. By the time the French guard units arrived on the scene, the planes were on fire and all they found was a dead Viet entangled in barbed wire.

Alarmed, General Cogny sent Major Bigeard and a small company of his paratroopers to Haiphong to reinforce the Senegalese guards at the Cat Bi air base there. Arriving on March 6, Bigeard told the officer in charge, Lieutenant Colonel Brunet: "General Cogny sent me to take command of the air base defense for a few days."

Furious at what he saw as interference with his command, Brunet shouted: "I don't give a fuck for Cogny or your paras! I don't want a shithouse on my base! Now get the fuck out!"

"My men and I are not a shithouse," Bigeard calmly replied. "I am six feet tall and I weigh seventy-five kilos, and if you want a fight, you'll get one."

Brunet calmed down and said Bigeard could station his men on the edge of the airfield. At midnight, bombs began exploding. "The base is attacked, the airstrip is on fire," someone shouted. Bigeard's men fired flares, which revealed a lone Senegalese hiding behind the wheel of a B-26. Outside their hangars, three B-26s were on fire. The paras found a dead Vietminh on the ground, wearing only a pair of black shorts with Molotov cocktails tied to his belt. They went after the others, killing three and wounding one. The commandos left one B-26 destroyed, two badly damaged, and another hit in one engine, plus six Moranes destroyed. Two teams of twenty commandos each had gotten through the barbed wire without being seen.

An angry Navarre wrote General Lauzin, commander of the Far East Air Force, that the officers in command at the two air bases "did not have a clear understanding of their responsibilities. Although they had been warned that the Vietminh would try to attack the bases, they did nothing to prevent it." Navarre intended to discipline the two officers. Stung by Navarre's criticism, Lauzin argued that the officers had brilliant records. Brunet, having served in Indochina since 1945, had eighteen citations and had been wounded three times in combat.

Finally, Giap's artillery was in place: his 675th Artillery Regiment had arrived from China with nine batteries of four 105s each. In all, he had forty-eight U.S.-made howitzers that had been captured in Korea. He also had sixty 75mm recoilless rifles, forty-eight 120mm mortars, and thirty-six Russian 37mm antiaircraft guns. Although he had no 155s, he had a total of about a hundred and fifty pieces of artillery, while the French had sixty. Giap's men continued to dig trenches that allowed them to bring troops and light artillery closer to the Dien Bien Phu perimeter, which they placed on high points that looked down on the base.

Where Do You Put Them?

In March, Castries was shocked by his February losses: 52 dead, 314 wounded, 14 unaccounted for, and 3 deserters. The total since CASTOR was 128 killed and 604 wounded, most of them on patrol. The garrison had more than ten thousand men forming twelve battalions, who required seventy tons of supplies a day; a tank squadron; a battery of 155s; and four companies of 120mm mortars. Each strongpoint was surrounded by a fifty-yard wide field of booby-trapped barbed wire. On March 2, four U.S.-made M45 Quadmounts arrived, each with four .50 caliber machine guns on a single base firing together. Each one weighed a ton and a half. Each Quad could fire about 1,600 rounds a minute and were devastating against a human-wave attack. The base was divided into three subsectors: North, commanded by Lieutenant André Trancart; South, at Isabelle, led by Colonel André Lalande with his Legionnaires and Algerians; and Center, with Lieutenant Colonel Jules Gaucher and his Legionnaires.

Navarre, now certain that the Vietminh would soon attack, flew in on March 4 with Cogny. As the two of them toured the strongpoints with Castries, Navarre still saw glaring weaknesses in their construction and in the isolation of Isabelle, about three miles south of Claudine. When they spoke to Piroth, he maintained his aplomb, saying that every square yard of jungle had been photographed, and he had thousands of shots of every possible objective. "The Viet artillery will be destroyed in a few hours," he promised.

Nonetheless, Navarre had nagging doubts, and as they drove around in Castries' jeep, he offered to send three more battalions and to build a new CR between Isabelle and Claudine. Castries said he didn't have room for additional men, and that they would only require more supplies to be flown in. Navarre insisted, saying that if the Viets saw a new strongpoint being built, they might postpone the attack until the rains came and fighting would stop. "We must push them into attacking," Castries replied, "so as to get it over with quickly." Cogny agreed, saying, "It would be a catastrophe from the point of view of morale if the Viets failed to attack."

At the 1955 commission of inquiry, General Catroux asked Castries: "Did not General Navarre express a certain anxiety over the outcome of the battle, and did he not tell you that bringing in three more battalions would create a problem for the Vietminh, and did you not reply: 'It is not necessary to send in more battalions. It would be hard, but we will see it through.'" Castries frowned and said he did not recall.

Catroux: "If he had proposed more battalions, what would your reaction have been?"

Castries: "I would have replied, 'Where do you want me to put them?' I was not about, on the eve of the attack, to place three battalions uncovered in the open, without shelters. . . . I had dwindling reserves of munitions and rations. I didn't need three more battalions to use up my reserves." Castries did not seem to grasp that Navarre's aim had been to bluff Giap into delaying the attack.

Dien Bien Phu was rapidly becoming a suburb of hell. The vise was tightening. The Bearcats photographed networks of trenches close to the northern centers of resistance: Béatrice, overlooking RP41 and consisting of three hills divided by ravines the Vietminh could infiltrate; and Gabrielle, a single strongpoint on a spacious plateau. On March 3, Lieutenant Colonel Gaucher, in command of both northern CRs, sent a patrol of Algerians about half a mile north of Gabrielle. They returned with four killed and ten wounded. On March 5, the Legionnaire paras at Béatrice tried to take a nearby hill and had three killed and thirty-five wounded. The Viets were everywhere.

Bad weather restricted the supply runs. On March 10, only four C-119 Flying Boxcars took off from Cat Bi in Haiphong. One of them had engine trouble sixty miles from Dien Bien Phu and started losing altitude. The pilot dropped his six tons of fuel in the jungle and managed to land on the airstrip on one engine.

On March 11, the Legionnaires at Béatrice went out again to chase away the Viets digging trenches in broad daylight. Lieutenant Bedeaux was standing next to his radioman when a bullet hit him in the spleen. Carried to Dr. Grauwin's surgical unit, he died from loss of blood. His last words were: "I'm sorry to give you so much trouble." Bedeaux was twenty-nine, married with a daughter. On that same day, mortar fire showered the airstrip and hit a Flying Boxcar that was being repaired. The plane caught fire and tipped over on its nose, sending up black smoke "like ten locomotives," as an eyewitness put it. Its blackened carcass was pushed to the side of the airstrip.

On March 12, Major Kah, who had recently arrived to command a battalion of Algerians, wrote his wife, Nicole: "Dien Bien Phu is under siege. All day we've been firing at Viets less than five hundred meters away. I saw some jump in the air when hit by our artillery. Others hiding in the bushes were incinerated by napalm. Last night they dug trenches within a hundred meters of the perimeter. They dug with rounded shovels that looked like scoops and covered the trenches with branches and straw."

There was such intense shelling of the airfield that twelve of the fourteen Bearcats stationed in sandbagged dispersal pens were sent to Laos. The weather was fine when General Cogny flew in on his last visit. He exited the Dakota, shielding his face from the dust, and jumped into Castries' jeep. As always, Cogny's thoughts were on the Red River Delta, and he told Castries that the Viets were cutting the road and sabotaging the trains with mines between Hanoi and Haiphong, which would affect the flow of supplies for Dien Bien Phu coming by sea.

The two generals went to look at Béatrice. What if it fell? Cogny asked. Did Castries have a plan for a counterattack? Castries said he had two battalions in reserve for that purpose. Cogny did not wish to linger and left at 3:30 in the afternoon of March 12. As he waved to Castries through the window of the Dakota, he saw a Morane burst into flames as it was hit by a shell. He could tell the shell was a 105.

Captain Noël, the intelligence officer, informed Castries that the villages near the post had been evacuated by the Viets. At 5 P.M., Castries summoned his officers and told them: "Gentlemen, it's for tomorrow."

In the hills where Vietminh troops had gathered, in the hidden artillery emplacements, in the camps where coolies kept their shovels and baskets, men and women gathered to hear commissars read General Giap's proclamation: "Officers and troops, the battle of Dien Bien Phu is about to begin. . . . It is not Dien Bien Phu or Hanoi, but the whole of Vietnam that is the prize of this battle."

Lieutenant Colonel Gaucher that morning wrote his last letter to his wife: "We're in a state of alert, surrounded by Viets who seem to want to attack us. Yesterday and today there was some serious fighting, and in my battalion I've lost six officers. It's hard to take. Planes are on fire from incoming artillery. Finally the long wait is over and hopefully it will end in a positive way."

ACT IV

The Battle

. . .

Ho Chi Minh tipped his sun helmet upside down on the bamboo table. . . .
His hands plunged to the bottom of the helmet. "That's where the
French are." Then he ran his fingers around the rim of the helmet and
said, "That's where we are. They will never get out."

WILFRED BURCHETT

• • •

Scene 1: The Ides of March

ON NOVEMBER 19, 1953, in a forest in Thai Nguyen Province, north of Hanoi, General Giap convened his commanders. Some had come on foot from the south. A day later came Operation CASTOR. Giap realized that "the parachute drop over Dien Bien Phu creates a favorable situation for us. It exposes a contradiction within the enemy between occupying the Northwest and reinforcing the Delta." Giap decided then that "the Northwest will constitute our principal front." The forces to be used were two or three divisions.

According to Chinese sources, it was General Wei Guoqing, Giap's top Chinese adviser, who first suggested that Vietminh troops encircle Dien Bien Phu. In January 1954, Giap proclaimed that "this will be the greatest positional battle in the annals of our army. Up to now, we have attacked fortified positions with one or two regiments. Now we will use several divisions, coordinating infantry and artillery. We will destroy a fortified camp defended by thirteen [sic] battalions."

The connection between the battle and the Geneva Conference, which was due to open in April, with China participating, was underlined in Peking. Chou En-lai instructed Giap's advisers: "In order to achieve a victory in the diplomatic field, you should follow our experience on the eve of the Korean armistice and win several battles in Vietnam."

The United States had detailed intelligence on the degree of Chinese involvement with the Vietminh, the number of advisers, the artillery and antiaircraft guns operated by Chinese gunners, the Chinese drivers at the wheels of Molotova trucks that brought in armament and other supplies.

What they did not know was that the Vietminh had learned from the Chinese experience in Korea the method of hiding their artillery from air strikes and counterbattery fire. The Vietminh dug tunnels in the sides of mountains to conceal their guns, bringing them out to fire twenty rounds and wheeling them back in before they could be spotted.

The attack, scheduled for January 26, was called off that very morning. Giap later wrote that "this was the most difficult decision I ever had to make." There was some grumbling among the advisers, one of whom accused Giap of "lacking the Bolshevik spirit." Another said he was not always candid with them. But Peking soon came around to Giap's way of thinking. And so, thousands of *bo dois* waited in the jungle, sleeping on mats of bamboo sticks softened by banana leaves. Mosquito nets were a luxury, so many of the troops caught malaria, and quinine deliveries were episodic. Usually the fever lasted seven days, though it could last a month. The diet was rice, sometimes with a bit of wild pig or monkey, washed down with tea. They were attack troops with no position to defend, inspired by an absolute conviction in the justice of their cause. They never questioned the barrage of simplistic slogans: "Zealously to build roads for artillery is zealously to work for victory. To build fortifications an inch thicker is to create more favorable conditions." There was a slogan for every aspect of the battle.

On February 22, the high command met in Giap's cabin at the edge of a forest. There, it was decided to follow the principle of "progress with a sure step." The reasoning in Giap's report was as follows: The French, unable to evacuate Dien Bien Phu over a long distance, had to keep reinforcing it. But the Vietminh maintained superiority in manpower and firepower.

> If we attack in stages, we will reinforce our position with each stage. We will keep the initiative, attacking when we want, where we want. But we will attack only when we are ready, and we will only occupy the positions we have taken when necessary. We

will exploit the enemy's essential difficulty—its supply lines. The longer the battle lasts, the more wounded he will have. Supplying the garrison will grow more difficult.

Our troops have never attacked positions held by more than two battalions. This time they will proceed with a series of attacks. Sector by sector. We must prepare for a relatively long campaign. We should not fear the enemy air force or artillery as long as we maintain secrecy and camouflage. During the transfer of our artillery pieces, we were able to hide for twenty days tens of thousands of men on a stretch of road within enemy artillery range.

When the rains come, our troops will suffer. But we are on the slopes, and we can dig drainage ditches, while the enemy in the plain will be submerged. The enemy is surrounded on the ground, and if its air supply is hampered, it will encounter insurmountable difficulties, due to the losses in food and munitions and the increases of wounded. The morale of this army of mercenaries will collapse. We will also suffer losses. Battles are won with blood and sacrifice. But if we attempt a rapid attack to avoid further losses we will end up with greater losses.

Here, in revealing detail, was Giap's battle plan, which he carried out to the letter. The French battle plan could be summed up in one sentence: Wait until the enemy attacks, and then defend yourselves. Here, nine years into the nuclear age, was a return to siege warfare that went back to medieval times. And although the French had tanks and airpower, it turned out that long lines of coolies were more dependable. The French were trapped in Cartesian syllogisms:

The Vietminh have no roads.
Cannon must be hauled over roads.
Therefore the Vietminh have no cannon.

The Vietminh have no experienced gunners.
Artillery requires experienced gunners.
Therefore the Vietminh artillery will fail.

Ignoring their own intelligence, the French remained enamored of their certainties. And yet doubt is an essential component in military planning. As H. L. Mencken put it: "One horse-laugh is worth ten thousand syllogisms."

The Vietminh Are Fortunate in One Thing: They Have No Pentagon to Deal With

In Saigon in early 1954, General Navarre felt that he was fighting a two-front war, one against the Vietminh and one against American encroachment. The personification of U.S. interference was Lieutenant General John W. "Iron Mike" O'Daniel, who had made three trips to Saigon, each more annoying than the previous one. At the age of sixty-one, Iron Mike made up in command presence what he lacked in stature—he was five foot six, but jut-jawed and gravel-voiced. His entire adult life had been spent in the army. At Saint-Mihiel in 1918 he was shot in the face by a German machine gun, which contributed to his bulldog appearance. In World War II, he was in charge of amphibious operations for the Fifth Army and conducted landings at Salerno and Anzio, leading the troops of the 3rd Infantry Division all the way to Rome. His motto was, "Sharpen your bayonet." On April 20, 1945, he took part in the capture of Nuremberg and hoisted the Stars and Stripes as the band broke into "Dogface Soldier." The flag flew at half-mast, in mourning for FDR. O'Daniel was one of those Patton-like officers who operated on guts rather than intellect, a distinction that Eisenhower perceived when calling him "one of our outstanding combat soldiers."

In Korea, O'Daniel commanded the U.S. Eighth Army and supervised the programs that were credited with training the lackluster South Korean army to the level of an effective fighting force. It was his success as an instructor that led to his being named head of the Military Assistance Advisory Group in 1954, at a time when the United States was still hoping for the formation of an effective Vietnamese army. O'Daniel's appointment was a reminder to Navarre that he should be pushing harder in that direction. Navarre resisted O'Daniel's efforts, not realizing that the MAAG boss was a blessing in disguise. His upbeat reports on the war contributed to increases in aid and a positive climate of opinion within the administration, which was not shared by Congress.

On January 28, 1954, not yet having been named head of MAAG, O'Daniel arrived in Saigon on short notice. Navarre said he didn't have much time for him, since he was conducting four military operations at once. Oblivious to Navarre's situation, Iron Mike proposed to come to Saigon on monthly visits and act as his link to the Joint Chiefs, thus bypassing Pentagon red tape. Navarre acidly replied: "The Vietminh are fortunate in one thing: They have no Pentagon to deal with."

In early February, Ambassador Heath sent a top secret letter to Philip W. Bonsal, the State Department director for Southeast Asia, saying that he was against O'Daniel becoming a counselor to Navarre. Heath had accompanied O'Daniel to the January meeting with Navarre, and was taken aback when Iron Mike laid out his plan to win the war. O'Daniel proposed they "build additional block-houses around the periphery of the Tonkin Delta at quarter-kilometer intervals and in front of that, have a whole wall of barbed wire. This would largely solve the whole question of pacifying the Delta, since the Vietminh could neither get in nor get out."

"This suggestion," Heath observed to Bonsal, "voiced with Iron Mike's usual positiveness, was so preposterous in view of the balance of forces between the Vietminh and the Vietnamese, that I merely stared at him and finally said mildly that the French didn't have the force necessary to garrison such a wall of block-houses and accomplish its other tasks."

O'Daniel, however, felt that he had won a major victory when Navarre agreed to having five U.S. liaison officers assigned to his headquarters. Iron Mike hoped they would "correct French weaknesses." On February 2, 1954, O'Daniel toured Dien Bien Phu with a group of American officers, among them veterans of Korea. In a cable to the White House on February 10, he concluded: "I feel they can withstand any kind of attack the Vietminh are capable of launching." But he added this prescient caveat: "If I were charged with the defense of the area, I would have been tempted to have used the high ground surrounding the area."

General Trapnell, chief of MAAG prior to O'Daniel, disagreed with him, and at a February 11 National Security Council meeting, Eisenhower lamented "the extraordinary confusion of the reports. . . . There are almost as many judgments as there are authors of messages." But he seemed to react favorably to General O'Daniel's views, for on February 19 he cabled Dulles in Berlin: "General O'Daniel's most recent report is more encouraging than is given to you through French sources. I still believe that . . . most needed for success [is] French will."

On March 2, 1954, Eisenhower's special committee on Indochina recognized for the first time that in spite of O'Daniel's optimism, direct U.S. action might be needed if the situation deteriorated drastically. At the time, the committee felt that the United States had done all it could to help the French win at Dien Bien Phu. By March, the Defense Department had spent more than $123 million beyond the funds allocated for 1953–54, and now the French were asking for $100 million more. The committee suggested that the Department of Defense develop "a concept of operations involved in the use of U.S. Armed Forces in Indochina, should such involvement be determined upon." Admiral Radford wanted O'Daniel permanently assigned to Indochina to monitor developments. In view of the massive U.S. aid, Navarre was not in a position to object. In early March, he told Heath that he was "very willing" to accept General O'Daniel as head of MAAG and would be happy to hear "any good ideas the general might produce," but it would be understood that MAAG "was to have no powers, advisory or otherwise, in the conduct and planning of operations, or in the training of national armies and cadres."

Navarre had another condition. O'Daniel would have to surrender a star, so that he would not be superior in rank to the French commander in Indochina. General Ridgway, the army chief of staff, bristled at this demand. Why should a distinguished senior officer be demoted to satisfy the general of another army? The United States would suffer a loss of prestige without any commensurate advantage. But O'Daniel magnanimously accepted the loss of one of his three stars and the Defense Department announced his appointment to MAAG on March 12. Soon after O'Daniel's arrival in Vietnam, Navarre had a change of heart and agreed to accept twenty-five to fifty Americans to help train native forces.

I Count Fifty Shells per Minute

"On the eve of the attack," General Navarre later wrote, "the fortified camp at Dien Bien Phu was the most powerful ever seen in Indochina." On March 11, officers on Béatrice, the CR covering the northeast of the perimeter and overlooking RP41, could see the Vietminh infantry in their green uniforms gathering by the hundreds on the hills opposite theirs. On March 12, Major Paul Pégot, commander of the four strongpoints that made up Béatrice, drafted his daily intelligence bulletin: "During the night, our forward observers were fired upon and had to pull back. Enemy approaches to the north are at fifty meters from our positions. The Vietminh seems to have completely encircled our positions." Castries knew the Vietminh were attacking on the March 13, and it should have been obvious that Béatrice was the target, but he did nothing to reinforce the 437 Legionnaires who held the three hills separated by gorges that formed the triangle of Béatrice.

Major Pégot had volunteered for service at Dien Bien Phu after suffering a personal tragedy. He was finishing his tour with a desk job in Saigon when he decided to bring his wife over. She left France on an ocean liner, and sent him a letter postmarked Suez describing her stopover in Egypt. A few days later Pégot received a telegram marked CONFIDENTIAL. It said: "Wife disappeared at sea." When the ship docked at Saigon, the consternated Pégot was waiting. The purser told him that his wife had fallen overboard in the Indian Ocean. Pégot inspected her cabin and took her luggage back to his room at the base. Soon after, he asked to command the 3rd Battalion of the 13th Foreign Legion Demi-Brigade (DBLE), an elite unit that had fought Rommel in Africa, and that now held Béatrice. It was said that he was "doing Camerone." When the Austrian archduke Maximillian accepted the offer of the Mexican throne in 1863, he was escorted by units of the French Foreign Legion, who fought a battle to the last man at Hacienda Camerone. This act of suicidal heroism was memorialized by the Legion. If Pégot had a death wish, he had come to the right place.

On the morning of Saturday, March 13, the daily life of the base, this network of overlapping little fortresses, this labyrinth of barbed wire and sandbags, went on as usual. Before the fog lifted, the patrols went out to pick up supplies dropped by parachute. Men on the banks of the Nam Yum washed their clothes and cut one another's hair. Beyond the perimeter stretched a flat landscape sprinkled with hills, and beyond that the jungle. Within the perimeter, the base in its preparations looked like a "before the battle" movie set.

The French were at a disadvantage, for they were closely watched by the Vietminh, who were not visible, and who did not reveal their firepower until the day of the attack, when they began shelling the airstrip with 105mm projectiles. Castries was expecting human-wave attacks over flat ground. His strategy was to hold two battalions in reserve, so that he could order a counterattack when needed.

According to a Vietminh officer, Béatrice had been chosen for the initial attack for three reasons: it was somewhat isolated on the northeast corner of the perimeter, more than a mile from central command (at Claudine); it protected the airstrip, the destruction of which was Giap's principal goal; and it was the closest base to the Vietminh regiments' line of approach. For weeks, Giap's scouts had been making nocturnal recon patrols, mapping out each belt of barbed wire and fold of ground. Giap had the initiative, choosing not only the site but the timing and cadence of the battle. His strategy was to pick off the strongpoints one at a time, engaging in a series of small battles, nibbling away at the French perimeter rather than taking it in one big but costly bite.

Béatrice, the most endangered center of resistance, was also the most seriously undermanned. The high command seemed to think that the reputation of the Legionnaires would make up for their scarcity in numbers. The battalion had a ration strength of 517, but on March 13, only 437 were present. Ten were in the hospital, sick or wounded, and seventy had been assigned to other duties in the central camp. The remainder of the four companies, occupying four strongpoints on three hills, were down to a single officer each, who if disabled would be replaced by a noncom.

The companies were stationed as follows:

On Béatrice 1, the northernmost hilltop, the 9th Company, led by Lieutenant Carrière.

On Béatrice 3, the southernmost hilltop, close to RP41, the 11th Company, under Lieutenant Turpin.

The longest and westernmost hill, with a strongpoint at each end, was held at the north by Captain Philippe Nicolas' 10th Company atop Béatrice 4, and at the south by Captain Lemoine's 12th Company on Béatrice 2. The battalion command post under Major Pégot was also on Béatrice 2.

For 437 men armed with ten mortars and a few machine-gun nests to hold four separate strongpoints against Vietminh regiments about to attack with heavy artillery was folly. They were so few in number that they had only one line of defense, and once that was breached, the post would be lost, since there were no reserves. It was like a game of toy soldiers, where a single hand brushes away the line of defenders at the top of a rise. Castries should have reinforced Béatrice, the obvious target for the first attack. But he was a tank commander, unseasoned in fixed-position warfare.

By the night of March 12, Vietminh sappers had dug trenches with emplacements for mortars to within two hundred yards of Béatrice 1 to the north and Béatrice 3 to the south, overlooking the road. The final trenches, going right up to the French barbed wire, would be dug under the cover of artillery preparation.

At 9 A.M. on March 13, a Dakota had no trouble landing on the airstrip with medical supplies, including stretchers and forty coffins that were stacked in the morgue, a square pit open to the sky. The nearby cemetery had recently been enlarged to accommodate more graves. To one side, a big C-119 Flying Boxcar with engine trouble was being repaired, while nine Bearcat fighters were stranded in their sandbagged dispersal pens due to polluted fuel.

At 10 A.M., the Vietminh artillery began firing at the airstrip. A shell burst hit the steel plating of the C-119, which lay on one side like a beached whale. The crew, on board waiting for takeoff, scrambled out. Supply planes continued to fly in, but kept their engines running in case they had to take off in a hurry. Captain Amanou recalled that as he landed his supply-laden Dakota, "a shell landed behind our left wheel. Everyone jumped out and as I ran, another shell broke a wing. I ran like hell to get away from the mortars. It was absolutely terrifying." Two of the stranded Bearcats were able to take off, and flew napalm missions on the way to air bases in Laos. One of the fighter pilots who made it out wrote to his parents: "I was at Dien Bien Phu on the 13th and I was able to take off, but I had to leave everything behind, my clothes and my checkbook. I'm sitting in Luang Prabang in my underpants. I'm worried about my checks; maybe I should put stops on them. I also left some mail there, which I didn't have time to read." Three other Bearcats were able to fly out the next day, but four were destroyed.

On the morning of the thirteenth, four C-119 Flying Boxcars with mixed French-U.S. crews and one with an American crew flew over Dien Bien Phu for airdrops, but the plane with the Americans turned back, on the grounds that their contract didn't cover encountering enemy fire. The involvement of American pilots from Civil Air Transport had begun on January 2, 1954, when Navarre's deputy, General Pierre Bodet, had shown his shopping list to Major General Trapnell, then the head of MAAG: more B-26s, more U.S. ground crews, and U.S. pilots to fly the Flying Boxcars on loan from the air force. Trapnell gave the go-ahead to Bodet's request with the proviso that the pilots come from CAT. Formed in 1946 in China by General Claire Chennault as an air-freight line, CAT had been taken over by the CIA in 1950 for operations in Korea and various covert projects. CAT pilots were freelancers rather than U.S. Air Force personnel.

On January 29, the Pentagon approved the French request for twenty-two B-26s with two hundred mechanics, and twenty-four CAT pilots to fly the twelve Flying Boxcars. By mid-February, the French had not made a formal request for pilots. In Saigon, Ambassador Heath asked if the pilots were still wanted. General Henri Lauzin, commander of the Far East Air Force, said he wanted them but was unable to pay for them. He needed $100,000 a month for the project. Heath cabled the State Department: "We see no reason for the U.S. to pick up this check and regret the niggling attitude displayed by the French authorities here and in Paris."

On March 3, however, a contract was finally signed calling for twenty-four pilots to operate a dozen Flying Boxcars with French markings. The pilots were paid seventy dollars per flying hour, with a monthly guarantee of sixty hours. That came to a minimum monthly pay of $4,200 a month, pretty good money in 1954, comparable when adjusted for inflation to salaries earned by today's Blackwater security contractors, now renamed Xe.

The first CAT contingent arrived in Haiphong from Formosa on March 9. They brought their own refrigerator. The French crews were astonished. The pilots stayed at a hotel near the harbor, called the Pot de l'Arrivée (the First Round of Drinks), and they set up a bar in Eric Shilling's room, where the music started blaring. Rain and fog kept them grounded until March 12, when they flew familiarization missions with French pilots over Dien Bien Phu, which seemed strangely quiet. They saw the damage to the airstrip, and the plane whose engine was being repaired. The CAT pilots reported that airdrops would be "a piece of cake." The crew that had turned back on the thirteenth decided upon reflection to fly the next mission.

As more planes were damaged that morning, six single-seat Grumman Hellcats off from the carrier *Arromanches* in Ha Long Bay (the bay of three thousand islands off Haiphong) and flew over Dien Bien Phu firing rockets and wing guns to silence the flak and dropping five-hundred-pound bombs. But lacking any information from ground control, they failed to do much damage. The skinny-barreled 37mm antiaircraft guns were hard to spot under their camouflage.

Colonel Piroth had prepared in advance a series of targets uncovered on the aerial photographs, but as his intelligence officer Lieutenant Verzat pointed out, there were no Vietminh batteries among the targets. The Viets had changed their emplacements.

Piroth, with his surface optimism, told his battery officers, "Don't worry, boys, they will have to reveal their location when they fire, and five minutes later, no more Viet artillery."

French armies going back to Napoleon had always fought "under the umbrella of artillery." Piroth had taken the risk of open emplacements that could fire *tout azimuths* (in a 360-degree circumference). He couldn't camouflage his guns or build protective casemates without restricting his field of fire. The Dien Bien Phu perimeter had to be protected on all sides.

But as the days wore on in February and March, Piroth became increasingly preoccupied by the inability of his 155s to find targets, and by the jeopardy of his firing teams in their open pits. While maintaining an upbeat joviality, he finally poured out his feelings to Major Guy Hourcabie, who asked him: "How can our batteries maintain their fire when the men have no cover?"

"Only artillery can save Dien Bien Phu," Piroth told Hourcabie, "but we're in the open, firing blind, while the Viets have observers in forward positions. The situation may be irreversible. Not even God can help our cannoneers." Then, growing agitated, he said, "In what kind of shit did the high command dump us? Do you realize, Hourcabie, the position I'm in?" Quieting down, he added, "Swear you won't breathe a word of this. It would be terrible for morale." The Vietminh gunners, on the other hand, had been studying their targets for weeks and knew the exact range and angle for each of their hidden guns. Firing on targets long observed, they did not need Piroth's intricate calculations. They simply fired at what they saw.

In midmorning on May 13, Lieutenant Colonel Gaucher of the 13th DBLE drove to the low hills of Béatrice to see how the 3rd Battalion was doing. The three hills rose about sixty feet above the plain. The Legionnaires had cleared the slopes of undergrowth, but not the gorges that divided them. Across RP41, thick scrub was backed by forested hills. The weather had cleared, and from Béatrice 3, overlooking the dirt road, Legionnaire officers could see Vietminh infantry in their green uniforms through their binoculars, up the road that veered eastward toward Tuan Giao.

Gaucher found Major Pégot at his command post on Béatrice 2. "The men are tired and tense," Pégot told him. "Tell them to wake up," Gaucher said. "It's tonight for sure." Gaucher had noticed gaps in the fields of barbed wire that encircled the three hills. Pégot protested that he had to fight for every yard of barbed wire, not to mention mines. Gaucher also pointed out that the overhead protection on the shelters was insufficient to withstand 120mm mortars. "Entrench yourselves well," he said, "for Béatrice is the little goat that the tiger eats for breakfast."

Touring the strongpoints, Gaucher found the Legionnaires making final preparations, cleaning and loading their weapons, making sure the machine-gun emplacements had plenty of ammunition, and fitting niches into the trenches to store grenades. He pointed out defects and chewed out Legionnaires. This was the irascible Gaucher they knew. His presence was almost comforting. On Béatrice 3, the hill to the south, the 11th Company cook, Stary, had prepared a hot lunch. "Who wants some goulash?" he asked. "Eat your fill. If the Viets attack, no more hot meals. Who wants more wine?" "Don't drink too much," Corporal Krauss warned. "If the Viets attack, you won't have time to piss."

By 3 P.M., the shelling of the airstrip was coming in at an increasing cadence. Standing outside the open door of the hospital, Dr. Grauwin told an aide: "I count eight bursts."

"It's a 105," said the aide.

"They hit the Packet," said Grauwin. The C-119 was lying to one side from an earlier hit.

"One shell to the left," said the aide, "one to the right, the third a direct hit." The Flying Boxcar was on fire, and other planes on the runway took off and circled overhead.

Grauwin looked at his watch: "They're firing sixty shells a minute."

The last Dakota to land that afternoon brought in a trio from the army press service: the cameramen André Lebon and Jean Martinoff, and the reporter Daniel Camus. "We saw below us what seemed like thousands of bomb craters," recalled Camus. "We jumped out of the plane under mortar fire. Lebon and Martinoff were shooting on the airstrip. I stopped running to look behind me and saw them both lying on the airstrip." In their eagerness to film the burning plane, both had been hit by mortar fire. Martinoff was killed and Lebon was taken to the hospital. One of Lebon's feet hung from his leg by the tendon, and he kept saying, "The bastard, the bastards!" Dr. Grauwin knew a plane was leaving for Hanoi ten minutes later. Lebon had to be operated on at once. Grauwin amputated and bandaged the foot, and two hours later Lebon was recovering at Lanessan Hospital in Hanoi.

After the Martinoff-Lebon incident, another journalist, Moissinac, asked Castries if he could visit his friend Colonel Lalande, who commanded the southernmost post of Isabelle. Castries told Moissinac, who was the editor of the aviation magazine *Caravelle:* "All right, but avoid eccentricities like your two pals who just got hit." By the time Moissinac found a jeep to drive him to Isabelle, the artillery barrage on central command and Béatrice had begun. Lalande told him: "You may have to stay awhile."

Surrender, Legionnaires!

At 4:45 P.M., Captain Yves Hervouet, the commander of the tank squadron, briefed his crews. "In fifteen minutes we'll know," he said. "Either Giap launches his offensive or it's a bluff like January." Giap was not bluffing. He was waiting for the fading light of dusk when his artillery crews had finished registering their targets. They would begin firing when it got dark enough so that French artillery firing counterbattery missions could not locate them. Half an hour after Hervouet's briefing, a shell burst outside the squadron shelter. The crews ran to their tanks and moved into positions where they could fire their 75mm guns.

The Vietminh artillery preparation began at 5:18 P.M. One third of Giap's artillery pounded the four strongpoints of Béatrice, while the rest was aimed at the central command post at Claudine, where the airstrip, the artillery, and the tanks were concentrated. The intensity and precision of the artillery barrage shocked the French. It started as a distant drumroll out beyond the perimeter, and then the shells began hitting their targets.

Piroth's artillery crews were in their pits waiting for orders on direction and angle to come from the central firing post. From the shelter inside his pit, Major Alliou felt the earth vibrate. The map on the wall was shaking. The Viets seemed to be firing all their guns at once. "This is like the Italian campaign," he said, "but then we were doing the firing." As Giap's 105s relentlessly pounded central command, Piroth's four 155s were incapable of doing their job. What surprised him was the cadence of the fire, as if the Vietminh had an unlimited supply of shells. Dakotas were in the air, dropping flares, but unable to locate the gun emplacements.

As the air force general Dechaux later told the 1955 commission of inquiry: "We tortured our brains to find ways to locate their artillery. Some guns were in tunnels six meters from the embrasure. They were moved up to fire, then pulled back."

Colonel Langlais, the commander of the paratroop reserves, was outside his bunker naked, taking a shower under a pierced fuel drum, when he heard the bursts close by and ran inside. It reminded him of the Black Forest in 1944, the kind of sustained shelling that scatters the most disciplined units when bursting shells sent fragments of steel whirling through the air. A thick fog of dust and cordite hung over central command. The barrage destroyed blockhouses and shelters and knocked out several artillery pits. The cables of field telephones were torn up, interrupting communications. Only a few sappers were visible, splicing the cables. The Viets hit a depot where five hundred mortar shells were stacked, killing twelve men.

On Béatrice 2, Captain Nicolas of the 10th Company was in his bunker, reading a letter from the Ministry of Finance informing him that his pay would be enjoined unless he paid his back taxes. Then came the sound of incoming shells like the whoosh of a passing express train, followed by the boom and flash of explosions.

At the hospital, Dr. Grauwin's field phone was ringing. It was an officer on Béatrice: "I've got twelve wounded, can you send an ambulance?" The stretcher cases started coming in and were lined up in the hall. One of the wounded men said, "Just my luck. I got here yesterday." Given the intensity of the shelling, Grauwin worried about capacity. He had forty-two beds in his surgical unit plus room for one hundred stretcher cases.

On the Béatrice strongpoints, the Legionnaires hunkered down in their trenches, heads sunk between their shoulders. The 10th and 11th companies, which were close to RP41, were the hardest hit. An aide told Gaucher at central command: "Colonel, Béatrice is asking for the counterbattery." Gaucher called Castries, who was dug into his own underground bunker. Castries replied, "You have priority." The artillery observers on Béatrice relayed the targets, but Piroth's gunners were drawing more fire than they sent out. They fired four or five rounds, then jumped back into their shelters, waiting for the reply. Two 105s had already been rendered useless with damage to their oil-filled recoil cylinders.

On Béatrice 3, the Legionnaire Franz Fischer saw the first shells explode on the hilltops, sending up fountains of earth, caving in trenches, vaporizing parapets. No one thought the Vietminh had that many guns, thought Jacques Leude, the twenty-eight-year-old doctor at the command post on Béatrice 2, where Major Pégot was in charge of the defense, in close contact with Colonel Gaucher.

At 6 P.M., a shell made a direct hit on Pégot's command post, killing him and the two lieutenants he was with. The Béatrice Legionnaires lost their commander when they most needed him. The radio link with Piroth's batteries was also knocked out. No more instructions came to guide his gunners, who had to improvise. The Legionnaires on Béatrice could only crouch in their trenches and wait it out. All their mortar teams had been killed.

It was not until seven that a liaison agent reached Captain Nicolas on Béatrice 4 to tell him that Pégot was dead and he was in command. Nicolas made his way up the hill to the command post, leaving a noncom in charge of the 10th Company. What bad luck, he thought, three officers killed before the Viet ground assault had begun. Could the battalion still be called operational?

At the command post, he saw the mangled bodies of Pégot and the two others. More bad news came from all sides. On Béatrice 3, Lieutenant Turpin, commanding the 11th Company, had been thrown against the wall of his blockhouse and lay unconscious with a broken arm and blood streaming from his head. Master Sergeant Fels had taken over the company. On Béatrice 1, the narrow northern hilltop, Lieutenant Carrière had been killed when a shell hit his command post, and on Béatrice 2, Captain Lemoine was temporarily out of commission. Captain Nicolas had to deal with a chaotic situation in which no unit could communicate with any other.

Back at central command, the last radio message Gaucher got from Béatrice was a guttural German voice saying: *"Alles tod."* Gaucher took the mike: "Here sector commander. Let me speak to an officer."

"Alles tod."

"Tell me your unit, goddammit." There was no reply. Realizing that the assault had begun, Gaucher said: "I hope they can last until dawn." A counterattack at night with tanks in that kind of terrain was hopeless.

Finally word reached Gaucher that Pégot and the two lieutenants were dead. "I always said those shelters were flimsy," he said. Minutes later, he suffered the same fate. His number two, Major Martinelli, recorded in his diary: "The colonel was sitting at a folding table and examining a map with his two aides [Lieutenants Bailly and Bretteville]. I was in the back on a chair directing the mortar fire over Béatrice on the phone. . . . A 105 shell came through the roof and exploded at about 7:45 P.M. and I was projected across the room and landed on my stomach. I felt something heavy on my legs and I shook myself loose. I headed toward the light through a cloud of smoke. Then I realized that my right leg was not folding at the knee but at the tibia. I heard Gaucher say, 'My God, my God.' "

Gaucher lay in the rubble with his chest torn open. "Wipe my face and give me something to drink," he said. Those were his last words. The death of Gaucher, the hardened survivor of so many battles, was a blow to the Legionnaires, one of whom said, "Things will not be the same." It was as if his loss of *baraka* (luck) was also theirs. Castries called Langlais and told him: "Gaucher has been killed. Take his place at once in command of the central sub-sector." But with Gaucher gone, so was his battle plan, and Langlais had to improvise.

At the hospital, outside the operating room, the phone kept ringing and bodies lay side by side on stretchers. Sergeant Sammarco, watching over Gaucher's coffin, said: "I wonder if we're going to end up eating rice." Bare-chested and bathed in sweat, Dr. Grauwin operated on broken men. Another surgeon replaced him when he was summoned to the triage center, where 150 wounded waited under a tent, some screaming, some groaning, some unconscious, some dying. If the triage center is hit, there will be a massacre, he thought. From the center emanated a nauseous compound made up of all human secretions, which he could almost feel sticking to his skin as well as entering his nostrils.

Grauwin and his orderlies treated seventy men on the spot and sent them off. Eighty more were kept for evacuation to Hanoi, and fifty of those had to be operated on right away, in an unending procession of blinded eyes, broken jaws, chests blown open, and fractured limbs. Grauwin filled out forms, which he pinned to each patient. Taking a break, he went outside for a smoke. Night had fallen and he could see a purple haze over Béatrice, where shells were still bursting, as the Dakotas dropped flares. In the morgue pit, more than a hundred corpses had piled up, some wrapped in parachute silk, others in gray bags, still others unwrapped and frozen in contorted positions, mouths gaping, eyes wide open. Above the pile buzzed a cloud of flies.

At around 7 P.M., the artillery preparation stopped and the infantry assault began upon the four Béatrice strongpoints simultaneously. The Legionnaires, in disarray from the pounding, were unable to mount a coordinated defense that might have allowed them to hold until daybreak. The companies were decimated by artillery fire, and the number of officers killed and wounded left them leaderless. French artillery support was compromised by the loss of radio communication, and once the single line of defense was breached, there were no reserves to plug the holes.

Two regiments of the elite 312th Division attacked the strongpoints, outnumbering the French twenty to one. When the shelling stopped, the Legionnaires raised their heads. They saw that trenches had been dug to within fifty yards of the fields of barbed wire. Vietminh sappers crawled out of the trenches carrying bamboo tubes filled with explosives to clear lanes through the barbed wire. The Legionnaires fired machine guns and poured down grenades, but when one Viet fell, another stepped over his body. As the sappers cut through wire and defused mines, the *bo dois* massed for the assault. One regiment attacked Béatrice 2 and 4 on the westernmost hill, while another moved on to the strongpoints on RP41, Béatrice 1 to the north and 3 to the south. Many of the point men lost their lives opening the way for others.

On the southernmost hilltop of Béatrice 3, Franz Fischer and Emile Krantz, two gunners in Lieutenant Turpin's 11th Company, fired their FM 24/29 automatic rifle down the slope at the oncoming Viets, but it was heating up. Close by, they saw the roofs of other gun emplacements collapse as bodies flew through the air. The dust made breathing difficult. A Legionnaire stood up and aimed his flamethrower at the advancing Viets. Shrapnel hit the fuel cylinder on his back, igniting him into a human torch, "jumping and screaming like an animal," as Fischer recalled.

A shell dropped through the roof of their dugout. It did not explode, but it hit Krantz in the back, killing him. Fischer crawled out and jumped into a nearby trench crowded with wounded. His friend Kuntz sat in a corner, groaning. His hair, eyebrows, and eyelashes had burned off and strips of burned flesh hung from his face. Fischer could hear the Viets shouting *"lai dai"* (come on) as they streamed up the hill, throwing grenades. Then he passed out.

At the northernmost post, Béatrice 1, the commander, Lieutenant Carrière, was dead, but the men of the 9th Company held out when French artillery halted the progression of the Viets, who were forced to lie on their stomachs. But when the Legionnaires were about to be surrounded, they ran down the slope to avoid capture. About a hundred made it to the central camp, looking like whipped dogs.

On the big hill to the west, at the southern strongpoint of Béatrice 2, where Pégot's command post had been hit and Captain Lemoine of the 12th Company had been killed, the survivors surrendered. "I was groggy," recalled Lieutenant Cruz, one of those captured. "They disarmed me, took my watch, tied my hands behind my back with telephone wire, and took me away." Captain Nicolas, who had taken command of the battalion, was in his shelter. "I could hear them throwing grenades in our trenches and I decided to come out," he recalled. "I saw the Dakotas dropping flares and I felt they were actually helping the Viets by lighting their way." At the northern end of the big hill, Béatrice 4, manned by the 10th Company, which Captain Nicolas had commanded before being called away, was the earliest taken, at 8:15 P.M.

On Béatrice 3, the southernmost strongpoint, the 11th Company still fought. Lieutenant Turpin had regained consciousness just as the Viets were storming through the wire, but he could not move his broken arm. Dr. Leude's medical team bandaged his head. Turpin got the radio working and sent out a message: "Here at the 11th we're holding." By 9 P.M., Turpin had only twenty-five men still able to fight. Another assault was stopped by a well-placed machine gun, but the Viets brought up a bazooka and destroyed it.

When Turpin and Dr. Leude heard Vietminh officers shout "Surrender, Legionnaires," they gave themselves up. Dr. Leude was mortified that "the Viets wouldn't let me stay with my wounded. They took my surgical instruments, my syringes, my bandages, my ampoules." In the trench where he had lost consciousness, Franz Fischer woke up as a bayonet poked his stomach. He heard a *bo doi* saying in French, "Stay put." He was lined up on the ground with the other wounded. *"Wasser,"* moaned the man beside him. When you're wounded, thirst can kill, Fischer thought.

Vietminh officers knew that the battalion command post was located on Béatrice 3, and knew the name of the commander. One of them asked Dr. Leude where Major Pégot was. Leude told him the major was dead. The

Vietminh officer did not believe him. "I personally saw him decapitated by a shell that flew through the shelter," Leude said. "Go get proof that Pégot is dead," the officer said.

By this time the captives had been marched off the hill. Accompanied by an escort of four, Leude returned to Béatrice 3, passing an interminable column of Vietminh stretcher-bearers. Leude led his guards to the command post where Pégot's headless body was half buried in the rubble. The guards took the major's stripes and his wallet. Dr. Leude felt nauseous.

When Lieutenant Turpin had first surrendered on Béatrice 3, everyone was milling around in the dark, and he quietly slid along a wall, holding his broken elbow with his left hand. He pulled his lieutenant's metal bars from one shoulder, but couldn't reach the other. Dazed, he sat on the edge of a trench, where a *bo doi* found him. They chatted in French. The *bo doi* seemed friendly and they talked about their families.

"What's your rank?" the *bo doi* asked.

"Sergeant," Turpin said, not wanting to admit he was an officer.

"You didn't think we had artillery."

"We knew you had 75s and 105s."

"Can you walk?"

"I can try."

"President Ho has told us to be humane to the wounded. Go back to Dien Bien Phu."

The *bo doi* gave him a safe-conduct pass and a letter offering a truce on the morning of the fourteenth from nine to twelve so the French could pick up their wounded. One of the conditions was that during the truce, the French air force would not intervene.

Castries relayed the offer to Hanoi, where it was approved. Two Dodge trucks and a jeep marked with red crosses arrived at around 9 A.M. at the designated spot on the edge of the forest, where they found only twelve wounded and three dead. The "truce" was a ruse to give Giap time to prepare his next attack. He pretended to be doing the French a favor. This was not a Truce of God but a Truce of Giap.

At the 1955 commission of inquiry, Castries said: "Personally, I did not want to agree to a truce."

General Magnan, surprised, asked if he had said so to Hanoi.

Castries: "I didn't reach Cogny himself, but I spoke to his chief of staff, Colonel Bastiani, who told me, 'You must accept.' "

"At what time was that?"

"Seven, seven-fifteen."

"And how many wounded were you able to recover?"

"Around thirty."

The correct number was twelve wounded and three dead.

General Valin: "You knew there would be an attack that night?"

Castries: "Certainly."

"Had you prepared a counterattack?"

"The elements were in place."

However, no order was given. Castries said: "Each time the Viets mounted a major attack, they chose a time of bad weather when the aviation could not intervene. From March 13 to 16 it rained. No counterattack was possible without aviation. I couldn't recover Béatrice with two battalions."

Valin: "But the initial attack was critical, it killed the officers in command. You could have reinforced then. . . . This was your principal position about to fall! With Béatrice lost, you would have trouble using the airstrip."

Castries: "Any reinforcement would have had to fight its way to reach Béatrice."

"Did you have confidence in the troops on Béatrice?"

"It was my best battalion. Losing it was a hard blow. . . . The following morning I did prepare a counterattack, but I was told, 'The planes can't fly because of bad weather.' "

The result of Giap's first attack was four strongpoints lost, the airstrip threatened, 125 killed and wounded, about 200 taken prisoner, and 112 survivors. On the Vietminh side, 600 were killed and wounded, but an important part of the Dien Bien Phu defense perimeter had been taken. Giap's meticulous preparation and supremacy in artillery had won the day. He did not occupy the strongpoints he had captured. "After a battle," he later explained, "we would not defend, we would wage another one immediately if possible, or we might take a rest to reorganize our forces and make better preparations for the next battle."

The Bastards Want to See Us Dead

On the morning of March 14, the sky over Dien Bien Phu was gray and a drizzle dampened what was left of the crater-pocked base. At the command sector, men repaired the damage of battle, using the steel cases the 155mm shells were delivered in to patch the roofs of the torn-open shelters. Castries and his chief of staff and bridge partner, Lieutenant Colonel Keller, had not left their underground command post during the artillery pounding. They urinated in cans to avoid going outside. Keller sat hunched in a corner of the office with his helmet on, motionless. He had suffered a nervous breakdown and later had to be evacuated. The one-armed Piroth wandered among his batteries, staring at poncho-covered corpses. It was not a time for words of reassurance.

At 8 A.M., a small, twin-engine Siebel NC-701 landed with six liters of blood and medical supplies. It flew out with three wounded, including Lieutenant Turpin, who had brought the truce offer, as well as Castries' secretary, Paule Bourgeade.

Atop Gabrielle, which was expected to be attacked next, the battalion commander, Major Roland de Mecquenem, broke out the champagne. A stickler for discipline, he had been nicknamed "von Meckenheim" by his Algerian fusiliers, but this morning he was in a festive mood. He believed that Gabrielle was the model CR. It was the northernmost, almost two miles from central command, between the Pavie Trail and the Nam Yum River, and consisted of four strongpoints on a single oblong hill, which was steep-sided and flat-topped. Nicknamed "the Tornado," the heavily forested hill had been cleared of every tree and bush. De Mecquenem had driven his Algerians to reinforce their sandbagged bunkers with logs of ironwood they had chopped down. The men of his 5th Battalion, some of whom were veterans of the battle of Monte Cassino in World War II, won the cash prize for the best built center of resistance. It had a double perimeter of trenches, dug in zigzag formation. With its 877 men and 14 officers and noncoms, de Mecquenem's battalion was close to its normal complement. He had twice as many men as had fought on Béatrice. In addition, Gabrielle had a heavy-weapons section of eight 120mm and four 81mm mortars, manned by Legionnaires under Lieutenant Clerget. From their hidden positions, the Legionnaires had fired test rounds to bracket the range where the Viets would emerge from their trenches.

The plateau on top of the hill was 700 yards long and 275 wide, running in a north-south direction, rising at its northern tip to 200 feet. Surrounded on all sides by paddy fields, the battalion was distributed as follows: 1st and 4th companies to the northwest and northeast, and 2nd and 3rd at the southeast and southwest. Each company had its machine-gun nests positioned to fire down the slope. This hill, higher and steeper than those of Béatrice, was surrounded by flat terrain, devoid of helpful undulations for the Vietminh. With all of Gabrielle's attributes, Mecquenem was convinced he could hold.

Back at central command, the hospital was overwhelmed with wounded from Béatrice. The plan was that most of the wounded, as soon as they were brought in and triaged, would be flown out. But that was not possible on March 14, when bad weather halted most flights. The wounded piled up in every room of the surgery unit. All night, Grauwin and his fellow surgeon Dr. Gindrey operated. The two performed twenty-three amputations, plastered fifteen fractured limbs, and sewed up ten abdomens, ten chests, and two craniums. The floor was littered with bloody bandages. In a trash-filled bucket, a lone leg stuck out, toes pointed skyward. "Piles of hands, arms, legs and feet mixed together as in some foul bouillabaisse," Grauwin wrote in a memoir. "The maggots swarmed in blankets, in sheets, in bandages, even in plaster casts. . . . At night, you could see these repulsive white worms on the hands and faces of sleeping men." The incoming wounded lay on stretchers in the hall, waiting their turn. Those who had been operated on were sent to the recovery room, which was hit by a 105mm shell, killing nine of the twelve men waiting there with notes pinned to them. One of them, who had been wounded on Béatrice, had told Grauwin: "If you could have seen it, thousands of them, jumping over each other when one was hit."

When the attack came on Béatrice, Castries asked Hanoi for reinforcements. General Cogny sent the 5th BPVN, the battalion of Vietnamese paratroopers who had previously been dropped on Dien Bien Phu, but had been flown out on January 28. The 588 men of the battalion were not considered an elite unit, but their commander, Captain André Botella, was well regarded. He was a forty-year-old Algerian *pied-noir*, with one leg shorter than the other from a World War II wound. What he lacked in mobility he made up in combat experience. When the men were told they were going back to Dien Bien Phu, some who had families in Hanoi deserted.

Prior to departure aboard C-47 Dakotas, Botella briefed his company commanders: "As soon as you hit the ground, get off the drop zone. Don't take the time to fold your chutes. There will be firing from all sides."

The unit jumped at 2:45 in the afternoon of March 14, over a drop zone near Isabelle, to the south. Fearing Vietminh fire, they jumped from six hundred fifty feet, so that they would be hanging in the air as briefly as possible. Looking out the open door of the C-47, Lieutenant Lalanne saw puffs of smoke that made the Dakota tremble.

Jumping at that altitude meant that the parachutes had only thirty seconds in which to slow the men's descent. Some chutes did not fully open, and on top of that, the day was windy, and the featherweight Vietnamese were pulled across the ground by their chutes after landing. The result was two killed and thirty wounded. One of those killed was the orderly of the battalion doctor, Pierre Rouault, the stubborn redheaded Parisian who had performed the tracheotomy in the jungle.

Captain Botella checked in with Colonel Langlais at central command. "So what are they saying in Hanoi?" Langlais asked.

"Cogny believes Dien Bien Phu is finished and didn't want to send me," Botella said.

"The bastards want to see us dead."

Langlais took Botella to see Castries, who was sitting behind his desk, hollow-cheeked and baggy-eyed. "Do you think we can hold?" Castries asked. Then he answered his own question. "Certainly, we'll hold." Botella was told to take his unit to Eliane 4, to the east of the command sector, and dig in. It took the battalion another couple of hours to get there. They dug protective shelters but they hadn't brought enough shovels, and some had to use their helmets. They hadn't been fed, it was raining hard, and after their rough landing, they had marched from one end of the perimeter to the other. Neither officers nor men were in a happy frame of mind. It was dusk by the time they settled in under their tents, and soon they heard the sound of artillery fire coming from the direction of Gabrielle.

The Vietminh followed the same plan of attack on Gabrielle as on Béatrice: artillery preparation at dusk, between 5 and 6 P.M., followed by an infantry assault at 8, after nightfall. In his command post, Major de Mecquenem heard thunder in the slate-gray sky. When shells began bursting on his positions, he raged at headquarters: "They're hitting their targets. Where is your counterbattery fire?" Piroth had promised him that his gunners could drop a shell on a pocket handkerchief.

Once again, Piroth's batteries were unable to locate the guns firing at the strongpoints. Piroth had become strangely alienated from the battle, since his artillery had proven incapable of modifying the course of events. He left the firing to his battery officers, until Castries himself took over, later telling General Cogny: "From the evening of the thirteenth, Piroth was defective. On the fourteenth, I did not leave the artillery command post and more than six thousand rounds were fired." Castries was no more successful than Piroth in targeting the Vietminh guns.

At the 1955 commission of inquiry, he was asked why. "Even if I had located them," Castries replied, "they were buried in such a way that ordinary shells couldn't reach them. I would have needed a rolling thunder of perforating shells. Our 105s were useless."

At 8 P.M., the men of the Vietminh 308th Division, codenamed "Viet Bac," jumped out of their trenches and charged the northern face of Gabrielle in a wave, like the incoming tide, like the Argonne in World War I, as if hallucinated, driven forward by whistle-blowing commissars. The Algerians in their bunkers, through clouds of smoke, saw Vietminh sappers with their bangalore torpedoes in the barbed wire and columns of infantry climbing out of the trenches, led by "death volunteers" carrying explosives to blow up machine-gun nests.

When the Vietminh riflemen started up the slope, cutting into the barbed wire, the artillery, now under Castries' command, was able to provide accurate fire as close as twenty yards from the French lines. As the men in green looked for gaps in the wire, they were cut down by artillery fire and the machine guns and mortars of Gabrielle. The Algerian gunners could see Viets hanging on the barbed wire, while others stepped over the fallen. Having taken heavy losses, the 88th Regiment was pulled back and replaced by the 165th Regiment of the 312th Division.

At midnight Gabrielle still held, while the Vietminh trapped in the barbed wire continued to take losses. The Viets took a pause at 2:30 A.M., but came back an hour later with another artillery barrage and fresh troops. The Vietminh 165th Regiment charged up the southwestern slope held by the 3rd Company, where the command post was. Around 4 A.M., the Vietminh infiltrated the northern slope. At 4:30 A.M., Lieutenant Clerget, in charge of the mortar company, reported that his last 81mm mortar was *hors d'usage* (out of commission).

It was then that two shells in rapid succession hit the command post, wounding Major de Mecquenem and knocking him out as he was blown against the wall. Major Kah, recently arrived as the replacement for de Mecquenem, whose tour was over, was hit in both legs. Captain Gendre of the 3rd Company took command of the battalion, and moved into the damaged command post.

The four companies atop Gabrielle were now engaged in hand-to-hand combat in isolated groups. On the northern slope, the Viets had reached the top on their fourth assault. Lieutenant Monneau of the 3rd Company, to the southwest, had six men left. The Viets were suddenly upon them and ordered them out of their trench. Monneau had been hit by shell fragments, but instead of helping him the Viets took his shoes. Barefoot, with a rope around his neck, he started on the long march. Only on the third day, when he joined the captives from Béatrice, did Monneau happen upon Dr. Leude, who cleaned his wounds with boiling water.

Lieutenant Fox, of the 2nd Company, on the southeastern stronghold, was killed alongside one of his Algerians. In his last letter to his father after a skirmish on March 5, he had written that he had a slight wound "no worse than a shaving cut. . . . God is protecting me."

Major de Mecquenem, wounded and unconscious, awoke in the rubble of his command post and felt his fatigue jacket. It was drenched in blood. He looked at his watch: 5:30 A.M. It was still dark, and the air was thick with yellow dust. A Dakota was dropping flares, and he could see men in green coming up the slope. He decided to head for the next-closest strongpoint and started walking inside a trench. At the first corner, two Viets jumped him and took him behind their lines, where the *bo dois* spat on him. He had shrapnel in the thigh and elbow, and his wounds were getting infected, but a Vietminh medic told him the wounds would heal themselves.

At around 5 A.M., when the sky had only begun to turn from black to gray, Castries called Captain Botella, whose Vietnamese were snatching a few hours sleep under their tents on Eliane 4, and asked him for "one more small effort." Castries was planning a counterattack to retake Gabrielle, and he wanted Botella's battalion to proceed to the Pavie Trail and join up with a unit of Legionnaires and tanks to storm Gabrielle. Botella couldn't believe he was being asked to go into combat on such short notice. He'd just arrived, his men were exhausted, they'd dug trenches until midnight, it was raining hard, and now they were supposed to march almost three miles to Gabrielle under enemy fire.

Curled up in a foxhole in the fetal position, with a few planks over his head from a case of medical supplies, the exhausted Dr. Rouault slept through the artillery barrage. When he awoke at 4 A.M., he found shrapnel from a mortar shell embedded in one of the planks, which had probably saved his life. An hour later, he was told, to his vexation, that they had to get ready to march on Gabrielle.

By 5 A.M. on Gabrielle, the Vietminh flag had been planted on the northern crest and the two northern strongpoints had been overrun. Two companies of the 1st BEP (Legionnaire paratroopers) were on the Pavie Trail, commanded by Major Maurice Guiraud. He was hoping to reach Gabrielle before sunrise, but was held up waiting for the tanks and the Vietnamese paratroopers to arrive.

The Vietnamese were stumbling around in the dark getting their gear together. They proceeded northward toward Gabrielle, but as it got light they took some artillery fire. Some men ran into a drainage ditch in single file, while others found shelter in shell craters and refused to move. Captain Botella had to pull them out bodily and kick them to get them going. One of his aides drew up a list of those who should be shot for cowardice. Instead of shooting them Botella decided to expel them on the spot from his battalion. He disarmed about twenty men and told them to make a run for it. They joined the "Rats of Nam Yum," the community of deserters who vegetated on the riverbank in the no-man's-land between the French and Vietminh positions and lived off scavenged supplies that fell their way. Botella later wrote: "Can we blame our little Vietnamese for having been overcome with hesitation while high-ranking officers hid out under triple layers of lumber with their helmets on their heads?"

Then at six came a new order from Castries. The purpose of the counterattack was no longer to recapture Gabrielle. Its new mission was to "recover the companies remaining on Gabrielle." At the imperiled command post, Captain Gendre picked up the radio message and tried to pass the word to the men still fighting that they should try to get down the hill and reach friendly lines. On the Pavie Trail, the paratroopers had been joined by seven tanks commanded by Captain Yves Hervouet.

Now that the mission had changed, Major Guiraud decided not to wait for the Vietnamese battalion. His men moved on Gabrielle behind the tanks. The sun was up, and Guiraud could see "the little men in green" running across the plateau, while Algerians sprinted down the southwest corner into the arms of his Legionnaires. An artillery barrage stopped the Viets from pursuing them.

It was after seven when survivors heard the comforting sound of tank engines and linked up with the rescue column. Captain Gendre told the Legionnaires: "From the top of Gabrielle until I reached you my feet never touched the ground. I walked over the cadavers of Viets killed by our artillery." The wounded who managed to get off Gabrielle were transported to the central sector on the back platforms of tanks. Returning to headquarters with the tanks and survivors, the Legionnaires came upon the point company of the Vietnamese battalion and told them the counterattack was over. Blood streamed down the sides of the tanks covered with wounded. Major Guiraud returned to headquarters an angry man, convinced that Gabrielle could have been saved had the order not been changed. The high command was not up to the task.

Castries later told the 1955 commission of inquiry: "The Legionnaires and the tanks reached Gabrielle at the very moment that the last defenders were leaving and gathered them in."

Your Artillery Dispositions Were No Good

By 8:45 on the morning of March 15, Gabrielle was in the hands of the Vietminh. The estimate of losses for the 5th Battalion of Algerian Rifles was 540 dead, 220 captured, and 114 survivors. Aerial photographs of Gabrielle produced an estimate of 1,000 dead and 2,000 wounded Vietminh. But how many had been carried away? In two successive days, two centers of resistance had been taken and two battalions had been wiped out. The only remaining CR on the northern perimeter was Anne-Marie, manned by the problematic Thai battalion. The Vietminh could now move their antiaircraft guns and artillery closer to the airstrip.

That morning, the central sector was quiet, except for a little mortar fire to remind the French that they were surrounded. The area looked as if it had been hit by a hurricane. Key officers had been killed, and the hospital was crowded with wounded who lay unattended. Two Bearcats out on napalm missions were shot down by Giap's antiaircraft guns. The air command in Hanoi changed its tactics: no more napalm drops at low altitude.

Captain Hervouet, who commanded the tank squadron, thought Dien Bien Phu was like a boxer who has been knocked out but is still standing. The Legionnaire survivors of Béatrice who'd been at Stalingrad said it was like Stalingrad. The Algerian survivors of Gabrielle who'd been at Monte Cassino said it was like Monte Cassino.

Lieutenant Moreau of the 6th Battery, inspecting his howitzers, was amazed to see that the paint had burned off the barrels, exposing the bare steel. His commander, Colonel Piroth, had been going around offering mea culpas. He told a chaplain, Father Michel Trinquand, "I'm responsible for our inferiority in artillery. I turned down more guns." Piroth had never been included in the tight camaraderie of the higher-ranking officers, he wasn't asked to play bridge, and perhaps he compensated with overconfidence. Now that his boasts had turned to dust, he went to the other extreme and placed all the blame for the defeat on himself. Overcome by a deep sense of shame, Piroth broke down.

At some point in the early hours of March 15, air force major Jacques Guérin was at the central command bunker when he heard two men shouting in an adjacent office. One was Colonel Langlais, more irascible than usual from loss of sleep, and the other was Colonel Piroth. Repelled by the wreck Piroth had become, Langlais said: "And what's more, your artillery dispositions were no good. The artillery on Isabelle was of no help to Gabrielle."

"Everyone knows the distance between Isabelle and Gabrielle," Piroth replied, his ire aroused. "The choice of the Isabelle position was made before your arrival and before the decision to occupy the Torpedo [Gabrielle]. Ask any of my artillery officers if they were twiddling their thumbs all night."

Major Guérin came out into the corridor to see Piroth, his ruddy face chalk white, stride by him without saying a word. Piroth walked over to his artillery shelter and lay down on a cot. He always had a few grenades hanging from his belt and he grabbed one with his remaining hand. He pulled the pin with his teeth, clasped it to his chest, and released the lever. The last sound Piroth heard was the spring in the lever.

Castries was told that Piroth had blown himself up in his shelter. He called a chaplain, Father Heinrich, and said: "Padre, come at once, Colonel Piroth is dead." Together they went to the shelter and saw what remained. Castries asked the chaplain not to divulge the circumstances of Piroth's death. Morale was bad enough already. The chaplain found some men to dig an unmarked grave in the shelter where Piroth had died. Castries informed General Cogny in Hanoi: "Accusing himself of everything, Piroth became a shred, and after dragging himself around for several days, he ended up as I told you."

A few days later, the daily intelligence bulletin from the base reported: "Mystery at Dien Bien Phu. Colonel Piroth hasn't been seen for three day. Official version: he was killed by a shell in his bunker." News of Piroth's suicide, however, could not be kept quiet for long, and within a week the story appeared in a Paris newspaper. On the base, it became common knowledge, and a young officer said: "If all those responsible for what's happening decide to kill themselves, it's going to be quite a crowd in Paris as well as Dien Bien Phu." Dr. Grauwin overheard a conversation at the hospital between the dentist and a noncom:

"Is he dead?"

"He killed himself with a grenade."

Grauwin asked, "You're talking about a suicide?"

"Colonel Piroth."

Grauwin found this hard to believe, and yet a few days before, he had run into Piroth and asked, "Not too tired?"

"I've got a right to be tired, don't you think? You see, *toubib* [slang for "doctor"], I always get the dirty job."

It was inevitable that the debacle of Dien Bien Phu would lead to finger-pointing among the high-ranking officers responsible for operations. This came out repeatedly at the 1955 commission of inquiry. When Langlais was asked, "And what was the role of Coloniel de Castries?" he replied: "He transmitted the telegrams to Hanoi."

Castries responded to Langlais' derision in his own testimony. "If Langlais had been in command," he said, "the battle would not have lasted fifty-six days. . . . His contempt for logistics, his prodigality in the use of artillery munitions, and his demand that the garrison of Isabelle should be reduced were proof of his ignorance."

Castries also stressed his difficulties with officers who fell apart. Piroth committed suicide, and Castries' chief of staff, Keller, "sat hunched in a corner with his helmet on, completely depressed," and had to be evacuated. Even the admirable Dr. Grauwin was sometimes "as depressed as those officers I sent him for treatment."

General Cogny told the commission he had mixed feelings about Langlais: "I have great respect for Colonel Langlais as a soldier. But he was much too high-strung. For instance, he wanted to arrest Major Pierre Tourret of the 8th Choc. He sent me a virulent report. . . . I waited a bit and a few days later he praised Tourret to the skies."

As Castries summed it up: "Everyone has his ups and downs. Langlais was obstinate and a braggart. . . . It was always, 'I did this,' and 'I did that.' . . . But he never made a decision without consulting me first."

I Had a Smaller Perimeter, Which I Thought I Could Hold

The Anne-Marie center of resistance, a mile southwest of Gabrielle, was held by the 3rd Thai Battalion, commanded by Major Léopold Thimonier.

It consisted of four dispersed strongpoints: Anne-Marie 1 and 2, at each end of the crescent-shaped hill surrounded by rice paddies. Anne-Marie 3 and the 12th Company, under Captain Guilleminot, were at the northern end of the airstrip. Anne-Marie 4 and the 9th Company, led by Captain Michel Désiré, were on a rise six hundred yards to the west, surrounded by brush.

The battalion had a splendid badge—a pair of crossed silver war-axes with a scarlet python curled around the handles. But among the 735 Thais, the warlike spirit was lacking. The men came from different tribes in the high country who spoke a dialect close to Laotian. Trained to trek through the jungle in guerrilla units, they took a dim view of being buried in bunkers under artillery fire. They were trail runners and mountain men, not static defenders under siege. Many of the men had families in nearby villages held by the Vietminh. Beguiled by propaganda that they would be welcomed with open arms, they were tempted to go home.

"Our Thais have lost the will to fight," Major Thimonier reported. "Their morale is low. The Viets tell them, 'You still have time to leave and join your brothers.' " Castries knew there was a point when panic spreads. He'd seen it in 1940, when his regiment, still on horseback, fled before the German tanks.

The battalion's doctor, Lieutenant Sauveur Verdaguer, an intellectual with an anticolonial bent, wrote down his thoughts: "We are now the last battalion on the north. We are well aware that our Thai battalion is far from matching the elite units on Béatrice and Gabrielle. Our dispersal over four separate strongpoints, several of which are more than a kilometer apart, can only help the enemy. Also, our Thais have witnessed the assault on Gabrielle and the massive concentration and maneuverability of the Vietminh troops. Every night, our sentries in the barbed wire receive messages telling them that the only way out is to desert."

The men on Anne-Marie expected to be attacked on March 15, but no attack came. In the afternoon, the *sonnettes* ("doorbells," or forward observers) saw Vietminh units arrive on the Pavie Trail in trucks and set up mortar emplacements on what had been Gabrielle. That night the Viets were close enough to the crescent-shaped hill to make direct appeals over loudspeakers in the Thais' own language, inciting them to desert, and also placed leaflets in the barbed wire.

Giap did not attack at once because he too was burdened with casualties. He had only six doctors behind the lines to tend hundreds of wounded. Due to the lack of steel helmets, there were numerous head injuries, while the field hospitals east of Dien Bien Phu teemed with ticks and maggots and yellow flies that lay eggs in open wounds. The weather did not favor either side. Rain on the fifteenth delayed the hauling of Giap's mountain artillery.

On the afternoon of March 16, an Algerian who had been wounded and captured on Gabrielle showed up outside the barbed wire at Anne-Marie with a message from the Vietminh, again proposing a truce to pick up wounded the next morning. At 8:00 A.M. on the seventeenth, Dr. Verdaguer and twenty-five stretcher-bearers arrived at a spot on the edge of the forest about eight hundred yards north of Anne-Marie. A *bo doi* was waiting with eighty-six Algerian wounded. Captain Dr. Pierre Le Damany, the chief medical officer, picked them up in trucks and brought them to the hospital.

By this time, the hospital was as crowded as a Tube station during the London Blitz. The surgeons on duty had never seen wounded like this—faces with no jaws, bodies with no legs, abdomens with intestines hanging out, men with the tops of their heads blown off, terrified men screaming from pain. The doctors were overcome with feelings of powerlessness. And yet they had to carry on. Dr. Gindrey had just heard from his wife that their baby son had been stillborn, but that she was all right. Worried that the news would affect him, Gindrey worked twice as hard to block it out, trying to fix up as many as he could for evacuation to Hanoi, and knowing that he was a world away from the lessons of his combat surgery course in Saigon.

There was some relief on March 16 when a seven-men surgical unit, all volunteers, under Lieutenant Dr. André Rézillot was parachuted in. The unit was sent to Isabelle to reinforce the small hospital there headed by Lieutenant Dr. Guy Calvet, which could now relieve the congestion in the central sector. On March 17, a second surgical team of seven was dropped in. Lieutenant Dr. Jean Vidal, young, muscular, and blue-eyed, introduced himself with the broad smile of the uninitiated. But where to put them? Grauwin found a hut on the other side of the Nam Yum, with room for thirty beds. He didn't want too much concentration of his medical units. His foresight saved lives, for later that day, a 105mm shell hit the X-ray room, where three stretcher cases had been placed. One survived. A second shell hit the room where twelve abdominal cases were waiting. Nine were taken directly to the morgue.

Meanwhile, on Anne-Marie, the Thais began disappearing into the jungle during the night of March 16. On the morning of the seventeenth, rumors flew that the attack was coming in the evening. Dr. Verdaguer was eating sardines out of a can at 2:00 P.M. when the artillery barrage began. "I left my shelter," he recalled, "and saw bunches of Thais at the turnstiles in the barbed wire elbowing aside a few veteran noncoms who tried to prevent them from fleeing into the rice paddies. In a few minutes, of the companies holding Anne-Marie 1 and 2 [on the hill], there remained only a few grizzled veterans and some French cadres." Verdaguer's medical orderlies stayed by his side, but his aide, Cheng, told him: "Lieutenant, now the time to depart."

The battalion commander, Major Thimonier, was on the phone pleading for reinforcements, which never came. The battalion had to abandon Anne-Marie 1 and 2, destroying what they could not carry. Verdaguer had to part with his most valuable belonging, his microscope. It had been left to him in 1945 by the departing Japanese, and now he was leaving it to the Viets. On Anne-Marie 3, to the north of the airfield, there had been massive desertions. Only the 9th Company on Anne-Marie 4 held, but they were ordered to proceed to Isabelle. Verdaguer and his orderlies headed for Huguette, a mile south, as the Viets doused them with mortar fire. "I have to admit I was scared shitless," he recalled. Moving from shell hole to shell hole, he reached Huguette in the late afternoon. Aside from being exhausted and depressed, he harbored a feeling of guilt at having abandoned his post that he could neither dismiss nor understand.

Vietminh radio broadcast the news that "our comrades the Thais who abandoned their positions have been reclaimed, according to President Ho Chi Minh's policy of clemency. Volunteers have been incorporated into our

ranks, while others were returned peacefully to their homes and families."
The Vietminh said they had processed 232 Thais, but many other deserters headed for the hills without passing through their hands.

In warfare, trouble does not come as single spies, but in battalions. With the losses of Béatrice, Gabrielle, and Anne-Marie, the entire northern perimeter was wiped out and the airstrip was left unprotected and exposed. The Vietminh could now bring forward their antiaircraft guns, mortars, and howitzers so that it became extremely hazardous to evacuate the wounded. Supplies now had to be dropped by parachute. The twelve battalions defending Dien Bien Phu were down to nine, although reinforcements were expected.

At the 1955 commission of inquiry, Castries was asked what his state of mind was after losing his three northern centers of resistance. "I did not think that the battle was lost," he said, "but I thought it would be harder now that I had to depend on supplies by parachute."

Catroux: "What were the reasons that gave you confidence?"

Castries: "I had a smaller perimeter, which I thought I could hold."

The C-47 Dakotas now had to drop their supplies over this shrunken perimeter from two thousand feet, making ten to fifteen passes under enemy fire, and flying acrobatic four-leaf clovers as they waited their turn. Many Dakotas returned to Hanoi with flak damage. The supplies were shoved out the side doors with cargo chutes that opened automatically. When the chutes landed, PIMs ran out to unfasten the straps and load the bundles onto trucks, when trucks were available. The chutes could only be used once, and they were using so many that supplies were running short.

Catroux then asked: "Did the morale of your troops increase your confidence?"

Castries: "No . . . but Langlais and I tried to build up their morale. . . . One of the main reasons for low morale was the piling up of the wounded in the centers of resistance."

One gauge of morale was letters home. After the March debacle, there was a tendency on the part of some to stress Vietminh losses, in order not to alarm their families. Colonel André Lalande, the commander of Isabelle, wrote his wife, Marie-Françoise on March 17: "The Viets have taken colossal losses, totally out of proportion to ours. . . . Have no fear, my big girl, not one hair will fall from my head."

Artillery lieutenant Yves Cloix, in a letter to his parents, was more candid. His battery of 105s, he wrote, had lost one gun, four gunners killed, and three wounded. "It's hard to fire when you're fired at. The noise is deafening. In twenty-four hours our battery fired 2,500 rounds. At night I was so scared I was shaking and my teeth were chattering."

Dr. Verdaguer, writing to his wife, Arlette, after his flight from Anne-Marie, saw political implications in the battle: "What worries me the most is the delirium of the French press. Really, for all sorts of reasons, it's high time this ended! But these fucking Americans want to torpedo the Geneva Conference. Out here, we have more sympathy for the Viets than for them."

As for Castries, a more honest appraisal than that given before the commission of inquiry was expressed in a letter to General Cogny: "It's a little like Verdun, but without the depth and above all without the Voie Sacrée [the Sacred Way, the one open road to Verdun that proved to be a lifeline for the encircled French during the ten-month-long battle]." In other ways as well—the sandbagged trenches, the fields of barbed wire— Dien Bien Phu had begun to resemble a World War I battlefield.

The view from Saigon, which Ambassador Heath cabled Washington on March 16, was that the situation at Dien Bien Phu "gives cause for concern." The French kept registers of Vietminh artillery, which was maintaining an average rate of fire of ten rounds a minute. The airstrip could no longer be used to land supplies. "Defense is thus heavily dependent upon airdrops from our loaned C-119s," which could drop one-ton pallet loads. But the garrison asked for smaller loads, which were easier to move under artillery fire. Seen from Hanoi, as Consul Paul Sturm informed Heath on March 17, the situation was alarming not only in Dien Bien Phu but around Hanoi itself. Heath had suggested evacuating the female staff at the Hanoi consulate and their dependents to Saigon. Sturm replied that "both civil and military authorities advise against using any roads that lead out of the city, all of which are under sporadic attack or subject to intensive mining. Hanoi–Haiphong highway is open to traffic only in the afternoon. Railway badly sabotaged twelfth, was restored to service yesterday only to have first three trains sent over the line blown up. Vietminh infiltration both of regulars and well-armed provincial troops has never before reached such proportions major population centers. Meanwhile, please keep all women and all visitors away from Hanoi."

The Central Task Is Now to Build Trenches

In a report on March 17, after the fall of Anne-Marie, Giap emphasized that taking the centers of resistance one at a time was the model to follow. Two elite enemy battalions had been destroyed. "Better to obliterate a company than rout a battalion," he observed. "An essential part of the peripheral defense has been demolished. The airstrip is directly menaced. Some still wish to launch a swift offensive, attacking simultaneously several positions. . . . Others do not see the need to safeguard our forces and would like to attack without interruption, instead of reorganizing after each attack. . . . But we are still in the second phase. We must finish our approach work and neutralize the enemy. This extra effort will save many lives."

Even though Giap talked about saving lives, Vietminh troops were taught that no victory was possible without sacrifice. In the human-wave attacks, as Giap later wrote, "there were always men prepared to sacrifice their lives for the superior interests of the revolution. What others called fanaticism was in reality the heroism of an army serving the people." The French, fighting a war that was increasingly unpopular at home, with an army largely made up of foreign troops, did not have the same motive. The best of them fought out of pride in their units.

Giap announced a pause that would last until the end of the month. He needed to replenish his supply of artillery shells from China. He planned to recruit 25,000 more men, not only to make up for the losses in the 312th and 308th divisions, but also to dig an extensive network of approach trenches around the posts he planned to attack next. The order of the day was: "Without trenches, no combat."

In his appeal to the troops on March 20, he said: "The enemy fears that if France loses the battle she will be in a disadvantageous position at the Geneva Conference. The day before yesterday, the reactionary ruling clique in France observed five minutes of silence to encourage the troops at Dien Bien Phu. What wretchedness! . . . I am told that you are burning with hatred. . . . We must pool our assets to complete the building of trenches. I know that you have spent many days doing this and that some of you are wearied. . . . The cooks will make an effort. . . . Rice and tea will be served hot. . . . Officers at all levels will supervise the digging. . . . Recently, due to superficial supervision, in many places the trenches were built carelessly and our casualties increased. . . . The central task now is to build trenches for attack and encirclement at a rapid rate and according to norms. This will enhance our strategy of 'advancing cautiously and striking surely.' "

A French prisoner who observed the trench diggers recalled: "At night in total silence, one team lined up bamboo stakes over the emplacement of the trench while a second team started digging to outline the trench and a third team dug deeper to the soldiers' height." The alluvial soil of the plain was soft at the start of the monsoon season, and the work advanced quickly. The French took aerial photographs that showed the trenches spreading like cracks in a windowpane. Castries sent out patrols to fill them, but reported: "We fill the trenches and they are reopened the next night and when we try again our units are met with mortars and artillery fire."

Top sergeant Cadiou and a platoon of Algerians came under fire when they tried to approach the Viet trenches. Cadiou wrote his brother Pierre: "The Viets are two hundred meters from our barbed wire, hiding in trenches. They look at us. We look at them. Yesterday we sent out a patrol to chase them away. We had one dead and one wounded. They harassed us with mortar fire. On top of everything, we've run out of wine."

You Are Not to Give Orders to Anyone in My Battalion

At 8 A.M. on March 15, General Cogny summoned Lieutenant Colonel Marcel Bigeard to his Hanoi office. Bigeard, whose 6th BPC had been the first to jump over Dien Bien Phu in the November 20 CASTOR landing, had led his unit in continual operations since then.

"Bruno, you're jumping tomorrow over Dien Bien Phu," Cogny said.

"It's a mess. The Viets in a surprise attack took Béatrice and Gabrielle. We lost two battalions. Our artillery is useless. Our counterattacks are deficient."

"My battalion has been fighting without interruption for twenty months," Bigeard said. "I'd like to give them a rest."

"No, Bruno, your battalion is indispensable. But don't let yourself get dragged into poorly planned attacks."

In the former seminary where Bigeard's men were garrisoned, news of their mission spread. Two of the paras discussed the failure of the counterattack.

"You could see it coming," said Lebrun. "If a Legion battalion was wiped out in a single night, it's not the lousy BPVN who can change anything."

"The BPVN are as good as any other," said Gadel. "It's cadres are French paras."

Lieutenant Jacques Allaire, who commanded the heavy weapons company, assembled his people and told them: "Tomorrow we're jumping over Dien Bien Phu. The morale there has taken a serious blow. You've been there. You know it's not healthy. You're four months from the end of your time. All I can tell you is I know how we're going to get in, but I don't know how we're going to get out."

Allaire left behind a letter for his wife. It was, he reflected, the kind of letter that is preceded by a phone call from the Ministry of Veterans' Affairs. He told her that "a soldier never really dies." As an example, he said with gallows humor, according to the veterans' office, unless two eyewitnesses confirmed a combatant's death, his wife had to wait seven years before she could collect his pension.

On the morning of March 16, Bigeard gathered his company commanders. "I know what you're thinking," he said. "We've got a lot of kilometers under our legs. But it's not going well. The Thais holding Anne-Marie are abandoning their positions without a fight. The colonel commanding the artillery committed suicide."

Lieutenant Hervé Trapp, whose 2nd Company had lost men in the CASTOR landing, said: "We're tired. We'd like to get back to France. But what we want doesn't matter."

The battalion of 613 men (of whom 312 were Vietnamese) was embarked aboard forty-six Dakotas at the military airport. The C-47s dropped them at 3 P.M. to the south, to avoid the Vietminh antiaircraft guns. Looking down at the cratered base below, Lieutenant Allaire wondered, "What happened to the charming Thai villages surrounded by green hills we saw in November?" They were, nonetheless, fired at over Drop Zone Simone, between the meandering Nam Yum and the Isabelle CR, with its trenches and artillery nests. Fifteen men were hit by mortar fire and fifteen more were hurt in jump accidents. Lecoq, the medic, tore off a pant leg to bind a broken leg, telling the *para:* "You've got the lucky wound."

Bigeard had a torn calf muscle, and after landing he could barely walk. He borrowed a jeep from Colonel Lalande at Isabelle and paid a call on Castries, while his battalion marched to their new home on Eliane 4, to the east of the central camp. He found Castries at his underground post, as usual freshly shaved and crisply uniformed, but nervous and uncommunicative.

At Eliane 4, situated on a small treeless hill that sloped down to the Nam Yum, the paras dug their trenches and foxholes. One of them, Garanger, said: "This reminds me of the boy who asked his mother, 'Why did grandpa go all cold,' and she said, 'Shut up and dig.' " The other Elianes were held by Moroccans of the 1st Battalion of the 4th Moroccan Rifle Regiment (RTM). Bigeard was astonished to find that since his departure in December, nothing had been done to occupy the nearby crests where the Vietminh had placed 75mm guns and mortars. Perhaps Castries wanted to draw the Viets closer so that he could pound them with artillery. But the troops he saw were demoralized from the recent attacks, and Castries didn't look well. Bigeard's friend Botella, who commanded the battalion of Vietnamese paratroopers with whom he shared Eliane 4, told him: "It's a mess here, hard to change." Dr. Grauwin gave him a shot for his calf, but did it stink in that hospital.

Bigeard's arrival coincided with Giap's pause in the fighting, and things were relatively quiet, except for the occasional shelling. On March 17, one of Bigeard's company commanders, Lieutenant René Le Page, was summoned by Colonel Langlais, who ordered him to carry out a recon patrol with his unit.

Bigeard exploded. Who was Langlais to give orders to one of his officers? He went at once to central command to have it out with Langlais.
"Colonel," he told Langlais, "you are not to give orders to anyone in my
battalion. I command the battalion, I give the orders. General Cogny
warned me that nothing here is done properly and I intend to make some
changes."

Both men were stubborn and high-strung. Langlais realized he had
overstepped his authority, and although he too was angry, he decided to
defuse the situation. "You are from Lorraine," he said. "I am a Breton.
We're both hardheaded. So let's knock heads and see whose is the hardest." They both burst out laughing and from then on Langlais kept his
mitts off Bigeard's battalion.

In his bunker, Bigeard wondered what he could possibly accomplish.
The battalions defending the base were of uneven quality. Vital positions
were held by second-rate troops. There was little serious preparation, too
few mines in the barbed wire, no connecting trenches between strongpoints. The airstrip and the artillery were useless, and six 105s were damaged.

On March 17, three sturdy American 105s were dropped from C-119s,
on platforms held up by huge chutes. One of Bigeard's officers, Lieutenant
Le Boudec, wrote home a dismal estimate: "Our twelve battalions that look
like olives on the map are far from being an impregnable bastion. No one
seems to notice the mediocrity of these poorly built little posts that have allowed the Viets to push their trenches right under our noses."

Jean Péraud, a reporter-photographer for the army's press and information service, jumped with Bigeard's battalion on March 16. He went
over to Castries' command center, which was overflowing with wounded
officers waiting to be evacuated. He snapped a Legionnaire lieutenant who
had a bandage soaked in iodine around his head, which made the cover of
Paris Match. Not much was happening and he was bored; in fact, he
wished he were on the Riviera. He ambled over to the telegraph office behind the hospital and sent a prewritten telegram: AM IN GOOD HEALTH AND
SEND AFFECTIONATE REGARDS.

He decided to take a look at the Thai village on the banks of the Nam
Yum. Passing the brothel, he heard the shrill voices of the Vietnamese

whores, who now worked as nurses. Down the river a ways, he found the "Rats of Nam Yum," a camp of deserters—Algerians, Moroccans, Senegalese, Thais, and Vietnamese—who lived off the parachute drops, particularly the cigarette cartons, for which there was a thriving black market.

Back at Bigeard's encampment on Eliane 4, Péraud told Lieutenant Allaire about this community of squatters. Allaire took six Legionnaires to check it out, and they encountered a group of Algerians who threw a grenade at them. Allaire and his men shot them all and searched their shelter. They found cases filled with blood for the wounded. Allaire could only guess who the customers for it might be.

It Is Hardly Necessary to Insist on the Necessity of Stopping This Carnage

Dien Bien Phu was no longer the hedgehog imagined by Cogny, or the ground-air base that would bar Laos to the Viets imagined by Navarre. Dien Bien Phu was a battle of attrition, where Castries' troops were being trampled trench by trench and strongpoint by strongpoint. They no longer fought for victory but for survival. They knew that they were expendable. Whether they lived or died, what would it change? In France, demonstrators spat on the wounded being removed from trains on stretchers. In Geneva, diplomats had already reserved their rooms at the finest hotels.

On the Somme, the Tommies of World War I defiantly sang, "We're here because we're here because we're here." It was the same at Dien Bien Phu. But between March 16 and March 28, a different battle took place, the object of which was not to kill the enemy but to save lives. This was a gallant venture by the French air force to evacuate the wounded. As the air commander, General Henri Lauzin, later put it: "We'd seen airlifts before in Burma and Berlin, but none that landed while fired on by enemy cannon."

On March 16, Sergeant Coudert, one of the pilots who had flown Bigeard's battalion over its drop zone, was asked to pick up some of the wounded who were piling up by the hundreds in the hospital. Just as he was about to land, mortar shells began hitting the airstrip and he was forced to turn back.

The French decided to paint some C-47 Dakotas with red crosses, in the hope that the Vietminh would respect the Geneva Conventions. In Hanoi, General Cogny broadcast a radio message asking that French planes with Red Cross markings be allowed to land and take off without being fired upon.

On March 17, Dr. Grauwin was told to have forty wounded in trucks on the airstrip at a designated time when the planes would land. Three Dakotas with markings on their fuselages approached for a landing. When the planes came in, the Vietminh antiaircraft guns started firing. The pilot of the first Dakota managed to land, but the others turned back. As the wounded were boarded, the able-bodied pushed aside the orderlies carrying stretcher cases. "I saw fights break out between blind men and amputees," recalled the reporter-photographer Daniel Camus. Under fire, the pilot started taxiing down the runway. The door was still open and several wounded hung on the frame until the *convoyeuse*, Michelle Le Sueur, scraped them off and closed the door. "I couldn't take pictures," said Camus, "because I wanted to throw up." Despite the tumult, Le Sueur was able to board thirty-two wounded.

Captain Le Damany and the other doctors were the first to realize why the Vietminh had turned over eighty-six wounded. What seemed like a humanitarian gesture was in fact a tactic to further weaken the base: They released the French wounded and then prevented their evacuation. Caring for the casualties became an ever-growing and insoluble problem that swallowed up resources and distracted the men from their duties. The Vietminh wanted the base to overflow with wounded, throwing it further into chaos. And, after all, the Vietminh had not signed the Geneva Conventions.

In Hanoi, Professor Pierre Huard, dean of the Hanoi School of Medicine, had kept in touch with his Vietnamese students, many of whom joined the Vietminh. He appealed to them over the radio to allow the French to evacuate their wounded. In Paris, Foreign Minister Georges Bidault wired Red Cross headquarters in Geneva to protest "the machine-gunning of Red Cross planes where the wounded about to be evacuated have been killed on the airstrip." The Voice of Vietnam, the Vietminh station, responded that the French were using Red Cross planes to bring in military personnel. This was true, in a limited way. For instance, the replacement for Piroth, Colonel Guy Vaillant, was flown in. He was a forty-nine-year-old widower with nine children, in good physical shape, affable if somewhat ponderous.

On March 18, General Lauzin authorized his pilots to take "exceptional risks." The weather was fine, and a Dakota landed, but Vietminh mortars forced it to take off before the wounded could board. This was the last plane to attempt a landing in daylight.

There was no end to the plight of the wounded, for that afternoon a shell tore through the tent that served as a roof for the triage center. As the sunlight flashed through rips in the canvas, the walking wounded stumbled out, but thirty-five of the fifty men on stretchers and benches were killed. Grauwin found a scene of devastation that made him thank God the wounded could only die once: broken limbs on broken stretchers, mangled bodies, blood everywhere. All night they operated, with blood spurting in their faces, applying plaster to the lucky ones who still had legs. The next day a unit of Moroccan sappers replaced the tent with a roof of steel plating covered by criss-crossing logs and five feet of sandbags. They also removed the dead. The stench was overpowering. That evening, Castries issued an order that men should be buried where their units were stationed.

In Hanoi, Lieutenant Colonel Descaves, who was in charge of the Gia Lam military air base, studied the possibility of night flights. A C-47 Dakota with a crew of four and a *convoyeuse* could load thirteen men seated and six on stretchers in less than three minutes. Those seated would be boarded first. Approaching the base, the planes would keep radio silence and douse their lights, cutting their engines and descending to the airstrip where the ambulances would be waiting. Once the plane was loaded it would be turned around by hand so that it could take off toward the south to avoid flak.

The initial flight of eight Dakotas, scheduled for the night of March 19–20, had the element of surprise. Descaves piloted the lead plane, but only five of the eight landed; the others turned back due to flak. All five flew out their nineteen wounded for a total of ninety-five. The *convoyeuse* Michelle Le Sueur said: "I couldn't help thinking of the distress of those who remained on the ground."

The night flights became an airborne form of Russian roulette. Some nights they landed, some nights they turned back, some nights they were shot down. On March 24, a C-47 caught by flak crashed in a rice paddy, killing the crew. On March 26, Major Maurice Marinet landed, but his *convoyeuse*, Elisabeth Gras, was a little slow pulling the wounded on board, and he took off with only six. Another C-47 was shot down that day, and two more on the twenty-seventh, while a third landed and took out nineteen wounded. The *convoyeuse* Paule Bernard, a survivor of the Ravensbrück concentration camp, recalled that "they were shooting us like rabbits. If the ambulance got on the airstrip first, they fired at the ambulance."

Reporting the loss of four C-47s to General Lauzin, each with a crew of four and a *convoyeuse*, Colonel Nicot, the commander of air transport, observed: "It is hardly necessary to insist on the necessity of stopping this carnage." The last night flight took off at 3:45 A.M. on March 28. The pilot was Captain Maurice Blanchet and his *convoyeuse* was Geneviève de Galard. Blanchet landed in fog, looking for the dimmed gooseneck lights on the runway. He was a little off the correct axis, and the plane grazed some barbed wire, which pierced the oil tank. As the wounded were being loaded, Blanchet's mechanic told him: "The oil pressure gauge reads zero. We can't take off." The wounded had to be removed. The stretcher cases were placed in a drainage ditch. Geneviève de Galard, marooned in Dien Bien Phu, asked to serve as a nurse. Later in the morning, when the fog had lifted, the stranded Dakota was destroyed by shell fire.

The airlift in the second half of March removed a total of 324 wounded, although more than 500 remained on the base. About 100 of those evacuated were taken out by helicopter, but the chopper flights stopped on March 23, when one that had landed on Isabelle lingered too long and was destroyed on the ground. An irate Castries told Cogny on March 24: "I feel great admiration for the crew of the transport planes, but the helicopter pilots are gutless. . . . Today not a single one came."

While Dakotas were rescuing the wounded, the Flying Boxcars flown by Franco-American crews made two three-hour round-trips a day, arriving over the base at 10 A.M. and 3 P.M. to drop tons of supplies. Due to flak, the drop altitude was increased to 6,500 feet, which meant that a percentage of the cargo fell outside the perimeter and ended up supplying the Vietminh. Still, the garrison collected an average of 126 tons a day, although the daily quota was 30 tons of food and 170 tons of ammunition.

In the second half of March, American crews of the Civil Air Transport made eighty-seven drops. Nearly every C-119 returned to its base pocked with 37mm antiaircraft fire. Flak peppered the fuselage and both engine nacelles of Hugh H. Hicks's C-119, but he completed his drop and made it back to the Cat Bi base in Haiphong, despite violent vibrations and loss of aileron control. Thomas C. Sailor also completed his round-trip with a damaged tail boom and rudder.

We Firmly Believe in Your Artificial Rain Project

By mid-March, Navarre was amazed that strongpoints were falling so fast and that the artillery was not doing its job. He was disappointed with the Hanoi command under General Cogny, with their "Come and get us!" posturing, and with Piroth's boasting. He knew he would get no more reinforcements from France. And yet he still saw Dien Bien Phu as *a* battle and not *the* battle. The grim situation there did not stop him from launching the second phase of Operation ATLANTE in central Annam, which involved thirty-three battalions. He did not realize that Giap had committed the major part of his army to what he considered the decisive battle. Navarre's principal fault was that he listened only to himself. He and Cogny had developed a mutual aversion to each other. When Navarre was in Hanoi, they rarely spoke, and communicated by memo. As for Castries, thought Navarre, he seemed to be in a daze, unable to mount a counterattack.

Mulling over the situation, Navarre decided that since he could not increase the size of his army, he would try to modify the weather. He had heard that there were ways to disperse substances on clouds that increased precipitation. By hastening the monsoons due in full force in early May, he could turn the Vietminh supply routes from China into a quagmire.

On March 14, he summoned from Paris Robert Genty, an air force colonel and meteorologist. Genty explained that it might be possible to provoke abundant rainfall by seeding the clouds with silver iodide, dropped by parachute in baskets of charcoal. Navarre wanted this done right away, but Genty told him he had to return to Paris for his equipment. He said, "Even if I went to every bistro in Hanoi and drank gallons of beer to fill my bladder, and even if I pissed out the door of the plane, I wouldn't have enough urine to start the rain," as a way of emphasizing his need to go back to Paris.

Genty returned to Hanoi in April and was told by Pierre Bodet, the air force general who was Navarre's deputy, "We firmly believe in your artificial rain project." But the high-altitude plane with the trap door to drop what Genty called his "bombs of carbolic snow" was not ready. Genty wondered why, if Navarre was so eager to try his method, they couldn't put a plane at his disposal sooner. The military bureaucracy in Hanoi was impenetrable. Finally, the preparations were made for some test flights, and Genty dropped his baskets over fat cumulus clouds and saw them darken. On one occasion, he provoked a violent hailstorm that shook the planes flying under it. In mid-April, he saw Navarre again and explained that the charcoal system worked and that a program for producing artificial rain was feasible, but that he had to return to Paris to prepare further tests. For it seemed that although his baskets had some effect on the clouds, the baskets were pushed by the wind outside the area where the precipitation was desired. From Saigon, an irate Navarre wired Hanoi on April 16: "I absolutely cannot understand why Colonel Genty wants further delays. . . . This method, if it succeeds, can have a decisive effect on the outcome of Dien Bien Phu. If it is not done by the end of April it will lose its interest. This affair must be pursued with vigor." After Genty again returned to Paris, however, the military in Indochina were absorbed in more urgent matters. Giap later admitted that the heavy rains of the monsoon season badly disrupted his supply lines. Already at the end of April there were stretches where the trucks were up to their bumpers in mud.

They Hope That the Vietminh Will Attack. As for Me, I Don't Share That Hope.

In Washington, in early March, optimism still reigned. Harold Stassen, back from a trip to Asia as director of the Foreign Operations Administration, told the National Security Council that he had found the French "hoping for a major enemy attack because they were so confident they could crush it." Senator Stuart Symington, a Democrat from Missouri and a member of the Armed Services Committee, saw Defense Minister René Pleven in Paris and asked him about the possible use of carrier-based planes armed with tactical nuclear weapons. Pleven replied that "he would prefer to have Secretary Dulles say at Geneva that Chinese planes flying over Indochina would be met by the U.S. Air Force." When Symington returned to the topic of nuclear weapons, Pleven stressed the lack of suitable targets.

After the attacks of March 13, however, the mood changed. At a meeting of the National Security Council on March 18, President Eisenhower remarked that "it was difficult to understand General Navarre's earlier statement hoping that he would be attacked . . . since he was sure of defeating them." Secretary of State Dulles said the Vietminh had attacked in preparation for a strong showing at the Geneva Conference, which was due to open in May. "The pessimistic French reports from Saigon might be designed," he said, "as a buildup to exaggerate the extent of their final victory." Dulles had a mental habit of doubting whatever did not fit in with his long-range strategic plans. The United States was now paying for 80 percent of the war and Dulles feared that the French would prop up their military position in order to negotiate their way out at Geneva.

A study was made by the U.S. Army and Air Force on the feasibility of using atomic weapons in Indochina. The army's Office of Psychological Warfare warned that even if they were effective there would be adverse effects on the reputation of the United States and on existing alliances. Intelligence officers in both services were also opposed to their use, prompting the army chief of staff, Matthew B. Ridgway, and one of his assistants, General James M. Gavin, to order a second study. The planners concluded that any such intervention would eventually lead to the commitment of ground troops and perhaps to Chinese retaliation.

In Paris, the mid-March events had thrown the Laniel government into a panic. If Dien Bien Phu fell, so would the government, and the antiwar left would come to power, which would mean a diplomatic tragedy at Geneva. Something had to be done at once. It was decided to send the French army chief of staff, General Paul Ely, to Washington, in response to an invitation from Admiral Radford. Ely was esteemed by the politicians, whom he rarely contradicted, as a diplomat among warriors. Short but erect, he was minus a right hand, courtesy of World War II, and his wife, who had been with him in the Resistance, had spent years in a wheelchair, courtesy of Buchenwald.

Named chief of staff in October 1953, at the age of fifty-three, Ely had found a hopeless mess in the way the various ministries ran the war, which did much to explain why he felt the French could not win. There was a labyrinthine distribution of responsibility, which seemed designed to obstruct decision-making. The minister of defense had no control over military operations in the only theater where the French were fighting. The army chief of staff was denied direct liaison with the commander in Indochina. A number of high-ranking officials called Indochina "the dirty war," which must be ended at any price so it would stop draining the defense of Europe. Ely tried to remedy the absurdities in the chain of command. It took him months to form a committee for war, which was responsible for its conduct. The committee's first meeting was held on March 11, 1954, two days before Giap first attacked. It came too late to prevent the deterioration at Dien Bien Phu. At least Ely could now communicate with Navarre via a special code. He also had to determine the goals in this distant war that did not directly threaten the security of France. It was not the kind of war where one side surrendered to the other.

Finally, there was an endless struggle to obtain the manpower Navarre needed, with interminable discussions regarding the length of deployment, and how to make up losses in combat. Navarre complained that commitments from Paris were not kept. Ely noticed a willful sluggishness to respond on the part of some government services. It was part of the tug-of-war between the needs of Europe and those of Indochina.

It was not, however, to Ely's credit that too often he sided with the politicians rather than with Navarre, even though he realized, as he put it, that calm reigned on the Elbe while in Indochina men were dying. When Navarre, in November 1953, asked for two hundred officers and a thousand noncoms to make up losses, Ely turned him down. To send those men, Ely said, would mean dissolving sixteen battalions and "sacrificing our other obligations, including the defense of Europe." The real man-power problem was that no conscripts could be sent to Indochina, since by law they could only serve in France. And so Navarre got nothing. It was like turning off the hydrants while fighting a fire.

Ely went to Indochina with Pleven from February 7 to 28, 1954, flying via Beirut and Karachi and arriving in Saigon on February 9. Navarre gave them the impression of calm decisiveness and outlined his strategy of continuing several operations at the same time. Ely and Pleven toured the sectors from the Red River Delta to Laos. They spent several hours at Dien Bien Phu, where all the men they spoke to, from private to colonel, ex-pressed the wish that the enemy would attack. Their only fear was that the Vietminh would back down. They showed off their strongpoints with pride, and it did indeed seem that they could withstand heavy shelling.

In the plane taking them back to Hanoi, Pleven expressed his ad-miration for the troops, then added: "They hope that the Vietminh will attack. . . . As for me, I do not share their hope." Ely replied: "Nor do I." Of course, publicly they expressed their full confidence in the garrison.

On March 11, Pleven reported to the Committee for National Defense that France had air superiority but the Vietminh had "inexhaustible" Chi-nese aid. The current military effort, he said, had taxed French troops to their limit. The Geneva Conference would provide an honorable way out. The United States, however, seemed to be counting on a quick victory.

Ely was given the mission of explaining the French quandary in Wash-ington. Without additional ground and air resources, there could be no military solution. He was also told to ask for U.S. retaliation should the Chinese conduct an air strike over Indochina. The Laniel government was committed to negotiation, which required a strong military posture at Geneva. Their inspiration for a negotiated solution was the cease-fire signed in Panmunjom on July 23, 1953. Dulles had tried to talk Foreign Minister Bidault out of negotiating later that summer, explaining that the U.S. obtained a cease-fire in Korea only because the enemy knew that a nuclear strike on Manchuria had not been ruled out. France, he said, must only negotiate from strength.

Ely also believed that, thanks to the extent of Chinese aid, time was no longer on the French side, and the best hope was to create military conditions for a political solution. By the time he left for Washington on March 19, events had cast a shadow on his mission. The telegrams from Saigon were pessimistic. Supply planes could no longer land on the airstrip and Navarre urgently needed cargo parachutes.

Ely spoke little English and Admiral Radford, his host, spoke only kitchen French. Ely took with him Colonel Raymond Brohon, who had attended the British staff college and spent four years at the Pentagon on the French delegation. He was an officer of considerable distinction who spoke fluent English.

On the plane to Washington, Ely studied his orders from the Committee for National Defense, which consisted of the highest civilian and military leaders in the government.

"Due to the very grave fall of Béatrice and Gabrielle," he was told, "which makes it possible for the Vietminh to capture all of Dien Bien Phu, it has become clear that the only solution is to continue defending Dien Bien Phu and particularly the central sector." In order to accomplish this, the French needed additional equipment, and Ely had been supplied with a shopping list.

Prior to his departure, he had received a cable from Navarre, telling him that were Dien Bien Phu to fall while he was in Washington, he should explain that this was a sideshow to lure Vietminh troops away from the Delta. He should also point out that Vietminh losses were much higher than French losses. Navarre concluded: "However, this positive attitude is at variance with public and official positions in France, part of which will find the reversal at Dien Bien Phu an argument for peace at any price in Indochina."

Give Him Everything He Asks For

Ely landed at New York's Idlewild Airport at 6:30 A.M. on Saturday, March 20, aboard TWA flight 931. The transatlantic voyage in those propeller-driven days took fourteen hours. Radford was waiting on the tarmac with his personal C-47 to shuttle Ely to Washington. Ely's week of high-level meetings was intended by his American hosts as a getting-to-know-you-and-your-policy occasion, and by Ely primarily as a shopping spree for specific military items. As matters developed, however, his visit became a catalyst for solidifying the two factions among highly placed administration figures, both civilian and military, that could be loosely described as interventionist and anti-interventionist. Aggravating the turmoil Ely's trip created were an accumulation of misunderstandings, false hopes, and translation problems. The Ely visit came to resemble the game of Telephone, where one player whispers something into the ear of a second, who whispers it to a third, and at the end of the line the message is garbled.

That Saturday evening, Radford had scheduled a stag dinner at his home. His guests were Vice President Richard Nixon, CIA chief Allen Dulles, Army Chief of Staff Matthew Ridgway, and Douglas MacArthur II, sitting in for John Foster Dulles. Ely recalled that the dinner had "a character of intimate cordiality." The high station of the guests showed him the importance the United States attached to his visit.

After dinner, when Nixon asked if the French were tired of the war, Ely replied that they were "determined not to capitulate to the Communists." But when he spoke of the situation at Dien Bien Phu, he found his audience "visibly pessimistic. They feared that the base would fall within days, if not hours."

Ely said the French wanted reassurances in case the Chinese air force intervened, since the planes provided by the United States were no match for the Chinese jets. He was told that something would be done, on the ground or in the air. But Radford noted that there was no intelligence indicating any Chinese air threat. Navarre, however, had told Ely that Chinese fighters had been moved closer to the border.

Ely found the time to explain to Radford the critical necessity of replacing cargo parachutes that could be used only once. "Raddy" said he would see to it that very night, and soon fifty thousand chutes were on their way from the Philippines. Radford had been a navy flier and commanded a carrier group in the Pacific. He was hard-charging and quick to act, an "Asia Firster" in the wake of MacArthur.

On Sunday, March 21, Ely relaxed. He was surprised to see that everywhere he went, he had a CIA escort. This had started in the car that took him from the Washington airport to his hotel, when an agent in civilian clothes slipped into the front seat, next to the driver, where Brohon the interpreter was supposed to sit. Even Radford, sitting next to Ely in the back-seat, was surprised. Brohon would have been more useful, for the French general and the American admiral had trouble communicating. At Ely's hotel, his guards occupied the adjacent room, and one of them stood in front of his door. On Sunday morning, he was asked which religious service he would like to attend. Ely felt sure the guard would have been offended had he demonstrated a lack of interest in performing his religious duties, and together they went to mass in a chapel next to the hotel.

While Ely was at mass, there was a high-level meeting at the White House at 12:16 P.M. to discuss the concept of "united action"—bringing in other allies besides France to forge security in Southeast Asia. The plan would be presented to Ely to see how the French would take it. No minutes were kept, but the meeting included Radford, Allen Dulles, and Douglas MacArthur II.

At 8 A.M. on March 22, Radford and John Foster Dulles spoke to a group of Republican congressional leaders who customarily met with the president for a legislative conference on Monday at nine. Dulles was carefully laying the foundation for his united action policy. The only mention of this meeting was in the diary of Eisenhower's press secretary, James C. Hagerty: "A restricted number of unnamed leaders." Later that day, however, Dulles spoke on the phone with three Republican legislators who served on their respective foreign policy committees: Senators Alexander Wiley of Wisconsin and H. Alexander Smith of New Jersey, and Congressman John M. Vorhys of Ohio. He asked all three to attend a further meeting that day at 5 P.M., "to discuss something discussed this morning at the White House regarding Indochina."

In his memoirs, Radford recalled that "with encouragement from the President, Mr. Dulles reviewed with congressional leaders the situation in Indochina and possible American actions. He told them the administration was considering a public call for united (free world) action and would appreciate their endorsement." The Republican leaders responded favorably, giving Dulles the support he needed to push the policy along. It was designed to avoid unilateral U.S. involvement in Indochina by bringing in the British, as well as Asian allies such as the Philippines and Thailand. Their participation would remove the stigma of colonialism from any military action in which the United States was involved, and act as a deterrent to the Communists—all with an eye on Geneva, in the hope of a reasonable settlement.

At 10:30 that Monday morning, Radford accompanied Ely to the White House for half an hour with the president. This was where the first misunderstanding took place. Eisenhower gave Ely the impression that he attached great importance, bordering on anxiety, to Dien Bien Phu, though Ike was only showing the empathy of one battle-tested veteran for another. Ely understood that Eisenhower was telling Radford "to furnish us with whatever we needed to save the entrenched camp without setting limits." Radford, however, understood that the words Ike used, "Give him everything he asked for," meant that the Defense Department should fill Ely's request to the extent it was able. At the photo opportunity, Eisenhower was overheard telling Ely, again soldier to soldier, that they had won World War II and would win again.

The United States Seeks to Control and Operate Everything of Importance

Between scheduled meetings, Ely and Radford conferred, with Brohon as interpreter. That afternoon Ely produced his shopping list. The French wanted 25 B-26 bombers, 14 C-47 transport planes, 20 helicopters, 20 landing craft, 550 flak vests, artillery shells, aviation fuel, and pierced steel plating for airstrips. Radford was able to promise everything except the C-47s and the helicopters. He felt, however, that Ely wanted "practically unlimited assistance," but was unwilling to make any concessions himself.

In their talks, which were conducted, he said, "in a spirit of confident cooperation," Ely expounded on the general conduct of the war. Was a military solution possible, he asked, such as had been obtained against Germany in 1918, and against Japan in 1945, and such as had been vainly sought against the Chinese in Korea? Like Korea, Indochina had a border with China. But even in Korea there had been a more or less classic war with a front, while Indochina was a new kind of war where a military victory did nothing to stop the political progress of the enemy. Whatever ground was gained by the French made them lose the hearts and minds of the population, while Vietnamese troops were portrayed by the Vietminh as collaborators. Even if a military victory could be achieved, Ely told Radford, it would not be until 1956, and it would require important means that only a coalition could furnish. It would also risk bringing in Chinese troops, which meant a war without end. The French policy was to improve their military position while urgently seeking a political solution in Geneva.

Getting down to specifics, Ely said that success at Dien Bien Phu had a fifty-fifty chance. It would not be possible to send troops overland to relieve the garrison. But even if the battle was lost, it would be a greater loss to the Vietminh due to their high number of casualties.

Franco-American relations were discussed "with great frankness," according to Ely. When Radford proposed U.S. trainers for the Vietnamese army, Ely asked what defects the Americans saw in the French training. Radford said there were too few recruits and that the French were not preparing them for the kind of war to be fought. Ely responded that if the Americans took a part in the training, Navarre's authority would suffer, since it would seem that the Americans were replacing the French.

Ely had a litany of complaints as long as his shopping list. Among them were:

- The United States seeks to control and operate everything of importance.
- The number of U.S. personnel in Indochina indicated an invading nature. (The United States at that point had 355 "technicians" in Indochina.)
- The French think McCarthyism is prevalent in the United States and is akin to Hitlerism.
- Many Americans appear to favor Germany over France.
- U.S. bureaucracy is wasteful, irritating, and paper-heavy.

Radford patiently absorbed the body blows and landed a few of his own: French behavior made Americans impatient. Americans were dynamic, while the French were slow, reticent, and indecisive. Falling back on French prestige in the case of trainers made Radford wonder how much prestige would be left if they lost the war.

President Eisenhower's Position Might Be a Little Different from That of the Secretary of State

On the morning of Tuesday, March 23, Secretary of State Dulles gave a radio and press conference at which he played down the importance of Dien Bien Phu, describing it as only an "outpost," where "a very small percentage of the French Union forces are engaged." He added: "There have been no military reverses as far as we can see, and none are in prospect." The unspoken subtext of Dulles's remarks was that military reversals would incite the French to make a deal at Geneva, upsetting his plans for "united action" in Southeast Asia, and thus should not be given credence.

Dulles's press conference was followed by lunch with Radford and Ely. The secretary of state and the French general were at cross-purposes. "I told Dulles," Ely recalled, "that a solution of the Indochina war was not possible without a political solution. Dulles did not give a direct reply." Ely felt that at the Berlin Conference, Dulles had been maneuvered into allowing Chinese participation at the Geneva Conference. It still rankled, which was why he seemed reticent.

"This was the heart of the problem," Ely recalled. "The American government was preparing for the Geneva Conference. Despite our common outlook, certain divergences began to appear. . . . France wanted to begin negotiating in an international setting, while pursuing the war vigorously if she failed. The American thesis was that negotiations should not be pursued unless there was a favorable military position."

Radford then raised one of the questions uppermost in Ely's mind, asking what the United States would do if the Chinese air force intervened in Indochina. Dulles replied that "if the United States sent its flag and its own military establishments, land, sea, or air, into the Indochina war, the prestige of the United States would be engaged and we would want to have a success. We could not afford to engage the prestige of the United States and suffer a defeat which could have repercussions." As for Chinese intervention, the U.S. reaction needed further study.

Ely, however, understood Dulles to say that "the free world would intervene in Indochina rather than let the situation deteriorate there through Chinese aid to the Vietminh." Ely saw this as an "allusion to the political alliance covering all of Southeast Asia that the Secretary of State already foresaw."

An added source of friction was Dulles's insistence that U.S. participation in the war "might involve a greater degree of partnership than had prevailed up to the present time, notably in relation to the independence of the Associated States and the training of indigenous forces." Ely later saw this as a demand for "getting rid of the last vestiges of colonialism," which he derided as the expression of "America's rather systematic and unnuanced anti-colonialism."

A dejected Ely, having obtained nothing from Dulles, left the lunch feeling that their meeting, "without becoming stormy or agitated, did not go without a few inevitable hitches. . . . Admiral Radford, sensing my malaise, conveyed the impression that President Eisenhower's position might be a little different than that of the Secretary of State." In his attempt to soothe Ely, Radford seeded his mind with another illusion.

Why Back a War with No Chance of Winning?

On the afternoon of March 23, Ely and Radford saw Allen Dulles and discussed guerrilla warfare and the possibility of the CIA taking over the funding of partisans behind Vietminh lines. Ely was noncommittal. Again, French prestige was at stake. From CIA headquarters in Langley, Virginia, they proceeded to the Tank, the famed conference room of the Joint Chiefs of Staff in the E Ring of the Pentagon. The chiefs were cordial but stern, going over Ely's equipment requests like accountants, questioning his need for every item on the list. They complained that the United States was consulted only when Navarre needed more planes or guns. Radford returned to the issue of using U.S. trainers for the Vietnamese army. Ely, trying to contain his anger, asked the chiefs if they wanted to take over the war. They replied that they had no intention of getting bogged down in Indochina, they merely wanted France to win, which was why Ely was getting everything he asked for (except the C-47s and helicopters). And they wanted a dynamic Vietnamese army that could take over the fighting within two years. More likely two centuries, Ely fumed, for France had reached the limit of its capacities, and its people were fed up with the war.

Once Ely had bid them good-bye, the Joint Chiefs continued the discussion among themselves. The curmudgeonly army chief of staff, Matthew B. Ridgway, said Indochina was a waste of the Defense Department's budget, which was already stripped down. Why back a war that was being fought halfheartedly, with no chance of winning? He rejected U.S. intervention of any kind, under any conditions. Following Radford's plan of air strikes, he said, would repeat the serious error of the first months of the Korean War. Battles were won by foot soldiers, and U.S. ground forces had been cut by 10 percent, despite an increase of worldwide commitments. He did not want his army dragged off to Indochina.

Following Ely's appearance and the discussion among the Joint Chiefs, Radford sent Eisenhower a memo to buttress his position. He said that "General Ely made no significant concessions . . . which would improve the situation in Indochina. . . . He submitted a request in writing as to what action the U.S. should take if aircraft based in China intervened in Indochina. No commitment was made. The matter is being referred to the Secretary of State. . . . I am gravely fearful that the measures being taken by the French will prove to be inadequate and initiated too late to prevent a progressive deterioration of the situation. The consequences can well lead to the loss of all of Southeast Asia to Communist domination. If this is to be avoided, I consider that the U.S. must be prepared to act promptly and in force possibly to a frantic and belated request by the French for U.S. intervention." Radford was parting ways with the Dulles advocacy of united action, instead proposing unilateral intervention.

France Is Creating a Vacuum in the World

At 8 A.M. on Wednesday, March 24, the secretary of state saw the president to press his case on Indochina in the light of Ely's visit. He told Eisenhower that the United States must not give any guarantees to the French. According to Dulles's memo of the conversation, "the President said that he agreed basically that we should not get involved in fighting in Indochina unless there were the political preconditions necessary for a successful outcome. He did not, however, wholly exclude the possibility of a single strike, if it were almost certain this would produce decisive results." Ike seemed to be trying to reconcile the diverging views of Dulles and Radford.

Dulles responded by proposing an alternative strategy of harassing tactics from Formosa and along the Chinese seacoast "which would be more readily within our natural facilities than actually fighting in Indochina." He added that he planned to address the issue in his March 29 speech, since he saw a "developing psychology in favor of 'appeasement' of Communist China, and something strong needed to be said to check it."

The president fully agreed, he added, "citing the misconduct of the Chinese Communists, their seizure and retention of American prisoners, etc." Dulles described the speech as "a paraphrase of the Monroe address," and Eisenhower gave his blessing to this extension of a doctrine previously limited to North and South America.

The president had in fact already asked the chief of naval operations, Admiral Robert Carney, to put the Pacific-based First Fleet on alert. Its commander, Vice Admiral William Phillips, was told on March 18 to be ready to defend Dien Bien Phu, with the caveat that no plan to intervene had been approved. The attack carrier strike group left Subic Bay on March 22 on a routine training mission in the waters off northern Vietnam. The Pacific Fleet commander, Admiral Felix Stump, was told to make the necessary preparations with General Navarre's staff for a naval-aerial intervention.

After his 8 A.M. meeting at the White House, Dulles went back to his office at the State Department, where he took a call from Radford, following up on the meeting with Ely. A transcript of the call was drafted by Dulles's secretary, who listened in: "The Secretary said we must do some thinking on the premise that France is creating a vacuum wherever she is. How can we fill that vacuum? One fellow [the Communists] is [already] trying."

Radford argued that the immediate crisis was Dien Bien Phu. If it fell, the French might walk out of Indochina, which they could do in two to three weeks, leaving a vacuum where "we look bad here to our own people." Radford might be obliged to give embarrassing testimony at a congressional hearing. "We have to do something to avoid the accusation we would not help them in their hour of need," Radford said.

"We must stop pleading," Dulles persisted, "and we must have a policy of our own even if France falls down. We could lose Europe, Asia and Africa all at once if we don't watch out." Dulles had reached a point of exasperation after putting up with French delays on Indochina and the European Defense Community. He wanted the United States to take the initiative.

At 10:30 that morning of March 24, a presidential news conference was scheduled in the Old Executive Office Building. An hour beforehand, James C. Hagerty called Dulles for guidance on handling the press. Dulles told him that "Ely has been trying to get us to say we would put planes in [if the Chinese air force intervened] but we have not made any such agreement."

Before two hundred reporters, Eisenhower was asked for his "soldier's appreciation of Dien Bien Phu." "Some of you were unquestionably at Anzio," he said, "and there the Allied forces were in an almost impossible position. They were lying on the plain, and the enemy had all of the observation positions to place all the artillery where they wanted to, and it is a terrible thing on morale, [but] as I see it, there is no reason for good troops to despair of coming out of things all right." The Allies had fought their way off the Anzio beachhead after a costly four-month battle, and Ike, who had a low opinion of the Dien Bien Phu position, was trying to put a hopeful spin on it.

Let's Forget About Indochina for a While

Ely was planning to leave on Thursday, March 25, but Radford prevailed on him to remain an extra day, since the president scheduled his National Security Council meetings on Thursday mornings at 10:30. This particular meeting, enlarged to include the full Joint Chiefs of Staff and the service secretaries, would discuss options on Indochina, of obvious interest to Ely.

Eisenhower kicked off the meeting at his most sardonic. Why, he asked, had the French not been able to close the one road leading from Laos to Dien Bien Phu, to prevent the 308th Division from taking part in the March 13 attack? If the Communists were preventing French forces from moving, except by air, it was no wonder they were popular with the Vietnamese.

Secretary of Defense Charles Wilson proposed that the United States "forget about Indochina for a while," and concentrate on a Pacific pact, echoing the line that Dulles was pursuing.

"The President expressed great doubt about the feasibility of such a proposal," according to the minutes of the meeting, "since he believed that the collapse of Indochina would produce a chain reaction which would result in the fall of all of Southeast Asia to the Communists." This was exactly what Radford had argued in his March 24 memo to Ike.

However, before the United States intervened, Eisenhower said, a number of conditions should be met. One was a request for assistance from the Associated States. He thought the United Nations might come aboard "if Vietnam [rather than France] called for assistance and particularly cited Chinese Communist aid to the rebels." He did not see "how the United States or other free world nations could go full-out in support of the Associated States without U.N. approval and assistance." In his mention of free world nations he was invoking the Dulles plan of "united action."

Doubts were raised as to whether the United Nations would be willing to intervene. Dulles did not want to bring a charge of aggression against Indochina before the United Nations, given the opposition of Russia and Third World nations.

Finally, Ike added that "the Congress would have to be in on any move by the United States to intervene in Indochina. It was simply academic to imagine otherwise."

At the risk of being academic, Dulles argued that "a lot more work needed to be done by the NSC on the problem before we were ready to take it up with Congress."

Playing for time, Dulles observed that the attorney general "was preparing an opinion with respect to the prerogatives of the President and Congress in the matter of using U.S. military to counter aggression." In addition, he said, "the fighting season in Indochina would end soon," and, he believed, "would end without a clear military decision." Thus, there would be enough time to secure U.N. backing. But the diminished role of France as a world power should also be considered: "We are witnessing the collapse or evaporation of France as a great power in most areas of the world. The great question was who should fill the void left by the collapse of French power, particularly in the colonial areas. Would it be the Communists, or must it be the United States?"

The Justice Department memorandum on war powers said that Congress and the president, acting together, could send armed forces outside the United States without resorting to a declaration of war. Under this "state of emergency," the president could exercise full powers for the duration of the conflict. This advice was sent to Dulles in late March or early April, but he did not discuss it with the president until April 19. Dulles thought it was "unduly legalistic," and that "the heart of the matter was that the government of the United States must have the power of self-preservation. If Congress was in session . . . concurrent action would be the preferred procedure. If the danger was great and imminent and Congress was unable to act quickly enough to avert the danger, then the President would have to act alone."

At the March 25 NSC meeting, conflicting views were expressed without being sorted out, so that the result was to put off any decision on Indochina until later. It was agreed that the NSC's Planning Board would make recommendations prior to the Geneva Conference on "the extent to which . . . the United States would be willing to commit its resources in support of the Associated States in the effort to prevent the loss of Indochina to the Communists, in concert with the French or in concert with others, or, if necessary, unilaterally." No option had been ruled out.

Eisenhower closed the meeting with a proposal that would be the genesis of the plan that was eventually adopted. A mutual defense pact had been signed in 1952 among the United States, Australia, and New Zealand. This pact could be extended to other nations, who could agree to intervene in Indochina, either under the auspices of the United Nations or through treaties with Vietnam.

"This latter offered the United States a good chance," Ike said, "since we could in all probability get the necessary two-thirds majority vote in

the Senate on such a treaty. There was the added advantage that this procedure avoided solely Occidental assistance to Vietnam." Of one thing at
least the president was "absolutely certain: The United States would not go
into Indochina unless the Vietnamese welcomed our intervention."

Ely Remembered Only What Was Favorable to Him

March 25 was Ely's last full day in Washington, and at some point after the
National Security Council meeting, Radford brought his fellow interventionist Vice President Richard Nixon to see the French general, according
to the interpreter, Colonel Brohon. It was the colonel who proposed that
the United States bomb Vietminh depots in the Tuan Giao area. Nixon
liked the idea, and Radford later asked the Pacific Command to make an
on-site study. This was the origin of the plan that Navarre called VAUTOUR
(vulture) when it was sent to him. He liked to give bird names to operations, as in MOUETTE (seagull).

Radford and Ely held their last tête-à-tête, which later turned into a
battle of the memoirs regarding what had been said. Ely recalled that "at a
time when Dien Bien Phu might be falling into the hands of the Vietminh,
we were naturally given, Admiral Radford and myself, to examining how
far American aid would go to avoid a defeat without precipitating an expansion of the war. . . . The danger that weighed on Dien Bien Phu came
from an unexpected increase in Vietminh artillery and anti-aircraft.
Heavy bombers could be used to counter this Chinese aid without seeming
to be a provocation. There was no question of attacking China, but only
loosening the noose around Dien Bien Phu."

Radford recalled in his memoirs that when Ely asked him how far
American aid would go to avert a disaster, he replied that "if the French requested such aid and our government granted it, as many as 350 aircraft
operating from carriers could be brought into action within two days," as
part of Operation VAUTOUR, which they had already discussed. Radford believed the air strike could be carried out without provoking the Chinese,
given their massive aid.

"This was a proposition whose importance could not escape me," Ely
recalled.

Four-engine B-29s from Clark Air Base in the Philippines, supported by naval jets from the First Fleet in northern Vietnamese waters, would conduct one or more night raids, carpet bombing to disrupt and destroy enemy positions around Dien Bien Phu. But Radford said he insisted that "the matter should be explored on a higher level in order to be ready."

Ely, in his memoirs, said that "at the time of my departure, no decision had been made. Neither Admiral Radford nor I had the necessary authority. It was agreed between us that if the French government made an official request for American intervention, Admiral Radford would strongly recommend it. It was obvious to me that he thought he had the support of President Eisenhower, and he assured me that our request would be quickly examined and acted upon by the American authorities."

This was where their recollections diverged. Radford, having read Ely's published memoir, commented in his own that Ely had attached too much importance to his brief get-together with Eisenhower, which was more of a social call than a serious discussion, while blanking out the cautionary remarks he had heard from Secretary of State Dulles. Ely did not seem to realize that the administration was divided between Radford and Nixon, the ardent interventionists, and Eisenhower and Dulles, who wanted the French to be more cooperative in exchange for U.S. help.

Ely interpreted Radford's offer as having the president's support, the admiral said, "even though I was very careful to explain that . . . action on the plans by U.S. forces could be instituted only on orders from the President, following consultation with Congress. I emphasized the time lag . . . to impress upon Ely that the French should not and could not expect quick action on emergency requests. But in spite of my precautions to be explicitly frank, he left with serious misunderstandings."

Nor had Ely achieved his principal goal, the promise of U.S. intervention in case of a Chinese air strike. But in his memoir, Ely wrote that he left with the impression that the United States would respond to a Chinese air attack. "No doubt could exist," he wrote, "of the intent of the United States to carry out the measures provided for if and when the time came." It was his understanding that "the appearance of any unidentified aircraft in the sky over Indochina should have automatically triggered the American response." Radford was convinced that Ely "remembered only the favorable (to him) things."

Radford thought it was ironic that Ely on his departure told him he was confident the United States would come through with an air strike but that "Paris was so fearful of provoking the Chinese that he would not hazard a guess as to whether his government would ask for our help to save Dien Bien Phu."

On this last point both men agreed, for Ely wrote, "Upon leaving Admiral Radford I had the feeling that he thought I would have more trouble getting my government to agree than he would. . . . I believed that Admiral Radford would finally get the approval of the American government. I remembered the speed and the firmness with which President Truman had decided to intervene in Korea . . . of course the problems are not the same, since there was no United States commitment directly involved in Indochina as there had been in Korea. But the fact remained that one decision was just as far-reaching as the other, with infinitely smaller risks." Radford thought the "smaller risks" part was a curious afterthought.

It should be said as a mitigating factor for both Ely and Radford that the French general knew very little about the process of presidential decision-making: how an idea germinated, gestated, was bounced back and forth in meetings, then was taken public for a flight test; how Eisenhower used his cabinet as a sounding board, how he weighed the conflicting opinions of his counselors, and how his offhand remarks might be trial balloons.

But all Ely saw was that the president greeted him effusively and that Dulles and Radford had different agendas. He could not have known that Eisenhower, like Dulles, seemed willing to take a chance on the rainy season. According to James Hagerty's diary for March 28, he told the cabinet: "You know, in rainy weather, a pack train will eat up all its food in 60 days. There's no useful food after that time." Chinese supplies, however, arrived most of the way by truck, not pack train.

Years later, in an oral history interview, Radford still believed the air strikes could have worked. "Whether these alone could have been successful in breaking the siege at Dien Bien Phu is debatable. If we had used atomic weapons we probably would have been successful. . . . That could have been decided one way or the other at the time of the specific military operation." But if conventional bombing had failed, "then the question would have come up." He neglected to mention that the French and the Vietminh were at such close quarters that nuclear weapons would have obliterated them both.

There were two things Ely did not understand, Radford said. One was that he lacked the authority to commit. The other was that France would not get the intervention without committing to united action: "Ely wanted us to come in, strike Dien Bien Phu, and break the siege . . . then withdraw and leave the fighting to them. . . . You can't just put one foot in and then pull out again. . . . We would have had to have a voice in the war—in the command—in the planning from then on. And the question was whether we should run it or not. I was in favor of running it."

In his report to the president's special committee on Indochina on March 29, Radford reviewed his five days of talks with Ely: In terms of expanding MAAG to assist in the training of the Vietnamese, which would get better results and release French officers for combat, "General Ely was most unsympathetic to any encroachment of French responsibilities . . . the French are disposed firmly to resist any delegation of training responsibilities. . . . Much the same attitude was manifested in regard to U.S. operations in the fields of psychological, clandestine, and guerrilla warfare [as discussed with Allen Dulles]."

Regarding Chinese air intervention, Radford said he and Ely had agreed on the following memo: "It was advisable that military authorities push their planning work as far as possible so that there would be no time wasted when and if our governments decide to oppose enemy air intervention over Indochina if it took place." Ely interpreted the memo as an agreement to intervene.

Committing U.S. Forces Would Lead to a War of Attrition Worse Than Korea

After seeing Ely off on March 26, Radford reported on his week of talks before a meeting of the State Department and the Joint Chiefs. His goal was to win over those present to the air-strike plan he had conditionally offered Ely. He stressed the desperate position of the French at Dien Bien Phu, and warned that their imminent defeat would bring the Communists into Southeast Asia. He read the text of his March 24 memo to Eisenhower: "The U.S. must act promptly and in force possibly to a frantic and belated request by the French for U.S. intervention."

Firm opposition to Radford's view came from an unexpected quarter, one of his Joint Chiefs. Army Chief of Staff Matthew Bunker Ridgway was a tough guy, relentless and outspoken, flinty and humorless, admired but not loved. Trim and in shape, he seemed to be never at rest, always bristling. He had led his airborne division in the assault on D-day and made the cover of *Time.* In Korea, he had taken command of the Eighth Army (which then meant all U.S. forces) after Lieutenant General Walton Walker was killed on December 23, 1951, when his jeep collided with a truck. There, his hard-driving style and penchant for attacking earned him the nickname "Wrong-way Ridgway."

Radford and Ridgway, both equally stubborn, were bound to clash. In July 1953, when Eisenhower had named Radford chairman of the Joint Chiefs and Ridgway army chief of staff, they clashed over the New Look plan, the Eisenhower administration's national security policy, which meant reducing the military budget and relying on the threat of nuclear retaliation. Thrifty by nature, Eisenhower had fond memories of the austerities of the Coolidge administration, when only the chief of staff had a government car, while other senior officers were given tokens for the trolley.

It took a soldier to grasp the wastefulness of war, and it was in the American grain to save manpower by improving technology. The Defense and Treasury departments backed the president in wanting "a bigger bang for the buck." Defense Secretary Wilson axed forty thousand workers from the Pentagon payroll. Secretary of the Treasury George Humphrey argued that the threat of nuclear weapons "kept peace in the world." And that "all the rest of these soldiers and sailors and submarines and everything else . . . could drop in the ocean and it wouldn't make a bit of difference." And hadn't Eisenhower called tactical nuclear weapons "just another weapon in our arsenal"? And had he not authorized the transfer of nuclear weapons for overseas deployment on the eve of the July 27 Korean cease-fire?

When Eisenhower asked the Joint Chiefs to write a report on the roles and missions of their respective services in the light of the New Look, Ridgway fought fiercely against budget cuts for the army. Radford sequestered the chiefs on the yacht *Sequoia* for a few days to iron things out. After long sessions on Thursday and Friday, "things began to fall into place" on Saturday, Radford recalled. "I suspect that Matt Ridgway, wanting to get home to his young bride for the weekend, began to see traces of merit in certain things he had opposed."

Ridgway felt he had been bulldozed into signing the report, and that Radford had turned it in without mentioning his dissenting views. As a result, when the army's budget shrank by 20 percent, he went around saying that weakening ground forces would be disastrous. Radford complained that Ridgway had agreed to the decisions, then went behind his back proclaiming his disagreement.

As recently as March 15, 1954, eleven days prior to Radford's meeting with the State Department and the Joint Chiefs, Ridgway had appeared before a subcommittee of the Senate Committee on Appropriations, where the following exchange with one of its members took place:

Senator Maybank: "I saw some articles in the paper that the Army was concerned they had been cut too much. Are you perfectly satisfied that the Army has sufficient funds?"

Ridgway: "That would be a pretty broad statement."

Maybank: "Were you consulted?"

Ridgway: "Yes sir."

Maybank: "And did you agree to these funds insofar as the Army was concerned?"

Ridgway: "It was not a question of agreeing to funds. It was a question of force levels, and then the costs followed."

Maybank: "Were you satisfied with the force levels?"

Ridgway: "I accept this program as a sound one."

In his memoirs, Radford wrote that Ridgway's speaking out of school "disturbed the President and the Secretary of Defense. He certainly disturbed me. . . . As a result, the President did not reappoint him when his two-year term expired."

Ridgway's stand on March 26 seemed to stem from a refusal to countenance another Korea and a lack of trust in Radford. No sooner had the admiral sounded the call for prompt intervention than Ridgway contested it. Committing U.S. forces, he said, would lead to a war of attrition worse than Korea. Ridgway was furious that once again, as in the report on the military, Radford in his memo to Eisenhower had made it seem that he was speaking for all the chiefs. But this time he would not let Radford get away with it. He demanded that an executive session of the Joint Chiefs of Staff be held at once. "I made the point," he wrote in a memo, that Admiral Radford's March 24 communication to the president "could very easily be misconstrued as the official expression of the corporate view of the Joint Chiefs," and could be interpreted "as advocating U.S armed intervention. The JCS must not, I added, advocate any such course."

Ridgway decided to send his own experts to Indochina to explore whether U.S. military intervention was feasible. He sent a team of seven officers from the Engineer, Transportation, and Signal corps on a covert mission to study the logistics and communications that an American intervention would require. The team was in Indochina from May 31 to June 22, but by then the war had been lost. Their report, however, stated that Indochina was devoid of the resources necessary for a substantial U.S. effort. Entering Indochina would mean five hundred thousand to a million men, forty engineering battalions, and a significant increase in the draft. The report reached Ridgway on July 12, confirming the folly of an intervention that never took place. But before it came in, Ridgway had appointed himself the whistle-blower revealing to the nation the high cost of intervention.

At a March 26 cabinet meeting, Secretary of State Dulles also disassociated himself from immediate intervention by declaring that the battle of Dien Bien Phu had little military importance. He predicted that Vietminh battle casualties would be so astronomical that even if they took the fort, it would be a Pyrrhic victory. It was a mistake to focus on this minor skirmish, Dulles said, when the real problem was the colonial issue. Victory would be won by building up a Vietnamese army and giving them a nation to fight for. Dulles did not realize that Navarre himself had lost hope in the Vietnamese army, and he also ignored the Laniel government's overwhelming desire for a negotiated peace.

Eisenhower did more listening than talking at the meeting, according to the notes kept by White House chief of staff Sherman Adams, although he showed his impatience when U.N. ambassador Henry Cabot Lodge (who had cabinet rank) compared the Indochina war to the Greek civil war, which brought about the Truman Doctrine in 1947. You couldn't compare the two, Ike chided. The Greeks were sturdy folk fighting for freedom, while the Vietnamese were a "backward people" who had lost faith in French promises. "France presents difficult questions everywhere you look," he snapped.

To Make Peace, Prepare for War

On March 27, Secretary of State Dulles showed the president a draft of the speech he would deliver two days later before the Overseas Press Club, in which he would unveil his "united action" policy. Eisenhower changed a few words and approved it. Dulles then called Carl McCardle, the State Department press officer, to tell him the speech had been okayed. Dulles said he had talked to Robert Bowie, director of the State Department Policy Planning Staff, who thought the country would not go along with a tough program. Dulles told Bowie, "If it won't go along with a strong policy, it won't go along on appeasement. Neither policy is popular—we better take the one that is right." Dulles told McCardle that the president agreed. He would now brief Senator Walter F. George, a Democrat from Georgia, about his speech "so the Democrats could not say they were not advised."

On the morning of March 29, the president and the vice president met with Republican congressional leaders for their weekly leadership conference. Eisenhower told them that if the military situation at Dien Bien Phu became desperate, he would consider the use of diversionary tactics—possibly a landing by Chiang Kai-shek's Nationalist forces on the island of Hainan, or a naval blockade of the Chinese mainland. What he said next alarmed the congressmen: "I am bringing this up because at any time within the space of 48 hours, it might be necessary to move into the battle of Dien Bien Phu in order to keep it from going against us and in that case I will be calling in the Democrats as well as our Republican leaders to inform them of the actions we're taking." The president sounded as if he was preparing to go to war.

That evening, Dulles spoke on "The Threat of Red Asia" to the Overseas Press Club. As he later told the *Life* writer James Shepley, he thought the use of air strikes was a poor way for the United States to get involved, "too narrow in its goals." He wanted a long-range allied defense of Southeast Asia, and the first step was to use his speech as a verbal deterrent, showing a readiness to fight.

He began by describing the extent of Chinese aid: the Chinese were delivering artillery shells obtained from the Czech Skoda works; they were training Vietminh cadres in China; in Giap's army, there were two thousand Chinese specialists in engineering, transportation, artillery, and communications, from the division level down.

This was followed by a grim prediction. In his best "prophet of doom" style, Dulles intoned: "If Communist forces were to win uncontested control over Indochina or any substantial part thereof, they would surely resume the pattern of aggression against the other free peoples in that area. The propagandists of Red China and Russia make it apparent that their purpose is to dominate all of Southeast Asia."

The grim prediction was followed by an explicit warning: "The imposition on Southeast Asia of the political system of Communist Russia and its Chinese ally, by whatever means, would be a grave threat to the whole free world community."

The explicit warning was followed by a call for united action: "The United States feels that that possibility should not be passively accepted, but should be met by united action. This might involve serious risks, but these risks are far less than those that will face us a few years from now. . . . The free nations want peace. However, peace is not had merely for wanting it. Peace has to be worked for and planned for. Sometimes it is necessary in war to take risks to win victories. The chances for peace are usually bettered by letting a potential aggressor know in advance where his aggression could lead him."

Editorial writers parsing Dulles's words wondered whether this call for action was also a call for war. Did united action mean military action? If so, bringing the other nations on board would be highly problematic. A *New York Times* editorial on March 30 said, "Dulles was as plain as words would allow in insisting that the United States look upon this struggle as vital to its interests and cannot stand passively by."

Senator H. Alexander Smith, a Republican from New Jersey, noted in his handwritten diary: "Went to Dulles at 6:15 P.M. Dulles showed me his speech . . . which he will give tonight. It is very stiff but it stands up. . . . It will probably upset the British and the French, but they should come along and stand by us."

Dulles did not think the speech had been well received by the press club audience, but as he told the Eisenhower aide C. D. Jackson, "They are 75 to 80 per cent Democrats." In any case, his real audience was Britain and France, "who are most eager for appeasement, and I felt I had to set it back." Concerned about the reaction in Congress, he was pleased to hear congratulatory remarks from the China lobby senator William Knowland. Dulles said the British and the French were "very unhappy" but that he had to "puncture the sentiment for appeasement before Geneva."

On March 30 in the Senate, however, John Stennis, a Democrat from Mississippi, who strongly opposed U.S. involvement in Indochina, expressed his feeling of dismay: "I followed Secretary Dulles' speech very closely, and I have not been able to decide exactly what he means by 'united action.' Exactly what is meant by 'united action,' and what is the necessity and case for it?" No other senator rose to offer clarification.

As for the unhappiness of the British, it was manifest in a phone call from Ambassador Roger Makins, who complained that Dulles had promised Foreign Secretary Eden that his speech would not imply any joint military action on the part of the Western powers. Eden was concerned that Dulles wanted to drag the British into Indochina. After all, Walter Bedell Smith had pledged to the Churchill government in February that the United States would never commit ground troops to the Indochina war. Was Dulles's speech a repudiation of that pledge?

The Only Way to Save Dien Bien Phu Was an American Air Strike

Meanwhile, General Ely had left Washington on March 26, in time to catch an 8:30 P.M. flight to Paris from Idlewild. Arriving in the afternoon of the twenty-seventh, he drove straight to Matignon, the residence of Premier Laniel, which he reached by 7 P.M. Pleven and Bidault were there. Ely briefed them on the VULTURE plan. "My impression," he said, "is that if the French government makes the request, the United States will send air strikes to bomb the terrain encircling Dien Bien Phu, where the Vietminh forces are concentrated." Ely did not believe there would be any response from China, since it would not be attacked on its territory.

This seemed to the ministers gathered a miraculous solution that could reverse the military situation just in time for the Geneva Conference. As Laniel later put it: "It had become clear that the only way to save Dien Bien Phu was an American air strike that would bury the enemy alive. The Americans had heavy bombers that could drop two-thousand-kilo bombs. All we had were three-hundred-kilo bombs. We needed to bomb them and then hose them down with napalm."

At the same time, the ministers worried that American intervention would be denounced by the antiwar crowd, and they wondered how efficient the air strikes would be. The only person who could address the second concern was General Navarre, but it would be unproductive to enter into long discussions by telegram. They decided to send the reliable Colonel Brohon to Saigon to consult with the commander. On March 29, the thirteen-member Committee for National Defense, which included Laniel, Bidault, Pleven, and Ely, deferred any decision on VULTURE until Navarre was heard from.

To describe the mood of the country, the old saw was truer than ever: France has fifty million subjects, not counting the subjects of discontent. For the first time, a parliamentary debate had been televised, and three hundred thousand viewers watched it. A vociferous exasperation with the Laniel government made itself heard: Enough of your sterile games! End the war! The opposition press was vitriolic, and in the army there were rumblings. France had been almost continually at war for fifteen years, but the army was taken for granted—it had become a pariah fighting a war the nation did not want. The civil service workers got salary raises, as did the workers who belonged to unions. The regular army did not. Infantry officers serving their third tour in Indochina were paid less than officers in other European armies. They left their wives and children behind in cheap hotels because the army did not provide housing for dependents. Recruitment had hit a wall, and one high military source was quoted as saying: "In twenty years we will have no more generals."

Pleven, the minister of defense, saw trouble coming when he told the Committee for National Defense on March 11: "I fear that we will soon have military demonstrations. If it wasn't for Indochina, I would resign. There may even be a spectacular coup d'état that will force the government to resign. I cannot remain as minister in charge of an army that is close to insurgence."

For Laniel, the European Defense Community had priority over Indochina. He heeded the warnings of the military that if France did not participate in a European army, "Germany will have obtained in one year what it failed to obtain in a thousand years of fighting—the subjugation of France." Laniel hoped that once the EDC treaty was ratified by the Chamber of Deputies, American generosity toward Indochina would know no bounds.

But what about Foreign Minister Bidault? He had done useful work in trying to incite the Soviets to prudence. Now, in mid-March 1954, after the reversals at Dien Bien Phu, Bidault seemed exhausted, a sad shred of a man on the verge of a nervous breakdown. He had been a brilliant history professor and a fearless Resistance hero, and in his political career he was admired for his intuitive brilliance. But he had ignored the rise of nationalism in the third world. He was determined to maintain the French Empire, not realizing that a nation's greatness no longer depended on its overseas possessions. However, because of the war, France was in a state of turmoil. What should be done? Negotiate at Geneva? Ask the Americans for an air strike?

Bidault talked a great deal. He tried out his thoughts on everyone he talked to, though the thoughts varied from day to day and even from hour to hour. On one hand, he refused to give up Indochina. He said the Vietminh must be destroyed, and that "Ho Chi Minh can go teach revolutionary tactics in Peking or Moscow." On the other, he hoped to negotiate a peace agreement at Geneva that would end the war. He lived and breathed inside a conundrum.

The Vietnamese Army Cannot Replace the French

When the Vietminh attacked Dien Bien Phu on March 13, General Navarre was in Saigon. The attack did not surprise him or cause anxiety. He kept to his schedule and flew to the Laotian air-ground base of Seno on the fourteenth for an inspection tour. At midnight in Seno, he was informed that Béatrice had fallen. He was not unduly concerned, for it had been agreed that the three paratroop battalions held in reserve at central command would immediately counterattack any center of resistance taken by the Viets. Arriving in Hanoi on the afternoon of March 15, he found Cogny waiting on the tarmac, and was "astounded" to learn that there had been no counterattack, even though Gabrielle had also fallen. The reason Cogny gave, that the fog had prevented air support, seemed flimsy, for artillery support would have been enough. Then Navarre was told that the forces involved in the counterattack could not be assembled in time.

Navarre was dumbfounded. The inability to assemble reserve battalions demonstrated an inexcusable lack of preparation. The desertion of the Thais on Anne-Marie did not surprise him. They were mediocre fighters, though useful for their knowledge of the terrain. As for the truce offered by Giap to pick up the wounded, it was an obvious trick intended to delay a counterattack, and should not have been accepted.

One of Navarre's aides, based in Hanoi, later told him: "It seemed that the initial success of the Viets at Béatrice struck the Cogny command in Hanoi with stupor. My feeling was that their main concern was to absolve themselves of any blame. The atmosphere was charged with unpleasant undercurrents, in shocking contrast to the confidence and optimism of the previous two months." Castries asked for three of the five paratroop battalions Cogny was holding in reserve. Two were dropped on March 14 (the 6th BPC) and 16 (the 5th BPVN). Navarre thought of relieving Cogny, Castries, and Langlais. But the latter two were splendid soldiers who had faltered momentarily, he decided, while Cogny knew the Delta and there was no one to replace him, so he left all three where they were.

Navarre's pique extended to the press, particularly the journalist who described the paras as "disorderly heroes whose only destiny is to get themselves killed." He did all he could to have the vilifier tried before a military tribunal but, as usual in Paris, nothing was done.

It was, however, undeniable, thought Navarre, that after the mid-March attacks there was a decline in morale at the base. Castries' chief of staff had to be evacuated. Piroth committed suicide. Deserters fled to the banks of the Nam Yum and formed a rat's nest that grew to several hundred, living off plunder.

Navarre surveyed the situation: Trenches had begun appearing all around the post, particularly to the east. The evacuation of the wounded had become nearly impossible. Most of his transport planes—one hundred C-47 Dakotas and twenty-four Flying Boxcars flown by CAT pilots—were assigned to the supply of the base by parachute. Two thirds of his B-26 bombers, as well as many of his Hellcats and Bearcats, flew strikes in the vicinity of the base. Dien Bien Phu was absorbing a major part of his resources.

Was the battle lost? On March 21, Navarre wrote his friend and mentor Marshal Juin: "Several days ago, the Chinese delivered a very great quantity of munitions to the border, enough to double the Vietminh's present supply." It was clear another attack was coming. But French transport planes were also air-dropping munitions into the base, so each side was making up its armament losses from the first attack. Even though Piroth's counterbattery operations had been ineffective against the Vietminh guns, he had fired sixteen thousand rounds, which slowed down the human waves.

Navarre stayed in Hanoi from March 14 to 22, and again from March 25 to 28, coping with the logistical problems of Dien Bien Phu: the supply drops, the wounded, and the loss of manpower due to casualties. But Dien Bien Phu did not absorb his full attention. Other operations were unfolding in other regions, such as central Annam, where ATLANTE kept twenty battalions busy. There was also the vexing problem of the Vietnamese army, with the Americans constantly prodding him. Recent reports from his officers in the field showed that it was at a standstill. He wrote Ely on March 26: "As skeptical as I was when Pleven, during his February visit, asked me if I thought the Vietnamese army would soon replace the French, I still overestimated the possibility. . . . They will not be capable of doing anything serious for several years." Thus the plan named after him was badly behind schedule.

I Feel the Situation Can Only Deteriorate Further

The mid-March reverses made Castries short-tempered and depressed. In an uncharacteristic scene, the normally debonair cavalry colonel lashed out at a sergeant, a helicopter pilot named Duhoux. As the Sikorskys began to arrive in Indochina, the French were short of pilots. Duhoux, although only a sergeant, showed an aptitude for flying choppers, and after his training, he was allotted on March 10 a brand-new Sikorsky H-19, with Sergeant Dauce as his copilot and Sergeant Maranger as his mechanic.

On March 13, Duhoux was sent to Dien Bien Phu to evacuate wounded. He arrived on the afternoon of the Vietminh attack. On the next day, the morning of the truce, he was told to pick up wounded from the various strongpoints and bring them to the hospital. But when he examined his helicopter, he found that two of the blades on the main rotor had been hit by shell fire. Unable to take off, he and his crew were stuck in Dien Bien Phu in the midst of battle. All three were astounded when they were given helmets and submachine guns and told to join one of the fighting units. Dauce and Maranger protested vehemently that they were not in the infantry. Duhoux found Castries in his bunker on March 15 and told him: "We're going to try to reach Muong Sai [the helicopter base in Laos]."

Castries threw a fit, ordered them to stay put, and called them slackers and worse. In the ensuing discussion, Castries offered to let them leave if they took with them six of the gravely wounded,

"I've got two badly damaged rotor blades," Duhoux said. "It will be a risky flight. Your six wounded are better off at the hospital."

"Take it or leave it," a furious Castries replied.

On March 16, Dauce and Maranger told Duhoux that if he waited any longer, they'd leave without him, before their chopper attracted the attention of Vietminh gunners. Duhoux tried to repair the blades with adhesive plaster used in thoracic wounds. He lowered the pilot's seat, so that he was barely visible, while Dauce and Maranger climbed onto the tail and applied the plaster to the rotor blades.

When they were ready to leave, instead of loading wounded, they summoned the three-man crew of a chopper that had been destroyed on the ground earlier, who were also stranded, and took them along, without giving notice. As he looked back, Duhoux saw that the airstrip was lined with dozens of corpses, some covered with blankets, some not. This cemetery without tombs was a sight that lingered in his mind's eye.

Once in the air, the chopper vibrated badly. The damaged blades were out of balance, the weather was bad, and Duhoux wasn't sure they had enough gas to reach Muong Sai, since he hadn't been able to fill up. He'd been on reserve fuel for seven minutes when they saw the Muong Sai airstrip.

As he came to terms with the loss of three centers of resistance, Castries' pessimism heightened. On March 19, he cabled General Cogny: "I must envisage the hypothesis of the fall of Dien Bien Phu. The fall of Isabelle seems imminent. I plan to order its commander Lt Col Lalande to destroy his artillery and try to reach Muong Khoua. Need your agreement." Any attempted breakout to the Laotian post sixty miles to the west through Vietminh-infested territory would have been suicidal. Cogny disagreed, but promised reinforcements. Castries' gloom persisted, and he wrote Cogny on March 22: "I feel the situation can only deteriorate further, unless there are new elements I cannot foresee." Again, on March 24: "What I am most pessimistic about, the morale of the garrison, cannot be improved without the evacuation of the wounded." He knew another attack was coming, for the aerial photographs dropped each day by parachute showed the weblike spread of Vietminh trenches.

Cogny was slow to keep his promises. His attention was divided between Dien Bien Phu and his cherished Delta, where Vietminh ambushes and sabotage on the vital Hanoi–Haiphong rail and road axis were diverting troops. The bulk of supplies for Dien Bien Phu arrived by sea at Haiphong. On March 22, an ambush in the southwestern Delta posts destroyed thirty-one military vehicles and ten trucks. But when he asked Navarre for reinforcements in the Delta, Cogny received a curt reply: "I can only repeat what I have told you many times: I am the only one who decides how I distribute my forces. . . . I ask you to remember that you are part of a team and that your command extends over all Tonkin. Thus, for now, the Delta must momentarily lose its priority in your preoccupations."

Have the Tensions of Battle Made Him Lose His Reason?

While Castries marinated in despondence, Colonel Langlais was brimful of fighting spirit, refusing to admit defeat. He now had all the troops in Dien Bien Phu under operational command, as head of the Groupement Opérationnel du Nord-Ouest (GONO). During the lull, Langlais put the garrison to work strengthening the centers of resistance. As he later described it, "Communication trenches were dug linking strongpoints. Field telephone wires were placed underground, and more mines were added to the barbed wire. Thousands of mines were parachuted in, and our two companies of sappers made a prodigious effort. I remember particularly the work of the sappers under Major Sudrat around the dangerous unoccupied hill we called the Bald Mountain, which dominated Eliane 2. Under enemy shelling, it was truffled with mines in record time." Langlais also built two new centers of resistance, one at the southern end of the airstrip called Epervier (Sparrowhawk), held by Major Pierre Tourret's 8th Choc, and one to the southeast called Junon (Juno), held by Major Maurice Guiraud of the 1st BEP.

The base now depended completely on supplies dropped by parachute, which averaged 120 tons a day in the second half of March. The PIMs (Vietminh prisoners) handled much of the heavy lifting from the drop zones to central command. When 155mm shells were dropped in cases of two, weighing more than two hundred pounds, they ran out to unfasten the harnesses and hauled them to the trucks. Then the shells were driven to the ammo dumps, where other PIMs unloaded them. The cases were pushed out the tail doors of Flying Boxcars. When they were dropped into thin air the planes' noses hiccupped upward and had to be leveled before the next package could be released. The CAT crews flying the C-119s spoke no French and ignored instructions from air traffic controllers. This problem was solved by using British Legionnaires as air controllers. The CAT pilots complained that they had been led to expect air cover, but French fighters were rarely seen below ten thousand feet. U.S. Air Force intelligence in Washington received reports that the pilots "were unhappy and wanted to quit."

Pleased with Langlais' efforts, Castries wrote Cogny on March 22 that "he has been remarkable—he took the defense in hand, reshaped it, and helped me greatly in lifting morale. I have designated him as my successor." And yet Langlais was adversarial, drank too much whiskey, and wanted to settle arguments with his fists. Cogny put it more tactfully before the 1955 commission of inquiry: "Langlais is an admirable lad as a fighter, but he's . . . I won't say difficult to command—but he forms many opinions which are subject to revision."

Langlais was in a state of permanent anger, and one of his targets was the hospital, where the wounded were piled like cordwood in the halls. One day he was nosing around looking for ways to enlarge the space when he came upon a mysterious office occupied by two lieutenants, several French civilians, and a few Thais. They told him they were running a "secret service," which was a secret even to him. "These useless services took up a lot of room," he recalled, "but when I asked them to move out and take their place on the strongpoints, they declined. I was stupefied to learn that they communicated directly with Hanoi and Saigon without going through Castries. I rounded up a commando of Legionnaires and threw the bastards out."

Dr. Grauwin was able to add fifty beds. Geneviève de Galard, who had taken up her duties as the only female nurse on the base, was allotted a narrow cell furnished with a cot and a rattan chair, its walls hung with parachute silk. Her mother, the widow of an army officer, wrote: "In a way, I'm glad you're in Dien Bien Phu. That way, you don't risk one of your planes crashing."

Cogny did not appreciate having his personal secret service thrown out on its ear. He cabled Castries: "Please use all your authority to settle this unacceptable incident between Langlais and the special services. It would be regrettable to have to apply sanctions. Have the tensions of battle made him lose his reason."

Langlais planned an operation against the "Rats of Nam Yum," who looted unburied bodies and came out at night to steal parachuted supplies.

They were particularly fond of cases of Vinogel, a concentrated wine to which water was added. He decided against the operation because the troops he would have to use would hesitate to fire on men they had served with.

Under the new system approved by Castries, Langlais was now in command of a division. As he pointed out in his memoir, "Although I was only a simple paratroop Lieutenant Colonel, I had directly under my orders more than ten thousand men." No higher-ranking officer in Hanoi, he noted, seemed eager to replace him. It was later said in some quarters that Langlais had engineered a veritable putsch when the para mafia took command, while Castries was relegated to serving as an intermediary between the paras and Hanoi. And yet Castries continued to praise Langlais.

What's the Use? We're Being Butchered.

Castries had asked Hanoi to speed up the delivery of aerial photographs of Viet positiions so that they could be dropped on the same day they were taken. This was the job of a detachment of six Morane Crickets at the Laotian base of Muong Sai, eighty miles southeast of Dien Bien Phu. They began taking pictures in the morning and flew back to the base, a three-hour round-trip. There the pictures were developed and interpreted, flown back to Dien Bien Phu, and dropped.

On the afternoon of March 19, a storm beat down on Muong Sai, and hailstones crashed through the cloth fuselages of the Moranes on the airstrip. A Cricket had gone out that morning with Lieutenant Asselineau and his copilot, Le Coz. They had been gone five hours. The base, having received no messages, was in a state of high anxiety.

That night, a message came from Dien Bien Phu: "Two officers who say they're named Asselineau and Le Coz. Are they yours?" Le Coz later recounted:

> Once our mission over Dien Bien Phu was over, we headed back to Muong Sai. Before us, a stormy black sky barred the way. With only an hour of flight time left, we couldn't go back to Dien Bien Phu. When we flew into the storm, we lost visibility and our alti-

tude dropped. I had trouble controlling the plane because of heavy rain and wind turbulence. Even though we saw forests all around us, we knew more or less where we were. Suddenly on the left we saw a clearing of rice paddies about a hundred meters long with a cabin on piles in the middle. The plane was shaking and we decided on a crash landing. As we hit the ground, I aimed at the cabin to stop the plane. We hit it at seventy kilometers an hour. Neither of us had a scratch. I cut the engine and closed off the gas supply. We dismantled the radio and hid it in the forest. We took our weapons and headed south through a driving rain, following a trail at the edge of the valley that we hoped would lead to Muong Sai. We came across a lone Vietnamese who kept his hands deep in his pockets. Asselineau held him and I found a grenade in each pocket. As we approached the village, we were charged by a water buffalo— apparently they don't like the smell of whites—but we ducked into the forest. In the village we found only a few women and children hiding in their houses on piles. Fifteen kilometers later, we reached the post.

The helicopters that evacuated the wounded from Isabelle were also based in Muong Sai, once a picturesque village on a hill with houses on stilts, now an improvised airstrip with landing zones for helicopters, flanked by mortar emplacements, where the crews ate off ammunition cases. The Sikorsky H-19s could carry five wounded and a crew of two, but had to take off from Isabelle through heavy flak. On March 23, Captain Maxime Fauroux said on returning from a run: "What's the use? We're being butchered." He had just seen a Vietminh mortar shell hit a Red Cross helicopter after it had loaded a wounded Legionnaire officer from Dr. Rézillot's bunker hospital.

The wounded officer, with a bullet in his knee, was Lieutenant Alain Gambiez, who happened to be the son of General Fernand Gambiez, Navarre's chief of staff. The stout and amiable Gambiez was one of the few officers Navarre had brought with him from France. He was the perfect office manager, rarely mentioned in dispatches, though it was he who had approved, in Navarre's absence, the March 14 truce to tend the wounded.

By coincidence, General Gambiez was flying over the base on March 21, the day before his son was wounded, coordinating supply flights in his Dakota. Gambiez had made it clear that he did not want his son to receive preferential treatment.

That instruction was not obeyed, for two helicopters were sent out from Muong Sai on March 23. By then, all the helicopters had concentrated on Isabelle, offering a target that Vietminh gunners could prepare for in advance. The first one, piloted by Captain Fauroux, landed close to the hospital with a letter for Dr. Rézillot, but had taken off right away due to shell fire.

The second was piloted by Warrant Officer Henri Bartier, who had been in Indochina since 1945. Bartier flew without a mechanic, to make more room for the wounded. His veteran copilot, Sergeant Bernard, had flown 262 missions in the Delta and evacuated 616 wounded. Bartier was flying his thousandth combat mission. They were bringing in medication and had only one wounded to take out, Lieutenant Gambiez, with his leg in plaster.

Around 12:30, Bartier's Sikorsky landed at the landing zone near the hospital. Bartier installed Gambiez and took off. He was about thirty feet above the ground when a 105mm shell exploded directly beneath him. Shrapnel hit the gas tank, which caught fire. Bartier's left leg was torn off below the knee. The chopper crashed and Sergeant Bernard was thrown out through the windshield. Despite his broken ribs, he crawled back to the cockpit and pulled Bartier out by the arms, helped by a Legionnaire.

As they extracted Bartier, they heard the anguished shouts of Gambiez, immobilized by his wound, but they couldn't get near him through the flames. He was burned alive. Bernard and the Legionnaire extinguished Bartier's flight suit, which was on fire. Bartier was taken to Rézillot's surgery unit and operated on at 1:30—amputaion of the left leg, burns on the right leg. The chopper's tail rotor was found forty yards from its incinerated hulk.

Bartier was then taken to the main hospital. On March 26, he was flown to Hanoi in one of the last planes to leave the Dien Bien Phu airstrip. The much-decorated warrant officer was awarded the Legion of Honor and promoted to second lieutenant. Was it worth a leg?

Captain Fauroux sent his copilot, Captain André Butor, to Hanoi on March 25 with a proposal, which was explained to General Lauzin of the air force. What if the helicopters took off in the afternoon, arriving at Dien Bien Phu at dusk? They would land, load the wounded, and take off in the dark, guided by a Dakota, since they were not equipped for night navigation, which would lead them into Luang Prabang.

Fauroux and Butor decided on a trial night landing at their Muong Sai base on March 27, dimming the landing field with shrouded lamps. They recruited three noncom volunteers as stand-ins for the wounded. The night was clear enough to distinguish the outline of the surrounding mountains. The Sikorsky took off toward the southwest and gained altitude. The spectators on the ground heard an explosion and then saw one of the nearby hills catch fire. When it was light, a rescue team, hacking through the jungle with machetes, found five bodies. They were buried in unmarked graves with their names in bottles. General Lauzin announced: "The accident on March 27 has led me to consider dissolving the Helicopter Detachment."

To Command Is to Anticipate

The pause in the second half of March was a pause in name only. Castries wrote Navarre on March 24: "Each day costs me around ten killed and forty wounded." He was not getting any reinforcements to make up for his losses.

Cogny responded on the same day with a lengthy directive that demonstrated the complete disconnect between the Hanoi command and the men on the ground. This exercise in wishful thinking deserves to be quoted at some length:

> The enemy has suffered heavy losses and is having difficulty filling his units. His logistical services are unable to assure supplies in munitions and rice.
>
> The rainy season soon to come will compromise his supply lines. His buried emplacements will turn to mud.
>
> If new losses destabilize your positions, I will be able to send you immediately another battalion of paratroopers.

On the day that the enemy, dislocated or exhausted by your aggressive resistance, abandons the battle, I can place at your disposal an airborne group being kept in reserve, which will confirm your victory with hot pursuit.

Our air attacks are more efficient each day, and I am counting on massive drops of napalm and continued raids on enemy artillery. The enemy is far from holding the decisive cards that will guarantee victory. . . . You must use all possible means to interfere with his preparations, and confuse his intelligence services by shifting your artillery positions. This way you will be able to delay the attack until the monsoons make it unworkable.

In order to avoid being smothered, you must go after the enemy antiaircraft by launching surprise attacks to make these over-impetuous gunners turn tail. These raids will benefit from artillery and air support.

To prepare for the rainy season, you must move all encampments subject to flooding to higher ground, away from the Nam Yum. If the enemy decides to attack prior to the monsoons, you must maintain the integrity of your positions.

This harsh struggle demands from the troops under your command an inflexible morale. Your personal influence is priceless. You will, I know, convey to the garrison that the stakes of this battle are nothing less than our keeping Indochina. Thus, you will win the battle and clear the enemy from Dien Bien Phu.

Instead of pressing his demands for more troops, Castries asked Hanoi for specialists and equipment in combat engineering for trench warfare. He also wanted four copies of the French army siege manual for the defensive organization of terrain, which had not been revised since 1916. His request raised eyebrows. Why had he not asked for the manual sooner?

Letters home from the men on the base became more graphic. The Legionnaire captain Chevalier wrote his wife on March 24 that he had seen "human waves of Viets drunk on *choum* [rice alcohol] marching over their own dead and attacking with flamethrowers. I've seen our men with bloodied uniforms and ravaged, ghostlike faces, immediately reincorporated into the fighting units that make up this horrible spectacle."

Colonel André Lalande, the commander of Isabelle, who had written his wife on March 17 that not one hair would fall from his head, was less certain of his invulnerability a week later: "I'm no hero, and I wish I were brave by nature. . . . I feel lazy and heavy of heart. . . . You say I'm in my element, but that's both true and false. War does not suit me, but the camaraderie and human contact are a joy."

While preparing for the next attack, the post was busy with its daily chores, such as opening the road that linked central command to Isabelle, the southernmost center of resistance. This three-mile stretch of RP41 followed the right bank of the Nam Yum through several villages. Although self-sufficient, with its own airstrip, artillery, tanks, and hospital, Isabelle stood in splendid isolation from the rest of the base. Keeping the road secure for supplies and transfers of personnel and wounded was a small daily victory that Castries was able to report to Hanoi. Usually, there were no incidents, as companies of Legionnaires, preceded by a couple of tanks, moved quickly past the first village of Ban Lai, which was beyond the halfway point, and on to Isabelle. On March 19, Warrant Officer Carette, riding in one of the U.S.-built Chaffees named after famous French battles, such as Douaumont and Mulhouse, raised nothing but dust.

On March 20, however, a unit of the Vietminh 304th Division evacuated the villages and took up positions in and around them. When the Legionnaires, led by Captain Michaud, were two hundred yards from Ban Lai, they were hit with a barrage of mortar and automatic fire. It was then that Lieutenant Gambiez was hit in the knee and evacuated to Isabelle. Several other wounded were close to the village. One of the tanks advanced, firing its machine gun and 75mm cannon, followed by Legionnaires who hustled the wounded onto the tank's sloping platform behind the turret. Michaud gave the order to fall back.

On the morning of March 22, the tank crews were eating breakfast and filling their canteens. They were more often thirsty than hungry, and they rarely touched the U.S. rations stored in the Chaffees. A thick fog hung over Dien Bien Phu, but the tanks were ordered out to win back control of the road to Isabelle. As they approached the village of Ban Lai, the tanks stopped. The Vietminh had dug a trench across the road, filled with *bo dois.* The lead section of Legionnaires, crouched along a bamboo hedge, took serious losses. Although the tanks fired streams of tracers, the Legionnaires could not outflank or break through Vietminh positions.

Stalled, they called Isabelle for help. Lieutenant Henri Préaud's three tanks, Lieutenant Wieme's Thai auxiliaries, and two companies of Algerians soon attacked from the south, but they too found that the Vietminh had dug a trench to block their advance.

The Vietminh stood and fought for five hours, while the tanks hammered their positions. Around 2:00 P.M., Vietminh fire became episodic, and the Legionnaires stormed the trench, finding 175 dead *bo dois*. The rest had fled into the hills. The French had 15 dead and 72 wounded. They took 9 prisoners and captured piles of weapons, including two bazookas. General Giap was prepared to take serious losses in order to attain a tactical objective—in this case, making the opening of the road to Isabelle too costly for the French to maintain.

On Tuesday, March 23, the Vietminh lay low. The 8th Choc, under its admired leader, Major Pierre Tourret, opened the road without incident. This was the day that Lieutenant Gambiez was burned alive at Isabelle.

On March 24, expecting trouble, Langlais sent a company of Bigeard's 6th BPC to open the road. The paras led by Lieutenant Hervé Trapp started out while it was still dark, supported by Sergeant Fernand Ney's tank platoon. Bigeard told Ney: "You'd better be there *mu-len* [on the double] to disengage my men if they fall on a bone [get into trouble]."

When two platoons, led by Lieutenants Samalens and Corbineau, advanced from different directions on the village of Ban Lai, they were met with heavy firing. Caught in the open, Samalens ordered an attack. Corbineau, who was a hundred feet away, saw men around Samalens fall, until Samalens stood alone, surrounded. Ney rumbled up with his three Chaffees, caved in the Vietminh's freshly dug trenches, and knocked down the bamboo hedges. One of the tanks, on the edge of a trench, was hit at close range by a bazooka and had to be towed back to the base. Trapp's 120 paras and Ney's two remaining tanks stormed a jerry-built blockhouse manned by a battalion of Vietminh. In these road-opening battles, the tanks made the difference.

Back at Bigeard's command post on Eliane 4, Trapp wiped the dust from his face and examined his combat vest, which had three dents in it.

He told Bigeard: "We've got to do something. We can't keep taking it on the chin without fighting back."

Now that the French had to fight their way through to Isabelle, the road-opening troops were rotated. On Thursday, March 25, it was the turn of a company of Moroccan fusiliers. They were stopped by Vietminh units at Ban Lai and summoned Warrant Officer Carette and his three tanks. The Moroccans were slow-moving veterans of the World War II Italian campaign. They didn't have the para élan. Their captain had pulled them back into defensive positions, waiting for tanks and artillery support.

From Isabelle, Lieutenant Préaud moved north with his tanks and stormed through a Vietminh-held village to help the Moroccans, who had taken serious losses. The two tank platoons coordinated their movements and swept the Vietminh from the road. Returning to Isabelle, Préaud took stock of the hits that had scarred his tanks.

Back at central command, a spectacular napalm drop on March 23 that set fire to outlying hills raised morale, though it was more of a fireworks display than a serious blow to the enemy. Another morale booster was that Captain Alain Bizard had parachuted in to take command of a company of the 5th BPVN. Bizard, a good-natured cavalryman, broader from chest to back than from shoulder to shoulder, had been serving as an aide to General Ely in Paris. He volunteered for a third rotation in Indochina. Upon his arrival in Saigon, he asked to be sent to Dien Bien Phu, which must have seemed both suicidal and cheering to the garrison. Since he did not have his paratroop certificate, he went to Hanoi for the required seven jumps, and was dropped into the retrenched camp on March 28. He had become a legendary figure in his first two tours, and was welcomed by the garrison.

Another outstanding officer was Major Pierre Tourret of the 8th Choc Battalion, which was dug in south of the airfield at Epervier and served as a reserve unit. Tourret had been in Indochina on and off since 1948. He'd served under Bigeard in the 6th BPC until he was given his own paratroop battalion. "He wasn't a Rambo, but he had a natural authority," one of his men later recalled. Slight and wiry, with a narrow, lined face and a "bird of prey" look, Tourret was the stereotype of the short-tempered leader with a heart of gold. Out on patrol, his eighteen-year-old sniper, Bernard Bryard, spotted a Viet in a tree through his telescopic sight. He fired two rounds but the Viet remained in the tree. An exasperated Tourret said: "Give the baby his bottle and take away his rifle." Later they found the dead Viet, who had tied himself to the tree. A contrite Tourret promoted Bryard from private to corporal.

Tourret was critical of the general organization of the strongpoints, but kept this to himself. His principal gripe was Dominique 2, an elongated hill east of RP41. At a height of 1,715 feet it dominated the airstrip and the central command post of Claudine, where Castries' bunker and the hospital were located. And yet it was defended by only two companies of Algerian fusiliers, worn out after three years in Indochina, and armed with antique Reibel machine guns. Their captain, Jean Garandeau, was ill with the flu. It was folly, Tourret thought, to have only two companies of Algerians manning this vital CR, when both Béatrice and Gabrielle had fallen despite being defended by battalions.

Tourret's motto was "To command is to anticipate," but the command at Dien Bien Phu had failed miserably, he thought, waiting until the knife was at their throat. He alerted Langlais to the deficiency at Dominique 2. On the afternoon of March 25, Tourret was ordered to take two companies backed by two tanks and fill the trenches the Vietminh had dug near the strongpoint. Lieutenant Colonel Maurice Lemeunier, a veteran Legionnaire, watched through binoculars and was impressed by the way Tourret handled himself, impervious under fire, standing with gloved hands, calmly ordering tank and artillery support, and pulling back only once the trenches were filled. As the companies moved out, they came under intense fire and lost sixteen killed and fifty-seven wounded. Tourret was offended that the same shell that killed Lieutenant Garoutaigt had also wounded Lieutenant Legrain. His two company commanders should not have been so close together. Lemeunier asked Langlais: "Who was that young captain who almost got himself killed?"

Other officers wondered what the point was of losing men to fill trenches that would be dug up again every night. They derided the Hanoi command, which kept promising light planes and helicopters to evacuate the wounded, while knowing that aircraft were no longer able to land. Hanoi seemed to be counting on the monsoons, which would of course persuade the two Vietminh divisions to pull out so that the Dien Bien Phu garrison could move to higher ground. The officers shook their heads and wondered how Hanoi could be so oblivious to reality. Captain Hervouet, the tank commander, said that if they were counting on the monsoons, they should have sent him landing craft instead of tanks.

On Friday, March 26, Jean Péraud, the reporter-photographer, summed up the day's impressions in his notes: "Attacks on the trenches with grenades provokes grenades from the Viets. . . . Our tanks are firing. . . . A terrifying atmosphere! I must have some good pictures. . . . Two Dakotas hit by Vietminh AA. . . . I gave some film to the pilot of the second one that went down. . . . But my morale is excellent."

On Saturday, March 27, there was a final road opening. Captain Hervouet, who'd been hit in the hand while out of the turret in one of the trench-filling operations, was proud of his squadron, and the road opening gave his tanks a chance to show what they could do. This time he went himself, linking up with Lieutenant Préaud, coming up from Isabelle. If Hervouet was disabled, Préaud would take his place. When they met, neither one wanted to break off their conversation, as if realizing that they might not see each other again.

They're Like Oysters on a Rock

Major Bigeard and his 6th BPC had been posted to Eliane 4, to the east of central command, which they shared with Bigeard's friend Botella and the Vietnamese paratroopers of the 5th BPVN. They were well dug in, and Bigeard's artillery officer, Lieutenant Allaire, constantly moved his mortars and 75mm guns so the Viets would think he had more than he did.

At 7 P.M. on March 27, Bigeard was summoned by Colonel Castries, at his most urbane: "Bruno, how are you, will you accept a whiskey? How is it going on Eliane 4?"

"Morale is five out of five, my colonel." Five out of five was the customary signal for clear reception on the radio—the best possible.

"Here's why I called you in. Hanoi has ordered me to do the impossible in order to wipe out the enemy antiaircraft guns on the west of the basin, which are endangering our supply drops. Consequently: You must seek them out tomorrow. You have carte blanche. Take whoever and whatever you need, and get hopping."

"Will do, my colonel, on two conditions: One, you must be ready to accept heavy losses among the two or three battalions capable of succeeding. Two, you must leave me enough time to plan a swift and precise operation."

"I understand, Bruno, you have my entire confidence."

Bigeard at once retired to his office and worked out the plan on the big map spread over the plank held up by two sawhorses that served as his desk. His aide, Master Sergeant Martial Chevalier, typed out the order, which took up only a single page.

At 2 P.M. on March 28, Bigeard held a briefing for the commanders of the units involved: Captain Tourret of the 8th Paratroop Shock Battalion (Choc); Major Maurice Guiraud, of the 1st Foreign Legion Parachute Battalion (BEP); Captain Thomas of the 6th Colonial Parachute Battalion (BPC), taking Bigeard's place; Major Clémençon, of the 2nd Foreign Infantry Regiment (REI); Colonel Vaillant, the artillery commander; Captain Hervouet, the tank commander; and Major Jacques Guérin of the air force.

"Castries asked me to go after AA guns that are firing on our planes and make them shut up," Bigeard said as he placed his finger on the outspread map. "Over here to the west. The principal batteries are near the two villages of Ban Ban and Ban Ong Pet." Martial Chevalier handed out typed orders on onionskin paper to each unit leader.

"The 8th Choc will handle Ban Ban, and the 6th BPC Ban Ong Pet. The 1st BEP will be held in reserve to the west, and the 2nd REI to the east. Troops in place by 5:30 A.M., three hundred meters from the objective."

To Vaillant: "How many tubes have we got?"

"Twenty-two 105s, two 155s, and a dozen 120mm mortars. This is half the base artillery. They can fire successive volleys of five minutes each, with intervals to let the Viets believe the preparation is over and they can stick their noses out."

Major Jacques Guérin said his only problem was the weather.

The unit commanders left to prepare for battle, while Bigeard tested his radio signals. He began to realize that the single page he had handed out was in fact the first offensive action against the enemy, the first time the French at Dien Bien Phu would benefit from the element of surprise, and it was planned by a mere major in command of two thousand men. He felt weighed down by the responsibility Castries had entrusted him with. Would it be a terrible mistake provoked by our useless losses, he wondered, or a brilliant success that would eclipse the memory of those who died in the battle? *Mektoub!* (God wills it!) The dice had been thrown. Captain Hervouet, looking for a cot to snatch a few hours of sleep, thought that Castries had been right to pick Bigeard. In his small, badly lit office, hovering over the makeshift table covered with maps and aerial photographs, Bigeard had shown that he was not only a warrior but a tactician. There was nothing pedantic or École de Guerre about it. He spoke to the other commanders with a reassuring concreteness, using the familiar *tu* form.

In the alcove next door to Hervouet, a Vietnamese intelligence technician was transmitting to Hanoi what he'd heard over Vietminh radio: "The detachments of 'courageous warriors' are to be dissolved. The phase of fighting by small units has come to an end. The political commissars are ordered to mobilize the enthusiasm of the comrades in order to accomplish the new mission."

At 5:30 in the morning on Sunday, March 29, at the end of a moonless night, Warrant Officer Carette sat on the turret of his M24 Chaffee and watched the long columns of men from the 8th Choc gather at the departure point. The clicking of their equipment blended with the scuff of marching feet. Carette was glad to be fighting alongside the best units on the base. He spotted the battalion commander, Tourette, who waved at him to follow. Carette had his orders and called out: "I can't leave until the artillery preparation begins, in order not to alert the Viets."

At 5:55, dawn was breaking, and Bigeard was on the radio, calling each unit—Are you in position? He took his command team into the field. The Legionnaires under Major Clémençon were east of the airfield, in reserve. The men of Bigeard's battalion, the 6th BPC, were waiting at Eliane 4 like runners at their starting blocks. For Lieutenant Michel Le Vigouroux, a platoon leader, the worst part was the waiting. One of his men, Berthumerie, was a true "bounding Basque," a noted jai alai player.

He was a wizard at throwing grenades, using the same motion he mastered with the *chistera.*

Bigeard, waiting for the TOT (Time on Target), counted backward from thirty, and the batteries start firing in rotation, so that shells fired from different distances hit their objectives at the same time, the most distant firing first. At 6 A.M. came the detonations of the first salvo, their converging trajectories exploding on Vietminh positions. In the distance, the eastern hills were tinged with orange. For half an hour, at intervals, the artillery preparation pounded the two villages, as the paratroopers advanced toward trenches where the Vietminh had embedded their light antiaircraft guns, only about two miles from the base.

Tourret's 8th Choc moved on Ban Ban on the right. The 6th BPC, under Captain Thomas, moved on Ban Ong Pet on a parallel line. The artillery fired for five minutes, then fell silent for three minutes, and the shells exploded three hundred yards beyond where the paras waited in ditches or streambeds.

This was the kind of fighting they had trained for on their obstacle courses, but it was a very long three hundred yards as they slogged through paddies, crouched along low dikes, and ducked around clumps of bamboo. The 6th BPC met stiff resistance from enemy trenches at the edge of Ban Ong Pet. At 9 A.M., the Bearcats arrived as the fog lifted and the day turned bright and clear, diving, turning, diving, strafing, and dropping their napalm, setting the hills on fire. The paras advanced, sometimes crawling, sometime flat on their stomachs, as streams of tracers darted above them, and finally reached the parapet of the main Vietminh trench, which was intact.

Lieutenant Le Vigouroux's platoon was in the lead. "Berthu," he called to the Basque, "twenty meters to the left, a machine gun." The Basque flung a grenade that flew over the trench parapet and exploded. Then he threw two more. When these too had exploded, Le Vigouroux and his men jumped into the trench. The antiaircraft machine gun was a pile of mangled metal, surrounded by six dead Vietminh.

Le Vigouroux, like a kid who's scored a goal and wants to tell his coach, got on the radio to Bigeard and said: "Bruno, it's going great. I've taken a few losses, but I've reached my objective and bagged a machine gun."

Bigeard congratulated him but got no response. Le Vigouroux had fallen to the ground. Someone else got on the line and said: "The lieutenant just took a bullet to the head."

Another promising young officer gone, thought Bigeard, while our great leaders in Hanoi are sleeping in their beds or getting laid. He was in radio contact with each company, and brought them into the fray as needed. Each enemy trench had to be occupied at the forward end, with the men fighting their way to the rear. When the 6th BPC was faced with a Vietminh counterattack, Sergeant Ney brought in his three tanks from central command, their 75s at the lowest elevation, and fired into the trenches, sometimes crawling over the parapets to crush the *bo dois* with their treads.

Around noon, Lieutenant Préaud's three M24s coming up from Isabelle reached the 8th Choc outside Ban Ban and opened the way by pounding its bamboo walls and thatched-roof houses. Vietminh artillery, dug into hillside caves, had limited sectors of fire, and were unable to shift toward the tanks, which had suddenly appeared in an unexpected location. Two of Préaud's M24s took bazooka hits, but kept firing. The speed and coordination of the attack, incorporating six tanks with two elite battalions, took the Vietminh by surprise.

The mobility and firepower of the Chaffees gave the paras confidence, although the five-man crews inside the World War II–era tanks were as cramped as circus clowns in a miniature car. The poor ventilation was further fouled by fumes from fired shells. But the tactics used on that day closely resembled those adopted by American air-land command in terms of agility, depth, initiative, and synchronization.

An account of the battle was later written in orderly paragraphs, but the actual fighting was chaotic. Each antiaircraft gun was protected by a Vietminh company. Trenches were taken and retaken in hand-to-hand combat. The two sides were at such close quarters that the artillery and air support could not intervene. The villages were barely visible under the dust and smoke. Inside the trenches, the Vietminh had dug protective pits from which they had to be routed by grenade and bayonet. One of the Bretons in Lieutenant René Le Page's 1st Company of the 6th BPC, said: "They're encrusted like oysters on a rock." Le Page's company took the heaviest losses, ten dead (including Lieutenant Vigouroux), and twenty wounded. Le Page took Vigouroux's wedding ring, glasses, and wallet to send to his wife, Marguerite, but all were subsequently lost in the fighting.

South of Ban Ong Pet, Lieutenant Francis de Wilde's 4th Company of the 6th BPC stormed through enemy lines and took one of the trenches where antiaircraft machine guns were placed. He knew the Viets would throw in reinforcements.

Lieutenant Jean Jacob, whose platoon thirty yards away had come up against an enemy unit, found six men and a machine gun to block a Vietminh thrust. When Vietminh reinforcements were sent in, he mowed them down as they crawled out of their trench. But Jacob was killed in the course of the skirmish and de Wilde's right hand was blown off by a heavy machine gun. Lieutenant Jacob was about to go home. His wife, Marcelle, had given birth to a son. "I know it's long," he wrote in his last letter, "but try to be patient."

At 3 P.M., Bigeard ordered his troops to fall back. My God, these balance sheets, he thought, medals for some, wooden crosses for others. He had 20 killed, including 2 officers, and 70 wounded, as well as two tanks hit by bazookas. The Vietminh, however, had 350 dead, while many of their wounded had been carried away and could not be counted. Captured and destroyed weapons added up to five 20mm antiaircraft cannons, a few 12.7mm machine guns, two bazookas, fourteen light machine guns, and a pile of small arms. It was not a decisive victory, however, for the paras were unable to penetrate deeper behind the Vietminh lines and knock out the 37mm antiaircraft guns that were doing the most damage to incoming flights.

Préaud and his three tanks were sent back to Isabelle. Captain Tourret, whose 8th Choc had broken through the defenses at Ban Ban, was mortified: "I felt that if they hadn't taken away my tanks, I could have captured the officer commanding the 308th Division. If I'd had all six, I would have caught Giap himself by the scruff of the neck."

Although exhausted by nine hours of fighting, the French battalions returned to Dien Bien Phu in high spirits. They had proved that they were capable of inflicting heavy losses on the enemy, reversing the equation by assaulting them in their defended positions. They regained some of their lost confidence. "Bravo, Bruno," Castries told Bigeard. For once, Castries had good news to report, on the same day that Cogny was telling two reporters from *Paris Match*, "In Dien Bien Phu, the carrots are cooked."

In the What If? department, it has been argued that the March 28 surprise attack showed that if the garrison had been sent more tanks, they could have held out longer. More tanks might have enabled them to keep the airstrip open, facilitating the evacuation of the wounded, which would have raised morale. More tanks could have kept the road to Isabelle open. Combined teams of infantry and tanks could have kept after the Vietminh antiaircraft positions. In the final analysis, what is a conjecture but an attempt to make history more palatable?

Dancing the Last Dance

At the Ritz nightclub in Hanoi on March 28, a Hawaiian band played its island tunes, and a starlit ceiling softly bathed the dance floor, which was also lit from below, so that the long white dresses of the Vietnamese taxi girls glowed and swirled like the sails of a sampan. When the lights were turned up at the end of each dance, they shone on a table where three spahi (cavalry) officers in light khaki uniforms, accented by gold and scarlet epaulets, sat with one of those ineffectual angels who are rented by the ticket. The spahi captain was with two lieutenants from his unit, taking a brief respite from protecting the Hanoi–Haiphong road.

All three vied for the favor of the taxi girl, and it soon became clear that she preferred the handsome young lieutenant, who was also the best dancer.

The captain, to get rid of the competition, sent the young lieutenant on a midnight mission. "My chauffeur will drive you to the Citadelle," he said, "where you will find a detachment of tanks and half-tracks, and you will patrol the city to reassure the population." The lieutenant arrived at the Citadelle muttering under his breath that he'd been sent on a contrived mission in order to further the captain's romantic expectations. At the head of his caravan, he drove down empty streets, crossed the Red River, circled the lake, and entered the Chinese quarter, telling himself, "If I hurry, I can get back to the Ritz to dance the last dance."

We Must Strike at Many Places at a Time

By the end of March, Dien Bien Phu was surrounded. The only way in was by parachute, and there was no way out. The battle had become a siege. Castries wondered whether Giap would attack or employ the less costly method of stifling the base.

Giap was planning on mounting an attack on several centers of resistance at once. The trench work accomplished during the pause was the key. Axial trenches coming from the north spread east and west in zigzags to within two hundred yards of the centers of resistance. As Langlais later put it, "Giap understood Vauban." Sébastien Le Prestre de Vauban, a military engineer who rose to the rank of marshal under Louis XIV, was a master of both defensive and offensive warfare. He built a wall of 160 fortresses around France to secure its borders. The French passion for breastworks went back to Vauban, and one might see in Dien Bien Phu, by way of the Maginot Line, an atavistic reflex. But Vauban was also skilled at taking fortresses. At the siege of Maastricht, in Holland in 1673, he elaborated a system of parallel trenches connected by zigzag trenches that allowed the French troops to approach with relative safety. This was exactly what Giap was doing 281 years later. In nearly three centuries, the armament had changed but not the tactic. Surround the fortress. Cut off supplies and reinforcements. Prevent sorties by the garrison. Assault the weakest points of defense under cover of artillery.

On March 27, Giap summoned his commanders and delivered his instructions: "Destroy the entire eastern sector. Occupy the heights to the east and turn them into attack positions from which we can threaten the centers of resistance Claudine and Huguette on the left bank of the Nam Yum. . . . Until now, our army has limited its battles to a single night. . . . The attack on Eliane will be part of a coordinated attack on all eastern strongpoints, as well as an indirect attack on the central command post. Our artillery will be spread out to hit several objectives."

On Monday, March 29, low clouds hid the hills surrounding the base, and rain turned the ochre ground to mud. The rain prevented the arrival of the daily quota of aerial photographs, but thanks to the protection of two tanks, some of the most severely wounded were evacuated by ambulance from Isabelle. The tank crews wondered why they weren't fired upon. Maybe for once Giap was respecting the red crosses. The wounded were added to the pile of 175 packed in Dr. Grauwin's infirmary.

Giap was otherwise occupied, addressing the troops: "Today our positions are ready. That was an immense labor indeed. It has enabled us to tighten our encirclement. The central sector is now under the range of our mortars. . . . A big attack has been decided. . . . We must strike at many places at a time to wipe out as many enemy as possible. . . . We must destroy and occupy his artillery positions, and we must occupy and hold such places that will threaten the remaining enemy. . . . This is not a general assault but will create the conditions for one. . . . Once this attack is won, we will have the conditions to wipe out the whole French force at Dien Bien Phu."

In Hanoi, U.S. consul Paul Sturm reported to Washington a conversation he'd had with Navarre, who had said that the Vietminh seemed to believe that by piling up the wounded at Dien Bien Phu they would cause him to end the battle for humanitarian reasons. "Even if I had three thousand wounded," Navarre had said, "that fact would not cause me to yield."

On March 30, Major Clémençon, commander of the Legionnaire battalion holding Huguette 6, which was formerly one of the Anne-Maries deserted by the Thais, went to see Castries to ask for reinforcements. He had the impression that the base commander was barely listening to him. Dien Bien Phu is like a spool of wool unraveling, Clémençon thought. Someone has to tie a knot to stop it.

Scene 2: April Is the Cruelest Month

The entrenched base at Dien Bien Phu, surrounded by Giap's infantry, had lost the initiative. The Vietminh chose the time and the place of attack, deploying as much equipment and as many troops as required. For the French, it was a guessing game. Where and when would the enemy strike? Everything depended on the unpredictable moves of the attacker. Giap had three divisions to throw into the battle, while Castries suffered an acute manpower shortage; his remaining strongpoints were thinly manned. His solution was to hold battalions in reserve, to be moved to critical points as needed. This stopgap measure prolonged the outcome, but did not change it.

The strongpoints most vulnerable to attack were the most weakly defended. It was fine to say, as some did, that war was like a chess game. But in chess you had time to ponder your next move, while here it was a matter of rapid response.

Buried in his bunker, on the phone with Hanoi, Castries argued and beseeched for reinforcements, but they did not come. As one officer put it: "When they were discussing in Hanoi how to get our finger out of the gears, they didn't realize we were already in them up to the shoulder." In Hanoi the high command argued about dropping men at night over a limited drop zone. They argued about sending volunteers who had never jumped. Every hour counted, but they spent days arguing. Add to that General Cogny's reluctance to move troops out of the Red River Delta for what already seemed like a lost cause, and a self-fulfilling prophecy resulted.

Until now, Giap's army had never fought a battle for more than a single night. Night meant protection from planes, tanks, and artillery. The goal was to destroy French strongpoints, take the equipment, remove the wounded, and fall back. The operation launched on March 30, however, was a new departure—simultaneous attacks on the so-called Five Hills, which formed an arc twelve hundred yards long on the eastern face of the French perimeter. Dominique 1, the northernmost point and the closest to the meandering Nam Yum, was a vulnerable hill only 180 feet high, seriously undermanned by unreliable Algerian fusiliers. Dominique 2, about four hundred yards to the southeast of Dominique 1, was a towering, elongated hill fifteen hundred feet high and three hundred yards long, which needed a full battalion to cover its many approaches, but was held by only two companies of Algerian fusiliers. Three hundred yards due south of Dominique 2 stood Eliane 1, only sixty feet high, with a bare and dusty dome, held by a single company of Moroccans. Behind Eliane 1 stood Eliane 4, where several reserve battalions were posted. The last and southernmost of these eastern hills was the indispensable Eliane 2, a massive egg-shaped bluff cut by ravines, with one end higher than the other. The lower end, to the east, as broad and gentle as a beginner's ski slope, was called the Champs-Élysées, and made a tempting entryway for the Viet-minh. Eliane 2 had only two companies of Moroccans to cover its many gullies and outcroppings. At the top were the ruins of the former provincial governor's domicile. All that remained of it was the concrete cellar where the officer in charge located his command post.

Giap hoped to take all five hills in a single night, using his customary tactics: artillery preparation at dusk, no longer concentrated on a single target, as it had been in mid-March, but firing on all five hills at once, since he now had more guns, positioned at closer range. As night fell the infantry would pour out of the lattice of recently dug trenches and storm the hills. Giap was throwing five regiments of three battalions each into the initial assault: the 141st and 209th from the 312th Division, the combat-tested veterans who had taken Béatrice; the 98th and 174th from the 316th Division; and the 102nd from the 308th Division. In all, between ten thousand and twelve thousand men. The capture of any one of the five hills, defended by a total of two thousand men, would offer the Vietminh a balcony over the central command post, with its batteries and transmission center, as well as the capability to install artillery at closer range.

If the Viets Have Dug Trenches, It's Not to Plant Peas

On the morning of March 30, the rain came down in sheets, turning the base into a swamp. Colonel Langlais stepped out into the sticky, tenacious mud that covered his jump boots and made every step an effort. The latest intelligence said that the Viets would attack in the afternoon, probably at one of the strongpoints to the east. He was concerned about the 3rd Battalion of the 3rd Regiment of Algerian Fusiliers (RTA), which was holding Dominique 1 and 2. Major Pierre Tourret of the 8th Choc, whom Langlais considered a pain in the ass, albeit a valuable pain in the ass, had recently told him that the crucial hill of Dominique 2 was poorly defended. After thirty months of campaigns, the men of the 3rd RTA needed a rest. The battalion should have been commanded by a major, not Captain Jean Garandeau, who, incidentally, had come down with the flu. It should have had twenty officers and fifty noncoms, not ten and twenty. Some platoon leaders were corporals.

An annoyed Langlais had told Tourret: "If I understand you correctly, you're trying to tell me that Garandeau doesn't know what he is doing." Tourret said, "If you don't believe me, go see for yourself." Then Lieutenant Colonel Maurice Lemeunier, Langlais' number two, told him, "Dominique is weakly held and poorly defended." Just the previous night, Langlais had played bridge with Lemeunier and the Legionnaire major Michel Vadot in Castries' bunker. For a few hours, they forgot the battle, except for the occasional shell. There had been a clang on the steel roof of the bunker. "That one didn't explode," Vadot said.

"Playing the two of clubs was a mistake," Castries admonished.

"I'm sure I was right to play it," Vadot said.

Langlais, his helmet pushed down between the ears of his vulturelike head, decided on the morning of March 30 to inspect the eastern positions. Lemeunier had seen the trenches coming up to the barbed wire of Dominique 2, and told him: "If the Viets have dug trenches that close, it's not to plant peas." Langlais was not a man who dealt in nuances. He divided all other soldiers, whatever their rank, into "good" and "no good." Yet he was the commander whom the men in the strongpoints saw and respected, while Castries was a hidden presence inside his bunker. As Franceschi, a paratrooper of the 8th Choc, put it: "By exposing himself to enemy fire, he wanted to show us why we were here—to get ourselves killed. But he always acted as if we would win, whether he believed it or not."

That morning on the high hill of Dominique 2, Lieutenant Lucien Aubert, a young doctor assigned to the Algerians, found that the rain had flooded his poorly insulated infirmary. As the orderlies mopped up, Aubert was aware of a drop in morale among the fusiliers. It had begun in mid-March, when they witnessed the rout of their fellow Algerians on Béatrice.

On Eliane 2, the southernmost of the eastern centers of resistance, Lieutenant Dr. Henri Premillieu reflected that each stronghold had its own personality, its own strengths and weaknesses. The strength of Eliane 2 was its massive size, its jagged slopes and escarpments, and four rows of barbed wire that encircled it. Its weakness was the open slope of the Champs-Élyseés, directly across from the two unoccupied hills, Mount Baldy and Mount Phony, that could easily be invested by the Vietminh.

Mount Baldy was less than a hundred yards away. Premillieu spent the morning preparing stretchers and bandages.

Langlais, huffing a bit as he climbed the hills, was not happy with what he saw. Dominique 1 was held by a single pared-down company, Lieutenant Jean Chataigner and his ninety Algerians of the 3rd Battalion of the 3rd RTA, supported by a Legionnaire mortar company. Many of this battalion's Arabic-speaking officers had been either killed or sent home. Those were the officers who knew their men, who read the illiterates their letters from home, and respected their religious holidays, and knew how to tie a *chechia* (head scarf). Several platoons, as Tourret had warned Langlais, were commanded by noncoms, and in February, sixty-five veteran fusiliers had been replaced by young recruits who had never seen combat.

On Dominique 2, the highest hill, Captain Garandeau, still down with the flu, had two companies, the 9th and the 10th, commanded respectively by Lieutenants Lensch and Marie. Each company had been allotted a Reibel machine gun, with a camembert magazine that belonged in a museum.

There was an urgent need to beef up these strongpoints, which the base could not afford to lose. Stationing only ninety men on Dominique 1, the most exposed of the eastern posts, was folly. Langlais drove over to Eliane 4, the hill directly behind Eliane 1, where Major Bigeard's 6th BPC and Major Botella's 5th BPVN were being held in reserve. The two majors had their command post in a cave at the base of the hill. Botella broke open a can of beer that they passed around. "I think they'll hold on Dominique 2," Langlais said, "but I'm worried about the isolated company on Dominique 1." Botella said he'd send over his 4th Company in the afternoon to relieve the Algerians.

From Eliane 4, Langlais went to the key CR, Eliane 2, three hundred yards to the southeast, held by Captain Jean Nicolas with two companies of Moroccan fusiliers of the 1st Battalion of the 4th RTM. Nicolas didn't have the men to occupy Baldy and Phony, and was counting on artillery to keep the Viets away. All they had to do was walk across from Baldy and up the Champs-Élysées.

On Eliane 2, Langlais found Captain Nicolas well dug in at the concrete cellar of the former governor's house. "How's your morale?" he asked. "Will your men hold?" Nicolas knew his Moroccans, tough Berbers from the Atlas Mountains, whose language he spoke. "If their officers hold, they'll hold," Nicolas said. Langlais said he would send the 1st Company of the 1st BEP, under Captain Lucciani, in reinforcement. With his system of borrowing companies from positions not immediately threatened, Langlais had improvised what amounted to a second line of defense. But instead of counterattacking with full battalions, he was plugging gaps in multiple locations with a limited pool of reserves. It was like a bucket brigade with too few men putting out too many fires at once.

Giap's units left their staging areas around noon on March 30 under heavy rain, advancing in single file through the trenches that had been dug in the last two weeks of March. At his surgery unit, Dr. Paul Grauwin reflected that the French, like the Vietminh, had improved their networks of trenches. You could now go from the hospital to the staff bunkers of Castries and Langlais through a minelike tunnel without exposing yourself to shell fire over open ground. But the stretchers still arrived in the open, and the bearers couldn't run while carrying wounded. When a Thai bearer was killed just outside the hospital, Grauwin asked Langlais for a covered trench on the approach.

Dr. Grauwin now had six shelters with rooms for 250 beds. Double-decker bunks had been dropped in, along with the contents of a U.S. field hospital: three hundred blue pajamas with mother-of-pearl buttons, three hundred sheets and white wool blankets, folding cots, and hundreds of vials of antibiotics. He was not accustomed to such luxury. His mail, which came intermittently, was dropped with the supplies. His only letter asked: "Please let us know if you would like your monthly pay sent to you or if we should hold it for you."

Dr. Grauwin was in charge of triage, which gave him the power of life and death. It was he who decided on the priority of operations, since an abdominal took longer than five amputations. He was particularly pleased with two new aides, who had literally dropped in on him. One was Fleury of the 8th Choc, who had volunteered to be his jack-of-all-trades. Fleury was a private, and not just any private, but one of those rare beings who can solve problems, a fixer, a *debrouillard* (disentangler). It was Fleury who went out at night to pick up steel strips from the runway to reinforce the roof of the surgical unit. It was Fleury who dug niches in the sides of communication ditches, like the alcoves for statues in Romanesque churches, where the wounded could lie down when all the beds were filled. Dr. Grauwin was so thankful, he gave Fleury his signet ring. The other new aide was Geneviève de Galard, who, being stranded on the base, volunteered to be a nurse. At first the orderlies grumbled. "What do we want with a girl? She can't even lift a stretcher." But they were won over when they saw that she didn't shrink from any task. She cleaned the raw wounds of amputees, of men with abdomens showing their intestines; she changed the shit-filled bandages of men with artificial anuses; she calmly went down the rows of wounded, doing what had to be done and saying what had to be said. The orderlies gave her a pillow and sheets, and a change of clothes.

It Was Like the End of the World

At 6 P.M. on March 30, the artillery barrage came down on all five hills with the roar of a hundred lions. "I've never seen anything like it," recalled Lieutenant Allaire, in charge of Colonel Bigeard's mortar company on Eliane 4. "It was like the end of the world. I thought the sky was falling. We were glued to the ground like suction pads. The earth was trembling. You couldn't see ten feet in front of you for the smoke."

Lieutenant Le Boudec, one of Bigeard's company commanders, had found some mortar-shell cases to cover his trench. "Suddenly the shells began flying," he recalled, "at high density and in quick succession. I jumped into my narrow trench and waited for the shelling to end. When I climbed out of my hole the ground was ploughed and pitted. I saw the decapitated head of my medical orderly, Thissen, and the corpses of a mortar crew, three French and three Vietnamese."

The shelling was unrelenting on central command, where Colonel Guy Vaillant's batteries were responding. In the first twenty-four hours, nine gunners were killed and sixty-five were wounded. Vaillant had three 155s, twenty-one 105s, and seventeen 120mm mortars. Ammo stocks had been built up during the pause and repair crews had patched up damaged oil cylinders and punctured wheels.

At the hospital, Dr. Grauwin's unit was hit and the lights went out. Wounded Moroccans were coming in from the Elianes. They didn't like the dark, and Grauwin did the rounds with a flashlight to reassure them. In a rare moment of discouragement, Geneviève, lying on her cot, told him, "I wish I could go to sleep and never wake up." This time, he reflected, it was much worse than Béatrice. More wounded were coming in sooner.

Fleury had volunteered to be a *sonnette* (lookout) to the west of the airstrip, an area infiltrated by the Vietminh. He was hunched in a trench with a flamethrower. When he was attacked, he fired until his reservoir was empty. He saw men aflame rolling in the dust. He climbed out of the trench and fired his submachine gun before being hit by a dozen bullets.

Not only was Dr. Grauwin affected by Fleury's death, not only were the wounded piling up as never before, but he also had a water problem. The water purifier, on the bank of the Nam Yum near the Bailey bridge, was under fire. Another trench had to be dug from the hospital to the purifier, under the barbed wire in zigzag. Two trips a day, at 6 A.M. and 5 P.M., brought in fifty gallons.

In the late afternoon of March 30, Major Botella sent his 4th Company of Vietnamese paratroopers to relieve the Algerian 11th Company on Dominique 1. When they arrived they saw the Algerians, soaked and exhausted, getting their gear together. From their ashen faces all hope had been drained. Lieutenant Martinais, in command of the 4th Company, presented himself to Lieutenant Jean Chataigner, commander of the 11th Company, and inspected the strongpoint. He found the defenses in poor shape. The barbed wire was falling down, no mines had been laid, the containers of napalm had been buried and couldn't be used, the trenches and dugouts had turned to mud. Martinais called Botella to ask for sappers, who soon arrived. He and the sapper officer were drawing up a plan to improve the defenses when a deluge of shells began to fall.

Lieutenant Reboul's mortar crew of Legionnaires took a direct hit, killing Reboul and most of his men. Panic spread among the Algerians. One platoon fled down the slope. Martinais fired a few volleys, but that didn't stop them. Then the Vietminh infantry appeared, having covered the barbed wire with earth-filled mats. There remained about thirty Algerians, along with forty surviving Legionnaires from the mortar company, and Lieutenant Martinais' company of Vietnamese paratroopers, perhaps two hundred in all, up against the Vietminh 209th Regiment. "The position gave way bit by bit," Martinais recalled, "and as night fell I was taken prisoner. The Viets separated me from my men, who were 90 percent Vietnamese. I never saw a single survivor. I was told they paid dearly for being on the wrong side." Lieutenant Chataigner was also taken prisoner. Dominique 1 fell at 9:45 P.M.

Dominique 2, across RP41 from Dominique 1, three hundred yards to the southwest, was an elongated hill, towering more than 1,250 feet and wider at the eastern end facing the Vietminh, where Captain Garandeau had his command post. Langlais had sent no reinforcements, hoping that the two companies of Algerians would suffice.

The artillery preparation on this easternmost CR was so intense that it blew holes through the barbed wire. At 7 P.M., the Vietminh infantry poured into the breaches, outflanked two machine-gun nests, and overran Lieutenant Marie's 10th Company.

From his vantage point on Eliane 4, three hundred yards to the south, looking through his binoculars, as the sun sank behind him, Colonel Bigeard saw Algerians running down the western slope of Dominique 2. Lieutenant Lentsch of the 9th Company called headquarters to say that his men refused to fight. Some ran toward their attackers with their arms in the air, while others sat in their trenches with their hands behind their heads. With his few remaining loyal men, Captain Garandeau continued to fight in the 9th Company blockhouse until he too fell, as did the highest hill, around 8:30 P.M. The fall of the two Dominiques opened a wide gap in the defense perimeter that led straight to the main command post of Claudine.

Two hundred yards due south of Dominique 2 stood Eliane 1, the most vulnerable of the five hills, being only sixty feet high, and defended by a single company of the 4th RTM, Moroccan fusiliers. They had seen the flight of the Algerians, which had a contagious effect. The hill was quickly overrun, and its loss was reported by 8 P.M. In the first night of the attack, three of the five hills had been lost.

Debouch at Zero

In their simultaneous attacks on multiple fronts, the Vietminh overlooked Dominique 3, a forward artillery position nestled in a dead arm of the Nam Yum under a canopy of trees. For further concealment, it had been placed astride a six-foot-deep drainage ditch, which served as a corridor that the officers and men used to remain unseen. The drainage ditch continued northward past the base and at its tip a tangle of booby-trapped barbed wire kept infiltrators out.

The 4th Battery of the 4th Colonial Artillery Regiment (RAC) was commanded by Lieutenant Paul Brunbrouck, seconded by his firing officer, Second Lieutenant Baysset. The battery consisted of four 105mm howitzers manned by Senegalese crews in sandbagged pits. For protection, a company of Algerians under Lieutenant Filaudeau and a heavy machine-gun company were dug in at the northern end.

Dominique 3 was situated three hundred yards southwest of Dominique 2, and two hundred yards north of the Bailey bridge that led straight to Castries' bunker. RP41 ran north–south along its eastern edge. Its mission was to provide artillery support for the Dominiques and to protect central command against a Vietminh assault on RP41, in the gap between Dominique 1 and 2.

Although only twenty-seven, Brunbrouck had shown promise at Na San, that other hedgehog base, where he had commanded a company of mortars. He was tall and athletic, with a beaky nose and a narrow face. His sandy hair stood straight up, like a cartoon character showing fright. His motto was "Always ready, never hurried" and he displayed an instinctive tactical ability and a natural coolness under fire.

On Dominique 3, on the morning of March 30, the men were cleaning their rain-soaked gunpits.

Sergeant Bernard Laurent, in charge of howitzer number three, said, "The Viets haven't attacked in fifteen days. Maybe they're short of ammunition."

That afternoon came the barrage on the Dominiques. Sergeant Laurent said, "Good God! Do you see what I see? On Dominique 2 the Algerians are running down the slope."

Lieutenant Brunbrouck called Colonel Langlais on his radiophone. "The garrisons on Dominique 1 and 2 are falling back in my direction."

"Negative," came the reply. "The strongpoints are holding."

"I repeat: Fusiliers in disorder are arriving on RP41."

Sergeant Laurent shouted: "Fourth Battery at your stations."

Brunbrouck was worried about his own Algerians, whose compatriots were scurrying down RP41. Lieutenant Filaudeau reassured him: "My company is solidly commanded." Brunbrouck did not want fleeing Algerians stampeding his position and sowing confusion. He called headquarters: "The situation is getting worse. We can see the Viets chasing the Algerians. I'm going to have to open fire."

From afar, the Algerians and their pursuers seemed to form a solid mass, but as they approached, the distance between them became visible. Brunbrouck gave the order as the Algerians dispersed toward the river and the Vietminh were a hundred yards away: "For automatic and individual weapons, fire at will." The Vietminh, surprised by the small-arms fire, halted in their tracks. Brunbrouck had time to prepare the classic World War I tactic, which was to lower the barrels of his howitzers to the horizontal and use them as if they were rifles, aimed directly at the enemy over flat ground.

When the Vietminh reached the barbed wire strung along RP41 to protect the northern approach to the battery, he ordered: "Cannoneers at your pieces! Debouch at zero!" The fuses were set to explode at a short distance. Four shells burst in the midst of the *bo dois*, followed by a salvo every ten seconds. The Vietminh were taking losses, but kept coming, and night was falling. Brunbrouck moved from gun to gun, saying, "It's going to be a long night, so stay awake." He wondered how long his gunners could keep firing. It was a complicated and exhausting business, requiring a crew of twenty for each gun. The fifty-pound shells had to be carried from the ammo dump to the gun pit. The fuse had to be adjusted with a wrench-like tool either for detonation on impact or time delay. Only then could the round be lifted and pushed into the open breech. The muddy pit piled up with shell casings that had to be removed, and the gluey muck that accumulated in the breeches had to be cleaned. Instead of falling back, the Vietminh attacked repeatedly. In addition to the gun crews, the Algerian fusiliers were firing, and every man on the post—radio operators, drivers, cooks—had picked up a weapon.

Brunbrouck called Langlais and asked for reinforcements, but Langlais said, "If you're in danger, fall back."

"And my guns?"

"Blow them up."

"Out of the question. I'll hold."

Langlais hung up, but said, "I like that young man."

Brunbrouck was getting some help from two Quads commanded by Warrant Officer Lemeur, positioned under parachute camouflage along the airstrip, parallel to the drainage ditch. Lemeur caught the Vietminh, who were trying to outflank Brunbrouck, in enfilade. Each quad consisted of four Browning .50 caliber machine guns, mounted one above the other on both sides of a one-ton carriage. Two Quads added up to eight machine guns firing a thousand rounds a minute with deadly efficiency when the Vietminh came into the open. These meat grinders had been offered at the urging of U.S. officers who had seen what they could do in Korea. Around the Quads there was a carpet of cartridges a foot thick.

Mowed down by the Quads, the Vietminh fell back to RP41 and came upon the drainage ditch. Cutting through the barbed wire, they jumped into the ditch. Lieutenant Filaudeau triggered the explosive charges he had buried there, killing an estimated two hundred Vietminh.

The Vietminh momentarily pulled back, but at 2 A.M. came another attack from the southeast. Brunbrouck had to swing his guns to face them, and Lieutenant Laurent's number three gun took a hit that damaged the recoil mechanism, but the other three kept firing. The barrels of the .50 caliber machine guns got red hot, and no one had time to fetch water. Second Lieutenant Baysset ordered the Algerian crew: "Piss on them." Baysset saw that the Senegalese gun crews, covered with sweat and powder, were so exhausted that they were practically sleepwalking. He helped carry shells from the ammo dump to the guns.

Brunbrouck lasted through the night. The Vietminh had attacked over flat terrain without artillery, expecting an easy victory compared to the uphill climb for the other hills. Brunbrouck had beaten them back, firing eighteen hundred shells. At dawn on March 31, taking advantage of the mist, he pulled his howitzers back to the base over the Bailey bridge, one by one with his single Dodge truck.

Brunbrouck was awarded the Legion of Honor for disobeying orders to pull his guns back and blocking a Vietminh attack that could have ended the battle.

That Swine Is Betraying Me Every Day

A little after 10 P.M. on March 30, in the transmission room of the Hanoi Citadelle, a report arrived for General Cogny. But General Cogny was not there. He had left for a social engagement and couldn't be reached. No one knew where he was spending the night. This became known as Cogny's "Night at the Opera."

The report said: "Dominique 1 and 2 and Eliane 1 have fallen. . . . The situation remains difficult to reestablish without reinforcement. We will do what we can. Castries." Someone went over to the big wall map and x-ed out three small circles. General Bodet, the low-slung air force general with the black mustache and legs that formed a bracket, was there with several other officers. There was nothing they could do, but they were unable to leave the room. They sat around the radio set the way close relatives sit around a hospital bed to monitor the patient, recalled Navarre's aide Jean Pouget.

Navarre was in Saigon when he was told that Giap had attacked. He flew to Hanoi, arriving at the Citadelle a little after 1 A.M. on March 31. An anguished Bodet briefed him. Navarre was impatient for Cogny to take the necessary measures, but was told that Cogny could not be found.

In the meantime, Navarre drafted secret orders for Castries, commending him for defending the honor of France under the world's admiring gaze. The mounting enemy casualties and the approach of the monsoons, he said, offered every hope that Vietminh forces bogged down at Dien Bien Phu could not be used elsewhere. Reinforcement would be limited to a single paratroop battalion and a battery of 75s. This was at a time when Navarre's pet operation in central Vietnam, ATLANTE, was failing despite the commitment of forty battalions.

When Cogny arrived at eight, Navarre took him into a private office and they had a heated discussion. Their shouts could be heard in the hall-way. Navarre later told the writer Jules Roy: "I exploded. I bawled him out. And he told me to my face what he had been telling others for some time." In a letter to his wife in Paris, Navarre wrote: "That swine Cogny has been betraying me every day." Navarre thought about replacing Cogny, who kept asking for more troops for the Delta, while orchestrating a campaign of pessimism about the fate of Dien Bien Phu, but the question was, With whom? Even though, when it came to Dien Bien Phu, as the military historian Henri Le Mire put it, "Cogny was like a lifeguard who, seeing a man drowning, instead of throwing him a lifebuoy, gives him advice on how to improve his stroke." Navarre no longer trusted his Tonkin commander, who was in charge of the battlefield at Dien Bien Phu.

There was another small matter to attend to. Navarre had asked the Ministry of War in Paris to promote Castries from colonel to general. But Paris dragged its feet, no doubt thinking that if Dien Bien Phu fell, better it should be a colonel than a general taken prisoner. However, Castries' wife lobbied for her husband among her political friends, and spread the rumor that he would resign unless he had stars on his kepi. This was absurd on the face of it, for resigning in mid-battle amounted to desertion. But now Navarre was pleased to see that the promotion had just come in. He would have good news for a change. The gesture might seem meaningless in the middle of a catastrophic struggle, but that was not the case for men who measure their careers not in years but in rank.

Nicolas Is Still Holding

The outcome of the battle depended on Eliane 2, which loomed over central command. On March 30, Major Jean Nicolas, commander of the two companies of Moroccans who held the many-faceted hill, had come back from the morning staff meeting with Castries and announced: "It's for this evening." The artillery came in right on time. Some of the firing came from Mount Phony, a mere three hundred yards away, where the Vietminh had installed 75mm cannon and mortars. They also had staging positions for their infantry in the gullies, from which they advanced to Mount Baldy, one hundred yards away from the gentle eastern slope of Eliane 2 known as the Champs-Élysées. The bulk of Mount Baldy had prevented the Vietminh 98th Regiment from digging approach trenches up to the French wire. But moving under the cover of artillery preparation, *bo dois* had invested Baldy by 6:30 P.M. The Vietminh commander moved two battalions through a dry streambed toward the beckoning slope of the Champs-Élysées.

That afternoon, Langlais had sent Lieutenant Lucciani and his 1st Company of the 1st BEP over to Eliane 2 to reinforce Nicolas' Moroccans. The Legionnaires were posted in the first line of defense on the eastern slope, above the Champs-Élysées, but found the trenches too shallow. They dug deeper, cursing "those fucking Arabs." Lieutenant Nicod, an Arabic-speaking veteran of Monte Cassino, and his company of Moroccans held the line. During the artillery preparation, a shell had blown off the log roof of Nicod's command post. "Since it's rare for a shell to fall twice on the same spot," he recalled, "we didn't budge."

Lieutenant Dr. Premillieu, who had trained as a military doctor because his math wasn't good enough to get him into Saint-Cyr, was behind Nicod in a field infirmary and had a fine view of Mount Baldy. He flew a Red Cross flag, which turned out to be an obvious target, for he heard the whistling of shells, and he just had time to grab a knapsack and fill it with some of his medical equipment. He climbed up to the main command post at the summit. There he joined Major Nicolas and Captain Lacroze in their concrete bunker with a thick roof of logs, where they were directing the defense.

At 8 P.M., a Moroccan noncom called out to Nicod that he saw Vietminh units advancing on the Champs-Élysées. Through his binoculars, Nicod noticed that instead of keeping intervals, they were marching in tight groups of a dozen. Night had fallen, but the glowworm planes were dropping flares, lighting up the targets.

Nicod called in artillery, and accurate fire from the 155mm howitzers decimated the Vietminh ranks. They left several hundred dead on the Champs-Élysées. The shells had timed fuses that burst above the ground, sending deadly fragments into the advancing infantry.

Nicod and Lucciani were also taking losses in their shallow trenches from the Vietminh guns that had been moved to Mount Baldy. At around

9 P.M., Major Nicolas told them to pull back to the stronger positions at the top. Nicod burst into Nicolas' command post and said, "That's it, they've outflanked us." The roof of the CP vibrated from shell bursts that were blowing up machine-gun emplacements. The Vietminh 98th Regiment was charging up the slope. There was so much firing that the French defenders were suffocating from the smoke, and had to move out to establish a temporary command post on the reverse slope.

When Major Nicolas moved out of his bunker, he maintained radio silence. Langlais, unable to reach him at 10 P.M., wrongly concluded that the Vietminh had taken Eliane 2. He ordered artillery fire on the summit. On Eliane 4, Colonel Bigeard habitually listened to all the radio frequencies to get an overall sense of the battle. He had followed Nicolas' messages and broke in on Langlais: "Nicolas is changing his position. He is still holding." Langlais called off the artillery. Bigeard said he'd send over one of his companies.

At 11 P.M., Bigeard summoned Lieutenant Le Boudec, commander of the 3rd Company. "Here's the situation," he said. "On Eliane 2, Lucciani of the BEP is still holding. He's asked for reinforcements. . . . I'm sending you. We're not going to give up Eliane 2."

Le Boudec briefed his platoon leaders, and soon his company was making its way two hundred yards due south to the western slope of Eliane 2. They came under fire as they made their way up the slope. Second Lieutenant Chevalier, a newly arrived young officer, was in the lead. He and his men dropped to the ground and threw grenades, and the Vietminh fell back. Sergeant Perrin spotted Chevalier sitting on the ground and said, "Lieutenant, we won," shaking his shoulder. Chevalier did not reply. A bullet in the neck had severed his spinal cord.

Continuing their climb, Le Boudec's company came under automatic fire from Vietminh trenches. Le Boudec crawled into a shallow trench with his radioman, Raymond Lemoine. In the dark, the engagement was chaotic. His company was "yellowed," and the only way he could tell his Vietnamese from the Vietminh was to see their faces, for the Vietminh wore gauze masks to protect them from dust and the stink of rotting corpses. Here and there were Moroccans without their officers, lost in the dark and waiting for orders. Le Boudec took charge of a 60mm mortar team and began firing at the Vietminh thirty yards away. The "glow-worm," he recalled, "the small plane that flew at high altitude to avoid flak, dropped flares every five minutes, giving us momentarily what a full moon would, but when the flare went out it was pitch-black again."

The fighting on Eliane 2 continued through the night. Le Boudec was reinforced by half of Lieutenant "Lulu" Martin's 3d Company, 1st BEP, and by two tanks, the *Mulhouse* and the *Bazeilles*. Five successive counter-attacks were mounted. Warrant Officer Carette, crew chief of the *Bazeilles*, chugged up the slope, where he found a good location from which to fire at gun emplacements on Mount Phony with his 75mm gun. But a crew chief inside a tank has limited peripheral vision, and the Vietminh had in-filtrated two antitank teams onto Eliane 2. Carette's turret was hit and he was knocked unconscious. His helmet saved his life. A second round hit the engine, which caught fire. The inside of the tank filled with thick black smoke. Unable to breathe, Carette and the rest of the crew jumped out and into a ditch. As Carette jumped, he was hit in the leg by a machine-gun burst. Behind him, the *Mulhouse* was hit in the turret by a 60mm armor-piercing bazooka rocket, and three of its five crew members were wounded.

Meanwhile, on the reverse slope near the improvised CP, Dr. Premillieu had set up another field infirmary in an alcove where the jeep had been parked. He began treating the wounded who lined up for bandages and morphine shots. A paratrooper was brought in with a leg mangled by a 105mm shell, bleeding profusely. And yet he didn't seem in pain and he couldn't stop talking. Premillieu was not a surgeon, but he had no choice, and he lay the man on the ground, injected Novocain into the sciatic nerve, and performed the operation with a scalpel and a pair of scissors. As the manual said: "Ligature of the arteries with linen thread. Cut away skin and muscle until you obtain a fine open wound." Premillieu ampu-tated at the thigh, but didn't suture, and gave the para antibiotics and morphine. He was evacuated by stretcher to the main hospital, where one of the surgeons there finished the job, and he survived.

At 3 A.M., Captain Lacroze appeared. He had just shot two Viets with a carbine right in front of his improvised CP. Before fleeing, a third Viet hit him in the arm. The wound was clean; the bullet had gone through without hitting an artery. All Lacroze needed was a bandage and a shot.

At dawn on March 31, an exhausted Premillieu was out of bandages and medication. He wanted to get back to his main infirmary at the summit, which was strangely silent. He was amazed to find there his three Moroccan orderlies, who had been taken prisoner by the Viets, but no live Viets around. The Viets had told them, "Wait here, we'll be back for you," and the Moroccans had obediently complied. Now they helped Premillieu carry his equipment to his improvised infirmary. All around them lay the dead. There was Warrant Officer Abdullah, with his Muslim-prophet beard, and the Legionnaire captain Russeil, who had sworn never to be taken prisoner—he'd already been through that in 1940. Then the sun came up.

Eliane 2 held during the night of March 30–31 thanks to the flow of reinforcements that Langlais threw in from all the units he could find. In so doing, he hit on the tactic of repeated counterattacks on hills that the Vietminh had taken or partly occupied. The tactic surprised the Vietminh and threw them off balance. On Eliane 2, Le Boudec's company of colonial paratroopers had launched the assault, followed by Lieutenant "Lulu" Martin's company of Legionnaire paratroopers, joined by Ney's tanks. After five counterattacks, the Vietminh 98th Regiment fell back at 4:30 A.M. At dawn, one fresh Vietminh battalion hung on to a sliver of the eastern slope. Lieutenant Hervé Trapp's 2nd Company of colonial paratroopers relieved Lieutenant Le Boudec at the summit. They looked down at the broad slope of the Champs-Élysées covered with corpses and wondered that they were still alive.

A Vietminh report on their inability to take Eliane 2 said: "Our high command had not expected that the enemy would shell within its own lines. A barrage of shells was fired into our attackers and also behind them, cutting off reinforcements. . . . At midnight more reinforcements were sent to join their comrades, but the enemy repeated its tactic, hammering us with artillery and then counterattacking with infantry." The 98th Regiment took such heavy losses that Giap had it relieved by two battalions of the 102nd Regiment. Giap had committed thirty thousand men to what he hoped would be the final battle, but tenacious French resistance on Dominique 3 and Eliane 2 made it necessary for him to bring in reserves.

At 2:25 A.M. on March 31, Castries had sent an urgent message to air force general Dechaux in Hanoi: "Need maximum fighters and bombers on Dominique 2 and Eliane 1 when dawn breaks." Five hours later, a squadron of Helldivers, each carrying four five-hundred-pound bombs and armed with 20mm cannons, took off from the military airport. The squadron leader, Lieutenant Commander Andrieux, was a veteran pilot who wore black Vietnamese pajamas under his flight suit, in case he had to bail out over enemy territory. Andrieux orbited over the base at eight thousand feet until he saw a hole in the clouds. In the midst of heavy flak, he followed RP41 at four thousand feet until he spotted Dominique 2 and dropped his bombs. His single engine was hit and caught fire and he and his gunner were killed when they crashed into a mountain.

Castries had decided to launch counterattacks on the captured hills, and was desperate for fresh troops, since the battalion of paratroopers promised by Hanoi had been held up by bad weather. At dawn on March 31, he asked for a sortie from Isabelle, three miles to the south.

Responding to Castries' distress signal, a column of three companies of Legionnaires and Lieutenant Préaud's three Chaffees left Isabelle at 7 A.M. on March 31. Midway, at the village of Ban Lai, the Vietminh were waiting. Two battalions of the 57th Regiment, backed by 75s and bazookas, conducted a pincer movement. A bazooka shell tore the machine gun from Préaud's tank and a second shell burst through the armor. The tank had to be towed back to the base by another tank. The Legionnaires took losses from machine guns concealed in trenches. Colonel Lalande, having lost fifteen killed and fifty wounded, called back the column. He regretted that Isabelle was so far from central command. It should have been built where the village was. But it was too late to recalibrate. There would be no rescue operations from Isabelle, which was now completely isolated.

That Day Was True Hell

On the morning of March 31, the day broke iron gray. Colonel Bigeard came out of his bunker in a bad mood. He hated wearing a helmet, but Eliane 4 was being constantly pounded by Giap's artillery. Major Jean Bréchignac and his 2nd Battalion of the 1st Parachute Chasseur Regiment (RCP) were stuck at the Hanoi airport, waiting to take off for Dien Bien Phu. Nothing in Hanoi ever went right, Bigeard fumed. Here they were with their noses in the shit while Navarre and Cogny sniped at each other, and Sauvagnac, that great expert on parachute training, didn't have a clue. Colonel Sauvagnac, the paratroop commander in Hanoi, was a stickler for the rules.

Colonel Langlais had sent Sauvagnac this message: "You have not understood that there is no more GONO no more Airborne Group no more Legionnaires no more Moroccans but only 3000 combatants whose core are the paras who at the cost of untold heroism and sacrifices are holding off three of Giap's divisions. Try to understand that the battle can continue only if reinforcements arrive. If you continue delay Castries will ask Navarre for everything you are refusing."

More bad news came from Castries, who called Bigeard to say that the rescue column from Isabelle had failed to get through. However, Castries said, he wanted Bigeard to use his reserve units to launch counterattacks on Eliane 1 and Dominique 2.

If war is like chess, strategists should think two moves ahead. But Castries, disappointed that Isabelle could not be of help, was acting on impulse. These counterattacks were later seen to be the worst mistake of the battle of the Five Hills. For if the troops were able to retake Dominique 2 and Eliane 1, they would have to be rapidly replaced with fresh troops, since they would be reduced in number by losses and exhausted from fighting. And unless Bréchignac's paras arrived in time, the troops on the hills would be unable to hold when the Vietminh attacked at night. Castries had no troops to relieve them, but felt that the hills were like pearls in a necklace. If one fell the rest unraveled, and so he acted at once.

Despite his misgivings, Bigeard deployed his reserves on Eliane 4. Two companies from Major Tourret's 8th Choc were sent to Dominique 2, Cap-

tain Pichelin's 2nd and Lieutenant Bailly's 3rd. For Eliane 1, Bigeard sent
three companies from his own battalion: the 1st under Lieutenant Le
Page, the 2nd under Lieutenant Trapp, and the 3rd under Lieutenant Le
Boudec. A company from Captain Botella's 5th BPVN joined them. Both
counterattacks had artillery, tank, and aerial support.

François-Xavier Pichelin was a popular officer: solid, even-tempered,
and good-humored. He would have had a great career ahead of him, had
he lived. The captain and his company moved off at 1:30 P.M. for Dominique 2, a good six hundred yards to the north of Eliane 4. He was
backed by three tanks, one to neutralize the artillery fire from the Vietminh-
held hill of Dominique 1, the others to open lanes up the slope. The massive height of Dominique 2 looked down on them when they reached the
western slope and started up under heavy mortar fire. Pichelin maneuvered well, using smoke grenades that made his men cough but kept the
Viets from seeing them. The Vietminh, also coughing, saw the paras suddenly appear out of clouds of smoke.

Master Sergeant Carré, who was on his third rotation, led the final assault, telling his men: "If you start firing while you're running, you either
miss or you slow down, and when you reach your objective, your clip is
empty when you need it most. Here's how we'll do it. The PM [*pistolet mitrailleur,* or submachine gun] in one hand, a grenade in the other to drop
in the trench."

Carré's men fought like wolves, each man fighting for the good of the
pack, each man knowing he could rely on the others. The Vietminh fled
down the slope, leaving behind four 81mm mortars and shells. But having
taken one side of the hill, Pichelin's company now came under heavy mortar fire. The men were flat on their stomachs. Pichelin and his radioman,
Souchard, were standing, alongside Carré. A mortar shell made a direct
hit. Pichelin fell without a word. Carré was also killed. Souchard lost an
eye. The bodies of Pichelin and Carré were carried on stretchers to be
placed on the back of a tank. Sergeant Franceschi, himself hit in the arm
without realizing it, carried one end of Carré's stretcher and looked down
at his famous mustache, encrusted with dried blood. Although Major
Tourret had banned mustaches in the 8th Choc, he had made an exception for Carré.

Castries, whose role was limited to sending hourly reports to Hanoi, wired Cogny at 1:30 P.M.: "Very hard fighting Eliane 2. Counterattack on Dominique 2. Linkup with Isabelle impossible."

An hour later, he wired: "Dominique 2 retaken. Very strong resistance Eliane 1. We are not sure we can remain on either. Send maximum planes." Hanoi had already advised him that no reinforcements would be dropped that day.

Tourret called Bigeard at around 3 P.M. "We're holding half of Dominique 2," he said. "The Viets keep attacking with half a regiment at least. It's bad at the top. Pichelin was killed. I can't hold without reinforcements." Bigeard looked up at the sky. Above the range of Viet flak, he saw C-119s circling. He knew they were dropping supplies, not men. He told Tourret, "I have no one to send you. If you can't hold, pull out."

Disgusted, the men of the 8th Choc fell back cursing. They had fought hard, they had taken the hill, they had lost Pichelin and Carré, two of their best-liked cadres, as well as many others, and for what? Only to be told to come back down. It was a costly attempt for nothing.

Bigeard had sent Le Page's 1st Company, Trapp's 2nd and Le Boudec's 3rd to the low hill of Eliane 1, even though Le Boudec had spent the night of March 30–31 fighting on Eliane 2. Reaching the base of Eliane 1, they scrambled up the muddy slope, which soon grew steeper, each company climbing from a different direction. The Vietminh fired from foxholes they had dug during the night. "Our first assault was pushed back," Trapp recalled, "and we waited a bit to recuperate and try again."

On the second try, after fierce close combat, they were hanging on to the top of the hill. Sergeant Cazeneuve of Le Boudec's company, his face blackened by mud, brought back Sergeant Gosse, who had been blinded by a grenade. Unable to direct himself, Gosse had stumbled toward the Vietminh trenches with his arms extended, looking for something to touch. Corporal Pingwarski, the humorist of the early days, whose lower arm looked like hamburger, guided Gosse down the slope, where an ambulance was waiting, full of men from the 8th Choc who'd been taken off Dominique 2. There was just enough space for Gosse and Pingwarski between the stretchers. Racing toward the surgical unit, the ambulance was hit by a 105mm shell and all those inside were killed.

Trapp's assault teams, led by Lieutenants Samalens and Corbineau, were near the top of Eliane 1 when the Vietminh fled from their trenches. His friend Samalens was hit by a grenade fragment. Trapp wrote Samalens' wife, Blanche: "That day was true hell. The Viets pounded positions held by their own men to keep us from advancing."

Lieutenant Le Boudec came up a different lane through bodies and debris, crawling and throwing grenades. With him were the cameraman Pierre Schoendoerffer and the photographer Jean Péraud, whose eagerness to shoot the action muffled any sense of danger. "I've got my scoop," Péraud exclaimed, beaming. "A bomb falling on a trench and Viets flying through the air."

When Le Boudec reached the top of the hill, he had taken losses and was low on munitions. He suddenly felt a punch in the chest and his mouth filled with blood. A bullet had nicked his chest, and with that on top of fatigue, he passed out.

By 3 P.M., Lieutenant Le Page, the only officer left who hadn't been hit, also reached the top of Eliane 1 and called Bigeard: "We've reoccupied three quarters of the position, but we can hold only with reinforcements." Bigeard told Langlais that Dominique 2 and Eliane 1 had been retaken. What was the news concerning the arrival of Bréchignac and his paratroopers? "Negative," replied Langlais. They had been delayed by bad weather. More to the point, Hanoi was afraid of daylight drops, since two planes had been shot down that morning—one a Dakota carrying supplies piloted by Warrant Officer Guiraud, the other Andrieux's Helldiver. Unable to send fresh troops to relieve his companies on Eliane 1, Bigeard called the companies back.

The Biggest Open-Air Cemetery on Dien Bien Phu

In Saigon, on March 31, the telegrams were flying. U.S. ambassador David Heath, briefed on developments by his military aides, sent Washington a secret night action wire at 6 P.M.: "Unfortunately weather this morning has been bad and French have been unable up to 1100 hours to take off from Hanoi either in heavy bombers or drop missions although fighter-bombers have been able to operate over battlefield and last night both

B26s and Privateers were engaged. Inability to drop is of critical importance as it is Navarre's apparent intent to drop one or two parachute battalions and one additional battery of 105s and 75s today. In last night's battle French lost seven guns at Central Redoubt [Claudine] and 6 out of 12 guns at Isabelle [it was actually five out of eight]. If by nightfall today these reinforcements have not been made available to de Castries our military feel that Vietminh may be able to overpower 'Eliane' which is a hill position and thus be in posture to a final assault. Navarre will then be faced with crucial decision whether to engage more forces or fight it out with what is left at Dien Bien Phu."

Navarre cabled Premier Laniel: "Although I am doing all I can do to avoid it the fall of the entrenched camp has become a possibility sooner or later." Lieutenant Colonel Levain, the head of the Deuxième Bureau in Hanoi, struck a more optimistic chord in a report to Cogny: "Even if the loss of our units engaged in Dien Bien Phu must be considered, it is hoped that they could inflict on the Vietminh losses that would prevent them from attacking the Delta before summer. . . . This would have a positive effect on army morale and on national and international opinion. Thus, in order to destroy the Vietminh divisions, we must reinforce the entrenched camp." Levain also said that General Giap was believed to be conducting the battle in person, with a Chinese general at his side, and that his intention seemed to be to continue pouring in troops until he took all five hills.

However, contrary to Giap's conviction that the French were demoralized, they launched furious counterattacks on the captured hills, and held on to Eliane 2, which obliged him to throw in his reserves. Giap's cardinal rule was to attack only when he was sure of success. He decided to postpone the human-wave assault planned for April 1 and return to the tactic of burrowing and asphyxiating one hill at a time. Above all, he had to take Eliane 2, the key to the entire defensive position.

At 10 P.M. on March 31, Langlais called Bigeard and said: "You be the judge. . . . If you think you can't hang on where you are on Eliane 4, fall back to the other side of the Nam Yum. I authorize you to give up all eastern positions."

"As long as I've got a man left alive," Bigeard said, "I'm not giving up Eliane 2."

The fighting raged all night there, and at dawn on April 1 the exhausted troops still held, though the front was fluid. Two platoons had arrived from the 1st Battalion of the 13th DBLE, commanded by Captain Krumenacker, who recalled, "There was a wavering in the Vietminh ranks and we took the slope. I was watching them fall back through my binoculars and I spotted an automatic rifle [*fusil mitrailleur*] covering their retreat. I was standing up and the FM hit an artery in my right arm and the blood spurted out. I was evacuated." With Krumenacker gone, Lieutenant Gerardin led the men down the slope and routed the Vietminh. "I was near a tank and caught fragments from a grenade," Gerardin recalled. "When I came to I was on a stretcher."

On the morning of April 1 the weather improved, and four Bearcats based in Laos took off, led by Captain Claude Payen. The planes were fitted with belly tanks and their engines and fuel reservoirs were reinforced with steel plates. Each Bearcat carried two thousand-pound bombs. Guided from the ground, Payen and his squadron went into their dives and dropped their bombs over Mount Baldy, and then climbed to a safer altitude. Three of the four made it back to the base. The fourth crashed into a mountain. In the officers' mess at Bac Mai airport in Hanoi, the topic was Dien Bien Phu. For the first time in the Indochina war, the pilots faced accurate antiaircraft fire. It was now a duel between planes and flak, strike and parry. The engagement began below eight thousand feet.

The naval pilots operating from the *Arromanches* developed a rapport with the men on the ground. Lieutenant Klotz dropped some whiskey, wrapped in the metal casings used to carry three grenades, at a low altitude in a small chute. On April 3, he announced, "I'm making a pass to drop a new kind of bomb." He dropped three bottles, and the next day air force major Jacques Guérin, who guided the pilots from the ground, told Klotz, "Your new bomb was greatly appreciated."

Despite the air intervention, the shelling of Eliane 2 continued. The Moroccans dug pits beyond their trenches to bury their dead, but when they tried to pick up the fallen, they were hit by mortar fire. The corpses were left to putrefy in the alternating rain and sun. Eliane 2 became "the biggest open-air cemetery on Dien Bien Phu," one officer said. The eastern slope was a scene of cratered earth, roofless blockhouses, trenches blown in, blanketed with corpses. The men on the summit fought not only the Vietminh but the urge to sleep. They ate emergency rations. Water, brought in at high risk by the PIMs, was running short. The trenches had become latrines and hygiene was a forgotten word.

I Don't Give a Shit About Huguette 7

When Giap launched his attack on the five hills of the eastern perimeter on March 30, he also sent troops in a diversionary attack on two centers of resistance west of the Nam Yum to the north and northwest of the airfield. These were the former Anne-Maries, which had been deserted by the Thais in the first wave of attacks in mid-March. Now manned by fresh troops, they were renamed Huguette 6 and 7.

Huguette 7, the westernmost position and closest to the Vietminh lines, was a hill in the midst of rice paddies, triangular in shape. It was held by three companies of Vietnamese paratroopers (BPVN), one at each point of the triangle. These strongpoints were linked by communication trenches to the command post where Captain Alain Bizard was dug in. Bizard was a big, hearty man with a thick chest and calves, an Indochina veteran who had fought in mud and jungle, with thirteen citations to prove it. Recently, he had been serving on the staff of General Ely in Paris, but he left the chestnuts in blossom to volunteer for Dien Bien Phu. Giving up a cushy job for a living hell made his men view him with a mixture of admiration and bafflement. He was dropped on March 28, two days before the final battle began.

Huguette 7 had two defects, Bizard recalled: "The exposed blockhouses to the north had embrasures facing the Viets, which made them vulnerable to direct hits from their cannons; and access to the hill from the south was exposed to enemy mortars. Only during the early morning fog could personnel be moved safely in and out."

At 11 P.M. on March 30, his northern position was under attack. Lieutenant Thély was killed by a shell that came through the embrasure of his command post. Sergeant Tournay was left in command and fought off the *bo dois* of the 36th Regiment of the 318th Division. Bizard called for reinforcements, at a time when Langlais was focused on the defense of Eliane

2. "I don't give a shit about Huguette 7," Langlais shouted, his nerves on edge. "I'm trying to save Eliane 2."

As Bizard recalled, "The attack was obviously intended to disperse our counterbattery fire from Eliane 2. Luckily we had filled the Viet trenches closest to us, so they had to attack from farther back." His Vietnamese paras fought well through the night, but the Vietminh redug the trenches until they came up to the barbed wire. Bizard decided on the morning of March 31 to pull back the troops at the northern strongpoint and divided the ninety men that were left between the southwest and southeast strongpoints.

The Vietminh installed themselves on the northwest point of the triangle, thinking they were safe there from French artillery and air intervention since the combatants were so close to each other; the hill was only 150 yards wide at its base. Bizard waited until nightfall on March 31 and called in the 155s, which fired with deadly accuracy. The Vietminh took heavy losses, and by daybreak on April 1, Bizard's BPVN had retaken the northwest strongpoint. Langlais, realizing that his low opinion of the Vietnamese paras was not warranted, sent Bizard a company of Legionnaires led by Lieutenant Spozio as a reward. Spozio took over the northwest strongpoint.

On the night of April 1, General Giap, seeing that due to the resistance on Eliane 2 he could not take all five hills, intensified his attacks on Huguette 7. The strongpoint held by Spozio and his Legionnaires had been so torn up by French and Vietnamese artillery that they could not withstand the attack when it came at 10 P.M. from two battalions of *bo dois*. By 4 A.M., Spozio was surrounded in his blockhouse. Bizard put together a rescue force of one hundred paras and Legionnaires, backed by three tanks. They made it up to the northwest strongpoint, where they found a badly wounded Spozio, with thirteen survivors. Thirty-three of Spozio's Legionnaires were unaccounted for, and some had probably deserted. Others had been taken prisoner. One of these was Sergeant Gerswitch, who had fought with the Wehrmacht on the Russian front, and who later recalled: "They made me take my shoes off and carry them around my neck by the laces. They tied my hands behind my back and I walked barefoot over corpses." Bizard realized that the northwest strongpoint, destroyed beyond repair, was now indefensible. With Langlais' approval, he pulled out under the cover of fog after dawn broke on April 2.

The Tracers Lit Up the Corollas of Our Chutes

At Hanoi's Bac Mai airport, the men of Major Jean Bréchignac's 1st Battalion of the 2nd (Choc) Regiment paratroopers were waiting to be dropped on Dien Bien Phu. The battalion had a total of 868 men, 422 of them Vietnamese, and 22 officers. Captain Robert Charles of the 3rd Company recalled that "waiting in Hanoi, we knew that all was lost, but no one said so. We agreed to go in the name of honor and camaraderie." His friend Lieutenant Ruiter got off a letter to his fiancée, Marguerite: "We're chewing our fingers up to the elbow. It's a terrific battle, and we're going to change its outcome."

But they were not dropped on March 30 or 31, when they could have changed the outcome of the battle. Hanoi argued bad weather, but it happens in wartime that personalities count more than the weather. Colonel "Toto" Sauvagnac, commander of airborne troops in Indochina, took umbrage at all that Langlais asked for. When Langlais demanded that the paras be dropped right away, Sauvagnac took umbrage at daytime drops. When Langlais asked that tank and artillery crews be dropped to make up for losses, Sauvagnac insisted they accomplish six jumps before being sent. Langlais got on the radiophone and told Sauvagnac: "It's no harder to jump by parachute than it is to get off a bus on the fly." It took fifteen days of "exhausting discussions," as he later wrote in a report, to get Sauvagnac to drop men who didn't have the proper number of jumps. "I sensed the determined will," Langlais wrote in his report, "to delay by all possible means the sending of reinforcements."

Sauvagnac also opposed night drops, claiming that they were too dangerous, but finally conceded that they were the only option. The drop of the Bréchignac battalion began during the night of April 1–2. Bréchignac summoned his officers at noon on April 1 and told them: "The first wave will jump tonight about midnight. You know the situation. Choose your order of departure." Captain Minaud of the 4th Company drew the short straw. That night the Dakotas flew over the narrow Claudine drop zone but dropped only four sticks of twelve men each before the flak made them turn back. These night drops were a drama of their own. The men jumped through tracers and flak and landed in barbed wire, in trenches, on the roofs of shelters, or in the Nam Yum. They shed their harnesses and hoped they would stumble on friendlies. That night, six men were wounded by accidents or shell fragments.

Langlais thought the night jumps were one of the great feats in French military history. One of those dropped, Lieutenant Fragonard, arrived in Langlais' bunker with letters from his family and a bottle of Muscadet. Langlais' sister wrote that her children were playing Dien Bien Phu in the garden, having built an entrenched camp. A few days later, Lieutenant Fragonard was killed. Another para, Warrant Officer Lanzac, came by the hospital to say hello to Dr. Grauwin. The two had first met in 1947, when Lanzac was a corporal and Grauwin extracted a bullet from his thigh in Hanoi. In 1949, at Bac Kan, he'd removed shrapnel from behind Sergeant Lanzac's left ear. In 1953, he'd cut open Master Sergeant Lanzac's stomach. A few days after dropping in to see Grauwin, Warrant Officer Lanzac was brought in on a stretcher with a leg mangled above the thigh, and he died a few minutes later.

On the night of April 2–3, before Captain Charles's 3rd Company jumped, twelve of his Vietnamese paras were listed as missing. Charles figured they were the ones who had families in Hanoi. The Dakotas came over the base when it got dark, but made only half a dozen passes before being chased away by flak. Only fifty-four paras were dropped, plus the artillery lieutenant Jean-Marie Juteau and thirty-one gunners from a howitzer unit. Langlais was in a rage. "All around us when we jumped," Captain Charles recalled, were "tracers and bursts from the Viet AA. The tracers lit up the corollas of our chutes. When we landed, we were welcomed by 120mm mortars. Regrouping took a while. We jumped at midnight, and I rallied my company by 3 A.M. One man was killed by mortar fire. It was quite a performance, considering the conditions." Lieutenant Juteau was sent directly to Eliane 2 to repair the gun on the damaged tank *Bazeilles*. "I arrived on a hill so pitted," he recalled, "that you could not believe grass had ever grown there. A narrow pass took us to the cellar of an abandoned house. Intense fighting had just ceased after Bigeard's counterattack, backed by air strikes with napalm. Lucciani's Legionnaires had thirteen dead and twenty-three wounded." As Juteau got on the radio to signal his arrival, shells burst nearby and he began to smell the corpses strewn on the Champs-Élysées, which had become a no-man's-land where neither side wished to venture.

On April 3, Colonel Jean-Louis Nicot, commander of the Indochina Air Transport Group, ordered: "A battalion of paratroopers will be dropped tonight." In fact, fewer than four hundred men were dropped, including Bréchignac himself. Twenty planes took off that night, each carrying twenty paratroopers, with drops spaced every thirty minutes, to allow each plane to make its passes. They arrived over the base at 7,500 feet, dropped to 2,700 feet over the drop zone, which was five hundred yards long, and by dawn on April 4 seventeen sticks out of twenty had been dropped—340 men. There were two dead and ten injured, no worse than for a daylight drop. This drop led to an argument between Langlais and an air force controller in one of the Dakotas. Langlais had set fire to a gasoline drum on the Nam Yum and told the pilots to target the flaming drum and its reflection in the water as a drop zone. The air controller said, "It's against regulations. There will be some breakage." Sauvagnac had insisted that the paras be dropped over properly marked DZs. "Merde!" Langlais shouted. "Tell Sauvagnac I take full responsibility. Drop those men!"

The stocky but compact Bréchignac landed in barbed wire, where he left his pants, and burst into Langlais' bunker half naked. At the sight, Langlais found himself laughing, as he thought of Sauvagnac, that stickler for regulations, while he was in the midst of total chaos, where improvisation was de rigueur. Captain Marcel Clédic of the 2nd Company, who had also landed in barbed wire, came into Langlais' bunker. "Any bones broken?" Langlais asked. "One twisted ankle," Clédic said. It had been a lucky night, thought Langlais. But there were about two hundred men in Bréchignac's battalion still waiting to be dropped.

When he'd first jumped into Dien Bien Phu the previous November, Clédic had been a lieutenant. Now he was a captain, and commander of the 2nd Company, which was at full strength—200 men, half of them Vietnamese. Some were sick or wounded, so that only 170 jumped. "By

7 A.M. on April 4," Clédic recalled, "I had gathered my men and we were ordered to Eliane 2, which we reached in the early afternoon." The 3rd Company, under Captain Charles, reinforced the Algerians on Dominique 3. Lieutenant Minaud's 4th Company proceeded to Eliane 3, between the west bank of the Nam Yum and RP41, which was held by Moroccans. It wasn't in the regulations to divide a battalion that way, but at Dien Bien Phu it was a requisite.

By the time Clédic reached Eliane 2, the Vietminh had fallen back from the strip they still held. It was the first time the People's Army had given up ground after an attack. French patrols counted fifteen hundred *bo dois* and three hundred French dead on the Champs-Élysées, rotting in the mud.

In his report, General Giap wrote: "On Eliane 2, in the first night, we occupied two thirds of the position. At dawn the next day, the enemy reoccupied the positions it had lost. At night on March 31 we attacked again and we again occupied two thirds of the hill. The enemy again counterattacked and at night on April 1 we attacked again. Every inch of ground was harshly disputed and the battle lasted until April 4, with positions passing from hand to hand. The enemy fought with tenacity and received reinforcements."

In a Battle, Men Are Like Fuel

Unable to take Eliane 2, General Giap probed for weaknesses on other lines of defense. He focused on the two Huguettes, which protected the airstrip, first attacking the westernmost one, Huguette 7. Huguette 6, only fifty yards north of the runway, was held by a company of Legionnaires under Lieutenant Rastouil. The hill was shaped like a scallop shell, with a broad curved face at the northeast, narrowing to a straight side at the southern end. Huguette 6 was first attacked close to midnight on April 1, but the Legionnaires held. On the night of April 2–3, Giap sent in fresh troops. Huguette 6 was under artillery fire from the captured high hill of Dominique 2, and its barbed wire was chopped up. Still, Rastouil and his eighty-six surviving Legionnaires held.

On the morning of April 3, the battle-weary Legionnaires heard a familiar language coming over the Vietminh loudspeaker. A German-speaking voice offered a cease-fire to pick up some of the wounded at the base of Huguette 7. A party of stretchers-bearers trudged six hundred yards to the northwest and found the mutilated corpses of four of Spozio's Legionnaires. Once again, Giap was playing mind games. The message was: "This is what awaits you." Later that day, twelve Legionnaires deserted Huguette 6 through openings in the barbed wire.

In the evening, the post was again attacked, by fresh troops of the Vietminh 165th Regiment, and Langlais at 7:30 sent a company of the 8th Choc under Lieutenant Desmons to reinforce it. They proceeded from the improvised quarters of Epervier, between the southern end of the airstrip and the left bank of the Nam Yum, up a drainage ditch, supported by two tanks and some mortars. A lucky shot from a mortar hit a Vietminh command post behind Huguette 6 and the Vietminh attack wavered. The tanks and Desmons' company hit the Vietminh flank and the men of the 165th Regiment retreated. Desmons and his men returned to Epervier, a jerry-built shantytown where the trenches covered by steel strips from the runway were called *"le métro,"* and where the field brothel was installed in shacks, though the girls now worked as nurses.

On Sunday, April 4, heavy rain in Hanoi prevented the remaining 212 men of the Bréchignac battalion from taking off. Giap had decided to go for broke to take Huguette 6. At the same time, Castries told Langlais that Huguette must be held to protect the airstrip, which remained essential as a drop zone.

Giap's artillery preparation lasted from 6 to 8 P.M. His guns were firing from the captured hills of Eliane 1 and Dominique 2. Bigeard called the tank commander Captain Yves Hervouet and said: "Send me a wagon to do a little cleaning." Hervouet sent over a twenty-two-year-old tank lieutenant, André Mengelle, who had volunteered for Dien Bien Phu and been dropped on April 2. Mengelle went to Bigeard's command post on Eliane 4, which was like the entrance to a mine, and found him at his desk. "Hit the 75s that are firing from Eliane 1 and Dominique 2," Bigeard said. Mengelle fired thirty rounds, hitting an artillery observation post and the blockhouse at the top of Eliane 1. Bigeard commended him for his marksmanship.

Giap moved three battalions of the 165th Regiment toward Huguette 6, a stronger force than in previous attacks. The flare planes reported the movement of flat helmets in trenches. By midnight, the People's Army had breached the northern slope of Huguette 6, and Rastouil and his Legionnaires pulled back to the narrow southern end. At 10 P.M., Langlais sent over a company of Legionnaires from Rastouil's 13th DBLE, under Lieutenant Viard. They were unable to take back any of the ground lost, and by midnight they were on the verge of being forced off the hill.

Langlais sent up Lieutenant Bailly's 3rd Company of the 8th Choc, who advanced at the edge of the airstrip, supported by two tanks. One of them, *Conti,* was piloted by the just-arrived Lieutenant Mengelle, who was hoping they would get to Huguette 6 in time to cover the openings the Viets had made in the barbed wire. His crew brought to his attention a change in the sound the tank tracks made over the steel plates of the airstrip. Then an explosion shook the tank. Mengelle thought it was a bazooka, but was told it was a mine. He jumped out to inspect the damage. The second tank, Sergeant Boussrez' *Douaumont,* rumbled out of the dark and Mengelle climbed on board, leaving his crew to protect the disabled *Conti.*

Two hundred yards from Huguette 6, Lieutenant Bailly's company, having lost the support of one tank, was stopped by a barrier of Vietminh armed with bazookas. Under sustained fire, the paras jumped into the culvert, which they called "the gutter." Bailly, the last to jump, was hit in the shoulder and thigh.

Mengelle manned the coaxial machine gun on the *Douaumont* and broke through with some of Bailly's paras, while others remained pinned down in the drainage ditch. The *Douaumont* took up a position at the angle formed by the Huguette 6 barbed wire and the end of the ditch. Mengelle fired the machine gun at moving shadows. Thirty feet away, he saw a man with his arm stretched behind him, about to throw a grenade, and hit him in the chest. The man stood motionless for a very long ten seconds before falling backward.

As the battle for Huguette 6 raged past midnight on April 4 into April 5, Langlais kept sending in reinforcements. When he heard that Bailly had been hit, he sent in Captain Clédic's 2nd Company from Bréchignac's battalion at 3:15 A.M. "The Viets were firing from the other side of the airstrip," Clédic recalled. "We jumped into the ditch, hoping it hadn't been mined. One of my platoon leaders, Defline, was hit by a burst in the thigh and the shoulder. The men in the ditch tried to reach him, but by then dawn was breaking and enemy fire held them back. Defline heard the sound of shovels. His men were digging a trench out to where he lay. One of them managed to pull him in and he was given a shot of morphine."

At 4 A.M., Langlais called Bigeard: "Bruno, our counterattack on Huguette 6 is stalled. I sent Clédic's company, but the Viets have blocked the access route. Can you do something?" In less than an hour, Bigeard had rounded up 160 men from his battalion, under Lieutenant René Le Page, who wasn't easy to like, being stubborn and uncommunicative, but he was a *fonceur*—he went in one direction: forward. He was also the luck-iest officer in the 6th BPC, the only one who hadn't been wounded. Le Page and his 160 paras got going at dawn, with the support of three more tanks. The French at Dien Bien Phu used tanks as an auxiliary to the in-fantry, a sort of field artillery, described as a "mobile platform on tracks for direct-fire weapons."

By 6 A.M., the paras of the Bailly, Clédic, and Le Page companies had broken past the Viets who blocked the airstrip and reached Huguette 6, where they found twenty able-bodied Legionnaires under Lieutenant Legros. "Where are the Viets?" Le Page asked. Legros drew a circle in the air. The paras had attacked from three directions and the *bo dois* panicked, throwing themselves on the barbed wire. At dawn on April 5, French air-power came out in strength. Once the fog lifted, six B-26s left Cat Bi airport in Haiphong and were joined by eight Hellcats. They hammered the Viet-minh retreating over open ground with napalm, bombs, and machine guns. "I've never seen such carnage," Captain Clédic recalled. An esti-mated five hundred Viets were killed, while another three hundred were found dead or dying on the barbed wire. Some surrendered. Many of the dead were very young. The French had lost two hundred casualties. The April offensive was costly for both sides, creating manpower shortages, though Giap could remedy his. The Dien Bien Phu hospital population was by then 590. The final thrust at Huguette 6 led to a respite in the battle, like the minute in the corner between rounds at a prizefight. Bigeard re-flected that in a battle, men were like fuel—you use a gallon here and a gallon there, you blocked out the human dimension. But *respite* might not be the right word, for the central redoubt of Claudine remained under persistent artillery fire, and it was hazardous to remain in the open.

Captain Hervouet's tanks were decisive in routing the Vietminh. Three more had been brought in, led by Sergeant Ney in the *Ettlingen*. Ney kept his turret open a crack for a better view and saw a *bo doi* thirty feet away point his bazooka. The turret clasp saved Ney's life, but crewman Farouil saw blood streaming down Ney's face. Ney heard Farouil reporting his death over the radio to the other tanks. The *Ettlingen* turned around and brought Ney to the hospital, where Dr. Grauwin said, "I knew I'd be seeing you soon," which he meant as a compliment.

How Would You Like to Return to Dien Bien Phu?

On April 5, Navarre wired Castries: "I've decided to parachute volunteers as reinforcements after an accelerated training. We will begin tomorrow with men who have never jumped. We will then drop men who have jumped once or twice." Navarre was hoping for 500 volunteers, but to his and everyone else's amazement, 1,800 came forward—800 French, 450 Legionnaires, 400 North Africans, and 150 Vietnamese. Some wanted to help their comrades in arms, some were bored, some were pressured, some were fearless, and some went because a friend was going. Dr. Verdaguer, who took a jaundiced view of the battle, recalled that "when the volunteers were dropped, I couldn't decide whether to praise their bravery or damn the high command for conducting such a useless sacrifice. They landed acrobatically in an area pitted with trenches and divided by barbed wire and shell holes, and yet there was little breakage. I heard that was due to the wine and rum they were given during the flight."

According to Colonel Sauvagnac, 709 men were dropped. One of them was the Legionnaire Franz Fischer, who had been wounded on Béatrice on March 13. At the hospital in Hanoi, Fischer was on penicillin for three weeks until the swelling in his cranium subsided. He was sent back to his base, but his unit had been disbanded. He went to see the officer in charge of paperwork, who was eating an omelet for breakfast, and asked, "So where am I? I'd be better off dead or taken prisoner by the Viets."

The officer looked him up and down and asked, "How would you like to return to Dien Bien Phu?"

"How, on foot?"

"They're training volunteers at Bac Mai. Guys who never jumped."

"Did they find any?"

"You won't believe this. Hundreds."

The officer took Fischer to the barracks of Major Hubert Liesenfelt's 2nd Battalion of Foreign Legion paratroopers, who were soon to be dropped, and introduced him to a captain. "I'm bringing you a recruit," he said. "He's already fought at Dien Bien Phu."

"You must be joking," said the captain.

"He was wounded at Béatrice and flown out. He's looking for a unit to join."

The captain picked up the phone and said, "Carpentier, I'm sending you a recruit."

Another volunteer, Second Lieutenant Georges Pinault, recalled, "I was wasting away in the Delta and I wanted to see what things were like in the high country, so I decided to go. My parachute training lasted an hour. When I was dropped I landed in barbed wire a yard away from the latrines of the 1st BEP. The next day I was turned over to an artillery unit."

After their training—which consisted of jumping down a cable from a tower and learning to roll on landing—when the volunteers were actually in the Dakotas on their way to Dien Bien Phu, the initial eagerness wore off. Some had second thoughts as they sat on the benches waiting. Once they were poised at the open door, looking down at shell bursts lighting the night sky, waiting for the order to jump, some balked.

Those who jumped at the word *Go!* dropped into the void and often fell in barbed wire. But for the battered, battle-weary men of the base, these new arrivals, freshly shaved, in clean uniforms, their submachine guns freshly oiled, their jump boots freshly polished, were emblems of hope. Dr. Grauwin met one who was carrying a newspaper with the headline: THE FORMIDABLE TACTICAL AND POLITICAL MISTAKES OF DIEN BIEN PHU.

"You read this and you volunteered?" he asked.

"Do you think I pay attention to these rags?"

Another one came in with a face as chalk white as the plaster Grauwin was applying to one of the wounded. He had landed in the morgue pit. "I fell on something soft," he said. "And then I felt a nose, a mouth, and I realized where I was." Grauwin gave him a shot of rum.

The Intervention Could Have a Decisive Result

General Giap's March 30 offensive had repercussions in a number of foreign capitals and was linked to the Geneva Conference, about to open on April 26. General Ely returned to Paris on March 27 from his trip to Washington. Although he had the reputation of being a little too cozy with the politicians, and lacked the charisma and brilliance of a de Lattre, Ely was entirely devoted to his country, and had paid the price, losing his right hand in World War II. His wife had been sent to Buchenwald, where she was so badly tortured that she was still in a wheelchair.

The news from Indochina was not good. The chances of saving Dien Bien Phu decreased daily, which lent a certain urgency to Radford's offer of U.S. intervention. Ely realized, as he wrote in his memoirs, that "neither Admiral Radford nor myself had the necessary authority" to make the decision. Their agreement was that the French would present an official request, while Radford would strongly recommend intervention to his people.

On the evening of March 30 in Saigon, Navarre was told that General Giap had launched a fierce attack on the eastern centers of resistance at Dien Bien Phu. He left at once for Hanoi, arriving after midnight on March 31. Cogny, who was usually on the tarmac to greet him, was not there, nor in his office at the Citadelle. His chief of staff said he was very tired and needed rest. Navarre stayed up through the night, staying abreast of developments. At 5 A.M., he called Cogny's home. He was told that Cogny was sleeping. Wake him up, Navarre said. He was then told that Cogny was not at home.

Cogny showed up at 8:30. "I reproached him vehemently," Navarre later wrote, "for having left his command post instead of following the developments in the battle." Cogny said there was nothing he could do at night. What about the hours before dawn, Navarre asked, when orders were given for air support? "It was an impassioned conversation, and I warned Cogny that once the battle was over I would have him replaced. I asked him to maintain complete silence on the change in our relations, so that it would not affect service matters."

On March 31, Navarre was shown a decrypted Vietminh message that said: "The Geneva Conference is a result of the moral weakness of our adversary and his disgust for the war. It is a success for the Vietminh. Since the Americans will try to sabotage the conference, the Vietminh must try to spread the desire for peace in the enemy camp. We must exploit our military successes and the confused military situation in France to demoralize the enemy." For Navarre, the connection between the battle of Dien Bien Phu and Geneva could not have been more clearly stated.

Arriving in Saigon on March 31, Colonel Raymond Brohon saw Commissioner General Maurice Dejean, who told him that Navarre was in Hanoi. They flew to Hanoi on April 1, and that evening Dejean hosted a dinner at the chic Maison de France for Navarre, his deputy General Bodet, Cogny, and Brohon. After dinner, Brohon outlined the Radford plan, an air strike with heavy bombers and carrier air support. Navarre said they would discuss it further the next morning.

When they met on the morning of April 2, Navarre expressed reservations about Radford's plan. What if the air strike led to Chinese retaliation? What if the Chinese bombed French planes on the ground? It was too risky, at a time when Dien Bien Phu might fall. Navarre's air force chief, General Lauzin, had told him the Chinese had two hundred planes within range of French air bases.

They also discussed an issue that Brohon had raised in Washington, the use of tactical nuclear weapons. How could they be used around the base, Navarre asked, with the combatants so close to each other? The spread of the thermal nuclear blast would endanger the garrison. And how effective would nuclear weapons be on an enemy dispersed through the jungle? Navarre later wrote: "Ely sent me Brohon, who told me the Pentagon felt that China's intervention at Dien Bien Phu justified an American intervention. Dulles had made a speech, relying on French decrypts, denouncing Chinese AA gunners and Chinese advisers."

Colonel Brohon left Hanoi on the afternoon of April 2, and with the thirteen-hour time difference reached Paris on Sunday, April 4. On landing, he went straight to the home of General Ely on the Rue Puvis de Chavannes. "To my great surprise," Ely recalled, "the reaction of the Commander-in-Chief was reticent. His reason was that the operation would risk a Chinese reaction."

As Brohon flew home, the battle of the Five Hills continued to be fiercely fought, and Maurice Dejean told Navarre that the danger of Dien Bien Phu falling was greater than that of a Chinese air attack. Navarre expected a final assault after Five Hills. Just as General Ely was being debriefed by Brohon, an officer came in with a wire from Navarre. The wire said: "It seems that the battle has reached a point of equilibrium. . . . I am reinforcing the garrison by dropping new units at night. Given these conditions, the intervention that Brohon mentioned could have a decisive result, particularly if it takes place before the Vietminh [final] assault . . . which may come toward the middle or the end of next week. Perhaps the intervention could come before then." An unspoken factor in Navarre's reasoning was that the Vietnamese National Army, riddled with desertions, was falling apart.

The Conditions for a Favorable Solution in Indochina No Longer Exist

In London, Foreign Secretary Anthony Eden was confused by what he felt were the contradictory elements of American foreign policy. In Saigon, Ambassador Heath had observed: "The French won't be allowed to skedaddle unless China gives absolute guarantees." And yet Undersecretary of State Walter Bedell Smith, head of Eisenhower's special committee on Indochina, had told Eden's ambassador in Washington that there was no intention of sending U.S. troops to Indochina. How could this bifurcated policy be resolved, Eden wondered. Nor was he happy about Indian prime minister Nehru's proposal that there be a cease-fire in Indochina prior to Geneva. A cease-fire would leave the people of Indochina at the mercy of the Vietminh, since this was a war without a continuous front.

Eden felt somewhat proprietary about the Geneva Conference, which he and Molotov had worked out at Berlin in February 1954, the first post-Stalin conference. Eden's chief concern was Malaya, where the British were fighting Communist guerrillas. If the Geneva Conference led to some form of partition of Indochina that brought about an end to hostilities, the British in Malaya would have a barrier to the north.

Eden thought French chances of victory in Indochina were slim, given the widespread opposition to the war, the failed Bao Dai experiment, and the shortcomings of the national army. Even more important, French conscripts were not allowed to serve their military service outside France, while British conscripts were fighting in Malaya. Thus, the French had a chronic manpower shortage. Dulles wanted to make it clear that having Red China at the table did not imply recognition of the regime. Eden in his memoirs called Geneva "the only worthwhile result of the Berlin Conference."

The March 29 Dulles speech on united action, however, confirmed the British in their opinion that "there was a gulf between French and American thinking," as one Foreign Office analyst put it. The British, no matter how often the president and his secretary of state pressured them, did not wish, prior to Geneva, to antagonize the Chinese. At the same time, they realized that the French were looking for a way out of Indochina.

The French, with their excessive "mental dexterity," as one Foreign Office man put it, exasperated the British. One example of tortured French logic was described in a March 16 analysis from the British embassy in Paris: The French were balancing the Indochina war against the European Defense Community and its integrated army. If the war ended, the National Assembly would ratify the EDC. But the Russians, who wanted the EDC to fail, would keep the war going. But if the war ended and the troops came home, there would be no need for the EDC, since the returned French divisions would suffice. Thus the Russians would want the war to end. Sir Ivone Kirkpatrick, the administrative head of the Foreign Office, lamented "the hopeless instability of French thought." Eden commented on March 26 that "the French become daily more helpless and contemptible."

A Foreign Office paper at the end of March entitled "Policy Toward Indochina" concluded: "There may no longer be a prospect of a favorable solution to the Indochina problem and the most we can do is strive for the adoption of the least disadvantageous course. Partition might salvage more from the general wreck than any other."

Geneva would open in less than a month, and Eden agreed that partition was the best solution. Partition would trace a continuous front, since "there was no love lost between North and South." Eden wired Ambassador Makins on April 1, echoing the Foreign Office paper: "The conditions for a favorable solution in Indochina no longer exist." This should be kept in mind in Geneva, since the Western powers might be "forced to accept a policy of compromise with the Communists."

Action by Our Forces Holds
No Significant Promise of Success

At the time of the battle of the Five Hills, President Eisenhower was trying to balance two contradictory elements: intervention to help the French and opposition to another Korea. He wrote a friend that intervention would "lay us open to the charge of imperialism and colonialism, or—at the very least—objectionable paternalism." He was also convinced that "no military victory was possible in that type of theater," with China and its limitless manpower across the border.

At his press conference on March 31, Eisenhower was asked whether the united action Dulles had announced in his speech meant that U.S. troops might be used in Indochina. The president replied: "I can conceive of no greater disadvantage to America than to be employing ground forces, and any other kind of forces, in great numbers around the world, meeting every little situation as it arises." Those words reflected only one compartment of his binary mind.

Admiral Radford, in the meantime, was trying to build support among the Joint Chiefs for an air strike to support Dien Bien Phu while it was under attack. But when he polled them on March 31, all four were opposed. On April 1, he tried again, pumping up the question with the phrase "if requested by proper civilian authority." The response was the same. The Joint Chiefs were smarting from the failure to win decisively in Korea. Their input was a thumb on the scales.

As a soldier, Eisenhower had long viewed the opinions of the Joint Chiefs with a pinch of skepticism, having once stated: "The JCS can have 872 agreements and only three disagreements . . . [but] these might well be the only really fundamental matters." A French defeat in Indochina was a fundamental matter.

At the regular Thursday meeting of the National Security Council on April 1, Eisenhower said he realized that all the Joint Chiefs but Radford had opposed an air strike. However, he saw "no reason for the NSC to avoid considering the intervention issue." Secretary of State Dulles asked what could be done to save the garrison at Dien Bien Phu. Radford said an air strike could be launched the next day. Ike said he would discuss the matter in his office later with "certain members" of the NSC.

No record was kept of the president's meeting with "certain members," but soon after it ended, Dulles called Attorney General Brownell to say that "something fairly serious" had come up and he was working on a memo to discuss with congressional leaders. He would show the president a draft the next morning. The "something serious" was a request for intervention for Congress to authorize.

In the meantime, Eisenhower had lunch with the press lord Roy Howard, of Scripps Howard, and his editor in chief, Walker Stone. Jim Hagerty recorded in his diary that Ike told them "the U.S. might have to make decisions to send in squadrons from two aircraft carriers off coast to bomb Reds at Dien Bien Phu." Ike, as was his habit, seemed to be trying out one policy against another as one would try on a suit for the fit.

Radford had decided to poll the Joint Chiefs yet a third time, this time in writing, prior to a meeting on April 2 at the White House. The question was: "If the United States government is requested by the government of France to render assistance in Indochina by committing USAF and/or naval forces in combat, what position do the Joint Chiefs of Staff take?" To give the question greater weight, Radford said it came from Secretary of Defense Wilson. The replies from the Joint Chiefs, reflecting the interests of their respective services, were not promising. The Joint Chiefs were sure to have seen the memo that Vice Admiral Arthur C. Davis, director of the Office of Foreign Military Affairs, had written on January 5 to General Charles H. "Tick" Bonesteel III, the military liaison to the NSC staff: "Involvement of U.S. forces in the Indochina War should be avoided at all practical costs," he wrote. "The U.S. should not be self-duped into believing the possibility of partial involvement—such as Naval and Air units only. One cannot go over Niagara Falls in a barrel slightly. . . . It is difficult to understand how involvement of ground forces could be avoided. Air strength to be of worth in such an effort would require bases in Indochina of considerable magnitude. Protection of those bases and port facilities would certainly require U.S. ground force personnel, and the force once committed would need ground combat units to support any threatened evacuation. . . . There is no cheap way to fight a war once committed."

General Matt Ridgway, who had commanded the Eighth Army in Korea, was a man who did his homework. He had been briefed on Indochina by the young CIA officer George Allen, who told him that if ground troops were required it would take five hundred thousand to a million men, forty engineering battalions, and an increase in the draft. Ridgway's reply to Admiral Radford's question was that an intervention at Dien Bien Phu would be disproportionate to the liability it would incur. It would not decisively affect the military situation there, but it would "greatly increase the risk of general war."

General Lemuel C. Shepherd, the Commandant of the Marine Corps, had been commander of the Fleet Marine Force in the Pacific during the Korean War. His reply to the question on intervention was an elaborate and resounding "No." "Air intervention would be an unprofitable adventure," he wrote. "We can expect no significant military results from an improvised air offensive against guerrilla forces. They simply do not offer a target which our Air Force will find remunerative. They are nowhere exposed at a vital point critical to their continued resupply and communications. . . . Action by our forces, if initiated today, would be taken in the face of impending disaster and holds no significant promise of success. . . . The inevitable result would be the necessity of admitting a fresh military failure [after Korea] on our part or intervening further with ground forces in an effort to recoup our fortunes. . . . It is with regret that I record conclusions which run so counter to my natural instincts to support our friends in their efforts to halt the Communist advance."

Admiral Robert Carney, chief of naval operations, had seen action in World War I against German U-boats. In World War II, in command of the cruiser *Denver,* he laid mines along the sea-lanes used by the Japanese in the Solomon Islands. As a result, he won the Bronze Star and was promoted to admiral. On the issue of intervention in Indochina he was a fence-sitter. He thought the Joint Chiefs should take the position that American air-power "would improve the French tactical situation," but not "that it would be decisive." Intervention, he said, had to be weighed against "the potential consequences of U.S. involvement in the Indochina War."

General Nathan Farragut Twining, the air force chief of staff, came from a Wisconsin family whose men had served in the army and navy since the French and Indian War. He had commanded B-29 bombers in the last push against Japan, and those bombers might now be used in Indochina. He had also commanded the unit that dropped the first atomic bomb. As an advocate of massive air retaliation, he gave what he called a "qualified yes" to Radford's question. But he made three conditions that turned his vote into a "qualified no."

- The United States should maintain command of its air and naval elements.
- The United States should train and organize an indigenous Vietnamese army under indigenous leadership.
- The French should grant "true sovereignty" to the Associated States of northern and southern Vietnam, Laos, and Cambodia.

The first condition could be easily settled by giving the United States tactical command while the French oversaw the operation from the ground. But the two other conditions were not in the cards.

In an oral history interview on March 16, 1965, General Twining said that "three small tactical A-bombs" could have saved the day. "It's a fairly isolated area, Dien Bien Phu," he said, "no great towns around there, only Communists and their supplies. You could take all day to drop a bomb and make sure you put it in the right place. No opposition. And clean those Commies out of there and the band would play the Marseillaise and the French would come swarming out of Dien Bien Phu in fine shape. And those Commies would say, 'Well, those guys may do this again to us. We'd better be careful.' " This was wishful thinking in the year of the American buildup in Vietnam. It sounded as if Twining was saying, "We might not have the problems we're facing now if we'd acted then."

On the morning of April 2, at the White House, the president met with

Dulles, Wilson, and Radford. Dulles showed Eisenhower his draft of a memo to Congress, which said: "The President of the United States is hereby authorized . . . to employ the Naval and Air forces of the United States to assist the forces which are resisting aggression in Southeast Asia, to prevent the extension and expansion of that aggression, and to protect and defend the security of the United States." The resolution did not explicitly exclude ground troops, since naval forces could include Marines. The draft set a time limit of June 30, 1955, and stipulated that intervention would in no way "derogate from the authority of Congress to declare war."

Eisenhower then had a skimpy majority in the Senate (49-47-1) and the House (221-212-1). The Republican right was fickle, the Democrats were restive, and the Army-McCarthy hearings were about to open. The "no more Koreas" feeling was strong in both houses. Eisenhower felt that it would be a better tactic to let congressional leaders do their own thinking on Indochina before submitting a draft. As Dulles put it in a memo: "The tactical procedure should be to develop first the thinking of Congressional leaders without actually submitting in the first instance a resolution drafted by ourselves." Eisenhower later said that Dulles wanted the resolution "not in order to intervene, but to avoid the need to intervene." Dulles also wanted to clarify his differences with Radford. He did not want an immediate air strike but instead a deterrent that would bring the allies into united action with the United States.

Radford said, "The outcome will be determined in a matter of hours, and the situation is not one which calls for any U.S. participation." Having received little or no encouragement from the Joint Chiefs, Radford was crushed. The air had leaked out of his balloon.

When Dulles asked Radford whether he had anything specific in mind on Indochina, he replied: "Nothing specific."

Eisenhower's tactic of giving Congress the initiative rather than forcing a resolution down their throats was an example of what Attorney General Herbert Brownell called "his preferred strategy: Operating through others to attain his political goals, having his cabinet officers serve as lightning rods, and projecting an image of being above the fray." It was at West Point, Brownell said, that Eisenhower had first developed his view of the president's place within the constitutional system. It was a system of divided but shared powers that worked best by establishing comity with the other branches, and not by embracing an imperial presidency.

The downside of passing the ball to Congress was that the pass might be incomplete or intercepted.

Dulles began his push for united action with the British on the afternoon of April 2, after the White House meeting. At 3 P.M., he and Walter Bedell Smith met with Ambassador Makins and his embassy colleague Robert Scott. Dulles came right to the point, asking for "a solid front to stiffen the French attitude at Geneva." Either by military collapse or by trying to reach a settlement at Geneva, Dulles said, the French could lose Indochina, which could lead to the loss of Southeast Asia. The U.S. government could not stand passively by and let Southeast Asia go by default to the Communists.

A Southeast Asia coalition, Dulles said, could convince the Communist Chinese that "stepped-up activities on their part could lead to disastrous retaliation on our part by sea and air." To underline what he meant by "disastrous retaliation," Dulles explained that "the atomic balance, which is now advantageous to us, might decline over the next four years."

Maintaining his diplomatic aplomb, Makins said that Dulles's argument "had merit." As he reported to London: "Dulles said if it was made plain to the Chinese that continuation of aid to the Vietminh was dangerous for China, they would desist, and the Russians would use their influence in the same direction."

Scott then asked whether air and naval action against China would have the desired result in Indochina. Would Peking yield to the pressure or would it mean a widening war, which would be bad for the British in Hong Kong.

Smith said that "the main factor in bringing about an armistice in Korea had been Chinese knowledge that the United Nations Command were contemplating bombing industrial bases in Manchuria [with tactical nuclear weapons]." He said that he "did not see how general war with China could ensue, without troops being landed in China," an option he did not favor.

Makins's reply was to read the wire he had received from Foreign Secretary Eden the day before, saying that a military solution was no longer feasible and united action should consist of finding a negotiated solution that could involve partition.

This seemed like a setback for Dulles, but Makins, advising Eden after the meeting, said he was in favor of narrowing what he saw as a widening gap between English and American views. He recommended that "we align ourselves with the administration" in order "to bring our influence continually to bear. . . . I believe the Americans will listen to our views."

Makins seems to have underestimated Dulles's tenacity of purpose, for as the secretary of state reported to his ambassadors in Paris and London: "Partition seems to London least undesirable solution. It was clear United Kingdom had not yet developed thoughts for dealing positively and constructively with situation which well may confront us if French determined to sell out." Dulles emphasized it was essential to maintain a solid Anglo-American front to "stiffen French attitude."

Given Churchill's absolute and oft-repeated hatred of nuclear war, however, Dulles's mention of it made it certain that English participation in united action was dead on arrival.

The Day We Didn't Go to War

Dulles and Radford met with eight congressional leaders at 9:30 A.M. on Saturday, April 3, in a fifth-floor conference room near Dulles's office at the State Department. Also attending were Walter Bedell Smith; Undersecretary of State Thruston Morton; Deputy Secretary of Defense Roger Kyes (who was against intervention in Indochina for fear "the Defense budget would skyrocket"), sitting in for Wilson; and Secretary of the Navy Robert Anderson.

The heavy hitters from the Senate were the California Republican and majority leader, William Knowland, who had not backed Eisenhower for the presidency and habitually wandered off the reservation; the Colorado Republican Gene Millikin, whose motto was "No one ever got to heaven in one jump"; and three Democrats, Minority Leader Lyndon Johnson, Richard Russell of Georgia, and Minority Whip Earle Clements of Kentucky. From the House, there were the Republican Speaker from Massa-

chusetts, Joseph W. Martin, and two Democrats, Minority Whip John Mc-
Cormack of Massachusetts and J. Percy Priest of Tennessee.

In the Senate there were two wings: the "strict constitutionalists" like
John Stennis of Mississippi, who said in January 1954, with regard to the
mutual defense treaty with Korea, "We are treading on dangerous ground
when we commit ourselves to take action thousands of miles from home
without giving Congress an opportunity to participate in the decision";
and the "internationalists," such as the Wisconsin Republican Alexander
Wiley and the Minnesota Democrat Hubert Humphrey, who believed that
Congress should not "tie the President's hands" and that its power to declare war should be balanced by the president's power as commander in
chief.

The April 3 meeting opened with a comprehensive briefing on the war
in Indochina from Admiral Radford, standing beside a wall map of Southeast Asia. He went into some detail on the battle at Dien Bien Phu, being
waged as he spoke, and was followed by Secretary of State Dulles, who said
Indochina was the key to Southeast Asia. If Indochina went, America
would be "forced back to Hawaii." Dulles urged that the president be given
"Congressional backing so that he could use air and sea power in the area
if he felt it necessary in the interest of national security."

Senator Knowland, a stalwart backer of Chiang Kai-shek, at first concurred, but was drowned out by the seven others, who were emphatic in
stating that there should be no congressional action until Dulles had obtained commitments from the allies. The standpoint was: "We want no
more Koreas with the United States furnishing 90 percent of the manpower." Aside from the lingering effects of Korea, the congressional leaders were still smarting from the decision to send two hundred air force
technicians to Indochina, made without their knowledge and carried out
over their objections.

Radford pointed out that no ground troops were contemplated. The
reply was that once the flag was committed the use of ground troops
would inevitably follow.

Dulles said he was working on united action with the allies. He had already spoken with the British ambassador and to Carlos Rómulo of the
Philippines (who had been president of the U.N. General Assembly and

ambassador to the United States), and he was going to meet with the French ambassador Henri Bonnet as soon as the current meeting was over. But he had to know from Congress whether the United States was ready to commit if the others responded.

Radford was asked if airpower could save Dien Bien Phu. He said it was too late for that, but that if it had been done three weeks ago the Red forces would have been beaten. The congressmen expressed little confidence in the French. Senator Russell was particularly hard on them. Russell, a skilled legislator, was considered liberal for a southern Democrat, but remained a man of his time, a die-hard segregationist. He viewed civil rights as a way of punishing the South for losing the Civil War. In 1957, when federal troops enforced a school desegregation order in Little Rock, Russell accused Eisenhower of "applying tactics copied from the manual of Hitler's storm troopers."

The congressmen were also hard on the British. Russell said that if they flinched, the United States would have to reconsider its entire system of collective security from the standpoint of dependability. Radford pointed out that the British also had responsibilities in the area and had deployed troops in Malaya and elsewhere.

The meeting concluded with Dulles promising that he would try to get commitments from the British and other nations. If those agreements were obtained, the congressmen said, a resolution could be passed, giving the president power to commit U.S. armed forces in the area.

The trouble with this agreement was that Dulles had lost the initiative. American plans now depended on the willingness of other nations to agree to some form of united action. What Dulles needed was a congressional resolution prior to consulting with the allies—to "fill his hand," as Secretary of Defense Wilson put it. Such a resolution would be the logical follow-up to his "united action" speech. It would strengthen Dulles's hand by showing that America was united in its commitment to action, without being specific about it, and would not be swayed by concessions and conditions demanded by the allies. With it, he had a full house. Without it, he had two pairs.

Eisenhower was spending the weekend at Camp David, playing golf. Dulles reached him on the phone in the afternoon and said, "On the whole it went pretty well—although it raised some serious problems. The feeling was that Congress would be quite prepared to go along on some vigorous action if we were not doing it alone. They want to be sure the people in the area are involved too."

Eisenhower and Dulles agreed that they couldn't blame Congress for seeing it that way. "You can't go in and win unless the people want you," Ike said. "The French would win in six months if the people were with them."

Dulles said the congressmen were worried about the British, and that it would be "hard to get the American people excited" if the British were not on board. He suggested that Ike contact "the PM" (Churchill), and the president said he would.

On Capitol Hill, four Democratic senators were impatiently waiting for Lyndon Johnson to brief them. One of the four, Albert Gore of Tennessee, recalled in 1978 that they waited until late afternoon in the Democratic Cloak Room. When Johnson showed up, "he gave us a vivid, muscular, and athletic recounting of the meeting. Admiral Radford . . . and Dulles were strongly in favor of intervention. . . . Eventually, the reactions of the Congressional representatives were solicited, and according to Senator Johnson's description, he outlined his opposition and told us that he pounded the President's desk in the Oval Office to emphasize his opposition." Either Gore's memory twenty-four years after the event or Johnson's account was faulty, for the meeting in question was held at the State Department and the president did not attend.

The secret meeting with the congressmen was kept out of the papers. But as the *Washington Post* columnist Chalmers Roberts later told an interviewer for the Congressional Research Service of the Library of Congress, he had convinced one of the participants to talk, meeting with him in an out-of-the-way office where they could confer unobserved.

The leaker was John McCormack, a strong anti-Communist, who had taken copious notes. McCormack was willing to share his notes with Roberts because he was alarmed that the United States might be heading for another war. As for his anti-Communism, he told Roberts: "It's one thing to make a speech about it in an Irish section of Boston and it's another thing to vote to send troops overseas to die in a foreign field."

Roberts's account appeared in *The Washington Post* of June 7, 1954,
under the title "The Day We Didn't Go to War." The story was so detailed
that the FBI investigated but came up empty. According to Roberts, the
plan that Radford had in mind once Congress passed the resolution was
to send two hundred planes from the 31,000-ton U.S. carriers *Essex* and
Boxer, already in the South China Sea for training. The carrier-based
planes would join U.S. Air Force planes from bases a thousand miles away
in the Philippines, for a single strike to save Dien Bien Phu.

If the strike did not succeed in relieving the fortress, a congressman
asked, would we follow up? Radford replied in the affirmative.

Would land forces then also have to be used? Radford's reply was in-
conclusive.

Earle Clements, a senator from Kentucky, asked the first key question.
"Does this plan have the approval of the Joint Chiefs of Staff?"

"No."

"How many of the three agree with you?" (There were actually four.)

"None."

"How do you account for that?"

"I have spent more time in the Far East than any of them and I understand the situation better."

Lyndon Johnson asked the other key question: Knowland was going
around saying that in Korea 90 percent of the men and money came from
the United States. Americans were now sold on the idea that this was
wrong. Hence, in any Indochina operation, we should know who was putting up the men. Had this been raised with our allies?

Dulles said it had not, and was forced to admit he had no dancing partners, which meant he would get no resolution.

Why didn't he go to the United Nations, as Truman had for Korea?

Dulles said it would take too long.

McCormack, the House minority whip, couldn't resist a dig at Dulles.
Hadn't the Democrats been called "the party of treason" by Joe McCarthy
in his Lincoln's birthday speech under GOP auspices? Why was Dulles
looking to them now to take the lead in a situation that might lead to war?
Dulles did not reply.

In the end, as McCormack told Roberts, all eight congressmen told

Dulles he'd better go shopping for allies. McCormack had also heard a rumor that Dulles was carrying a draft of the joint resolution he wanted Congress to sign, but if so he didn't produce it. Shopping for allies would take too long to make an air strike effective. The state of emergency that existed in Dien Bien Phu was not communicated to the congressmen.

The secret meeting had lasted two hours and ten minutes. As they left the Hill, the eight congressmen told reporters only that they'd been briefed on Indochina. In the May 1 *New York Times*, Tom Wicker quoted Senator Russell as saying: "I sat listening to him [Dulles] talk about sending American boys off to fight in a war like that and suddenly I found myself on my feet shouting, 'We're not going to do that!' " Russell denied being on his feet and shouting. "All of the discussion was vigorous," he later wrote, "and a bit of it might have been described as heated, but there was no shouting as I recall."

There is one major discrepancy between Dulles's notes and the Chalmers Roberts scoop. Dulles has Radford saying that it was too late for an air strike on Dien Bien Phu, but Roberts has him describing how the air strike would be conducted. Given the amount of detail that McCormack revealed to Roberts, Dulles must have been referring to the position Radford had taken on April 2, when he said in a moment of low spirits that the situation was no longer one that called for U.S. participation.

Undersecretary of State Thruston Morton thought that the president had outflanked Admiral Radford. "Hell," he recalled in 1979, "if we had let Raddy go, he would have been in there with a whole carrier fleet. . . . Raddy had it all figured out, how he could get carriers in the area and bomb the hell out of them and knock them out of this high ground. . . . Eisenhower put the quietus on that. Dulles accepted Raddy's estimate of the situation, but Eisenhower didn't." Ike also put the quietus on Dulles by telling him not to present the draft resolution, by declining to lobby influential legislators with phone calls and one-on-one meetings, and by going to Camp David for the weekend. He seemed to want Congress to block any unilateral American action.

After the meeting, Dulles called Ambassador Bonnet to explain what "united action" meant. A coalition would be formed, made up of France, Britain, the United States, Australia, New Zealand, Thailand, and the

Philippines. Dulles wanted the prospective participants to take some positive measures prior to the opening of the Geneva Conference, to demonstrate allied resolve. It was thought that this would make the Communist
powers renounce their aggressive designs and prevent them from demanding major concessions from France at Geneva. Dulles did not mention the meeting with the congressmen and their refusal to commit the
United States until the allies were on board.

After his talk with Dulles, Bonnet cabled Paris that the secretary of
state wanted a declaration signed prior to Geneva so there would be "no
ambiguity." The government in Paris agreed with the British that such a
declaration would jeopardize the conference and provoke the Chinese.

Back in Washington with his wife, Mamie, on the evening of April 4,
Eisenhower held a meeting at 8:20 P.M. attended by Radford, Dulles,
Smith, Kyes, and Douglas MacArthur II. When told of the congressional
conditions, he said he had his own conditions: the British, the Australians,
and the New Zealanders should contribute troops, and France should ac-
celerate the independence of the Associated States and agree to stay in the
war until the war was over. The president's position had hardened, creating further obstacles to U.S. intervention. It was at this meeting that Eisenhower once again took the reins, making it clear that there would be no
unilateral American action in Indochina and that he was in charge of
policy.

Eisenhower drafted a message to Churchill, which was sent at 11:47
P.M. If Indochina fell, it said, "the consequent shift would be disastrous."
The answer was united action. "I know of no man," Ike told his former
comrade at arms, "who has firmly grasped more nettles than you. . . . If we
grasp this one together . . . we could approach the Geneva Conference with
the position of the free world not only unimpaired but strengthened."

This was one nettle Churchill did not want to be stung by. The British
Army was already fighting an antiguerrilla war in Malaya, while in
Kenya the Mau Maus were acting up. The last thing the British wanted
was involvement in another Korea-type war, or a resounding declaration
prior to Geneva that might anger the Communists and scuttle the conference.

At that time in England there was an appalled reaction that the British had not been consulted when the United States started testing the hydrogen bomb, exploding one on the Pacific island of Bikini on March 1 and another on March 31. Evelyn Shuckburgh recorded in his diary for March 31 that "the Old Man [Churchill] vents his feelings by sending peevish telegrams to Roger Makins." Anthony Eden was at his wit's end and said "this simply cannot go on; he is gaga; he cannot finish his sentences."

It was in the context of an April 5 debate in the House of Commons over the H-bomb tests that Churchill received what Shuckburgh called "a very excitable message from Ike about immediate action in Indochina." The Eisenhower plan "worried everybody." The trouble was that "the Americans don't want to bargain and think any division of Indochina would be a disaster."

Winston didn't look well, Shuckburgh reported. He was ashen gray, and Eden thought he would have another stroke quite soon. When Churchill told Eden that it was "splendid news" that *Izvestia* had called for a cease-fire in Indochina, Eden rebuked him: "Don't you see it is a trap; there is no line there; it is a trap and they would overrun the place." On top of everything, Shuckburgh wrote, "Ike has announced that he will not make bigger H-bombs than he needs!" At his April 7 press conference, the president had been asked by Merriman Smith whether the United States was "going to continue to make bigger and bigger H-bombs." "No," Eisenhower replied. "We have no intention of going into a program of how big these can be made."

The British were preparing for the arrival of Secretary of State Dulles, though still not certain whether he would show. Roger Makins, Shuckburgh noted, "had infuriated" the Foreign Office "by appearing to share the State Department's belief that we are responsible for the many leakages about Dulles's plans." Makins, as we have seen, had called for cozying up to the Eisenhower administration.

He Who Defines the Battle Controls the Peace

In Peking, Mao Tse-tung was watching the battle of the Five Hills unfold no less anxiously than Eisenhower was in Washington. The Geneva Conference, seating Red China at the same table with the United States, was a diplomatic breakthrough. Mao felt sure that a victory at Dien Bien Phu would strengthen the Chinese position at Geneva.

Mao's involvement went back to September 1953, when Ho Chi Minh had rejected General Giap's plan to concentrate on the Red River Delta. Instead there was a push toward Laos, which led Navarre to build the entrenched camp at Dien Bien Phu. General Wei Guoqing was sent to Indochina as the head of the Chinese Military Advisory Group working with Giap. He gave Ho Chi Minh a copy of the Navarre Plan, which had been obtained by Chinese intelligence. Wei was instructed by the Central Military Commission in Peking to adopt the strategy of "separating and encircling the enemy and then wiping them out bit by bit. You should strive to eliminate one enemy battalion at a time. If you destroy four to five battalions, the enemy may lose confidence. Either development will be favorable to us."

In March 1954, Foreign Minister Chou En-lai sent a wire to the Chinese Military Advisory Group working with Giap, asking them to win some battles, which would give the Communist delegation at Geneva the initiative. In mid-March he wired Ho Chi Minh to start studying the issue of a demarcation line in the event of a cease-fire. Like the British, the Chinese saw partition as a possible solution.

Mao believed that he who defines the battle controls the peace. In March and April, he stepped up aid to the Vietminh. Four battalions trained in China and armed with 37mm antiaircraft guns were sent to Dien Bien Phu. Other Vietminh units were trained in sniper techniques by Chinese veterans of Korea. A dozen army engineers, also veterans of Korea, went to Dien Bien Phu to oversee the digging of hundreds of miles of trenches.

Although deeply involved in the tactical details of the battle, Mao preferred diplomacy. The precedent of the Korean War led him to mistakenly believe that the United States would intervene in Indochina, just as Dulles and Eisenhower mistakenly believed that Red China would swallow up Southeast Asia. For Mao, war was an interruption of his economic program. Already, Korea had set back his five-year plan. And now that Stalin was dead, the Soviet Union exercised a moderating influence.

Mao was not at all sure that the fall of Dien Bien Phu would end the war. He saw a protracted conflict that would last at least six months. A Vietminh victory at Dien Bien Phu, he hoped, would be followed by an attack on Hanoi. The best he could expect was that the victory would boost his bargaining power at Geneva. Thus, on April 3, as attacks and counterattacks on the Five Hills left the outcome in doubt, he called for the training of two more Vietminh artillery divisions and two engineer regiments. In a message to Peng Dehuai, deputy chairman of the Central Military Commission, he gave detailed instructions: The divisions should be regular Vietminh recruits. The instructors should be Korean veterans and include cadres at the division level. If the Vietminh didn't have enough guns, the Chinese army should supply them. Vietminh units should receive their equipment and complete their training within six months. The training should take place in Vietnam or in the Chinese border province of Kwangsi. These matters should be worked out at once by the general staff and the artillery command. Once the Vietminh had two additional artillery divisions on top of the one already fighting, it could, along with its five infantry divisions, attack Hanoi and Haiphong. Peng was instructed to prepare "*sufficient* ammunition and engineering equipment" for the new divisions. Mao's advice on Dien Bien Phu was limited to the view that an all-out attack must begin as soon as possible. Hanoi could be attacked in the winter of 1954 or the spring of 1955. In his aid and advice to the Vietminh, Mao had a distinct advantage over the United States—he didn't have to deal with Congress. He drafted his orders and they were promptly carried out. In addition, the Vietminh did not object to the degree of Chinese kibitzing, while the French constantly complained about U.S. meddling.

French Government Now Asking for U.S. Carrier Support

On April 4 in Paris, as General Ely received the wire from Navarre saying that he wanted an air strike after all, Premier Laniel and Minister of Defense Pleven attended a mass at Saint-Louis des Invalides in honor of the Indochina dead. As they left for a ceremony at the Arc de Triomphe, a colonel in the Invalides courtyard expressed the deep discontent of career soldiers at the conduct of the war by shouting, "Long live the army." Laniel thought his outcry was "very disagreeable," as if he, the head of the government, was not behind the army.

The terreplein of the Arc de Triomphe was packed with Indochina veterans when the ministers arrived in their Citroëns. As the ministers proceeded to the Tomb of the Unknown Soldier, the veterans shouted, "Down with Laniel, down with Pleven, long live the army." A police cordon quickly separated the ministers from the mob, and Laniel was able to climb into his car. Pleven, whose father had been a colonel in the Foreign Legion, and who agonized over the divorce between the army and the government, was assaulted by a high-ranking officer who broke through the police ranks. Pale, but trying to keep his dignity and his glasses intact, Pleven got away under police escort.

Upon receiving Navarre's wire that afternoon, General Ely informed Pleven and together they went to Matignon to see Laniel. The Committee for National Defense met after dinner, along with the Joint Chiefs of Staff and Colonel Brohon. Ely read Navarre's message. The committee agreed to request an air strike, and at 11 P.M., Ambassador Douglas Dillon was summoned to Matignon.

Dillon wired Dulles that Laniel and Foreign Minister Bidault had told him that "immediate armed intervention of U.S. carrier aircraft is now necessary to save the situation. Navarre reported that the Vietminh are bringing up the last available reinforcements which will way outnumber what the French can do by parachute drops. Ely brought back from Washington that Radford gave him his personal (repeat personal) assurance that if situation at Dien Bien Phu required U.S. naval air support he would do his best to obtain such help from the U.S. government. . . . French government now asking for U.S. carrier support at Dien Bien Phu. Bidault closed by saying that for good or evil the fate of Southeast Asia now rested on Dien Bien Phu. He said that Geneva would be won or lost depending on the outcome of Dien Bien Phu."

Indochina Is the First in a Row of Dominoes

On the evening of April 5, Dulles read Dillon's wire over the phone to the president, who was not pleased. Eisenhower gave Radford the benefit of the doubt that he had been talking to Ely in confidence—"but he should never have told a foreign country that he would do his best because they then start putting pressure on us," according to Dulles's notes on the conversation.

Eisenhower was now adamant that U.S. intervention at Dien Bien Phu was "impossible. In the absence of some kind of arrangement getting support of Congress, it would be completely unconstitutional and indefensible."

Dulles put in a good word for Radford, saying he was "quite reconciled" that it was a "political impossibility."

Ike told Dulles to find another way to help the French, but "we cannot engage in active war." The request for air strikes, he said, was just another "French whim."

Dulles at once replied to Dillon that "as I personally explained to Ely in the presence of Radford, it is not (rept not) possible for the US to commit belligerent acts in Indochina without full political understanding with France and other countries. In addition, Congressional action would be required. After conference at high level, I must confirm this position. . . . Such action is impossible except on coalition basis with active British Commonwealth participation. Meanwhile US prepared, as has been demonstrated, to do everything short of belligerence.

"FYI US cannot and will not be put in position of alone salvaging British Commonwealth interests in Malaya, Australia and New Zealand. This matter now under discussion with UK at highest level."

On April 6, however, Dillon cabled that the French, on further reflection, had fastened on Dulles's promise "to do everything short of belligerence." Bidault had called Dillon to say that since intervention was not immediately possible, the government of France would settle for a loan of ten to twenty B-29 bombers, flown by French crews but operating from U.S. bases in the Philippines and maintained by U.S. personnel. But this was turned down on the grounds that French crews could not fly the B-29s effectively.

To thrash out the Indochina dilemma, Eisenhower called an emergency meeting of the National Security Council (which normally met on Thursdays) on Tuesday, April 6. As it happened, three reports on intervention in Indochina had been prepared for discussion: one by the NSC's Planning Board, chaired by Ike's special assistant for national security affairs, Robert Cutler; one by the special committee on Indochina, headed by Walter Bedell Smith; and a brief memorandum from the army.

The Planning Board paper estimated that if the United States came in to help the French, 35,000 naval and 5,600 air personnel would be required, but that the operation "may turn out to be ineffective without the eventual commitment of U.S. ground forces." It also argued that even if Dien Bien Phu fell, a French cease-fire in Indochina was "not imminent."

But what stood out starkly in the report was its candid admission that atomic weapons "will be available for use as required by the tactical situation and as approved by the President." The estimated forces to be supplied by the United States in an intervention "are based on the assumption of availability" of nuclear weapons. "If such weapons are not available, the force requirements may have to be modified." In other words, the more A-bombs that were dropped, the less personnel would be needed.

The political fallout from the use of nuclear weapons was also discussed. The State Department, said the report, considered that "the military effect of the use or non-use of nuclear weapons should be made clear in the estimates of military requirements to assist in making a decision."

In the event of tactical nuclear weapons being employed, the report went on, "America's allies would lose their last hope that these weapons would ever be used again. Our allies would doubt the wisdom of the use of nuclear weapons in Indochina and this doubt would develop into strong disapproval," if it was done without their being consulted. Soviet reaction "would probably be substantially the same as in the case of no nuclear weapons. The Communists would brand the U.S. as an aggressor." As for the reaction of the Chinese, opinions of the Planning Board were divided as to what the United States should do.

The Planning Board report recommended that "if necessary," U.S. forces should be used to defend Indochina, and that contingency plans to that effect should be drawn up.

The army's brief memo, arguing against intervention, stated that "there are important military disadvantages to intervention in Indochina.

A military victory cannot be assured by U.S. intervention with air and naval forces alone. The use of atomic weapons would not reduce the number of ground forces required to achieve a military victory."

The report from the special committee on Indochina was more hawkish, arguing that the United States should continue to fight the war with or without the French, in order to stop the spread of Communism in Southeast Asia. The United States should oppose any negotiated settlement in Geneva.

Once the reports had been summed up, the NSC meeting opened for debate. Admiral Radford, Secretary of Defense Wilson, and CIA director Allen Dulles argued against the Planning Board's conclusion that the French would keep fighting after Dien Bien Phu. The loss of Dien Bien Phu, they said, meant that a military decision must be made on Indochina as a whole.

President Eisenhower disagreed. Dien Bien Phu, he said, could not be considered a French military defeat in view of the enemy's losses. The French thought otherwise, although Ike may have seen Bidault's "prophet of doom" rhetoric as a tactic to obtain swift U.S. intervention.

"Unilateral intervention is off the table," Eisenhower said. Even if it was tried, "we would have to take it to Congress and fight for it like dogs." He also expressed his "hostility to the notion that because we might lose Indochina we would necessarily have to lose the rest of Southeast Asia," for once ignoring the dominoes.

Eisenhower was now committed to united action for the defense of Southeast Asia, "even if Indochina should be lost. In any case the creation of such a political organization would be better than emergency military action." He felt strongly that it was wrong for the United States to "become the colonial power which succeeds France. The Associated States would certainly not agree to invite our intervention unless we had other Asiatic nations with us."

Secretary Dulles, whose plan Ike had adopted, said there was no need to decide at once, since "we know that under certain conditions Congress is likely to back us up." The next step was to organize the regional grouping prior to Geneva, so that they could go to the conference "strong and united," with "the Communists backing down." It was a "hopeless fight to try to overcome Congressional opposition," even though this might involve "an undesirable delay from the military point of view."

Eisenhower had to contend with the vox populi, which at the NSC meeting was expressed by an unlikely cabinet member, Treasury Secretary George Humphrey. Ike did not form friendships with most members of his cabinet. He admired Dulles for his dedication and tirelessness, but wondered about his brusque personality. Wilson was competent at Defense, under Ike's guidance, but unable to sell his program to Congress. Humphrey, however, had become a warm friend. They were the same age, sixty-three, and they were both bald. Ike said on meeting Humphrey for the first time, "I see you part your hair the same way I do." More to the point, Humphrey, a wealthy industrialist, owned a plantation in Thomasville, Georgia, that Ike sometimes visited to relax, play bridge, and shoot quail.

They rarely disagreed except over bridge hands, but now Humphrey, who thought military intervention would be disastrous for the budget, expressed a latent isolationism. He questioned the Dulles coalition by asking whether "every time the local Communist forces became strong enough to subvert free governments, would this not amount to a policy of policing all the governments of the world?"

That was too much for Ike, at a time when McCarthy was calling him soft on Communism. He pointedly told Humphrey that no free government had yet gone Communist by its own choice. The United States could no longer afford to say "that internal Communist subversion, as opposed to external Communist aggression, was none of our business. We have got to be a great deal more realistic than that."

The hardheaded Humphrey, instead of being silenced by the president, expressed his "very great anxiety over what looked like an undertaking by the United States to prevent the emergence of Communist governments everywhere in the world. I can see no terminal point in such a process."

This time speaking in a more equable tone, Eisenhower resorted to the dominoes he had earlier abjured: "Indochina is the first row of dominoes. If it falls its neighbors will shortly thereafter fall with it, and where does the process end? . . . It will end with the United States directly behind the eight ball.

"George," Ike beseeched, "I think you exaggerate the case. Nevertheless in certain areas we cannot afford to let Moscow gain another bit of territory. Dien Bien Phu itself may be just such a critical point." The president acknowledged that the United States was not prepared to take action at Dien Bien Phu. "But if we can secure this regional grouping for the defense of Indochina, the battle is two thirds won."

I'm Worried About Losing My Ass

On April 6, the same day as the emergency NSC meeting, the Senate discussed the Indochina situation, in the wake of rumors that the United States might resort to military action. Senator John F. Kennedy argued that united action would work only if the people of Indochina were granted independence. "To pour money, material, and men into the jungles of Indochina without at least a remote prospect of victory would be dangerously futile and self-destructive." But the French persisted in refusing independence for Indochina.

Kennedy's speech reflected the mood of the Senate. Only the staunch anti-Communist Democrat from the state of Washington, Henry Jackson, sounded the alarm that "we cannot allow Indochina to fall into Communist hands. . . . The administration should come to Congress with a resolution stating . . . the policy to be pursued . . . lest we lose Southeast Asia to the Communist forces which are about to take over."

As was often the case on the Hill, private debate was more probing than speeches for the gallery. Also on April 6, twelve influential Democrats who formed the Democratic Policy Committee met under the chairmanship of Lyndon Johnson. George Reedy, an aide to Johnson, who was present, recalled that "Walter George [of Georgia] was there, and very obviously there to play the devil's advocate, and to argue that we should go into Indochina. Walter George was a commanding personality in the Senate. Nobody liked to be disrespectful to him. And I have never seen a group of men explode like that, especially Bob Kerr [from Oklahoma]. George said something like, 'If we don't go in we will lose face,' and Bob Kerr slammed that big fist down on the table, saying, 'I'm not worried about losing my face, I'm worried about losing my ass.' " Reedy added: "When the thing was over, there was no doubt whatsoever where the Democratic Policy Committee stood. They were against [intervention]. And Johnson so reported back to the President."

Secretary of State Dulles was now focused on bringing the British on board. After Eisenhower had written Churchill, Anthony Eden had warned Ambassador Makins to say nothing at this stage. Eden did not want, he said, to "be hustled into injudicious military decisions." A collective defense of Southeast Asia would of course contribute to the security of Malaya and Hong Kong, but to proclaim it prior to Geneva would frighten off important potential supporters such as India. Threatening China prior to a conference with China was unsound. Dulles had not "weighed the consequences of his actions."

On April 7, Dulles received a wire from his ambassador to London, Winthrop Aldrich, who had seen Eden the day before. The thrust of Eden's view was that there was no need for any hurried decisions. Eisenhower's letter to Churchill was being discussed "at the highest level." Eden now believed that the seriousness of the military situation in Indochina had been exaggerated. He said that "the French cannot lose the war between now and the coming of the rainy season, however badly they conduct it." (This was also what Dulles thought.) Eden would consult with Churchill, the cabinet, and the military brass and "let you know soonest whether it is thought that you or Bedell Smith might profitably come here prior to meeting in Paris."

While the British stalled, the French were threatening to end the war. Dillon reported on April 7 that Bidault had told him that if Dien Bien Phu fell, "it was most unlikely that either Associated States or France would be willing to continue war even with full American military support." An exasperated Dulles replied on the same day that Bidault's reaction to the proposal for a coalition was "disturbing. . . . I sincerely trust that it was merely a preliminary and hasty reflex of a deeply harassed man. It hardly reflects a frame of mind conducive to effective collaboration between our two governments in this difficult period."

As Dulles prepared on April 7 to fly to Europe and put some starch into his allies, his assistant Douglas MacArthur II received a visit from Admiral Radford's aide, navy captain George W. Anderson, Jr., who wanted to discuss "a delicate matter." The Joint Advance Study Committee of the JCS had been looking into the use of atomic weapons at Dien Bien Phu. They had concluded that "three tactical A-weapons, properly employed, would be sufficient to smash the Vietminh effort there." (These were the weapons General Twining had mentioned in his oral history.) Radford wanted to know whether the Dulles regional pact would interfere with the use of those weapons, or whether, once the pact was formed, the French would agree to their use. Dulles, who was meeting with resistance from the French and the British, said he was not ready to discuss the matter. His assistant Roderic O'Connor noted: "Sec did not want to raise this now with Adm R——— & the latter I gather did not raise it with the Sec."

Also on April 7, Eisenhower gave a press conference. Asked about the strategic importance of Indochina, he spoke of "what you would call the 'falling domino' principle. You have a row of dominoes set up, you knock over the first one, and what will happen to the last one is the certainty that it will go over very quickly." In the case of Indochina, the risk was that Burma, Thailand, Malaya, and Indonesia would be lost. And after that, Japan, Formosa, and the Philippines.

Insulated by Congress and its refusal to intervene, the president had the luxury of giving vent to a frightening scenario based on the catchy but fallacious notion that nations were dominoes. Widely popular, it became a bipartisan fallacy, with Adlai Stevenson warning that "all Asia would slide behind the Iron Curtain" should Indochina be "absorbed into the Moscow-Peking empire." There were a few dissenting voices, like that of Paul Nitze, then in the State Department, who warned that we should not forget "that the majority of Asians are infinitely alien to us."

Eisenhower adopted an alarmist tone more to buck up the allies and placate the Republican right than to frighten the American people. His public remarks were at variance with what he said in private meetings. He told reporters he wasn't sure the Associated States of Indochina really wanted to be independent. In any case, independence was not a condition for U.S. intervention. He refused to say whether the administration would "go it alone" in Indochina, while knowing full well that this had become an impossibility.

The press fell for Ike's staged alarm. In an article entitled "Why U.S.

Risks War in Indochina," *U.S. News & World Report* stated that "the U.S. is putting the world on notice that it will tolerate no deal that gives the Communists Indochina."

Send Ho Chi Minh to Peking University

Neutral Switzerland, onetime host to the League of Nations, was now preparing to receive the Geneva Conference in the same building. Jean Chauvel, the French ambassador stationed in Bern, had found a peaceful backwater where he attended agricultural fairs and automobile shows. Suddenly, this meticulous and circumspect diplomat was asked to make preparations with the Swiss for the conference.

Chauvel went to Paris to sound out the principal cabinet ministers on government policy, and was astonished by what he found. At Matignon, Premier Laniel conveyed a joviality that one readily grants to men of massive girth. Of all the ministers Chauvel saw, he was the only one who listened more than he spoke. He believed that the Soviets would be willing to restrain the Chinese from helping Ho Chi Minh if granted credits from the French to consolidate their five-year plan.

Paul Reynaud, vice president of the Council of Ministers, was also at Matignon, sitting in a chair so high that his feet did not touch the ground. Short in stature but peremptory in manner, Reynaud instructed Chauvel that French policy at Geneva would consist of making a deal with the United States: France would ratify the European Defense Community and in exchange the Americans would take complete charge in Indochina.

Edgar Faure, the minister of finance, more easygoing than Reynaud, was no less assured: French policy would focus on making a deal with the Soviet Union. The French would negotiate a cease-fire with the Vietminh, and the Russians would drop their objections to a European army.

When Chauvel went to see Pleven, the minister of defense seemed pessimistic to the point of depression. He could see no way to solve the military problems he was faced with, the European army on the one hand and Indochina on the other. He was hoping to confer with the Vietminh at Geneva. He planned to appeal to their nationalism and ask them to free themselves from their Chinese guardians without succumbing to American influence.

At Chauvel's meeting with the foreign minister, Bidault confided that Pleven was "a broken man." Bidault was planning to have direct talks at Geneva with the Chinese. He believed that in exchange for the industrial equipment they badly needed, the Chinese might agree to put pressure on Ho Chi Minh to leave Indochina for a chair in political science at Peking University.

Chauvel returned to Switzerland with his mind whirling from the different options that had been presented. Most of it was pie in the sky. His own conviction was that France was not prepared to continue the war. It should have been turned over to the Americans, just as the British turned over Greece in 1947. This could have been done in 1950, but now it was too late. After Korea, the Americans wanted no more Asian forays. As things stood, Chauvel would wait for the Vietminh delegation to arrive in Geneva and then sound them out.

To Each His Ghosts

While the mills of diplomacy churned in foreign capitals, at Dien Bien Phu there was a pause in the battle between April 6 and 10. After three counterattacks, Huguette 6 had been saved. The estimated Vietminh losses of eight hundred dead led General Giap to change his plan of battle. He needed time to bring up replacements and take care of the wounded who had been carried off the field. On April 7, he gathered his senior officers to tell them that the conditions for an all-out offensive had not yet been reached. They would return to what he called *grignotage* (nibbling away) and resume the encirclement tactics.

The failure of the Vietminh to take the Five Hills showed that the French, with far fewer numbers, were using greater tactical skills. French artillery was now more effective, while the Vietminh guns hidden in the sides of mountains had limited fields of fire.

The garrison's brave stand against superior numbers was rewarded on April 17 with a collective citation from the War Ministry, which amounted to a Croix de Guerre with Palm for every man there. The reality, however, was that the garrison was exhausted. The drops of fresh units did not make up for the growing number of casualties. The size of the base had shrunk from 1,186 to 642 acres, so that supplies sometimes landed in

Vietminh territory. Colonel Langlais' private complaint was that he'd run out of whiskey and cognac. His relations with Hanoi were so strained that no one ever thought of slipping a bottle into a case of cargo.

The brief pause in the infantry battle did not extend to the Vietminh artillery, which kept pounding the French positions and airstrip. The Morane Crickets from the Muong Sai base in Laos continued to carry out reconnaissance missions over Dien Bien Phu, in order to report on and photograph freshly dug Vietminh positions. On April 6 at 3 P.M., Lieutenant Bertrand de la Mettrie and his pilot, Sergeant Jean Ribière, dove through the clouds a little too low. A 37mm antiaircraft shell hit the Cricket, seriously wounding de la Mettrie. Ribière didn't think he could make it back to Muong Sai in time to save de la Mettrie and radioed the Dien Bien Phu air controller: "My observer is badly wounded and my gas tank is leaking. I urgently need to land." He landed on the runway, which was strewn with torn-up steel plates and pocked with shell holes. Ribière tried to pull de la Mettrie from the cockpit, but he was unconscious. A shell burst behind the Cricket and Ribière stumbled away from the airstrip. After being hit by a shell, the Cricket caught fire, and two days later what was left of Bernard de la Mettrie was buried.

Contributing to the problems of air supply were the concerns of the twenty-four American Civil Air Transport pilots, who were flying twelve C-119s with French insignia out of Cai Bi airport in Haiphong. Their grumbling over lack of protection from French fighters had grown to near mutiny. On April 6, the CAT president, Alfred T. Cox, flew into Haiphong with the director of operations, Robert E. Rousselot. One of the pilots recalled that "the pitch consisted of a heavy dose of flag-waving and admonitions that we were doing a great service to the United States and the French government." Cox promised better fighter support and detailed daily briefings. The pilots returned to their Flying Boxcars with a renewed sense of dedication, though they later had cause to feel that Cox had flimflammed them. Hanoi reported to Paris on April 11 that the CAT crews were taking part in the airlift *"avec beaucoup de cran"* (with a lot of guts).

In Hanoi, Surgeon General Jeansotte was frustrated by his inability to evacuate the wounded from Dien Bien Phu. The situation was worse than his most pessimistic premonitions. During the April attack, which caused mounting casualties, the overcrowding got so bad that the surgical units stopped treating abdominal wounds, and were letting men die. Jeansotte dropped in an additional surgical unit on the night of April 5–6, under Captain Robert Caillaud. But the problem was insoluble, Jeansotte thought, particularly when there was such discord between Navarre and Cogny, the latter refusing to take any initiative and letting it be known that "Dien Bien Phu is finished." Jeansotte wondered why the army hadn't foreseen what should be done if the airlift was interrupted. The young doctors now being parachuted into the entrenched camp under truly appalling conditions were as heroic as any soldier. All that Jeansotte could do was drop medical supplies—more than 600 cots, 860 stretchers, 1,454 pajamas, 1,021 blankets, and case after case of medicine, from 17,000 ampoules of morphine to millions of units of penicillin.

On the night of April 7–8, another surgical team was dropped, under Captain Ernest Hantz, who took off from Hanoi with his team of seven at 11:30 P.M. At 1 A.M. on April 8, they saw the *T* of the drop zone lit up by fires in barrels filled with sand and oil. Hantz landed on the roof of a Dodge truck. An hour later, the team had retrieved their equipment and were led by the head doctor, Le Damany, to a former mess hall near an artillery battery, where they could set up their unit. They hung parachute silk on the walls and over the operating tables. Next door there was a room with beds for postsurgical patients. A covered trench linked the surgery unit to the main infirmary.

At 4 A.M., orderlies brought in the first stretcher cases. As soon as the news got out that a surgical unit had arrived, the other units sent their overflow—wounded who hadn't been processed yet, bandaged with scarves and old rags, their broken arms and legs immobilized by sticks or rifles used as splints. Each one had a handwritten label on him from the field infirmary describing his wound and the drugs already administered.

Hantz went to work, examining the stretcher cases; he found the men, aside from their wounds, thin and weakened. He later calculated that one out of ten men died before they could be operated on. Some had lost too much blood, often from internal hemorrhages. Others were turning blue from lack of oxygen, while those with head wounds or multiple wounds were beyond help, except by relieving their pain with morphine.

It was up to Hantz to do the triage, to decide who might live and who would not. An orderly marked their foreheads with a crayon, to indicate the order of priority, thoracic wounds before vascular, since the latter could be closed with a clamp prior to an operation. Orderlies cut away the wounded's filthy uniforms and washed off the mud and blood, then gave them antitetanus and antigangrene shots, and a presurgery anesthetic.

Operating bare-chested in the unventilated room, Hantz asked himself: "What am I doing in this hospital from hell?" and gave himself the answer: "I chose to be an army surgeon." And after a few days, even hell became banal when you performed thirty operations a day. He drank a cup of Nescafé and ate a bowl of rice and beef between operations, and in the corner there was a pile of parachutes where he could collapse for a few minutes at a time.

Hantz never knew the names of his patients, they were only mangled human forms with numbers on their brows. Years later, he was still haunted by the young lieutenant who, knowing his wound to be fatal, asked that his Moroccan orderly be treated first. And the Legionnaire who had deserted his wife in Germany, whose last words were that his bonus be sent to her in Tübingen. And the big Senegalese whose face was split in two, with the lobes of his brain pushing out of his broken skull, who survived for ten hours thanks to morphine. There was a saying among the doctors who survived Dien Bien Phu: "To each his ghosts."

Geneviève de Galard was in charge of the forty-bed room for the gravely wounded. As Dr. Grauwin told her: "No one can replace a young woman at the bedside of a wounded soldier." The wounded knew she understood what they were going through, and proudly showed her their marks of progress: "Look, Geneviève, I can move my big toe." She pushed a cigarette between the lips of eighteen-year-old Simon Marie, blinded by grenade fragments, whose head was encircled with bandages like an Egyptian mummy. She also had to light it, for he'd lost several fingers on each hand. A few days later, she found him trying to play the harmonica.

The Legionnaire corporal Heinz Haas had lost both arms and a leg. The stretcher-bearers who brought him in said, "He's fucked." But Dr. Grauwin, admiring Haas's will to live, wanted to save him. The triple amputation—

left arm at the shoulder, right arm at the elbow, left leg at the knee—took twenty minutes. With the help of transfusions, Haas lived. When he woke up, beaming, he said: *"Mein herren! Danke!"* He survived Dien Bien Phu and returned to civilian life in Germany, where he was twice married and twice divorced, and had two children.

The Only Chance for Us Is to Wait for a Cease-Fire

Colonel Bigeard, garrisoned with his 6th BPC on Eliane 4, was being harassed by the Vietminh on Eliane 1, which had been abandoned on March 31 by Moroccan fusiliers. Eliane 1 was only 150 yards to the northeast, and the snipers and grenade launchers and mortars were making his life miserable. "I'm tired of shells falling on my head," Bigeard said. Anyone who stuck his head out of a trench was fired at, and Bigeard had lost an officer that way. During the day, it was dangerous to move around. He decided it was preferable to take the initiative rather than sit there passively. He still thought that if Dien Bien Phu held, Hanoi would come to the rescue. After all, he told himself, "I'm fighting for the defense of the free world."

Always willing to learn from the enemy, Bigeard proposed a counterattack by digging an approach trench the short distance between Eliane 4 and the western slope of Eliane 1. Castries approved, but asked that Bigeard wait until the expected battalion of Legionnaire paratroopers was dropped, which gave Bigeard time to dig the trench by night.

Major Hubert Liesenfelt's 2nd Foreign Legion Parachute Battalion (BEP), consisting of 719 men, was dropped during the night of April 9–10. Three men from Lieutenant Fragonard's 7th Company were killed in the drop. One had his chute set on fire by a bullet. Captain Boulinguiez landed headfirst in a trench but recovered. The most admired officer of the battalion, Captain Charles Delafond, landed safely. A giant by French standards, well over six feet tall and massively built, he was called "Charles the Magnificent." At the airport before takeoff, he had sent a letter to his wife, Chantal. He had given her a boxer named Brutus, and ended his letter with the request, "Give Brutus a lump of sugar."

Liesenfelt's battalion was assigned to Eliane 3, the southernmost strongpoint on the eastern bank, between the Nam Yum and RP41. At dawn on April 10, Major Liesenfelt and Captain Delafond used a winding trench to reconnoiter the Eliane 3 position. As the major later wrote Chantal Delafond: "On that day, April 10, there was heavy firing from the mortars. Returning from our recon, we were following the trench when a mortar shell burst on the parapet. I was thrown to the ground, and when I looked around I saw Delafond lying unconscious with a hand on his helmet. A shell fragment had ripped through the helmet and he never regained consciousness." Years later, Chantal Delafond told an interviewer that her husband's death had been the culmination of a run of bad luck. Two weeks earlier, while she was staying at a hotel in Lyon, her engagement ring had been stolen. When she got home, she found that Brutus had been poisoned. Then she learned of her husband's death, and she was left to raise their daughter, Patricia, alone.

Meanwhile, at Eliane 4, on the night of April 9, Bigeard summoned three of his four commanders to his grotto. The companies were down to roughly eighty men each. "Hervé [Trapp], you start first with all you've got to the foot of Eliane 1, before daybreak. Don't load yourselves with heavy weapons, we'll back you up from here. As soon as the artillery preparation stops, storm the hill. Le Page, help out Trapp if it gets too hot. Allaire [commander of the mortar squad], position your mortars at the base of Eliane 4." Bigeard knew from previous counterattacks that due to losses and fatigue, the attacking units had to be replaced at once. He arranged for men from Bréchignac's recently arrived battalion to replace his men once they took the hill.

At dawn on April 10, the thunder of the artillery preparation roared over the camp. The French still had four 155s, twenty-one 105s, and sixteen 120mm mortars at Claudine and Isabelle. Combined, these guns fired eighteen hundred shells in ten minutes, mainly on Eliane 1. Mortar rounds were also fired to the north of Eliane 1 to prevent the sending of reinforcements from Dominique 1 and 2.

Bigeard directed the battle from a pit he had dug on the forward slope of Eliane 4, where he watched through his binoculars, surrounded by maps and radio sets. As his men moved through the trench to the foot of Eliane 1, four tanks fired their 75s into the embrasures, where the Vietminh had machine-gun nests, and Hellfires swooped in on the trenches that linked Eliane 1 with Dominique 2 to the north.

In Liesenfelt's battalion there were a number of volunteers, among them Fischer, the Legionnaire wounded on Béatrice who was returning to Dien Bien Phu. He landed on a bank of the Nam Yum, but it was the wrong bank, the one held by the Vietminh. They grabbed him, took his jump boots, tied his hands behind his back, and marched him up RP41 past Béatrice, the hill he knew so well, to their encampment. At dawn, he saw columns of coolies bringing back wounded from Bigeard's artillery preparation in hammocks tied to bamboo poles. Another column, carrying supplies on bicycles, was coming from the north. Later that day, Fischer was taken to a camp with thirty other prisoners.

By the time of the artillery preparation at 6 A.M., Trapp's and Le Page's companies had begun moving along the trench to the base of Eliane 1. At 6:10, Allaire fired smoke bombs on the western slope to mask the companies' advance out of the trench. The Vietminh had a battalion on Eliane 1, while the two companies added up to only 160 men.

Trapp's assault company followed the smoke bombs up the slope. But halfway up they were stopped, bracketed from above by a Vietminh machine gun, and from below by mortar fire from Dominique 2. Bigeard alerted Le Page, who had with him a unit of flamethrowers. Le Page and his men moved through half-destroyed trenches, each platoon using fire and movement to cover the others as they scaled the slope. A mortar shell exploded nearby and flung Le Page to the ground. He was covered by flying debris. A blockhouse above them was firing down. Le Page sent in a team of flamethrowers.

The modern infantry portable flamethrower had been invented by the Germans, who used it against the British in 1915's trench warfare with some success. The French had the American-made M2 model, which the Marines had found helpful in clearing Japanese trenches and bunker complexes. The M2 had a three-cylinder backpack—one cylinder held compressed nitrogen and the other two were filled with jellied gasoline. The gas propelled the fuel through a hose to the gun element, a small reservoir with an ignition system. Depressing the trigger allowed the flammable liquid to flow past the igniter so that it emerged as a stream of flame. Manning a flamethrower was one of the most perilous jobs that could be given to an infantryman. The backpack weighed seventy pounds, restricting mobility over difficult terrain and under fire. The range was limited—the operator had to get within forty yards of the target, which often meant exposing himself to enemy fire. The flamethrower, however, was a much feared weapon, evoking the horror of being burned alive at the stake. If the operator was captured, he had good reason to believe that he would be summarily executed.

Le Page recalled: "I will never forget the Legionnaire with the flamethrower, protected by two paras with submachine guns, the heavy cylinders on his back, advancing with amazing calm. I saw him point the muzzle, and the fulgurating jet of flame hit the blockhouse, which ignited like a match in dry stubble." Both companies, backed by Allaire and his mortars, then stormed the top of Eliane 1. "It was close combat under the burning sun," Bigeard recalled. "You're in a second state, you don't feel anything. Not a single Viet ran, they all had to be killed." Lieutenant Trapp looked at his watch. It was noon. They now had to improvise defensive positions, for the Viets were sure to respond. Bigeard's orders were: Don't concentrate on the summit, it makes you too easy a target. Spread out in different positions on the hill.

The situation report that Castries sent to Hanoi at noon said: "We took the summit on Eliane 1 at 11:30 after hard fighting. The Vietminh still hold a couple of blockhouses on the northern face."

At 2 P.M.: "Most of Eliane 1 is in our hands after extremely severe combat. Very violent reaction of Vietminh artillery. . . . Our losses are heavy and still being counted."

While waiting to be relieved, Trapp took out his notebook and drew up his casualty list: of eighty-five men, fifteen dead and twenty-two wounded. In the afternoon, two companies of Bréchignac's Legionnaires came to relieve Trapp and Le Page. It occurred to Le Page, whose company had forty casualties, that the Legionnaires would have to settle into a destroyed strongpoint, without shelters, trenches, or barbed wire. He was glad to have been assigned to the counterattack, so that now he could leave.

Lieutenant Dutel, commanding one of the relief companies, later described what he saw: "The hill was dug up by artillery fire, nothing remained of the shelters, and the trenches were filled with rotting corpses. When I tried to dig a pit, my shovel hit bones and debris. Imagine what that was like—men pulling disarticulated corpses out of the ground to dig a pit to sleep in, in the midst of an overpowering stench, blinded by dust and deafened by artillery fire."

It was harder to hold the hill than it was to take it. In their first night on Eliane 1, the Vietminh counterattacked and the Legionnaires lost 9 dead and 4 unaccounted for. As for Bigeard, his battalion, now down to 320 men, had suffered another 80 casualties. He wondered how much longer he could take these losses, among them veterans with whom he had fought for years—Sergeant Balliste, who'd been with him for five years, killed; Second Lieutenant Prigent, who led a squad of machine gunners, killed. Bréchignac's relief companies had to live with corpses.

April 11 was Palm Sunday. Langlais and Bréchignac inspected Eliane 1, where the Legionnaires were dug in, trying to make themselves invisible. Lieutenant Charles of the 3rd Company asked the two officers to keep their visit brief. "I don't want to have to take you out on stretchers," he said.

Despite the recapture of Eliane 1, General de Castries felt a growing pessimism that he described to the 1955 commission: "I didn't think we could hold out much longer. . . . Our perimeter was shrinking, the supply problem was growing, and I was contemplating getting the garrison out. Every day I asked General Cogny: 'How do we get out?' I never got an answer. He said it was up to General Navarre to decide. At one point, he said, 'We're preparing something.' I understood it had something to do with the American air force, but it was very vague. I remember telling him one day when I was more impatient than usual: 'When you come down to it, the only chance for us is to wait for a cease-fire.' "

General Giap's losses in the battle of the Five Hills created morale problems in his ranks. Although the battle had been indecisive, Giap remained certain of victory. "We had put out of action since the start a force equal to three battalions," he wrote. "Their remaining force was more than ten thousand, but their morale was sagging. We had neutralized the northern heights and most of those on the east. We moved closer to the airfield, tightening our encirclement, and cut off liaison with Isabelle. The eastern hills were turned into strong defensive positions, with mortars and mountain guns that kept the enemy under fire."

We Have Gotten Very Near
Having Cheated the Americans

John Foster Dulles had a passion for shuttle diplomacy. Phone calls and cables, instructions conveyed to ambassadors, were in his eyes inadequate. He had to get on a plane so that he could use his power of persuasion on foreign dignitaries. In 1956, Dulles boasted that in his three years as secretary of state, he had clocked 226,645 miles to thirty-four countries and met with their leaders, ranging from Franco in Spain to Tito in Yugoslavia, and from Queen Juliana of Holland to U Nu of Burma.

Dulles arranged to take his flights at the end of the business day, and used the plane as his arena, preparing for the diplomatic corrida with his picadors before relaxing with a highball or two of rye whiskey. He liked to tell the story of the three-year-old son of one of his security men who pointed to a newspaper photograph of a Lockheed Constellation and said, "This is where Mr. Dulles lives."

On April 10, Dulles flew to London with his team: Robert Bowie, director of the Policy Planning Staff; Walter Robertson, assistant secretary of state for Far Eastern affairs, and the deputy assistant, Livingston Merchant; and Douglas MacArthur II, the State Department counselor. This was the first of two frantic round-trips to Europe prior to the opening of the Geneva Conference on April 26, in a final push to urge France and Britain to join his Southeast Asia coalition.

Arriving on Palm Sunday, April 11, Dulles found London basking in glorious sunshine, with daffodils and forsythia in bloom in the public gardens. That evening, Anthony Eden and his undersecretary Denis Allen arrived at the U.S. Embassy for a dinner hosted by Ambassador Winthrop Aldrich. One of Eden's main concerns was Commonwealth relations, and in particular India, which would play, he felt, an important role at Geneva behind the scenes, given the influence that Prime Minister Jawaharlal Nehru had with the Chinese. "It was essential," Eden wrote in his memoirs, "not to alienate India by our actions in a part of the world which con-

cern her closely." Eden was disturbed to hear from the British high commissioner in Delhi that Dulles's speeches had created "the worst possible
impression" there. The feeling in India was that the United States was determined to scuttle the Geneva Conference. Eden's aim in his talks with
Dulles was to prevent this from happening.

After dinner, Dulles discoursed on U.S. policy in Indochina. "If some
new element were not interjected into the situation," he said, he feared
that "the French might be disposed at Geneva to reach an agreement
which would . . . turn Indochina over to the Communists." If Indochina
collapsed, he went on, Thailand, Malaya, Burma, and Indonesia might
also be absorbed by the Communists. Dien Bien Phu was at a crucial
phase, and the United States did not think much of its chances. The U.S.
Joint Chiefs of Staff had suggested a naval and air intervention. (In fact, all
but Radford had been against intervention.) Aircraft carriers were already
steaming from Manila toward the coast of Indochina. Dulles, however, did
not wish to act alone. Before a decision to intervene was taken, the French
must grant real independence to the Associated States. And, in addition,
the United States needed time to sound out the allies about forming a
coalition to defend Southeast Asia. Dulles handed Eden a draft outlining
the purpose of such a coalition.

Eden, who knew that the United States did not think much of Britain's
ability to defend Malaya if Indochina collapsed, responded that his nation
had "every intention of holding the position in Malaya," where security
was improving. As for "united action," Eden welcomed it in principle,
though further study should be made on the question of membership,
which should include India and other Commonwealth nations. Dulles, who
had no intention of being encumbered with Nehru's neutralist India, said
that inviting the Commonwealth Asians would raise the question of invit-
ing Korea, Taiwan, and Japan, which would overextend the fledgling organization. Eden responded that in order to counter the objections of the
Labour Party, he needed to say that "India was fully informed." Eden disliked the idea of balancing India against Formosa, and the question of
membership was left pending.

Eden's second major point was that Britain was committed to discussing Indochina at Geneva with the Chinese and the Russians. There

should be no question of Western intervention or bellicose warnings prior to the conference. The joint communiqué to be issued after Dulles's visits to London and Paris should say only that the work of the Geneva Conference must not be prejudiced by any Communist military action.

Dulles saw Eden's acceptance of the principle of united action as a breakthrough, cabling Washington: "Eden indicated a real willingness to consider defense arrangements in Southeast Asia, but not prior to Geneva, for he doubted whether sea and air support could turn the tide."

Talks continued at lunch on the the next day, April 12, with Dulles telling Eden that the situation in Indochina was analogous to the Japanese invasion of Manchuria in 1931 and to Hitler's remilitarization of the Rhineland in 1936. He was confident that if Britain and France backed him up, Congress would authorize President Eisenhower to use air, naval, and possibly even ground forces in Indochina. Eden said that the British Chiefs of Staff did not believe military intervention could be limited to air and naval action. He added that British public opinion was firmly opposed to any present involvement in a war in Indochina.

Attending the lunch for Dulles and his aides was Eden's private secretary, the irrepressible Evelyn Shuckburgh, who was moved to compare the work habits of the British and the Americans. Shuckburgh, who spent his leisure hours playing the violin and gardening, found himself "ashamed to discover how much less any of us work in the Foreign Office than people like Douglas MacArthur and Livingston Merchant," who began at 8 A.M. and kept at it until 7:30 P.M., with "only occasionally a Sunday free." Apart from his normal work, Merchant told Shuckburgh, he had "to be quizzed by Senators for hours on end." When Shuckburgh expressed his "horror" at this procedure, Merchant explained that foreign policy "could no longer be a matter handled by experts in secret, but must become the subject of continuous scrutiny by the masses." Shuckburgh, his Tory hackles rising, responded that "democracy could not survive if issues, as opposed to personalities, were to be put before the public for judgment."

Shuckburgh also chatted with the Far East expert Walter Robertson, whom he described as "a dreadful man." While he claimed to be an intimate friend of Chou En-lai's and Mao Tse-tung's, Robertson insisted that neither he nor Dulles had any intention of having a whiskey with the Chinese at Geneva. "When the court rises," he said, "you do not take a drink with the criminal at the bar." Shuckburgh pointed out that Geneva was not a court but a conference. "No," Robertson said, "we are bringing them before the bar of public opinion."

"I beg your pardon," Shuckburgh replied, "but you are not bringing them, they are coming." What a fool he was, thought Shuckburgh, "a wholly inelastic and opinionated man."

In Paris on April 12, the *New York Times* columnist Cy Sulzberger was invited to lunch at the home of his old friend General Pierre Billotte, who had been de Gaulle's army chief of staff. Also there was General Ely, who stressed the importance of Dien Bien Phu. He estimated that the Vietminh had lost twelve thousand men in the recent fighting. However, it was no longer possible for the French to bring in reinforcements overland. The only hope was to enlarge the perimeter so that more troops could be dropped. Commenting on Colonel de Castries' recent promotion to general, Ely said the reason it had taken so long was concern that it would remind people of Hitler promoting Friedrich Paulus from general to field marshal in the midst of the debacle at Stalingrad during World War II.

In Washington, at a National Security Council meeting on April 13, Walter Bedell Smith complained that while the American aid record was "almost miraculous," the French performance "was often worse than disappointing." Why, he wondered, had the French urgently asked the United States to airlift two battalions of troops from North Africa to Indochina and then stalled their departure by giving them two weeks leave? He also chastised their "niggardly" attitudes in trying to get the United States to pay the salaries of CAT pilots.

In London on April 13, Dulles remained optimistic about united action, ignoring the conundrum that he faced: to get congressional support for united action, he had to get the British on board. But Eden insisted that no action be taken prior to the Geneva Conference, and he wanted India and Burma to be members of the coalition. That morning, at their third and final meeting, Dulles and Eden agreed on a communiqué that avoided the sticking points of membership and pre-Geneva actions.

"We are ready to take part," said the joint communiqué, "with other countries principally concerned, in an examination of the possibility of establishing a collective defense . . . to assure the peace, security and freedom of Southeast Asia and the Western Pacific." This was vague enough in terms of timing and membership to satisfy both parties.

Eden, who had to appear before the House of Commons that afternoon, added a verbal condition explaining what he would say if the question of membership was raised in the Commons. He reserved the right to tell the House that "the whole question of membership was a matter for further consideration and that it would be discussed with the government of India as with the government of Pakistan and others."

Dulles, confident that he had Eden's agreement to take part in united action, wired Eisenhower: "Believe accomplished considerable in moving the British away from their original position that nothing should be said or done before Geneva. The communiqué issued today indicates a large measure of acceptance of our view of the danger and necessity of united action. . . . Despite differences in emphasis and timing feel satisfied that a very big step forward has been taken in bringing British thinking in harmony with our own." Dulles's appraisal went well beyond the phrasing of the communiqué.

Dulles left for Paris that afternoon elated by his success, and upon landing told reporters on the tarmac: "Mr. Eden said in London an hour ago that the Communist forces which fight the French Union in Indochina in fact endanger the peace and security of the entire of Southeast Asia and the Western Pacific. That is why I am here in Paris. For it is right that all those who are concerned should unite in common purpose. The purpose is the end of the war."

Even as Dulles was announcing that he and Eden were on the same page, Eden appeared before the Commons, where the Labour backbenchers lit into him for signing the communiqué. Aneurin Bevan, leader of the radical wing, accused him of "surrender to American pressure . . . for the purpose of imposing European colonial rule." Bevan was so angry that he resigned from the Labour Party's shadow cabinet.

Having warned Dulles that he might have trouble in the Commons, Eden responded to the Labour attack by saying: "I hope that those critics who thought that we were going to issue some sort of fulminating declaration before the Geneva Conference took place will realize that we are as anxious as they are—and perhaps more so—to see the Geneva Conference succeed." The question of membership was not raised, but Eden found it appropriate to say that he had made no commitment to join a Southeast Asia coalition or help establish one.

Meanwhile, Dulles was telling Ambassador Dillon that he had finally convinced Eden "to move ahead and really help the French." The next day, when he saw the transcript of Eden's remarks, he felt double-crossed. Robert Bowie, who had sat in on the Dulles-Eden talks, thought that Eden had caved in when Bevan and his cohorts denounced the communiqué. What Eden said in the Commons to placate them refuted every word that Dulles had spoken in Paris. Denis Allen, Eden's aide on Asian affairs, who had also sat in on the talks, felt that Eden "*did* indicate that he would be willing to start talks at once. . . . The American record showed that, but ours was obscure on the point." Allen felt that they had gotten "very near having cheated the Americans on this question." In any case, the incident poisoned relations between the two men in charge of foreign affairs in their respective countries. When the question of who was right was raised with Eden, he said, "His instinct was all against the slightest concession to Dulles."

Having failed to convince the British to agree to anything prior to Geneva, Dulles proceeded to try to convince the French in Paris. His call for a united front did not resonate, for the Laniel government wanted military aid with no political strings attached. They were counting on Geneva to end in negotiations and didn't want Dulles interfering.

On April 9, Laniel had made one of his infrequent appearances before the National Assembly to lay out France's "line of conduct" in Indochina: "First, to make all preparations for resisting victoriously at Dien Bien Phu and to maintain, with American material aid, our military effort; secondly, to approach the negotiations at Geneva in complete liberty, with the willingness to neglect no opportunity that could meet the sought-for result: peace with respect for the rights and the liberty of the people concerned." Implicit in his remarks was the incompatibility of united action and a negotiated solution. Laniel walked a tightrope, for his government would fall if Dien Bien Phu fell, and it would also fall if he accepted the conditions for U.S. intervention.

On April 10, that other frequent flier, Colonel Brohon, had returned from Washington, where he had seen Radford. The news he brought was not encouraging. Radford said there could be no U.S. intervention without the prior existence of a collective treaty.

Dulles and his team were in Paris on the evening of April 13 when Doug MacArthur was summoned to Matignon to see his old friend from the Resistance, Premier Laniel, who offered a swap: ratification of the European Defense Treaty by the National Assembly in exchange for American intervention. Laniel promised that on April 15 the cabinet would fix a date for the long-awaited debate. The mere scheduling of the debate, he said, would cause turmoil in the Assembly and might bring the government down. But if the United States came in to save the brave men at Dien Bien Phu, Laniel thought he could rally the anticolonial left. If Dien Bien Phu fell, however, "the situation with respect to both the EDC and Indochina would be virtually hopeless."

MacArthur reminded Laniel of his earlier promise that he would never be a party to turning Indochina over to the Communists. Laniel replied that he would keep his promise as long as he was premier, but that if Dien Bien Phu fell so would his government.

On April 14, Dulles had a full day of meetings with Laniel and Bidault, in the morning with Bidault in his office, continued conversations after lunch, and at 5:30 P.M. with Laniel. Dulles made his pitch for a coalition, saying that if the French joined he would have the leverage to go to Congress for a vote that would lead to U.S. intervention in Indochina. But there would be no intervention unless France granted independence to the Associated States.

Bidault responded that "French public and parliamentary opinion would not support the continuation of war in Indochina if the concept of the French Union were placed in any doubt whatsoever." The end of the war must be negotiated at Geneva, he said. "The war in Indochina has long been calumnied. It weighs on the French army and the nation's morale. Why fight Communism twelve thousand kilometers from France, since the war fans the flames of Communist propaganda inside France. Such is the reasoning of many political leaders. The need to negotiate an honorable peace, which would not be a victory for the Communists, is the government's aim. . . . This is not a question of peace at any price. At Geneva, we will put our cards on the table and study every aspect of the problem."

At Matignon, Dulles told Laniel that the British had "moved in considerable measure" toward the action. His tactic was to misrepresent the positions of each recalcitrant ally to get the other on board. Laniel saw through it, remarking that "this must be difficult indeed."

Dulles extracted from the French a joint communiqué, similar to the one with Eden, of studied vagueness: "In close association with other interested nations, we will examine the possibility of establishing . . . a collective defense." The communiqué added, however, that "no effort should be spared to make the Geneva Conference a success," and that any defense arrangement "would be profoundly conditioned by the outcome of the conference." Like Eden with the House of Commons, Laniel and Bidault had to reckon with the volatile National Assembly, though Eden's spats with Labour were trifling compared to the obstruction from the Communists and defeatists in the French parliament. Thus, the wording of the communiqué made it clear that there would be no united action until after the conference.

The well-connected and astute Cy Sulzberger had a chat with Walter Robertson, who had made such a poor impression on Shuckburgh. Sulzberger wondered about the paragraph in the communiqué that stated: "The independence of the three Associated States within the French Union, which new agreements are to complete, is at stake in these battles."

Robertson said that this phrase was "the toughest wrangle of the whole deal." The French objected to the words "new agreements" and Dulles objected to "within the French Union," so they ended up with both. Sulzberger told Robertson about his conversation with General Ely and asked if the French had requested air support. Robertson said they hadn't clarified their point of view yet. He was "distressed by French ineptitude." After "hysterically urgent French prodding," he and a group of experts had sat up until three in the morning, arranging an airlift to Dien Bien Phu with U.S. planes and French pilots. Once the airlift had been set, he got word from Defense Minister Pleven that it couldn't be done until mid-May because it would interfere with the vacation schedule of the pilots.

Sulzberger also saw Dulles, who "looked tired but in good humor." Over a whiskey and soda, Dulles said: "We foresaw at Berlin that if the subject of Indochina was put on the agenda of the Geneva Conference, it would probably lead to intensified military efforts by the Communists, to try and help their bargaining position at Geneva. Precisely that has happened." Dulles complained about the "misinterpretation" he'd been subjected to in London, where they thought he was advocating an ultimatum to the Chinese by threatening "the menace of war and atomic bombing." He never had such an idea in his mind, he said. He simply wanted to make the Communists realize they were up against "something strong enough" to keep them from trying to take over Southeast Asia. He hoped to start practical arrangements for a Southeast Asian alliance very soon, perhaps in the form of working committees. But "the stigma of colonialism" must be removed.

Sulzberger wondered how the stigma could be removed with two colonial powers as partners. Nehru would never fall for the idea that this was not a colonial enterprise. But Dulles said the French were sincere in wanting to give independence to the Associated States, even though the communiqué said "within the French Union."

Dulles was back in Washington on April 15, only to find that the Senate was up in arms over Indochina. On April 14, the Montana Democrat Mike Mansfield gave a speech entitled "Last Chance in Indochina." He argued the Dulles line for united action prior to the Geneva Conference in order "to prevent Communist seizure of Indochina without full-scale war." The United States had this "last chance" to keep the conference from "ending in disaster." The French, he said, must give complete independence to the Associated States. "The failure lies not in the military but in the political realm . . . [and the] failure to understand fully the power of nationalism in this struggle against Communism."

Hubert Humphrey said that Dulles must be made aware of the strong support in the Senate for Indochinese independence. But John F. Kennedy said united action was not the answer. The principal problem was recruiting "an effective native army to meet other native armies."

Senator Knowland, the Republican majority leader, agreed with Mansfield that the people of Indochina should be given the right to decide whether they wanted to remain in the French Union. "No matter how powerful their friends abroad may be," he said, "unless people desire freedom and have the will to resist, the resistance will not be effective."

Mansfield said Dulles was aware that nationalist demands had to be satisfied and was doing something about it. In fact, Dulles had failed to obtain commitments for prompt united action from either the French or the British. Like a traveling salesman with his foot in the door, Dulles continued to push a product that neither wanted. He was not giving up. Deaf to the protests of the allies, he was about to force the issue.

Targets Had Been Selected

Even though Congress had blocked unilateral intervention, and even though Dulles was finding the road to united action pocked with potholes, the Joint Chiefs continued to develop contingency plans for an air strike. With Geneva coming up, and with Panmunjom in mind, the United States needed to negotiate from a position of strength.

On March 19, Admiral Robert Carney, the chief of naval operations, ordered that the First Fleet, stationed at the Subic Bay naval base in the Philippines, be placed on twelve-hour alert and prepared to steam to the Gulf of Tonkin. Carney explained that there was no approval of a plan for Indochina, but that Dulles was "aware of the potential critical military situation in Indochina and the possible implications of serious French reversals."

The commander of the First Fleet, Vice Admiral William Phillips, was given the public mission to conduct training in the South China Sea. His classified mission was to maintain readiness for combat operations against China or in defense of Indochina. Phillips organized his ships into two task groups: the first, an attack carrier strike group (TG 70.2) commanded by Rear Admiral Robert Blick, consisted of two carriers, the *Wasp* and the *Essex*, eight destroyers, and a submarine; the second was a logistic support group.

The task groups set out on March 22, without informing the French, and steamed at flank speed to an area one hundred miles south of the island of Hainan. On March 29, Admiral Carney approved a proposal that carrier aircraft conduct reconnaissance of Chinese airfields and assembly points for the supplies flowing into Dien Bien Phu. On March 31, Carney told Admiral Felix Stump, commander in chief of the Pacific Fleet, that although no decision had been made, the possibility had been discussed of strikes against Chinese airfields and in support of French ground troops by bombers and carrier aircraft.

According to Dulles's biographer John Robinson Beal: "Targets had been selected; the aircraft carriers . . . were in the area with their tactical air groups and atomic weapons aboard. . . . The planes would strike at staging areas where Chinese Communists grouped the forces they were pouring behind the Vietminh, but would not attempt to carry warfare to the big Chinese population centers."

On April 8, Rear Admiral Herbert Hopwood, Stump's chief of staff, flew into Saigon to see Navarre. They discussed contingency plans. Navarre wired General Ely in Paris that "the plan is satisfactory and certain details still have to be worked out . . . in case of Chinese air intervention. No serious preparations have been made. . . . Radar installations would have to be built."

On the same day, the carrier task force was told to move within 125 miles of Haiphong so that its planes could take aerial photographs of Dien Bien Phu and Vietminh supply lines. On April 9, however, Secretary of Defense Wilson called President Eisenhower to ask whether the carrier task force should be sent back to Subic Bay. With the prospect of U.S. intervention fading, Ike said, "I guess we might as well let them come back."

It's Not Courage That Wins Battles

In Paris, General Ely was troubled by the information he was receiving. He wired Navarre on April 10: "I am struck by the anxiety that has become evident as the situation evolves. I still believe that the enemy attack was wished for, and that even if the garrison fell, it would be a military success in terms of the losses inflicted on the Vietminh. Are there new elements that render this view invalid?"

Among the new elements were these: The perimeter of the base was now reduced by half, from about three to about one and a half square miles. The manpower was 9,940, of whom 800 severely wounded were piled up in various shelters, getting muddier by the day as the monsoon season erupted, while 1,670 lightly wounded remained with their units. Having that many men trapped in a shrunken perimeter made them more vulnerable to artillery fire. The base was surrounded by twenty-eight Vietminh battalions, who received a steady stream of arms and supplies from China, while more and more of the French supply drops fell into the hands of the enemy as the base got smaller. In Hanoi, Colonel Guibaud of Navarre's Deuxième Bureau warned that Giap was preparing to continue the battle during the rainy season and that the Tuan Giao supply depot had stocked 3,400 tons of rice.

The week of April 11 to 18 was critical. Vietminh confidence was shaken by heavy losses and the possibility of U.S. intervention. Reinforcements arrived on both sides. Several battalions and more than three hundred volunteers were dropped into the base, while Giap received freshly trained battalions from China armed with 75s and rocket launchers. Lieutenant Allaire later recalled that this was the week when the battle could have gone the other way. "It's not courage that wins battles," he said. "The men at Dien Bien Phu showed magnificent courage, with only a few exceptions, but that wasn't enough to make up for the mental laziness of the high command. I'm quite willing to believe that there are no useless sacrifices, but why exonerate those responsible for our failure?"

Major Bréchignac, whose paras were fighting and dying for a few feet of churned-up trench on Eliane 1, told Allaire: "Cogny said that with the monsoon, the Viets will be trapped in the mud of their trails."

"Cogny hasn't read Joffre, who said, 'When it rains on the enemy, it rains on us,' " Allaire replied.

Morale remained high among the French forces, however, thanks to radio intercepts from People's Army commanders saying that their troops were not obeying orders. In addition, a Vietminh prisoner claimed that some *bo dois* had been forced into battle at gunpoint.

At the 1955 commission hearing, Castries was asked: "Did you take any prisoners? What did they say?"

Castries: "Not much. They were hardened cases."

"They told you nothing?"

"Some of them said, 'We're only fighting because the political commissars egg us on.' "

"Did you capture any officers?"

"None of them admitted being officers. At the end, we had fifty to sixty prisoners whom we placed in the center of the perimeter. Many wounded, whom we treated."

Also helping morale was the drop of Major Hubert Liesenfelt's 677-strong 2nd BEP on the nights of April 11 and 12.

Meanwhile, Castries drafted his almost-hourly situation reports. The last one on April 11, at close to midnight, said: "Counterattack on Eliane 1 reached summit 8 P.M. Elements of 2/1 RCP submerged, forming islands of resistance." The men knew they had to hold out until morning, when the aviation could operate. They dug up graves and threw out the corpses and took their place to protect themselves from mortars, fighting off the swarms of flies.

The situation report of April 12 at 11:15 A.M. stated: "The Vietminh detachments on Eliane 1 fell back at seven this morning, carrying their wounded and dead. Our losses are heavy." The wounded were taken to Captain Dr. Hantz's surgery unit. In the worst days of 1916, Hantz reflected, the wounded had been evacuated to the rear, but here there was no rear. They arrived on stretchers or astride the backs of fellow soldiers, who had carried them through mud-filled craters and half-crumbled trenches. Sometimes the lights went out in the infirmary and triage was done in the dark. Sometimes there was no room inside, and the stretcher cases were left outside in the mud, half naked.

At the isolated strongpoint of Isabelle, as on the rest of the base, the perimeter was shrinking. Vietminh trenches were creeping up to Colonel Lalande's barbed wire enclosures. He sent patrols out to ambush the trench diggers. His men killed fifty Viets and filled three hundred yards of trenches, but at a cost of twenty-three dead and wounded. And what was the point? As soon as the trenches were filled they were dug again. It was like emptying the ocean with a spoon.

Giap's attention was now focused on the six Huguettes, which flanked the airstrip and maintained the western end of the perimeter. Aerial photographs showed that Giap's troops were extending their web of trenches closer to the runway. Lieutenant Spozio, whose company of Legionnaires held Huguette 1, midway down the airstrip, was sent out with Lieutenant Legros on April 11 on a daylight sortie to destroy trenches. Three Vietminh companies sprang out from concealed shelters, flanked by machinegun nests. Two tanks were brought in for support and one was hit by a bazooka. Spozio was hit, lost an eye, and was carried off.

"The Viets were sixty meters away," Sergeant Pottier recalled, "and Legros ordered an assault. They started firing when we were within twenty meters. Legros was in the lead. I saw him fall five meters from me, and I crawled toward him. He had a gaping wound on the outside of his left thigh, and his radioman lay dead beside him. I applied a tourniquet to his thigh just as the Viets counterattacked with grenades. I wanted to carry him toward the rear, but he ordered me to regroup the platoon and pursue the attack." The French fell back, however, leaving the Vietminh in their positions dangerously close to Huguette 1.

On April 12, with the Vietminh closing in on the western side of the runway, Colonel Langlais reorganized the defense of the base, dividing it into five zones, each commanded by an officer who reported to him. Bigeard was placed in command of counterattacks. He left his cave at the base of Eliane 4 and joined Langlais in more comfortable quarters. He liked the new arrangement, which began each morning with a briefing of the commanders. Castries, a cavalry officer unaccustomed to this kind of fighting, was out of the loop. There should have been a three-star general in command of the base, but no one was volunteering. Bigeard thought of his wife, Gaby, and his daughter, Marie-France, but it was pointless to linger on family. Some of the other officers sent telegrams: MORALE GOOD. THINKING OF YOU. And the next day they were dead. Bigeard never sent telegrams.

Keep the Press Clippings for Me

In the March 31 fighting, Lieutenant Brunbrouck's order to "debouch at zero" had saved the day. He had pulled his howitzers back to the central camp across the Nam Yum and reconstituted his 4th Battery in muddy gunpits. In late March, when the mail was still going out, he had written his brother, Maurice: "The life of artillery gunners is hell. We are in open pits, vulnerable to enemy fire. As soon as the Viets see us move, the shells start raining. And yet we have to keep firing. Keep the press clippings for me, I'd like to look at them when this is over." To his sister Alix, who had raised her two brothers when they were all orphaned, he wrote: "I believe in my lucky star. But if anything happens to me, I leave you all my belongings."

On April 13, the morning fog allowed the resupply of Brunbrouck's 4th Battery, as his gunners repaired damaged 105s. Major Knecht, in command of the artillery unit, told an aide: "We've got to shut down the recoilless rifle that's showering us from Dominique 2. Ask the 4th Battery to handle it." The fog had lifted and Brunbrouck was not happy to draw fire by daylight. "It's going to be a downpour," he said. The recoilless rifle was well hidden at the top of Dominique 2. Brunbrouck, his helmet on, peered through his binoculars. The first shell went too far. When the recoilless rifle returned fire, Brunbrouck got off another round and made a direct hit.

That afternoon came a heavy counterbombardment on the 4th Battery. A shell fell through the roof of the command post, exploding in the center. The blast threw the men inside against the hard clay walls. Once the smoke and dust had settled, a voice said: "I'm wounded." Second Lieutenant Baysset saw Brunbrouck lying on the ground. "It's my back," Brunbrouck said. The others turned him on his stomach and saw a deep cut in the small of his back. The shell, with its short-delay fuse, had exploded after smashing through the roof. Brunbrouck not only had shrapnel in his back, he had been splashed with acid from the battery of a destroyed radio.

Brunbrouck seemed lucid, but they had trouble getting him onto a stretcher. Around the narrow entrance of the command post, a protective wall had been built. Baysset held Brunbrouck under the shoulders and pulled him backward, but Brunbrouck slipped and fell, grimacing with pain. Outside the command post, they placed him on a stretcher and carried him to the main infirmary. Dr. Gindrey was alerted and asked, "Paul Brunbrouck of the 4th Battery?" They had been in the same regiment in Tunisia in 1952. Gindrey wrote Brunbrouck's brother: "He recognized me and said, 'Old friend, I'm done for.' I saw his eyes close and I knelt beside him, and held his head. He died in my arms."

Too Many Men Are Getting Killed Supplying Huguette 6

Major Clémençon, in charge of the Huguettes, was worried about Huguette 6, to the north of the airstrip. Captain Bizard and his Vietnamese paratroopers and Lieutenant François and his Legionnaires, about three hundred men in all, were surrounded by Vietminh trenches.

On the night of April 13, Giap decided to send a battalion to dig a trench across the airstrip, to cut off Huguette 6 from the rest of the base. Battalion chief Nguyen Quio Tri was picked for this assignment. That afternoon, his regimental commander, Nam Ha, spread out a map and traced the line of the proposed trench with a red pencil. Nguyen thought of how close he would be to French lines. He thought of his wife and two children in his village of Do Luong. Would he see them again? He rid his mind of negative thoughts. The sun was sinking in the west and his helmet of cloth-covered bamboo kept it out of his eyes. The crests seemed to be swallowing the sun.

He summoned his company commanders over cigarettes and tea and showed them the map. The 1st Company would dig the trench. The 2nd Company would cover the 1st at the edge of the airstrip. The 3rd Company would stay in reserve. It was dark when they reached the airstrip. The sounds of shovels and hoes were mixed with occasional firing. By 11 P.M., they had dug two thirds of the way across and the men were resting when the artillery fire hit. Cries of rage came up from the trench. "Their mothers are whores! One third of the company is done for!" Nguyen jumped out of the trench to take stock of the wounded being bandaged. They had taken serious losses, and the stretcher-bearers further reduced their number. They built niches in the trenches and roofs a foot thick, made of planks and earth, indiscernible at ground level. On the airstrip they saw open parachutes lying in disorder with the cargo that the men of Huguette 6 had neglected to pick up.

The food wagon arrived—a man carrying two pails on a bamboo rod. Each ration consisted of rice with salted sesame, and a mouthful of buffalo meat. They prepared for combat as they heard the French reinforcements approach. Nguyen called headquarters for artillery support and the French fell back. Bua Xuan Chi, the food carrier, dropped his pails, hopped into the trench, and picked up some grenades. He said he was glad to finally be seeing combat.

Protected by machine guns and snipers, one team did the digging while another brought up planks, sandbags, and roof timber. By 4 A.M., they had dug a trench forty yards across. Their position was enveloped in clouds of smoke, and Nguyen's ears rang from the shell bursts. Once again, he asked for artillery, and the 75s and mortars responded. The French fell back, but Nguyen learned that his friend Khoi of the 1st Company had been killed. Khoi had been a weaver in Nam Dinh. When the war was over, he had planned to marry one of the female workers at his factory. "Every pan needs a lid, as they say," he had told Nguyen. The 1st Company had lost half its men. Nguyen could not continue fighting in daylight, so he pulled his men back, to complete the job the following night.

Huguette 6 was about a mile north of the main base of Claudine. But once the trench across the airstrip was completed, retrieving the daily supply of cases of food and ammunition and the twenty-five-gallon jerrycans of water became a costly battle. The paras and Legionnaires had to fight their way across the freshly dug trench, and through the machine-gun and mortar emplacements concealed on the west bank of the airstrip and in the destroyed Curtiss Commando.

On April 15, thirty-seven PIMs were moving up the drainage ditch when they were hit by heavy mortar fire. Twenty-eight were killed and only five jerrycans reached Huguette 6. Bizard dug a well but the water came up filthy. His men were dehydrated and their food was down to a cup of rice a day, if there was water to cook it, and maybe a can of sardines to share. The Vietminh had brought up mortars, and a shell hit the command post while the officers were in a meeting. Lieutenant Rastouil was killed but Bizard and François were unhurt. In the four nights from April 13 to 17, providing supplies to Huguette 6 cost one hundred casualties.

At 6:20 P.M. on April 17, Langlais told Castries: "Too many men are getting killed supplying Huguette 6." Castries had to agree, even though abandoning his northernmost strongpoints would further shrink his drop zone. Major Clémençon relayed the message to Bizard, speaking in English, since the Vietminh listened to their radio communications. Bizard was given the choice of surrendering or leaving behind his wounded and fighting his way out. "Do what you can," Clémençon told him. "If you surrender, no one will be offended—but no white flags."

The next day was April 18, Easter Sunday. It was also Bizard's birthday. He was twenty-nine years old. He decided he wasn't going to surrender on his birthday. A surge was better than captivity. It was almost dawn, but the fog had not lifted when he gathered the three hundred men about to storm through enemy lines. He told them: "Each of you take two sandbags and remove half the sand and place one on your chest and one on your back."

They leapt out of the southern trenches into the fog, flinging grenades. Lieutenant Latanne recalled: "Bizard was always in front and amazingly was never wounded. We were stopped by automatic weapons firing along a track we had to cross. I was crouched behind a knoll, quite close to Lieutenant Francois, who was hit by a bullet in the throat. I threw my arms under his head and his hands grabbed my combat vest, but I felt his grip loosen." Of the 300 men who fought their way out of Huguette 6, 106 were killed, 49 were wounded, and 79 were unaccounted for. Bizard ended his career with four stars and commanded the military academy at Saint-Cyr.

The Cigar-Shaped Pellets Were Very Effective

While Eisenhower had sent the carrier task force operating off the Indochina coast back to its base in the Philippines on April 9, the U.S. Far East Air Force (FEAF) in Japan continued to furnish logistical support to the French, in spite of pessimistic reports drawn up by its staff. One staff paper dated April 13 said the French still followed an "arrogant" colonial policy and had so alienated native loyalties as to make a military solution impossible. And rigid ceilings on manpower did not help. In addition, the French air force was incapable of interdicting enemy supply routes or properly using air strikes on the Vietminh concentrations ringing the fortress.

General Earle Partridge, who took command of the FEAF on March 26, 1954, directed "full, prompt, and effective" assistance. In early April, when the French commissioner general Maurice Dejean asked Ambassador Donald Heath for eighteen C-47s to replace losses, the planes were flown from Japan on April 9, on loan. Other deliveries included twenty-five B-26s, H-19 helicopters taken from Marine Corps units in the Far East, L-20 liaison planes borrowed from the air force, and twelve F8F fighter replacements diverted from Thailand. The carrier *Saipan* sailed from Japan with twenty-five Corsair fighters and reached the Indochina coast on April 18. U.S. pilots flew the Corsairs to the Tourane airfield and the *Saipan* steamed into the harbor to pick up the pilots by helicopter. The FEAF flew in large shipments of munitions, paraflares, and white-phosphorus bombs, while deliveries of heavier ordnance came by ship from Korea and Okinawa.

On April 7, the FEAF deputy for operations, General Jacob Smart, offered the French five million cluster projectiles, known as hail bombs or Lazy Dogs, which were stored in Japan. These lethal weapons, later outlawed in many countries (but not the United States), had been made to strike enemy troops in Korea, but were never used in combat. More than eleven thousand of the finned bullets were packed in containers about the size of a five-hundred-pound bomb; they were dropped from fifteen thousand feet and burst open at five thousand feet, gaining velocity as they descended on their targets. Five hundred of these bomb units arrived in Haiphong on April 16, but they weren't unloaded until the twenty-third. When the shipment was unpacked, some of the bullets were corroded and others had damaged fins. The French, instead of using them against enemy personnel, dropped a total of 369 bombs on antiaircraft emplacements. The results must have been positive, for the transport planes supplying Dien Bien Phu reported less AA fire and the Vietminh dispersed their batteries. A French officer later taken captive was told by his interrogators that "the cigar-shaped pellets" were very effective. Lieutenant Colonel William Saunders, an FEAF technical expert, observed that "the finned bullets were successful, but only due to volume rather than good delivery tactics."

When the air force general Jean Dechaux, head of the Northern Tactical Air Group in Indochina, testified before the 1955 commission, he said: "The Americans proposed to let us have some hail bombs. This was a five-hundred-pound bomb containing eleven thousand clusters. Dropped at high altitude, the container fell to five thousand feet before opening and releasing the polished and pointed darts at the speed of sound, or even faster.

"The Americans assured us that their trials showed the clusters were highly effective," Dechaux continued. He asked why they had not been used in Korea. He was told: "We didn't use them in Korea because we didn't want to be accused of using a weapon of mass destruction like an atom bomb." On a tactical level, Dechaux thought the hail bombs would be a way to get the Vietminh to pull out its antiaircraft guns, if they were bombed daily with clusters. "I forget the exact number of bombs the Americans gave us," he told the commission. "Between six hundred and a thousand. . . . We informed General de Castries that we were trying out new munitions. 'You won't see anything on the ground,' we told him, 'but you will hear a whistle.' The Americans had told us the darts produced a loud whistle. Castries saw nothing, absolutely nothing. However, the AA fire slowed down appreciably for forty-eight hours. I believed in the hail bombs. I knew the darts could burst through the hood of a jeep and destroy the engine. We used all the bombs they gave us."

Dechaux also believed in the efficiency of napalm. "We dropped it from C-119s," he told the commission. The big C-119 Flying Boxcars, on loan from the United States, were normally used for supply drops and were flown by American CAT pilots. Dechaux had to form French crews for night drops over Dien Bien Phu. "Each plane carried nine containers of ninety gallons each," he recalled. "But the C-119s were busy dropping supplies and were rarely available. We should have conducted an intense napalm drop, every day for a month around the base. It was worth trying. When fighters drop napalm, at an angle, it spreads over too great a surface. When it's dropped straight down, it starts huge fires. I've seen Viet munition dumps hit and explode. But the time to do it would have been December 15, not April 15, before the rains."

Lieutenant Colonel Felix Brunet, the commander of the Cat Bi airfield in Haiphong, took part in six of the eight napalm raids the French secretly conducted. On March 23, nine C-119s loaded with napalm were ready to take off from Cat Bi. The first one crashed at the end of the runway. The other eight took off and dropped their napalm. "I am certain," Brunet told the commission, "that the zones on which napalm was dropped were evacuated by the Viets. If dropped during the dry season, napalm can produce extraordinary results." However, the rules governing the loan of the C-119s were that they should not be used in combat, and the high command in Hanoi, concerned about U.S. reactions, called off the raids.

"The C-119s came from Clark Field in the Philippines," Dechaux said. "We had a workshop where we painted a cockade over the stars. At the Cat Bi airport in Haiphong there was an American team that forwarded our requests." This team of twelve men from the 8081st Quartermaster Air Supply and Packaging Company was headed by Captain Donald Fraser. They taught the French how to use the material they received. One less lethal form of U.S. aid was resupplying. The French had an aerial company for resupply (the 5th CAR) that depended entirely on U.S. supplies.

An Air Strike Is Militarily Useless and Politically Dangerous

On April 14, General Partridge arrived in Saigon for consultations. As Maurice Dejean recalled before the 1955 commission: "Partridge told me he had come to examine on a purely technical level the chances of success for an eventual operation against Vietminh positions around Dien Bien Phu by B-29s flying at high altitude. The general spent two days in Tonkin. Back in Saigon, he told me that if the conclusions of his report were accepted, he would send one of his aides to study the operation in greater detail."

Partridge flew over Dien Bien Phu at high altitude. In Saigon, he saw Navarre, who asked him about Operation VULTURE. In an April 16 wire to Ely, Navarre reported that Partridge "had heard nothing regarding VULTURE, other than one vague wire authorizing him to study it with us. He had no idea it was an urgent matter until I told him." Navarre asked Partridge whether B-29s could knock out the Vietminh guns around Dien Bien Phu. Navarre thought the supply base at Tuan Giao might offer a better target. Partridge said that that would have to be decided by a survey mission.

Navarre apparently managed to communicate his sense of urgency to Partridge, who, on his way back to Japan on April 18, radioed General Joseph Caldara, commander of FEAF Bomber Command, to meet him at Haneda Airport in Tokyo. Partridge told Caldara that Navarre was hoping for an air strike using B-29s, which he said had been cleared through diplomatic channels, although Partridge had received no directive to that effect. Partridge wanted Caldara to go to Indochina and examine whether B-29s would be effective, in case the flights were authorized. Caldara had available for a massive air strike a total of ninety-nine B-29s—thirty-two at Yokota Air Base in Japan and sixty-seven at Kadena Air Base in Okinawa. Bomber Command, or Bom Com, had flown thousands of missions in Korea, but B-29s were not suited to pinpoint bombing, since they dropped their loads from eighteen thousand feet. Short-range navigational radar (SHORAN), which could guide bombers from the ground with precision, was essential, and it took ground crews weeks to learn to use it.

Caldara and a team of eight other officers flew to Saigon on April 19 and conferred with French and U.S. embassy officials. The team inspected airfields and photographed Vietminh supply routes from the air. Caldara flew over Dien Bien Phu three times, once in a French Dakota and twice in his own B-17, and saw how embedded with each other the two armies were. In Hanoi, he saw the air force general Jean Dechaux, who said before the 1955 commission: "General Caldara told me that if the conclusions of his report were accepted, he would make available a fleet of ninety-nine planes within twenty-four hours. He asked me to set up at once radio guidance posts on high points within one hundred or two hundred kilometers of Dien Bien Phu."

Caldara was astonished when Dechaux told him that he had no radio guidance. Nor could he propose any high points held by the French. Caldara explained that the B-29s could not conduct a massive raid without radio guidance on the ground. He also pointed out that from the moment the French called Manila to ask for the intervention of B-29s, seven hours would elapse before the raid took place. "In seven hours the weather could change," Caldara told him. "We could not provide targets that would still hold up seven hours later. The Vietminh artillery could withstand five-hundred-pound bombs and even thousand-pound bombs. They changed their hidden locations, perhaps not every seven hours, but often."

The Americans were prepared to conduct as many raids as necessary, Dechaux told the commission, because carpet-bombing had to be repeated several times to do much damage. But there was another delicate problem: What if a B-29 crashed in Tonkin or China, proving the direct involvement of the United States in the war? And what if a B-29 had to make a forced landing at one of the three crowded French air bases? What technical help could the French provide? Neither France nor the United States wanted another Korea, with the appearance of Chinese "volunteers" in Indochina, Dechaux said. He informed Navarre that a U.S. air strike on Dien Bien Phu was "militarily useless and politically dangerous." Navarre agreed that without SHORAN, a massive strike close to the camp was impossible. He would rather have a strike on Tuan Giao, the supply base fifty miles northeast of Dien Bien Phu. Caldara informed General Partridge that the strike was impractical and left Saigon with his team on April 29. With the benefit of hindsight, Caldara recalled in a 1966 memorandum for the record that "the bombing raid could have effectively destroyed the entire enemy force surrounding Dien Bien Phu." However, the massive raid could have destroyed the French force as well. In his report to General Partridge, Caldara said that accuracy was beyond the capabilities of onboard radar. Partridge later recommended that carrier-based aircraft be used rather than B-29s, but by that time, it was too late.

The Administration Must Face Up to The Situation and Dispatch Forces

On April 16, two days after Dulles had returned from his trip to Europe, Vice President Nixon addressed the American Society of Newspaper Editors. He said that his remarks should be attributed to a "high administration source." But one of the editors in the audience told him it was ridiculous to insist that he was off the record when there were at least five hundred newsmen in the audience.

"There is no reason," Nixon said, "why the French forces should not remain in Indochina and win. They have great manpower and a tremendous advantage over their adversaries, particularly air power. . . . What can be done? . . . More men are needed and the question is where to get them. They will not come from France, for France is tired of the war. . . . If this government cannot avoid it, the administration must face up to the situation and dispatch forces."

Nixon's call for unilateral American intervention had repercussions at home and abroad. Was he floating a trial balloon or enunciating government policy? His belligerent tone prompted headlines in the British and French press, just as Dulles was in the midst of bringing the allies on board for united action. Dulles said in a phone call to a senator, "It was unfortunate, but it will blow over." The president, who was in Georgia on a golf vacation, was not overly concerned, and called Nixon to tell him not to worry. The uproar had been all to the good because it woke up the country to the seriousness of the situation in Indochina. However, Jim Hagerty wrote in his diary: "Think it was foolish of Dick to answer as he did but will try to make the best of it."

In Congress, there were expressions of alarm. At a private party at the home of Senator Estes Kefauver, one of the guests, the Colorado Democratic senator Edwin "Big Ed" Johnson, said: "I heard the Vice President whooping it up for war in Indochina. I am against sending American GIs into the mud and muck of Indochina on a blood-letting spree to perpetuate colonialism and white man's exploitation in Asia."

At the weekly meeting of Republican congressional leaders, with Eisenhower back from vacation, Charles Halleck, the House majority leader, said Nixon's remarks "had really hurt," and he hoped "there would be no more talk of that type." The president said it was important not to let the Russians think we would stand passively by if they stepped up their involvement in Indochina.

In the light of Nixon's remarks, Dulles felt the need to keep the momentum going on united action. This was the point where his shuttle diplomacy stumbled, although it stands out as one of the more intricate and absorbing efforts in recent U.S. diplomatic history. The triangulation of the talks left room for misunderstandings and false hopes, but the persistence of Dulles, the canny evasiveness of Eden, and the plight of the

French made the twists and turns as gripping as a car chase that ends in a wreck.

The French were in a state of permanent emergency, while British policy was to keep things vague so they couldn't be pinned down. British desires not to strain the American alliance were outweighed by the certainty that any action prior to Geneva would damage their relations with the Commonwealth nations. Dulles also wanted to keep things vague, in order to rope in the allies. But he was ready to turn any ambiguity to his advantage. As Churchill once put it: "Dulles is the only case I know of a bull who carries his china closet with him."

In their meetings in Paris on April 11 and 12, Eden had made a distinction between two features of the Dulles proposal: one was to form a lasting security system for Southeast Asia, which Eden approved of; the other was to apply that system at once to Indochina, which Eden disapproved of. Dulles showed Eden a draft of his final communiqué to that effect, but Eden responded that "it would be difficult for His Majesty's Government to give an understanding in advance of the Geneva Conference regarding action to be taken subsequently."

Dulles replied that a situation might arise where "Indochina was the place for such intervention" provided that the French gave independence to the Associated States and that the conflict was placed on an international basis. Victory would be possible "with the addition of outside air and naval support."

Eden refused to accept the Dulles proposal. He explained that "British public opinion would be firmly opposed to . . . becoming involved in what was an unpopular war in Indochina." Things might be different after Geneva, he said, which was why he did not wish to commit himself to any intervention in advance of the conference. And so it was that they hammered out a communiqué acceptable to both. The Foreign Office understanding was that preliminary talks with interested governments could begin at once, as long as no public announcements were made prior to Geneva. Eden agreed that he would allow Ambassador Makins to take part in this informal group. But who were the interested governments? Eden had reserved the right to discuss the matter with India and Pakistan.

I Am Not Aware That Dulles Has
Any Cause for Complaint

On April 16, the day of Nixon's speech, Dulles informed the British ambassador, Roger Makins, that he had invited the ambassadors of nine nations to start talks on April 20: Australia, Britain, France, New Zealand, the Philippines, Thailand, and the three Associated States—Vietnam, Laos, and Cambodia. Makins, who took it for granted that the talks had been cleared with Eden, sent him a wire ending with: "I assume that I can agree with such a proposal."

A furious Eden wired back that he certainly did not agree. He felt that Dulles had preempted the right to pick the members for his security organization, excluding India, Pakistan, and Burma. And this at a time when the British were about to hold their regional conference of Commonwealth nations in Colombo, Ceylon, on April 28. Dulles's plans were an insult.

On April 17, Eden wired Makins: "According to my understanding we reached no definite agreement in London on either (1) the procedure for examining the possibility of establishing a collective conference or (2) a definite list of states to be approached." Makins passed Eden's objections on to Dulles, only to be told that the invitations for the April 20 meeting had been issued and that the meeting had been announced in the newspapers. On April 18 at 6:41 P.M., Makins sent Eden a secret and personal telegram that said: "Dulles made no comment or complaint about the misunderstanding. Indeed he repeated how useful he had found your talks and said how much easier it was to talk a deux than a trois.

"However, there is no doubt that the State Department's full record on the point, which Australians and New Zealanders have seen, is clear and unequivocal, whereas the only record I have had (a draft only) is ambiguous.

"I hope you will be able to clear this misunderstanding up with Dulles and his advisers."

April 18 was Easter Sunday and Eden was in his country house at Binderton. Denis Allen, his undersecretary in charge of Far Eastern affairs, was inaccessible in Devonshire. There was only a skeleton staff on duty at the Foreign Office. When Eden received his dispatches, including the Makins wire, his mood was not improved. He resented that Makins seemed to be taking sides with Dulles, and he felt more acutely than ever that Dulles had pulled a fast one. It seemed clear that the countries Dulles had invited would be regarded as constituting the proposed organization. Instead of following the usual procedure of having an undersecretary draft a reply, he was in such an irritated state that he wrote around the margins of Makins's telegram in his spidery hand:

1. I am not aware that Dulles has any cause for complaint.

2. Quite apart from any question of texts, I should have thought anyone could have foreseen the reaction such a meeting must have on the Colombo Conference, to which we attach importance, to say nothing of Geneva.

3. Americans may think the time past when they need to consider the feelings or difficulties of their allies. It is the conviction that this tendency becomes more profound every week that is creating mounting difficulties for anyone in this country who wants to maintain close Anglo-American relations. We at least have constantly to bear in mind all our Commonwealth partners, even if the United States does not like some of them, and I must ask you to keep close watch on this aspect of our affairs and not hesitate to press it upon the United States. Nobody here regards Siam and the Philippines as truly representative of Asian opinion.

It was Makins's unpleasant duty to convey the gist of Eden's wire to Dulles. When he called on Easter Sunday, Dulles was in the hallway of his home with his sister, Eleanor, who also worked in the State Department. She recalled that when her brother picked up the phone he was "visibly disturbed." He turned to her and said, "Eden has reversed himself on our agreement." The meeting on April 20 was converted into an insignificant gathering of signatories to the Korean cease-fire. Any form of united action prior to Geneva had been effectively blocked by Eden. As Shuckburgh put it in his diary for April 19: "A. E. tells me he had 'a bloody weekend.' . . . The telegram related to the Dulles plan for S. E. Asia security revealed a divergence of opinion as to whether A. E. had agreed to the first meetings taking place before Geneva. Roger Makins seemed to be taking the American view that we had agreed, and received sharp reprimand drafted by A. E. himself round the edges of his telegram copies."

If Dulles had an escutcheon, the motto on it would have said: "Never Give Up." On April 20, he was off to Europe again for a final round of talks with his recalcitrant allies, a week before Geneva opened. Dulles thought that Eden's demands for wider Asian participation were merely a pretext for delay. There was little chance that India would join a security organization under the tutelage of the United States. Eden, however, could not alienate his Commonwealth partners by joining what they saw as a colonial war, particularly after Nehru had told him privately that the stumbling block for Asian leaders was French colonialism.

Prior to his departure, Dulles met with congressional leaders, who included Senators Knowland and Lyndon Johnson, to discuss Indochina and Geneva. He complained to Jim Hagerty that "those people on the Hill . . . are interested only in themselves and their own seat and apparently care nothing or less than nothing about our country." Hagerty confided to his diary on April 20 that he told Ike: "I was getting fed up with leaders not supporting us; that Knowland was trying to cut Dulles' heart out every time he had a chance and that other leaders, with the exception of Halleck, didn't have the guts to come out of the rain." Eisenhower agreed. Dulles had told Hagerty before leaving that "at present Communists do not know whether we will attack if they move into Indochina and we want to keep it that way."

Partition at the 16th Parallel

Shunned by the United States, the Communist Chinese were grateful to Molotov for having trumped Dulles at Berlin in February by arranging to have them invited to the Geneva Conference on Korea and Indochina. The ambassador to the Soviet Union from the People's Republic of China (PRC), Chang Wentian, was profuse in his thanks during an hour-long meeting in Moscow with Molotov on March 6. He said that "although the Americans will try to wreck the Geneva Conference," the PRC would try to lessen tensions. At the very least, "a path for active participation in international affairs is being opened up for the PRC."

Both men agreed that Geneva would be a lengthy and difficult process, since they had to establish the conditions for ending the war. Molotov said it might last two or three months, though it could drag on until November. One of the sticking points would be the partition line between North and South Vietnam. Chang, whose government was in close touch with Ho Chin Minh, said that the 16th parallel had already been mentioned and would be to Ho Chi Minh's advantage. It was quite a revelation that the Vietminh would be satisfied with the 16th parallel, since at the conference they started out by demanding the 13th, while the French wanted the 18th.

Chang said it was necessary to halt American aid, or the war would drag on. The strategy in Peking was being worked out, in terms of personnel and draft proposals. The Chinese would need help from the Soviets, since they had no experience in dealing with "the methods and techniques of bourgeois representatives." Molotov said that Deputy Foreign Minister Andrey Gromyko, who had abundant experience in international conferences, would be assigned to help them. Many procedural issues would arise—the chairmanship, the staff, the premises—and disputes were unavoidable. Chang asked if India could be a participant. Molotov said that this was inadvisable, since it would lead to a reduction of the role of the PRC, which ought to be on a par with the four other great powers, which India could not claim to be.

In April, Foreign Minister Chou En-lai went to Moscow three times to coordinate his Geneva policy with the Soviets. Ho Chi Minh also went to Moscow to talk to Khrushchev and Molotov. Indochina was not a Soviet priority. They were more interested in having France reject the European Defense Treaty. Undermining German rearmament was their aim. Neither China nor the Soviets wanted to press for maximum advantage at Geneva for fear of bringing the Americans into the war.

Khrushchev did not place much confidence in Geneva, but Chou En-lai argued that the presence of China was in itself important. "We must strive to achieve some results," he said. "We must recognize that imperialist countries are having a hard time." The Chinese and the Soviets should arrive in Geneva with a common policy, Chou said. Molotov suggested that the Chinese include in their delegation two master chefs in order to make friends at banquets.

The members of the Chinese delegation were announced on April 19. Their instructions were to set a precedent for solving international crises at great-power conferences, in order to counter the U.S. policy of isolation and embargo. Chou En-lai briefed the delegation on the importance of this initial conference. He had in his youth been a drama student, and he stressed the need to give a credible performance in their first appearance on the world stage. The delegation flew to Geneva via Moscow, where Gromyko briefed them on procedures and precautions, such as how to prevent their conversations from being bugged.

In Peking on April 19, Chou En-lai told the Indian ambassador that Washington's goal was to prevent a cease-fire in Indochina by putting pressure on France. Chou referred to Nixon's April 16 speech, where the vice president had said that if necessary the United States should dispatch forces. The Chinese, he said, were concerned that the United States might come into the war. They preferred an armistice, even if that delayed the unification of Indochina.

I Now Believe in an Immediate Cease-Fire

On April 15, Jean Chauvel, the French ambassador to Switzerland, who was in charge of the preparation of the conference, sent General Navarre a list of twenty-nine questions. Six of them concerned a cease-fire, which showed the way the French were leaning. Others had to do with the Vietminh in case of a cease-fire, and still others on how a cease-fire could be enforced.

Navarre replied on April 20 with a paper entitled "Note on the Opportunity for a Cease-fire in Indochina," which turned out to be prophetic. "The intensification of Chinese aid," he said, "began as soon as the Geneva Conference was announced." Thanks to Chinese aid, the French were now fighting a modern army, equipped with artillery, antiaircraft guns, and vehicles. The only elements they lacked were tanks and aviation. To fight this new kind of war, he needed ten additional battalions, and more planes, heavy guns, and tanks. "Is France prepared to make the effort?" he asked. If not, France would be progressively replaced by the United States, whose material aid would eventually allow it to control Indochina's economy, until Indochina became an American protectorate. This would mean, said Navarre, the end of French influence in Indochina, the end of one hundred years of effort and eight years of sacrifice.

Navarre, however, was hedging his bets, for he also sent a letter to General Ely, in which he was more emphatic, saying: "I now believe that an immediate cease-fire would be preferable to negotiations during which the fighting would continue. With the overlapping of positions, with our Vietnamese troops always ready to flee or desert, we may fall, after several weeks of talks in Geneva, into a hopeless situation that will help the enemy. Two months ago, I would never have agreed to a cease-fire, but now I realize that continuing to fight during negotiations would be a mistake."

Left unspoken was Navarre's fear of raids from the Chinese air force. In March, some MiG-15s had violated French air space. Navarre told the 1955 commission: "General Lauzin told me twenty times that if Chinese planes bombed our airfields we would lose two thirds of our aircraft. In parking our planes, we were not thinking of possible bombing raids but of commando raids on foot. Instead of dispersing the planes, we crowded them close together and surrounded them with barbed wire. We had no defense against Chinese bombers, no radar and no antiaircraft."

On April 21, Navarre wired Paris: "From now on, it is much more for the United States that we are fighting than for ourselves." Navarre's pessimism alarmed Paris. The British had indicated that they would not contribute to U.S. efforts to save Dien Bien Phu, where the situation was deteriorating daily after the evacuation of Huguette 6 on April 18.

On April 20, the five commanders at the base took stock. Bigeard pointed out that of the 13,000 men they had in the beginning, they were left with 2,300 able-bodied men, distributed as follows: Bigeard's 6th BPC, 250; Bréchignac's 2nd Battalion of the 1st RCP, 200; Tourret's 8th Choc, 250; Botella's 5th BPVN, 550; Legionnaires, 400; artillery, Moroccans, and Thais, 650.

The base's heavy armament was seriously reduced. Of the twenty-four

105s, nineteen were still serviceable, eight of those at Isabelle. The four 155s were down to two, and the thirty-two 120mm mortars were down to fifteen. Personnel losses in the artillery were such that infantrymen had to be hastily trained. The loss of officers was such—166 dead or disabled— that noncoms served as platoon leaders.

Morale was low, and the men said of Navarre: "He had bait for a trout and he hooked a whale." Lieutenant Latanne of the Vietnamese paratroopers recalled: "In April, the weight of bad news began to crush me. The deaths of men I loved like brothers, added to the anxiety and deprivations of our daily life, became almost too much to bear. Fatigue, lack of sleep, discouragement and fear, all played a part, until my only wish when I woke up was to stay alive one day longer."

The number of deserters increased. Some joined the Rats of Nam Yum, while others went over to the Vietminh. Castries reported: "Under the influence of Vietminh propaganda and, unfortunately, certain French radio programs and newspapers, morale is fluctuating in some units: we have had desertions and men hiding to avoid combat." A postbattle report listed 253 deserters, not counting the 907 Thais who had returned to their villages.

The erosion of mind and body in a situation of permanent combat took its toll in strange ways. Lieutenant Dr. Madelaine of the 2nd BEP recalled that some of the men in his unit had died, though they had no wounds. "These were war-hardened Legionnaires who had fought on the Russian front in the German army. You'd be chatting with them in the trenches, and after they'd eaten and rested, without anything seeming wrong, they were unable to finish the sentence they'd begun and they fell to the ground dead. We didn't have the facilities for an autopsy. All we could do was bury them."

But along with these unexplained deaths there were daily acts of courage. It amazed the young surgeon Ernest Hantz how many men returned to their units after being wounded. Michel Chanteux of the 1st RCP took a bullet in the arm. He was treated and sent back out, but returned to the infirmary when shrapnel removed a piece of his posterior. On his third visit he had three bullets in the chest, which made him unfit for further service.

"One of the worst crimes committed by Ho Chi Minh," Hantz recalled, "was to prevent the evacuation of the wounded, in order to undermine the morale of the garrison, beaten down by the spectacle of these disfigured and dying comrades." In mid-April came the monsoons, and the wounded were covered with sticky mud. The infirmary's roof of earth and logs was leaking. Men began coming in with minor wounds, but suddenly died, from exhaustion.

Who Will Be the Best Rifle Shot?

In his hidden command post twenty-five miles north of the base, General Giap planned the battles and stayed in touch by radiophone with his unit commanders. When the 316th Division came under an hour-long aerial bombardment, he called General Le Quang Ba about the damage and was told: "All we lost were the pants of a soldier who hung them up to dry."

Nonetheless, Giap had his own problems with the wounded. In April, the director of his health service, Vu Van Can, told him that the few doctors in the field infirmaries at the front were unable to treat certain wounds, such as skull fractures. In addition, the monsoons were affecting the troops. The alcoves dug into the sides of the trenches for the men to sleep in were turning to mud. Their meals were often cold rice. The smoke from artillery shells and the corpses left rotting on the field of battle polluted the atmosphere.

Giap held a meeting of his commanders, who said that nothing could be done about the conditions, for this was the nature of trench warfare. Giap replied that they couldn't let the abnormal become normal. The French were confined to a small space, whereas his army had plenty of room, including room for improvement. His great advantage was that the wounded did not pile up, and he could send most of them to field hospitals in the back country. The gravely wounded had to be treated at once at the front, Giap said, but they should be given fresh vegetables and hot tea, newspapers and playing cards.

Giap brought in additional doctors, including the noted surgeon Ton That Tung, known as "the man with the golden hands." Two deans of the Vietminh faculty of military medicine, Trieu and Huan, accompanied by some of their students, also arrived. The minister of health, Vu Diong Tung, tried to improve the deliveries of drugs and equipment. Giap later claimed that his field infirmaries had treated five thousand wounded who were able to return to their units.

Having captured Huguette 6 on April 18, Giap prepared his attack on Huguette 1, now the northernmost French strongpoint, midway down the airstrip. He chose a battalion of the 36th Regiment, known as the Bac Bacs, for its men came from the provinces of Bac Ninh and Bac Giang. In digging their trenches to encircle the post, the Bac Bacs wove six-foot-long bundles of straw, which they placed above the sides to deflect French fire. But as they approached Huguette 1, the straw shields could not protect them from grenades. The losses they took slowed them down, so they decided to dig tunnels leading to the forward blockhouses. Giap had positioned snipers close to the supply drops, preventing the French from coming out for the supplies. Intermittent mortar fire kept Captain Chevalier and his Legionnaires thinking that the Viets were about to attack.

By the night of April 21, Huguette 1 was encircled. Chevalier was losing men and asked for reinforcements. He discovered one of the tunnels inside his position and sealed it with explosives. Huguette 1 was only fifteen hundred yards from Claudine, but it took supply parties hours to fight their way through.

On April 22, Giap turned the sniper fire into a contest by asking: "Who will be the best rifle shot on the Huguette 1 front? Snipers should kill one enemy with one bullet." The winner would be rewarded. On April 22 at 10 P.M., with the Vietminh controlling most of the airstrip, small groups were sent into the tunnels to infiltrate the forward blockhouses. The men of the 13th DBLE were stupefied to see soldiers with leaves in their helmets coming at them with bayonets. In less than two hours, the Bac Bacs took Huguette 1. Captain Chevalier was killed, and 167 Legionnaires were taken prisoner.

Some Thought He Was Drunk

Secretary of State Dulles arrived in Paris on Wednesday April 21 with his wife, Janet; Livingston Merchant; Walter Robertson; and Douglas

MacArthur II. The ostensible reason for the trip was a NATO meeting on Friday, but in fact Dulles was still selling united action, though the French and the British weren't buying.

On the morning of the next day, Dulles saw Foreign Minister Bidault, who was in a state of high anxiety over the news of imminent disaster at Dien Bien Phu. General Ely was with Bidault and confirmed that the base was as good as lost. No breakout was possible, and in any case the wounded could not be left behind. Dulles did not realize that the French had decided to try for a quick cease-fire at Geneva, and asked Bidault to subscribe to the common defense of Southeast Asia. "Knowledge by the Russians that a common defense system was in prospect," Dulles said, "would strengthen our hands at Geneva." Bidault replied that such a pact would have no bearing on the outcome of the battle being fought. If Dien Bien Phu was lost, the French would have no interest in joining. There was a deadlock. The French wanted immediate U.S. intervention. Dulles refused to budge without a collective defense system. He cabled Eisenhower that Bidault's "impression was that if Dien Bien Phu fell, the French would want to pull out entirely from Southeast Asia."

Anthony Eden and Evelyn Shuckburgh flew into Paris later that morning and were met at the airport by Bidault, who took them to lunch with the Dulles entourage. It struck Shuckburgh at lunch that Bidault's prior meeting with Dulles had irritated him "beyond endurance." He seemed "worn out, garrulous, ironical, and obscure." He was "hysterical about the calamity at Dien Bien Phu," which "provoked an excessive reaction of complete French surrender." Shuckburgh concluded that "the Americans and French are being excitable and depressed, and the British, we think, steady and dour."

In the afternoon meeting at the Quai d'Orsay, Bidault made even less sense. "Some thought he was drunk," but Shuckburgh doubted it. Bidault read a "declaration of French intentions" to continue fighting in Indochina, perhaps to impress Dulles, but then said it was only *une tendance* rather than the position of the French delegation then on its way to Geneva.

That evening, Walter Robertson had dinner with the omnipresent Cy Sulzberger, who found Robertson "highly charged with an explosive mix of emotion and alcohol." Robertson compared Dien Bien Phu illogically with Valley Forge, in that the base had not actually fallen but its area was now so small that aid couldn't be sent in. He felt that the United States would have to intervene. For the moment, he said, they were stuck with the "horrid little Bao Dai, a rotten little Japanese collaborator," who claimed that malaria kept him from visiting the front. Geneva was opening on Monday. China would be there but not as a peer. It was a four-power conference with rotating chairmen. Otherwise, the United States would have walked out. Robertson said that Chou En-lai, the head of the Chinese delegation, was one of the most charming and intelligent men he'd met of any race, and a fine linguist who spoke French and English, but "he'll cut your throat if given the chance."

President Eisenhower flew to New York on April 22 to give a speech before the American Newspaper Publishers Association. The publishers said the public needed to be educated on Indochina, because the average citizen didn't even know where it was. American interests had to be clarified. Ike told them that "the words Dien Bien Phu are no longer just a funny-sounding name to be dismissed from the breakfast conversation because we don't know where it is." If Indochina fell, it would be a "mere additional pawn in the machinations of a power-hungry group in the Kremlin and in China."

The Friendlies Will Be Crossing the Airstrip

On April 23, at Dien Bien Phu, there was a sunny day for a change. At 7 A.M., only hours after the fall of Huguette 1, General de Castries summoned Colonel Langlais and Colonel Bigeard (recently promoted from major). "We must retake Huguette 1," Castries said. "It's vital for our drops."

"All our battalions are broken, dead from fatigue, reduced to a quarter of their strength," Bigeard said. "Our last reserve, the 2nd BEP, is holding the Elianes. Given these conditions, an attack on Huguette 1 could fail. Even if we succeed, we won't be able to hold on to it." Langlais was no more willing than Bigeard to sacrifice more men in a chancy counterattack.

But Castries, convinced that the base would be starved of supplies without Huguette 1, insisted that the counterattack be launched in the early afternoon with air and artillery support. "Do the impossible," he said, "and retake Huguette 1 before 4 P.M." Bigeard had to obey, although he knew that attacking a strongpoint ringed by Vietminh artillery in broad daylight would be costly in terms of manpower.

The plan was that Major Hubert Liesenfelt's 2nd BEP would retake Huguette 1. Although only recently dropped into the base, Liesenfelt's battalion had already lost one third of its men, who were spread out among several strongpoints east of the Nam Yum. They would have to be relieved before they could be redeployed. The success of the counterattack depended on timing. The paras of the 2nd BEP had to be in place by the time the aerial bombardment and the artillery preparation were completed.

Liesenfelt established his command post on Huguette 2, at the southern end of the airstrip, where he would have a good view of the deployment. Two companies, Lieutenant La Cour Grandmaison's 7th and Lieutenant Garin's 8th, would attack Huguette 1 from the east, proceeding up the drainage ditch. Lieutenant de Biré's 5th Company would gather at Huguette 2 and attack from the south, while the 6th Company, under Lieutenant Boulinguiez, was held in reserve at the base of Huguette 2. Two tanks were available to support the ground attack, the *Douaumont* and the *Mulhouse*. Liesenfelt's instructions to the tank commander, Captain Hervouet, were brief: "Position your tanks near Huguette 2 and help my men get across the airstrip." The French did not know that aside from the *bo dois* holding Huguette 1, there were hundreds of Vietminh hidden in a lattice of trenches on the western side of the airstrip, armed with machine guns and mortars.

The planes were scheduled to arrive at 1:45 P.M. Once they had dropped their bombs, there would be a twenty-minute artillery preparation. The four companies of the 2nd BEP were supposed to have reached their departure points by that time so that they could initiate the counterattack. The flaw in the plan was that there were too many parts to coordinate. The aircraft, artillery, and tanks had to be synchronized with the assault on the ground.

By the time the air strike was due, it became apparent that it was taking the Legionnaires much longer than expected to proceed from their strongpoints on the Elianes to the operational points of departure. Liesenfelt told Langlais that his men were not ready because they had been slowed down by having to proceed through narrow trenches to avoid enemy mortars. But it was too late to delay the air strike.

At 1:45 P.M., the two companies of the Vietminh 88th Regiment that were holding Huguette 1 were eating their bowls of rice when they saw planes in the sky. Company Commander Viet Thieng told them to prepare for combat. Four B-26 bombers circled overhead and dropped thousand-pound bombs on the post and on suspected sites of antiaircraft batteries. They were followed by six single-seat, single-engine F6F Hellcats, known as "the little trucks that fly," which dropped their bombs and rockets. The target was well defined and the bombs exploded with remarkable precision, inflicting heavy losses on the two companies holding the position.

Liesenfelt then asked that the artillery preparation be delayed, but it was already under way. It was, however, interrupted to give the Legionnaires more time to move into position.

At 2:15 P.M., a second squadron of Hellcats swooped in to bomb and strafe Vietminh positions around Huguette 1. One of the pilots, Lieutenant Bernard Klotz of the navy, a veteran of many missions, came in at eight thousand feet, pleased with the fine visibility. He dove on a slant, found his targets through the flak, dropped his two bombs, and veered upward to the left. He didn't realize he'd been hit until he saw yellow flames spurting from his engine. Then his dashboard exploded. He opened the cockpit and jumped. "My worst scenario," he recalled, "was parachuting behind Viet lines." He saw his Hellcat crash and hit the ground three hundred yards south of Eliane 2. The wind carried him and he made a hard landing on his shoulder. He crawled through rice paddies to a low dike as bursts of enemy fire blew clumps of mud into his face. He seemed to be in a no-man's-land. But nearby, a patrol of Legionnaires had seen him fall. They came out through the barbed wire and brought him in. He was taken to the hospital, where Dr. Grauwin treated his dislocated shoulder.

In the meantime, the ground operation turned out to be as haphazard as a game of tag. By 2:30, the 7th and 8th companies were moving up the drainage ditch, but where were the 5th and 6th? Castries, in his bunker, couldn't tell what was going on. He called Bigeard, who hadn't slept in days, and was taking a catnap. "Bruno," he said, "I have a feeling the attack has no punch." Bigeard hopped into his jeep and drove over to Huguette 2 to talk to Liesenfelt.

Liesenfelt told him, *"Ca doit coller"* (It must be going well). "I haven't heard anything." Bigeard tried his radio and found it wasn't working. Liesenfelt said it was because of the steel plates on the runway, which Bigeard doubted, since this had not happened before with troops near the runway. And why hadn't Liesenfelt sent someone on the ground to see where his units were? Bigeard fixed the radio, which was on the wrong frequency. He called in a five-minute artillery preparation, and hundreds of 120mm mortar and 105mm howitzer shells pounded Huguette 1. Half of the artillery's supply of shells had already been fired in the earlier, aborted preparation.

As soon as Liesenfelt's four companies got going, they were in trouble, for during the lag the Vietminh had brought in reinforcements. Lieutenant Garin, who led the 8th Company across the runway, was pinned to the ground by automatic fire. A shell fragment sectioned his carotid artery. Liesenfelt later wrote his brother Marcel: "He was buried in the shellpit where he died. I gave the order not to bring his body back so as not to risk more losses." The reality was not so simple. When Garin saw his men coming to retrieve him, he blew his brains out to spare them.

Lieutenant de Biré's 5th Company moved up the runway from Huguette 2, flanked by the two tanks. Second Lieutenant André Mengelle, in the *Douaumont*, saw them take their positions, but he could also see Vietminh units hastening to reinforce Huguette 1. Up ahead was the carcass of the twin-engine Curtiss Commando glistening in the sun. It didn't seem possible that anyone could be hiding inside it, but as Mengelle approached, a ball of fire rose from the ground and landed directly behind him. It was an antitank bazooka rocket. He put his tank in reverse, and another rocket hit Second Lieutenant Pradine's *Mulhouse*, wounding one crew member. Mengelle fired his 75mm gun into the belly of the Curtiss and the firing stopped.

The 5th Company was fighting its way from trench to trench to reach Huguette 1. Lieutenant de Biré was in one of the trenches when he was hit in both knees. He told Liesenfelt on the repaired radio that he couldn't walk. Captain Léonce Piccato, who was in the command post with Liesenfelt, volunteered to replace him. When Piccato reached the trench, he was killed by a sniper's bullet and buried in a corner. Piccato often said that his wife, Madeleine, and his two children, Georges and Michelle, were more important than his military career, and yet he had not hesitated to take the place of his wounded comrade. In his last letter to his wife, he had written: "For some time now, I've been in a state that's hard to define. I do everything mechanically, like a robot. The alive part of me is with you. Sometimes I'm frightened when I think of the place that you hold in my heart."

By 3:30 P.M., all four companies were stalled. The 7th and 8th company commanders said that their men were being slaughtered. At 4 P.M., Mengelle in the *Douaumont* got a message from Bruno: "What is your position?"

"A hundred and fifty meters north of Huguette 2 at the level of the Curtiss. The area is in the hands of the Viets."

"Okay. Wait."

A few minutes later, another message: "The friendlies will be crossing the airstrip. Assure their protection."

Mengelle was astonished. Bigeard had ordered a pullback. Both tanks covered the retreat. They saw about a hundred paras jump out of shell craters and trenches, cross the runway, and vanish into the drainage ditch. Mengelle was so overcome with disappointment that he momentarily forgot his own discomfort. It was like an oven in the tank.

Among those who made it back was Lieutenant de Biré, commander of the 5th Company, who was using shovels as crutches. But the pullback under fire was as costly as the attack. The failed counterattack decimated Liesenfelt's 2nd BEP. There were 152 dead and 72 wounded. The losses were such that the 2nd BEP was fused with 1st BEP into a single battalion of Foreign Legion paratroopers. As for Liesenfelt, he was stripped of his command and resigned from the army in 1956, at the age of forty-three.

In his memoirs, Colonel Langlais summed up the counterattack: "The aviation had done a terrific job, and if the position was not taken it was due to the lack of synchronization between the end of the bombing and the launching of the attack. Liesenfelt said the radio interruption was due to the steel plates on the airstrip. Bigeard said Liesenfelt had not arranged his frequencies correctly." Bigeard cursed himself for having been so exhausted that he left Liesenfelt in command of the operation, when he himself was in charge of all counterattacks. It was said, however, that Bigeard had wanted nothing to do with the operation, which he did not approve of. In any case, there were no fresh troops to hold Huguette 1 had it been retaken.

Whoever was to blame, the counterattack on Huguette 1 was the last important operation the garrison undertook. The Vietminh had also showed signs of fatigue, and there was a period of respite, though they kept up the artillery barrages and the digging of trenches. With the loss of Huguette 1, a new strongpoint called Ópera was jerry-built on the edge of the drainage ditch to the east of the runway and became the first line of defense. It was manned by one of the five zone commanders, Major Pierre Tourret, and his durable 8th Choc, and every day it received two to three hours of shelling. It was like Walpurgis Night, Tourret recalled—the night when witches were believed to rendezvous in Walburga, Germany.

The British Must Not Shut Their Eyes and Then Plead Blindness

News of the failed counterattack compounded the gloom and doom among French leaders. Dulles cabled Eisenhower: "The situation here is tragic. France is almost visibly collapsing before our very eyes." The NATO Council meeting was in full session that Friday, April 23, at the Palais de Chaillot, and Bidault was the chairman. Although it was supposed to be devoted to NATO affairs, hanging over the meeting was the storm cloud of Indochina. When Shuckburgh got there he was told that Bidault was "drunk again" and had kept the meeting going for hours over trivialities. Shuckburgh found the French foreign minister "loquacious, sentimental, bitterly ironical, and weary. He gave a frightful impression of moral collapse, coupled with a histrionic show of courage and morale," saying, " 'Today the chestnut trees are in flower. When we meet again in October, who knows, I hope they will not all have lost their flowers.' " The news from Dien Bien Phu must be pouring in, thought Shuckburgh, and all bad.

It was in this charged atmosphere that Dulles rose to speak at 6 P.M. His topic was atomic weapons, due to the furor over the H-bomb tests in March, and also in line with his tactic of keeping the Russians and the Chinese guessing. He said that since the West did not have anywhere near the manpower the Soviets had, nuclear weapons should be considered part of its "conventional" arsenal. It was, he said, "our agreed policy" in both a general or local war to use atomic weapons "whenever or wherever it would be of advantage to do so, taking account of all relevant factors." There would of course be consultations with allies, except for "certain contingencies" when time would not permit consultation.

Could Indochina be considered a contingency? Dulles was not saying. But on the same day, Douglas MacArthur II was invited to see Premier Laniel, who was with French undersecretary of state André Bougenot. The undersecretary proposed that the United States commit naval aircraft to Dien Bien Phu for an isolated action lasting two or three days. The planes could carry French insignia so the Americans would not be accused of committing a belligerent act. As it happened, on that very day in Washington, Admiral Phillips's attack carrier strike group (TG 70.2) in the Philippines was placed on twelve-hour notice for the possible resumption of operations in the South China Sea. The carriers *Boxer* and *Philippine Sea* were on alert in Subic Bay.

This sense of extreme urgency was communicated to Dulles at the NATO Council meeting when Bidault approached him with a wire from General Navarre warning that the fall of Dien Bien Phu was imminent and that only a massive U.S. air strike in the next seventy-two hours could save it. Dulles said that a "B-29 intervention as proposed seems to be out of the question under existing circumstances."

Bidault responded that it was pointless to make a U.S. intervention conditional on British participation, which would only slow things at a time when fast action was needed. The British contribution would not "amount to much of anything." But if Dien Bien Phu fell, the French people would want to end the war, and would have no use for a coalition that would be seen as a sinister way to keep them fighting indefinitely.

In his cable to Eisenhower, Dulles reported that "Bidault gives the impression of being a man close to the breaking point. His mental state this morning was much better than yesterday, but it was painful to see him preside over the long afternoon session. He is obviously exhausted and is confused and rambling in his talk."

Despite his apparent exhaustion, however, that evening Bidault hosted a dinner for the NATO foreign ministers at the Quai d'Orsay. Before dinner, Dulles drew Eden aside to tell him about the wire from Navarre, asking for an air strike to save Dien Bien Phu. Navarre also wanted the Vietminh supply line bombed, although it was dispersed over an area of eight square miles. Eden said he found it hard to believe an air strike could have much effect. Intervention could not save Dien Bien Phu and might have far-reaching consequences. Dulles read Eden parts of a wire from Eisenhower, which said that "the British must not merely shut their eyes and then plead blindness as an alibi." Eden objected to the insinuation that the United Kingdom was "somewhat indifferent" to the situation. He was convinced that the remedy was not outside interference prior to Geneva. The situation was all too reminiscent of French demands for the last RAF squadrons in 1940, to stop the German invasion.

Dulles and Eden were joined by General Alfred Gruenther, the NATO supreme commander, who said he had never seen French morale so low. He feared that the collapse of Indochina would lead to the fall of the Laniel government.

Dulles said the collapse of France as a world power would create a vacuum. If Eden stood with him, he would ask Eisenhower for "war powers."

Gruenther reported to Walter Bedell Smith in Washington that the situation in France was "very unstable. . . . French military view is that the whole thing is washed out unless we can intervene."

After dinner, Eden wired Prime Minister Churchill: "I told Dulles that I trusted that no action would be taken in response to the French appeal without consultation with us. It might have far-reaching consequences for us all, and we must have an opportunity to consider these in advance. Dulles reassured me on this point."

Eden thought of himself as hardened to crises, but went to bed that night a troubled man. The thought of another Korea haunted him. He did not want the United Kingdom in "the wrong war against the wrong man in the wrong place."

Forget About the Rainy Season

On April 24, the battle of Dien Bien Phu suffered its first American casualty. CAT pilot Paul Holden was in the right-hand seat of a Flying Boxcar when it took off from Cat Bi airport in Haiphong at 9:49 A.M. The copilot, on his left, was Wallace Buford. Thanks to increased fighter protection and improved time-delay fuses on the parachutes, so that they deployed closer to the ground, the C-119s were dropping bigger loads and landing more of them within the shrunken French perimeter—250 tons on April 15 with only a 15 percent loss—the biggest single-day total since the start of the siege.

As Holden's aircraft approached the drop zone, Vietminh antiaircraft guns sited on high ridges started firing. The C-119, dropping to five thousand feet to release its load quickly in a single pass, was caught in the murderous cross fire of 37mm flak. One shell tore through the tail boom but did not explode. A second shell exploded inside the cockpit, destroying the escape hatch. Holden's antiflak vest saved his life, but shell fragments badly wounded his right arm. The plane made it back to Cat Bi, where French surgeons offered to amputate his arm. Holden asked to be flown to the military hospital at Clark Air Base in the Philippines, where U.S. Air Force surgeons saved the arm.

Several French sources later wrote that after Holden was wounded, the CAT pilots refused to fly between April 26 and 30. But three of the men who served at Cat Bi and were later interviewed denied there was a stand-down, and one of them, Rousselot, said the accusation was "a goddamned lie."

Naval lieutenant Bernard Klotz, who had been shot down on April 23, had no choice but to remain on the base. He told Castries: "I have no ship and I have no plane, but I can fire a weapon." He was detached to Castries' headquarters staff, as the number two for airborne operations, under air force major Jacques Guérin. Klotz took his meals with Castries, Langlais, and the zone commanders, and was able to assess their morale. He found it to be neither complacent nor beaten-down, but expressing the realism of professional soldiers who continued to do their jobs while aware of the outcome. There was still some hope that the monsoons would turn Dien Bien Phu into a lake that would make the battle a draw.

The French trenches were turning to mud. But so were the Vietminh trenches. At the 1955 commission, General Catroux asked Castries: "Had you already been subject to abundant rainfall?"

Castries: "Yes, in the trenches we were in mud."

General Valin: "In France there was a kind of propaganda that went, 'If only we can hold out until the rainy season, everything will be all right.' But the exact opposite happened!"

Castries: "May I say that not only was this the opinion in France, but also in Hanoi . . . where it was said: 'The Viets have never conducted a campaign during the rainy season.' Which, incidentally, was true. But this time Ho Chi Minh and Giap said: 'Forget about the rainy season, since we are on the high ground and they are in the basin.' "

Would You Like Two Bombs?

April 24 was Dulles's last day in Paris before leaving for Geneva. He had been unnerved by Bidault's threat that the French would pull out of Indochina. He wanted to make one final effort to bring the British aboard for some form of intervention before the conference opened, but Eden was busy that morning. The two decided on a postlunch meeting at Ambassador Dillon's residence. Dulles would be joined by Admiral Radford, who had flown in to add a heavy hitter to the team. Eden and his entourage arrived at 3:30 P.M., thinking it was more of a social call to discuss "assorted and harmless questions," as Shuckburgh put it. They found Secretary Dulles and Mrs. Dulles in the garden, along with assorted brass who were playing with the ambassador's dogs. Dulles and Radford led Eden and his people into the study, where Livingston Merchant joined them.

Dulles stated that the United States was ready to give immediate military help to the French provided the British joined in and subject to Congress giving the president war powers. Shuckburgh observed in his diary that "Radford, whom we did not think was very intelligent, and who is obviously raring for a scrap, said the only thing to do to stop the French and Vietnamese morale from collapsing when Dien Bien Phu falls (as it must do in a day or two), is for the US/UK more or less to take over the conduct of the war and push the French into the background."

Eden asked what was wanted from the United Kingdom.

Radford said a prompt British contribution might involve sending RAF squadrons to Tonkin and perhaps an aircraft carrier.

Eden said there was a carrier sailing in Malayan waters, but he didn't see how air strikes would improve the picture. The danger was that the Chinese might retaliate. Had Radford forgotten that the Chinese were allied with the Russians? Going into Indochina might mean heading for a world war.

Radford said air strikes would stabilize the military situation, and that "a limited Chinese intervention" could be dealt with. If the Chinese attempted air action, the United States would bomb vulnerable Chinese airfields. The Vietnamese, he said, "were angry with the French" for their "terrible leadership" and would welcome U.S. and British help. If the United States intervened, Navarre might be relieved of his command and Americans could have "a considerable voice behind the scenes."

Eden said the British felt the French could carry on after Dien Bien Phu.

Radford said the fall of the base would lead "to growing defections" from the Vietnamese army and the possible massacre of French civilians. The only way to stop that was to demonstrate that France had powerful allies on her side.

Eden said there would be "hell to pay at home" over intervention. He would have to return to London to confer with Prime Minister Churchill and the cabinet.

Dulles chimed in: "Our military authorities say that if Indochina goes, the only effective deterrent measures open to us would be those directed at Communist China itself. Our military were thinking in terms of a blockade of the China coast, the seizure of Hainan and other measures." Dulles was threatening a war with China unless the British cooperated.

Eden repeated that there was an alliance between China and the Soviet Union. Radford thought the Soviets would stay out of it. They would not start a world war now. They would do so only at a time of their own choosing. And, in any case, "the acceptance of risk is necessary in order to avoid being nibbled to death."

Near the end of the meeting, Sir Harold Caccia, the British deputy undersecretary for foreign affairs, dropped a disturbing bit of news. "The difficulty in the French presentation of the problem to the British and Americans," he said, was that they were telling the British one thing and the Americans another. Bidault had told the British ambassador Gladwyn Jebb that France would go on fighting after Dien Bien Phu fell. Yet he had told Dulles the exact opposite.

The meeting ended because Eden and Dulles were due at the Quai d'Orsay for a final talk with Bidault. Shuckburgh felt that the British were "pressed by a dilemma. If we refuse to cooperate with the American plan, we strain the Alliance. If we do as Dulles asks, we provoke the bitterest hostility of India and . . . destroy the Commonwealth. . . . We are quite clear we cannot undertake any commitment in advance of the Geneva discussion, and we are sure it would be folly to try and save Indochina by force of arms."

The crucial, Rashomon-like meeting with Bidault makes it difficult to determine what was actually said. All three principals were under the strain of what the fall of Dien Bien Phu might bring. Dulles, Eden, and their experts were led into one of the formal Quai d'Orsay drawing rooms called the Salon du Perroquet, where Bidault and his aides were waiting.

Eden recalled that "Dulles began by telling Bidault that if the French could give an assurance that they would continue the struggle after the fall of Dien Bien Phu, the United States would at once set about organizing the defense of the entire region." It disturbed Eden that Dulles was implying that the United Kingdom was already committed to armed action in Indochina. He broke in to state that this was not the case. Bidault said he understood. He did not give a direct reply to Dulles's request, said Eden, but "merely emphasized the catastrophic results of the fall of Dien Bien Phu."

Dulles, in his cable to Smith after the meeting, said he confronted Bidault, who at first equivocated, saying that he and Laniel wanted to continue to fight but would have to contend with adverse military and psychological reactions. Dulles wrote: "In all honesty and frankness he could not guarantee what position the government would take if Dien Bien Phu falls."

Dulles, who had been stung by the disclosure that Bidault had a forked tongue, retorted that at the previous night's banquet, Minister of Defense

Pleven "told me that the cease-fire which Navarre envisaged in his letter covered all of Indochina and not just Dien Bien Phu." Bidault admitted that this was correct and veered off into "a self-flagellating discourse" on how the whole battle had been a mistake. Dulles asked Bidault "point blank" if the Laniel government planned to declare a cease-fire before the start of the Indochina phase of the Geneva Conference. Bidault promised it would not. Eden said he was not committed to intervention, but would refer the issue to his government in London. Bidault then caved in and said that anything that could be done to assist the French troops would be appreciated.

It was at this point, according to Eden, that Dulles produced the draft of a letter, which Eden was allowed to glance at briefly. As far as Eden could make out, "the sense of the letter seemed to be that although it was unfortunately now too late for American support to be provided at Dien Bien Phu, the United States was nevertheless prepared, if France and the other allies so desired, to move armed forces into Indochina and thus internationalize the struggle to protect Southeast Asia as a whole."

According to Dulles, the letter was a response to Navarre's wire asking for U.S. intervention. Dulles explained that this response would amount to "active belligerency" and required congressional authorization, which could only be obtained in the framework of a political understanding. There was no reason why the fall of Dien Bien Phu should alter the French military position in Indochina or require a plea for a cease-fire.

The Dulles letter was less an offer of intervention than a pep talk from the coach at halftime. It concluded: "We believe that it is the nature of our nations to react vigorously to temporary setbacks and to surmount them. That can be done if our nations and people have the resolution and the will. We believe that you can count on us, and we hope that we can count upon you."

Dulles told the State Department that the purpose of the letter was to "establish the record clearly since the French might pin on us the responsibility for their withdrawal from Indochina."

After reading the letter, Bidault hesitated several minutes before announcing that Dulles should send it to him officially. Bidault's version of the April 24 meeting in his memoirs was that he told Dulles, "If, in response to Navarre's request, the Americans bombarded the surrounding area [of the base] extensively this would save the garrison and boost the morale of all our troops." Bidault recalled that Dulles "looked glum," for he knew how difficult it would be to get the president and Congress to accept his proposal. Dulles did not even offer to transmit Bidault's request in Washington. "What he did do," Bidault wrote, "was to ask me if we would like the United States to give us two atomic bombs." To this offer, Bidault said he replied: "If those bombs are dropped near Dien Bien Phu, our side will suffer as much as the enemy. If we drop them on the supply line from China, we will be risking a world war. In either case, far from being helped, the Dien Bien Phu garrison will be worse off than before."

There is no mention in the Dulles cable traffic of an offer of atomic bombs. Dulles was pleased to have obtained a promise from Bidault to keep fighting until Indochina was discussed at Geneva. In a cable to the president after seeing Bidault, Dulles said, "It would seem that we will at least enter the Geneva Conference without the French government definitely committed to some disastrous course of action."

As for Eden, after leaving the Quai d'Orsay, he cabled the Foreign Office: "It is now quite clear that we shall have to take a decision of first-class importance, namely whether to tell the Americans that we are prepared to go along with their plan or not. It seems essential that I should discuss this with my colleagues, and I am therefore returning to London tonight."

Bidault's claim that Dulles offered him atomic weapons has been called "highly implausible" by a number of scholars in the field, who argue that there is no corroboration from American or French sources. In fact, corroboration does come from three separate French sources.

The chief source is Jean Chauvel, an eyewitness to the exchange. Chauvel, the ambassador to Switzerland who was making preparations in Geneva for the French delegation, was a skilled, trustworthy diplomat not given to hyperbole. He happened to be at the Quai d'Orsay conferring with Bidault when Dulles and Eden arrived on April 24. He said in his memoirs that at some point the three decided to leave their aides and pursue their talks in a small private salon, and Chauvel followed. In the hall leading from one salon to the other, Chauvel heard Dulles say in a low voice: "Would you like two bombs?" It was clear to Chauvel that he meant atom bombs, which would be dropped by French pilots. Chauvel recalled that emotions had been running high. In the small salon, Bidault collapsed into an armchair. Eden, who may or may not have heard the exchange, said: "Am I asked to do anything?" Chauvel told Bidault that this required an answer, since Eden was leaving for London, but nothing came of it.

A second source is Maurice Schumann, who was the French deputy minister of foreign affairs. He recalled that "Bidault came into my office, which was unusual. Since he was my superior in rank, he usually summoned me to his. He was chalky-faced, and blurted out, 'Can you imagine what Dulles told me? He proposed atomic bombs to save Dien Bien Phu.'" Schumann replied, "Calm yourself, it was only hypothetical. If you had agreed, he'd really be worried." Schumann could not see how two atom bombs, which could have annihilated both armies, might save Dien Bien Phu. He couldn't believe the offer had been made seriously. Was it a spur-of-the-moment whim? Or was Dulles testing the French will to keep fighting? Schumann wasn't sure, "But Bidault's all-too-visible reaction to the offer showed that he had no intention of following up."

News of the offer of atomic weapons spread to other high-ranking members of the French government. General Ely wrote in his diary on April 25 that he had mixed feelings about "the offer of two atom bombs. The psychological effect would be tremendous, but the effectiveness was questionable and it carried the risk of generalized warfare." In any case, he thought, the Laniel government was too weak to take on the responsibility.

The Dulles offer was common knowledge at the Quai d'Orsay. Later that year, in August, the State Department drew up a document on the history of French requests for aid to Indochina. The document came across the desk of Roland de Margerie, director of political affairs in the French Foreign Ministry. He notified Ambassador Dillon that the document should be revised, for "it omitted all mention of your offer of atomic bombs to Bidault." Dillon, who knew nothing about the offer, asked if Dulles could have been speculating on the effectiveness of atomic weapons. Margerie said that Bidault had told him of the offer shortly after it had been made.

Dillon cabled Washington on August 9: "Our judgment is that Margerie fears that if Bidault should feel that publication of the statement [on aid] as drafted placed him in an unfavorable light . . . he might respond by publishing his version of the conversation regarding atomic bombs and might attempt to take credit for preventing their use." This was tortured logic indeed.

Dulles replied on the same day that he was "totally mystified" and that he had no recollection of making the offer. "It is incredible that I should have made [the] offer since the law categorically forbids it as was indeed well known not only to me but to Bidault because it had been discussed at NATO meetings." Margerie did not insist on the point and agreed with Dulles's suggestion that Bidault had been "overwrought."

Despite his demurral, Dulles had a long history of using the nuclear deterrent as the centerpiece of his diplomacy of brinkmanship, a term that was coined in the controversial interview published in *Life* magazine on January 16, 1956. It was an election year, and President Eisenhower was recovering from a heart attack. Dulles was being blamed by the Democrats for his failed foreign policy. He responded by arranging with his friend and fellow Presbyterian Henry Luce to be interviewed by the compliant James Shepley. The interview ran under the headline: HOW DULLES AVERTED WAR: THREE TIMES, NEW DISCLOSURES SHOW, HE BROUGHT U.S. BACK FROM THE BRINK. Dulles was described as having "probably devoted more thought to the subject of war and peace than any other man alive."

Three examples—Korea, Formosa, and Indochina—illustrated his confrontational policy of brinkmanship, which he claimed had saved the world from war. In all three cases, the threat of atom bombs was involved. In Korea in June 1953, when the Panmunjom negotiations broke down, he had exercised the "Manchurian option." He went to India and saw Nehru to let the Chinese know that "the U.S. would lift self-imposed restrictions on its actions, and hold back no effort or weapon to win." Thirty-nine days later, Dulles said, the Panmunjom truce was signed. Nehru, however, denied any involvement as go-between, and there was no evidence that a threat to use the bomb ended the stalemate. Mao Tse-tung did not need Nehru to tell him that the United States had a nuclear option. However, Dulles had convinced the president that relying on the threat of atomic bombs as a deterrent would make containment work. As Dulles later said: "We had already sent the means to the theater for delivering atomic bombs. This became known to the Chinese through their good intelligence sources and in fact we were not unwilling that they should find out."

As for the Formosa crisis of 1955, Dulles said he was instrumental in drafting the resolution passed in January by Congress that allowed the president to use force if Formosa was attacked. This was indeed quite an achievement, the first time a president had been given a blank check to start a war whenever he wanted. The resolution came about after the Chinese Communists began shelling the Nationalist-held islands of Quemoy and Matsu, two miles off the Chinese mainland. Chiang Kai-shek had garrisoned seventy-five thousand men on the islands, seeing them as stepping-stones for his return.

Dulles said in the interview that Eisenhower believed an attack on Quemoy and Matsu would be an attack on Formosa. This was a distortion of the record, for the Formosa Resolution made a point of *not* mentioning Quemoy and Matsu, which Eishenhower privately called two indefensible specks "within wading distance of the mainland."

Formosa developed into a crisis, which Dulles made more serious with his bomb-rattling. At a meeting of the National Security Council in 1955, Dulles said that to defend Quemoy and Matsu, "we'll have to use atomic weapons" to hit mainland airfields. On March 12, he said in a speech: "The United States has new and powerful weapons of precision which can utterly destroy military targets without endangering unrelated civilian centers."

This was all part of Dulles's belief, expressed in the interview, that "the ability to get to the verge without getting into war is the art. . . . We walked to the brink and looked it in the face." The crisis ended when the Chinese stopped shelling the two specks in May. Dulles thought it was his doing, but the Chinese had been held back by the Soviets, who refused to assist them in any attack on Formosa.

It was on his Indochina policy that Dulles made the most questionable claims. "In April of 1954," he said, "the French situation in Indochina had become desperate. The French pleaded for American intervention in the form of a carrier strike against the forces besieging the fort of Dien Bien Phu." After "careful reflection," he concluded that a carrier strike was "a poor way for the U.S. to get involved." But then he decided that "if Britain would join the U.S. and France would agree to stand firm, the three Western states could combine with friendly Asian nations to oppose the Communist forces on the ground in Indochina, just as the United Nations stepped in against the North Korean aggression in 1950. There was of course the risk that Peking would send its armies openly into Indochina as it had done in Korea."

Dulles said he recommended that the risk be faced. "If the Chinese Communists intervened openly, their staging bases in Indochina would be destroyed by U.S. air power." Dulles went to London on April 10 to enlist the British. At the same time, he said, two carriers, the *Boxer* and the *Philippine Sea,* steamed into the South China Sea. "On board were their tactical air groups armed with atomic weapons. It was a version of the classic show of force designed both to deter any Red Chinese attack on Vietnam and to provide weapons for instant retaliation if it should prove necessary."

In fact, Admiral William Phillips's strike group consisted of the carriers *Wasp* and *Essex,* eight destroyers, and a submarine, the *Bluegill.* They proceeded to the South China Sea on March 22 with orders to recon Chinese airfields, assembly points, and roads where Chinese matériel was brought in. Admiral Robert Carney, chief of naval operations, said on March 31 that although no commitment had been made, the possibility had arisen of carrier aircraft strikes against Chinese airfields, and support of French ground forces by carrier aircraft and air force bombers. When Congress nixed intervention on April 4, however, the carrier force was told to complete its recon by April 12 and returned to the Philippines in the second week of April. On April 23, in view of alarming developments at Dien Bien Phu, the carrier task force in Subic Bay, now consisting of the *Boxer* and the *Philippine Sea,* was placed on twelve-hour notice. Admiral Phillips was designated commander of a new Southeast Asia Defense Command with headquarters in Saigon, but the command was never activated. The modest naval movements in March and April had no bearing on the fall of Dien Bien Phu or the loss of Indochina.

Dulles said in the interview that he thought he had commitments from the British and the French, "but all plans were suddenly arrested on the afternoon of Easter Sunday [April 18] when it became apparent that the British had had a change of heart." This was "the first major frustration Dulles had encountered as Secretary of State," said the *Life* article, "and for several days he was at a loss. Friends who observed Dulles at the time observed that the nervous blinking which is the only outward evidence of the severe strain under which he operated, was noticeably intense.

"Dulles regarded the Geneva Conference with extreme misgivings," the article went on. That much was true, since he left the conference after the first week, before the Indochina part had begun, and was replaced by Walter Bedell Smith. "But again the policy of boldness impressed the Communists. He had seen to it that the Chinese and the Soviets knew that the U.S. was prepared to act decisively to prevent the fall of all Southeast Asia." As a result, instead of negotiating from their own weakness, the French and the British "found themselves able to bargain from Dulles' strength." But Dulles was not present and the American delegation at the conference remained aloof from the wheeling and dealing, being opposed to the partition of Vietnam.

Thus, thanks to Dulles's "strength, half of Vietnam was lost to the Communists, but southern Vietnam, Laos, and Cambodia were saved," said the article. Dulles was snatching victory from the jaws of defeat. Far from being elated with the outcome of the negotiations, the U.S. delegation refused to sign the final agreement.

General Navarre was particularly upset by Dulles's version of events. As it happened, Navarre's memoir, *Agonie de l'Indochine,* was also published in 1956, after Dulles's *Life* interview. Navarre said in the memoir that Dulles was rewriting history. He felt sure that the Chinese had not been informed about any U.S. action. Instead of saving southern Vietnam, Laos, and Cambodia, "exactly the opposite happened. The American bluff and subsequent pullout definitely shattered the positions of the Western powers." The interview, Navarre said, was "a dishonest performance based on specious claims."

He concluded: "We now have proof that we were fighting alone. America wished to take only very limited financial risks."

In the United States, the interview created an uproar. Several members of Congress called for Dulles's resignation. A London paper called him "an edgy gambler." James Reston in *The New York Times* said he had "added something new to the art of diplomatic blundering." However, 1956 was an election year, and Eisenhower called Dulles "the best Secretary of State I have ever known," in spite of some "unfortunate expressions."

The bizarre mix of bragging and inaccuracy was part of what George Kennan called Dulles's "emotional anti-Communism." Kennan left the State Department in 1950 after Dulles, who was then on the Policy Planning Staff, told some reporters that Kennan was "a dangerous man" for advocating the admission of Communist China to the United Nations. Another object of Dulles's ire was Paul Nitze, the brilliant head of the Policy Planning Staff, who was part of a May 1953 purge in which Dulles brought in "reliable people." Dulles's people, Nitze recalled, "seemed to me like Cossacks headquartered in a grand old City Hall, burning the paneling to cook with." Nitze thought that Dulles viewed foreign policy as if he and the other powers were opposing attorneys engaged in cunning maneuvers.

With regard to Dulles's offer of atom bombs to Bidault, the *Life* interview sheds some light. The pattern running through his three crises—Korea, Formosa, and Indochina—is the threat of using nuclear weapons. This was central to his penchant for brinkmanship, which had become the answer to every crisis. It does not seem at all implausible that it would have come to mind with Bidault. It was part of Dulles's vocabulary. Chauvel, the eyewitness, was a reliable source, one whom Eden described as having "a quick and lucid mind. . . . I respected his sense of purpose and his firmness in maintaining it."

In French government circles, it was taken for granted that the offer had been made. Premier Laniel told the National Assembly on May 4: "There has been talk in the press of an aerial response to Chinese intervention. It's true that there were discussions with our allies and that *all* military solutions to improve the situation at Dien Bien Phu were discussed. But we preferred not to do anything that would broaden the conflict prior to the conference."

General Bodet, Navarre's number two, told the 1955 commission:

"They talked about dropping an atomic bomb to free up Dien Bien Phu, but that was nonsense, technically. Where would it have been dropped? You couldn't drop it on the entrenched camp. Where else, in the mountains?"

We Were Furious at Being Used as Whipping Boys

After leaving the Quai d'Orsay in the late afternoon of April 24, Eden and his aides went to the British embassy to go over the day's events. Denis Allen summed up the British position in eight points, the gist of which was that the British would not take part in any Indochina intervention in advance of Geneva. After a quick supper they flew to London, landing at 10:30 P.M., and drove straight to Chequers to see Churchill, now seventy-nine and recovering from his stroke in June 1953. He met them in the hallway, wearing silk pajamas under a silk dressing gown. He took them in for a cold supper and went over the telegrams, but his mind wandered. When Eden explained the eight-point policy, Churchill said, "We have thrown away our glorious Empire, our wonderful Indian Empire." The thought being, Shuckburgh supposed, "why should we fight for the broken-down French colonial effort?" When the conversation turned to Ho Chi Minh, Churchill said, "Of course when I go to see him I shall talk atomics." He was referring to President Eisenhower, and his planned visit to Washington in May.

Eden was finally able to focus Churchill's attention on Indochina, and they agreed it was inevitable that Dien Bien Phu should fall. Eden explained that Dulles and Radford wanted some dramatic gesture of intervention to prevent the general disintegration of Indochina. They wanted the British to intervene in order to obtain the approval of Congress. Churchill summed up by saying the British were being asked to assist Dulles in misleading Congress into approving a military operation that would in itself be ineffective and might bring the world to the verge of a major war. Eden and Churchill agreed to decline any military assistance to the French in Indochina and to refuse to join any military intervention in advance of Geneva. The best hope now was partition. Then Eden said he was tired and would like to go to bed, and Churchill also "toddled off,"

Shuckburgh wrote, "looking like an old granny of about 100 smoking a cigar."

President Eisenhower, after his speech to the editors in New York on April 22, had flown back to Washington that night. The next day he went to Kentucky. Back in Washington on April 25, he was briefed on developments by Walter Bedell Smith, the acting secretary of state, while Hagerty wrote in his diary: "The British are getting weak-kneed on cooperative effort" while the French were "really wilting. The French have put all their eggs at Dien Bien Phu. . . . Why I'll never know."

Smith told Eisenhower that Eden "had grave doubts that Britain would cooperate in any activity" in Indochina. Ike's first reaction was irritation at the British unwillingness to help. He instructed Smith that Radford should tell the British "baldly" that they should help the French now rather than wait until they had lost two hundred thousand men. Eisenhower was torn between wanting to help the gallant garrison and realizing that the French had made a mess of things, for he then asked Smith to draft a message he could read when Dien Bien Phu fell. He told Smith that "the French want us to come in as junior partners and provide materiels, etc., while they themselves retain authority in that region." He was more explicit in a letter to his old friend "Swede" Hazlett, accusing the French of using "weasel words in promising independence and for this one reason as much as anything else, have suffered reverses that have been really inexcusable." They had lost the war in the same way the British had lost the American War of Independence, by treating the majority of Loyalist Americans as "colonials and inferiors."

At 11 A.M. on April 25, there was an emergency cabinet meeting at 10 Downing Street, the first in years on a Sunday, with the British Chiefs of Staff also attending. Churchill, who was not a domino player, said the fall of Indochina would have no decisive effect on the British in Malaya. Eden told those present that the situation at Dien Bien Phu was grave, and that the garrison would soon be overwhelmed. Dulles, said Eden, fearing a collapse of French resistance, wanted a dramatic Anglo-American intervention. But Eden did not believe that intervention would be effective. The Chiefs of Staff agreed. Eden's recommendation to his colleagues was "that they should decline to give any immediate undertaking to afford military assistance to the French in Indochina. . . . The best hope for a lasting solution lay in some form of partition. Our object should therefore be to strengthen the negotiating positions of the French at the Geneva Conference."

A directive was drafted stating that the British would undertake no action prior to Geneva. It was approved unanimously. It was now clear that the United States and Britain would arrive at the conference with entirely different agendas.

Eden and his aides prepared to leave for Geneva aboard an RAF plane that Churchill insisted they take. There was, however, an unwelcome interruption. Evelyn Shuckburgh, who was at the Foreign Office while Eden was having lunch with Churchill at the Carlton Club, took a call from the French ambassador to London, René Massigli. The ambassador said that he must come at once to deliver an important message from Bidault. Massigli arrived at 2:30 P.M. and Eden kept him waiting until 3:15. When Massigli produced the message, Eden "got a bellyful," according to Shuckburgh.

The message was the text of Bidault's reply to Dulles's letter and it said: "The advice of our military experts is that a massive intervention of the American Air Force can still save the garrison. . . . The Vietminh have concentrated an exceptional number of troops and armaments around the base. The Vietminh are providing for the first time an opportunity to destroy from the air a great part of its forces. This action could also interrupt their supply lines . . . this could be a decisive blow."

Massigli told Eden that Henri Bonnet, the French ambassador in Washington, had discussed the letter with Smith, who told him the United States could do nothing alone, but that if the British and other allies came in, Congress would pass a war-powers resolution and U.S. naval aircraft could go into action at Dien Bien Phu.

Eden disliked having his arm twisted by the United States via a French intermediary. Why hadn't the State Department informed Makins, his ambassador in Washington? Nonetheless, it was a new development that required a second emergency cabinet meeting at 4 P.M. Eden told the cabinet "that intervention would be the first step toward a third world war." "Her Majesty's Government decided to reject the American proposal," Eden re-

called, "and I was advised to inform Mr. Dulles and M. Bidault of our decision." Shuckburgh thought the Massigli ploy was a way of "all the blame
being put on us. . . . We were furious at having ourselves used as whipping
boys." At the cabinet meeting, "everyone was quite clear that [interven-
tion] would be folly, ineffective, fatal to our relations with Asiatic opinion,
fatal to the Geneva Conference, and liable to rend our own public opinion
in half. A.E. thought the UK Government would fall if it tried to agree."

After the cabinet meeting, Shuckburgh recalled, "we gave Massigli the
slip, swept off to Heathrow, and got into our shining Queen's Flight Has-
tings." They had to stop in Paris to pick up Eden's wife, Clarissa, and
Bidault was there standing beside her on the tarmac. They all went into a
waiting room decorated with pots of hydrangeas, and Eden informed
Bidault of the British government's decision. "Deep gloom," Shuckburgh
reported. They left "poor Bidault" and went on to Geneva.

During the flight, Eden's thoughts turned to the international conferences he had attended in Geneva in the days of the League of Nations: The
crisis in 1934 when the French foreign minister, Jean-Louis Barthou, was
assassinated in Marseilles with King Alexander of Yugoslavia, and war
seemed imminent; he had had to handle the dispute at the request of the
League Council. And the other crises, the Italian invasion of Abyssinia,
the murder of the Austrian chancellor, Dollfuss, by the Nazis, Hitler's
growing power, and the threat of war. And now, twenty years later, he was
returning, under the threat of a new catastrophe, and to the same building, now the Palais des Nations.

At 9:45 P.M., the British delegation arrived at their hotel, the Beau Rivage, and Eden was shown to the same room that he had previously occupied, looking out on the lake. Ah, that was the professional courtesy of the
Swiss, he thought, but his pleasant memories were interrupted by the ir-
ruption at 10:15 of Dulles, who had arrived in Geneva with his aides earlier in the day.

It was a "disagreeable session," Shuckburgh recalled, with Eden firmly
laying down the United Kingdom line. Eden asked Dulles why the United
States had failed to tell the British what they had told the French, and
Dulles denied what Smith had proposed to Bonnet, saying he was against
an air strike on Dien Bien Phu. "We do not yet have the political basis for

taking military action," he said. Shuckburgh still felt that "the whole Bedell Smith incident was little more than an attempt to bounce us and shift the blame for the fall of Dien Bien Phu on us."

Eden once again repeated what he had already told Dulles a number of times, though it never seemed to sink in: there would be no armed intervention on the part of the United Kingdom prior to or during the Geneva Conference.

After their meeting, Dulles reported to the State Department: "I met with Eden this evening at 10:15 P.M. . . . He said that the United Kingdom is strongly opposed to any intervention at Dien Bien Phu." Eden was, however, prepared to join Dulles in a "secret study" for the defense of Southeast Asia if the French capitulated.

"I said to Eden that while I had reservations myself about air intervention at Dien Bien Phu . . . his reply was most discouraging in that it seemed to give the French nothing to fall back on. If the French are to stand [the] loss of Dien Bien Phu they must be strengthened and a declaration of common intent would do this. . . . I said to Eden that I doubted there would be French will to stand up to their adversaries in Geneva. Eden made it quite clear that the United Kingdom is opposed . . . to becoming directly involved in any way with the Indochina War."

Eden told Dulles there was no parallel between Indochina and Malaya, where the British had the situation "in hand" with twenty-two battalions and a hundred thousand native police. He showed Dulles a map prepared by the British Chiefs of Staff, indicating that "virtually all of Vietnam, Laos, and Cambodia are under or subject to imminent control by the Vietminh."

"I said to Eden," Dulles concluded, "that . . . it would be a tragedy not to take steps now which would prevent Indochina from being written off. Eden said 'there was obviously a difference in the United States and the United Kingdom estimates . . . but this was as far as the British Government could go.' "

The weeks of shuttle diplomacy, the pressuring of Bidault and Eden, as insistently repetitive as water torture, the behind-the-scenes intrigues involving Massigli, all this had amounted to nothing. The Americans and the British were hopelessly at odds. The British objected to Dulles's moral rigidity, his intolerance of opposition, and the vehemence of his language when he spoke of "massive retaliation" and "agonizing reappraisal." In one cable to Eisenhower, Dulles said, "After dinner I hit Eden again," which was the language not of diplomacy but of boxing. In Dulles's brinkmanship, the British saw a willingness to take risks to keep his anti-Communism pure. As for Dulles, he had told the National Security Council on April 6: "The paralysis of the British government is almost as serious as that of the French." But despite Dulles's fiasco, one has to admire his conviction, shared by the president, that diplomacy mattered, and unilateral action was out of the question. Dulles may have cursed his allies, but he never stopped working with them, or on them.

Eden's stay at the Beau Rivage was short-lived, for he was informed that there now existed what he called "gadgets for overhearing others," which had not existed in the thirties. A Swiss friend loaned him a secluded villa, Le Reposoir, on the lake, with a garden, to which he moved with his chief aides, Denis Allen and Harold Caccia, both Far East experts. Caccia was "tough and persistent," while Allen was "enormously resourceful."

What About Fortress America?

In Washington on Monday, April 26, Eisenhower held his weekly meeting with Republican congressional leaders and told them the French were "weary as hell" and the fall of Dien Bien Phu could have "enormous consequences." If the United States put "one combat soldier" into Indochina its prestige would be at stake. "The French go up and down every day," Ike said. "They are very voluble. They think they are a great power one day and feel sorry for themselves the next."

Senator Knowland warned that "they'll say we're not facing up to the situation."

"Well, they've said that before," the president replied.

Vice President Nixon said the United States had to face the question of whether to act without its allies.

Eisenhower said, "If allies go back on us, we would have one terrible alternative—we would have to attack with everything we have."

Knowland said Congress needed a thorough briefing on Soviet atomic potential.

Senator Eugene Millikin of Colorado said that if America was deserted by its allies it might have to return to "fortress America."

"Listen Gene," Ike testily replied, "Dien Bien Phu is a perfect example of a fortress and the Reds are surrounding it and crowding the French back into a position where they have to surrender or die. If we ever come back to the fortress idea for America . . . we would have to explode an attack with everything we have. What a terrible decision that would make."

On the same day, Eisenhower wrote his old friend and deputy chief of staff in 1944, Al Gruenther, now, as NATO commander, Eisenhower's most reliable link to French leaders, that "it seems incredible that a nation which had only the help of a tiny British army when it turned back the German flood in 1914 and withstood the gigantic 1916 attacks at Verdun could now be reduced to the point that she cannot produce a few hundred technicians to keep planes flying properly in Indochina." Ike wanted Gruenther to impress on the French that a loss at Dien Bien Phu did not mean the loss of the war.

That Horrible Thing—the Atomic Bomb

In London on Monday, April 26, Admiral Radford met with the British Chiefs of Staff but found that "their approach [was] strictly in terms of local United Kingdom interests, without adequate regard for other areas of the Far East." Field Marshal Sir John Harding told him that whatever happened in Indochina, the British would hold Malaya.

Radford reported to Washington, via Ambassador Winthrop Aldrich, that he didn't think the British were "squarely facing up" to the prospects for Southeast Asia. "I am having dinner with Sir Winston tonight," he said, "and will continue . . . to emphasize that a united front might afford the only opportunity to take any positive action to save Southeast Asia." He would also "make it evident" to Churchill that the British defection on united action would have an adverse effect on the U.S. Congress and public opinion.

Prior to the dinner, Churchill had received French ambassador Massigli, who was making a final stab at getting the British involved, at Premier Laniel's urgent request. Churchill said: "Tell President Laniel that I have measured the tragedy of this crisis to save the Dien Bien Phu garrison. My government is unanimous in thinking that only in Geneva can the situation in Southeast Asia be resolved. It is painful for me to tell you this, but I cannot tell you anything else."

Radford recalled that evening at Chequers as "one of the most interesting of my career. Sir Winston was the genial and fascinating host, full of stories and reminiscences that often kept his small audience in gales of laughter." And yet Radford could not have been amused by the substance of Churchill's remarks. "The PM went into an emotional discourse that Indochina could be saved only by 'that horrible thing—the atomic bomb.'

"I have known many reverses myself," Churchill went on. "I have not given in. I have suffered in Singapore, Hong Kong, Tobruk. The French will have Dien Bien Phu."

In his memorandum of the dinner, Radford wrote that Churchill "was determined to commit forces and to incur risks only to hold Malaya. . . . He repeatedly referred to the loss of Empire, making the point that since the British people were willing to let India go, they would certainly not be interested in holding Indochina for France. . . . He discoursed at length on the threat of atomic weapons to the United Kingdom, citing this as a factor which required the utmost caution in dealing with the situation in the Far East. Now that the Soviets had atomic and hydrogen weapons, there was no point in provoking them. East-West problems should be solved at conferences. It was folly to squander our limited resources around the fringes."

Radford's hope of plugging united action came to nothing, and his warning that Churchill's position might have an adverse effect in the United States fell on deaf ears. What Churchill told Radford privately at dinner he repeated publicly before the House of Commons on the following day when he announced to applause from both benches that "Her Majesty's Government are not prepared to give any undertaking about United Kingdom military commitments."

Molotov Had the Face of an Angry Pekinese

In Geneva on the afternoon of April 26, the conference on Korea and Indochina opened. It would last almost three months, until July 21. While the men on the ground in Indochina continued to fight and die, the diplomats argued.

Accustomed to conferences, the residents of Geneva took them in stride, but this one had some surprises. The Chinese, who saw Geneva as a chance to establish their rightful place as the fifth world power, brought a delegation of more than two hundred. In April 1954, the People's Republic of China was less than five years old. It was recognized by the communist bloc; the Asian states of India, Burma, and Pakistan; and the European states of Sweden, Denmark, Finland, Switzerland, and Great Britain. Thus, China had a consul in Geneva, who made the preparations for this throng of delegates, dispersing them among seven hotels.

The principal delegates, headed by Foreign Minister Chou En-lai, rented a splendid villa four miles from the city, Le Grand Mont-Fleuri. They had the villa emptied, for they had brought their own furniture, carpets, and art objects, so that it looked like a museum of Chinese decorative arts. All this showed the importance they attached to the conference. For Chou, it was an opportunity to show that the "New China" was a player in world affairs. He was happy to have at last a pulpit where he could preach peaceful coexistence to gain the approval of the neutrals. He let it be known that he was speaking for all of Asia, and during breaks in the sessions he lobbied the New Dehli and Rangoon diplomats.

Jean Chauvel, number two in the French delegation after Foreign Minister Bidault, had served in China from 1924 to 1927 and was fascinated by Chou, whom he placed in the category of wise ancients, since he came from a family of mandarins. Although he wore the austere, high-necked tunics of his compatriots, Chauvel envisioned Chou in a long robe with his hands in its sleeves. Aside from a stay in France as a youth, Geneva was probably Chou's first trip to the non-Communist world.

A Quai d'Orsay note on April 24 outlined the Chinese position: "In Asia no problem can be solved without China. Its policy is based on the independence of the Asian people. American policy is to encircle China with military bases. . . . In Indochina the U.S. wants to take the place of France. . . . France's interest is to separate itself from America's policy and conclude the peace."

Anthony Eden and his people were moving into Le Reposoir, one of the finest villas on the lake, where King Leopold had lived while in exile from Belgium. Chauvel had known Eden since the League of Nations in the thirties, and thought of him as "elegant, hardworking but doing his best to hide it, a good listener. He looked for solutions with patience and ingenuity." Chauvel was told that Eden "was given to inexhaustible grouchy fits, but none of that showed in public."

The Russians were in a pretty eighteenth-century house outside Geneva, but Foreign Minister Molotov refused to stay there, wanting to be close to the Palais des Nations, where the conference was held. Chauvel found Molotov "immovable. He had the face of an angry Pekinese and spoke in a neutral voice, showing neither pleasure nor displeasure, but sometimes a sense of irony. At one meeting, for instance, Bidault began a discourse on the fish of Lake Baikal [a Siberian lake that held one fifth of the world's fresh water]. Thereafter, whenever there was a lapse in the conversation, Molotov would say, 'We can talk about the fish in Lake Baikal.' "*

The Americans, as if to show that they were in transit, had not rented a villa, but stayed at the Hotel du Rhône, Chauvel noted. Dulles was there with his wife, who was always smiling and devoted. They both loved planes. "The world for him was like a city to whose neighborhoods he would fly when he needed to bring insubordinates into line. He seemed to have a mania for displacement, and his only policy was the struggle against Communism, which he saw as a battle of good versus evil. His power of invective in the service of his faith was such that an English humorist wrote: 'There is no situation so bad that Mr. Dulles cannot make it worse.' " Still, Chauvel saw Dulles as "a fine man, the opposite of an opportunist, but remarkably inopportune."

---

* When I joined the Paris bureau of the *New York Herald Tribune* in 1961, my bureau chief was Don Cook, who had covered the Geneva Conference. He told me that the U.S. press corps passed around the following joke about Molotov: President Eisenhower tells Stalin: "My secretary of state is so stubborn he can sit on a block of ice until it melts." Stalin replies: "Mine is so stubborn he can sit on a block of ice—and it doesn't melt."

The mood of the conference from the outset was antagonistic. The United States refused to recognize the presence of the Chinese. The French, however, were in luck. Chauvel had on his team a former military attaché in China, Colonel Guillermaz. Not only did Guillermaz speak the language, but he recognized in the Chinese delegation an old friend, Wang Ping-nan, who turned out to be secretary-general of foreign affairs, the number-two man in the delegation. Chauvel and Wang Ping-nan began to meet secretly at the home of the French consul general, which had a splendid view of Mont Blanc. "But we did not try to scale its heights," Chauvel recalled. "We kept things simple and concrete."

When Eden and his entourage arrived at the conference hall for the first plenary session at 3:30 in the afternoon, Shuckburgh was struck by the murals, although another observer described the decor as inspired by the public rooms of a transatlantic liner. The seating arrangement was a double horseshoe, with the advisers sitting behind the delegates. The British nodded to the Soviet delegates they had met in Berlin. When the Chinese arrived in lockstep, all wearing their high-collared suits, Shuckburgh "almost felt a common feeling with these white men, amongst all the yellow fellows who teemed on every side—Burmese, North Korean, South Korean, Siamese, Philippinos, Chinese."

One of the "yellow fellows," Prince Wan Waithayakon, the foreign minister of Thailand, took the chair. This first session dealt with such procedural matters as the adoption of five official languages—English, French, Russian, Chinese, and Korean. Even on this point there were arguments on including Chinese. As the conference went on, it became clear that plenary sessions would be devoted to speechmaking. The U.N. secretariat provided simultaneous translations of the verbiage and distributed copies to the media. There were eight plenary sessions, but the real work was done in private meetings outside the conference hall. The Chinese and the Russians worked in close coordination on negotiating tactics. Molotov spoke often with the French and the British. The British spoke to the Russians, the Chinese, and the French. Only the Americans were left out, although they tried to promote their policies by leaning on the British and the French.

The conference had two tracks, Korea and Indochina. The plan was to begin with Korea, where there was a cease-fire but no peace treaty. All twelve of the states that had sent troops to Korea under the United Nations were participants, as well as the Big Four, Communist China, and the two Koreas—for a total of nineteen states. The Korean part of the conference was soon deadlocked regarding proposals for the unification of Korea based on elections. South Korea wanted U.N.-supervised elections. North Korea, which had one third of the Korean population, insisted on an election commission with equal representation from North and South, which would give it a veto. Molotov argued that the United Nations had no standing to supervise elections since it was one of the combatants. The Korean part of the conference sputtered along until the conference recessed on May 14. The fighting in Korea had stopped, so there was no urgency for unification. When it became clear that unification could only be achieved by force, Korea remained divided.

In any case, the tragic situation at Dien Bien Phu had placed Korea in the shadows and brought the Indochina phase to the forefront. The initial problem was who should be asked to participate. Bidault conceded that the Vietminh could come only "if the Soviets insisted." The composition of participants was not agreed upon until May 2. There would be nine members: the Big Four, Communist China, the Vietminh, the Vietnamese government of Bao Dai, and Laos and Cambodia. The Vietminh delegation arrived on May 4, led by Pham Van Dong, who was described by Chauvel as having "a tormented face, hollow-cheeked, with burning eyes. Under the table his knees jumped compulsively. Bidault noticed that his gymnastics stopped when he spoke to the Russians."

Another procedural matter dealt with at the opening session was who would chair the plenary sessions. Dulles objected to a rotating chair that included the Chinese. Before the conference began, Eden went to see Molotov and they agreed that the chair would rotate among the Thais, Molotov, and Eden. "Dulles was rather put out when he first heard of it—but played up well," recalled Shuckburgh. However, "Eden is so anti-American that it is hard to get him to look for positive ways of bringing Dulles to a more patient frame of mind."

The first plenary session lasted only forty minutes, and as the delegates left the conference there was some socializing in the large reception hall. Eden asked Molotov to introduce him to Chou En-lai. Dulles appeared with one of his aides, U. Alexis Johnson, then ambassador to Czechoslovakia, but also a China expert. Johnson saw Chou move toward Dulles with his hand outstretched, but Dulles, seeing photographers flitting about, turned his back on Chou. He didn't want to be snapped shaking hands with the Communist Chinese foreign minister. It wouldn't look good at home, and he'd already been burned in Berlin. Chou, who had wanted to be courteous, as the foreign minister of one great nation greeting another on neutral ground, was left standing there with his hand in the air. Johnson later recalled that the snub "deeply wounded Chou and it deeply affected his attitude. It was a loss of face that I could see reflected through the rest of the conference." When Dulles's press spokesman, Carl McCardle, was asked whether Dulles planned to exchange views with Chou, he said: "Not unless their limos crash into each other leaving the hall."

That afternoon, Bidault asked to see Eden and Dulles at his villa. As Dulles reported that night to Washington, "Bidault launched into rather confused discussion of problem his government faces with regard to establishing position for Indochina negotiations which he said was extremely difficult during progress of Dien Bien Phu battle." The range of possibilities Bidault mentioned included collective defense, a cease-fire, and partition.

"Eden picked up the question of cease-fire," Dulles continued, and encouraged Bidault to respond to it "with the cryptic remark that a month ago British had felt cease-fire was dangerous due to general infiltration but that now . . . they were not so sure.

"I pointed out that cease-fire at Dien Bien Phu locally would be in fact surrender and that cease-fire generally would involve serious risk of native peoples' resisting with resultant massacre of French."

Bidault said he had heard from Navarre that there must be either a final cease-fire or further reinforcements at once.

Dulles and Eden, supposed allies, expected to work together, were in fact at antipodes. "In my judgment," Dulles went on, "Eden has arrived with instructions actively to encourage the French into almost any settlement which will result in cessation of hostilities in Indochina." Dulles had already heard via Chauvel that "Eden's instructions are to press actively for a cease-fire," and now he heard it from Eden.

Dulles "made clear to Bidault privately that we could have no (repeat

no) part in settlement at Geneva which constitutes surrender of Indochina to Communists, and that France had better chance by fighting on
rather than attempted withdrawal." Dulles's frustration with British policy was palpable when he added: "I intend to see Eden alone tomorrow
morning to talk with extreme bluntness to him expressing my dismay that
British are apparently encouraging French in direction surrender."

ACT V

Diplomacy, Defeat, and Captivity

. . .

• • •

I Reject the Moral Value of Sacrifice

THE OPENING OF THE GENEVA CONFERENCE changed the nature of the battle at Dien Bien Phu. Navarre, who was counting on a cease-fire, hoped to hold the base until it could be negotiated. Giap, sure of the advantage the Vietminh delegation would draw from victory, planned the final attack.

Giap's instructions from the military committee on April 22 were: "From May 1 to May 5 we must conquer the last hills the French occupy on the east of the Nam Yum, and we must also take the strongholds on the west bank. From May 6 to 10 we will consolidate our efforts." Giap announced that he had received enough supplies to allow him to keep fighting until June.

Meanwhile, Navarre in Saigon and Cogny in Hanoi continued to spar by wire. On April 22, Cogny, who thought Dien Bien Phu was a lost cause fought at the expense of the Tonkin Delta, wired Navarre: "The fall of Dien Bien Phu would have grave repercussions in the Delta."

Navarre replied on April 24: "I am aware of the critical situation in the Delta but I consider no less critical the fall of Dien Bien Phu and its repercussions on the rest of Indochina."

Before the 1955 commission, Cogny admitted that "my constant pressure on the commander in chief came close to lack of discipline." One example came in his reply to the April 24 wire: "Dien Bien Phu can last two to three weeks with reinforcements unless there is a general assault. If reinforcements cease now it can last eight days due to drop in morale. I absolutely reject the moral value of sacrifice. Only military honor defended to the end would be lost if the base fell. We must either send reinforcements or obtain a cease-fire before the base falls."

Navarre replied on April 26: "I believe that military honor even without the certainty of a favorable outcome justifies an additional sacrifice. A favorable outcome can be hoped for as a result of the Geneva Conference which may produce a cease-fire or American intervention. Am therefore determined to prolong resistance in Dien Bien Phu as long as possible."

Navarre later wrote in his memoirs that, seeing the end coming, he studied several plans to save the garrison. One was dropping paratroopers outside the base so they could hit the Vietminh from the rear. "This was absolutely impossible," he concluded. "The jungle terrain did not permit parachute drops. We would be sending out battalions to a certain death."

Another action contemplated "intercepting the supply line from the Chinese border to the depot at Tuan Giao. But experience had taught us that the Vietminh supply line was extremely flexible and capable of quick changes. It was divided into thirty sectors of thirty to fifty kilometers each. Each sector had its trucks that shuttled back and forth to load and unload. The sectors were limited by natural obstacles. If one sector was damaged, a parallel sector was ready. Columns of coolies handled the supplies. Cutting off the supply line would have required placing troops at key points."

One operation that Navarre did attempt was a rescue of the base from Laos, dubbed Operation CONDOR. Around April 6, Navarre sent a small staff to Colonel de Crèvecoeur, commander of land forces in Laos, to plan the operation. The rescue force in Laos, amounting to three thousand men, consisted of four battalions under the command of Lieutenant Colonel Yves Godard (three Laotian and one Foreign Legion), joined by an element of eight hundred lightly armed and skimpily officered Meo partisans. The force started moving on April 14 toward the Laotian post of Muong Khoua, about seventy miles southwest of Dien Bien Phu. They were supposed to continue to Sop Nao, the halfway point, where three battalions of paras would be dropped. This combined force would then proceed through a pass in the mountains that would bring them six miles south of Isabelle. Godard's progress was slowed by a shortage of porters and pack animals, and he did not reach Muong Khoua until April 25. By that time, all available planes were needed for Dien Bien Phu. Dropping three battalions of paras over Sop Nao would mean diverting the entire fleet of Dakotas for twenty-four hours. CONDOR was stillborn due to the lack of planes.

If Found Guilty, They Faced the Firing Squad

On April 25 came the roaring winds and torrential rains of the full-blown monsoon season. Navarre, who had experimented with artificial rain, got a deluge at Dien Bien Phu. The garrison waded in a slimy mud marsh. The Vietminh could no longer take their dead from around the Elianes that the French still held, and the stink of corpses was overwhelming. The decomposing bodies drew swarms of flies. At the central command post of Claudine, the mud was hard on gunners in their pits, who were knee-deep but had to keep firing. Reminding themselves that "the weapon of the artillery is not the cannon but the shell," they moved hundreds of shells to dryer ground.

The young surgeon Ernest Hantz operated with boots on. The roof of his surgery unit leaked and a parachute had to be placed under it to collect the water and the mud. It was on April 25 that he first noticed men coming in with mud in their wounds. As he operated, from inside the laceration came spurts of muddy blood. Bandages, infested with maggots, had to be changed more often. Plaster casts refused to dry, and infections led to gangrene. An emergency shipment of DDT had to be dropped to disinfect the surgery unit.

It happened in battles that men hoped for the "good wound," one that would take them off-site. But here there were no good wounds, since the men could not leave the base. They were stranded in the "catacombs," the vile, intestinelike, candlelit passageways honeycombed with niches dug in the walls, where the surfeit of wounded were placed. Some of the men in these underground trenches drowned. The amazing thing, Hantz thought, was that volunteers were still being dropped. Those young men, some of whom had never seen combat, had to pass a full medical exam, including a Wassermann test for syphilis, for the privilege of being allowed to die at Dien Bien Phu. They were stamped HEALTHY and flown straight to hell.

Pierre Bonny, a paratroop corporal on Eliane 1, watched new volunteers drop out of the sky and figured that they had cushy jobs such as cooks and chauffeurs. They were bored and wanted to fight, Bonny thought. They weren't fanatics, like the Vietminh "volunteers of death" who threw themselves on barbed wire with twenty pounds of TNT strapped to their chests. It was more likely the foolishness of the young, or a kind of contagious enthusiasm: "You're going to volunteer? Hey, I'll come too."

On the morning of April 26, the sky cleared and the sun came out. Castries' underground bunker was under a foot of water, but Castries remained dapper, freshly shaven, wearing a clean and pressed white shirt with the red spahi foulard. When the day's intelligence report arrived, it identified twenty-eight Vietminh battalions encircling the base, plus four armored battalions, in addition to thirty thousand coolies.

He also had the casualty figures for April: 701 killed, 1,948 wounded, 375 unaccounted for, and 47 deserters. The Rats of Nam Yum were multiplying. Castries had on the base a total of 3,000 wounded, 947 of them seriously. The latter needed to be evacuated, but could not be. He had 3,620 able-bodied men left, plus 1,300 at Isabelle, three miles south. And now his intelligence told him that he was encircled by thirty thousand *bo dois*, half of them fresh troops, their morale improved by the arrival of supplies and the start of the Geneva Conference.

Castries reported to Hanoi that "certain articles in the press are catastrophic for the morale of our troops." He had in mind a story in the April 22 issue of the Paris daily *Le Figaro*, under the headline CAN 100 PLANES STILL SAVE DIEN BIEN PHU? The article had been mentioned over one of the radio stations the troops had access to, and quoted a French pilot as saying, "I flew 17 hours today . . . we need 100 more planes to change the situation." The reporter, Max Olivier, interviewed a general (probably Cogny) who unrolled a map of the Tonkin Delta and said: "This is what I call the leprosy map. What you see in red is totally controlled by the Vietminh. . . . In pink is what we occupy by day and they occupy by night. In white is what we control." The map was almost entirely red. "My best battalions are at Dien Bien Phu, encircled," the general said. "And those I've got left open the road daily between Hanoi and Haiphong."

This plea for the primacy of the Delta was Cogny's theme song, but at Dien Bien Phu there were still men who believed in the defense of the base. One of them was Colonel Langlais, the operational commander. It was said that his head was as hard as the granite of his native Brittany. To those who cursed Giap's refusal to let the wounded be evacuated, Langlais replied: "Giap is waging war, and in a war, there is no sentiment. He knows the wounded are our heaviest handicap. If I had the choice between a fresh battalion and the evacuation of the wounded, I'd take evacuation. But the responsibility for the tragedy of the wounded cannot be blamed on the enemy."

How dangerous this myth of Geneva was, Langlais thought. He warned his officers not to expect a miracle. To win, they had to hold on another month, when, because of the rain, the Viets would run short of supplies. Langlais asked Dr. Grauwin if perhaps some of the lighter casualties might be persuaded to return to their units. Langlais went through the wards making the offer and, to his surprise, "I saw men missing an arm or a leg or an eye, raise their hands. I couldn't believe it." Men with missing limbs, as well as others with their arms or legs in casts, returned to their units and fought alongside their comrades. Men who could not stand or sit lay down in trenches and fired their weapons.

Langlais realized, however, that holding on another month was less a matter of men than supplies. They were running short of rice and munitions. Thirty percent of the drops were lost to the Viets. Each day it was worse. All their vehicles were destroyed and they could gather supplies only on foot.

The last jeep they had was Bigeard's. Two of his men, Cruzille and Decupper, were the supply team. "It's like a game," Cruzille said. "We come to pick the stuff up, they try to stop us. I've got to bring back enough grenades, shells, rations, and bags of rice so we can hold." Zigzagging back to the base to avoid mortar shells, the jeep got stuck in mud. The two men jumped into a shell hole moments before the jeep was hit and overturned, its wheels in the air. Bigeard shrugged when they told him. "It had to happen," he said. He refused to consider defeat, saying: "We still hold good positions."

The good weather over the base on April 26 prompted a supreme effort from the air force, but it also proved to be a banner day for the Vietminh antiaircraft gunners. All day the B-26s, navy Hellcats, and huge four-engine Privateers came and went. The B-26s, equipped with Norden bomb sights, dropped their four thousand-pound bombs from ten thousand feet, with greater accuracy than the dive-bombers. Six B-26s took off from Cat Bi airport in Haiphong at 8:30 A.M. and targeted antiaircraft emplacements on strongpoints formerly held by the French. They were followed by six Hellcats, carrying five-hundred-pound bombs, which came in at twelve thousand feet and dropped to eight thousand to unload their cargo. The flak was heavy, and the Hellcat piloted by twenty-year-old petty officer Daniel Robert was shot down during a strafing run. Robert bailed out and landed behind enemy lines. Surrounded by men in green battle dress, he was brought before an officer.

"Why are you doing this war work?" the officer asked.

"Because I'm a soldier like you and I obey orders," Daniel Robert replied. He died in July during the long march to the prison camps, of dysentery and beriberi.

Between 10 A.M. and noon, eight Privateers on flak-suppression missions, each carrying twelve five-hundred-pound cluster bombs, hit antiaircraft emplacements northwest of the airstrip. Each container held 11,200 bullets and covered an area the size of a football field.

Two Privateers and four B-26s were hit by 37mm flak at nine thousand feet. Lieutenant Iteney's left engine caught fire. The cockpit filled with smoke, the plane was vibrating, and the crew of four donned their chutes. Three bailed out, but the fourth man, Lieutenant Tharaud, went down with the plane. The Vietminh found his charred body.

Lieutenant Caubel had piloted one of the morning B-26 missions and as he came over Isabelle once again in the afternoon, he heard on the radio that the flak was "particularly virulent." One B-26 had already gone down. His objective was an antiaircraft emplacement. His bombardier, Lieutenant Baujard, was lying down in the plane's glass nose with his eye on the sight. His two tons of bombs were dropped, the bomb hatch closed, and Caubel, seeing heavy tracer fire, tried evasive tactics. It was too late; the right engine caught fire, and the fuel tank was hit. Caubel headed toward Laos, where the rescue column was supposed to be, and gave the order to jump.

Sergeant Texier, the flight engineer, bailed out and was taken prisoner. Baujard tried to jump from his normal position but the right wing was on fire, so he climbed to the back, and jumped from there. He landed in a clearing and folded his chute. That left the pilot, Caubel, who jumped as the stricken B-26 nose-dived. He had no parachute training, and when he pulled on the handle, it came off in his hand, which was normal, but he didn't know that. He saw the jungle below, still in free fall, and thought, "I've had it." But then his chute blossomed and he was reminded of a World War II story: A Resistance fighter is dropped over Belgium where a bicycle has been left for him. But his chute isn't opening and he thinks: "Just my luck, and when I get there the bike will have a flat tire."

Caubel landed on a hill, where he found Baujard. They figured they were about twenty miles from Dien Bien Phu and walked west toward Laos. Children collecting roots in a field fled when they saw the downed airmen. That night they were taken prisoner by Montagnard tribesmen and turned over to the Vietminh.

The inundation of the base on April 25 was particularly hard on Isabelle, which was built on flat ground on both banks of the Nam Yum and surrounded by rice paddies. Colonel Lalande's positions did not allow for deep trenches, though the four strongpoints were well built, with thick roofs that resisted howitzer shells. The command post, hospital, and artillery pits were on slightly higher ground. To the northwest, Captain Jeancelle and his Algerians were dug in; to the southwest, Lieutenant Wieme's Thais; to the southeast and northeast, the Legionnaires. Because of its small size, Isabelle was difficult to supply, for it took a Dakota only two seconds to fly over it. Food shortages were made up for by the resourceful Thais, who killed the occasional water buffalo.

On April 26, Isabelle was heavily shelled and so badly cratered it looked like the moon surrounded by water. Vietminh 75s were less than two miles away. The trenches inched closer, and from them the Vietminh infantry sprang forth, screaming and firing.

Colonel Lalande felt he had to respond and asked Major Jeancelle to send a company of his Algerians to take out a trench near their positions. The major sent Lieutenant Choulet's 7th Company. They reached the trench at dawn, but after an hour of fighting they realized there was a second trench. When the *bo dois* in both trenches leapt up, the Algerians panicked and limped back to Isabelle with six killed and twenty-two wounded.

Concerned about low morale and a lack of combativeness among his Algerian and Thai troops, Colonel Lalande decided to convene a court martial. He told Major Jeancelle to pick two men from each of the platoons of the 7th Company to be tried on charges of cowardice in the face of the enemy. If found guilty, they faced the firing squad. Jeancelle recalled: "I was able to make him change his mind, but it wasn't easy. He'd never commanded Algerian troops. I was helped by [the company commander] Lieutenant Belhabich. We argued that if Lalande insisted on a firing squad it would be catastrophic for the battalion. It would lead to mutiny and desertions." Lalande saved face with a quick trial and acquittal.

The condition of the main base on April 26 as seen by General Giap is worth noting: "The area the enemy occupied was narrowing. His aircraft could not fly at low altitudes and part of his supply fell into our hands. We appropriated his goods and ammunition. We used his cannon shells to fire back at him." But the monsoon season was hard on his men as well. "Our fighters had to spend long periods in trenches and dugouts in periods of heavy rain."

The crucial difference between the two sides, said Giap, was that "although the surface of the French base grew smaller, the zone reserved for the wounded and the dead kept growing. More and more of the wounded had to remain with their units. The only bulldozer left was used to dig graves. DDT was added to the supplies, for horse-flies and dung flies lay their eggs in wounds. In double-decker bunks, those who occupied the upper bunk leaked blood and pus on those below. In the common graves they threw in all sorts of waste, amputated arms and legs, empty medicine vials, and the torrential rains flooded the pits and its contents floated out. . . . The men in the trenches were living in the dark like rats. Cogny was asked to supply periscopes so they could see without sticking their heads out of the trenches."

Our Relations Are Very Bad

On the morning of April 27 in Geneva, Evelyn Shuckburgh complained that clouds prevented him from seeing Mont Blanc. He made up for his disappointment at lunch with Livingston Merchant with a *truite au bleu*. Prior to lunch, Bidault had come by to report to Eden on his talk with Molotov. Bidault and Molotov had discussed who should attend the Indochina conference. Molotov wanted the Vietminh to attend. Eden told Bidault he should agree—at a price. Why not ask for the evacuation of the wounded? Bidault said he would try this.

Prior to Bidault's visit, Dulles had dropped by to lecture Eden on what a frustrating ally the British were. Dulles reported to Washington:

> I said I considered it a great mistake to push the French in direction cease-fire which I believed would be a disaster.
>
> Eden replied with some heat . . . that all he had been thinking of had been a cease-fire with adequate safeguards and controls.
>
> I replied that I wanted immediate plans covering Southeast Asia if Geneva failed but the British were against this. The French I said had in effect no government and were at a loss as to what to do. They were drifting toward disaster. . . . The British seemed to think that plans for a joint defense were more apt to spread conflict than absence of any plans. Eden said we must see how things go here in the next few days and do what we can to buck French up.
>
> I said . . . the fall of Laniel might result in a left-of-center government coming to power which would exist by Communist sufferance. . . . At this point Bidault arrived and we broke off our conversation.

The more Dulles pressured Eden, the more Eden resented it.

President Eisenhower wrote in his diary for April 27: "The situation at Dien Bien Phu looks a bit brighter than it has for the last ten days. Apparently there has been some resupply of ammunition and food, but so far as I know, the difficult problem of the care of the wounded had not been alleviated. There has likewise been some evidence of a resurgence of French courage and determination. We just received a request for some perforated steel plate for two airfields and for some additional POL [petroleum, oil, lubricants]. They want also a few experts in the laying of steel plate. In addition they want a small quantity of earth-moving machines." Ike did not seem to realize that these requests were not intended for Dien Bien Phu, where the airstrip was in control of the Vietminh, and where there were no functioning vehicles except for a single tank.

The president's reaction to the Dulles cable on Eden's cease-fire policy was that "the British are afraid that if the fighting continues we—and possibly other countries—might become involved and tend to increase the danger, in the British opinion, of starting World War III. . . . The British government is showing a woeful unawareness of the risks we run in that region."

As Jim Hagerty put it, U.S. aims at Geneva were to keep the French from negotiating a cease-fire and to form an anti-Communist coalition with France and without the British, without giving in to "so-called French prestige."

On the morning of April 28, the British were still at their hotel, waiting to move to the villa, and Shuckburgh reported that Eden was in a "dreadful state," owing to the scooter detonations in the streets of Geneva that started at 5:30 A.M. and woke him up. Eden wanted to buck up Bidault before his meeting with Molotov. Eden and Shuckburgh found Bidault with Dulles, who lost his temper with Eden over the remarks Churchill had made in the House of Commons the day before. "Dulles stalked out without a word," Shuckburgh wrote. "Our relations are very bad, and we shall have to be very careful."

That afternoon, Eden and Shuckburgh attended the plenary meeting, at which the two adversaries, Dulles and Chou En-lai, were scheduled to speak. Chou attached great importance to Geneva, seeing it as a chance to break out of the U.S.-imposed policy of embargo and isolation and claim great-power status for China.

At the same time, the Chinese feared that the United States would intervene in Indochina. Chou stressed peaceful coexistence. While in Moscow, he had told Khrushchev that China had refused Ho Chi Minh's request to send troops to Indochina. "We've already lost too many men in

Korea," Chou said. "That war cost us dearly. We're in no condition to get involved in another war at this time."

At the plenary meeting, Dulles spoke first, and Shuckburgh found him "disagreeable but not overly violent." Dulles called for a united Korea and the withdrawal of Chinese troops. The highlight of Dulles's speech, which Shuckburgh found baffling, was: "We know that those who live by faith prevail over those who live by calculation."

Then Chou took off his headphones and began to read a long speech in Chinese script in his "bird-like voice." China has been subjected to "impermissible discrimination," he said, and the conference "should mark the beginning of change." Soon, however, Chou was attacking "influential circles in the United States." It seemed to Shuckburgh that he was giving "a very false history of the Korean aggression," and that, with his "violent self-confidence," he spoke for "hundreds of millions of yellow men . . . who have become our enemies." In a way, Shuckburgh reasoned, "it is the fault of the Americans . . . for being so damned contemptuous of them."

He looked across the room at "poor Bidault, pale and apprehensive, doomed," and after Chou had finished he noticed "the ashen anger of Dulles." As the plenary session broke up, Molotov told Eden that Dulles and Chou had given "two very wise speeches. It is just as well that two different points of view should be clearly expressed." Shuckburgh was tempted to think of Molotov as "a sort of benevolent middle-man."

That evening Bidault had dinner with Molotov and made his bid for the evacuation of the wounded on humanitarian grounds, according to the traditional laws of war. He urged Molotov to intervene with the Vietminh at once. Molotov said: "The solution of this matter, as well as the opening of the Indochina phase, depends on France. The presence of the Vietminh is the condition that will open the conference and solve the local problem of the wounded." Molotov was linking the wounded to French acceptance of the Vietminh delegation. As he put it, he was "willing to contribute to the matter of evacuation but that it was subordinate to the participation of the Vietminh at the conference."

Bidault concluded that the Soviets were exploiting the tragic situation of the wounded to force the French to accept the presence of the Vietminh.

He wired Paris: "They want to obtain an invitation to the Vietminh without any qualifications or conditions."

Without Allies the Leader Is Another Genghis Khan

In Washington on April 28, the National Security Council meeting focused on Indochina. Allen Dulles summarized a National Intelligence Estimate on the consequences of the fall of Dien Bien Phu as "very serious but not catastrophic." Admiral Radford told Dulles that he was too optimistic. Walter Bedell Smith read a just-arrived cable from Secretary of State Dulles: "The decline of France . . . and the considerable weakness of England create a situation where . . . we must be prepared to take the leadership. . . . I believe our allies will be inclined to follow."

The president seemed to think that Secretary Dulles was giving up on united action, for he observed that he did not see how the United States "could intervene with armed forces in Indochina unless it did so in concert with some other nations. . . . This seems quite beyond my comprehension."

Radford then reported on the desperate situation of the garrison, and he must have made an impression, for the notes of the meeting said that his remarks were followed by "a brief interval of silence."

Harold Stassen, head of the Foreign Operations Administration, proposed that "if the French folded, and if the British refused to go along, the United States should intervene alone in the southern areas of Indochina in order to save the situation." It was better to defend part of Indochina than none at all, Stassen concluded.

Eisenhower told Stassen: "If the French collapse and the United States move in, we will in the eyes of many Asiatic peoples merely replace French colonization." To go it alone, Ike said, echoing what his secretary of the treasury, George Humphrey, had told him in January, "amounted to an attempt to police the entire world. . . . We should be everywhere accused of imperialist ambitions. . . . Without allies and associates the leader is just another Genghis Khan."

Backed by Vice President Nixon, Smith said there was a way to avoid doing too much or too little. That way was to conduct air strikes even if Dien Bien Phu fell, to encourage the French to keep fighting. Perhaps the situation could be saved without committing ground forces. "General Navarre, however, would have to go," Smith added, since he had proved incompetent. "We should also have absolute assurance from France for the complete independence of the Associated States."

Smith had been Eisenhower's chief of staff in the major operations of World War II, and the president respected his military insight. Ike agreed that the plan might be feasible and said he would ask Congress to consider it. The meeting concluded with a presidential warning: "Let us not talk of intervention with U.S. ground forces. People are frightened and opposed to this idea."

Later that day, the NSC Planning Board discussed the meeting that had just been held and decided that it was "impossible to meet the President's requirement that the indigenous peoples invite and actively desire U.S. intervention. This has been told to the President." Thus, no sooner did Smith propose his plan than it was scrapped. U.S. policy remained united action.

On April 29, Eisenhower followed up on Smith's proposal of an air strike in a discussion with the Joint Chiefs. He later wrote that "although the three service chiefs had recommended against this course, there was some merit in the argument that the psychological effect of an air strike would raise French and Vietnamese morale and improve, at least temporarily, the entire situation." No air strike, however, was ordered.

The Almost Pathological Rage of Dulles

In Geneva on April 29, Shuckburgh reported that "Bidault's discussion with Molotov (who has incipient flu) last night over dinner led nowhere." The British were finally moving into their villa, Le Reposoir, and Eden was a happy man. The following day members of the British delegation were having lunch with Molotov and Chou.

Dulles wired Washington that "developments have been so rapid and almost every hour is filled with high-level talks that evaluation has been difficult.

"Present French government holding on because their Parliament is in [three-week Easter] recess and probably no one eager to take over at this juncture. . . . We do not have anyone on the French side with whom we can make any dependable agreements. After deputies return and Dien Bien Phu falls, there may well be a change of government, probably to the left, committed to liquidate Indochina." Dulles's pessimism was increasing daily, and his prediction was accurate.

Dulles thought that a plan to have French forces withdraw to defensible enclaves in the Delta, where they would have U.S. air and naval protection, might offer the French the best hope of staying in the war. But the British were not on board. "UK attitude is one of increasing weakness. British seem to feel that we are disposed to accept present risks of a Chinese war and this, coupled also with their fear that we would start using atomic weapons, has badly frightened them."

How lovely it was at the villa, thought Shuckburgh on Friday, April 30, waking up to the singing of birds in the chestnut trees and a cowbell in the fields. For once, Eden had slept soundly, and there was cherry jam for breakfast. Dulles came around before lunch, wanting "half an hour alone" with Eden. He had sunk to a new low of crabbiness, saying that no one at the conference had supported the United States against Chou's attacks. Asia was lost, France was finished, and the alliance was nearly at an end. Shuckburgh was reminded of King Lear: "We have seen the best of our times . . . and the bond cracked between father and child." Dulles wanted someone to make a speech at that day's session attacking Communism. After Dulles left, Eden said that it wouldn't be him. "They would think in London I was mad."

Then came lunch at Molotov's villa. The Russians, beaming with hospitality, introduced the British to the grinning Chinese. Shuckburgh couldn't tell one from the other, except for Chou. The meal was a feast of twenty courses, including caviar, eel, duck, and ice cream, "served by extremely hygienic-looking Russian maidservants with comely rustic faces." When Molotov got up to propose a toast, the chairs scraped the parquet floor.

The word was out that Dulles was leaving Geneva, and this was the first topic of conversation. Why was he leaving? Eden was asked. Eden did not have an answer. He then took Chou to task: "You were very rough to us yesterday. You called us a wicked colonial power. Look what we did for India, Burma. We recognize you. I wonder if you recognize us."

"You don't recognize us in the U.N.," Chou replied.

Molotov chimed in: "That undermines the U.N."

Chou expressed his "disgust" with Dulles for planning to leave on May 3, seeing in his departure a refusal to join in an Indochina settlement.

After lunch, Molotov, Chou, and Eden went off on their own, with interpreters, and were joined by Shuckburgh and Andrey Gromyko, the deputy foreign minister.

Eden raised the question of the wounded at Dien Bien Phu.

Molotov said it should be possible to arrange a truce, but it must be done "by the two parties concerned."

Molotov then expounded on how useful conferences were for making personal contacts.

Eden said, "Certainly I am glad to meet Mr. Chou En-lai. Of course Mr. Molotov and I know each other well. I always know when he is cross with me and when he is pleased."

"In that case," Molotov said, "I am a bad diplomat. I should conceal my feelings."

Everyone laughed, and Shuckburgh, a big, strapping fellow, leaned back in his chair and cracked it.

"That is a bad diplomat, to break his host's chair," Eden said.

Shuckburgh thought the chair had been weakened by the insertion of microphones.

Chou's preferred topic seemed to be bitterness toward Americans. "They hate us and are jealous of China," he said.

"On the contrary," Eden said, "they have loved China, and when relations went wrong it was an emotional disappointment."

Shuckburgh reflected that so far Eden had handled things well. Their only worry was "the almost pathological rage of Dulles," which would not be easy to allay, for Eden "is fed up with Dulles . . . and almost resents seeing him."

That afternoon, Dulles and Eden tried to cheer up a despondent Bidault. With the loss of Dien Bien Phu approaching, Bidault deplored that he had "hardly a card in his hand, perhaps just a two of clubs and a three of diamonds." He was against any talk of partition, nor was a cease-fire possible, since the two sides were so inextricably mixed that the result would be a massacre. The best course was to work for an armistice.

Bidault was a man of strong emotions, and he keenly felt the hopeless situation of the wounded at the base. He wanted to keep Indochina French, and he had never been willing to recognize the Ho Chi Minh regime. But on April 30, he realized that the only way to help the wounded was to open negotiations with the Vietminh, which amounted to de facto recognition. He summoned to Geneva the Indochina hand Colonel de Brébisson, who met secretly in a hotel with Colonel Ha Van Lau, a member of the Vietminh military delegation. Their talks were the true beginning of the Indochina phase of the conference. Between April 30 and June 8, they met six times. At first they discussed the evacuation of the wounded and the improvement of conditions for prisoners of war, but eventually they dealt with the military modalities for a cease-fire. Bidault also opened a private line of communication with the Chinese thanks to the connection between Jacques Guillermaz and Wang Ping-nan.

But all this took time, and Bidault wanted to help the wounded at once. He had General Ely wire Navarre on April 30: "The best way to resolve this painful problem is for General de Castries to ask for a truce [to evacuate the wounded]. If they do not change their attitude their moral position at Geneva will be weakened. . . . I have several reasons to believe that this solution has Soviet support."

There were, however, a number of practical problems, not the least of which was that there weren't enough helicopters to fly out the 914 seriously wounded, which meant fixing the airstrip, now occupied by the Vietminh. It would take forty-eight hours to repair the airstrip, and three or four days to take out the wounded. This meant a weeklong truce.

Navarre replied that "asking the Vietminh for a truce of this length and for the use of terrain which it controls is not a right but a favor that can be refused for valid motives. We could however agree to cease aerial attacks during that period, so that it would amount to a sort of cease-fire." This complicated matter could not be arranged overnight, added Navarre.

In Washington, on the morning of April 30, Robert Cutler, Eisenhower's special assistant for national security affairs, brought the president the draft of a National Security Council paper that explored the possibilities of using atomic bombs in Indochina. The president said: "I certainly do not think that the atomic bomb can be used by the United

States unilaterally. . . . You boys must be crazy. We can't use those awful things against Asians for a second time in less than ten years. My God!"

I Was in the Toilet Bowl up to My Neck

At first, when the French troops occupied Dien Bien Phu in November 1953, they called it *le camp retranché* (the entrenched camp). After the battles of March and April, they called it *le merdier* (the shit hole). With the coming of the monsoons, it became *le bidet*. During most of the last five days of April, the spigots in the sky were on full blast, except for a brief intermission at dusk. The men in the trenches were submerged in stinking, muddy puddles up to their waists. The time of burying the dead was long past, and they lay rotting beside the living, who had little to eat, no access to clean water, and no way to stay dry. In his underground bunker, Castries splashed back and forth in a foot of water that had to be mopped daily. Luckily, there was little fighting, except for the back and forth of the rival artillery, like two angry drunkards roaring at each other.

Everyone was convinced that the end was coming. On April 25, French intelligence picked up Vietminh radio traffic announcing the arrival of two hundred vehicles at the Tuan Giao depot, carrying twenty-four hundred drums of gasoline. On April 27, it was reported that an important shipment of medical supplies, enough to cover Vietminh needs for an entire month, had left Tuan Giao for Dien Bien Phu. This was soon followed by a report on the shipment of a month's supply of rice.

Colonel Langlais was an angry man. There was plenty of blame to go around. Some strongpoints had been carelessly built. "We know perfectly well that one meter of earth and logs over a trench two meters deep provides protection," he recalled, but that guideline was seldom followed. He derided comparisons between Dien Bien Phu and the trench warfare of World War I. The shelling of 1916 may have been worse, but the poilus did not remain on the line for more than a week and the wounded were bundled to hospitals at the rear.

What angered Langlais the most was the lack of cooperation from Hanoi. "The fight I had with Hanoi for reserves wore me out more than the enemy," he said. In Hanoi, "they did not understand the true nature of the battle." Thus the long arguments and the units that did not arrive in time for counterattacks. Later, when he went to the Ministry of Defense in Paris and appeared before the 1955 commission, sitting at the long table facing four generals and an admiral, he said: "I was a simple lieutenant colonel, and I had under my command ten thousand men. I was in the fucking toilet bowl up to my neck but I didn't see any generals in Hanoi offering to take my place. If there had been a general in command, a general with authority, who didn't have to beg for supplies and reinforcements, things would have been different." Langlais damned Hanoi for "acting like grocers" and parceling out reinforcements by the ounce.

As for the wounded, there were now more than a thousand, jammed into makeshift shelters in the various surgical units. Desperate for help, Dr. Grauwin had recruited some of the ladies from the two brothels to serve as nurses. Grauwin was happy to have them, since they were trained in giving comfort to men.

In Hanoi, given the plight of the base, the high command discussed a possible sortie. On April 30, however, Colonel Dominique Bastiani, Cogny's chief of staff, wrote a report condemning the idea. Exhausted troops would have to break though the ring of Vietminh divisions and it would turn into a rout, at night, in the jungle, and they would suffer terrible losses. He stressed that "we cannot abandon more than a thousand wounded after having solicited the help of the enemy for their evacuation. We cannot tarnish the glory of six weeks of battle with a shameful and disorderly flight. The base can hold as long as it remains supplied. As long as it holds it inflicts losses on the Vietminh and fixes Giap's army in place. Any commander who signs an order of flight will be dishonored. We must accept the consequences of our acts."

Navarre came to Hanoi to discuss the matter with Cogny, while Colonel Bastiani took notes. Although reluctant to continue the battle, Navarre was still hoping for a cease-fire at Geneva, and wanted the base to hold out a bit longer. As a mark of confidence, he had decided to send in another battalion. But to keep his options open, he decided that a sortie might eventually be necessary and should be planned. "General Navarre decided to abandon the wounded with a medical team," Bastiani wrote in his notes. "He is convinced the Vietminh will allow the evacuation."

Navarre knew that in Geneva, Bidault was discussing the matter of the wounded with various parties. Navarre said that at the proper time, he would give Castries the order for a sortie called Operation ALBATROSS. Cogny disagreed, stating that "it is more than likely that only a small fraction of the garrison will be saved. The decision to abandon the wounded is a serious one that can only be made by the government in Paris."

Navarre at once sent a wire to General Ely in Paris: "If the government has a moral or political objection to the abandonment of the wounded please let me know urgently. I will not pursue the sortie if a cease-fire is in the immediate perspective at Geneva." Ely replied the same day, papering over the moral predicament of leaving the wounded behind, which went against a hallowed tradition of the army, with meaningless qualifications: "All measures must be taken to assure the protection and care of the wounded by maintaining with them a commanding officer, doctors, nurses, and stretcher-bearers."

On April 27, the air force dropped three hundred U.S.-supplied flak jackets, with priority for the artillery. It was yet another example of Hanoi's desultory attitude. Had the jackets been requested earlier and delivered in a timely fashion, they would have provided protection from the thoracic wounds that had been keeping the surgeons so busy.

On April 28, monsoon rains flooded the camp and no supplies could be dropped. On April 29, the garrison was placed on half rations. The men ate their *singe* (canned beef, which they called "monkey") and sardines, and reflected that though they were short on food, there was no shortage of shells pouring down on them along with the rain. That night, the last functioning tank, the *Douaumont*, was hit by a 105mm shell, and the entire crew was killed. The Chaffee was thereafter used as an artillery emplacement.

On April 30, Castries wired Hanoi: "As of today I do not have a single available tank." April 30 was also the day the Civil Air Transport pilots decided to resume their flights. They joined a total of about a hundred planes that dropped 212 tons of supplies, half of which were not recovered. For the Legionnaires, April 30 had a special meaning. It was the day they celebrated Camerone, a battle fought in Mexico on April 30, 1863, during the war against the emperor Maximilian, who had been sent to rule the country by Napoleon III. In the pueblo of Camerone, sixty-two Legionnaires and three officers, who were stationed there to protect the passage of a convoy, were surrounded by a force of two thousand. They stood their ground and died almost to the last man. Impressed by their bravery, the Mexicans spared the lives of three survivors, and returned the wooden hand of their commander, Captain Danjou, which was embalmed like a splinter of the true cross at Legion headquarters in Sidi Bel Abbès, Algeria.

Lieutenant Colonel Maurice Lemeunier, the senior Foreign Legion officer at Dien Bien Phu, put on a clean uniform and recited the tale over a loudspeaker. The Legionnaires, sitting on sandbags in their bunkers, kept their heads down so as not to offer targets for snipers, ate their warmed-over rice and canned peas, and drank thimblesful of Algerian red wine sent over by Castries. It cannot have escaped them that, like the men of Camerone, they were fighting a sacrificial holding action.

Finally, on April 30, the weather was fine. Six Hellcats bombed Vietminh artillery positions and flew back to their carrier, the *Arromanches*. This was their last flight. They were down to ten pilots. Of the squadron's nine officers, three had been killed or were missing. A fourth had been shot down over the base, and a fifth was a prisoner of the Vietminh. Captain Patou, the squadron leader, wrote the admiral commanding naval forces in the Far East: "The flotilla needs time to recover and make up for its losses."

On April 16, General Navarre had wired Marc Jacquet, secretary of state for the Associated States of Indochina, that "a great weariness is manifest in the enemy units, some of which give the definite impression of being worn out physically and morally." Navarre's estimate was based on the interrogation of captured Vietminh after the battle of the Five Hills. His views coincided with the concerns expressed by General Giap regarding "rightist tendencies" among his troops, which had to be repressed with reeducation and improved conditions. In this army of peasants, Giap's strongest argument to boost morale was extolling agrarian reform, so that every soldier could feel that he was fighting for the right to own a few acres.

On April 27, Giap convened the divisional political commissars and told them to get to work lifting morale. On April 29, he insisted that the principal theme should be agrarian reform. As an officer of the 312th Division put it, "At that moment every soldier thought: 'Now my wife, my mother, and my brother will have enough food.' "

Giap, like Castries, had an underground bunker, which was dug into the mountain at his headquarters, with a gallery three hundred yards long, offices and assembly rooms, and a direct link to China, as Castries had with Hanoi. There, at a bamboo table covered with maps, he planned the final attack, though he too was afflicted by the monsoons, which did more damage to his supply routes than French bombs. Entire strips of road were washed down the sides of mountains into ravines, and avalanches caused by the rain blocked the passage of supplies. However, Giap recovered five thousand shells from French drops.

Giap's attack force of fourteen thousand men outnumbered Castries' three thousand able-bodied men by nearly five to one, but his dilemma remained the big hill of Eliane 2. The 174th Regiment proposed using its sappers to dig a tunnel under the hill and then fill it with dynamite. A special group of twenty-four sappers led by the military engineer Nguyen Phu Xuyen Khung approached the southern side of the hill at the end of April and started digging with hand tools through solid rock. The first night they advanced less than three feet, protected by several companies. It took three nights to dig the entrance. Once inside the tunnel, the men suffocated and had to be replaced. When it was ten yards long, the lack of light and oxygen slowed their progress, as well as the disposal of earth and rocks. They were out of sight of the French, who could hear digging but did not investigate.

Giap's plan was to launch the final attack with a three-hour artillery preparation, by far the most intense yet, starting at 5 P.M. At 8, he would throw his divisions at strongpoints on both sides of the Nam Yum, except for Eliane 2, which would be stormed only when the tunnel was finished and filled with dynamite. On the eastern bank, the 316th Division would attack the low hill of Eliane 1 and then cross over to Eliane 4. On the western bank, the 308th Division would attack the two remaining Huguettes, 4 and 5, bringing Giap's troops within a hundred yards of the French camp.

We Were Consuming a Hundred Men a Day

May 1 was a Communist holiday, and at Giap's mountain headquarters, red flags flew to the strains of "The Internationale." It was also the day that Giap attacked, with a massive artillery and mortar barrage that began at 5 P.M. and pounded the base for three hours. From his surgical unit, Dr. Verdaguer reckoned that the cannonade's "apocalyptic density" was due to the Viets' artillery positions on strongpoints they had captured from the French. Verdaguer realized that night that the battle was lost. The Crèvecoeur relief column was blocked. The Geneva Conference was stalled. The Americans were nowhere in sight. Verdaguer had two hundred men under his care at the central hospital, and every day more men died. Verdaguer wanted it to end, "just as one hopes that a man struck by an incurable disease will find deliverance."

Captain Pierre Tourret, commander of the 8th Choc, stationed on Epervier, on the western bank of the Nam Yum, was stunned by this "terrifying bombardment, all the more intense due to our shrunken perimeter, so that even small-caliber mortars could reach our positions." Inside his command post, the teak roof held, but the wall panels for maps were knocked down and the lights went out.

The force of the artillery preparation unsettled Castries, who wired Colonel Sauvagnac, the paratroop commander in Hanoi: "Why are you hiding behind General Navarre to hold up my reinforcements? For the last time I demand that you line up with the other Hanoi officers. We will win this battle in spite of you. This is the last message I will send you."

As Langlais told the 1955 commission: "What I hold against Colonel Sauvagnac was his refusal to drop non-paratroopers. They wanted us to hold on, which meant more men, for we were consuming a hundred men a day. Thus we needed a hundred fresh troops a day. All they had to do was ask for volunteers, put a parachute on them, and push them out of the plane.... But Sauvagnac wanted them to have a certificate, which was absurd. It would have set their arrival back a month when we needed them right away."

At 8 P.M., as the artillery barrage ended, Giap threw his divisions against four strongpoints on both sides of the base—Dominique 3 and

Eliane 1 to the east of the Nam Yum, and Huguette 4 and 5 to the west. Each regiment had three battalions of about five hundred men, divided into three companies. The 316th Division attacked Eliane 1, the low, sausage-shaped hill. To its west was Dominique 3, wedged between RP41 and a dead arm of the Nam Yum, where Lieutenant Brunbrouck had made his stand on March 30–31. On the western bank, the 308th Division moved on Huguette 4 and 5, about five hundred yards west of the airstrip. In his simultaneous attacks on four strongpoints, Giap was counting on the French scarcity of manpower, assuming that they would have to constantly move men from one emergency to another.

Eliane 1 was manned by units of Major Jean Bréchignac's paratroopers. Bréchignac, in command of the eastern bank, was stationed at the base of Eliane 4 in a cave he shared with Major André Botella of the 5th BPVN. Bréchignac's battalion had been reduced to three meager companies, which he rotated every forty-eight hours for the arduous duty on Eliane 1.

On May 1, Captain Marcel Clédic's 2nd Company came down from Eliane 1 and was replaced by Lieutenant René Leguère's 3rd Company. Clédic was red-eyed from lack of sleep. Eliane 1 was so churned up by artillery fire from three hundred yards to the southeast that the men of the 2nd Company could not protect themselves. As Warrant Officer Cordier recalled, "It became impossible to dig shelters in the plowed-up ground. Every time you stuck a shovel in you hit a corpse."

Lieutenant Leguère was in a command post with a roof of sandbags and logs. A mortar round went right through it. In the trenches the mixture of mud and dust made it hard to breathe. At around half past eight, spotters in the forward trenches told Leguère they were seeing what looked like an entire battalion scaling the slope. It was led by Le Van Duy, commander of the 811th Company of the 98th Regiment of the 316th Division. Leguère asked for machine-gun fire from Eliane 4. The reply came: "Impossible. The Viets are attacking everywhere."

As the Vietminh fought their way up to the command post on the summit, the *bo doi* carrying the flag fell ten yards from the top. His friend picked up the blood-stained flag, covered his comrade with a blanket, and kept going. By this time, Bréchignac had sent over Lieutenant Yves Périou and the 1st Company, who fought their way up Eliane 1's southwestern slope. Périou appeared at the command post, Colt in hand, out of breath, and said: "The Viets are right behind us. We've got to get out." They were forced off the summit and led about fifty survivors to the reverse slope. The only way out was the trench back to Eliane 4.

Leguère led the way with his radioman, followed by Périou and the surviving paratroopers. Inside the trench, the dead and the wounded littering the ground had attracted multitudes of flies that got into their nostrils and stuck to their lips and the corners of their eyes. The Vietminh flung grenades into the trench, killing Périou and the radioman and wounding Leguère, who made it back to Eliane 4 with seventeen others, all that was left of the two companies of paras. Eliane 1 had fallen.

Dominique 3, positioned between the Nam Yum and RP41, barred the access to the Bailey bridge and controlled the gap between Eliane 1 and 2. Manning the strongpoint were Captain Filaudeau and the same two companies of Algerians who had been stationed there since the "debouch at zero" epic of March 30–31. Then a lieutenant, Filaudeau had by May 1 been promoted to captain. He had seeded the barbed wire with six hundred mines, but needed more men. Major Maurice Chenel and his company of Thais were sent in.

Colonel Langlais, who didn't trust the Algerians or the Thais, and who hoped to prevent the Vietminh from attacking central command down RP41, sent over the 3rd Company of Bigeard's 6th BPC, led by Captain Robert Perret. By the time Perret got there, mortar fire had churned the wire. Perret asked for more wire. "I didn't want to be swallowed like a raw egg," he recalled. By nightfall, Filaudeau said, "we could see the coolies digging trenches toward us. The *bo dois* came out of the trenches and threw grenades in our wire to blow up the mines."

The first Vietminh assault was thrown back, but a second wave broke through the wire and into the trenches, where Perret could see shadowy forms shouting in Vietnamese, while the Algerians jumped from trench to trench trying to escape. Perret radioed that the blockhouse had been destroyed. He hid in a muddy shell hole but was captured. Dominique 3 fell before dawn on May 2.

On the western face of the perimeter, Giap's 120mm mortars had been installed on the former French strongpoints of the Anne-Maries, about a mile north of the Huguettes. The northernmost French-held strongpoint, Huguette 5, defended by two platoons of Legionnaires commanded by Second Lieutenant Alain de Stabenrath, took a pounding. At 2 A.M., the men of the Vietminh 88th Regiment, who had dug the trenches across the airstrip, came right up to the wire and attacked. Lieutenant Pierre Jauze, holding a crenel facing west, had prepared twenty grenades and twenty submachine-gun clips. "Then a bunch of Viets jumped me," he recalled. "I didn't know where they'd come from. They tied my hands and took my jump boots and I walked barefoot for two hours and found myself in a clearing with some Moroccans."

Lieutenant Stabenrath, hit in the stomach, got tangled in the barbed wire while trying to escape and couldn't get up. Three of his Legionnaires dragged him back to central command, where Dr. Hantz operated on him, but he died of dysentery a few days later.

Huguette 5 having fallen, Huguette 4 now became the northernmost strongpoint, held by Captain Lucciani and his Foreign Legion paratroopers. That night Huguette 4 fought off three assaults from the 88th Regiment. Lucciani had been blinded in one eye, and his head was bandaged. But at dawn, Huguette 4 still held.

In a single night, May 1–2, the garrison had lost 331 killed or missing, 168 wounded, and three centers of resistance—Eliane 1, Dominique 3, and Huguette 5. In the surgical units, Dr. Gindrey recalled, "we were veritable zombies. I operated in a second state. Sometimes I had to be held up. Amputations were performed on stretchers with the surgeon on his knees. There was mud everywhere and no place to put the wounded. If we put them in trenches, the trenches collapsed."

Separated from the main base, Isabelle had a distinct personality, situated on flat terrain in the middle of rice paddies, astride the Nam Yum. Its garrison of thirteen hundred, made up of Thais, Algerians, and Legionnaires, was uneven in quality. They had already shown that if they were sent up the road to reinforce Castries, they would take serious losses. Thus, Isabelle played only a small part in the final battle.

Isabelle was divided into five strongpoints, one of which, across the Nam Yum, was manned by Lieutenant Wieme and his Thais. On May 1, Isabelle was pounded by Viet artillery like the rest of the base, and the shells sent up geysers of mud. At nightfall the Wieme strongpoint was attacked and fought over, but held with the help of Lieutenant Préaud's tanks. Isabelle still had tanks, though the main base did not. By dawn, however, the strongpoint was so torn up that it became indefensible. Colonel Lalande pulled the men back across the river and abandoned the stronghold. Isabelle had nine killed and forty-two wounded, and only six of its howitzers were still firing.

On the morning of May 2, Castries reported what he saw on his wall map: "We have lost Eliane 1, Dominique 3, and Huguette 5 and the Wieme stronghold at Isabelle, but we are launching a counterattack. The strongpoints were literally swamped by the Viet assaults. We have no reserve troops and we ask for a reinforcement battalion."

Giap's intelligence told him that on May 2, Navarre flew to Hanoi for an urgent meeting with Cogny and other officers. Giap wondered whether Navarre had finally realized his mistake in spreading his forces thin by sending them to irrelevant fronts in central Annam and Laos, leaving him no reinforcements for Dien Bien Phu.

In Hanoi, Navarre decided to send Castries an elite battalion, the 1st BPC (colonial paratroopers), led by Captain Guy de Bazin de Bezon. The battalion was alerted at 9 A.M. on May 2 at their barracks, but because of bad weather, heavy flak, and supply demands, only two and a half companies were dropped over the next four days.

Captain Jean Pouget had arrived in Indochina in 1953 as Navarre's aide-de-camp, and could often be seen standing behind Navarre in official photographs. Pouget decided in January 1954 that he wanted to be in a combat unit. He was transferred to the 1st BPC, the battalion that Navarre had just designated to jump over Dien Bien Phu. Pouget was told on the morning of May 2 that he'd be jumping that night.

At lunch at the officer's mess in the Hanoi Citadelle, Pouget spotted General Pierre Bodet, Navarre's man in Hanoi, who had just been promoted to four stars. Pouget, noticing that Bodet had bags under his eyes from lack of sleep, joined him at his table with the intelligence officer Lieutenant Ferrandi.

"Navarre is arriving at four this afternoon," Bodet said. "I'll go to the airport. But it's all over. Dien Bien Phu will fall tonight or tomorrow."

"I didn't see General Cogny this morning," Ferrandi said. "As usual he was in his office with his favorite reporters, Lucien Bodard and Max Clos."

"Cogny tries to imitate de Lattre by talking to the press," Bodet said, "but he has neither the grandeur nor the talent. . . . It took Navarre a long time to lose his confidence in Cogny. He could not believe the degree of duplicity."

"Giap doesn't have the same scruples," Ferrandi said. "If anyone disobeys, it's the firing squad."

In fact, on that very day, Navarre threatened Cogny that he would have him investigated by military security for defeatist press leaks.

Pouget rose and excused himself.

"Join us tomorrow," Bodet said.

"Tomorrow I'll be in Dien Bien Phu."

Bodet's face reddened with anger: "Why didn't you say anything?" he asked. "All this is so stupid. The French people don't give a fuck, the government is hopeless, the generals don't believe in victory, and the volunteers jump into the jaws of the monster. No, it's too stupid!"

Pouget did not jump that night. No planes were available. But his unit waited at Hanoi's Gia Lam airport, and the next day, 135 of them jumped, the 3rd Company of the 1st BPC.

The United States and Britain Are in Complete Disarray

On May 1 in Geneva, the weather was lovely, and Shuckburgh spent the morning taking the sun on the terrace of Le Reposoir. At noon, he and Eden went to Bidault's villa, where Dulles had already arrived. Most of the talk was about who should take the chair when the Indochina part of the conference opened in a week's time. Eden proposed the prime minister of Ceylon, in order to bring in a member of the Colombo Conference of Britain's Asian allies.

With Dulles was Walter Bedell Smith, who had just arrived to lead the U.S. delegation. Eden had known Smith since the Second World War, when he had been Eisenhower's chief of staff, and from the first had liked him. He was touched when Smith greeted him effusively, after the rough treatment he was getting from Dulles, who resented having gotten Congress and public opinion steamed up over united action, with no results. *The*

Washington Post wrote of "a major defeat in American diplomacy," and there was a tendency to blame the British. But as they left Bidault's villa, Smith said in an aside to Eden, "Don't pay too much attention to the stupid things being said in the U.S.A."

Eden and Shuckburgh speculated whether Eisenhower, who was close to Smith, might be in sympathy with the British line. Eden hoped he would oppose Admiral Radford's plugging of air-sea intervention. He now wanted Dulles to leave as soon as possible. There was no doubt, Shuckburgh felt, "that they have got thoroughly on each other's nerves and are both behaving like prima donnas."

The French also saw Smith as an improvement over Dulles. As Jean Chauvel described him, "Smith was rather short and thin, with a face of bumps and hollows that gave him the appearance of having swallowed a bitter pill. As I later learned, he had stomach trouble, which led to brief outbursts of anger. He liked authenticity, he didn't take wooden coins. I had nothing but praise for his candor at a time when his government had a tendency to lead us on a wild goose chase. He had no confidence in Geneva or its outcome, and was suspicious of what he called 'intellectual generals,' by whom he meant Navarre."

As Eden prepared for a final dinner that evening with Dulles, Chou En-lai was sending Mao Tse-tung a report on his meal with Molotov and Eden at the Soviet villa the day before. The conference that day, he said, had adjourned in less than thirty minutes. "Although the U.S. fired many blanks, they could not scare anyone but themselves. The U.S. is attempting to form an alliance of invader nations of Southeast Asia. However, Britain is still hesitating. . . . Dulles [has] decided to run away [from the conference] and leave the problem to [Smith]."

Chou said Eden asked him whether the Soviet and Chinese sides could push for the withdrawal of the wounded from Dien Bien Phu.

Chou replied: "It is better to have the two belligerent parties discuss this directly." He refused to get involved.

Molotov said during the postprandial talks that Britain and the United States spoke the same language.

Eden responded: "We have nothing in common with the U.S. except the same language."

Chou concluded: "Since the U.S. is not reconciled to the loss of China it uses every means at its disposal to threaten and massacre people. . . . The American way of doing things only makes its own people nervous."

The farewell dinner for Dulles did not go well. The principal members of the U.S. delegation were there—Smith, Livingston Merchant, and the bibulous Walter Robertson. As Eden put it, he and Shuckburgh "were subjected to a prolonged and somewhat heated onslaught."

Dulles said the situation between the two countries was "very disturbing." The United States and Britain "were in complete disarray."

Eden said he did not understand what steps he was being asked to take.

Dulles said he was asking only for moral support in any action the United States might take.

Eden asked what sort of action Dulles had in mind.

Dulles said that that had not been decided.

Smith said that Dien Bien Phu could not be saved, but that they should find a way to defend Thailand, Burma, and Malaya.

Eden said that if the Americans went into Indochina, the Chinese would step up their participation, and the next thing you knew, the Americans and the Chinese would be fighting each other, and that could be the start of a third world war.

In the meantime, according to Eden, Walter Robertson, "whose approach to these questions is so emotional as to be impervious to argument or indeed to facts, was keeping up a sort of 'theme song' to the effect that there were in Indochina some 300,000 men who were anxious to fight against the Vietminh."

Eden told him, "If they are so anxious I cannot understand why they don't do so. The Americans have put in nine times more supplies of matériel than the Chinese, and plenty must be available for their use."

Dulles and the others then introduced the topic of training Vietnamese forces, which they admitted would take two years. The problem was what would happen in the meantime. Dulles said they would have to hold some sort of bridgehead, as had been done in Korea prior to the Inchon landings.

After dinner, Eden told Shuckburgh that he could just see himself getting up in the House of Commons after U.S. forces landed in Indochina "to direct and train the Vietnamese," and being asked, "Did you know and approve this move?" Eden was convinced the Americans wanted to replace the French and run Indochina themselves.

He reported to London that night that "the Americans are deeply aggrieved by our refusal to support them in such military measures as they think advisable. . . . At the same time they have no plan of their own, but are searching about for some expedient."

The following evening, May 2, a conciliatory letter arrived from Dulles, asking for a five-power meeting in Washington—the United States, Britain, France, Australia, and New Zealand—to get back on track for united action. Eden saw the invitation as a trap and stuck to the British line that there should be no discussions until after Geneva. He reported: "We cannot give the Americans the moral support they seek. . . . They have not worked out their ideas at all clearly. . . . We must refuse to be drawn into the Indochina war."

According to Bidault, when Dulles left Geneva on the evening of May 3, he had briefed Smith on the U.S. position regarding Indochina: "No cease-fire and no partition." Bidault saw Dulles's "verbal belligerence" as his only bargaining chip. As long as Dulles made threats, Bidault might be able to coax the Vietminh into an "honorable" cease-fire. But after Dulles left, Bidault felt that Washington was sending mixed signals. Eisenhower was saying that the United States could not be "the gladiator to the world," and should seek a middle ground between an unacceptable loss of Indochina and an unattainable victory over the Vietminh.

Prior to his departure, Dulles had a final meeting with Jean Chauvel, and asked him whether France could hang on in the Tonkin and Mekong deltas, with the help of U.S. airpower, for the two years it would take to form a Vietnamese army that could reconquer all of Indochina. Dulles seemed to be hoping that the intransigence of the Vietminh at Geneva would make agreement impossible.

Chauvel took in every word that Dulles uttered, not knowing quite what to make of it. He was also told by his military aides that tens of thousands of U.S. Marines were available to help the French during the two-year interim. Where was all this coming from? he wondered. When he questioned Smith about the Marines, the reply was that they did not exist. Chauvel asked what the United States would do if the Geneva talks broke down. Smith said: "Nothing." Chauvel realized that France was alone.

As for the Vietnamese army, the high command in Hanoi had finally accepted that it was a mirage, because it lacked the will to fight. In the fall of 1953, it had a total of 112 battalions, more than 200,000 men. The plan was to reach 330,000 by the end of 1954, but the units were being formed too fast to be well trained. The officers were mediocre. Troop morale was low, for they were despised by most of the population. The Vietminh were seen as fighting for independence, while Bao Dai's men were viewed as French stooges. The recruitment campaign of 1954, announced on April 12, drafted all able-bodied men from the ages of twenty to twenty-five. It failed completely. Half of those called joined the Vietminh. Most of the others hid in their villages or changed their names or bought exemptions. Only one in ten of those called joined.

In the meantime, Shuckburgh had persuaded Eden to see Dulles off at the airport. Eden agreed, but said he was giving no ground on any meeting until Geneva was over. "My instinct is all against any concession to Dulles," he said. He thought he might find an ally in Smith, whom he invited to dinner at Le Reposoir after Dulles's departure. Smith told him: "American ground forces will go into Indochina over my dead body." Shuckburgh hoped that the entente between Eden and Smith would heal the rift in Western ranks.

Why the Fuck Did They Send Us Here?

At Dien Bien Phu on May 2 and 3, there was a pause in the battle as the Vietminh divisions regrouped and took stock. The rain continued to fall, as did the artillery shells, but there were no major battles. Despite heavy rain, at 1:15 A.M. on May 3, the first elements of the promised paratroop battalion (the 1st BPC) were dropped over the base—107 men of Lieutenant Marcel Edmé's 2nd Company.

Made up of French and Vietnamese paras, the 1st BPC had been fighting in Laos for two straight months when they were called back to Hanoi in March for guard duty at Gia Lam airport. They were still close to exhaustion, and their commander, Guy de Bazin de Bezon, resented being chosen for what he thought of as a futile mission.

For Edmé, jumping involved a personal dilemma. His wife, Maryse, was eight months pregnant and he was haunted by the conviction that he would never know his child. As Edmé's company flew over the base, each Dakota carrying two sticks of eight, recently installed Vietminh search-lights crisscrossed the sky. The drop zone, lit up by a fiery beacon, was so small that the Dakota had only six seconds to drop the first stick of eight paras attached to the static line. It took another pass to drop the second stick, and there were three who refused to jump, all young Vietnamese.

Back at the Hanoi airport, Pouget and his 3rd Company were waiting. On the evening of May 3, Colonel Sauvagnac himself arrived to tell them they would be jumping that night. He gave them a lecture on the difficul-ties of the jump: no real drop zone, approximate beacons, violent flak. Pouget's Dakota, flying over the clouds, arrived at the base around 3 A.M. on May 4 and plunged into the midst of tracers and flak. Pouget saw the tracers rising, and realized that the Viets knew the route the Dakota had to take to cover the DZ. He could see the flaming cross below him. He jumped, floated down, and landed in the mud. That night, 121 men were dropped.

Pouget headed for Langlais' command post and found Langlais at his desk, looking haggard. Bigeard was there, standing against the wall, and told Pouget: "Assemble your company at dawn." Castries came in, walking with a cane and looking ten years older than when Pouget had last seen him.

A loudspeaker in Langlais' office, which relayed the radio traffic from the remaining strongpoints, crackled. The report was from an officer on Huguette 4, held by Captain Lucciani, who had suffered multiple wounds. Reinforcing Lucciani's Legionnaires was a platoon of Moroccans. Huguette 4, now the northernmost strongpoint, only seven hundred yards from Castries' bunker, had come under attack by Vietminh compa-nies emerging from flooded trenches.

The Vietminh seemed to have timed their assault with the drop over the central camp, during which the *luciole* (firefly) flares had to be extin-guished. Taking advantage of the darkness, the Viets overran Huguette 4.

Suddenly, over the loudspeaker in Langlais' office, a desperate voice was heard. It was the lieutenant commanding the platoon of Moroccans.

"Where are the reinforcements?" he asked. "The Viets are attacking. I can hear them coming down the trench. . . . Here they are." And then a shout: "Aaahhh!"

"It's Huguette 4, isn't it?" Castries asked. Then, turning to Pouget: "What in the world are they doing in Hanoi? How long do they think we can hold?"

"Negotiations have opened in Geneva," Pouget said. "An armistice could be signed in a few days."

"Tell them to get moving," Castries said.

By 4 A.M. on May 4, Huguette 4 had fallen. All Castries had left on the west bank of the Nam Yum was a network of improvised small strong-points to defend the Bailey bridge and the central command area. On the east bank, Eliane 2, 3, and 4 still held. The night had cost 164 dead and missing and 58 wounded. Castries' message to Hanoi at 9 A.M. reflected the exasperation of this unusually equable man after being an auditory witness to the death of an officer: "Our provisions of all kinds are at their lowest. . . . We don't have enough ammunition to stop enemy attacks. . . . I am told of the risks to air crews, but every man here runs infinitely greater risks—there cannot be a double standard. . . . I have an absolute need of provisions in massive quantities. The very small size of the center of re-sistance and the fact that the elements holding the perimeter cannot leave their shelters without coming under fire from snipers and recoilless guns, means that more and more cases are no longer retrievable. . . . I cannot count on recovering even half of what is dropped. . . . This situation can-not go on."

Castries' critique of the air force was vigorously rebutted by the air commanders. In a postbattle report, Colonel Jean Nicot, in command of air transport, said: "If I refused to send pilots in at low altitude on daylight flights to a certain death, it was because their sacrifice would have been useless, since their planes would have crashed with the cargo they were carrying. I couldn't spare the planes and I couldn't spare the pilots."

Before the 1955 commission, General Jean Dechaux, commander of the Northern Tactical Air Group, explained: "They didn't understand the aerial photographs we sent them. They were in their shelters and didn't grasp the extension of the enemy trench network. The photographs were an essential source of information, taken, developed, and dropped on the base within twenty-four hours."

In addition, Dechaux said, when the planes flew over the base with designated missions, Castries would often give them a different, more urgent mission, which created confusion. The air force planned its targets carefully and did not like improvisation. Castries wanted bombs dropped just outside the barbed wire of positions under attack, but in the thick haze of battle the targets were clouded. The planes had to drop their bombs with precision while avoiding flak. And what was the point of dropping a thousand-pound bomb on a small number of men? It was like using a pile driver to kill a mosquito.

It was held against Castries that he didn't mingle with the men, that he never left his bunker. But that morning of May 4, he decided to visit the hospital. Perhaps he had been moved by the last words of the young officer on Huguette 4. He wanted to lift the morale of the wounded by awarding decorations, though the medals lay unretrieved in a case in no-man's-land.

Dr. Grauwin was his guide through the two main infirmaries from which spread out twenty overcrowded trenches, steaming, putrid, rat-infested bowels that stank of rotting flesh. It was hot in there, and Castries wore shorts and a short-sleeved khaki shirt. "I've come to see the wounded," he told Grauwin. "I don't have the decorations. They were dropped during the night behind Viet lines."

Castries was thorough. He visited every man in the trenches. Sometimes he slipped in the mud, but he righted himself. He stopped before each man, who told his story, where and when he was hit. Then, with a forced smile he said: *"Médaille militaire"* or *"Légion d'honneur."* Then he explained that he did not actually have the medals.

It was a disturbing scene—the mud, the bloody bandages, the naked men on stretchers, the jump boots under beds, and the despair of those whom no medal could salvage. In a hallway, he came upon the Legionnaire sergeant Carnot, who had been hit in the spine. It was clear that Carnot did not have long to live. His belly was swollen, his eyes half-shut, he was sweating and unable to speak.

"Take his name," Castries told an aide. "I'm giving him the *Médaille militaire* with Palm, but make sure it's not awarded posthumously."

He stopped before another stretcher, where a man was laying motionless, eyes shut. "How do you feel?" Castries asked. There was no reply.

"The general is talking to you," Grauwin said.

The man tried to sit up and said, "My respects, my general."

"I give you the Croix de Guerre with Palm."

The next man was Corporal Simon Marie, a paratrooper who explained that a bullet had hit a grenade on his belt.

"How do you feel?"

"I'm fine, but my right eye . . . "

"How old are you?"

"Eighteen."

"We'll take care of you. Tomorrow you'll be in Hanoi."

This was of course impossible. Castries wanted to shake Marie's hand, but both hands were bandaged.

Castries saw them all and told them they would soon be in Hanoi: the man whose fractured jaw had been reassembled with wire and who had to be fed through the nose; Heinz, the triple amputee. Castries held out his hand, but there was no hand to shake.

On the way out, they passed through the surgery unit where Dr. Gindrey was operating. Castries stopped and watched for a long time.

Captain Pouget had been told that he should take his 3rd Company to Eliane 3, where it would be held in reserve for Eliane 2 across RP41. He assembled his company at dawn on May 4 and started out through the trenches. It was raining hard and their brand-new camouflage uniforms were soon filthy. They were up to their knees in mud and corpses. The mud stuck to their legs and they had to stop every few feet due to artillery fire.

Eliane 3 was one of the "low Elianes," dug into the riverbank flats between the Nam Yum and RP41, two hundred yards west of Eliane 2. On Eliane 3, Pouget and his men found troops of all ranks and races, dirty and unshaven, who had formed improvised small units. The post looked like a hobo jungle. The men had been pushed to the limit of their endurance and had what American units in the Pacific during World War II had called the "thousand-yard stare." They were running out of water but still had some Vinogel. Eliane 3 was the most spread out of the strongpoints, where Dr.

Vidal's hospital, which had posted a SOLD OUT sign, had to accommodate three hundred wounded. Those who weren't stretcher cases manned gun emplacements. Pouget saw amputees behind machine guns, being fed ammunition by other amputees.

At 2:40 A.M. on May 5, another batch of paras were dropped over the base. Five Dakotas unloaded seventy-three men of Captain Trehiou's 4th Company, plus the command unit of Captain Bazin de Bezon's. The captain was in a foul mood, and when he showed up at Langlais' command post, he said: "Why the fuck did they send us here? My men are tired and it's over."

Tempers were short all around and Bigeard told him: "We're not asking your opinion. We're asking you to get mangled like us." That did not take long, for a few hours later, a shell burst mangled Bazin's thigh.

Trehiou had broken his ankle prior to the jump and had it plastered in Hanoi. When he presented himself at the command post, Langlais said, seeing his leg: "Jumping at night did not bring you luck. But they fixed you up fast."

"It was plastered in Hanoi," Trehiou said, "and it held."

"Are you trying to tell me," Langlais asked, "that you jumped into this battle at night with a broken leg?"

"I wasn't about to let my company leave without me."

On the morning of May 5, Pouget and his 3rd Company were sent to Eliane 2 with Lieutenant Edmé and his 2nd Company to relieve the Legionnaires under Captain Coutant. Again, it took two hours to get through the trenches. Pouget arrived at the hulking Eliane 2 and was taken in charge by the round-faced and avuncular Coutant. Like Pouget, Coutant had been stationed in Saigon behind a desk, running the Legion's social services. After Béatrice fell in mid-March, he volunteered for Dien Bien Phu.

Coutant took Pouget on a tour of the many-sided hill with its broken shelters, ruined trenches, and soggy sandbags. On the flat slope known as the Champs-Élysées, Pouget commented on the smell. "There are fifteen hundred Viets buried here," Coutant said. Coutant then debriefed Pouget, saying he would need three thousand grenades a night. He told Pouget about the "death volunteers," with twenty pounds of TNT strapped to their chests, who came out of the trenches and threw themselves at the blockhouses. The Legionnaires had only seconds to fire before they reached their targets. Coutant also mentioned the digging noises.

When Coutant's Legionnaires left Eliane 2, they were so happy they sprinted down the hill. Pouget and his company occupied the summit, where the carcass of a tank was half sunk in the mud. Edmé's company was positioned on the southern and eastern slopes. The defenses were shredded and had to be rebuilt. Master Sergeant Chabrier, in Edmé's company on the southern slope, heard digging and reasoned that the Viets were not ready to explode the tunnel. He sent a patrol out to blow up the tunnel, but the Vietminh company defending the entrance stopped them at the wire and wiped them out.

That day, Giap got the word from the 174th Regiment that the tunnel had been packed with fifty packets of dynamite weighing forty-five pounds each—more than a ton of dynamite. The explosion of the tunnel would be the signal for the general offensive.

All of Vietnam Will Be Lost Except for Some Enclave

On May 4, conditions at Le Reposoir improved with the arrival of a new chef, who gave Eden and Shuckburgh an "exquisite lunch." Eden was irritated over an article in the *Journal de Genève* that said he was "mediating" between East and West. He used rugby terms to explain his tactics to Shuckburgh: "I am inside right, the Americans are outside right. Molotov is inside left, Chou is outside left."

Bidault and Chauvel came to dine at the villa. Eden recalled that the two Frenchmen were too worried about the Laniel government going down in defeat to focus on the immediate problem of the conference. Shuckburgh described Bidault as "half in despair, half courageous; half helpless, half vigorous. Terrible descriptions of Dien Bien Phu."

May 5 was "gloriously sunny." The Russians came to dinner and Eden was pleased that Molotov and Gromyko didn't try to score points. Eden said this was the most difficult conference he had ever taken part in. The main thing to work for regarding Indochina, he proposed, was an armistice. Molotov agreed but added that conditions must be attached. It was during dinner that they agreed to rotate the chair between them when Indochina started rather than among the nine participants. The implication was that the success of the conference depended on the collaboration of the British and the Soviets. Each had allies whose views were more extreme. Eden described the "strong view" the Americans had regarding China. Molotov said it was pointless to build up Chiang again and the Americans should get used to it. Molotov added "with a frosty smile" that Dulles had succeeded in never once acknowledging that Chou existed. Both men agreed that if matters weren't settled in Geneva, it could mean the start of World War III.

Shuckburgh, who was suspicious of the Russians, blamed Eden for drinking too much wine and doing all the talking. Eden's theme was the moderate position of the Soviets and the United Kingdom, with implications that the Americans were unreasonable and the French were hopeless. Afterward, Eden said: "I really enjoy talking to Molotov, he has mellowed." Then: "Have I done wrong?" There was, of course, replied Shuckburgh, something in the idea that Molotov wants peace in Korea and a settlement in Indochina. Eden said it was because he feared that a continuation of the fighting would lead to a world war. If that was the case, said Shuckburgh, his fear should be encouraged.

On the morning of May 5, back from Geneva, Dulles reviewed the crisis with the president at the White House. He blamed the British and the French for undercutting his position. He said the French had never formally asked for a U.S. air strike. There had been only "one or two oral and informal requests." And yet, as the record showed, how much more formal could one get than a letter from Foreign Minister Bidault and a direct verbal request from Premier Laniel?

"What the French fear," Dulles said, "is that if the U.S. is brought into the struggle, France will not have a free hand to sell and get out." As for the British, they wanted partition. They wanted the removal of all foreign troops followed by an election. "All of Vietnam would be lost," he said, "except for some enclave." Dulles concluded that "conditions do not justify the United States entry into Indochina as a belligerent at this time." Eisenhower willingly agreed, since that had been his policy all along.

That afternoon, Dulles briefed congressional leaders for an hour and a half at the State Department. The usual suspects attended: Knowland and Saltonstall and five others on the Republican side of the Senate, Lyndon Johnson and Richard Russell and three others from the Democrats. From the House, Speaker Joseph Martin and six other Republicans were there, along with John McCormack and four other Democrats.

Dulles repeated what he had told Eisenhower. Lyndon Johnson, the Senate minority leader, asked a probing question: Had not the first request from the French come after General Ely had been given the impression in Washington that the United States would intervene? Did Ely get that impression from Dulles or from the Pentagon? Dulles replied that it definitely did not come from him. He could not really say where Ely might have gotten it, and did not mention Radford.

On May 6, Dulles attended the weekly meeting of the National Security Council. He mentioned that the French were preparing to offer a cease-fire in Indochina. Robert Cutler, the special assistant to the president for national security affairs, said some members of the Planning Board were opposed to a cease-fire. General Charles Bonesteel argued that Southeast Asia might be lost unless the United States intervened. Others said a cease-fire would destroy the French will to win and that the Vietminh would "covertly evade cease-fire controls." Then other arguments were expressed: that the French government was incompetent, that the United States had no business "bailing out colonial France," and that the United States should not rush into every trouble spot on the globe alone. Still others advocated U.S. military intervention under the usual conditions— freedom for the Associated States and training of the Vietnamese army by the American military.

In Geneva, discussions on Korea continued to be deadlocked until June 15, when that part of the conference disbanded. It was clear that no action would be taken without starting another war. Korea remained partitioned, and remains partitioned to this day.

On May 6, the secret conversations on the Dien Bien Phu wounded resumed. Wang Ping-nan, the secretary-general of the Chinese delegation, told Colonel Guillermaz that "the situation of the wounded can be discussed as soon as the Indochina conference opens by direct contact between the French and the Vietnamese delegations." The Vietminh wanted to be sure that there would be no last-minute objections to the seating of their delegation. Bidault wired Paris: "The Chinese gave us the same reply as Mr. Molotov eight days ago." He sent out a press release saying: "Our contact with the Chinese delegation has received no other answer than to put off this urgent and humanitarian matter until the plenary sessions of the conference."

Looks Like This Is It, Son

On the morning of May 6 at Dien Bien Phu, the sun broke through the mist and a clear day allowed twenty-nine Dakotas and twenty-five Flying Boxcars to drop 196 tons of supplies over the shrunken perimeter, none of which were recovered. A massive air strike of forty-six B-26s protected the transport planes on their final drop. Castries had sent an urgent wire to Hanoi that morning: "We have to limit our artillery fire due to lack of munitions. Enemy artillery, mortars, and recoilless 75s have caused additional losses due to the trenches collapsing because of rain."

One of the American CAT pilots who volunteered for the daytime drops was Arthur Wilson, who was unloading artillery pieces over Isabelle, fastened to three parachutes, when he took a 37mm hit in the aft section of the port tail boom and lost elevator control. He was able to make it back to the Cat Bi airport in Haiphong.

Another C-119 took off at 3:15 P.M. carrying ten thousand pounds of artillery ammunition. The pilot was James McGovern, with copilot Wally Buford. A French crew of four "kickers"—led by Second Lieutenant Jean Arlaux—were assigned to toss the cases from the back of the C-119.

McGovern was a picturesque character. He weighed over three hundred pounds, and with his aloha shirts and shorts, and his hair in a military cut, shaved on the sides and short on top, he looked like a Honolulu beachcomber. He had flown for the Flying Tigers during the Second World War and boasted that he had shot down nine Japanese Zeros. His plane had gone down over Japanese-occupied China, which led to the running joke that the Japs had freed him so they wouldn't have to feed him. His bulk, however, made him averse to parachuting from a stricken plane.

This was his forty-fifth mission over the base, and as he headed for Isabelle, he knew that the cargo had to be dropped close to the ground to fall within the diminishing perimeter. His C-119 plunged through the hail of flak. A metal shard hit the left engine, which began leaking oil. McGovern feathered the engine and a second shell ripped off a tail section. Unable to hold his altitude, he restarted the engine.

Steve Kusak, piloting a C-119 near McGovern, suggested that the crew parachute over Isabelle. McGovern said he was flying too low to jump. He headed northwest into Laos, looking for a spot to crash-land. Kusak stayed in radio contact. After a while, McGovern saw a winding stream in a narrow valley where he could attempt a belly landing. They were about a hundred miles northwest of Dien Bien Phu on the Nam Het River. When McGovern came down, his wingtip touched the side of a hill and the plane flipped over and exploded as it hit the ground. His final message to Kusak was: "Looks like this is it, son."

The C-119 had broken in two. In the back, two of the four "kickers" survived, Arlaux and an Algerian named Moussa. "I remember the explosion when we hit the ground," Arlaux recalled. "When I woke up I was on a sampan, with Moussa beside me moaning." They had been captured by Pathet Lao regulars, who were taking them downriver to a camp. Arlaux had terrible back pains. He didn't know it, but he had fractured four vertebrae. "My ring finger was bleeding," he said. "One of the Pathet Lao had pulled off my wedding band." Moussa died in captivity, but Arlaux survived. When he was freed he weighed ninety pounds.

For You the War Is Over

On the morning of Thursday, May 6, it became clear to Langlais and Bigeard, from both the unnatural calm and intelligence reports, that Giap was about to launch a massive attack. They studied what was left of their defensive positions: To the north, Tourret on Epervier with the remains of the 8th Choc. To the west, Major Guiraud and 160 Legionnaires hung on to what was left of the Huguettes, renamed Lili, to which were added Major Nicolas and his Moroccans. To the southwest, the two Claudines, dangerously close to central command, were held by Major Clémençon's Legionnaires. On the east bank, Pouget and the 1st BPC were on Eliane 2.

On Eliane 4, Bréchignac and what was left of his paras of the 2nd Battalion of the 1st RCP, and Botella and his Vietnamese. On Eliane 3, between the river and RP41, some Legionnaires and a platoon of Moroccans. The situation was extreme but not hopeless, Bigeard said.

At noon, Castries summoned his battalion commanders to discuss the possibility of a breakout—the plan known as Operation ALBATROSS. Bigeard inauspiciously called it *"percée de sang"*—the bloodletting. As Castries told the 1955 commission: "When you're fighting people who know the jungle and who hold the points of passage, it would be like fighting in a tunnel. Since we could not maneuver outside the trails, it would be easy to stop us, but part of the units up front might get through."

The ALBATROSS plan called for dividing the breakout units into three detachments: Colonel Lalande at Isabelle; Lieutenant Colonel Maurice Lemeunier with the Legionnaires; and the paras with Langlais and Bigeard. "I would stay behind," Castries recalled, "with three battalions and the artillery and make as much noise as possible to cover their departure and protect the wounded . . . but it was a desperate solution." The sortie was planned for nightfall on May 7.

That morning, the 255th Battalion of Giap's 174th Regiment fell back from Eliane 2, where it had been protecting the sappers. Their work was now done. Giap decided not to wait for the explosion but to attack at once. The 249th Battalion, commanded by Vu Dinh Hoe, divided into two wings, one for the southwest of Eliane 2, and the other on RP41, to block reinforcements and isolate the big hill.

Each of the men on the base prepared for the battle in his own way. Some wrote letters that couldn't be mailed. Captain Yves Hervouet asked Dr. Grauwin to remove the plaster cast from his broken arm, so that he could climb back into the turret of a disabled tank, if only to fire its 75. In the afternoon, Langlais and Bigeard visited the remaining strongpoints. They saw walking wounded, waiting for the end. Behind the last two Elianes on the east bank, 2 and 4, were a batch of low Elianes, strung along the Nam Yum, dug into the flats, the last barriers to the Bailey bridge and the central camp. These low Elianes, 3, 10, 11, and 13, were mostly improvised posts manned by mixed units that had been cobbled together. Eliane 10, just west of RP41 and two hundred yards from Eliane 4, was commanded by Lieutenant Hervé Trapp, who had thirty-two men left in his company of the 6th BPC. The Viets advancing down the riverbank were so close that at 4 P.M. Trapp could see their bamboo helmets sticking up from the trenches.

At 5 P.M., thick clouds overhead began drenching the French positions. A strange silence hung over the base, like the silence in a theater when the lights go out and the curtain rises. Then it seemed that every cannon in the Vietminh arsenal was firing at once. The French heard a screeching sound they had not heard before. The Chinese-made rockets had arrived, sets of six rockets in two layers of three tubes each that fired all at once. The German Legionnaires were reminded of the "Stalin's Organs" from the eastern front in World War II. One of them compared their sound to the mewing of a cat. What the rains had not destroyed, the rockets did. A weary Bigeard, his battalion decimated, told Trapp: "Hervé, if you can't hold, fall back."

At Pouget's command post at the top of Eliane 2, they were listening to news from Geneva over Radio Hanoi. The Vietminh delegation had arrived. The talks on Indochina would begin on May 8. Then at five came the rolling thunder of 105s, 75s, and 120mm mortars fired from Mount Baldy, only a hundred yards to the east.

It was still light when the Viets attacked Eliane 2 at 6:45 P.M. A thousand men from the 98th Regiment avoided the trap of the Champs-Élysées and stormed the barbed wire on the western face. Pouget called in artillery, and when the smoke lifted there were more than a hundred bodies in the wire. The two platoons defending the western slope, commanded by Lieutenant Julien and Second Lieutenant Paul, held their ground.

Artillery support dwindled as night fell, for some of the howitzers firing from Isabelle had been knocked out. The ammunition depot for Eliane 2 was fifty yards away, but the trench from the base of the hill to the depot had collapsed. The men carrying cases of ammunition were under heavy fire. Out of a party of twenty, only one made it back to Pouget's command post with a case of grenades.

The Vietminh attacks were coming every half hour, with a seemingly unlimited number of troops. Pouget had thirty-five men at the summit and was running out of ammunition. He called headquarters and said:

"Unless you send me a company, I'm going to try and reach Eliane 3." He got the Legionnaire staff officer Michel Vadot, who told him: "I don't have a single man, not a single shell. Try to hold on until dawn."

On the southern face, another Vietminh battalion deployed under supporting fire from the fifty mortars on Baldy. They waited for the tunnel to explode. At 9:30 P.M., it seemed to Pouget that the entire hill shuddered. A slice of the hill at the southern end blew into the air. In his command post, Lieutentat Edmé was covered by an upheaval of earth and rocks, but he was not directly over the tunnel. His second platoon, however, was buried alive.

The Vietnamese sappers had miscalculated, for the tunnel did not reach the northern side where Pouget had his command post. The explosion did succeed in destroying the obstacles that had blocked previous assaults, though, and replaced them with a crater through which several Vietminh units climbed. Their advance was slowed by the ground strewn with boulders, while machine-gun fire peppered them. Pouget's men on the summit, where the destroyed tank *Bazeilles* was half sunk in the mud, got its machine gun working and fired straight down.

Edmé saw the Viet infantry come up the hill, maneuvering to the whistles of their officers, three battalions up three faces of the rise. Lieutenant Nectoux recalled: "It was impossible to be everywhere at once. The explosions, the flames, and the rain beating down on us projected us into a world that had lost all meaning." Viets jumped over the trenches and dropped grenades. Bodies lay in the mud, and it was impossible to tell which side they were from. The Viets advanced methodically, firing at every trench and opening.

At midnight, the commander of the 174th Regiment, Nguyen Huu An, ordered the final assault on Eliane 2 and broke through the last lines of defenders. "There was a flash and I knew I was hit," said Nectoux. "I heard shouting in Vietnamese and men removed my belt and took my Colt. Someone applied a bandage to my chest. I was dragged to the crest where the Viets were assembling prisoners."

Pouget saw the Viets appear on the crest, hunched over, side by side, above his command post. It took him a moment to grasp the situation. With ten men, he formed a sort of barricade made up of mud and corpses.

They threw grenades. Then something hit his helmet and his head hurt. A Viet grenade had bounced off it, burning the camouflage netting and denting the steel. Pouget threw his last grenade and passed out. When he came to, a *bo doi* stood over him and said: "You are a prisoner of the Vietnamese Popular Army. For you the war is over."

Eliane 4, sandwiched between Eliane 1 and 2, now both in the hands of the Vietminh, came under attack at around 9 P.M. It was the last bastion that could keep the Viets from crossing the river. If Eliane 4 fell, there were no more eastern defenses, except for the low Elianes along the riverbank, which were easier to overrun. Eliane 4 had a potpourri of defenders: Botella's Vietnamese paratroopers were down to a single company of 150 men. Their shelters were open to the sky, and the trenches from one shelter to the other had caved in. Bréchignac's light infantry paras (of the 2nd Battalion of the 1st RCP) were down to a hundred able-bodied men under Captain Clédic, plus Lieutenant Cesarini and his mortars.

Captain Trehiou, his ankle in a cast, was sent over on the afternoon of May 6 with his seventy-three-man 4th Company of the just arrived 1st BPC. The first wave of the Vietminh 174th Regiment was chopped up by Cesarini's mortars. The second wave ran over the corpses of the first wave. "When they came through the barbed wire," Trehiou recalled, "we shot them like rabbits, but they kept coming. We pushed back the assaults with heavy losses, then the attacks stopped and they hit us again with artillery." Bréchignac asked for counterbattery fire but the French guns were low on ammunition. Instead he was sent sixty Legionnaires, who took two hours to get across the bridge and through the trenches, suffering losses. Bréchignac launched counterattacks that held off the *bo dois* until midnight.

Under the artillery pounding, Eliane 4 was smoking like a factory chimney. Lieutenant Latanne, on the eastern crest, saw small teams begin to infiltrate. "Around three in the morning, it became impossible. Total chaos. You couldn't get anyone on the radio. I took my men down the hill. Screams and explosions . . . I was hit but I didn't know where and tried in the dark to find blood. It was my right knee. I was in a trench and couldn't move. I applied a tourniquet to my right thigh and limped along." Latanne found Rouault, the BPVN doctor, who operated on his knee and bandaged it.

At dawn on May 7, they were still fighting. On the northern face, Captain Trehiou climbed out of his trench and saw Vietminh infiltrators cleaning up the terrain. "They seemed to be firing at everything that moved. I came out with my arms in the air. I was taken prisoner and when I saw men of my company and the state they were in I realized that we had regressed into a category that was less than human."

At 7:30 A.M., the Vietminh 216th Battalion, stationed on Eliane 1, divided into three groups to storm Eliane 4. The southern tip of Eliane 1 was only 150 yards from Eliane 4's northwest façade. Clédic could see the hill swarming with *bo dois.* "They came down the hill straight at us," he recalled. "There weren't many of us left, and we'd had a hard night. We blew up our mortars and started back to central command. Grenades rained down on our trench and we realized there were Viets at both ends. Lieutenant Cesarini took shrapnel under the shoulder blade, but he could walk. Then the Viets disarmed us and took us before an officer who bragged he'd captured Colonel Bréchignac." Clédic was glad to hear it. He thought Bréchignac had been killed.

From his command post at the base of Eliane 4, Captain Botella heard soldiers speaking Vietnamese. He told one of his men to go and talk to them. "Tell them we have wounded and not to throw grenades." From a loudspeaker Botella could hear in French: "Surrender, your lives will be saved." Before surrendering, Bréchignac messaged Bigeard: "It's the end. Don't shell us. There are too many wounded."

Eliane 10, between the riverbank and RP41, was one of the most exposed of the low Elianes, but it was also the last barrier to Castries' bunker across the bridge. It was manned by what was left of Bigeard's 6th Battalion of paras. Under Captain Thomas, Lieutenants René Le Page and Hervé Trapp commanded what was left of the 1st and 2nd companies. Between them they had sixty men. "Every day the store faces bankruptcy," Trapp said. At the headquarters unit, Le Boudec was out of the hospital with his wounds barely healed. He had just been promoted to captain; he was one of those in the initial drop of November 1953. Also on hand was Lieutenant Allaire with what remained of his 81mm mortars. The paras were backed up by so many wounded men from other units that Eliane 10 was nicknamed "the strongpoint of the wounded."

When Eliane 10 came under attack at 10 P.M. on May 6, Langlais sent over from Epervier on the west bank two forty-man platoons commanded by Lieutenants Jacquemet and Bailly of the 8th Choc. Jacquemet's platoon was annihilated, and it took Bailly until 3 A.M. to reach a reduced enclave of three blockhouses where Captain Thomas was still holding. A Vietminh officer later recalled: "The battle of Eliane 10 was particularly difficult. Three assaults, three counterattacks. One of our battalion chiefs reported that his men were faltering."

At the Hanoi airport at 10 P.M., five Dakotas were lined up for boarding by the 1st Company of the 1st BPC. They would be the last group to jump over the base. Before his departure, Lieutenant Gibeaux got off a letter to a friend: "The DZ is small so we're dropped by sticks of eight. We have no illusions about the outcome of the battle. I don't have the courage to write my parents. If you don't hear from me again, you know what you have to do."

It took hours to complete the dangerous drops over intense flak. When the last planeloads came in with the company commander, Lieutenant Faussurier, it was 5:20 A.M., still dark. The *luciole* parachute flares dropped from small planes had to be doused before the men could come down. But on Eliane 10, the blockhouses still held. René Le Page called Langlais at the base headquarters to insist that without *lucioles* his men would be overrun in the dark. It was a catch-22: maintain the flares and cancel the drop or douse the flares and lose Eliane 10.

Langlais and Bigeard asked each other: Should we let them jump? The drop zone was so narrow the company might land on enemy-held ground. It wasn't worth the risk. Langlais told the planes to turn back, even though Faussurier was bringing two bottles of cognac. Disappointed at not leading his men into battle, Faussurier did not realize that he'd won the lottery. In all, between May 3 and May 7, of the 383 men in the 1st BPC, 301 were dropped, including 155 Vietnamese.

Among those who jumped in the early hours of May 7, before Faussurier's drop was cancelled, was Lieutenant Dr. Staub. Staub went to the hospital to introduce himself to Dr. Grauwin, who asked: "What do they say in Hanoi?"

"They say it will be over soon," Staub said.

"Then why did the 1st BPC jump?"

"You know the paras. We win or we die together."

An orderly burst in. "Are you Staub? Hurry up, your battalion is on its way to the Elianes." Grauwin never saw Staub again.

Grauwin wondered what was left of those elite battalions, the 1st BEP, the 6th BPC, the 8th Choc? Maybe a hundred men in each? Vidal's hospital on Eliane 3 was now on the front line. He had hundreds of wounded there and was up to his ankles in mud, with no electricity, down to ten candles. He couldn't even apply a bandage correctly. Where Grauwin was, at the main hospital, they had more than thirteen hundred wounded.

At dawn on May 7, Eliane 10 still held. Small, isolated groups were surrounded by Vietminh. It got to the point where they didn't know if a trench was held by the Viets or friendlies. Captain Trapp, left with nine men, was hit in the tibia and immobilized. In another trench Le Page and Le Boudec saw the palm-topped helmets approach. A grenade burst near them and mangled Le Boudec's arm. It was his fourth wound. They pulled back and made it to the Bailey bridge with Lieutenant Rivier, the doctor for the 6th BPC. Rivier told Dr. Grauwin that a mortar shell had blown up his infirmary and his battalion had been liquidated. "I haven't eaten in two days," he said. "I drank a little rainwater that collected in empty shell cases." Grauwin gave him an orange.

Grauwin told Vidal on Eliane 3 to bring back his team and those wounded who could walk. It took Vidal an hour to cross the bridge, carrying sixty-five-pound bags of medical equipment. He arrived covered with mud with some Legionnaires, one of whom said, "We kill them but they just keep coming. *Alles Kaput!*" Eliane 3 still held, but Eliane 10 had fallen. Grauwin examined Le Boudec, who told him, "A bullet in the arm. I can't move my fingers." Grauwin sent him to surgery, where Hantz and Gindrey were still operating. Le Boudec was the last man operated on.

By the morning of May 7, three crucial Elianes—2, 4, and 10—had been taken on the east bank of Nam Yum. On the west bank, only three hundred yards from Castries' bunker, the Vietminh attacked the westernmost of five strongpoints that formed a protective ring around central command. This was Claudine 5, situated on flat terrain in a rice paddy on the Hong Phong stream. It was held by a company of Legionnaires under

Captain Schmitz, with two platoons of Moroccans. During the night of May 4–5, some of the Moroccans had cut a lane through the barbed wire and gone over to the enemy. The Vietminh began firing into the gap. Captain Schmitz sent Master Sergeant Kosanovic and seven Legionnaires to repair the breach. All were killed trying to close it. Angry Legionnaires disarmed the remaining Moroccans and told them to go and join the Rats of Nam Yum. Claudine 5, with two fewer platoons, was surrounded by the 108th Regiment of the 308th Division. At daybreak on May 7, Claudine 5 fell.

Has Castries Been Taken?

May 7 was a fine day—no rain, not a cloud in the sky. The good weather brought out twenty-five B-26 bombers to pound the hills where the Vietminh were entrenched. On the base itself, however, the orderly landscape of the entrenched camp, with its airstrip, its tanks, and its artillery emplacements, was a shambles of craters, wounded men, and destroyed positions.

At the command post with Langlais, Bigeard recalled, "It was hallucinating. We didn't eat, we didn't sleep, we lived on coffee and tobacco. Corpses everywhere, the wounded moaning in the trenches, shelters caved in, mud up to our ankles." In his own cherished 6th Battalion of seven hundred paras, forty able-bodied men were left.

He studied the situation that morning with Langlais. Eliane 10 had fallen shortly after dawn, but two of Bigeard's officers, Le Page and Le Boudec, had made it back to headquarters. At 9 A.M., on the east bank of the Nam Yum, there was nothing between the Vietminh and the river but the riverbank posts of Eliane 3, 11, and 12. The latter two were muddy pits held by Algerians and Moroccans under Major Chenel.

As news of the fighting continued to trickle in, Langlais and Bigeard learned that the Moroccans on the front line of Eliane 12 were waving white cloths from the barrels of their rifles. They were quickly overrun by the Vietminh 141st Regiment, which then moved against Eliane 11. Its defenders leapt from their trenches and fled. East of the Nam Yum, only Eliane 3 was left, for the moment ignored by the Vietminh, since it was three hundred yards south of the Bailey bridge. Here too the Moroccans fled, leaving only the Legionnaires of the 13th DBLE.

In his bunker at 10 A.M., Castries reported to Cogny on the radio-phone: "For the two battalions of BEP [Foreign Legion paras], two companies each remain. . . . Three companies of RTM [Moroccan fusiliers]. But they're worthless. . . . These are companies of sixty to eighty men." He went down the list of units he had left.

"We're doing all we can, fighting foot by foot, we hope to stop the enemy on the Nam Yum. . . . If we cannot hold the eastern bank, we'll run out of drinking water. . . . I will try to send men toward the south."

"At night, probably?" Cogny asked.

"Yes, of course."

"What about munitions?"

"We're almost out of munitions. . . . But we'll hold on as long as we can."

Cogny returned to Castries' previous remark regarding a sortie to the south. Did he really intend one?

"Certainly," Castries said, "by way of Isabelle. And after that, good Lord, I'll keep those units who don't want to go."

"Yes, that's it."

"How can I put it? Of course, the wounded, though many of them are already in the hands of the enemy, since they remained on their strong-points. The wounded of Eliane 4 and Eliane 10."

"Yes, of course."

"And then, you see, I'll keep all those people under my command."

It was gallant of Castries to stay behind, but all Cogny said was: "Yes, old fellow, good-bye, old fellow."

"I may call you again . . . before the end."

Cogny prudently confirmed in writing these verbal instructions: "Proceed with 'Albatross' for the retrenched camp and Isabelle. I ask you to let me know your intentions and what aerial support you need."

Langlais and Bigeard were studying the latest aerial maps dropped by a Corsair. The way south along the river showed thin white lines indicating Vietminh trenches that had not been there three days before. At around noon, Langlais gathered at his command post the officers leading the units involved in the breakout. Given the information that their escape route was blocked, they unanimously said that the remnants of their units, perhaps 650 men in all, were too exhausted to attempt it. Castries was informed at 1 P.M. that a breakout was not feasible.

By noon, all the Elianes had fallen except Eliane 3. Monitoring the battle from his mountain hideaway, Giap's thinking was: There are still a lot of fighting men down there, but they're not going to fight to the last man. He knew that some of the units were laying down their arms. Enemy radio reports told him that the base had asked Hanoi not to send more supplies. His observers told him that transport planes had flown over the base and then turned back. Over the radio, his men heard French aviators saying good-bye to the men on the ground.

Early in the afternoon, Giap was told of a possible French collapse, given the number of deserters in the east-bank positions. He sent out the following order at 3 P.M.: "The Commander of the Front to the divisional commanders—Commence immediately general offensive—pointless to wait until nightfall." Units of the 312th Division fought their way across the Bailey bridge to the west bank, where they joined up with the 308th Division advancing from the west. French resistance was collapsing, while the Stalin's Organs kept up their screeching dirge.

Castries' last communication with Hanoi was on the radiophone at 4:30 P.M. He got General Bodet on the line, who said: "We're not abandoning you. In Geneva there may be a solution within days."

"Would that we could hold out until then."

"That's what we wanted, that's what Navarre wanted. It's not your fault. You were magnificent."

"We did what we could. . . . I'm sending out negotiators at 5:30 P.M. We have wounded everywhere. We can't even bandage their wounds."

"What about Albatross?"

"Isabelle will try, my general."

"Perfect."

"Alert my wife. Tell her not to worry. I'll be back."

"Of course. We will never abandon you. . . . I'm putting René on."

Cogny came on and said: "Listen, old fellow, I realize it's all over, but avoid any form of capitulation. That is forbidden. We must have no white flags. Any capitulation would spoil the magnificent things you have done."

"Fine, my general. But I must take care of the wounded." Castries seemed to be implying that he might raise a white flag over the hospital, which led Cogny to insist:

"Yes, but I've got my orders. I do not have the right to authorize you to capitulate. Do the best you can. . . . But it must not end with a white flag."

"Yes, my general. . . . My general, it would be nice of you to go see my wife."

Cogny's emphasis on white flags was foolish as well as profoundly inappropriate, for white parachutes had been dropped all over the base. As Captain Bienvault later observed, "There were, alas, some discreet white chiffons among the Moroccans and the Vietnamese." In many cases, for men who were in trenches or shelters, unseen by the enemy, waving a bit of white cloth could mean the difference between life and death. There was in any event something deeply incongruous about these polite chitchats, with General Bodet conveying to Castries "my best wishes," as if he were seeing him off on a train, when the suffering and death of thousands was at stake. And beyond that, Cogny was saying that what mattered most was not the corpses littering the ground or the survival of the living, but the display of a symbol of surrender. It was like a dying man's family worrying about the suit he should be buried in.

Langlais came into the bunker just as Castries was finishing his last talk with Cogny. He could hear Cogny's voice saying, "*Au revoir,* dear friend." Langlais told Castries: "The enemy is crossing the Nam Yum. No sortie is possible. Any more fighting will kill the thousands of wounded piled up in the shelters. The fighting must stop." Castries agreed, and told Langlais to inform each unit commander to cease firing.

When the final attack came, Giap's commanders reported that there was very little firing from the French. Forward observers saw white foam rising from the Nam Yum. The French were throwing gasoline, shells, and the breechblocks of big guns in the river. Explosions could be heard in the center of the camp, where they were blowing up ammunition dumps. Lieutenant Redon blew up his quads. Captain Hervouet drained the oil from his tanks and ran the engines. Men fired one last round from their rifles with the barrel in the mud. In his office, Langlais burned his archives and his red beret. Bigeard, however, took the precaution of tying a silk map of Tonkin around his ankle. Other officers removed their stripes and thought of what to take into captivity: hidden weapons and compasses, cameras, pills to disinfect water, cigarette lighters, razor blades, anti-malaria tablets, an extra pair of boots.

The end of a battle is as disorderly as a battle itself, but less noisy. Silence descended on the camp after fifty-six days of uproar. For Lieutenant Allaire, the mortar platoon commander in Bigeard's battalion, the silence was "deafening." He was on Eliane 3, when he contacted Bigeard and suggested an escape attempt. He was told not to try anything. The cease-fire was fixed for 5:30. Allaire unreasonably insisted that he wanted an order in writing. Bigeard sent a runner carrying a crumpled note written with a ballpoint pen that said: "For Allaire—Ceasefire at 17.30—Don't fire anymore—No white flag—See you soon—Bruno." Then, Allaire recalled, "they came down on us like a hive of bees." Allaire kept that bit of paper and eventually returned it to Bigeard.

How quickly they took over. Thousands of men swarming into the heart of the base, jumping and running, a tremendous clamor. Their officers did not wear stripes but could be recognized by the number of pens in their chest pockets. Lieutenant Duluat, who was with a Thai unit, heard one of them speaking French and asked him what his rank was. The reply was a burst from a submachine gun at Duluat's feet.

"I had long known the battle was lost," the artillery officer Lepinay recalled, "but that was a mental attitude. When the moment came, the moment when you lift your arms—it's not easy. This was it. We had lost. I was overcome by a feeling of impotence."

Bernard Klotz, the navy pilot, buried his Colt in the mud "and soon the Viets arrived. What does one feel in a moment like that? Deep physical pain. Those who fought had reached their limit. And now we climbed out of our holes, and we saw other men guarded by *bo dois.* It was unbearable to have been transformed from a fighting man into a captive. It was like a wound that never heals."

Corporal Bonny of the 4th Company of the 2nd Battalion of the 1st RCP (light infantry paras) was brought "before an excitable pol com [political commissar] who asked what my unit was. I told him and he nodded and recited the names of all the officers in the battalion. He knew every operation the battalion had been on since it had been dropped in April. He was showing off how well informed they were. Then, in spite of my fractured arm, he ordered a young coolie to tie my hands behind my back, and the long end of the rope was placed between my legs, and I was pulled like a poodle on a leash to join the other captives."

In Dr. Gindrey's surgery unit, Le Boudec had just been operated on for grenade fragments in the forearm when the blanket over the door was set aside and a helmeted Viet burst in shouting *"Di di maolen"* (Come out fast). Dr. Grauwin went outside looking for a pol com. He wanted to explain that the former brothel girls were voluntary nurses. The Chinese madam had already been found and taken away and shot. The Vietnamese girls were also removed and Grauwin suspected they too were shot.

Loudspeakers blared: "Surrender. You will be well treated. Show white flags and come out of your shelters in good order. Those carrying rifles, point the barrel toward the ground."

Hundreds of men arrived at a gallop and surrounded Castries' bunker. He was waiting outside, wearing his red *calot,* his general's stars, and his decorations. Giap asked his chief of staff, Le Trong Tan, who was at the bunker: "Has de Castries been taken?"

"We are told he has been arrested."

"How can you be sure? We have to be sure they didn't bring in a substitute." A captured French general was unprecedented in the Indochina war, where they were rarely seen on the front lines. Castries was Giap's star prisoner and he didn't want an understudy.

"Verify his ID and his decorations. Have you ever seen a photograph?" Le Trong never had, so Giap found one and sent it to the bunker.

Soon, Giap called again: "Did you see de Castries with your own eyes?"

"I did. They are all standing in front of me. De Castries has his cane and his forage cap."

Giap left his headquarters and toured the battlefield. Close up, the valley seemed much bigger. Every inch of ground, he mused, was impregnated with the blood of the enemy. Unburied corpses were covered with flies and gave off an unbearable stench. On Béatrice he was shown the emplacement of a submachine gun with an infrared light for firing in the dark. When he inspected Castries' bunker, he saw more clearly how the French had trapped themselves inside their barbed wire and minefields, losing all mobility. The floor was covered with paper, including a letter from Castries to his wife. Giap told Cao Van Khanh, the second in command of the 308th Division, to collect the paper, which might have historical value. Khanh said that the underground shelters used as hospitals were in a terrible state, filled with mud. Giap told him to get some lime and disinfect them.

Only after the mines had been cleared did Giap cross the Bailey bridge, which he noted was American-made, and inspect Eliane 2, the key to the battle. Every inch of ground showed signs of combat, from the destroyed tank at the top to the red earth, its vegetation replaced by cartridges, bits of barbed wire, and shell fragments. The tunnel his men had dug and dynamited was fifty yards long, but badly positioned. Even so, it had blown up a French platoon. From the top, Giap could see the network of trenches. He did not promise decorations to the wounded as Castries had done, but he singled out heroic soldiers: Be Van Dan had offered his body as a machine-gun support. Hoang Van No had died as he bayoneted an enemy. Yo Vinh Dien died protecting an artillery piece. Drivers of supply trucks had stayed at their steering wheels after being wounded. Medical orderlies had plunged into heavy fire to carry away wounded.

When he later read that some of Castries' men had died without showing any apparent wounds, Giap concluded that "their endurance had failed, because they did not know what they were fighting for." Navarre's defeat at Dien Bien Phu, Giap believed, had come from "an error in judgment in that he did not understand his adversary. He didn't realize it was a people's war. For the French elite troops, war was their profession. But what were they fighting for? Navarre's mistake was that he couldn't believe illiterate peasants could become good artillerymen, or that cadres who hadn't graduated from Saint-Cyr could solve strategic and tactical problems."

When Navarre testified before the 1955 commission, General Valin asked him, "Did Castries not abdicate his command?"

"No, not at all," Navarre said. "Castries never abdicated his command.

I called him every two or three days. Cogny called him twice a day. He was always the commander. He was a cavalryman, and he understood that combat troops such as paras and Legionnaires must be given a lot of leeway. You could not hold them on a tight rein. He trusted officers like Bigeard, who had already shown his ability. Was that an abdication? He made, however, a number of tactical errors."

A government report based on questions the wounded had been asked upon their return concluded: "All survivors seem to think that General de Castries and his headquarters staff were incompetent all the way down the line. Praise is reserved for the battalion commanders and Colonel Langlais."

I Can No Longer Communicate

Three miles down the road, the isolated post of Isabelle had not been attacked on the morning of May 7, though the artillery bombardment was unrelenting, and some of the outlying positions moved back to Colonel André Lalande's strongpoint. It got so crowded that Dr. Rézillot had to move his infirmary to the officers' mess. He had 250 wounded. The May fighting had killed 160 and Isabelle had about 750 able-bodied men left.

At 2 P.M., the Legionnaire Jean Dens was in Lalande's office and overheard a radio conversation between Lalande and Lieutenant Colonel de Séguin-Pazzis, Castries' chief of staff. They spoke in English, which Dens understood, in case the Vietminh were listening. Lalande was told that the cease-fire would come at 5:30 P.M. It was not a surrender, but a mutual cease-fire. He was advised to hold out as long as possible in order to organize a sortie at night. In principle they might be able to link up with the CONDOR column, which was supposed to be about twenty miles to the southwest in Laos.

Lalande knew that an entire Vietminh division, the 303rd, would attack at nightfall. It was pointless to stand and fight, so he would try the sortie. He had to improvise, since his maps were not specific enough. At 5 P.M., he summoned his company commanders. Lieutenant Wieme and his Thais would take the lead, followed by a company of Legionnaires, down one bank of the Nam Yum. An hour later, more companies would start down the other bank. If there was an ambush on one bank, the rest of the garrison would follow on the other. In the meantime, destruction of matériel that could not be carried was to start at once. Lalande told Dr. Rézillot: "GONO [the main garrison] has surrendered, tonight we'll try a sortie, but you and Captain Calvet must remain with the wounded." Rézillot was in shock. Busy with his wounded, he hadn't realized things were that bad.

As teams began to dismantle the tanks and howitzers, dumping the parts in the river, a heavy artillery barrage began at 6 P.M. The surgical unit took a direct hit while Rézillot was operating. It filled with smoke and had to be evacuated. The bamboo walls of the infirmary caught fire and thirty wounded were carried out and dumped on parachutes outside. The orderlies formed a bucket brigade.

Jean Dens, the Legionnaire, was wounded by artillery fire and headed for the infirmary. On the roof, bags containing parachutes had been placed for protection. The nylon caught fire and flames fell like a waterfall down the side of the entrance. He managed to get in and his wound was bandaged. He'd lost a lot of blood and passed out.

At 8 P.M., Lieutenant Wieme and his Thais started out in the perilous dark over a destroyed landscape, tripping and sinking in the mud slick, followed by Captain Michot and a company of Legionnaires. Each man carried a submachine gun, grenades, and two days' rations. Some of the walking wounded wanted to join them. Michot warned: "When you can no longer walk we won't carry you."

They went down a track broken up by shell craters, along the bank of the river. An hour later, a second column made up of a company of Algerians under Captain Pierre Jeancelle, a company of Legionnaires, and Lieutenant Henri Préaud and his Thais started out on the right bank. They had gone about a mile and a half when they fell into an ambush. Captain Jeancelle, fearing a massacre, shouted, "Cease-fire." They dropped their weapons and were surrounded by Vietminh, who separated officers and men. Those units who tried to follow in their wake found the southern exits from Isabelle blocked by Vietminh.

Lalande realized that his men could not keep fighting after having destroyed their heavy weapons. The enemy was still half a mile away, but had captured a lieutenant, Jean-Pascal Tymen, who was now being used as a go-between and had proceeded to the base carrying a white flag. It was pitch-black and Tymen was sure he'd be shot by a sentry, but a Legionnaire recognized him. Lalande agreed to a cease-fire and soon the Vietnamese streamed into the base. At 2 A.M. on May 8, Lalande sent his last wire: "I can no longer communicate."

When the *bo dois* came into his infirmary, Dr. Rézillot wondered why they wore face masks. "Did they think we were conducting biological warfare?" They took his surgical instruments and penicillin. The one in charge told him: "From now on, we'll take care of your wounded. You are a prisoner of war." Eight men were waiting for surgery, and two had gangrene, but Rézillot wasn't allowed to operate. They stripped the infirmary, taking everything from soap to electric wire. Later, they brought in one of their surgeons, who performed an amputation while reading from a textbook. The amputee died during the night. As for the unconscious Jean Dens, hit by multiple shell fragments, he awoke to find himself looking into the face of a Vietnamese surgeon, who said he would remove the fragments, but had no anesthetic. Nor did he have catgut to sew up the wounds, but he applied bandages.

The Wieme-Michot column had continued along the left bank, meeting no resistance thanks to their early start. They were now about six miles from the base, at a point where the track left the plain and verged toward wooded hills. They marched in single file in the dark, each man touching the shoulder of the man in front of him. Suddenly a voice from the top of the hill barked out, *"Nadai?"* (Who's there?)

The column dispersed off the path and followed a stream that took them to a cliff from the top of which came automatic fire. The Legionnaires fired back. In the dark, confusion reigned. Men were hit and fell into the stream and were carried away by the current. Others tried to climb the cliff. Lieutenant Wieme got up about three yards with one of his Thais climbing above him. The Thai was hit and in falling dragged Wieme down with him. Wieme found himself in the stream, having lost his weapon, and let the current carry him for about six hundred yards. At that point the cliff was more gently sloped, and he was able to climb it. Without his weapon or his backpack, he wondered what to do next.

Michot and fifteen Legionnaires headed toward Laos, but Michot kept losing men until he was left alone. He hesitated to approach Thai villages, and he was dying of hunger and thirst, his feet bloodied, when he was captured in a field of bamboo on May 8, exhausted, bareheaded, clothes torn. Lieutenant Wieme was also captured in a field of bamboo on May 8. During his captivity, Wieme thought back to January, when Castries had sent planes over Vietminh positions to drop tracts: "What are you waiting for to start the battle that you think is decisive? Do you doubt that you will succeed? Have you lost faith in your general and your troops? Come, I await you."

Back in the defeated valley, the Vietminh were facing the dilemma of victory, which had mainly to do with numbers. The cost of the battle to France, since its start on March 13, was sixteen battalions, eleven of them elite units, seven battalions of paras and four of Legionnaires. In addition, two artillery groups, a squadron of tanks, and a battalion of engineers were lost. These totalled 15,090 men. On March 13, the base had a garrison of 10,813, to which were added 4,277 dropped during the battle.

Casualties were recorded until May 5, as follows:

- 1,142 dead plus 429 who died of their wounds in infirmaries and surgical units
- 1,606 unaccounted for, most of them presumed dead
- 1,161 deserters, including the Rats of Nam Yum, mainly Algerians, Moroccans, and Thais
- 4,436 wounded

But many more were killed and wounded on the lethal days of May 5, 6, and 7.

The army's evaluation of those taken prisoner on May 8 is as follows: A total of 10,261, of whom 2,257 were French, 932 Moroccans, 804 Algerians, 221 Africans, 2,562 Legionnaires, and 3,585 Vietnamese and others, such as Thais. The French expeditionary force was less than 25 percent French. Roughly half of those captured had been wounded.

The Vietminh were unprepared to deal with these numbers. The victory had come more suddenly than Giap had expected. Never before had the Vietminh taken anywhere near that many prisoners. The number of wounded was far in excess of anything Giap had imagined, even though he had prevented their evacuation as a way of breaking down morale. He proceeded to remove the wounded from their filthy trenches and place them under tents made from parachutes in groups of twenty. They emerged from their burrows blinded by the light of day. Keeping the seriously wounded would provide a bargaining chip at Geneva. The rest could move out with the POWs.

Giap's plan was to disperse his divisions quickly, leaving only a regiment of the 308th Division to take care of the wounded. The 316th Division would take the POWs on foot to Vietminh camps hundreds of miles away. The battle was over but the war went on. He would move his other divisions to the Delta in trucks, which could take two or three weeks. The Vietminh had an estimated seventy-six thousand men minus the Dien Bien Phu casualties, while the French in the Delta had about two hundred thousand. But they were enclosed in forts and their morale was low.

In their haste to get moving, the Vietminh conducted a triage of captured French that was far too simplistic. Those wounded below the waist who couldn't walk would be kept in the tents. Those wounded above the waist were presumed to be capable of walking. In the process, many of those who were near death with chest or abdominal wounds compounded by gangrene and dysentery were forced to join the long march. It was a form of cruelty based on haste and indifference to suffering. One glaring example was Captain Trehiou, who had jumped with his leg in a cast. He could barely walk on his broken ankle, but could not get medical attention and was sent on the long march although he had been hit below the waist.

On the evening of May 7, the POWs were marched to the northeast corner of the valley after being searched. Senior French officers, major and up, were piled into trucks and driven to a transit camp. Castries had a jeep to himself. The rest were herded up RP41 to a clearing, where they were separated by nationality and rank.

The doctors were at first pushed into columns for the march, but when the Vietminh saw how many gravely wounded men there were lying in the mud—amputees without crutches, head wounds without bandages—

they retrieved the doctors and brought them back to the base. Dr. Gindrey climbed up on the roof of the surgery unit, rolled up in a parachute, and slept for twenty-two hours. Other doctors helped with the triage, trying to see to it that the gravely hurt stayed behind.

At midnight on May 7, Giap lay down on his grass-filled mattress, but he could not sleep. He was kept awake by the thought of the Vietnamese people when they heard the news, by the thought of the delegation in Geneva waiting hour by hour, by the thought of Navarre, his plan in tatters. Dien Bien Phu was over. What was next?

I Don't Blame Castries, I Blame the High Command

In Saigon, Navarre wired General Ely on May 8 that he was expecting two new Vietminh divisions in the Delta, coming from Dien Bien Phu. Due to the rains, the daily bombing of RP41, and the fatigue of the men, he did not think they would arrive for thirty or forty days, depending on whether they traveled by truck. Therefore, the northern front of the Delta would be threatened by mid-June. If worse came to worse, he would have to abandon part of the Delta to increase the density of French forces elsewhere. Areas in the south would be given up in order to maintain the Hanoi–Haiphong corridor. For the time being, he would wait, since retrenchment in the Delta would impact on the Geneva negotiations.

In Paris, given the seven-hour time difference, news of the defeat arrived at noon on May 7. At the National Assembly, so bitterly divided over the war, the deputies discussed the disaster in hushed tones as they filed into the main chamber. Premier Laniel asked for a minute of silence, then said: "The government has just learned that the retrenched camp of Dien Bien Phu has fallen after twenty hours of violent fighting."

Interrupting his remarks, the entire six-hundred-odd Assembly, except for the Communists, rose in a collective gesture of regard for the garrison. "Isabelle is still holding," Laniel continued. "The enemy wanted to obtain the fall of Dien Bien Phu before the [Indochina part of the] Geneva Conference opened. He thought that this would be a decisive blow to French morale. . . . The enemy sacrificed thousands of men to defeat the heroes who in fifty-five days have won the admiration of the world and covered themselves with glory. . . . The fall of Dien Bien Phu will in no way modify the conduct of our representatives in Geneva. . . . The heroism of our soldiers should incite our adversaries to take measures in favor of the wounded. No better way could be found to establish a favorable climate for peace."

A front-page editorial in *Le Figaro* the next day, signed by its editor in chief, Pierre Brisson, judged the conduct of the war severely: "The men of Dien Bien Phu died because we lied to ourselves. They died because we did not know how to fight this war and because we were incapable of not fighting it. During these nine years of war, opportunities to win, as well as opportunities to negotiate, were lost because of our weakness. By giving in to Communist blackmail, we fought this war shamefully. The conduct of operations was a series of excuses."

This harsh though credible appraisal was the exception, however, for in their collective self-regard, the French were compelled to turn the defeat into an act of heroism. Dien Bien Phu was a perfect failure that had to be converted into an admirable feat of arms. The feel-good outlets in the media sounded the trumpet. The popular weekly *Paris Match*, in its May 8 edition, said: "A clearing in the Indochina jungle has become the capital of heroism." Dien Bien Phu was compared to Verdun, the most celebrated victory of World War I. The comparison was absurd, for at Verdun the wounded were evacuated on the Voie Sacrée, the only road still open, and men on the front lines were replaced after eight days. At Dien Bien Phu, it was Giap who held the "voie sacrée," RP41, moving thousands of men and tons of matériel to the front. In creating the myth of a second Verdun, it was forgotten that a poll of the French public in February 1954 showed only 8 percent in favor of the war. Heroism at Dien Bien Phu became a bumper to absorb the shock of defeat, and the "honor of our soldiers" was a way of hiding political cowardice.

Castries was turned into a triumphant warrior. Not since he had broken the world records for the equestrian high jump (2.38 meters in 1933) and long jump (7.60 meters in 1935), had he known such adulation. The daily *France-Soir* wrote on May 9 that he was "one of the most prestigious heroes of French military history, which boasts so many." The French embassy in Washington reported that "General de Castries has become for the citizens of this country a sort of national hero." All this was cold comfort for the general in his prison.

For the survivors, the wounded under their tents and the POWs on the long march, Castries represented inertia and confused tactics. The men recalled that he was never seen on the strongpoints, that he ordered useless counterattacks, that he turned the command over to Langlais and the para battalions. He said himself that an infantry officer would have done a better job than someone from the armored cavalry. Men from every rank down to private said they missed feeling the charisma of a great leader like de Lattre. Ernest Duffort, a private, said: "Before the battle, he was always driving around in his jeep, wearing his red forage cap and white scarf. But once the battle started, we saw him no more."

And yet Castries had proved his courage in June 1940, when with sixty men he held off a German battalion, surrendering only when he was wounded and out of ammunition. He then escaped from a POW camp in 1941, by digging a tunnel with twenty other officers. By the time he was named to the command of Dien Bien Phu, he had twenty-one citations for bravery. Bigeard, who saw him daily, recalled: "I felt affection for him. He was a cavalryman with a brilliant past, this battle was not his. But there he was among us, while there should have been a three-star general. . . . I don't blame Castries, I blame the high command." That is to say, the blame should be placed on Navarre, with his multiple operations and his inability to grasp that Giap could bring in artillery and cut off the airfield, and Cogny, with his bizarrely lackadaisical attitude, his priority for the Delta, his leaks to the press, and his sniping at Navarre.

At a conference in 2004 entitled "Dien Bien Phu Between Memory and History," one of the military experts present, General de Bire, observed: "When the quarreling started [after the battle], when the blame game ran its course, only one high-ranking officer maintained the dignity of silence, General de Castries." But were the thousands of men who died there heroes? Victims, rather, ignored by a government of bunglers in Paris and a high command in Saigon too divided to do its job.

On May 9, Navarre adopted the requisite tone of heroism in a message to the troops: "The glorious conduct of our army gives us a new reason to fight. The war will continue." He expounded on the aid the

Vietminh had received from China, which had changed the nature of the war.

The previous day, Ho Chi Mihn had congratulated his troops by asking for the avoidance of hubris: "Our victory is brilliant but it is not decisive. We must not be too proud of our success. We must not underestimate the enemy."

The Baby Would Be Rapidly Devoured

When it became known in Washington on the morning of May 7 that Dien Bien Phu and its ten thousand defenders had fallen, the reactions in the Senate showed two poles of thought. The Montana Democrat Mike Mansfield opined that "to withdraw now, to negotiate a settlement laying open all of Indochina to the conqueror's heel, would be to break faith with those of Dien Bien Phu who gave us so much."

The Oregon Republican Wayne Morse responded that "the next time we go to war, we will find that we were plunged into it by events and then the Congress will be called upon to draft a declaration of war, simply to make it legal. . . . We must make clear to France that we are not going to enter into any agreement which will result in shiploads of coffins draped in American flags being shipped from Indochina to the United States in any attempt to support colonialism in Indochina."

That night, over nationwide radio and television, Secretary of State Dulles pronounced on "the issues at Geneva." "An epic battle has ended," he said. "But great causes have, before now, been won out of lost battles. . . . If hostilities continue, the need will be even more urgent to create the conditions for united action in defense of the area." That morning, Dulles had spoken to the president, who insisted once again that the United States would not act alone. Eisenhower sent a wire to the French president, René Coty, extolling French gallantry.

At noon on May 7 in Geneva, Anthony Eden and Walter Bedell Smith went to see Georges Bidault, who had heard the news, according to Shuckburgh, and "was unable to decide on anything, waiting for orders from Paris. . . . Poor chaps, poor French there," Shuckburgh observed. "Very gloomy." The opening of the Indochina portion of the conference was delayed while the delegates argued over the matter of who should be seated. Molotov wanted a Democratic Republic of Vietnam (DRV) delegation. Bidault and Eden argued that seating the DRV should be tied to cooperation on the evacuation of the wounded.

Smith came by Le Reposoir before dinner to see Eden. Smith had just left Bidault, and said he was in a bad way, "weaving and wringing his hands," and fearing instructions from Paris demanding a cease-fire. Bidault deplored the influence of some of his defeatist colleagues. Smith wanted Eden to call Bidault and buck him up, but Eden was annoyed with Bidault's hesitations and delays. "Oh, come off it, Anthony," Smith said, "you can bring yourself to do a little of that stuff, can't you?" Eden said he would. Smith said, "I'm getting too old for this."

On Saturday, May 8, Shuckburgh spent the morning enjoying the glorious sunshine on the terrace of Le Reposoir. The two-hundred-year-old chestnut trees were in flower, as were the lilacs. Young greens were sprouting around the house, and around the lake and mountains beyond. He had a lunch of eggs and cheese and waited for the opening session of the Indochina talks at 4:30 P.M. at the Palais des Nations.

This initial session was high drama, with the defeat at Dien Bien Phu and the ongoing war in the background. "It was infinitely more alive and explosive than the Korean talks," Shuckburgh noted. Bidault had agreed that the DRV delegation should be seated. "The Chinese and the Russians came in with the Vietminh in tow," Shuckburgh said, "with Chou looking more and more like a monkey with a nasty savage bite."

The nine participants were the United States, the Soviet Union, Britain, and France, plus China, the DRV, the Bao Dai government of Vietnam, and the royalist governments of Laos and Cambodia. Eden was in the chair, and Bidault was scheduled to speak when Molotov proposed that the Communist "governments" of Laos and Cambodia, the Pathet Lao and the Issarak Front, be allowed to seat their delegations as well. But the representatives of those two groups missed their cues and Eden tabled the motion.

Bidault spoke as if enveloped in a funeral shroud. He evoked "the most cruel battle of the war . . . and the hardening that has until now refused to allow the evacuation of the wounded, contrary to the laws of war and the principles of the civilized world." The French proposal, he said, was re-groupment of both armies under the supervision of an international control commission.

Pham Van Dong, the deputy prime minister and foreign minister of the DRV, and the head of his delegation, wore the crown of victory and demanded full independence for the Associated States, the withdrawal of all French troops, and the holding of free elections. He also reiterated Molotov's request that the Pathet Lao and Issarak Front be seated. Shuckburgh, who described Pham as a "thin-faced, thick-lipped, bespectacled little bastard," was shocked by the thought that "these two puppet stooges might attend the conference." Smith intervened, saying it was the business of the four inviting powers to decide who should attend.

Meanwhile, in Washington, Dulles was making another stab at united action. He told the French ambassador, Henri Bonnet, that the United States was prepared to talk about "internationalizing the war." He realized that the French were put off by the idea, but they might change their minds when "the full harshness of probable Communist terms were revealed."

Chou En-lai diligently reported on each session to Mao, starting with the first: "The nine-country meeting on Indochina was finally convened yesterday. Bidault was the lead speaker and denied that the Democratic Republic of Vietnam was an opponent in the war. He called it a rebelling force. The essence of his proposal represented a preparatory step by the U.S. for collective security in Southeast Asia." Bidault "revealed the great role that America's intrigue played."

Between the opening session on May 8 and the closing session on July 21, there were eight plenary sessions. The real work was done at informal meetings away from the table. The plenary sessions accomplished nothing. As Eden put it, "They merely provided a stage for the striking of attitudes on both sides."

On the Sunday, May 9, break, Eden and Shuckburgh wondered whether the Communists were going to discuss seriously the question of stopping the war. Shuckburgh did not think they had any incentive to stop, since "it is going nicely for them." Eden said his strategy was getting close to Molotov, to enlist his help in controlling Chou.

On May 10, the French and the Vietminh reached an unofficial agreement on the evacuation of the seriously wounded. The French, according to Smith, were "very gloomy." They feared that the Laniel government would fall, and that the government replacing it would want an armistice in Indochina.

That afternoon at three there was a plenary session, with Molotov in the chair. Shuckburgh reported that Pham Van Dong gave "a long, insolent, and bloody-minded speech, hurling every insult at the Americans, but produced a plan baited to French opinion." The plan called for a cease-fire, followed by the withdrawal of foreign troops and a general election. In effect, Shuckburgh estimated, the plan meant "withdrawal of French forces and the total Communization of Indochina." He wondered how the "war-weary, divided, defeatist French" would respond. Behind it all was the military deterioration of Indochina.

Smith responded by cabling Washington that Pham's plan would "result in the rapid turnover of Indochina to the Communists." At 3 P.M., Dulles called Admiral Radford to tell him that he had heard that morning from Ambassador Dillon in Paris. "For the first time," Dulles said, "they want to sit down and discuss the military situation. They seem willing to do business with us so we can get Congressional support."

"Too bad it wasn't done two months ago," Radford replied. Acting without the British would be a big hurdle, Dulles said.

Dulles saw the president at 4:30 P.M. and told him that Premier Laniel had asked Dillon what military action the United States was ready to take. This new point of view had come about because the Laniel government was walking a tightrope. Eisenhower agreed to respond to Laniel's initiative by sending General Trapnell, the former head of MAAG in Indochina, to Paris. Dulles prepared a list of the usual conditions for U.S. intervention—independence for the Associated States and the training of native troops. Eisenhower agreed to pursue a truncated united action that did not include the British.

Dulles said they were on "the horns of a dilemma." The United States had to show that it was not supporting colonialism, but the Associated States were not ready for full independence. They had no trained personnel and their leaders were no good. "It would be like putting a baby in a cage of hungry lions," he said. "The baby would be rapidly devoured."

At lunch on May 11, Eisenhower told Dulles that the forces sent by the

United States should be described as "principally sea and air." Dulles was pleased to be moving ahead without the British. That afternoon he replied to Dillon's cable with the seven-point list of conditions. The conditions, however, were intended to be rejected, while creating the illusion of forward movement.

In Geneva on May 11, Shuckburgh reported that Eden was getting letters from friends at the Foreign Office telling him "how wonderfully popular he was for standing up to the Americans." There was no session on Indochina that day because the conference was still alternating between Indochina and Korea.

On May 12 there was another plenary session on Indochina during which Chou En-lai enunciated his reply to Dulles's united action: a policy of mutual respect and noninterference among Asian countries, in order to avoid "the neocolonialist exploitation of Asians fighting Asians." Shuckburgh thought Chou had been very rude to the Americans. The speechmaking lasted until midnight.

Could the Americans Use the H-Bomb?

Bidault was hanging tough, saying: "We must keep saying no to Chou's proposal until the last minute." He had gotten wind of the latest U.S. proposal, which he thought he could use as a threat. He told Smith: "We must prepare the thunder, but we don't want it to clap during the conference. We must content ourselves with a few distant rolls to warn our adversaries of the risks of intransigence."

As Dillon reported to Washington, "The French wish to use possibility of intervention primarily to strengthen their hand at Geneva." The State Department saw the game the French were playing, and played along, not wanting a sellout at Geneva, but only up to a point, since they didn't mind if the conference came to nothing as a result of Communist intransigence.

On May 13, Bidault and Smith paid Eden a morning visit. Bidault mentioned that in the afternoon in Paris there would be a vote of confidence on the continuation of the Laniel government. Bidault said: "They would not dare to oust me," meaning that the Laniel government would survive because he was the indispensable man in Geneva. Laniel won the vote of confidence by the paper-thin margin of two votes, 289 to 287. The two votes meant nothing. The reporters who covered the National Assembly said the lack of confidence was palpable. Laniel was not a lame duck but a dead duck, though he didn't want to give up his job as premier. He was a vain man who believed that without him France would go Communist.

Eden asked Smith and Bidault whether he should go and see Chou to tell him that "if he keeps coming to meetings to make rude remarks about the Americans, he is playing with fire." Both said it was an excellent idea. Smith had met with Molotov, who said he wasn't so worried about Korea "because there at least we are not shooting each other." But in Indochina there was a situation of grave danger.

Eden was suffering from conference fatigue. The plenary sessions were getting nowhere. He asked Bidault and Smith to back him in asking for restricted sessions, consisting of the heads of all nine delegations, with two or three advisers each, and no press, and he asked them to bring it up with Molotov and Chou. The main difficulty was that the Chinese and the Russians wanted a blanket settlement for all of Indochina, while Eden, the United States, and the French wanted only to settle the war in Vietnam.

Chou reported on May 14 to Mao that Eden had come to see him that morning with two aides and an interpreter. Eden said "it was dangerous for everybody to be delivering speeches accusing each other. He wanted to propose restricted sessions to get down to actual negotiations."

Eden told Chou: "I'm afraid that the major powers will insist on their positions, which could lead to international dangers."

Chou replied: "Many people want peace, but some people want to continue the war."

"Everyone wishes that the war would cease," Eden said.

Chou asked Eden to clarify his proposal for troop concentrations on both sides.

Eden said it was to avoid conflicts.

Chou said the United Kingdom should exert its influence on the French and the Americans.

Eden said the press would not be told about the restricted meetings. This had worked well at the Berlin Conference. Eden then said: "We hope to see the four great powers—excuse me, I made a mistake. We hope very much to see the five great powers work together to decrease international tensions. . . . Indochina should not affect relations among the five great powers."

"China deserves the status of a great power," Chou said. "This is an existing fact."

"I am worried," Eden replied, "that Ho Chi Minh might be asking too much. He might be able to get it, but it would affect the relations between the great powers."

"The person who is asking too much is Bao Dai," Chou replied. Bao Dai's proposal of one government and one army was "very familiar. Chiang Kai-shek made the same demands and we all know how he wound up." Eden wanted a military armistice first. Chou wanted to discuss military and political matters at the same time. Eden said they should meet again, adding, "Now I will go meet with Mr. Molotov." Eden's private sessions with Chou and Molotov, who both agreed to restricted meetings, were the first breakthrough of the conference.

May 14 was Shuckburgh's last day as Eden's private secretary. He had been promoted to assistant secretary for Middle East affairs. Eden said he was depressed about the state of the conference. Shuckburgh had his doubts, since Eden was really running the show and enjoying it all. The Chinese called him "the king of the conference." That morning, Eden received British reporters, who praised him for standing up to the Americans and keeping Britain out of Indochina. Among the headlines in the London press were EDEN SPEAKS FOR BRITAIN and EDEN'S LONE HAND AGAINST ODDS. Shuckburgh reflected that for the British, Indochina was "something remote and nasty, like Czechoslovakia."

Shuckburgh flew off to London in the evening and Eden was at the front door to see him off. Shuckburgh was glad to be going back to England, to his family and his garden. Eden wasn't always easy to work with. Shuckburgh was pleased, however, when he received a note that said: "I enjoyed every hour of our work together. I could not have survived physically or politically without your wisdom and guidance."

On May 15, Eden read in the Geneva papers that Franco-American talks were taking place on the military intervention of the United States in Indochina. He was startled that the issue had been resurrected and that he was being kept out of the loop. Smith said he knew nothing about it. Eden went to see Bidault, who offered a vague denial. Bidault was with one of his advisers, Roland de Margerie, who took Eden aside and showed him Dulles's letter listing the seven conditions.

"Then what the newspapers say is true," Eden observed.

"Very much so," Margerie replied.

Eden raised the matter again with Smith, "who exploded with indignation and deplored Washington's inability to keep anything secret." Eden said he was surprised at having to learn about it from the newspapers.

Smith said, "Of course you should have been told."

In Paris, the Committee for National Defense, consisting of eight cabinet ministers and the French Joint Chiefs, met on May 14 to discuss the Dulles offer. There was general agreement that a negotiated solution to the war must be found at Geneva. But there was some uncertainty concerning the American offer.

Maurice Schumann, the number two at Foreign Affairs, took the Bidault line: "We must consolidate our military positions, affirm our resolution, and bring in our allies. In other words, use the threat of internationalizing the war to win the battle for peace in Geneva."

Paul Reynaud, vice president of the Council of Ministers, did not think things were that simple. "The eventual intervention of American forces is still distant," he said. "It supposes a decision from Congress, which is presently unfavorable, and a determination from the government, whereas the statements from Dulles betray his uncertainty. . . . Therefore what should our policy be? If Geneva fails, we should think about asking the Americans to use the H-bomb against China, which would bring the Communist block face-to-face with the prospect of a world war."

Reynaud's remark showed the disarray in French thinking in the last days of the Laniel government. Dropping the H-bomb on China was certain to start a world war, not prevent it. And he was unaware of Eisenhower's reluctance to consider any sort of military intervention and any use of nuclear weapons, particularly in Asia.

Bidault was now shuttling between Geneva and Paris, trying to get some decisiveness out of his government. "My situation as negotiator has become literally unbearable," he said.

In Washington, one of the results of the Dien Bien Phu defeat was a discarding of the domino theory. With Indochina on the verge of collapse, what had been described as the first of a disastrous chain of events was now seen in a different light. At a press conference on May 11, Dulles was asked: "Do you think, Mr. Secretary, that the Southeast Asia area can be held without Indochina?"

"I do," Dulles replied. "The situation in that area . . . was that it was subject to the so-called 'domino theory.' . . . We are trying to change it so that would not be the case. . . . You generally have a whole series of countries that can be picked up one by one." But with those nations coming together for collective security, "the domino theory ceases to apply."

On May 12, Eisenhower backed up his secretary of state at another press conference. "Mr. President," he was asked, "a couple of weeks ago you told us your theory of dominoes in Indochina. . . . Since the fall of Dien Bien Phu . . . is Indochina still indispensable to the defense of Southeast Asia?"

"The great idea," Eisenhower replied, "is to set up an organism so as to defeat the domino results. When each is standing alone, and one falls, it has the effect on the next, and finally the whole row is down. You are trying, through a unifying influence, to build that row of dominoes so they can stand the fall of one, if necessary."

The domino theory, a vivid rhetorical device that had no basis in reality, was now laid to rest, and united action became a "one size fits all" policy.

I Want to Thank You for Your Compassionate Attitude

At Dien Bien Phu, on the evening of May 7, when the Vietminh had begun the triage among the wounded, Lieutenant Cesarini, who had been hit by shrapnel in the ribs while trying to get his mortars off Eliane 4, was told that only those with leg wounds would stay behind. He asked Sergeant Réale, the medical orderly for his company of Legionnaires, to plaster his leg. As he soon saw, the triage was swift and arbitrary. He was not the only one to develop a sudden leg wound. Men with wounds in both lungs were sent on the long march. On the morning of May 8, Captain Charles, the

Legionnaire who had fought on Eliane 1, thought the base looked like a battleground from the Napoleonic Wars, with hundreds of bandaged men, abandoned and helpless, filthy and skeletal, some still lying in the mud. The Viets had been forced to bring back doctors. The wounded were being moved to tents held up by bamboo poles, under torrid heat and rain, but they were better off than underground. Thousand of coolies were stripping the base, taking everything—including medicine out of the infirmaries—down to belt buckles and matches. Medical orderlies started moving out to the strongpoints to recover more wounded and roll the dead in parachutes.

Geneviève de Galard was given permission to help in the tents. She changed the bandages of the men with abdominal wounds. The Vietnamese doctors were polite, but stingy with gauze and medication. And yet in Hanoi, General Jeansotte, the director of health services for the Far East, continued to drop medical supplies on the base, while realizing, as he wrote in a report, that "it could be used all or in part for other wounded than ours." He expected that the Vietminh would want to negotiate the return of the French wounded, but what would they ask for in exchange?

One sign that the Vietminh were preparing a prisoner exchange was that they had begun to clear the mines from the airstrip, though they had no planes. They used teams made up mainly of Vietnamese prisoners from the French garrison, who were considered traitors and were thus expendable. Mine removal without maps indicating their location was an invitation to have a foot blown off. Dr. Hantz was assigned to perform amputations like a mechanic on the assembly line, with rusty Chinese scalpels. His own equipment had vanished.

Nor would the Vietminh allow French surgeons, aside from Hantz, to operate on their own men. Lieutenant Jacques Defline of the 8th Choc, one of whose thighs had been gouged out, woke up on May 8 hemorrhaging under his cast. He was taken to a unit manned by a Vietminh surgeon. Seeing Defline's obvious hesitation, the surgeon told him in French: "I will leave it to you to decide whether you want me to operate." Defline had no choice, he was bleeding to death, and the surgeon tied his femoral artery.

As for the evacuation of the wounded, there was a breakthrough in Geneva on May 11, when Pham Van Dong announced that the DRV had decided to proceed with their return. The French should send delegates by helicopter to Dien Bien Phu and land on the northern end of the airstrip, so that the two sides could confer. Pham scored a propaganda coup, appearing generous and lacking a spirit of revenge. In addition, agreeing to negotiate on this matter would constitute de facto recognition of the DRV. For the French, the return of the wounded was a humanitarian necessity. For the DRV, it was a political stratagem. From Paris, General Ely cabled Navarre, urging him to go ahead. Ely added a sinister proviso: "You should know, however, that the Vietminh for the moment excludes the Vietnamese wounded from the evacuation. Insofar as you can, please do not object to this exclusion." The French were throwing to the wolves the Vietnamese, such as the paratroopers of the 5th BPVN, who had fought by their side, often gallantly.

As it turned out, the discussions over the wounded turned into a crude gavotte—one step forward and two steps sideways, then do-si-do and circle back. The key French figure was Dr. Pierre Huard, tall and thin, dramatic and quixotic, and deeply drawn to the Vietnamese. He had mastered the language and married a Vietnamese woman, who helped him develop a circle of Vietnamese friends. Huard was an old Indochina hand, having been sent there as a doctor for the navy. He then practiced surgery at Lanessan Hospital, which he left to teach at the Hanoi School of Medicine. There he encouraged the recruitment of Vietnamese students to fight alongside the French. After 1946, some of his students, upon graduating, joined Ho Chi Minh's forces. When Huard became the head of the Red Cross in Hanoi, his contacts with the Vietminh were often with former students. Huard was a man astride two cultures, who believed that the only way for the French to remain in Indochina was to give the people their independence.

His opinions did not endear him to the military. In 1950, when de Lattre was in command, the general became convinced that Huard was a Vietminh agent and had him fired from the Red Cross. But Huard was reinstated, and now he was seen as the providential figure, capable of negotiating with the enemy. The Vietminh were hostile to the Red Cross, which they saw as an agent of international capitalism. Nor did they trust French aircraft with Red Cross markings, which had been used in deceptive maneuvers. But they would talk to Huard, an outspoken adversary of French policy. He was chosen to head the French negotiating team.

On May 11, General Cogny, with Navarre's approval, broadcast a message over the army's station, Radio Hirondelle, calling for the evacuation of the wounded "as quickly as possible, under the following conditions: A first group of 450 wounded, 250 of them seriously . . . with the possibility of further evacuations. . . . In view of the condition of the runway, evacuation by helicopter and Beaver. . . . During the evacuation, all other air activity will be suspended in an area of ten kilometers around the base. Also suspended on RP41 between Son La, Tuan Giao, and Dien Bien Phu."

Later that day, a reply came from the Voice of Vietnam: "The high command of the Vietnamese Popular Army authorizes the French to come for their wounded in Dien Bien Phu. A delegation should be sent at once to meet with our delegates and discuss the conditions of transfer. The French helicopters should carry the sign of the Red Cross."

Dr. Huard was ordered on a "Mission of Liaison with the Vietminh High Command." On the morning of May 12, accompanied by two other doctors and an expert in air transport, he flew from Hanoi to Luang Prabang, where the group boarded a Sikorsky for Dien Bien Phu.

They arrived on a repaired area of the runway marked by four parachutes. On both sides of the runway, hundreds of coolies wearing gauze masks buried the dead. Dr. Huard introduced himself to the Vietminh commander of the conquered base, Colonel Cao Van Khanh of the 308th Division, a puffed-up martinet strapped into a Soviet-style uniform with shiny boots. He had power of life and death over the wounded, for he drew up the lists of those to be evacuated, based on the reports of his chief doctor, Nguyen Thuc Mau.

Colonel Khanh led Huard into one of the Viet-erected wigwams for a tête-à-tête. While Khanh got down to business, the others in Huard's party examined the runway, pocked with craters and twisted steel strips that stuck up in the air. No Dakota could land there.

Khanh told Huard that they planned to release, as stipulated in Cogny's message, a first group of 450 wounded. The possibility of a second group would be studied later. Khanh insisted that the bombing of RP41 would have to stop, as also stipulated in Cogny's message, "in order to allow the Vietminh health services to evacuate their own wounded." He particularly underlined the stretch of RP41 between Son La, fifty miles east of Dien Bien Phu, and Tuan Giao, farther north, where the Vietminh had their main depot. This happened to be the route Giap was taking to move his divisions to the Tonkin Delta. French aerial photos showed Molotova trucks already on the move, pulling artillery. The evacuation of the wounded was a transparent tactic for obtaining the suspension of bombing on RP41, so that Giap could launch operations in the Delta.

Dr. Huard said he was not authorized to sign Khanh's agreement. He and his team left Dien Bien Phu at 4 P.M. and Huard was in Cogny's office at the Citadelle by 9:30. Despite his radio message of May 11, Cogny was having second thoughts about stopping the bombing of RP41, which would create a dangerous military situation in the Delta. He also wondered why Colonel Khanh had made no mention of including Vietnamese wounded in the evacuation. However, after a conversation with Navarre, they agreed to suspend bombing on RP41.

Huard was told to go back to Dien Bien Phu on the morning of May 14, with two helicopters and a Beaver, and a letter of agreement from Cogny. They flew in from Luang Prabang in the early afternoon, but the single-engine Beaver, a small bush plane, skidded on the torn-up runway and slammed into one of the choppers, damaging the Beaver's propeller and the helicopter's cabin. The Beaver had to stay on the base overnight, awaiting repairs.

Huard showed Colonel Khanh Cogny's letter. When the colonel said evacuation could begin that very day, Huard signed an agreement. Due to logistical problems, only eleven wounded men were flown out, at 3:30 P.M. The eleven consisted of three Algerians, one of whom, Mohammed Chouise, had lost both legs; three Legionnaires, one of whom, Louis Zucotti, was also a double amputee; and five paratroopers, mostly amputees. On the way to Luang Prabang, where they were to spend the night, they were bounced around in a violent storm. Visibility was reduced to forty yards, which compelled the tiny squadron to land at the military post of Nam Bac. The next day, the eleven were flown to Hanoi. At Lanessan Hospital, some of them were interviewed by Radio Hirondelle. Casimir Pekarsy of the 6th BPC said: "I was wounded on May 1 and my bandage wasn't changed for ten days. It was full of worms and pus." He had no idea why he was one of the first eleven evacuated. It seemed that Colonel Khanh had deliberately chosen mainly Algerians and non-French Legionnaires.

Dr. Chippaux, a member of Huard's team, had tried to talk to the wounded in the tents but was driven back. He made notes of what he saw: "Many cases of gangrene, many thoracic wounds, an estimated 250 amputees. We hope to get them all out."

Radio intercepts showed that wounded officers were asked to write letters that were read over the Voice of Vietnam, such as this one from the Legionnaire captain Capeyron: "Coming out of our trenches we could finally breathe fresh air. . . . Our Legionnaires were singing and shouting with joy. Now our only hope is that the success of the Geneva Conference will return us to our families."

On May 15, Navarre wired Cogny that he was altering the evacuation agreement out of concern for the military repercussions. He felt that he had been duped. The Vietminh would not allow French teams to repair the runway for the landing of Dakotas. By using only Sikorskys and Beavers, which could carry six men on stretchers and three seated, or three on stretchers and seven seated, the evacuation would take weeks. During that time, the Viets would have free use of RP41 to move their battalions and heavy weapons.

Navarre asked that negotiations be started over from scratch along the following lines:

- Repair the airstrip so Dakotas can land, to speed up the rhythm of evacuation.
- Accept the neutrality of RP41, while verifying it be used only to take out Vietminh wounded.
- Specify that Vietnamese must be released along with other wounded.

"Until these negotiations bear fruit," Navarre concluded, "I will continue air action over RP41. The Vietminh command is hereby notified."

Back in Hanoi, Dr. Huard was told on May 15 that the agreement he had signed had been cancelled. He was in shock, feeling that he had been sorely used. Cogny wired Navarre on May 15: "Dr. Huard objects to change in attitude and refuses to continue." Navarre agreed to delay the start of the bombing until May 18.

French intelligence reported that the Vietminh were in no hurry to reach an agreement—they could continue to move their divisions up RP41 as long as the bombs did not fall. The pilot of the Beaver stuck for repairs, Lieutenant Arrighi, had counted the number of trucks he saw leave, loaded with equipment.

At Lanessan Hospital, when the first wounded came in, the surgeon Jacques Aulong made a point of chatting with them. In a letter to his parents, he wrote: "The paras have a grudge against Castries. They say he never came out of his hole. The Legionnaires have a grudge against the North Africans, who they say ran like rabbits. The Legion and the paras did the fighting."

Dr. Huard had a change of heart and decided to return to Dien Bien Phu on the morning of May 18. Colonel Khanh scoffed at the French shuffle. "Is your mission official?" he asked. "Do you represent General Navarre or General Cogny? If we sign an agreement as we did the other day, will it remain valid? We are concerned that an agreement from General Cogny would be countermanded."

"This time we will ask General Navarre to sign it," Huard said. And yet, Colonel Khanh did not seem concerned by Navarre's threat to resume bombing, and released nineteen wounded. That night, B-26s bombed a truck convoy on RP41. And yet the evacuations continued on May 19. The explanation was twofold: The Vietminh figured they had played a trump card at Geneva by announcing their humanitarian gesture and did not want the benefits canceled. General Giap closely monitored the progress of the conference, and his policy was based on enhancing its success for the DRV. Also, he was happy to get rid of the French wounded, whose presence slowed down his departure from the base. So, as it turned out, it didn't matter whether Navarre bombed or not—the evacuations were not interrupted, and Huard did not have to resign his commission.

In Geneva, however, Chou En-lai was incensed, and reported to Mao on May 19 that the French were using the issue of sick and wounded soldiers "as a means for political blackmail and have conducted a series of slanderous propaganda activities. . . . [The fact] that the French military resumed bombardment on the 18th and killed fifteen French prisoners had caused heated repercussions." If this in fact happened, it was not reported by the French.

May 19 was Ho Chi Minh's birthday, and there was a parade in his honor at Dien Bien Phu, complete with two French tanks that Colonel Khanh had repaired. The Viets handed out cigarettes and wine. A large birthday evacuation was announced, and the choppers flew in. Geneviève de Galard had been asked to write Ho a birthday greeting, which she did, thinking it would help the wounded. It was, she said, just a letter from a nurse: "I want to thank you for your compassionate attitude toward the wounded that you have freed. . . . I will try to encourage greater understanding between our two peoples." But when the Vietminh newspaper published the letter, de Galard was criticized by the French command. After the feast, 78 men were evacuated, among them Haas, the triple amputee, and the blind lieutenant Simon Marie, of the 3rd Battalion of the 3rd RTA (Algerian fusiliers).

On May 20, Navarre bombed RP41 again, and 52 wounded were flown out. On May 21, bad weather limited the number of flights, and only 17 left the camp. On May 22, Vietminh radio declared that the bombing "proves that the French have no interest in the condition of their wounded," but 108 were flown out. On the night of the twenty-third, a B-26 dropped its bombs only four miles from the base, but 136 were flown out.

And so it went. On May 24, Geneviève de Galard was the first of the medical staff to be freed, flying out with 141 wounded. She felt guilty leaving the others behind. In Hanoi, where the publicity-conscious Cogny was at the airport to greet her, she found herself a media star, and gave a press conference. "Were you afraid of dying?" she was asked. She was on the cover of *Paris Match* that week.

In another first, those evacuated on May 24 included 8 Vietnamese and 4 officers, including Liutenant Defline, who'd been operated on by a Vietminh surgeon. Waiting on a stretcher by the side of the airstrip while the whirring blades of the choppers raised clouds of dust, Defline kept count—he'd been on the base 185 days. In Luang Prabang, he was offered a beer. But in Hanoi, his leg had to be amputated.

On May 25, 4 officers and 9 Vietnamese were among the 153 evacu-

ated. On May 26 came the final evacuation, 142 wounded, including 67
Vietnamese. In that last batch was Lieutenant Rondeaux, 1st Company,
5th BPVN, who had been badly wounded in the fighting of March 28. He
had an artificial anus and his weight was down from 170 to 90 pounds. In
Hanoi, he was operated on but did not survive. On May 27, Huard and his
team were back in Hanoi. They felt they had done the best they could: a
total of 858 evacuated: 624 Europeans, 150 North Africans and Africans,
and 84 Vietnamese. Another agreement was reached to exchange the 27
noncoms and officers in the Dien Bien Phu medical service for 575 Vietnamese prisoners of the French. Three doctors, including Grauwin, and
24 orderlies were picked up on June 1.

The evacuations stopped abruptly after Giap's divisions had been
trucked out, and the 200 remaining wounded were sent to POW camps:
some in trucks, like Lieutenant Lucien Le Boudec, men with fractures and
amputees, crowded together over bumpy roads that made them howl with
pain; and some on foot, like Sergeant Monchotte, who had several bullets
in his kidneys that couldn't be extracted and walked bent over with two
sticks.

I Seem to Have Been Lied To

After the defeat at Dien Bien Phu, there was a lull in fighting on all fronts,
and Navarre had time to study an endgame strategy. In the Delta, the
Hanoi–Haiphong corridor was calm. The five divisions that had taken the
camp, the 304th, 308th, 312th, 316th, and 351st, had started toward
the Delta but were slowed by French bombing from the air. Needing rest,
they stopped in safe zones to recuperate.

Navarre suspected Cogny of spreading pessimistic rumors in the
French press. Cogny was predicting a catastrophe in the Delta, where
"the human anthill" would rise up in insurrection. He proposed evacuating Hanoi. Among the headlines that Navarre traced back to Cogny
were:

TWO BATTALIONS OF VIETMINH HAVE ARRIVED IN HANOI DISGUISED AS

FISHERMEN AND TAXI DRIVERS

HANOI IS ENCIRCLED BY 100,000 VIETMINH WHO BLOCK ALL ENTRIES
   IN BROAD DAYLIGHT
THE MORALE OF THE TROOPS HAS DETERIORATED TO A PSYCHOSIS THAT
   COULD TURN TO PANIC

Navarre warned Cogny that he would be held responsible for the de-featist atmosphere in the Hanoi command. There was one man in the army that Navarre trusted, and that was General Paul Ely, the armed forces chief of staff in Paris, who was so scrupulous he was known as "the hairsplitter." The two men kept up a regular correspondence and Ely acted as Navarre's lobbyist with the government. Navarre wrote Ely that he wanted to fire Cogny. Ely replied that he would be difficult to replace.

In his candid letters, Navarre wrote that the Vietnamese National Army had become a rabble, deserting right and left. He needed reinforce-ments from France, since Giap was moving his divisions into the Delta. Navarre was in effect asking for three divisions, Ely decided. That would mean sending conscripts, who could not be ready until at least October. In France, young men at the age of eighteen had to perform two years of mil-itary service, but under the law they could not serve outside France. The law would have to be changed by the National Assembly. Sending three di-visions to Indochina would also reduce France's contribution to the de-fense of Europe under NATO and under the still unratified European Defense Community.

Ely let Navarre know that he was asking for the impossible. Navarre replied that he would try to hold on in the Delta, but that it was becoming more difficult to keep the Hanoi–Haiphong road open. He would eventu-ally have to abandon French-held territory while Geneva was ongoing, which would weaken the French negotiating position and lead to further desertions.

The Committee for National Defense met on May 14 and 15, after Laniel's narrow victory in the National Assembly, to discuss what could be done for Navarre. René Pleven, the minister of defense, said he did not op-pose a pullback, but he wanted it to look like a consolidation, not a retreat. It was decided to send Ely to Saigon to tell Navarre that his first concern must be the safeguard of the expeditionary corps. There must be no more

Dien Bien Phus. The commander in chief "must avoid the dispersion of our forces," the committee instructed, "in order not to risk the attrition of the expeditionary corps." Navarre should regroup his forces in the "useful Delta."

As for the three divisions of conscripts, that was put on hold by Premier Laniel. However, their formation would be announced to help the French cause at Geneva. This breathtaking bluff was deemed a "psychological necessity" that would also impress the Americans, since the United States had sent an army of draftees to Korea.

Ely arrived in Saigon on May 18 with General Raoul Salan, the old Indochina hand. He found Navarre still balking at launching the pullback while Geneva was on. Ely was impressed by the argument that a pullback would provoke mass desertions. He left Saigon on May 23 intending to tell the government to delay the pullback and still hoping for a positive decision on the three additional divisions.

On May 25, Ely reported back to the committee. His secret report was leaked to the press. He sketched a somber situation: heavy losses, lack of offensive spirit, unreliable Vietnamese troops. Giap had one hundred battalions ready to attack the Delta, which was defended by sixty-three French battalions. By late June, Giap could launch an offensive. Navarre had insisted that he must remain in command. But Ely, with his "on the one hand but on the other hand" caution, proposed that Navarre be replaced by an illustrious commander who could start anew, without the burden of a crushing defeat. If such a commander could not be found, it would be risky to change the Navarre-Cogny command, in spite of their disagreements.

Ely, who had no inclination for the job, did not realize that he was nominating himself. The Council of Ministers had soured on Navarre, and also on Commissioner General Maurice Dejean, who was said to be "good at giving dinners." On May 28, both men were relieved of their duties, and on June 2, Ely was named to fill both positions, like de Lattre before him. Ely told a friend: "This is the worst mishap of my career."

On June 3 in Hanoi, Dr. Jacques Aulong was invited to the annual celebration of the 8th Spahis, a tank unit stationed near Lanessan Hospital, whose commander was General Navarre's brother. Navarre was there, and Aulong introduced himself. Navarre told him, "What comforts me is the knowledge that the wounded were treated in conditions comparable to those at Lanessan." Aulong could not believe what he was hearing. He decided to tell Navarre about the crowding, the improvisation, the mud, the pestilence, the men sent back to their units after amputations, and the flooded trenches full of dying men. Navarre listened impassively, then turned to his orderly and said, "Have Grauwin and Le Damany returned? I want to see them both tonight." Then, looking off into the distance, he said, "I seem to have been lied to."

Ely was back in Saigon on June 6 with Salan as his number two. He found Navarre to be unduly optimistic. Of course it was natural for a departing commander to want to leave a favorable impression on his successor. There was in fact a pause in the fighting. At 2 A.M., however, Ely was awakened by heavy firing. It was a Viet ambush on the outskirts of the city, which brought home to him that there were no "calm zones," although the regulars continued to order their aperitifs daily at the Grand' Rue Café. From Geneva, Bidault wired Ely asking for a rundown on Vietminh progress in the Delta. Bidault was worried that the hardening attitude of the Vietminh delegation signaled a coming offensive. The secret talks with Colonel de Brébisson were tending toward partition, which Bidault could not accept, since that would endanger the two million Vietnamese Catholics in the north. Ely replied that from what he had seen, partition was the only solution, although the French would try to keep the enclave of Haiphong for as long as possible. One of the characteristics of the war was the imbrication of the two armies in Tonkin. A cease-fire required separating them into two clearly defined zones, as had been done in Korea.

Bad Afternoon, Much Confusion

At Geneva, the restricted sessions proceeded at a halting pace. They were held in a carpeted room, smaller than the chamber for the plenary sessions, with nine tables arranged in a rectangle. At each table sat a delegate, flanked by a couple of advisers and a translator. Each speech had to be translated into every language of the conference, and the multilingual drone went on for hours. Since U.N. personnel were not admitted to these sessions, each delegation had stenographers sitting behind the tables on leather benches under the windows.

Eden had hoped they could get down to business, but the speech making went on unabated, such as Pham Van Dong's tendentious exposé on the history of Indochina during the previous ninety years. The Soviets and Chinese seemed to be exchanging carbon copies of each other's speeches. Nor was there any variance in the positions of China and the DRV, which were in lockstep. Bidault reported "a narrow cohesion among our adversaries."

Walter Bedell Smith believed the Communists were stalling so that the Vietminh could win further victories in Indochina to enhance their position at the conference. He wanted to go back to plenary sessions, where they would have to stall in public before the press. Eden was "flabbergasted" when Smith proposed this idea to him on May 19. It had taken three weeks to get the secret sessions started and it was pointless to abandon them after only two days. Eden felt that, given the aloofness of the Americans and the difficulties of the French, he would have to handle the personal diplomacy. Smith reported to Washington that "the British believe, either honestly or for political effect, that they can continue to play the role of mediator."

It was, however, Eden's personal diplomacy that resulted in the minimal progress that had been made. His plan was to work through Molotov and Chou, who, he hoped, would lean on the DRV. At first he found Chou inaccessible and bitterly anti-American, but when Molotov brought Eden and Chou together on April 29, he saw that Chou was much friendlier outside the conference, where he did not have to pose. Eden was invited to the grandiose Chinese villa and admired the porcelain to break the ice. He then asked Chou to dinner, not to discuss the conference, but simply to get to know each other and find areas where their sympathies concurred. Eden knew he was making headway when Chou reminisced on the hardships of the Long March of 1934, when the Chinese Red Army covered six thousand miles on foot.

There was progress when Eden's cochairman, Molotov, agreed to discuss military and political problems separately. This was a major concession to Eden. There was further progress when, on May 19, Molotov raised the problem of "regroupment zones." This was a sticking point, for the term was a euphemism for partition. Bidault was opposed to partition and called for "leopard-spot" regrouping of troops wherever they were currently stationed, in isolated islands. Bidault had written Bao Dai on May 6 that the French goal was to seek a cease-fire followed by elections. "Nothing could be more contrary to our intentions than the establishment of two states." The DRV position, expressed by Pham Van Dong on May 29, was that the armies be regrouped on either side of a line of demarcation.

Despite his aversion to partition, Bidault did not rule out secret meetings with the Chinese and the DRV, where, as it turned out, much of the real work was done between Colonel Jacques Guillermaz and Wang Ping-nan. Wang was a much-traveled and sophisticated diplomat who had married a German aristocrat, Anna von Kleist; she became a Communist and wrote a book called *I Fight for Mao.*

At their first meeting, Guillermaz asked Wang to help out with the wounded. They met again on May 18, and Wang assured Guillermaz that everything they discussed would get back to Chou. "We are not here to back the Vietminh," he said, "but to end the war." Emphasizing that China's role was not to spur on the DRV but to guide it, he said: "China is not necessarily encouraging military action in the Delta." This was good news for the French, at a time when the defense of Hanoi and Haiphong was uppermost on the French military agenda.

The secret meetings with the Vietminh—between Colonel Michel de Brébisson and Colonel Ha Van Lau, both military members of their respective delegations—had begun over the issue of the wounded. They met on May 19, and continued to meet, though making little headway.

The procedure at the restricted meetings was to hit a hurdle, then try to get past it to the next hurdle. One hurdle was partition. Another was separate agreements for Laos, Cambodia, and Vietnam. A third was the composition of the armistice control commission. Eden pushed to include the Colombo powers: India, Pakistan, Burma, and Ceylon. Molotov agreed on India, but wanted Poland and Czechoslovakia. Long discussions ensued on whether a Communist armistice controller could be neutral.

At every restricted session, Eden worried what the political weather would be like. On May 27, he noted "bad afternoon, much confusion."

Chou was grandstanding again, calling for a complete cease-fire in all of Indochina. However, after the session, Wang met with Guillermaz and said the Chinese were serious about reaching a settlement. "When we speak of negotiations," he said, "that means both sides need it."

Smith felt that he was being outflanked by Eden. The United States was still trying to reach an agreement with the French on intervention, in order to keep them in the war and avoid partition. General Trapnell had seen General Ely on May 27, but nothing had been decided. American policy seemed to have reached a dead end, which may explain Smith's cable to Secretary of State Dulles after the session of May 29. Eden, he said, "gave a startling public exhibition of impatience and pique. . . . His performance was absolutely shocking to me. . . . The British attempt to distract and deceive was so obvious that even Molotov could not swallow it."

In Paris, Laniel was hanging by a thread, which made it impossible for him to comply with American conditions. In Washington, at a meeting with the president on May 19, Dulles continued to blame the British for allowing the Communists "to consolidate their position throughout Indochina." Eisenhower, who was expecting a visit from Churchill in June, said he might tell his old friend that the British were "promoting a second Munich." Dulles said the situation was deteriorating to the point where it might be necessary to have Chiang Kai-shek's forces conduct diversionary operations on the China coast with U.S. naval and air support. This was just the kind of brinkmanship that Eden was trying to avert at Geneva. Dulles showed the draft of a congressional resolution to that effect to Senator Knowland, who objected that "it would amount to giving the President a blank check."

At around that time, General Ridgway, the army chief of staff, prepared a report for the president that outlined the disadvantages of sending ground troops to Indochina. He said the cost would be greater than in Korea. "Every telephone lineman, road repair party, every ambulance and every rear-area aid station, would have to be under guard or they would be shot [at] around the clock." Ike remained convinced that the United States should not intervene in Indochina on any basis except united action.

On May 30, the authoritative military correspondent for *The New York Times*, Hanson Baldwin, reported that two Vietminh divisions had infiltrated the Red River Delta in the south and would soon attack. Their strategy was to bring down the Laniel government in the hope that its successor would want peace at any price.

Peace Is Like the Pyrenees

In Geneva, arrangements were being made for Bidault to hold his first private meeting with Chou. At 10 P.M. on June 1, Bidault, along with Jean Chauvel and Colonel Guillermaz, arrived in secrecy at a friend's villa on the outskirts of Geneva. Chou soon arrived with his aides and apologized for being late.

Bidault said the conference was at "a critical juncture." He proposed that a military commission from each side determine regrouping areas for the troops. "Time is running out," he said. "If the quarreling continues, the situation will get worse. . . . The commanders must quickly determine the areas on their maps where the forces of both sides shall be regrouped. . . . An enlarged war [an allusion to U.S. intervention] will hurt everyone."

Chou replied: "The risk exists—American intervention. . . . That is what we are concerned about."

"We are a country with a long military tradition," Bidault said, "and we don't like failure. If we can't obtain a reasonable settlement, I will suggest to my government a laissez-faire policy [meaning anything goes]."

Chou: "There is no need to mention a laissez-faire policy. . . . The restoration of peace is glorious for both sides. . . . The French people are peace-loving [an allusion to their opposition to the Indochina war]."

Bidault: "Yes, the French people love peace. However, we have to live with our history and tradition."

Chou: "If the war broadens, it will not help the glory of France. It would be nothing but what we Chinese call a 'fisherman's catch.' The people of Indochina and France will suffer miserably."

Bidault was using the threat of U.S. intervention to get Chou to compromise on troop resettlement, but Chou wasn't buying it, so Bidault tacked: "The newspapers say that I came to Geneva to prepare World War III. This is so naïve! But we can't accept just any kind of agreement. . . . I have experienced two world wars. During the first war I was a corporal. During the second war I was a sergeant. I don't want to be promoted to master sergeant in the third war." What he wanted was, first, to have the commanders on both sides draw a map of regrouping areas and, second, to solve the armistice commission problem.

Chou said Bidault's points could and would be solved soon.

Bidault offered Chou a rare book as a gift.

Chou thanked him and warned that "some people intend to use threats." He suggested they should keep up their meetings. Their joint efforts would improve the situation and the national status of France would be furthered "through your peace efforts."

"We are neighbors," Chou said. "It is very convenient to see each other."

"Our opinions are pretty close, just like next-door neighbors," Bidault said. In fact, next-door neighbors often quarrel, and Chou had politely rebuffed Bidault's advances, knowing that the conference was moving toward partition. Bidault asked Chou not to talk to the press about their meeting. He did not want the Americans to find out about it. At a banquet given by Eden on June 2, Chou did compromise on the armistice commission issue by saying he did not back the inclusion of Poland and Czechoslovakia. He preferred a mix of Asian and European nations.

At the June 3 restricted session, Bidault said: "Communist nations cannot be neutral." On June 4, Smith proposed Switzerland, Sweden, India, and Pakistan for the armstice commission. The conference was deadlocked on the issue. Eden was fed up because session after session resulted "in mutual recrimination and endless argument."

On June 5, Chauvel and Guillermaz went to the Chinese villa for a secret meeting with Wang Ping-nan. At the meeting, Chauvel said: "The conference has not made much progress in the past several days. The discussion went around in circles. We are running out of time and we should move faster." The critical issues were still troop regroupment and the armistice commission. The French military had met with the Vietminh several times but they had not addressed specific issues.

Wang Ping-nan agreed that military staff contacts had gotten nowhere and that days had been wasted on the supervision issue. "If you argue that a Communist state cannot be neutral," he said, "then neither can a capitalist state be neutral. If so, there is no neutral nation in all the world."

When they met again on June 7, Wang told Chauvel that the main obstacle to progress was Smith, who kept saying, "No objection, but no acceptance." "This continuing negative attitude doesn't do any good," Wang argued.

Chauvel agreed, saying, "We have noticed recently that Molotov, Chou, and Eden all looked for a common position. The U.S. shows the most distrustful attitude." The French quandary, Chauvel explained, was that they could only offer solutions endorsed by their allies.

"The Chinese delegation does not have any selfish purpose," Wang said. "What we want to see is not a continuous bleeding of France and Vietnam, but a normalization of French-Vietnamese relations."

"Peace is like the Pyrenees," Chauvel observed. "Sometimes they look dark, sometimes bright. As long as we have confidence, we will eventually see bright Pyrenees."

Wang replied, "The Chang Bai Mountains always stand tall without any change. Clouds and rain are temporary conditions."

In Washington, Dulles continued to believe that the Communists were stalling until the Red River Delta went down the drain. At a press conference on June 8, he said, "The United States has no intention of dealing with the Indochina situation unilaterally," unless there was open armed aggression from China. Afterward he told Ambassador Bonnet that he deplored the French game of asking for U.S. help at their convenience. Laniel's request for two Marine divisions was "vain and without object."

On that day, Eisenhower received a letter from General Gruenther at NATO, who had been called in by Defense Minister Pleven to discuss the new divisions the French were promising to send to Indochina. Gruenther had his doubts and wrote, "Maybe!" Pleven told Gruenther, "If we should lose the Delta, it would start a wave of anti-ally outbursts in France because the allies let us down."

Eisenhower replied to Gruenther that the French asked for help but refused to meet the conditions. The United States had sent draftees to Korea, but the French refused to send conscripts to Indochina.

As for Dulles, he had lost all faith in the French and told Ambassador Bonnet on June 9 that the U.S. was not interested in making commitments the French could use "for internal political maneuvering or negotiating at Geneva." His offer was not one that could "lie indefinitely on the table to be picked up one minute before midnight."

I'll Bet the Vietminh Is Hiding in There

The sputtering talks between the French and Vietminh military commands got going again. The French team was now headed by a general, Henri Delteil, backing up Colonel de Brébisson. The Vietminh brought in Deputy Defense Minister Ta Quang Buu to reinforce Colonel Ha Van Lau. On June 9, Brébisson approached Ha Van Lau and proposed to discuss what Pham Van Dong had meant on May 25 by "an exchange of territories." The two teams met secretly that evening at a villa outside Geneva. Buu unfolded a map of Indochina and placed his hand over northern Vietnam. He said they would claim the territory of Tonkin and northern Annam down to Hue, at the 16th parallel. In addition to a state, they needed a capital and a port, meaning Hanoi and Haiphong.

This was the first specific declaration of what the DRV wanted. The French asked what they would get in exchange. Buu gave no answer, saying only that he hoped to continue the secret talks, given the "inconveniences" of the conference.

On June 9, at the National Assembly, a debate on Indochina had begun. The left-wing deputy Pierre Mendès France, long regarded as the leading figure opposed to the war, called Bidault a warmonger who wanted the United States to intervene in "this infernal poker game in which millions of lives are at stake." Mendès said: "There is only one solution . . . direct negotiations." As Bidault put it, "Mendès attacked the government untiringly, displaying much stubbornness, shrewdness, and treachery."

On June 12, the Laniel government fell, by a vote of 306 to 293, over the failure of its Indochina policy. Laniel resigned on June 13, and the following day Mendès France was invited to form a government. Bidault remained in Geneva until that happened. His nerves were shot and he drank too much. He fell asleep in mid-session. On June 16, he and Chauvel went up to a group of Chinese at a buffet next to the council chamber. Bidault shook hands, saying, "I'll bet the Vietminh is hiding in there." He then turned to Chauvel and said: "It's not the first time I've shaken hands with a murderer."

If You Chase Two Rabbits, You Miss Both

For Dulles, the fall of Laniel meant that the Geneva Conference was now pointless. He wired Walter Bedell Smith on June 14: "Final adjournment of the conference is in our best interest." Perhaps the British would now be willing to discuss united action. As for the French, it might be "best to let them get out of Indochina entirely and then try to rebuild from the foundation."

Dulles's pessimism mounted when Smith wired that secret military talks were being conducted by the two sides. On June 17, he wired Smith that "QUOTE underground military talks UNQUOTE, even more than conference proceedings, are pointing toward de facto partition under conditions such that Communist takeover of all Vietnam looms ahead clearly. . . . French may end by accepting any Vietminh proposition which offers hope of extricating Expeditionary Corps. There can of course be no repeat no question of U.S. participation in any attempt to QUOTE sell UNQUOTE a partition to non-Communist Vietnamese."

As Smith reported to Dulles on June 18, with the rise of Mendès the French were abandoning Bidault's "leopard-spot" solution for repositioning troops. Also, if they had to give the Vietminh an enclave in southern Vietnam in exchange for keeping Haiphong, they would give up Haiphong. The line the French had in mind for partition was vaguely described by Chauvel as "the line of the chalk cliffs," Smith reported, which corresponded to the 19th parallel. Chauvel added that the "underground military talks" Dulles was concerned about had thus far been unproductive.

On June 19, Smith wired Dulles that he had gone to the Russian villa to tell Molotov he was leaving, and they talked for an hour and a half. Molotov said that Walter Robertson's outburst at the previous day's restricted session seemed to show that the United States did not want to find a solution. Smith replied that he was not convinced by Pham Van Dong's remarks about withdrawing Vietminh "volunteers" in Laos and Cambodia. If Laos and Cambodia agreed not to allow any American bases, they should also keep out the Chinese. The United States did not want those two small countries "handed over to the Chinese." As for the Vietminh, they were demanding too much—the entire Delta, including Hanoi and Haiphong. Molotov said there was an old Russian proverb that said if you chased two rabbits, you missed both. In wanting both the northern and the southern part of Vietnam, the French were chasing two rabbits. Smith said partition was "repugnant" to the United States, and that the Vietminh were chasing two rabbits in wanting both Hanoi and Haiphong. Molotov said the U.S. aversion to partition could be solved by holding elections at once. The important thing was to be realistic, and "to avoid putting out one-sided views or extreme pretensions."

Smith commented that "the raising of the ante by the Communist side probably reflects an estimate on their part that our intervention is improbable and that they are safe to go ahead. . . . The determining factor will continue to be their estimate of the likelihood of U.S. or joint intervention and nothing short of a conviction on their part that this intervention will take place will stop them from . . . taking all of [Indochina] eventually." Smith's alarming conclusion was a misreading of the role that China and the Soviets were playing in restraining the Vietminh. He was out of the loop in the private discussions and took a position guaranteed to please his boss in Washington. As a former U.S. ambassador to Moscow under Stalin, he had also formed a habit of suspecting anything the Communists said.

The coming to power of Mendès France, with his program of cease-fire and partition, rippled out to Geneva, where there were sudden changes in the Chinese and Soviet positions. On June 15, Eden saw Chou, who said he could convince the Vietminh to withdraw from Laos and Cambodia. China would recognize their royalist governments, as long as there were no American bases, and Vietminh "volunteers" would pull out. This was a huge step toward the French and British positions, as well as an implicit admission that the Vietminh had invaded both countries. Laos and Cambodia were in the same situation as Vietnam, attacked by outsiders. Chou's offer showed how far the Chinese were prepared to go to keep American troops out of Indochina. That afternoon, at the twenty-first restricted session, Chou presented his plan. Pham Van Dong was unhappy about it, and made some noise, but had no choice. Chou was his godfather, making an offer he couldn't refuse. At this same session, Molotov gave up his insistence on an equal number of Communist and non-Communist members for the armistice commission, and proposed adding a fifth member, Indonesia.

In Paris, Mendès France addressed the National Assembly on June 17. France would not accept peace conditions contrary to her interests, he said. He would set himself a deadline of four weeks, until July 20, to reach a settlement. If he failed, he would resign. The National Assembly gave him 310 votes, a majority, but he refused to accept the 99 Communist votes. In a second vote he obtained a majority of 419 votes to 47, with 147 abstentions, and became the Fourth Republic's sixteenth premier. On June 19, he formed his cabinet, placing Jean Chauvel at the head of the French delegation in Geneva, and serving as his own foreign minister.

Bidault argued that by setting a July 20 deadline, "Mendès threw himself at the mercy of the Communists. All they had to do was wait until the time limit expired. . . . It was like an engineer's decision to remove the rail beyond a certain point in order to guarantee that a train will stop exactly there." The counterargument was that Mendès had made a clever move, for if he did not meet his deadline and resigned, what kind of government would Ho Chi Minh then face? Better the known than the unknown. For Ho, this was a onetime opportunity. It seemed to General Delteil, who was conducting negotiations with the Vietminh military, that they wanted to settle. The war was costly for them too, and the civilian population was burdened with taxes.

The Cease-Fire Should Come First

After more than six weeks of boondoggling, the foreign ministers in attendance at Geneva were ready for a summer break, and off they went— Eden to London, Molotov to Moscow, Chou on a goodwill visit to India and Burma, and Bidault back to Paris without a job. Smith left too, replaced by U. Alexis Johnson, who later recalled that he was given no instructions.

In Washington on June 23, Smith told members of Congress that Vietnam would be partitioned and that if there were a free election, Ho Chi Minh would get "80 per cent of the vote," since "Bao Dai was corrupt and the French still continue to impose colonialism."

"We now have a Far Eastern Munich," Senator Knowland said.

Smith responded: "We haven't given up anything that wasn't first occupied by force of arms, which cannot now be retaken."

On June 21, Churchill wired Eisenhower: If the French had wanted to fight for Indochina, why didn't they send troops conscripted for two years? Instead they had fought for eight years "with unworthy local troops . . . and with the Foreign Legion, a large proportion of whom were Germans. . . . Mendès France, whom I do not know, has made up his mind to clear out on the best terms available. If that is so, I think he is right." Three days later, he and Eden flew to Washington in the Stratocruiser *Canopus*. They were hoping to convince Eisenhower and Dulles to give Mendès a chance. Eden was exhausted from his six-hour sessions in the chair at Geneva. Churchill would be eighty in November, and though his face was pink and unlined, he had suffered a stroke and was increasingly deaf.

On the flight over, Eden expostulated on Dulles, how foolish he had been to walk out in Geneva, how stupid the Americans were to never exchange a word with the Russians and the Chinese. "You cannot expect to get anything out of people if you won't speak to them." Churchill grunted his assent. Eden said China was a formidable power, and unlike the Russians, "they did not seem to be frightened by the hydrogen bomb." Churchill, who was back in the days of the Boxer Rebellion, talked about "the little yellow men."

They landed on June 25, with Churchill hoping that, in their talks, Eden and Dulles would not kill each other. It all went rather well. Dulles now accepted the partition of Vietnam, given conditions on the ground. But whatever the settlement, he said, the United States would not endorse it. Congress would never guarantee the Communist domination of northern Vietnam. On June 29, they drafted a seven-point agreement on the minimal conditions for an armistice. The four most pressing conditions were:

- Integrity of Laos and Cambodia and withdrawal of Vietminh forces
- Preservation of the southern half of Vietnam and if possible an enclave in the Delta
- Transfer of those wishing to be moved from one zone to the other
- International supervision of the agreement

The United States and United Kingdom issued an innocuous communiqué: If there was not an acceptable agreement at Geneva, "the international situation will be seriously aggravated." For once, the two Western powers were in tandem.

Back in Geneva, Chou reported to Mao on June 22 that Eden had come to see him before leaving for London on June 19. Eden said that Vietminh forces should not engage in large-scale hostilities while the negotiations were under way, and that if an agreement was reached hostilities should cease on the spot. He had heard that the Vietminh were attacking French posts. Chou replied that the French should also restrain from large-scale campaigns. Chou said he had just met with Chauvel, who had seen Mendès France in Paris. "Mendès' mission is to quickly reach a peaceful solution by the deadline he has set for himself," Chou reported. To that effect, Chauvel told Chou, Mendès wanted to meet Chou secretly.

They met in Bern on June 23, and Mendès thanked Chou for postponing his trip to India. Mendès had to solve his problem quickly. Chou summed up: The first requirement to a peaceful resolution was a cease-fire. The three Indochinese states all had different problems. Vietnam needed an election for unification after the war. Chou had spoken to Pham Van Dong, who said he would respect the independence of Laos and Cambodia. He had also spoken to the foreign ministers of those two countries, who assured him they did not want American bases. Mendès replied that though the goal for Vietnam was unification, there could not be an election immediately after the cease-fire. Nor did he want any American bases in the region.

Chou said he was glad to hear that. He agreed that the cease-fire should come first and the political settlement second. "It should be two steps, not one step."

Mendès said, "The focus is on the military issues but there is not much progress." He would be returning to Paris that night to see General Ely, who was back from Saigon. They were hoping to move into the practical phase of regrouping areas. There would be a horizontal dividing line from west to east, but the proposed Vietminh line was much more to the south than the real situation reflected.

"We should solve the problem of regrouping first," Chou said.

"Three weeks should be the maximum time," Mendès replied.

General Ely had arrived in Saigon on June 8, with General Salan and his faithful aide, Colonel Brohon, intending to get some idea of what to do next. When Navarre left, Ely detected relief rather than bitterness. Navarre had been promised a high position commensurate with his rank, which never came through.

Ely left for Hanoi on June 10 and spent two days visiting the troops in various Tonkin sectors. His job was to prepare the pullback to "the useful Delta," which would allow the French to concentrate their forces and reduce their imbrications with the Vietminh. He promised Cogny that he would not abandon Hanoi without a fight. His other priority was the Hanoi–Haiphong axis, which had to be kept open for vehicles and trains. Vietminh guerrillas had infiltrated the villages along the route and attacked French convoys day and night. Ely ordered the bombing of the villages, after warnings to the villagers, in an operation called BULLDOZER.

The pullback was due to start on June 20. Ely visited Laos and Cambodia, leaving Salan with Cogny. Back in Saigon on June 15, he was told that Laniel had fallen and Mendès was now premier. Ely left for Paris on June 17, hoping that Mendès' deadline would make him receptive to sending conscripts to Indochina.

Ely's arrival in Paris came at a time when the chiefs of staff had begun to consider the deterioration of Indochina as a burden on French national defense. The war had become an afterthought. Ely resolved to change their thinking. On June 28, Ely attended a meeting of the Committee for National Defense—its first under the new government—with some trepidation. Still hoping to get two divisions of conscripts, he showed those gathered Cogny's "leprosy map" with the Vietminh-controlled zones in red. The map made a strong impression, in showing that a pullback to the "useful Delta" was essential. As for the conscripts, he was promised that the committee would ask the National Assembly to pass a law before July 20 allowing them to serve in Indochina.

Ely flew back to Saigon on July 2, after having been informed that the pullback was a success. Colonel Paul Vanuxem had by July 4 evacuated a total of 68,000 military and civilians, with a loss of 38 dead, 129 wounded, and 26 missing.

In Saigon on July 4, Ely was met by Bao Dai's new premier, Ngo Dinh Diem. Ely recalled that "[Diem's] intransigent nationalism, his aura of mysticism, gave him the certainty of carrying out a divine mission." He was opposed to the Delta pullback, and on one occasion became so strident that Salan came close to slapping him, which may be one of the reasons why Diem preferred Americans.

Dulles was convinced that the French were keeping Diem in the dark about negotiations in Geneva. He wired the embassy in Saigon on July 2 that they should pressure the French to divulge their intentions to this "uncompromising nationalist" in order to "minimize his resentment."

I Can't Feel My Feet

On the night of surrender at Dien Bien Phu, May 7, navy lieutenant Bernard Klotz lay in a clump of grass and looked at the stars, glad to be alive. He took a deep breath, suddenly aware that there were no sounds of firing.

Lieutenant Gildas Fleury of the 8th Choc thought of escaping, but he had no map and no money, and he didn't speak the language, so he decided to help with the stretcher cases. He was convinced that being a prisoner would be like the massacre in the Katyn forest in the spring of 1940, when 4,250 Polish officers who had been taken prisoner were shot on Stalin's orders.

For the Vietminh, ten thousand captured French troops were an immense logistical problem. They had been taking prisoners since 1946, but never in such numbers. Their prison camps were near the Chinese border, close to rice depots, but 375 miles from Dien Bien Phu. The Vietminh needed their trucks to move men and equipment to the Delta, so aside from the thousand or so hospitalized in the hasty triage, the prisoners would have to walk to the camps, even though it would take weeks. The officers were intentionally separated from their men, leaving them without guidance. Those above the rank of captain were taken in trucks to Camp No. 1.

The subaltern officers had to walk. Several hundred men were left behind to serve on mine clearance and other details.

The Vietminh command wanted the prisoners off the base by nightfall, so that the coolies could strip the camp. Nine thousand men were divided into groups of a hundred and marched across the Bailey bridge and up RP41 in single file. Their guards shouted, *"Mao len, mao len"* (Quick, quick). They marched past the strongpoints of Dominique and Béatrice, as the sun dropped between two hills in the west. They marched past hundreds of coolies heading toward the base, men and women wearing gauze masks.

"Is it the smell?" one man asked.

"It's to avoid catching the colonial virus," another replied.

The sky darkened, and there was a chill in the air. To the prisoners, the *bo dois* looked as alike as bowling pins in their baggy green uniforms and flat helmets.

At 10 P.M., the first groups came to a clearing about nine miles from the base. Rain began to fall and they found shelter under the trees. Here they were searched. Lieutenant Pinault recalled that Vietminh soldiers took his watch and his money. Men hid their wedding rings in the lining of their uniforms. A triage was now performed by rank and nationality. The Vietnamese prisoners were removed and sent to reeducation camps. Each group of one hundred men was divided into subgroups of twenty. Then came a little speech from the *can bo* (political commissar): "You will learn to light a fire and cook rice. You will learn to march, the way our soldiers do. You will meet civilians who do not like you, for you have bombed their villages. It will be long and hard, but the difficulties are not insurmountable."

As they trudged northward, they were passed by trucks carrying Giap's divisions. The schedule called for covering around twelves miles each day. Reveille was at 5 A.M., departure at 5:30, march until 10, prepare meal, eat second meal before starting out at 3 P.M., and march into the night.

In one of the officers' trucks, Bigeard's fellow prisoners were mostly colonels. They were squeezed in, some already suffering from malaria and dysentery, bumping over bad roads with their broken dreams: a good meal, a pretty woman. Langlais had grown old overnight. Vaillant, the short, olive-skinned artillery colonel, often spoke about his nine children. Lieutenant Colonel Voinot, who'd commanded the western sector, had lost an eye under de Lattre; aside from that he was strong and husky. He'd once quarreled with Langlais, who'd thrown a glass of Scotch in his face—what a waste! They drove at night and hid in the forest by day. Sometimes they got a banana—what luxury! After crossing the Red River, Bigeard and Bréchignac and Voinot were sent into the jungle with machetes to cut wood. They made a run for it, but two days later were caught by Viet irregulars, and were brought back to the truck under arrest. The others were a little angry; they'd been punished too. They came before the *can bo*, and Voinot placed his glass eye on the *can bo*'s desk.

"Why did you escape?" the *can bo* asked.

"To continue the battle against Communism."

The *can bo* told Voinot he would be shot. Then turning toward Bigeard, he said, "You led your comrades into escaping. You will be shot." Bigeard wrote it off as bluster, correctly.

The daily stops for those on foot were near rice depots, and each group of twenty was responsible for fetching the rice and cooking it, though it was hard to find dry wood during the rainy season. Jean Dens, who was glad to see that his shrapnel wounds weren't infected, volunteered for the rice brigade, which meant opportunities for barter in the villages. He traded his watch for two catfish, an egg, and tobacco, then, back on the line, he traded the tobacco for another watch. If you ate nothing but rice you lost weight.

The men were overmarched and underfed, with only about a pound of rice a day (it varied from day to day), little or no salt, no minerals, no fat, no protein. This went on for six weeks, until they were on the edge of famine, reaching the zombielike state of vertical corpses, still breathing but devouring their own bodies. Despite warnings not to drink unboiled water, they did, and there was an epidemic of dysentery.

There were other escape attempts—it was fairly easy to fall away from the line of march—but they rarely succeeded, for without a map and a supply of money you didn't know where you were and couldn't buy food in the villages. In any case the villagers were not to be trusted.

Dr. Verdaguer, who had not been called back to the camp with the other doctors, was on the long march with his friend the Legionnaire captain Sterman. "He was terrified of captivity," Verdaguer recalled, "having survived the German occupation as a Jew. I tried to improve his morale, but he got worse, he caught dysentery and could hardly walk. We got him as far as the Claire River and the hospital in Tuyen Quang. I later heard that he had died on July 14. The ordeal of captivity was more terrible than the battle."

It got to the point where men stopped washing, then they stopped eating, then they stopped marching, and they sat by the road and died. An Italian Legionnaire recalled: "I had shrapnel in my back, which a Viet orderly removed with tweezers. Bandages are for our wounded, he said, not for yours. One of my pals, a Spaniard, had a razor blade. His knees were swollen and he couldn't walk. He slit his wrists and the *can bo* finished him off with a pistol shot."

The Spanish Legionnaire was one of the many wounded sent on the march after the hasty triage based on if wounds were above or below the waist. In the absence of medical care, the long march, for those with thoracic or abdominal wounds, or head wounds, or open wounds, or open fractures, or for those who were blind, was a death sentence.

When they reached the Meo Pass in the dark of night, Lieutenant Fleury recalled, their column came to a halt at the edge of the road. "The landscape seemed to come to life. First we heard the voices of several hundred women, singing a melancholy dirge, over and over. Then we saw a long, scintillating caterpillar twisting around the corkscrew turns. It was the women plugging the craters left by our bombs. They carried baskets on bamboo rods filled with rocks and dirt, one behind the other, filling each hole as they sang, then returning to their camp to sleep during the day."

Captain Yves Hervouet, the tank commander, had a broken arm in a cast but was deemed able to walk. He removed the spongy plaster from his infected arm. His feet were swollen. One of the men in his group became a stretcher case and Hervouet volunteered to help carry the stretcher, even though he had amoebic dysentery and bled while walking. On July 6, a mile or so from the prison camp, Hervouet collapsed. "I can't feel my feet," he said, and died that afternoon. The *can bo,* who kept a mortality list, said, "I'm surprised he lasted as long as he did."

The French command suspected the Vietminh of intending to kill as many prisoners as possible before they reached the camps. Their goal, it was held, was the elimination of the vulnerable and the weakening of the fittest, so that there would be no escapes or mutinies.

Colonel de Sury, the president of a commission that interrogated the survivors upon their release, reported on October 12, 1954: "The prisoner of war camps offered a method of slow extermination that left no traces. Deaths were due to the long marches, and the lack of food and medication. Some cases were identical to those observed among the political deportees in Germany."

A question arose: Why did the high command in Saigon not protest? General Ely gave the answer: "I intentionally did not protest regarding the deplorable state of our returned prisoners, feeling it was inopportune as long as all the prisoners of war were not returned. Any protest might incite the enemy commanders to allow to die those prisoners whose state was grave."

If You Were a Prisoner, Wouldn't You Try to Escape?

By May 26, Giap had moved his divisions off the base, and the evacuation of the wounded was terminated. The remaining wounded, as well as the men who'd been kept behind on various details, such as burials and repair of the airstrip, were now sent on the long march. They were 400 in all, divided by ethnic origin into twenty groups of twenty—160 North Africans, 120 Foreign Legion (subdivided into German and non-German), 80 Africans, and 40 French. Each group had a leader to prevent escape and assign the rice detail.

Off they marched in single file, *mao len, mao len,* spreading out and compressing like an accordion, depending on the state of the road, losing all sense of time, the body on automatic pilot, under a monsoon downpour that soaked them through. They stopped at a clearing bordered by shit-filled latrines and tried to sleep under shelters topped by braided bamboo. At dawn they started marching, and covered an average of twelve miles a day. On the fifth day they reached the Vietminh depot of Tuan Giao, sixty-two miles from Dien Bien Phu, and were given a day of rest before climbing up the Meo Pass, which was at twenty-four hundred feet. During the pause they were asked to sign a petition asking for clemency. The captives were divided on this. Some said, "Tell them to stick it up their ass." Others argued, "It will let our families know we're alive." A few signed and a group leader showed the petition to Dang, the *can bo*, who said, "Everyone or no one." Their refusal to sign would be seen as an insult to the benevolence of Ho Chi Minh. No one signed. That night they didn't get their rice ration.

The next morning, they started up hairpin turns to the pass, which they reached by nightfall. It had been bombed so often it was like walking on the moon. Going down at dawn was harder on the knees. After twenty-three hours without food, water, or sleep, they stopped at a clearing next to a mosquito-infested stream. Then they marched into the valley that led to the onetime provincial capital of Son La, where every trace of French presence had been expunged. They had been marching for ten days and already seven men had died. Their camp on the Chinese border was still 250 miles away.

When they reached the Black River, a paratroop lieutenant and his sidekick, a private, managed to drop away from the line. Their plan was to float down the river to French-held territory. But in June the river was swollen and the swift current hurled them against the rocks. They came to a dozen fishermen's huts on stilts. Several pirogues were tied up at a dock. "I don't see any oars," the lieutenant said. Pirogues didn't have oars; they operated with poles. They found a pole, untied a pirogue, and started downstream. It was like a toboggan ride; they couldn't control the boat. Then the river widened and the water calmed. As night fell, they were caught in a net that had been strung from bank to bank. Soon they saw dozens of flashlights approaching, and armed Vietminh in boats told them to raise their hands. With their nets, the Viets controlled navigation on the river.

They were locked up and told they would be brought before a people's court, charged with theft. Among the eight members of the court was a woman who spoke French. "An officer should not steal," she said.

"If you were a prisoner," the lieutenant replied, "wouldn't you try to escape?"

"Stealing a pirogue from a fisherman is an act of aggression," the woman said.

When the jury deliberated, the lieutenant, who spoke kitchen Vietnamese, heard the word *chet*—death—several times. The prisoners were on their knees with their hands tied behind them. It was painful, and the jury took its time.

The woman told them they were sentenced to death for war crimes. They were taken to a freshly dug ditch, where two coolies stood bent over shovels. Two *bo dois* armed with submachine guns appeared and told them to get on their knees. The lieutenant said he wanted to die standing up. One of the *bo dois* hit him in the stomach with the butt of his weapon. The lieutenant's friend thought: "It's like a parachute jump. In three seconds the chute will open." He heard a burst of automatic fire but felt nothing. Then he heard laughter. The Viets had fired into the air.

Back at the Black River, it took four rotations of many rafts to get the convoy and its escorts across. Captain Duan, who commanded the two companies that relayed each other, wanted to hurry the pace, even though twenty-six men had died. They covered eighteen miles a day on forced marches and reached the Red River in a week. During that week, thirty-four men died.

One of them was Captain Trehiou, who had jumped in the last days of the battle with his ankle in plaster. He did not make the cut in the evacuations and was sent on the long march. Trehiou walked with a cane, and he was spitting blood. One night he died, "as silently as a candle that's blown out," said one of his friends.

They crossed the Red River and marched through a bamboo forest, then followed the Yunnan railroad track near the Chinese border, its rails and traverses gone, and turned right on a macadam road chopped up with "piano keys," as the cuts made to stop the passage of trucks were called.

That evening the *can bo* told them they were a week away from the camp. "Where are we going, China?" someone asked.

"Departure in a quarter hour."

At 4 A.M., they crossed the Song Chay over a bridge built by Eiffel, and saw a stone marker that said: HANOI—140 KM. They stopped at a so-called hospital where the patients lay on a sloping platform, two to a mosquito net. By this time Mendès France was premier and an Algerian told the new arrivals: "Things are moving in Geneva. Mendès is willing to make concessions."

They crossed another river and came to a small market town on the side of a hill, then down a narrow trail through a forest of bamboo that formed arches over their heads, reaching a clearing where the camp stood, on a stream the color of urine. The broken-down huts, with roofs supported by four stakes, were thick with green flies, and the smell of rot stuck in their nostrils. They thought, This stink-hole is a prison camp? It must be a mistake. The death toll was eighty. Colonel Robert Bonnafous, who wrote a doctoral thesis on the prisoners of war, called the long march "the start of genocide."

In Washington There Is Much Suspicion

For Chou En-lai, the Geneva Conference had multiple goals, one of which was to secure China's role as a dominant power in Asia. India, though nominally neutral, was a natural ally, and Chou left for New Delhi in late June and spent three days there talking to Prime Minister Nehru, who followed the Eden line on Indochina. Chou pledged to support the independence of Laos and Cambodia and make sure the Vietminh got out of both countries. At Eden's suggestion, Nehru warned Chou that fresh offensives in the Delta would compromise the conference. In their joint press conference, they agreed that the Chinese revolution "cannot be exported," for Nehru had his problems with Indian Communists. Chou then went to Rangoon and saw U Nu. Like India, Burma was a Colombo nation under British influence. Once again, Chou promised that revolution was not an export item. Chou's widely discussed travels prompted Chauvel to say that China was now a major player in Asia.

Chou used his newly gained prestige to exert influence on Ho Chi Minh and General Giap. He arrived on July 3 in Liuzhou, a Chinese town on the border with northern Vietnam, and apologized for being a day late, due to "careless eating and an upset stomach." Giap showed Chou his own "leprosy map," where the French held only two areas—Hanoi and its environs and the coastal area around Haiphong. In Annam, they had a few provincial capitals and coastal cities. Chou asked Giap how long it would take to win the war if the French brought in more troops. Two to three years, Giap said. Chou said it was better to get an agreement now, to avoid such complications as U.S. intervention. Peace was beneficial to both sides. They had to be flexible on the partition line, so that elections could be held, reuniting the two zones. "We must help Mendès France and prevent him from stepping down. . . . We must obtain peace before the November elections take place in the U.S. Now they have misgivings about intervention, but after November we don't know what their position will be." Ho and Giap were taken aback. In view of the forces on the ground, they felt that the 13th parallel was reasonable. The 17th was unacceptable. If they were forced to make concessions, they would go only as far as the 16th. Chou said he would discuss the partition line with Molotov. The Chinese and the Soviets, he said, wanted the war to end. If the Americans came in, when would it end? Indochina needed peace to rebuild its capital and harbors.

Chou's visit paid off, for in a July 5 directive, the DRV Politburo instructed Pham Van Dong to propose a dividing line at the 16th parallel. This was described as a bargaining position probably unacceptable to the French, since Route Coloniale 9, a vital link from the Laotian border to the sea, was north of the 16th parallel.

Chou and Eden were both back in Geneva on July 11, and met with each other the next day at Chou's residence. Chou said the sticking point was the partition line. The DRV was willing to make concessions, but Mendès was insisting on the 18th parallel.

Eden asked Chou about his talk with Ho Chi Minh, but Chou was reticent, saying only, "We discussed the issues covered in these talks."

"Everyone hopes for a solution," Eden said. "When I say this, I include Washington."

"We only have a short amount of time left," Chou said. "Everyone must make an effort."

Eden: "Should Mendès fall, it would be very bad for all of us."

Chou: "But some people are hoping that he will fall."

"I know what you mean," Eden said. "In Washington I found that there is much mutual suspicion. The United States thinks that China has ambitions in Southeast Asia, not for now but in the long run. . . . You also think the United States has ambitions in Southeast Asia."

Chou: "We have no ambitions, and even in the future we will have no ambitions." But Chou was worried about Dulles's Southeast Asia defense plan. If it included any part of Indochina, "peace would have no meaning other than preparation for new hostilities."

Chou also saw Pham Van Dong on July 12, having been told that he still insisted on the 14th or 15th parallel. Chou urged Pham to be flexible and explained the dialectic as one step back and two steps forward. He tried to convince Pham to give up any hope of keeping Vietminh-controlled enclaves in southern Vietnam. Ho Chi Minh wired the stubborn Pham to heed the Politburo directive.

Molotov, also back in Geneva, had seen Mendès France, who told him that the French were "deeply disappointed" at the DRV's insistence on the 13th parallel. Molotov told Mendès there were regions in that area under Vietminh control. Mendès said there were regions in northern Vietnam that were still under French control, making it a tradeoff. Mendès felt that the 18th parallel was reasonable, allowing the French to keep RC9. Molotov had begun to act as a referee between the French and the DRV.

The Line Will Be That Geneva Is a Failure

On July 6, Dillon reported to Dulles that Mendès was asking when the secretary or undersecretary of state were returning to Geneva. Mendès said he was about to tell the National Assembly that if he missed his deadline of July 20, it would be necessary to draft the law to send conscripts to Indochina. Mendès claimed that the shipping to move the first group of conscripts would be ready on July 25.

On July 7, Dulles wired Eden that Mendès was asking about his return. "It is my present feeling that it would be better if neither Smith nor I were back," he said. "Our high-level presence might prove an embarrassment to all concerned." On July 8, he wired Alexis Johnson in Geneva that he was maintaining representation at the present level "because we do not want to be the cause of any avoidable embarrassment by what might be a spectacular disassociation from France." However, Dulles went on, "since starting to dictate this," he had received a message from Mendès via Bonnet "strongly urging" that either he or Smith should go back. Dulles repeated that he did not wish "to do irreparable harm to Franco-American relations," although his decision not to go was not "irrevocable."

Mendès needed Dulles in Geneva to serve as a bogeyman to frighten the DRV into making concessions. He argued that "if Americans on a high level are absent, the Communist side will automatically and inevitably draw conclusions that there is a split between the Western powers." Mendès was planning to be in Geneva on July 10.

Dulles discussed the matter with Vice President Nixon, who felt strongly that neither Dulles nor Smith should go. "The line will be that Geneva is a sellout—a failure of diplomacy."

Dulles said, "They want us to give respectability to what they are going to do." Nixon said the United States shouldn't "be part of a deal we don't believe in."

On July 10, Dulles sent a message to Dillon for Mendès, saying that he had spoken to the president, and that they were both "greatly moved by your earnest request" that either he or Smith return to Geneva. However, he did not want to put himself in the position "where we would seem to be passing moral judgment on French action."

Dillon replied on July 11 that he had spoken to Mendès, who said that he would not do anything unacceptable to the United States. Mendès described a frightening situation if no settlement was reached in Geneva. There would be a debate on sending conscripts to Indochina in the National Assembly on July 22 and 23, and if approved, the first division would leave on July 25 and the second division about ten days later. It would take a month to get to Indochina and three weeks more to prepare the troops for action. The Vietminh were sure to learn about the reinforcements, and would launch a massive assault in August prior to their arrival. This business of the conscripts was highly dubious, if not deceptive. Mendès had pledged to resign if he did not meet the July 20 deadline, and the National Assembly would be in no mood to pass such an unpopular law. Voting for the use of conscripts outside France would lead to a public outcry and street demonstrations. But the Mendès strategy was to show French resolve and bring Dulles to the table.

Mendès pleaded with Dulles to meet him in Paris, "to allay the rising feeling in France that the United States is deserting France in her hour of need." Dulles flew to Paris on July 12 and remained there for the next two days, as he put it, "in practically continuous meetings with Mendès France and Mr. Eden from the time of my arrival to my departure."

Mendès argued that if the United States were not at Geneva "at the ministerial level," the French people would feel abandoned, and all hope for the passage of the EDC would vanish. Eden backed Mendès, saying they were "on a knife-edge," with only a week before Mendès' deadline.

To win over Dulles, Mendès made promises he could not keep. He promised to abide by the pesky seven points the French had always balked at. He promised to send the two divisions of conscripts by September if the talks failed. When Dulles said the U.S. public "was getting short-tempered on EDC and that Congress might terminate aid to NATO," Mendès promised that he would get a vote by early August, even though he knew that he did not have a majority in the National Assembly. Mendès' own defense minister, General Koenig, was a leading opponent of the EDC. Given these promises, Dulles agreed to send Smith back to Geneva for the endgame.

Eden reported to London that "Mendès fought his corner brilliantly," while "Dulles cut a sorry figure," by which he may have meant that he was overly suspicious of his allies.

Back in Washington on July 15, Dulles told the National Security Council that he didn't want to get "into the Yalta business of guaranteeing Soviet conquest," but that blocking a solution would have led to French hostility. "There would have been more talk of too many stiff-necked Presbyterians. . . . The whole structure of Franco-U.S. friendship might have been destroyed, and that would have been the end of any hope for EDC." And so, he gave in "to the very strong pressure on us to return to Geneva."

The next day, Dulles reported on his Paris meeting in an executive session of the Senate Committee on Foreign Relations. When the question of partition was raised, Dulles said that "we are not as urgent about elections here as we would be in Germany or Korea, because as things stand today, it is probable that Ho Chi Minh would get a very large vote." He was hoping for elections at a more favorable time. On July 17, Dulles told Henry Luce over the phone: "It will not be a sellout, but it will be a partial surrender."

Nature and the Population Are Our Guards

The Vietminh had been taking prisoners since the start of the war in 1946. The first was said to be a civil servant, René Moreau, captured in late 1946. At first, when the Vietminh were skirmishing as guerrillas, the prisoners taken were few and could be kept in villages. But the more intense the battles, the greater the number of prisoners. In 1950 came the evacuation of Cao Bang, when the columns led by Colonels Le Page and Charton failed to link up and were annihilated. In that one catastrophe, three thousand French prisoners were taken. By 1954, these men had been prisoners for four years.

A profusion of camps were built in two principal locations, both close to rice depots in Vietminh-held territory. The first was only about a hundred miles north of Hanoi, near the Chinese border. The other, about a hundred miles south of Hanoi, was in Thanh Hoa Province, on the lower Song River. Both camp areas were about three hundred miles from Dien Bien Phu, which made the long march necessary. While the nine thousand captured French slogged toward the camps, preparations were made for the huge influx of prisoners.

For weeks after Dien Bien Phu, the trails leading to the highlands were crowded with a pitiful procession of prisoners, who reached their camps with fatalities of up to 30 percent. These were not the camps of World War II movies, with tidy barracks, barbed-wire enclosures, watchtowers, and searchlights. They were ramshackle bamboo huts in the jungle. "Nature and the population are our guards," the *can bos* said. There was no need for walls—the jungle did the job.

The men arrived in a state of exhaustion, and had always suffered weight loss. Among the diseases incurred on the march or in the camp itself, where rats as big as rabbits carried typhus in their urine, were amoebic dysentery, which led to dehydration and death; beriberi, where the extremities swelled, the lungs filled with liquid, and people died looking like a fairground doll; nematode worms that came up from the intestines into the larynx, bringing death by suffocation; and the skin disease called yaws. There was no medical care to speak of—the infirmary was known as "the morgue." Men went there to die, with their foul-smelling bandages that were never changed and their abdominal wounds that burst open.

The diet was rice and more rice, about a pound a day. A soldier needs twenty-five hundred calories a day, and the rice delivered a thousand, so the men's bodies fed on themselves. And, in any case, for a Frenchman, a diet without bread was a calamity. The Lord's Prayer, as Jean Pouget pointed out, says, "Give us this day our daily bread, not our daily rice."

Drinking unboiled water was a sure way to get dysentery. It was hard to stay clean without a razor or a toothbrush, and the men spent hours each day delousing themselves. The mornings were taken up by rice and wood details, for the rice depots were miles away.

In the afternoons the prisoners attended brainwashing sessions, called reeducation. One of the reasons the men had been separated from their officers was to end all hierarchical influence and make them more amenable to propaganda. They soon learned to go along to get along, and obediently recited the catechism:

"What do you think of this war?"

"It is an unjust and criminal war."

"Why is this war criminal?"

"Because it is an armed aggression against the Vietnamese people."

They said in unison, "We are all murderers," and sang "The Internationale."

Laziness Is Counterrevolutionary

The 400 men who left the base after the prior evacuation of the 858 wounded arrived at their camp in July. The camp director, small and thin and soigné, sat at a desk on a platform and addressed them as follows: "Here you can recover from the long march. Those of you who are wounded will receive care in our infirmary. You must not forget that you are prisoners of war. Obey your guards, particularly in matters of hygiene. I realize that you are accustomed to a temperate climate. That is why you must be vigilant in cleanliness. Wash your kitchen utensils and put them on a flame to kill the germs."

The men nicknamed the camp director Monsignor. They were about six miles from the Claire River, not that far from the Chinese border. Some thought of escaping down the Claire on bamboo rafts, but those who tried it vanished.

Reveille was at 5 A.M. After a soup of recooked rice, the men assembled on the esplanade bordering the stream and were divided into work teams. Ten men for the rice depot, bringing back thirty-three pounds each. Another team to cut bamboo and repair the huts. A team to fix up the camp cemetery. The rest cleaned the latrines and collected firewood. Hauling thirty-three pounds of rice wasn't that bad. They carried it in pairs of pants with the legs tied, wrapped around their necks, like life buoys. The bamboo detail was a bitch, hauling bundles of long and rigid branches on a twisted trail. The cemetery was the worst, with corpses half out in the open, gnawed by rats, and the wooden crosses eaten by termites. In the afternoon were the reeducation lectures.

Monsignor said: "Laziness is counterrevolutionary." But many never recovered from the march. The death rate was staggering. In the first three weeks, 207 prisoners died. On July 14, 15 died. It was Bastille Day, with a special meal, and the men gathered to sing "La Marseillaise."

The Wedding Band Is Not a Commercial Object

The trucks taking the officers to Camp No. 1 drove at night and stopped under the dense foliage during the day. When the truck carrying Bigeard passed through Son La, he was reminded of a holiday he had spent there with his wife, Gaby. Moving northward, the trucks crossed the Black and the Red rivers heading for Tuyen Quang, about sixty miles from the Chinese border.

Camp No. 1 was on a stream at the bottom of a hill, a pretty location if you were vacationing, and consisted of two long bamboo dorms. About a hundred officers were already there, most of them having been captured at Cao Bang, including the two colonels, Le Page and Charton, who weren't on speaking terms. The arrival of two hundred officers from Dien

Bien Phu (including the captains and the lieutenants, who came on foot) caused serious overcrowding, and some of the new arrivals were sent to live with villagers across the stream.

All the doctors, except for the two who had been evacuated in May, were sent to Camp No. 1, since they were officers, and since the Vietminh did not want their moral presence in other camps. Officially, they were not allowed to practice, but they resorted to what they called "capitalist medicine": Don't sleep bare-chested. Pull down your sleeves and pant legs for protection against malaria-carrying mosquitoes. Pass a piece of flaming bamboo over the inclined platform where you sleep to kill the mosquitoes hiding in the cracks. Burn eucalyptus leaves to smoke up the barracks. In the absence of soap, wash with sand from the river. Never leave food uncovered; typhus-carrying rats piss in it. Always boil your water, and eat on parachute cloth. The doctors had among them one pair of scissors, and two of them doubled as barbers. Getting a haircut and a shave was part of survival. And had there not been a time when surgeons were barbers? Dig the latrines deep and keep them clean by covering them daily with earth and burning straw over them every few days. The doctors sought out local healers who showed them what they used—lilac bark for intestinal parasites, guava leaves for dysentery, sesame for fat, pimento for vitamin C.

The officers' camp had a mortality rate of 25 percent, while in the other camps it was 67 percent. This was not only due to the presence of the doctors, but to greater solidarity and discipline. There was less snitching and ass-kissing. The enlisted men came from all over—Waffen-SS, dirt-poor and illiterate Arabs and Africans, ex-convicts, the unemployed. The officers, however, had graduated from a military academy, where they learned esprit de corps. They formed an authentic fraternity, with a professional code of honor and a higher intellectual level.

Bigeard, designated as a group leader, was determined to stay fit. At 6 A.M. ever day, he ran and exercised for an hour. At noon he took a long bath in a stream, followed by sunbathing to keep his tan. He had lost ten or twelve pounds but was still muscular. As a colonel, he got about two pounds of rice a day, while majors got a little under a pound and three quarters, and subaltern officers a little less than that. The Viets professed egalitarianism, he mused, but practiced discrimination. He wanted to protest, but the other colonels talked him out of it: esprit de corps had its limits. Bigeard volunteered for the detail to the rice depot six miles away, for it meant a few bananas. He wondered why, in a zone where bananas were abundant, they weren't added to the prisoners' diet. When he took it up with the *can bo*, he was told: "Rice is the blood of the people. You eat what our soldiers eat."

When they first arrived, the officers' watches and wedding rings had been taken from them, since they could be sold during an escape attempt. Bigeard hid his ring, which he had bought in Nice in 1942 when he married Gaby. Captain Jean Pouget kept his on his finger and told the *can bo*: "In our society, sir, the wedding band is not a commercial object but a religious symbol. It cannot be sold or exchanged, and from the day of our marriage until the day we die, it never leaves our finger." The *can bo* let him keep it, but called him "a vile colonialist."

The old-timers advised the newcomers from Dien Bien Phu to appear attentive at the indoctrination sessions. During the self-critique portion, they should proclaim a list of crimes committed against the Vietnamese people, the more terrible the better. To the newcomers, the old-timers seemed a little too cooperative. They had even formed a committee for peace and repatriation.

The reeducation sessions introduced the officers to a Manichaean world where there was a side for peace and a side for war, where democracy fought imperialism, where the white colonizers were the exploiters and the yellow colonized were the exploited.

The *can bo*, scholarly and didactic, gave the sermon, followed by questions. "Can the democratic camp stop the war?"

A hand went up. "Yes, because the forces on the side of peace are growing daily." Had the old-timers learned their lesson too well?

Then came the self-critique: "My contribution to the collective is a disgrace. My firewood bundles are too small." The newcomers threw in a little irony. "My only excuse is that I was raised by a nanny, who took me to the Bois de Boulogne and told me not to touch the trees." One officer was punished for saying, "I regret stealing a chicken. Do not do as I did. Do not get caught."

The day came when the *can bo* told them that to redeem themselves they must sign a manifesto. The officers convened and decided, "Oh, what the hell." They hammered out a text affirming their desire for peace, condemning imperialist policy, and expressing gratitude to Ho Chi Minh for their excellent treatment. When they showed it to the *can bo,* he said, "You remain bourgeois and egotistical in your reasoning. You must kill the bourgeois within you. You must define the character of the war." The officers discussed what to do. One of them said, "Our enemy is the amoeba, dysentery, malaria. The manifesto will protect us."

Another replied, "This manifesto will be published in France. We cannot sign."

"Those who read it will see through it."

"If we sign one there will be another."

They ended up signing and the *can bo* was so pleased he passed out cigarettes. They were allowed to send a postcard to their families, but no petit bourgeois outpourings were allowed: Health good, War wrong, signed ————————. The rumor circulated that at dinner there would be one banana for four and a chicken for twelve. Someone asked, "Who gets the neck?"

The officers discussed Dien Bien Phu in the light of World War II operations, such as Kesselring's defense on the Italian front in 1944, which held the Allies at bay for months with counterattacks. They were split over Navarre: He knew nothing about Indochina. His mind was on logistics; he ignored the enemy. Pouget, who had been Navarre's aide-de-camp, spoke up on his behalf, and said, "Dien Bien Phu was installed to protect Laos."

One day, Castries, who kept to himself, showed up for lunch. Bigeard stood and called, *"Garde-à-vous"* (Attention). *"Repos"* (At ease), Castries said, "and thank you, my lords." Bigeard had to admit that he did not feel at ease in Castries' presence.

We Have Ended an Eight-Year War

In Geneva, the final week before Mendès France's deadline was hectic, with mutual suspicions overcome by a will to settle the issues. Secretary of State Dulles's brief trip to Paris was enough to strike dread in the hearts of the Chinese delegation. Mendès France had no doubt that there would be a settlement by July 20. "On the night of the nineteenth," he told Chauvel, "they will all lay down their cards." Chauvel thought Mendès had taken command with clearheaded authority. He was the only head of government to personally conduct negotiations, and the Vietminh were surprised at how tenaciously he fought over the partition line.

Anthony Eden, back from his talk with Dulles in Paris, passed his time "in a flurry of meetings, often as many as five a day." The military subcommittees were "working feverishly and an immense number of draft agreements accumulated." The three key issues still being fought over were the partition line, the date of elections, and the members of the armistice commission. These were, as Mendès told Molotov and Eden on July 16, the holes in the tapestry.

After his meeting with Chou En-lai, Ho Chi Minh warned his stubborn delegation by wire that "some people intoxicated with our victories want to fight on at all costs, to the finish. They see only the trees, not the forest. . . . They see the French, but not the Americans."

It had become clear to the British and the French that they had to go through Chou En-lai and Molotov to make an impression on the DRV delegation. At a dinner Molotov gave for the French premier on July 15, Mendès brought up the timing of the elections. An early date could cause chaos, while too late a date would upset the people of Vietnam.

Molotov said that although Vietnam would be divided in two, its people would want to be unified. Both men agreed that they should step up their meetings with Chou and Eden, but without the Americans. Mendès again brought up the issue of the elections. Laos and Cambodia should be dealt with separately from Vietnam, he said. They had their own governments and institutions and could hold their elections right away. "The situation is not so convulsive." Whereas in Vietnam, "there were a number of complex operations" required prior to elections, "in particular the evacuation of troops on both sides." There was also the evacuation of the Delta to be dealt with. "Months will be required," Mendès said, and more months to relocate the population that wanted to resettle. Political parties had to be formed. For all these reasons, "it is impossible right now to set an exact date."

Molotov replied that though it might be difficult to set an exact date, they should set a deadline.

The talk turned to partition. Mendès unfolded a map and showed Molotov the line of the 18th parallel proposed by the French. This was the traditional boundary between Tonkin and Annam, he said. It was a natural boundary in terms of topography and history. The DRV, with its offer of the 13th parallel, wanted to keep a narrow coastal strip about ninety miles long under its control, but giving up this strip was a counterpart to the French giving up the Delta. In either case, Mendès explained, thirty thousand troops would need to be evacuated, so it came out even. France wanted to keep Hue, the political and spiritual capital of Annam, as well as the port of Tourane (present-day Da Nang), which had no military value, and RC9, the only road linking Laos to the sea. Mendès said he would be unable to convince his government to reject the 18th parallel, which would mean abandoning Hue and RC9. The region between the 16th and the 17th parallels had always been occupied by French troops, and the DRV had no grounds for demanding it.

Molotov reminded Mendès that the DRV was leaving all of southern Vietnam to the French. In the area between the 16th and the 18th parallels, it was common knowledge that the French controlled only a small strip of land along the coast. The backcountry was in the hands of the Vietminh. Nor did the French have full control over RC9, which stretched from the border of Laos and Thailand to the South China Sea. In addition, Pham Van Dong had agreed to compromise from the 13th to the 16th parallel, "a great step forward in reaching an agreement." It would take "great force of conviction to get the DRV to give up its longtime region," Molotov said, but he was willing to take it up again with Pham Van Dong. Molotov and Mendès talked until one in the morning.

On July 16, in a meeting with Chou and Pham, Molotov said the French were set on partition north of the 16th parallel. Mendès also objected to elections being held in 1955. Chou proposed a deadline of June 1955 to resolve the matter. He had discussed the election date in detail with Ho Chi Minh, who had agreed to the deadline.

What most concerned Chou was the creation of an American-led military bloc in Southeast Asia. He had always stressed that there should be no foreign bases in the territory of Vietnam, Laos, and Cambodia. Molotov said he would take this up with Mendès. He mentioned that the French were asking for a period of 380 days to move their troops out. He proposed that the time could be reduced by transporting them not only by sea but by rail and highway.

Chou observed that the movement of enemy troops was hampered by road conditions and the problems of food supply. The French, he said, intended to keep their troops in southern Vietnam for a while. "Such a delay is to our advantage," he said, "inasmuch as the presence of the French can serve as an obstacle to the establishment of military and political collusion between the Americans and Bao Dai." For Chou, the American threat overrode the independence of Vietnam.

The three met again at 3:30 P.M. on July 17. Pham had met with Eden, who told him the United States did not intend to establish military bases in Indochina. Molotov asked where Chou and Pham stood on the question of partition. Chou said that in a conversation with Wang Ping-nan, Colonel Jacques Guillermaz had proposed the joint use of RC9. The line must be drawn north of the road. As for elections, they insisted they be held in two years.

Molotov asked both men what their final position would be.

Pham said the DRV was willing to concede RC9 and draw the line to the north. In return he would demand that the French not turn Tourane (Da Nang) into a naval base and set a precise date for elections. He would not oppose an extension of the date, to give the DRV a chance to campaign among the population. Chou agreed with the partition offer and asked Molotov whether Mendès would compromise on the elections. Molotov wasn't sure. However, regarding partition, an exact line must be drawn, he said. Pham said he would have his military experts prepare a map.

They discussed the commission that would supervise elections. Chou said he had heard from V. K. Krishna Menon, the head of the Indian delegation at the United Nations, who was in Geneva, that the French would accept a commission consisting of India, Canada, and Poland. On the question of regrouping time for the French, Chou proposed 240 days rather than 380.

Later that day, Chou saw Mendès, a few days after Mendès' meeting with Dulles. Mendès had to assure Chou that the United States did not plan to set up bases in Indochina. "Please trust me on this," he said. "You have my word without reservation." Mendès complained that the DRV demands on partition were unrealistic. They wanted an area stretching six hundred miles from north to south. "This is difficult to accept," Mendès said. "I hope, Mr. Premier, that you can give Pham Van Dong some advice as you have done on many occasions, and ask him to advance more realistic proposals."

Chou, who had just heard Pham say he was willing to concede RC9, said, "If you make a step, the other side will make a step." Mendès was getting his information from General Delteil, who had told him the Viets were sticking to the 13th parallel. He asked Chou to elaborate, and was told, "If France gives a little, the DRV will give a lot."

Mendès lost no time setting up a meeting with Pham, who started out by proposing the 16th parallel as the line of partition. Pham said the Vietminh would be giving up important areas they controlled, such as Qui Nhon, only two hundred miles north of Saigon, and Quang Ngai, in the central highland area.

Mendès argued that the partition line should be at the narrow neck dividing northern from southern Vietnam, so that the French could keep Hue and Tourane, as well as the vital RC9, the only road linking Laos to the South China Sea.

Pham said an arrangement could be made for French use of RC9. Mendès said the Berlin corridor showed that arrangements like that did not work. Mendès felt that the give in the Vietminh position was the result of his meeting with Dulles. The talks continued between the DRV and General Delteil, who told Mendès that the DRV agreed to settle above RC9.

On July 18, at the twenty-third and final restricted session, Molotov was in the chair and said private talks were moving toward agreement. Walter Bedell Smith, who had returned the previous day, announced that the United States was not a belligerent and did not want to impose its views. "The United States would refrain from the use of force to disturb the arrangement made." The Chinese were certain that Smith had returned in order to scuttle any agreement. He reported to Washington, however, that the three members chosen for the control commission—India, Canada, and Poland—were "much better than we obtained in Korea." The brief session on July 18, he said, was "the strangest performance to date." Nothing had been prepared. While Molotov said they were close to an agreement, everyone was in the dark. In reality, Smith was the one in the dark, due to his absence and his being left out of the private meetings.

On the same day as the last restricted session, Eden sent his trusted deputy undersecretary, Harold Caccia, an old Etonian with a forceful personality, to talk to Chang Wentian, a member of the Chinese delegation who was also his country's ambassador to the Soviet Union. Caccia wanted to do a little horse-trading. He said the French were giving up a great deal in the north and needed some give from the DRV. The French would never allow the Vietminh to control RC9, he said. "Fortunately, this route does not fall on the 18th parallel or we could all buy our tickets home."

Chang made no comment and changed the subject to the elections. A deadline must be set, he said.

Caccia said it was pointless to make promises that could not be kept. India, once it got its independence, took two or three years to hold elections.

Chang said a definite date was needed to give the Vietnamese a goal for reunification. "We can always set a realistic timetable," he said. "Time, after all, cannot be unrealistic."

It was on July 18 that Eden first felt that "the tangled ends began to sort themselves out."

On July 19, the day before the deadline, there was a round-robin of private meetings. Smith had a long talk with Mendès, and told him the United States would not be part of any agreement, but would do nothing to scuttle one. Smith pointed out that the results of partition could be the same as in Germany and Korea, "deeply wounding the Vietnamese people, provoking trouble throughout the country, and threatening the peace so dearly acquired." In reality, there could be no peace without partition.

Mendès also met with Chou, and said he wanted to maintain three thousand French troops in Laos, not to continue the war but because the Laotians need help in forming their own army. "They are not aggressive and do not threaten anyone," Mendès said. "Would your Excellency agree?" Chou replied that although French troops in Laos would be anathema to the DRV, "this could be considered. . . . We are willing to have Laos become a buffer zone as described by Mr. Eden."

At the Chinese villa, talks resumed between Caccia and Chang, who were narrowing the gap increment by increment. Chang asked whether the French would accept a line south of the 18th parallel. Caccia said the French had two main concerns: one, they must keep RC9; two, they must have enough space above RC9 to provide minimal security for those who used it. There were two rivers between RC9 and the 18th parallel. Perhaps one of the rivers could provide protection for RC9.

Chang, who would report Caccia's proposals to the DRV, needed Caccia to be precise. Did Caccia mean, he asked, that as long as RC9 was safe, the partition line to its north would be acceptable to the French?

Yes, Caccia responded, but it must not be a "preposterous" line; there must be a topographical feature such as a river.

Did the French insist on RC9? Chang asked.

"Absolutely," Caccia said. "If this can't be negotiated, we can all buy our tickets home."

After Chang had spoken to the DRV, he and Caccia met again at 5:45 P.M. Chang said the DRV agreed to a line six miles north of RC9, with a demilitarized zone of three miles on each bank of the river.

Caccia was afraid that this would be too narrow a demilitarized space.

Chang and Caccia decided they had gone as far as they could on the question of the line and that Pham and Mendès would have to thrash it out.

Chang said the DRV was ready to make a concession on the election, which could be held two years after the cease-fire. A final point of contention was the timetable of the departure of French troops, which Chang wanted to be completed in 245 days. Caccia said that given the capacity of the railroads and the ports, and the possibility of inclement weather, Mendès would have to "trust all his hopes to good fortune" to get the job done in 245 days.

Chang responded that the figure of 245 days took mishaps into account, and that in any event Mendès was a man who had so far had almost nothing but good luck.

The talks on July 19 continued into the night, when Eden met with Molotov. "We have done what we could," Eden said, "and now we leave with a clear conscience."

Molotov said he didn't understand the French. Even though they had set a deadline of July 20, they didn't seem to be in a hurry. Perhaps they intended to extend the deadline.

Eden was concerned about Vietminh aggression in Laos and Cambodia. Molotov said the real problem was the patience of the people of Indochina, who had been fighting for eight years. He added that the positions of the French and Americans were clear, but what was the position of the British?

Eden waggishly replied that the British had no position. The French should decide for themselves. The British couldn't tell them how to act.

Molotov recalled that at the restricted session on July 18, when Chou proposed that the nations of Indochina should be neutral, the French and the Laotians had said his proposal deserved attention, Walter Robertson had lashed out at them. Did Robertson "want to be more French than the French and more Laotian than the Laotians?" Molotov wondered. It was obvious, he said, that "Dulles did not favor the Geneva Conference from the start."

Eden, who was annoyed by the secretary of state's absence, noted that Dulles had agreed in Berlin to convene the conference. He was, however, impressed by Chou's resolve to reach a settlement.

"China wants calm south of its borders," Molotov said.

Eden said Chou had convinced him that China had no ambitions regarding Laos and Cambodia, both of which could lead a happy life as neutrals with no foreign military bases on their territory.

Molotov said the French did not seem that interested in Laos and Cambodia.

"The French governments," Eden said, "are different [from other governments] in that they exhibit great energy only in the first weeks of their existence."

On July 20, Chou reported to Mao that the night before, Pham Van Dong and Mendès France had cleared the major hurdles. They agreed to a partition line at the 17th parallel, which happened to be the border of two provinces, Quang Binh and Quang Tri. Mendès agreed to elections in two years and troop withdrawal in 245 days. Chou and Molotov pressured the DRV to accept. It seemed that the deadline had been met. There would be a plenary session that afternoon and a closure ceremony at 9 P.M., and everyone could go home.

Later that morning, Chou received the Cambodian foreign minister, Tep Phan, for a courtesy visit. Phan told him that Cambodia was a peace-loving nation, where the military and the monks were not allowed to vote. "There are about 60,000 monks in our country and none of them partic-ipate in elections," he said.

And why was that? Chou asked.

"Because they renounced the world and stand aloof from worldly af-fairs," Phan said. "They are not interested in politics. The monks wear the yellow *Kasaya* robe. In our country everyone is Buddhist."

Chou sounded him out on the presence of French troops, and Phan said: "France is no better than the Vietminh."

"But being pro-American is even worse," Chou said.

At the plenary session that afternoon, Molotov was in the chair, han-dling procedural matters. During the intermission, the delegates retired to the bar. Smith ambled over to chat with Chou, whom Dulles had ignored, and introduced himself. Eden came over and said he hoped what was left of the session would not be too polarized. Smith told him that the inflam-matory Walter Robertson was sick and had to go home.

Everything seemed set. But when the heads of the delegations met at the British villa at 8:30, a last-minute demand by Cambodia threatened to scuttle the entire conference. Sam Sary, the envoy of the king of Cambo-dia, said that the prohibition of foreign bases was an insult to the govern-ment of his country. Chou was confounded. He had spent two hours with Tep Phan that morning, and no objections had been raised.

Molotov suspected that the Americans were behind the Cambodian de-mand, in order to sink the conference. He was partly right, for Sam Sary, who believed that Cambodia must rely on the United States for protection, had been conferring with the American delegation. On July 16, he had met with Philip Bonsal, the State Department director for Southeast Asia, who was in Geneva. Bonsal told him that if the cease-fire did not prevent

Cambodia from cooperating with other non-Communist states, he was "confident the U.S. and other interested countries" could discuss security matters. On July 18, Sam Sary called Smith, who recommended that he should state at the conference that Cambodia had no intention of having foreign bases on its territory, in order not to tip his hand. However, Smith asked that Cambodia would be free to import arms and employ French military instructors. Some of the weapons might be American, and some of the instructors American-trained. Smith stated in his wire to Washington that Cambodia's position was to "emerge from the conference . . . with maximum freedom of action . . . to assure its defense." Smith privately encouraged Sam Sary to leave the door open to Western military help. This was a little backroom dealing on the part of the Americans that matched the ad hoc meetings of the other delegations. Cambodia and Laos would later be brought within the security perimeter of the Southeast Asia Treaty Organization, which came into being later that year. Cambodia's last-minute objection was a solitary but major achievement of the Americans at Geneva.

At the British villa, the more they talked, the more Sam Sary refused to budge. It wasn't that Cambodia wanted foreign troops, he said, but they didn't want to be denied the right to have them. The clock was running, and it was past midnight, past the deadline, when Sam Sary announced that he had seventeen other demands. He had to be appeased. At 2 A.M. on July 21, it was agreed that Cambodia could have foreign military bases for its security. This amendment was extended to Laos. Thus the independence of those two countries was preserved and the Vietminh forces would be withdrawn.

The final gathering at the Palais des Nations was held at 3 P.M. on July 21, when the backdated agreements were signed. Eden, who was in the chair, said in his closing statement that they had all come to the end of their prolonged and intricate work. They had ended an eight-year war and reduced international tension. The achievement was worthwhile, though the result was not entirely satisfactory. Mendès France did not attend the gathering. He said his heart was broken. In Paris, he told the National Assembly, "I have no illusions concerning this agreement. The text is cruel because the facts are cruel."

The agreements were signed by all nine participants except the Americans. Smith said the United States would not resort to arms to modify them. When the Ngo Dinh Diem government in Saigon denounced the agreements, Mendès told Jean Chauvel that they were "spitting in the soup," for, after all, they had gotten half the country. In Saigon, the flags were at half-mast. The United States backed free elections, but at the same time respected the right of the South Vietnamese to "full freedom of action."

Vietnam was "temporarily" partitioned at the 17th parallel until after the elections scheduled for July 1956. The French would hand over Hanoi and Haiphong within three months. A date was set for exchanging the captives of both sides. Hostilities in Vietnam would cease on July 27, for it took time to notify the units in the field. It was not like World War I, when all the men rose from their trenches simultaneously on Armistice Day.

In the DRV ranks, particularly among Pham Van Dong and the other delegates, resentment was felt at having to bend to the will of their allies. The big boys in the playground had pushed them down the slide of partition. Their resentment was long held in, but flared into the open in 1979 when the DRV issued a white paper charging that "the Chinese leaders betrayed the revolutionary struggle of the peoples of Vietnam, Laos and Cambodia."

In a CIA study later commissioned by Defense Secretary Robert McNamara, entitled "Asian Communist Employment of Negotiations as a Political Tactic," there was one interesting remark: "The events of 1953 and 1954 had an influence on the attitude of Ho Chi Minh and his principal lieutenants regarding the war. They realized that they had been induced by Moscow and Peking [at Geneva] to stop half-way to a total victory. . . . It is impossible to overestimate the impact of this historical lesson on Ho Chi Minh. He was [thereafter] hostile to any suggestion that he stop half-way on the road to total control of all Vietnam."

The Chinese, while giving the impression of being fully behind the DRV, exercised a moderating influence. Their primary concern was to obtain an agreement that would prevent U.S. intervention. They were like jockeys who give their horse the whip while pulling on the reins. In addition, a Communist North Vietnam offered security on their border, where they had historically sought buffer states. Chou En-lai was seen as the master diplomat of the conference. One writer said he was to Geneva what Metternich had been to the Congress of Vienna in 1815.

Molotov and Eden were not far behind, and had formed their own entente cordiale. The Soviets wanted to avert a major war in which they would be forced to assist the Chinese. They were satisfied with the creation of a Communist enclave in Vietnam. A happy side effect would be the removal of French troops from Indochina, which would increase French troop levels in Europe and offset the need for the EDC. Preventing German rearmament was a Soviet priority. Part of the fallout from Geneva was that Mendès was accused of making a deal with Molotov: success at Geneva in exchange for the defeat of the EDC. There was no convincing evidence of such a deal, though Mendès was less than candid with Dulles, using the promise of EDC ratification to get Smith back to the table in the last hectic days. In August, however, the National Assembly killed the EDC on a procedural vote. Dulles said it was a "shattering blow to U.S. policy."

France lost the crown jewel of its colonial empire, which had a domino effect on its North African colonies. Its commercial and financial interests in Vietnam were ruined, although Cambodia remained a French satellite until 1970. In the south, Ngo Dinh Diem turned to the United States for support.

On July 22, Eden drove to the Geneva airport with Smith, "a splendid friend throughout." On the flight back to London, he felt relieved that the fighting had stopped. But he knew that Indochina's problems were not over. He wondered what part the United States would play in its destiny. He hoped America's assistance would not be resented.

That Terrible Agreement in Geneva

In Washington, U.S. aid to the French had been winding down. On July 13, Secretary of Defense Charles Wilson ordered the suspension of all shipments to Indochina. The U.S. Air Force had ceased deliveries and recovered its aircraft on loan, the B-26s and the C-119s. Eisenhower later wrote in *Mandate for Change* that U.S. assistance had been unable to cure the "unsound relationship between the Asiatics and the French," and had been "of only limited value."

At a press conference on July 21, the president said: "The agreement contains features we do not like, but a great deal depends on how they work in practice. . . . We will not use force to disturb the settlement."

Question: "A number of Congressmen today are branding the Geneva settlement an appeasement."

Eisenhower: "I hesitate to use such words. . . . I would say that this agreement . . . is not satisfactory. It is not what we would have liked to have had. [But] if I have no better plan, I am not going to criticize what they have done."

Years later, in an oral history, Eisenhower referred to "that terrible agreement in Geneva."

Although promising not to use force, the United States sent its mighty fleet alarmingly close to Chinese maritime boundaries. On July 22, the day after closure in Geneva, Vice Admiral William Phillips took the aircraft carrier *Hornet* for training exercises in the South China Sea, in the company of another carrier, the *Philippine Sea,* and twelve destroyers. On July 26, three planes on a recon mission from the *Philippine Sea* were attacked by two Communist Chinese fighters, which opened fire but failed to score any direct hits. The U.S. planes fired back and hit one of the Chinese, causing it to roll over on its back and crash into the sea. The second Chinese plane, also hit, crashed near a fishing junk. Also on July 22, Chinese fighters twenty miles off the coast of the island of Hainan shot down a small British passenger plane going from Bangkok to Hong Kong with eighteen on board. Admiral Phillips heard the distress call and ordered Rear Admiral Harry Felt, commander of a carrier group in the area, to search for survivors, nine of whom were rescued. Felt was aboard the *Essex,* which had a special weapons officer responsible for tactical nuclear weapons.

On July 29, Chou En-lai was in Moscow on an urgent mission to see Georgy Malenkov, the chairman of the Soviet Council of Ministers. Chou was distraught and angry over the incident in the South China Sea. "Having suffered a defeat in Indochina," he said, "the U.S. government is trying to provoke conflict in other regions of the Far East. . . . With the support of the Chiang Kai-shek pirates, they are infringing upon the freedom of navigation in the open ocean and plundering ships headed for China. . . . Recently the Americans moved aircraft carriers to the maritime boundaries of China. Several days ago, aircraft operating from the carriers shot down two Chinese aircraft in the area of the island of Hainan."

Chou said that in order to strengthen its coastal defense, China needed to develop a navy and air force, which he would start doing at once when he returned to Peking. The Soviets were recommending a division of its long-range Tu-4 heavy bombers. "In the opinion of the Chinese military," Chou went on, "these aircraft are obsolete." What China needed, he said, was "jet technology."

Malenkov said his military comrades would look into it.

I Beg to Send My Gratefulness

On July 21, Secretary of State Dulles briefed the House Foreign Affairs Committee on the Geneva agreements and the Vietnamese elections to come in 1956. One member observed that North Vietnam had a population of twelve million to South Vietnam's ten million. If the two million Catholics in the north moved south, the shift in population would give the south a majority enabling it to win the 1956 election. "That is right," Dulles replied.

The Geneva agreement stipulated that "until the movement of troops is completed, any civilians residing in a district controlled by one party who wish to go and live in the zone assigned to the other party shall be permitted and helped to do so by the authorities in that district."

No sooner were the agreements signed than thousands of refugees began pouring into the Hanoi–Haiphong corridor, where eighty thousand French troops were preparing to evacuate. Thousands of Catholics had already been removed from the Delta to refugee camps, and the French were swamped. On August 5, Ngo Dinh Diem asked Ambassador Donald Heath if the United States could help to relocate refugees. Indeed it could, in two ways, by organizing a sealift called Operation PASSAGE TO FREEDOM, and by launching a psychological warfare campaign to "stimulate" relocation. United States Information Service officers printed posters that said "Come to the South for Happiness and a Good Life." Leaflets appealing to the Catholics were titled, "God Has Gone South."

As for PASSAGE TO FREEDOM, it was run by Rear Admiral Lorenzo Sabin, who flew to Haiphong in early August to confer with General O'Daniel and the French. Sabin offered a fleet of twenty-four LSTs (tank landing ships), eight AKAs (attack cargo ships), four LSDs (dock landing ships), and eight APAs (attack transport ships). The first ship, an APA, arrived on August 14 off the chosen beach site. A French landing craft ferried the refugees alongside it, a gangway was lowered, and aboard they came, nineteen hundred of them, and three days later they disembarked in Saigon.

When refugees came aboard the AKA *Montague*, carrying balance poles with a basket at both ends holding their belongings, they brought on deck a barrel of pungent *nuoc mam* fish sauce, the essential Vietnamese condiment. The ship's doctor took one sniff and ordered the barrel thrown overboard. Navy cooks gradually learned Vietnamese recipes.

The U.S. Navy was landing three thousand refugees a day, and by September had reached the one hundred thousand mark. A total of ninety births aboard ship were recorded. The numbers tapered off in October, for once the French had removed their troops the "bamboo curtain" fell: the Vietminh restricted group travel and the sale of homes; Vietminh troops forced travelers back, clubbing them with rifle butts; a badly beaten priest staggered into a Haiphong camp with chopsticks jammed into his ears.

The Geneva agreement stipulated a deadline of May 18, 1955, for the movement of civilians. By then, since August 1954, PASSAGE TO FREEDOM had evacuated 310,848 passengers, all but 17,846 civilians. Combined with French sea and air operations, about 800,000 got out of North Vietnam. One of them, Vong Phu Dan, wrote the captain of the ship that carried him: "I beg to send my gratefulness. Your are nursery my people with vigilance. I never forget together on this ship, because you are very goodness."

The Angel of Dien Bien Phu

If there was any way that a military defeat could be turned into a public relations triumph, the answer was Geneviève de Galard. On May 19, when de Galard was still in captivity, Representative Frances Bolton, an Ohio Republican and a member of the House Foreign Affairs Committee, called Secretary Dulles and urged that she be invited to the United States upon her release.

When she landed in New York on the morning of July 26, 1954, de Galard discovered the travails of celebrity. Mayor Robert Wagner was at Idlewild Airport to greet her, and two hundred well-wishers applauded when she descended from her plane. Mrs. Bolton introduced her as a "symbol of heroic femininity in the free world." She had been given a wardrobe of Jacques Fath dresses so that she would look presentable. Fath himself chose the evening gown, gray organza with white polka dots, a low neckline, and a wide belt of blue satin. He insisted that he didn't want any publicity, and that this was just his homage to the army.

De Galard kept telling herself, "I don't deserve this," as she recited the brief remarks she had learned by heart in English. She took questions from the press, pronouncing *th* like *z*. Ze armistice will stop ze level of casualties. Yes, she had ze rank of an officer, but she didn't want to be called "lieutenant." Asked about her letters to Ho Chi Minh, she said the first was from a nurse wanting to help the wounded, and the second was to thank him for her freedom and ask that the rest of the medical team be released. The newspapers called her "The Angel of Dien Bien Phu" and "Sweet Geneviève."

Then came the ticker-tape parade down Broadway in an open Cadillac, before cheering crowds estimated at 250,000, and a reception at City Hall.

On July 27, de Galard was flown to Washington on an air force plane and taken to the Capitol for lunch in the Speaker's Dining Room. She stopped to look at the House gallery, where, by coincidence, an amendment to an appropriations bill for Indochina was being debated. Laurence Smith, a Wisconsin Republican, had moved to reduce the allotment for Indochina from $712 million to $500 million. Walter Judd, a Minnesota Republican, spotted her and said he wanted to welcome "the Angel of Dien Bien Phu." This led to applause and some hilarity, for Judd was breaking House rules, which called for ignoring guests. The amendment, however, was defeated, 98 to 63.

At the White House, President Eisenhower presented her with the

Presidential Medal of Freedom and called her "the woman of the year." Mamie Eisenhower steered her around like an attentive grandmother. After three days in the capital, de Galard was taken on a whirlwind tour of six states. She was put up in the best hotels, there were flowers in her room, but the hospitality was overwhelming. She was exhausted. In Cleveland, Mrs. Bolton's bailiwick, at a dinner for three hundred, the finale was an enormous cake shaped like the Arc de Triomphe. Then Chicago, then Denver, then San Francisco, then Dallas, where she was given a diploma: "Qualified to wear spurs and a Stetson." In New Orleans, she found familiar residues of French civilization. Back in New York, she attended a solemn high mass at St. Patrick's and had lunch with the pink-cheeked Cardinal Spellman, who compared her to Joan of Arc. The French ambassador, Henri Bonnet, accustomed to the disdain of his country in the American press, was ecstatic, and wired Paris that her visit was "an exceptional success."

In Free Vietnam There Is Political Chaos

The uplifting interval of Geneviève de Galard's visit to the United States gave way to deep post-Geneva hangovers in official Washington. It seemed that America's Asian policy was in shambles. On August 6, a National Security Council report stated that Geneva "completed a major forward stride of Communism which may lead to the loss of Southeast Asia. . . . It was a serious loss for the free world, the psychological and political effects of which will be felt throughout the Far East and around the globe."

In a follow-up report on August 12 called the "Consequences of the Geneva Conference," the NSC declared that "the Communists have secured possession of an advance salient in Vietnam. . . . The loss of prestige suffered by the U.S. . . . will raise further doubts in Asia concerning U.S. leadership and the ability of the U.S. to check further expansion."

The situation in South Vietnam looked grim: "In Free Vietnam there is political chaos. The government of Prime Minister Diem has only one virtue—honesty—and is bereft of any practical experience in public administration. The Vietnamese National Army has disintegrated as a fighting force. Free Vietnam is the seat of three rival private armies and security services have, by decree of Bao Dai, been handed over to a gangster sect, the Binh Xuyen, whose revenues are derived from gambling, prostitution and extortion."

In Saigon, General O'Daniel, the head of the U.S. military mission, saw a great opportunity for the United States to take over from the departing French. This would require "U.S. advisors in all functional activities to assist Free Vietnam officials and government agencies."

In Washington, Secretary Dulles was still working on the Southeast Asia treaty, and still complaining that the British and the French "are blocking everything we want to do." He was due to leave for Manila for the treaty conference, but worried that "going into a treaty of this sort will limit our freedom of action. . . . They are more concerned with trying to annoy the Communists rather than stopping them." However, he attended the meeting and the treaty was signed on September 8.

In 1956, when Diem refused to abide by the elections, Dulles said, "Dien Bien Phu was a blessing in disguise."

President Eisenhower's achievement was keeping ground troops out of Indochina. "The United States never lost a soldier or a foot of ground in my administration," he later said. "We kept the peace. People asked how it happened—by God, it didn't just happen, I'll tell you that." Eisenhower remains America's wisest post–World War II president because he understood that there were limits to the deployment of U.S. power.

What Was Your Attitude During Captivity?

While Geneva dragged on, and Geneviève de Galard received the keys to the city, the men in the prison camps continued to die. Their release date was set for August 20, a month after the signing of the Geneva agreement. With the cease-fire on July 27, a mixed commission was formed to determine the conditions of the prisoner exchange. One of the articles was that no blood should be taken from the prisoners prior to their return, for the Vietminh had an urgent need of plasma. Another condition was that men of all nationalities must be freed. The main point of exchange was Viet Tri, on the Red River, only forty miles northwest of Hanoi, where teams from both armies processed the returned men. French landing craft deposited Vietminh prisoners, picked up the French, and took them to Hanoi.

As an example of Uncle Ho's clemency, one hundred men were

granted early release on Bastille Day, July 14. Their condition was such that Reuters quoted the naval captain René Bardit, who had ferried a boatful of them to Hanoi: "The Vietminh internment camps are veritable Buchenwalds." As for the treatment of Vietminh prisoners, they were neither underfed nor refused medical treatment. But a top secret report established that nine thousand Vietminh had died in captivity, and that a high percentage had been executed. Most of the Vietminh prisoners in Indochina were guarded by Vietnamese troops.

The landing craft arrived at Viet Tri, the front ramp was lowered, and the Vietminh hopped onto bamboo rafts that took them ashore, as a crowd of villagers cheered. When their turn came, the French were transferred to the landing craft. By nightfall, they were at Lanessan Hospital, sleeping in real beds on real mattresses, near a bathroom with clean water, and on their night tables were stacks of mail from their wives and families.

More than ten thousand other French prisoners were released between August 21 and October. About one third had been captured at Dien Bien Phu. The procedure was to take them to a holding camp on the grounds of a former racetrack at Tuyen Quang, sixty miles north of Hanoi, in one of the provinces east of the Red River that had long been occupied by the Vietminh. There they were barbered and fed, and dressed in green uniforms, light bamboo helmets, and Chinese rubber sandals too small for European and African feet.

Taken by truck to Viet Tri, these unrecognizable phantoms, at half their normal weight, vacant-eyed, many unable to walk, came upon a grotesque operetta setting: an orchestra playing French tunes, smiling young women carrying trays of fruit, nurses in white handing out pills, a huge banner proclaiming PEACE AND FRIENDSHIP, singing schoolchildren pinned with the Picasso dove, with the entire scene being filmed. Major Millot, commanding the French exchange team, expressed his disgust at these "exasperating excesses."

Behind a table piled high with watches and bundles of piastre notes sat an affable *can bo*. "You have a right to an indemnity for what you have lost," he told Lieutenant Louis Stien.

"I didn't lose anything," Stien replied. "It was stolen from me."

"Let us say, confiscated," the smiling *can bo* said.

"My watch, my wedding ring, twelve hundred piastres, my wallet."

"Will you accept twelve hundred piastres and choose among the watches one similar to yours? We have no wedding rings."

Stien realized that the pile of watches had been taken from the dead at Dien Bien Phu. Nonetheless, he accepted.

Dr. Jacques Aulong, a surgeon at Lanessan Hospital, first saw the released POWs arrive by truck on August 22. Many of them had to be carried in on stretchers. General Cogny was there to greet them, and those who could walk lined up to shake his hand, then stood at attention. It was a horrible spectacle, Aulong thought, these barefoot men with swollen feet, their bony legs protruding from their shorts. Some had died on the short hop in the landing craft. Others died at Lanessan.

Aulong's job was to save the dying. Captain Désiré, a popular officer wounded on Anne-Marie, was sent to the infirmary. One of the last radio messages on May 7 had been for him—his wife had given birth to a girl. On the long march, he was left by the side of the road to die, but his fierce desire to see his newborn daughter saved him. He named her Anne-Marie, after the strongpoint he had defended and lost. Of those hospitalized, sixty-one died within a week, and forty-nine of those were from Dien Bien Phu.

Ely came by to see the prisoners, and Dr. Aulong took the pale, soft-voiced, ascetic general around. Ely was shocked at what he described as their "terrible state of degradation." Two out of three had been hit by shrapnel. The real catastrophe of Dien Bien Phu, Ely thought, was that far more died after the defeat than during the battle. Many could have been saved by the penicillin that was dropped, but the Viets kept it for themselves.

In ten days, Dr. Aulong calculated, five thousand POWs came through Lanessan; nine hundred had arrived in a single day. The hospital was swamped and the overflow were sent to facilities in Saigon and Haiphong. What had happened to the rest? Aulong wondered. What had happened to the Vietnamese?

One of the wounded at Kie Nan Hospital in Haiphong recalled that a military intelligence officer came into his dorm and asked: "Tell me frankly, what was your attitude during captivity?" From his bed, a man called out: "Why weren't you there to see for yourself?" The man took the wash basin on the chair next to his bed and flung it at the officer, who left the room without a word.

The officers were the last to be freed. At Camp No. 1, in mid-September, Colonel Langlais found a spoonful of sugarcane molasses in the boiled rice he ate out of a palm frond, and wondered about the reason for the improvement in his diet? A *can bo* appeared at the door: "Departure in ten minutes. You'll soon know where." A few days later they were in Hanoi. General Cogny invited Langlais, Bigeard, and a few others to his home for dinner. When they arrived there were flowers, a white tablecloth, and fine wines. Bigeard was not in a festive mood. "Why was there not a single general at Dien Bien Phu?" he asked. Cogny did not reply. An embarrassing silence hung over the table.

Among the officers returned from captivity since 1946 were thirty-five doctors who were questioned by Major Dr. Martin. He asked: "Were the [French] POWs sentenced to death because the Vietminh government had not signed the Geneva Convention in 1949?" The reply was affirmative.

From the start of the war until the armistice, the French lost 45,013 captured or missing. In the prisoner exchange, 10,752 were turned over. That left 34,261 unaccounted for. Of the surviving 10,752, 3,290 were from Dien Bien Phu, out of 10,863 taken prisoner there.

The French military came to believe that the towering mortality rate among the POWs was due to a deliberate policy that amounted to a refinement of the Nazi death camps. Comparisons were made: at camps like Dachau or Buchenwald, 80 percent had died; among the Dien Bien Phu prisoners, 70 percent had perished. Instead of the gas chamber, the men died of malnutrition, disease, and their neglected wounds. Colonel Bonnafous, however, who wrote the authoritative study on the prisoners, concluded: "It cannot be established that this was a deliberate plan." It was Bonnafous who obtained the documents showing that nine thousand Vietminh prisoners of the French were killed in camps with no nutritional or medical problems.

Questions were asked: Was it the Asiatic attitude to human life? American POWs had also suffered and died as prisoners of the Japanese on a death march in the Philippines during World War II. Was it a form of political conditioning? Was it a refusal from national pride or suspicion to open the camps to the Red Cross?

Pierre Bonny, a para corporal, believed that the long march, which he had experienced, was not a deliberate attempt to kill prisoners; it was imposed by circumstance. In the space of a single day, the Viets found themselves with ten thousand additional mouths to feed, and they were overwhelmed by the logistics. Cruelty was inherent in the nature of the long march, and pity would have interfered with efficiency. Rather than a cynical policy of extinction, there was an absence of nutrition and medical care. A May 17 directive uncovered by French intelligence, under the rubric of "Prisoners of War," said: "Towards the officers, there must be no mistreatment. We must behave in a way that they will not despise our soldiers and our people." The inference was that mistreatment should be limited to non-officers.

The question remained, even if it was not a deliberate policy, was there an absence of humane behavior toward a hated enemy? Why did they not free the seriously wounded once the armistice was declared? In August and September, on the eve of freedom, men were still dying. Colonel Ducruix, who in mid-March had replaced the psychotic Colonel Keller as Castries' chief of staff, was one of the five high-ranking officers who did not survive captivity. He died of leptospirosis on the road to Viet Tri. Captain Gendre of the Algerian fusiliers, a survivor of the Gabrielle battles in mid-March, died of an abdominal hemorrhage in August. And there were others.

On October 9, 1954, French troops under the command of General Salan crossed the Paul Doumer Bridge and exited Hanoi on their way south. Their departure precipitated the flight of Vietnamese Catholics and French businessmen. Signs went up in store windows: 50% OFF ENTIRE STOCK. Some regiments were sent directly to North Africa, which was in a state of rebellion. They were professional soldiers. Their duty was to fight colonial wars, one after the other.

The survivors of Dien Bien Phu and the prison camps returned to France aboard troop transports, except for some officers and wounded who were flown home. Aboard the ships, a sense of relief—"the nightmare is over"—mixed with a sense of failure and sorrow for those left behind.

An officer said: "France treated Indochina as a colonial problem, without enlisting the enthusiasm of the nation."

Upon arrival, they found a nation more divided over the war than when they had left. Many of the transports docked at Marseille, where the longshoremen's union was militantly antiwar. As they descended the gangplanks, they were met with curses and rocks, and needed a police escort to leave the harbor for their transit camp, where they were given civilian clothes for travel by rail. In some cases they were disembarked at night.

In their home towns, they were made to feel unwelcome. In the street, antiwar activists insulted men in uniform. In a restaurant, a waiter told an officer: "The tip is not included. Have you forgotten the customs of your country?" The officer wondered whether "this rotten soulless place is still my country." It took time to readapt, in spite of the baguettes, the Camembert, the *frites*. It took time, as Bigeard put it, "to learn to be civilized again."

Even in their families, they felt isolated and estranged. In some cases marriages broke up. In others, there was a point where questions posed about their captivity began to feel like voyeurism. Misunderstood themselves, they stopped trying to understand. One officer said, "The kids leaving school, the women shopping, the traffic cop, the delivery boy on his bicycle whistling, the taxi driver honking his horn, I tuned them all out." They trusted only their comrades in arms, who knew what they had been through.

The way the army treated them was scandalous. Their combat bonuses were withheld for the time they had been prisoners. Many of them were no longer fit to serve, but when they filled out the forms for a medical discharge, they were asked for documentary evidence of how their disease was contracted—as if the Vietminh kept records. One man suffering from dysentery was told, "After all, you could have contracted it while touring the country on leave."

Major Dr. Martin, who had written a report based on his questioning of the wounded, had to remind the military bureaucrats that "every single surviving prisoner is suffering from malaria, amoebic dysentery, intestinal parasites, or some other form of deficiency. This must be taken into consideration in responding to the indemnities solicited by former prisoners lacking the paperwork concerning their infirmities."

Many of those who could no longer serve were crippled for life by physical and psychic wounds. They had recurring attacks of malaria, intestinal infections, and rheumatism, and had to be repeatedly hospitalized. There were mental traumas that never healed. What we now know of as post-traumatic stress disorder had not yet been identified. The army doctors had neither the understanding nor the antidepressants to treat it. Men suffered from combat flashbacks, insomnia, hallucinations, and fits of rage. Some began to drink heavily, and kept weapons at home, and some used those weapons on themselves.

Epilogue

...

Even today, in the light of subsequent wars, the defeat at Dien Bien Phu resonates. How could it all have gone so wrong? That was the question the commission of inquiry tried to answer when it convened in 1955 for twenty-two sessions, and heard its long list of witnesses. General Catroux, who presided over two other generals, an admiral, and a civilian official, turned in his report on December 3 to the minister of defense, General Koenig. The report remained secret until 1969.

To sum up, there was not one mistake but a plethora of mistakes. The French Joint Chiefs accepted the Navarre Plan. But Navarre failed to consider the crucial factor of accrued aid the Vietminh received from China. He still thought in terms of bands of ragged guerrillas. When he did not get the reinforcement he asked for, he should have modified his plan.

Lacking instructions from the government regarding the defense of Laos, he took the advice of Commissioner Dejean, who said: "Not to defend Laos is inconceivable." Catroux's report faulted Navarre for failing to see that the tactical value of the Dien Bien Phu base was lost against a heavily armed Vietminh force. Navarre was wrong in assuming that the base could be defended when it was only accessible from the air. And in any case, the base was incapable of barring access to Laos.

The jungle and the mountains surrounding the base favored enemy maneuvers. The location of the base, 185 miles from French airfields, was unfavorable. Navarre should have given up the base on December 10 at the latest. He let time pass when it was still possible to give it up because he had not correctly measured the logistical capacity of the Vietminh and the opportunities the topographical setting of the base gave them. As General Giap put it: "From the end of December, when our troops had encircled the basin, evacuation would have resulted in severe losses."

General Cogny shared in the responsibility for the defeat. "Navarre, who had no personal experience in jungle warfare," said the report, "did not find in General Cogny the wise counselor capable of alerting him to the danger. The government was at fault for picking a commander who was unfamiliar with the conditions of the operation he was about to launch." Navarre was seen as having gone through three phases: over-confidence in seeking the battle; fearing the outcome, but declining to change the situation by evacuation or diversionary operations; and further dispersing his forces with the major operation of ATLANTE in central Vietnam. In addition, "the intervention of a powerful air force, hammering enemy positions day after day, could have saved the base. But the commander in chief did not have a powerful air force."

General Cogny was a divisive element who leaked information to reporters to put across his own point of view. Cogny was in daily contact with Castries, but did nothing to alter Castries' tactics of static defense, nor did he warn Castries of the Vietminh tactics of hiding their artillery. "Before the commission," said the report, "General Cogny covered Colonel de Castries and took the blame for mistakes made. However, a better tactical sense and a more energetic spirit of initiative could have helped. De Castries did not improve his dispositions for the defense of the base." Another problem was that Castries seemed to take a passive role and leave operational decisions to Colonel Langlais. Of course Castries was in constant liaison with Langlais, "but the men, who saw him rarely, were inclined to judge him unfavorably. . . . De Castries was mistaken in giving operational control to Langlais, which he should have kept for himself." He was a tank commander unsuited for the defense of a base supplied by air.

Navarre was expelled from the active ranks in 1956 and took a position with a brick manufacturer. Cogny was named military governor of the city of Metz, then sent to Morocco, and ended his career in French West Africa. He was killed in a plane crash in 1968. Castries retired from the army in 1959, after a car accident, and continued to ride horses in the Bois de Boulogne.

It was Homer, in *The Iliad*, who wrote: "After the event, even a fool is wise." It's tempting to march in step with the conventional wisdom on military folly, but there is another way of looking at Dien Bien Phu—as a cemetery where thousands are buried, with heroism and gallantry on both sides. Think of the bicycles carrying the rice to Giap's troops. Think of the thousands of coolies opening roads for the artillery. The Vietminh had the advantage of being in their own country, with a seemingly unlimited human reservoir. Think of the young *bo doi* who planted a flag on the airstrip so the artillery could adjust its fire and was killed on the spot. Dien Bien Phu was one of the great epics of military endurance. On the French side, think of the tenacious small-unit combat on the strongpoints against human waves of attackers. Think of the doctors who continued to operate under inhuman conditions, and the men who volunteered to carry stretchers on the long march.

And think of Major Pierre Tourret of the elite 8th Choc, a much-admired officer who was said to think only of his men. Tourret was awarded a field promotion from captain to major on April 16. He observed that it was a salute for those about to die. But he survived with his sense of irony intact, and when he was trucked to Camp No. 1, he said it was an example of the Asian respect for the elderly.

He survived, but he was disgusted. He served in Algeria but left the army in 1961. In 1989, he was at the Val-de-Grâce Hospital in Paris after surgery. He asked for Dr. Grauwin, who dropped by. Tourret said: "A friend is someone to whom you can say, 'Come, I need you.' " They talked of the battle, a bottomless pit of discourse. Grauwin grumbled about the slightly wounded who came begging for treatment ahead of the more urgent cases. Tourret said: "No need to be a card-carrying Communist to say that Giap ran rings around M. de la Croix de Castries."

After being released from the hospital, Tourret was told that his close friend Bréchignac had died. He went to the cemetery where Bréchignac was buried, in Fréjus, in the south of France. Night had fallen by the time he got there. He had a flashlight, and when he found the grave, he stood there for a long time with his hand over his heart.

Shortly afterward, Colonel Thomann, who was commanding the 8th Choc at that time, invited Tourret to the regiment's annual anniversary, as a veteran of Dien Bien Phu, thirty-five years after the event, and introduced him. At first, the applause was slow and hesitant, but it quickly exploded with the power of a clamorous war whoop, until it rose to the ceiling of the gymnasium where the ceremony was being held. It was a display of collective memory, on the part of men not yet born when the events took place. Later that year, Tourret died at the age of seventy.

Acknowledgments

. . .

This book could not have been written without my wife, Eileen, who did the Internet and library research, found the books and journals I needed, copyedited the text, shared the rigors of our trip to Dien Bien Phu, and took the photographs. She was my sustaining force.

I would also like to thank the following:

My editor, Rob Cowley, for his enthusiasm and sound advice.

Nguyen Tien Man, our indefatigable guide at Dien Bien Phu.

David Chandler, the eminent scholar of Southeast Asia, for his helpful reading of the text.

John Prados, for sharing his out-of-print articles.

Thomas Reynolds, archival specialist at Texas Tech University's Vietnam Archive, for supplying Vietnamese periodicals.

Harold Menheit, for his December 1970 Cornell paper on Japanese intervention in Vietnam, for which he got an A.

Jonathan Randal, for his sound advice.

And Will Murphy of Random House, who guided the battleship through the canal.

Bibliography

. . .

Documents

"L'armée Française dans la Guerre d'Indochine." Colloque du 30 Novembre et 1er Decembre 1998, Centre d'Études d'Histoire de la Defense sous la direction de Maurice Vaisse.

John F. Melby. Oral History, November 1986, Truman Library.

"The Documentary History of the Truman Presidency, vol. 32: The Emergence of an Asian Pacific Rim in American Foreign Policy." Ed. Dennis Merrill. Bethesda, Md., 2001.

Paul Mus. "Le Vietnam, Chez Lui." Conference at the Collège de France, June 26, 1946, published by the Centre d'Étude de Politique Étrangère.

The Pentagon Papers, vol. 1. Boston, 1971.

Russian Documents on the 1954 Geneva Conference, *Cold War International History Project Bulletin,* Issue 16.

New Evidence from Archives of the Ministry of Foreign Affairs of the People's Republic of China, *Cold War International History Project Bulletin,* Issue 16.

"The 1954 Geneva Conference." A top secret document declassified in 1979. Vietnam Project at Texas Tech University.

"Presentation of the Insignia of Knights of the Legion of Honor to Seven CAT Pilots at Dien Pien Phu," February 24, 2005. Vietnam Project at Texas Tech.

Major Vincent J. Goulding, Jr., Marine Corps Command and Staff College, Quantico, Virginia, Seminar on Dien Bien Phu, April 1, 1985.

Articles

Bloomer, Maj. Harry D.: "The French Defeat at Dien Bien Phu." *Global Security, Org,* 1991.

Champaux, Jacques de: "Un centre d'interrogation Vietminh à Dien Bien Phu." *Revue Historique des Armées,* 1989.

Chen Jian: "China and the First Indochina War." *The China Quarterly,* no. 133, March 1993.

Defourneaux, René: "A Secret Encounter with Ho Chi Minh, as Told to James Flowers." *Look,* August 9, 1966.

Dinh Van Ty: "The Brigade of Iron Horses." *Vietnamese Studies,* no. 43, 1976.

Duncan, David Douglas: "The Year of the Snake: A Time of Fear and Worry Comes over Warring Indochina." *Life,* August 3, 1953.

Fall, Bernard: "Communist POW Treatment in Indochina." *Military Review,* December 1958.

Herring, George, and Richard Immerman: "The Day We Didn't Go to War Revisited." *The Journal of American History,* vol. 71, no. 2, September 1984.

Hess, Gary: "Franklin Roosevelt and Indochina." *Military Review,* vol. 59, no. 2, September 1972.

Hunt, Peter: "A Field Guide to Hanoi and Dien Bien Phu." The Hong Kong Society of Wargamers, August 1, 2008.

Kikoyo Kurusu Nitz: "Japanese Military Policy Toward French Indochina During the Second World War." *Journal of Southeast Asia Studies,* vol. 14, September 1983.

La Feber, Walter: "Roosevelt, Churchill, and Indochina, 1942–1945." *The American Historical Review,* vol. 80, no. 5, December 1975.

Leary, William: "CAT at Dien Bien Phu." *Aerospace Historian,* September 1984.

McCoy, Alfred, ed.: "Southeast Asia Under Japanese Occupation." Yale University Southeast Asia Studies, Monograph Series no. 22.

Melby, John: "Memoir: Vietnam 1950." *Diplomatic History* 6, no. 1, Winter 1982.

Meulendijke, Pieter: "Shifting Images of the Dien Bien Phu Crisis of 1954." Catholic University, Nijmegen, Holland, September 2001 newsletter.

Qiang Zhai: "China and the Geneva Conference of 1954." *The China Quarterly,* no. 129, March 1992.

Seals, Bob: "Peace in a Very Small Place." Military History Online, May 17, 2006.

Shepley, James: "How Dulles Averted War." *Life,* January 1956.

Simcock, William: "Yesterday's Battlefield." *Canadian Army Journal,* July 1958.

Spector, Ronald: "Allied Intelligence and Indochina, 1943–1945." *Pacific Historical Review,* 1981.

Vietnamese Studies, no. 3: "Contribution to the History of Dien Bien Phu."

Vietnamese Studies, no. 43: "Early History of Dien Bien Phu."

Woodgerd, Michael: "French Armor at Dien Bien Phu." *Armor,* September–October 1987.

Zervoudakis, Alexander: "Franco-Vietnamese Intelligence in Indochina, 1950–1954." *Intelligence and National Security,* vol. 22, February 2002.

Books

Abramson, Rudy: *The Life of Averell Harriman.* New York, 1992.

Accoce, Pierre: *Médecins à Dien Bien Phu.* Paris, 1992.

Acheson, Dean: *Present at the Creation.* New York, 1969.

Adams, Sherman: *First-Hand Report.* New York, 1961.

Anderson, David: *The Eisenhower Administration and Vietnam, 1953–61.* New York, 1991.

Artaud, Denise, and Lawrence Kaplan: *Dien Bien Phu.* Lyon, France, 1989.

Bail, René: *Dernier baroud à Dien Bien Phu.* Paris, 1990.

Bartholomew-Feis, Dixee R.: *The OSS and Ho Chi Minh.* Lawrence, Kans., 2006.

Bayle, Claude: *Prisonnier au Camp 113.* Paris, 1991.

Beal, J. R.: *John Foster Dulles.* Paris, 1959.

Bergot, Erwan: *Bataillon Bigeard.* Paris, 1977.

———: *Convoi 42.* Paris, 1986.

———: *Deuxième Classe à Dien Bien Phu.* Paris, 1964.

Bidault, Georges: *D'une résistance à l'autre.* Paris, 1965.

Bigeard, Marcel: *Pour une parcelle de gloire.* Paris, 1975.

Billings-Yun, Melanie: *Decision Against War.* New York, 1988.

Bird, Kai: *The Color of Truth.* New York, 1998.

Bodard, Lucien: *The Quicksand War.* New York, 1967.

Bodin, Michel: *Les Africains dans la guerre d'Indochine.* Paris, 2000.

———: *Les Combattants Français en Indochine.* Paris, 1998.

———: *Soldats d'Indochine.* Paris, 1997.

Bohlen, Charles: *Witness to History.* New York, 1971.

Bonnafous, Robert: *Les prisonniers Français dans les camps Viet Minh.* Montpellier, France, 1985.

Bornert, Lucien: *Dien Bien Phu, citadelle de la gloire.* Paris, 1954.

———: *Les éscapés de l'enfer.* Paris, 1954.

Brancion, Henri de: *Des artilleurs dans la fournaise.* Paris, 1993.

Brownell, Herbert: *Advising Ike.* Lawrence, Kans., 1993.

Bruge, Roger: *Les hommes de Dien Bien Phu.* Paris, 1999.

Burchett, Wilfred: *The Furtive War.* New York, 1963.

Buttinger, Joseph: *Vietnam.* New York, 1977.

Byrnes, James: *Speaking Frankly.* New York, 1947.

Cable, James: *The Geneva Conference.* London, 1986.

Cameron, Allen, ed.: *Vietnam Crisis.* Ithaca, N.Y., 1971.

Catroux, Georges: *Deux actes du drame Indochinois.* Paris, 1959.

Césari, Laurent: *L'Indochine en guerre.* Paris, 1995.

Chandler, David, and Christopher Goscha: *Paul Mus, l'espace d'un regard.* Paris, 2006.

Charmley, John: *Churchill, the End of Glory.* New York, 1993.

Chauvel, Jean: *Commentaire.* Paris, 1973.

Chen Jian: *Vietnam and China, 1938–1954.* Princeton, 1969.

Childs, Marquis: *The Ragged Edge: The Diary of a Crisis.* New York, 1955.

Clarke, Peter: *The Last Thousand Days of the British Empire.* New York, 2008.

Committee on Foreign Relations, United States Senate: *The U.S. Government and the Vietnam War. Executive and Legislative Roles and Relationships, 1945–1961.* Washington, 1984.

Currey, Cecil B.: *Victory at Any Cost: The Genius of Viet Nam's Gen. Vo Nguyen Giap.* Dulles, Va., 2005.

Dalloz, Jacques: *La guerre d'Indochine.* Paris, 1987.

Decoux, Jean: *A la barre de l'Indochine.* Paris, 1952.

Delpard, Raphael: *Les rizières de la suffrance.* Paris, 2004.

Delpey, Roger: *Soldats de la boue.* Paris, 1992.

Dennis, Peter: *Mountbatten and the Southeast Asia Command.* New York, 1966.

Dewey, Peter: *As They Were.* New York, 1946.

Duiker, William: *The Communist Road to Power in Vietnam.* Boulder, Colo., 1981.

———: *Ho Chi Minh.* New York, 2000.

Eden, Anthony: *Full Circle.* London, 1960.

Eisenhower, Dwight D.: *The White House Years,* vol. 1, *Mandate for Change: 1953–1956.* New York, 1963.

Elgey, Georgette: *La république des contradictions.* Paris, 1968.

———: *La république des illusions.* Paris, 1965.

Ely, Paul: *L'Indochine dans la tourmente.* Paris, 1964.

Fall, Bernard: *Hell in a Very Small Place.* New York, 1967.

Fenn, Charles: *At the Dragon's Gate.* Annapolis, Md., 2004.

Fondaumière, Georges de: *Le chagrin d'une armée.* Nice, France, 2004.

Friang, Brigitte: *Les fleurs du ciel.* Paris, 1955.

Futrell, Robert: *The United States Air Force in Southeast Asia: The Advisory Years to 1965.* Washington, 1981.

Gaddis, John Lewis: *We Know Now.* New York, 1997.

Galabru, André: *Un soldat au grand coeur: Capitaine Tourret.* Paris, 2003.

Galard, Geneviève de: *Une femme à Dien Bien Phu.* Paris, 2003.

Gallicchio, Marc: *The Cold War Begins in Asia.* New York, 1988.

Gandy, Alain: *Salan.* Paris, 1988.

Gardner, Lloyd: *Approaching Vietnam.* New York, 1988.

Gellman, Irwin: *Secret Affairs: FDR, Cordell Hull, and Sumner Welles.* Baltimore, Md., 1995.

Genty, Robert: *Ultimes secours pour Dien Bien Phu.* Paris, 1994.

Giap, Vo Nguyen: *Dien Bien Phu.* Hanoi, 2005.

———: *Unforgettable Months and Years.* Ithaca, N.Y., 1975.

Gras, Philippe: *Histoire de la guerre d'Indochine.* Paris, 1992.

Grauwin, Paul: *J'étais médecin à Dien Bien Phu.* Paris, 1954.

Greenstein, Fred: *The Hidden-Hand Presidency.* Baltimore, Md., 1994.

Griotteray, Alain: *Dien Bien Phu.* Paris, 1994.

Guillain, Robert: *La fin des illusions.* Paris, 2004.

Gurtov, Melvin: *The First Vietnam Crisis.* New York, 1967.

Halberstam, David: *The Coldest Winter.* New York, 2007.

Halifax, Lord: *The Life of Lord Halifax.* London, 1965.

Hammer, Ellen: *The Struggle for Indochina.* Stanford, Calif., 1966.

Hooper, Edwin, Dean Allard, and Oscar Fitzgerald: *The United States Navy and the Vietnam Conflict,* vol. 1: *The Setting of the Stage to 1959.* Washington, 1976.

Hoopes, Townsend: *The Devil and John Foster Dulles.* New York, 1973.

Journoud, Pierre, and Hugues Tertrais, eds.: *Paroles de Dien Bien Phu.* Paris, 2004.

Joyaux, François: *La Chine et le reglement du conflit d'Indochine.* Paris, 1979.

Jurika, Stephen, Jr., ed.: *From Pearl Harbor to Vietnam: The Memoirs of Admiral Arthur R. Radford.* Stanford, Calif., 1980.

Kahin, Georges: *Intervention.* New York, 1987.

Kail, F. M.: *What Washington Said.* New York, 1973.

Kaplan, Lawrence, Denise Artaud, and Mark Rubin, eds.: *Dien Bien Phu and the Crisis of Franco-American Relations, 1954–1955.* Wilmington, Del., 1990.

Karnow, Stanley: *Vietnam: A History.* New York, 1973.

Kennan, George: *Memoirs, 1925–1950.* New York, 1967.

Langlais, Pierre: *Dien Bien Phu.* Paris, 1963.

Laniel, Joseph: *Le drame Indochinois.* Paris, 1957.

Lawrence, Mark, and Fredrik Logevall: *The First Vietnam War.* Cambridge, 2007.

Leebaert, Derek: *The Fifty-Year Wound.* New York, 2003.

Leffler, Melvyn: *A Preponderance of Power.* Stanford, Calif., 1992.

Le Mire, Henri: *Epervier: Le 8e Choc à Dien Bien Phu.* Paris, 1988.

Leonetti, Guy, ed.: *Lettres de Dien Bien Phu*. Paris, 2004.

Lockhart, Greg: *Nation in Arms*. Sydney, Australia, 1989.

MacDonald, Peter: *Giap: The Victor in Vietnam*. New York, 1993.

MacGregor Burns, James: *Roosevelt: The Lion and the Fox*. New York, 1956.

Marr, David G.: *Ho Chi Minh's Prison Diaries*. Athens, Ohio, 1978.

————: *Vietnam 1945*. Berkeley, Calif., 1995.

Mary, René: *Les bagnards d'Ho Chi Minh*. Paris, 1986.

McCoy, Alfred: *The Politics of Heroin in Southeast Asia*. New York, 1956.

Mee, Charles L., Jr., *Meeting at Potsdam*. New York, 1975.

Mendès France, Pierre: *Gouverner, c'est choisir*. Paris, 1986.

Mengelle, Henri: *Des chars et des hommes*. Paris, 1996.

Meyran, Michel: *Merci Toubib: Dien Bien Phu: Trois médecins racontent*. Paris, 2000.

Moran, Lord: *Churchill: Taken from the Diaries of Lord Moran*. New York, 1966.

Mosley, Leonard: *Dulles*. New York, 1978.

Muelle, Raymond: *Combats en pays Thai*. Paris, 1999.

Mus, Paul: *The Vietnamese and Their Revolution*. New York, 1970.

Navarre, Henri: *Agonie de l'Indochine*. Paris, 1956.

————: *Le temps des vérités*. Paris, 1979.

Nitze, Paul H.: *From Hiroshima to Glasnost*. New York, 1989.

Nordell, John R., Jr.: *The Undetected Enemy: French and American Miscalculations at Dien Bien Phu*. College Station, Tex., 1995.

Paillat, Claude: *Dossier secret sur l'Indochine*. Paris, 1964.

Patti, Archimedes: *Why Vietnam?* Berkeley, Calif., 1980.

Pellissier, Pierre: *De Lattre*. Paris, 1998.

————: *Dien Bien Phu*. Paris, 2004.

Pettit, Clyde: *The Experts*. Secaucus, N.J., 1975.

Pissary, Jean-Pierre: *Paras d'Indochine*. Paris, 1982.

Porter, Gareth: *Vietnam: A History in Documents*. Paris, 1981.

Pouget, Jean: *Le manifeste du Camp no. 1*. Paris, 1969.

————: *Nous étions à Dien Bien Phu*. Paris, 1964.

Prados, John: *Operation Vulture*. New York, 2004.

————: *The Sky Would Fall*. New York, 1983.

Qiang Zhai: *China and the Vietnam Years, 1950–1975*. Chapel Hill, N.C., 2000.

————: *The Dragon, the Lion, and the Eagle*. Kent, Ohio, 1994.

Randle, Robert: *Geneva 1954*. Princeton, N.J., 1968.

Renald, Jean: *L'enfer de Dien Bien Phu*. Paris, 1955.

Renaud, Patrick-Charles: *Aviateurs en Indochine*. Paris, 2003.

Rioux, Jean-Pierre: *La France de la Quartième République*. Paris, 1980.

Rocolle, Pierre: *Pourquoi Dien Bien Phu?* Paris, 1980.

Rotter, Andrew: *The Path to Vietnam.* Ithaca, N.Y., 1987.

Rotter, Andrew, ed.: *The Light at the End of the Tunnel.* New York, 1999.

Roy, Jules: *The Battle of Dien Bien Phu.* New York, 2002.

Sainteny, Jean: *Histoire d'une paix manquée.* Paris, 1967.

Schoendoerffer, Pierre: *Dien Pien Phu.* Paris, 1992.

Shipway, Martin: *The Road to War: France and Vietnam, 1944–1947.* Oxford, England, 1996.

Shuckburgh, Evelyn: *Descent to Suez.* New York, 1976.

Simpson, Howard: *Dien Bien Phu: The Epic Battle America Forgot.* New York, 1994.

———: *Tiger in the Barbed Wire.* New York, 1994.

Smith, R. Harris: *OSS.* Berkeley, Calif., 1972.

Spector, Ronald: *In the Ruins of Empire: The Japanese Surrender and the Battle for Postwar Asia.* New York, 2007.

Starobin, Joseph: *Eyewitness in Indochina.* New York, 1954.

Stien, Louis: *Les soldats oubliés.* Paris, 1993.

Sulzberger, C. L.: *A Long Row of Candles.* New York, 1969.

Thevenet, Amédée: *La guerre d'Indochine par ceux qui l'ont vécue.* Paris, 2001.

Trinquier, Roger: *Le temps perdu.* Paris, 1978.

Truong Chinh: *Primer for Revolt: The Communist Takeover in Vietnam.* New York, 1966.

Vallaud, Pierre, and Eric Deroo: *Dien Bien Phu.* Paris, 2003.

Vandenberg, Arthur: *Private Papers.* Boston, 1952.

Von Tunzelman, Alex: *Indian Summer: The Secret History of the End of the Empire.* New York, 2007.

Wallace, Henry: *The Price of Vision.* Boston, 1973.

Windrow, Martin: *The Last Valley: Dien Bien Phu and the French Defeat in Vietnam.* Cambridge, Mass., 2004.

Zervoudakis, Alexander: *French Operational Strategy and Tactics in Indochina, 1951–1952.* London, 2002.

Notes

. . .

Act 1
The First Partition of Vietnam

5 **"It is understood":** Adolf A. Berle, *Navigating the Rapids.*
5 **"I am tied down to this chair":** James McGregor Burns, *Roosevelt: The Lion and the Fox.*
5 **"I really think":** Berle.
6 **Ickes told him:** Harold Ickes, *The Secret Diary,* vol. 3.
6 **FDR nomination:** Ted Morgan, *FDR.*

The Commissary Line

7 **Japanese invasion of Indochina:** Kikoyo Kurusu Nitz, "Japanese Military Policy Towards French Indochina During the Second World War," *Journal of Southeast Asia Studies* 14, 1983.
8 **Decoux:** Georges Catroux, *Deux actes du drame indochinois.*

We Mustn't Push Japan Too Much

9 **"glacially lofty Sumner Welles":** Ickes.
9 **"we mustn't push Japan too much":** Morgenthau Diaries, FDR Library, Hyde Park.
10 **"Give Cordell a few more days":** Ickes.

Those Two Fellows Looked Like a Pair of Sheep-killing Dogs

12 **"the Japanese running around like":** Morgenthau.
12 **Hull:** Irwin Gellman, *Secret Affairs.*
13 **"A pair of sheep-killing dogs":** Lord Halifax, *The Life of Lord Halifax.*

I Never Received a Greater Shock

13 **Japanese offensive:** Kikoyo Nitz.
15 **Vichy under Japanese:** Jean Sainteny, *Histoire d'une paix manquée.*

Asia for the Asians

16 **Vietnam:** Paul Mus, *The Vietnamese and Their Revolution.*

You Have Four Hundred Years of Acquisition in Your Blood

20 **"he is a little touched here":** Morgan.
20 **Churchill at Placentia Bay:** John Charmley, *Churchill, the End of Glory.*
21 **"That is the way we talked to her when we were wooing her":** Peter Clarke, *The Last Thousand Days.*
21 **"the president . . . uses conversation":** Halifax.
22 **the concept of "four policemen":** Halifax.
22 **Mountbattan:** John Terraine, *The Life and Times of Lord Mountbatten.*

France Has Milked It for One Hundred Years

23 **Cairo and Tehran conferences:** Morgan.
24 **"to deprive France of her economic stake":** Charmley.
25 **"The Fourth Term. Oh, God damn it":** Henry Wallace, *The Price of Vision.*
25 **FDR reminiscence:** Wallace.

A Spirit of Ruthless Go-Getting

25 **Second Quebec Conference:** Charmley.
27 **Stilwell and Frank Dorn:** Committee on Foreign Relations.
27 **FDR and Indochina:** Gary Hess, "Franklin Roosevelt and Indochina."

I Give Him Only a Few Months to Live

28   **Yalta:** Morgan, Hess, and Lloyd Gardner, *Approaching Vietnam.*

What Are You Americans Driving At?

30   **The last days of FDR and Indochina:** Hess, and Andrew Rotter, *The Path to Vietnam.*

A Voice in the Wilderness

31   **Ho Chi Minh:** William Duiker, *Ho Chi Minh.*

The Man Who Looks Always Angry

33   **Giap:** Cecil Currey and Peter MacDonald biographies, and Giap, *Unforgettable Months and Years.*

The French Had Lost Face

36   **Jean Decoux:** Decoux, *A la barre de l'Indochine.*

37   **Japanese coup:** David Marr, *Vietnam 1945;* David Chandler, *Paul Mus;* and Sainteny, *Histoire d'une paix manquée.*

37   **Raid on Indochina coast:** Edwin Hopper, *The United States Navy and the Vietnam Conflict.*

Suddenly We Were Able to Come Out of the Trees

40   **"After so many years":** Giap, *Unforgettable Months and Years.*

41   **Japanese and Vietminh in 1945:** Ellen Hammer, *The Struggle for Indochina.*

41   **Famine and Vietminh reaction:** Giap, *Unforgettable Months and Years.*

Would You Like to Work for the Americans?

42   **Charles Fenn:** Fenn, *At the Dragon's Gate.*

45   **OSS in 1945:** Dixee Bartholomew-Feis, *The OSS and Ho Chi Minh.*

45   **Archimedes Patti:** Patti, *Why Vietnam?*

46   **Deer Team:** Patti.

The United States Recognizes French Sovreignty over Indochina

50 **Trusteeship and Truman:** Marc Gallicchio, *The Cold War Begins in Asia.*

50 **1945 U.N. Conference:** Georges Bidault, *D'Une resistance à l'autre.*

The Dreadful Division at Potsdam

52 **Potsdam:** Rudy Abramson, *Harriman;* Charles Mee, *Potsdam;* and Martin Shipway, *Road to War.*

54 **Surrender tactics:** Gallicchio.

55 **Mountbatten:** Terraine.

France Means to Recover Its Sovereignty over Indochina

58 **Vietminh seize power:** Duiker, *Ho Chi Minh.*

59 **Mark Hatfield:** Committee on Foreign Relations.

59 **Sainteny in Hanoi:** Sainteny, *Histoire d'une paix manquée.*

Provisional Government Groping in the Dark

60 **Ho Chi Minh and Giap in Hanoi:** Giap, *Unforgettable Months and Years;* Duiker, *Ho Chi Minh;* Patti; and Sainteny.

62 **Ho's September 2 speech:** Duiker and Giap.

Ho Chi Minh Is Riding a Wild Horse Bareback and Holding Only One Rein

63 **OSS in Chungking:** Patti.

64 **Chinese occupation:** Sainteny, and Marr, *Vietnam 1945.*

64 **Ho Chi Minh toward Chinese:** Marr.

65 **Patti's days over:** Bartholomew-Feis; Ronald Spector, *In the Ruins of Empire;* and Peter Dewey, *As They Were.*

Americans Will Be Regarded with Suspicion

68 **British occupation and Gracey:** Marr, *Vietnam 1945;* and Hammer, *The Struggle for Indochina.*

It Was Like Wiping Your Ass with a Hoop

72   **State of Leclerc's army:** Michel Bodin, *Les Combattants Francais en Indochine;* Claude Paillat, *Dossier Secret.*

73   **Salan:** Alain Gandy, *Salan.*

One of the Finest Twelfth-Century Minds

74   **d'Argenlieu:** Sainteny, and Georgette Elgey, *La République des illusions.*

They Are Strong on Parades

75   **Ho Chi Minh forms government:** Duiker, and Greg Lockhart, *Nation in Arms.*

76   **Leclerc moves north:** Sainteny and Hammer.

The Moment Has Arrived to Teach a Hard Lesson

81   **The Haiphong incident:** Sainteny, Marr, and Hammer.

83   **Blum government:** Elgey, *La République des illusions.*

83   **Situation in Hanoi:** Duiker.

84   **"Vespers of Hanoi":** Sainteny.

The Concern About Communist Expansion Led to a Fixation

85   **Moffat:** Committee on Foreign Relations.

85   **Mus:** Mus, *The Vietnamese and Their Revolution.*

Act II
The Colonial War Becomes a Proxy War

91   **Vincent memo:** Gareth Porter, *Vietnam: A History in Documents.*

This Whore of a Tropical Country

92   **French army:** Bodin.

94   **French air force:** Patrick-Charles Renaud, *Aviateurs en Indochine.*

Get Up, You're Overdoing It

95 **Vandenburg:** Arthur Vandenberg, *Private Papers.*

96 **Acheson:** Dean Acheson, *Present at the Creation.*

96 **National Assembly:** Elgey.

97 **George Kennan:** George Kennan, *Memoirs.*

97 **Ramadier:** Elgey, *La République des Illusions.*

A Dangerously Outmoded Colonial Outlook

98 **Marshall:** Porter.

99 **Reed:** Porter.

100 **Salan:** Gandy.

101 **Bao Dai:** Elgey, and Stanley Karnow, *Vietnam: A History.*

The Jungle Is Neutral

102 **Giap tactics:** Cecil B. Currey, *Victory at Any Cost.*

102 **Salan tactics:** Gandy.

It Seems Definitely That Indochina Will Go Communist

103 **1948 Bangkok conference:** "Documentary History of the Truman Presidency."

Was Ho Chi Minh an Asian Tito?

105 **Acheson on Southeast Asia:** Committee on Foreign Relations.

106 **Schuman visit:** Acheson.

106 **Acheson on Ho Chi Minh:** "Documentary Histroy of the Truman Presidency."

You'll Learn on the Job

107 **Revers:** Elgey.

108 **Carpentier:** Elgey.

108 **NSC:** Pentagon Papers, vol. 1.

Getting Something Out of Stalin Is Like Taking Meat from the Mouth of a Tiger

110   **Chinese aid to Ho Chi Minh:** Duiker, *Ho Chi Minh.*
111   **Ho Chi Minh visit to Moscow:** Duiker, *Ho Chi Minh.*

We Are Not Exactly Popular Among These Native Peoples

112   **Allen Griffin mission:** "Documentary History of the Truman Presidency."
113   **Acheson:** Committee on Foreign Relations.

Truman's War

114   **Truman and Indochina:** "Documentary History of the Truman Presidency."

Do Not Show the Victor's Arrogance

115   **On Chinese advisers:** Chen Jian, *Vietnam and China,* and Qiang Zhai, *China and the Vietnam Years.*

We Found Vietnam More Confused and Irresolute Than Ever

116   **John Melby mission:** "Documentary History of the Truman Presidency."
120   **Melby and security investigation:** Melby, oral history.

Charton, We Will Cut Off Your Balls

120   **Battle of Cao Bang:** Philippe Gras, *Histoire de la guerre d'Indochine,* and Lucien Bodard, *The Quicksand War.*

The French In indochina Are Not Fighting

131   **Wake Island meeting:** Harold Gosnell, *Truman's Crises.*

Yellow Men Will Be Killed by Yellow Men Rather Than By White Men

132   **French reaction to Cao Bang:** Elgey.
133   **Joint State-Defense report:** Committee on Foreign Relations.

My Presence Is Worth a Division

134   **De Lattre:** Pierre Pellissier, *De Lattre.*

Alors! When Will This Incident Be Over?

137   **Giap and Chinese advisers:** see Qiang Zhai.
137   **De Lattre:** Pellissier.

Indochina Is a Key Area of Southeast Asia

138   **Acheson briefing:** Committee on Foreign Relations.
139   **Pleven meeting:** "Documentary Histroy of the Truman Presidency."
139   **NSC, February 25:** Pentagon Papers, vol. 1.

The French Have a Knotty Problem on That One

140   **De Lattre in Paris:** Pellissier.

Forgive Me for Not Having Been Able to Protect Our Son

141   **Giap attacks of 1951:** Currey.
142   **De Lattre and the death of his son:** Pellissier.

The Will and Genius of de Lattre Is Arrayed Against the Stalinist Dynamic

144   **Humphrey and Gullion:** Committee on Foreign Relations.
144   **De Lattre in Washington:** Gardner, *Approaching Vietnam,* and Pellissier.

I'm Going to Join Bernard

147   **Kennedy trip to Vietnam:** Committee on Foreign Relations.
147   **Radford trip to Vietnam:** Stephen Jurika, *From Pearl Harbor to Vietnam.*
148   **Death of de Lattre:** Pellissier.

The French Are Now in Good Shape

148   **Bruce to Acheson,** Porter.
148   **Melby:** "Documentary History of the Truman Presidency."

The Accumulation of French Government Neuroses

149   **Churchill on Truman's yacht:** Acheson.
150   **"If you fellows come in you will be pasted":** Committee on Foreign Relations.

The Ship Has a Helmsman at the Rudder but No Captain at the Wheel

151   **Salan:** Gandy.
152   **Gullion estimate:** Committee on Foreign Relations.
152   **Ho Chi Minh, "self-reliance" and land reform:** Duiker.
154   **Luo Guibo plan:** Qiang Zhai.

France Lacked the Will to Draft Its Own Men for Service in Indochina

154   **Acheson to Franks:** Acheson.
155   **"The now familiar line":** Anthony Eden, *Full Circle.*

In Our War, Where Is the Front?

156   **Giap and Na San:** Currey.
157   **Howard Simpson at Na San:** Howard Simpson, *Tiger in the Barbed Wire.*
158   **Starobin visit:** Joseph Starobin, *Eyewitness in Indochina.*

The French Should Stop Sitting in Their Beau Geste Forts on Champagne Cases

160   **Dulles on Indochina:** Committee on Foreign Relations.
160   **McClintock:** Simpson.
161   **René Mayer visit:** Elgey.
161   **Nitze and Vandenberg:** Committee on Foreign Relations.

You've Got to Write Eisenhower That It's Take It or Leave It

176 **Navarre in Paris:** Navarre.

177 **Laniel and Douglas MacArthur:** Elgey.

178 **Navarre and *Life*:** Navarre, and David Douglas Duncan, "The Year of the Snake."

179 **"You are pouring money down a rat hole":** Committee on Foreign Relations.

179 **Laniel gloats:** Elgey, *La République des Contradictions.*

This Plan Will Contribute to the Final Defeat of Colonial Rule

180 **Chinese and Vietminh strategy:** Duiker, Currey, and Qiang Zhai.

The War in Indochina Is Doomed. . . . We Should Spend the Money on Schools

181 **Operation** HIRONDELLE: Marcel Bigeard, *Pour une parcelle de gloire.*

182 **Navarre studies Dien Bien Phu:** Navarre.

184 **Navarre and Cogny:** Navarre.

You Cannot Bar a Direction

187 **Navarre studies Dien Bien Phu:** Navarre.

188 **Bastiani pessimism:** Pierre Rocolle, *Pourquoi Dien Bien Phu?*

188 **Cogny wire to Navarre:** Rocolle.

189 **Meetings with Cogny and Dechaux:** Rocolle.

No Unfavorable Opinion Was Expressed Before the Battle

190 **Jacquet arrives in Saigon:** Jules Roy, *The Battle of Dien Bien Phu.*

190 **Navarre and the defense of Laos:** Navarre.

190 **"Do you have any objections":** Rocolle.

191 **Alexander Smith visit:** Committee on Foreign Relations.

192 **Cabanier visit:** Navarre.

I'll Be Happier When You Have Found a Successor for Me

197   **The drop continues:** Rocolle.

198   **Dropping the bulldozer:** Windrow.

198   **"It landed as gently as a butterfly on a flower":** Roger Bruge, *Les hommes de Dien Bien Phu.*

199   **Cogny visits base:** Rocolle.

199   **Jeansotte visit:** Rocolle.

We Decided to Wipe Out at All Costs the Whole Enemy Force at Dien Bien Phu

200   **Navarre's explanation for the operation:** Navarre.

201   **As Giap saw it:** Giap, *Dien Bien Phu.*

201   **Evacuation of Lai Chau:** Rocolle, and Windrow.

That's What They Call Inflation

202   **Letters home:** Bruge.

203   **Cazeneuve and Pingwarski:** Bergot, *Bataillon Bigeard.*

204   **Building the bases:** Windrow.

It Is Impossible to Lay Down Arms Until Victory Is Completely Won

205   **Giap strategy:** Giap, *Dien Bien Phu,* and Qiang Zhai.

206   **Bonsal to Robertson:** Committee on Foreign Relations.

207   **Berteil in favor of CASTOR:** Roy.

I'd Rather You Picked Somebody Else

207   **Interview with *Expressen:*** Duiker.

208   **Navarre and Cogny pick Castries:** Navarre.

208   **On Castries:** Pellissier.

209   **National Intelligence Estimate:** Pentagon Papers, vol. 1.

Bidault Looks Like a Dying Man. Laniel Is Actually Dying Upstairs.

210   **Bermuda Conference:** Evelyn Shuckburgh, *Descent to Suez.*

210   **Churchill and Eden at Bermuda:** Lord Moran.

213 **Sturm:** Simpson, *Dien Bien Phu.*

213 **O'Daniel report:** Edwin Hooper, *The United States Navy and the Vietnam Conflict.*

I Have Decided to Accept the Battle

214 **Lalande to wife:** Guy Leonetti, *Lettres de Dien Bien Phu.*

214 **Navarre instruction to do battle:** Rocolle.

215 **Navarre and Thye:** Committee on Foreign Relations.

215 **Shaughnessey report:** John R. Nordell, Jr., *The Undetected Enemy.*

The Tamers of Iron Horses

216 **Dechaux to 1955 commission:** Bruge.

217 **Dinh Van Ty:** Dinh Van Ty, "The Brigade of Iron Horses."

If You Lose an Inch of Ground, You're Done For

219 **Gilles and Castries:** Windrow.

You Were Sitting on My Stomach

220 **Evacuation of Lai Chau:** Rocolle, Bruge, and Pierrre Langlais, *Dien Bien Phu.*

If I Were Your Father, I'd Spank You

223 **Castries briefs Navarre:** Rocolle.

224 **Piroth:** Henri de Brancion, *Des Artilleurs dans la fournaise.*

225 **Gaucher:** Pouget.

Is This What They Call Waging War? It Is Utterly Pointless

225 **On the march to Laos:** Andre Galabru, *Capitaine Tourret.*

226 **Commission of inquiry:** Bruge.

227 **Tanks:** Henri Mengelle, *Des chars et des hommes.*

À la Hussarde! *You Know What That Means, Castries!*

228 **Navarre:** Navarre.

228 **Castries and Gaucher:** Pouget.

228 **Letters:** Leonetti.

229 **Death of Guth:** Bruge.

229 **Navarre instruction:** Roy.

230 **Castries before commission:** Bruge.

230 **Jacquet and Dejean:** Elgey, *La République des contradictions.*

The Bombing Campaign Suffered from a Lack of Leadership

231 **Air force.** Partick-Charles Renaud, *Aviateurs en Indochine.*

232 **Bordellos:** Pouget.

232 **Gendarmes:** Langlais.

Dien Bien Phu Is Surrounded on All Sides by Enemy Forces

232 **Letters home:** Bruge, and Leonetti.

233 **Langlais to commission of inquiry:** Bruge.

234 **Death of Nénert:** Bruge.

234 **Sturm:** Nordell.

234 **Faure and Laniel:** Elgey, *La République des contradictions.*

Step by Step, We Are Moving into This War in Indochina

235 **NSC meeting January 8, 1954:** Committee on Foreign Relations.

236 **"Are we ready to go to war with China?":** Committee on Foreign Relations.

237 **Request for air force mechanics:** Robert Futrell, *The United States Air Force in Southeast Asia.*

237 **Senators irked:** Committee on Foreign Relations.

Our Men Died in Many Ways

238 **Giap's supply lines:** Giap, *Dien Bien Phu.*

239 **Bui Tin:** Windrow.

239 **Chinese advisers:** Qiang Zhai.

Eventually There Will Be Two Indochinas, as There Are Two Koreas

240   **Navarre:** Pellissier.
240   **Letters:** Leonetti.
240   **Distinguished visitors:** Windrow.
242   **Commission of inquiry:** Bruge.

Molotov Showed Great Pallyness

243   **Shuckburgh in Berlin:** Shuckburgh.
244   **Dulles in Berlin:** Shuckburgh.
245   **Bidault in Berlin:** Bidault.
245   **Navarre on Berlin:** Navarre.

The Geneva Conference Sealed the Fate of Dien Bien Phu

246   **Navarre before the commission of inquiry:** Bruge.
246   **Bedell Smith:** Committee on Foreign Relations.
247   **Radford:** Committee on Foreign Relations.
247   **Apologetic Dulles, Bonsal to Heath:** Committee on Foreign Relations.

The Navarre Plan Is a Bust

248   **Dien Bien Phu was the crucial front:** Giap.
248   **Dien Bien Phu surrounded by twenty-seven battalions:** Rocolle.
248   **Chevigné visit:** Windrow.
249   **Gaucher and Pichelin letters:** Leonetti.
249   **Grauwin arrives:** Paul Grauwin, *J'étais médecin à Dien Bien Phu.*
250   **Pleven and Ely visit:** Paul Ely, *L'Indochine dans la tourmente.*
250   **Pleven press conference:** Brigitte Friang, *Les fleurs du ciel.*
251   **Payen:** Renaud.
251   **De Galard:** Geneviève de Galard, *Une femme à Dien Bien Phu.*
251   **Gaucher and Pichelin letters:** Leonetti
251   **Guillain:** Robert Guillain, *La fin des illusions.*

Get the Fuck off My Base

252   **Bigeard to Haiphong:** Bigeard.
253   **Navarre to Lauzin:** Renaud.
253   **Giap artillery:** Giap.

Where Do You Put Them?

254   **Navarre March 4 visit:** Navarre.
254   **Castries at the commission of inquiry:** Bruge.
255   **Death of Lieutenant Bedeaux:** Grauwin.
255   **Major Kah to wife:** Leonetti.
256   **Gaucher to wife:** Leonetti.

Act IV

Scene I: The Ides of March

259   **Giap convenes commanders in 1953:** Giap, *Dien Bien Phu.*
260   **Criticism of Giap:** see Qiang Zhai.
261   **Plan of attack:** see Giap.

The Vietminh Are Fortunate in One Thing:
They Have No Pentagon to Deal With

262   **O'Daniel:** Futrell.
263   **Heath to Bonsal:** Committee on Foreign Relations.
264   **O'Daniel giving up the star:** Futrell.

I Count Fifty Shells per Minute

265   **Pégot bulletin and personal tragedy:** Bruge.
266   **Béatrice chosen:** Giap.
266   **Situation on Béatrice:** Rocolle.
267   **Difficulties of supply planes:** Renaud.
268   **Civil Air Transport:** William Leary, "CAT at Dien Bien Phu."
269   **Piroth's preparations:** Brancion.
270   **"The men are tired and tense":** Bruge.

Your Artillery Dispositions Were No Good

287   **Hervouet:** Mengelle.
288   **Piroth suicide:** Brancion.
288   **"Is he dead":** Grauwin.
289   **commission of inquiry:** Bruge.

I Had a Smaller Perimeter, Which I Thought I Could Hold

290   **The Thais at Anne-Marie:** Philippe Gras, *Histoire de la guerre d'Indochine*.
290   **Dr. Verdaguer:** Journoud.
293   **Commission of inquiry:** Bruge.
293   **Letters home:** Leonetti.
294   **"It's a little like Verdun":** Windrow.
294   **Heath and Sturm:** Simpson, *Dien Bien Phu*.

The Central Task Is Now to Build Trenches

295   **Giap strategy:** Giap.
296   **"At night in total silence":** Bruge.
296   **Cadiou to brother:** Leonetti.

You Are Not to Give Orders to Anyone in My Battalion

296   **Return of Bigeard:** Bergot, *Bataillon Bigeard*, and Bigeard.
299   **"Our twelve battalions that look like olives":** Bruge.
299   **Péraud:** Journoud.

It Is Hardly Necessary to Insist on the Necessity of Stopping This Carnage

300   **"We'd seen airlifts before":** Renaud.
300   **Picking up the wounded:** Renaud.
302   **The plight of the wounded:** Grauwin.
302   **Night flights:** Renaud.
303   **De Galard stuck on the base:** de Galard.
303   **Civil Air Transport:** see Leary.

We Firmly Believe in Your Artificial Rain Project

304 **The artificial rain:** Robert Genty, *Ultime Secours pour Dien Bien Phu.*

They Hope That the Vietminh Will Attack. As for Me, I Don't Share That Hope.

305 **Stassen and Symington:** Committee on Foreign Relations.
306 **Eisenhower and Dulles:** Committee on Foreign Relations.
306 **Ridgway and Gavin:** Committee on Foreign Relations.
306 **Ely:** Paul Ely, *L'Indochine dans la tourmente.*
308 **Ely to Indochina with Pleven:** Ely.
309 **Ely to Washington:** Ely; Jurika; and Lawrence Kaplan et al., *Dien Bien Phu and the Crisis of Franco-American Relations.*

Give Him Everything He Asks For

310 **Ely in Washington:** Ely, and Jurika.

The United States Seeks to Control and Operate Everything of Importance

312 **Ely-Radford talks:** Ely, and Jurika.

President Eisenhower's Position Might Be a Little Different from That of the Secretary of State

314 **Dulles press conference:** Townsend Hoopes, *The Devil and John Foster Dulles.*
314 **Ely sees Dulles:** Ely, and Jurika.

Why Back a War with No Chance of Winning?

315 **Ely sees Joint Chiefs, Ridgway reaction:** Committee on Foreign Relations.

France Is Creating a Vacuum in the World

316 **Dulles memo:** Committee on Foreign Relations.
317 **Seventh Fleet on alert:** Futrell.
317 **Dulles-Radford phone call:** Jurika.
318 **Eisenhower press conference:** Melanie Billings-Yun, *Decision Against War.*

Let's Forget About Indochina for a While

318   **March 25 NSC meeting:** Committee on Foreign Relations.
320   **Memo on war powers:** Committee on Foreign Relations.

Ely Remembered Only What Was Favorable to Him

321   **Brohon proposes bombing supply depots:** Kaplan.
322   **Ely and Radford differ:** Ely, and Jurika.
324   **Radford report:** Committee on Foreign Relations.

Committing U.S. Forces Would Lead to a War of Attrition Worse Than Korea

325   **Ridgway:** David Halberstam, *The Coldest Winter.*
325   **Clashes with Radford:** Jurika.
326   **"things began to fall into place":** Jurika.
327   **Ridgway sends team to Indochina:** Committee on Foreign Relations.
327   **March 26 cabinet meeting:** Billings-Yun.

To Make Peace, Prepare for War

328   **Dulles prepares speech and meets with Republican leaders:** Committee on
       Foreign Relations.
328   **Dulles speech:** Hoopes, and Billings-Yun.
329   **Alexander Smith:** Committee on Foreign Relations.
330   **John Stennis:** Committee on Foreign Relations.
330   **Makins and Eden:** Eden.

The Only Way to Save Dien Bien Phu Was an American Air Strike

330   **Ely back in Paris:** Ely.
331   **The mood of France:** Elgey, *La République des contradictions.*

The Vietnamese Army Cannot Replace the French

333   **Navarre discouraged:** Navarre.
334   **Navarre to Ely:** Ely.

I Feel the Situation Can Only Deteriorate Further

335 **Duhoux incident:** Renaud.

336 **"I must envisage":** Rocolle.

336 **Ambush in the delta:** Windrow.

336 **"I can only repeat":** Pellissier.

Have the Tensions of Battle Made Him Lose His Reason?

337 **Langlais and fighting spirit:** Langlais.

337 **CAT pilots:** Leary.

338 **"Langlais is an admirable lad":** Bruge.

338 **"These useless services":** Langlais.

338 **Raid on Rats of Nam Yum:** Langlais.

339 **The para mafia:** Langlais, and Windrow.

What's the Use? We're Being Butchered.

339 **Cricket incident:** Renaud.

340 **Gambiez incident:** Renaud.

342 **Fauroux incident:** Renaud.

To Command Is to Anticipate

342 **Castries to Navarre:** Rocolle.

342 **Cogny directive:** Rocolle.

343 **Chevalier to wife:** Leonetti.

344 **Lalande to wife:** Leonetti.

344 **Opening the road to Isabelle:** Windrow; Rocolle; and Gras.

345 **Bigeard opens road:** Bigeard.

346 **Arrival of Bizard:** Journoud.

346 **Tourret:** Henri Le Mire, *Epervier: Le 8e Choc à Dien Bien Phu.*

348 **Hervouet on landing craft:** Mengelle.

348 **"Attacks on the trenches":** Bruge.

348 **Hervouet and Préaud:** Mengelle.

They're Like Oysters on a Rock

348   **Bigeard counterattack:** Bigeard.
350   **Hervouet:** Le Mire.
350   **Carette on his turret:** Mengelle.
350   **Le Vigouroux:** Bruge.
352   **Préaud's tanks come up:** Mengelle.
352   **Le Page company:** Bruge.
353   **Bigeard orders fallback:** Bruge.
353   **On Tourret:** Galabru.

Dancing the Last Dance

354   **Ritz nightclub:** Lucien Bodard, *The Quicksand War.*

We Must Strike at Many Places at a Time

355   **Giap:** Giap.
356   **Sturm:** Simpson, *Dien Bien Phu.*

Scene 2: April Is the Cruelest Month

356   **Giap battle strategy:** Giap.

If the Viets Have Dug Trenches, It's Not to Plant Peas

358   **Langlais and Tourret:** Langlais.
359   **Bridge in the bunker:** Langlais.
359   **Aubert:** Bruge.
359   **Premillieu:** Bruge.
360   **Nicolas:** Langlais.
361   **Grauwin:** Grauwin.

It Was Like the End of the World

362   **Le Boudec:** Bruge.
363   **Grauwin and Fleury:** Grauwin.
363   **Martinais:** Journoud.

Debouch at Zero

365 **Brunbrouck:** Brancion.

367 **The Quads:** Windrow.

367 **Baysset:** Bruge.

That Swine Is Betraying Me Every Day

368 **On Navarre and Cogny:** Navarre, *Le temps des vérités.*

369 **Navarre letter to his wife:** Pellissier, *Dien Bien Phu.*

Nicolas Is Still Holding

370 **Nicod and Premillieu:** Bruge.

371 **Bigeard and radio frequencies:** Bigeard.

371 **Le Boudec:** Bigeard.

372 **Battle for Eliane 2:** Bruge.

374 **Castries calls for air support and Andrieux goes down:** Renaud.

374 **Isabelle:** Windrow.

That Day Was True Hell

375 **Bigeard fuming:** Bigeard.

375 **Sauvagnac:** Langlais.

375 **Counterattacks:** Bigeard.

376 **Carré:** Bruge.

377 **Castries to Cogny:** Rocolle.

377 **Le Boudec:** Bigeard.

The Biggest Open-Air Cemetary on Dien Bien Phu

378 **Heath to Washington:** Simpson, *Tiger in the Barbed Wire.*

379 **Intelligence report:** Rocolle.

The Tracers Lit Up the Corollas of Our Chutes

383 **Charles:** Journoud.

383 **Ruiter:** Leonetti.

383 **Langlais to Sauvagnac:** Langlais.

384 **Lanzac:** Grauwin.

384 **Juteau:** Journoud.

385 **Langlais argument:** Langlais.

385 **Clédic:** Journoud.

In a Battle, Men Are Like Fuel

386 **Huguette 6 and 7:** Rocolle.

387 **"Send me a wagon":** Mengelle.

388 **Mengelle in the *Conti*:** Mengelle.

388 **Clédic:** Journoud.

389 **Bigeard:** Bigeard.

389 **Le Page:** Bruge.

390 **Ney:** Bruge.

How Would You Like to Return to Dien Bien Phu?

390 **Navarre to Castries:** Rocolle.

390 **Verdaguer:** Journoud.

390 **Fischer:** Leonetti.

391 **"You read this and you volunteered?":** Grauwin.

The Intervention Could Have a Decisive Result

392 **Ely and Radford:** Ely.

392 **Navarre and Cogny:** Navarre, *Le temps des vérités.*

393 **Brohon to Saigon:** Ely.

394 **Wire from Navarre:** Ely.

The Conditions for a Favorable Solution in Indochina No Longer Exist

394 **Eden confused:** Eden.

395 **"there was a gulf":** Kaplan.

395 **"mental dexterity" and "instability of French thought":** Kaplan.

395 **"Policy Toward Indochina":** Kaplan.

396 **Eden to Makins:** Eden.

Action by Our Forces Holds No Significant Promise of Success

396   **Eisenhower press conference:** Billings-Yun.

396   **Radford polls Joint Chiefs:** Jurika.

397   **Eisenhower and JCS:** Fred Greenstein, *The Hidden-Hand Presidency.*

397   **April 1 NSC meeting and Dulles to Brownell:** Committee on Foreign Relations.

397   **Ike lunch with Roy Howard:** Greenstein.

397   **Polling of Joint Chiefs:** Committee on Foreign Relations.

400   **Dulles draft:** Committee on Foreign Relations.

400   **"Nothing specific":** Jurika.

400   **Ike operating through others:** see Herbert Brownell, *Advising Ike.*

401   **Dulles sees Makins and Scott:** Kaplan.

402   **Makins recommends:** Kaplan.

The Day We Didn't Go to War

402   **Millikin:** Sherman Adams, *First-Hand Report.*

403   **April 3 meeting:** Committee on Foreign Relations.

404   **Russell:** Adams.

405   **Dulles to Ike:** Committee on Foreign Relations.

405   **Secret meetings of congressmen:** Committee on Foreign Relations.

405   **Chalmers Roberts's account:** Committee on Foreign Relations.

405   **John McCormack:** Committee on Foreign Relations.

407   **Thruston Morton:** Committee on Foreign Relations.

408   **Ike to Churchill:** Kaplan.

409   **"the Old Man vents":** Shuckburgh.

He Who Defines the Battle Controls the Peace

410   **Mao and Chou:** François Joyaux, *La Chine et le reglement du conflit d'Indochine.*

411   **Mao message to Pen Dehuai:** Qiang Zhai, *China and the Vietnam Years.*

French Government Now Asking for U.S. Carrier Support

412   **Laniel and Pleven jostled:** Elgey, *La république des contradictions.*

412   **Dillon to Dulles:** Committee on Foreign Relations.

Indochina Is the First in a Row of Dominoes

412   **Dulles calls Ike:** Committee on Foreign Relations.

413   **Dulles to Dillon:** Committee on Foreign Relations.

413   **April 6 NSC meeting:** Committee on Foreign Relations.

416   **Humphrey:** Adams.

I'm Worried About Losing My Ass

417   **"I'm worried about losing my ass":** Committee on Foreign Relations.

418   **Dulles copes with British and French:** Committee on Foreign Relations.

419   **Eisenhower April 7 press conference:** Billings-Yun.

Send Ho Chi Minh to Peking University

420   **Chauvel in Paris:** Jean Chauvel, *Commentaire.*

To Each His Ghosts

422   **Death of de la Mettrie:** Renaud.

422   **CAT pilots:** Leary.

423   **Hantz:** Michel Meyran, *Merci Toubib.*

424   **Haas:** Grauwin.

The Only Chance for Us Is to Wait for a Cease-Fire

425   **Bigeard counterattack:** Bigeard.

425   **Delafond:** Journoud.

426   **Bigeard directing counterattack:** Bigeard.

427   **Capture of Fischer:** Leonetti.

428   **On Le Page and flamethrower:** Bruge.

429   **Giap morale problem:** Giap, *Dien Bien Phu.*

We Have Gotten Very Near Having Cheated the Americans

430   **Dulles to London:** Eden, and Hoopes.

432   **Lunch with Dulles:** Shuckburgh.

433   **Sulzberger:** C. L. Sulzberger, *A Long Row of Candles.*

433   **Eden and Dulles in London:** Kaplan.

435   **Laniel before National Assembly:** Elgey, *La République des contradictions*.

436   **Bidault and Dulles:** Bidault.

437   **Sulzberger sees Robertson and Dulles:** Sulzberger.

438   **Senate up in arms:** Committee on Foreign Relations.

Targets Had Been Selected

439   **First Fleet movements:** Hooper.

It's Not Courage That Wins Battles

440   **Ely to Navarre:** Ely.

441   **Allaire and Bréchignac:** Journoud.

441   **Castries to commission:** Bruge.

442   **Castries' situation reports:** Rocolle.

443   **Pottier:** Bruge.

443   **Bigeard in charge of counterattacks:** Bigeard.

Keep the Press Clippings for Me

445   **Brunbrouck's death:** Brancion.

Too Many Men Are Getting Killed Supplying Huguette 6

445   **Giap battalion digs trench:** Giap, *Dien Bien Phu*.

446   **"Too many men":** Langlais.

447   **Bizard:** Journoud.

447   **Latanne:** Bruge.

The Cigar-Shaped Pellets Were Very Effective

447   **Partridge sends planes:** Futrell.

448   **FEAF offers cluster bombs:** Futrell.

449   **Dechaux testifies:** Bruge.

450   **Brunet testifies:** Bruge.

An Air Strike Is Militarily Useless and Politically Dangerous

450   **Dejean before commission:** Bruge.

450   **Partridge to Saigon:** Futrell.

451   **Caldara to Saigon:** Futrell, and John Prados, *The Sky Would Fall.*

The Administration Must Face Up to the Situation and Dispatch Forces

452   **Nixon to editors:** Committee on Foreign Relations.

453   **"Big Ed" Johnson:** Committee on Foreign Relations.

453   **Halleck:** Committee on Foreign Relations.

454   **Eden and Dulles in Paris:** Kaplan.

I Am Not Aware That Dulles Has Any Cause for Complaint

455   **Eden to Makins:** Eden and Kaplan.

456   **Dulles to sister:** Hoopes.

Partition at the 16th Parallel

457   **Chang Wentian and Molotov:** Joyaux, and Qiang Zhai, "China and the Geneva Conference."

459   **Chinese delegation:** Qiang Zhai.

459   **Chou to Indian ambassador:** see Qiang Zhai.

I Now Believe in an Immediate Cease-Fire

459   **Navarre note on cease-fire:** Chauvel.

460   **Navarre to Ely:** Ely.

460   **Navarre before commission:** Bruge.

460   **Commanders takes stock:** Bigeard.

461   **Latanne:** Bruge.

461   **Castries' report on deserters:** Rocolle.

461   **Madelaine:** Journoud.

461   **Hantz:** Meyran.

Who Will Be the Best Rifle Shot?

463   **Giap attack on Huguette 1:** Giap, *Dien Bien Phu.*

Some Thought He Was Drunk

463   **Dulles in Paris:** Bidault, and Committee on Foreign Relations.

464   **Eden and Shuckburgh in Paris:** Shuckburgh.

464   **Sulzberger and Robertson:** Sulzberger.

465   **Eisenhower to publishers:** Billings-Yun.

The Friendlies Will Be Crossing the Airstrip

465   **"We must retake Huguette 1":** Bigeard.

468   **Failed counterattack:** Bigeard, and Langlais.

469   **Mengelle in the *Douaumont:*** Mengelle.

The British Must Not Shut Their Eyes and Then Plead Blindness

470   **Dulles to Eisenhower:** Committee on Foreign Relations.

470   **Bidault "drunk again":** Shuckburgh.

471   **Dulles speech:** Shuckburgh.

471   **Bidault close to breaking point:** Committee on Foreign Relations.

472   **Eden to Churchill:** Eden.

472   **"the wrong war":** Eden.

Forget About the Rainy Season

473   **CAT casualty:** Leary.

473   **Klotz:** Renaud.

Would You Like Two Bombs?

474   **Meetings at Dillon's residence:** Shuckburgh.

476   **Meeting at Quai d'Orsay:** Eden; Bidault; and Chauvel.

479   **"Bidault came into my office":** Elgey, *La République des contradictions.*

479   **Ely's mixed feelings:** Ely.

479   **De Margerie and Dulles:** Committee on Foreign Relations.

480   **Dulles on brinkmanship:** *Life*, January 16, 1956.

483   **Navarre reaction:** Navarre, *Agonie de l'Indochine.*

484   **Uproar over interview:** Hoopes.

484   **Kennan, "a dangerous man":** Kennan.

484   **Dulles's people like Cossacks:** Paul Nitze, *From Hiroshima to Glasnost.*

484   **Laniel to National Assembly:** Elgey, *La République des contradictions.*

484   **Bodet before commission:** Bruge.

We Were Furious at Being Used as Whipping Boys

485   **Denis Allen sums up:** Eden.

485   **Supper with Churchill:** Eden, and Shuckburgh.

486   **Ike to Walter Bedell Smith and "Swede" Hazlett:** Billings-Yun.

488   **Eden recalls League of Nations:** Eden.

488   **Eden-Dulles meeting:** Committee on Foreign Relations.

That Horrible Thing—The Atomic Bomb

492   **Radford sees Churchill:** Jurika.

Molotov Had the Face of an Angry Pekinese

493   **Opening of Geneva Conference:** Joyaux, and Chauvel.

494   **Eden arrives:** Shuckburgh.

495   **The first session:** James Cable, *The Geneva Conference.*

497   **Dulles snubs Chou:** Leonard Mosley, *Dulles.*

497   **Dulles sees Bidault:** Committee on Foreign Relations.

Act V
I Reject the Moral Value of Sacrifice

501   **Giap's instructions:** Giap, *Dien Bien Phu.*

501   **Navarre and Cogny:** Pellissier, and Bruge.

502   **"The jungle terrain":** Navarre, *Agonie de l'Indochine.*

502   CONDOR: Windrow.

If Found Guilty, They Faced the Firing Squad

503   **Hantz:** Meyran.

504   **Bonny:** Journoud.

504   **Castries:** Pellissier.

505   **Langlais:** Langlais.

505   **Bigeard's jeep:** Bigeard.

506   **Daniel Robert:** Renaud.

506   **Caubel and Texier:** Renaud.

507   **Lalande at Isabelle:** Windrow.

508   **Conditions as seen by Giap:** Giap, *Dien Bien Phu.*

Our Relations Are Very Bad

509   **Shuckburgh at Geneva:** Shuckburgh.

509   **Dulles to Washington:** Committee on Foreign Relations.

509   **"The situation at Dien Bien Phu":** Eisenhower, *The White House Years.*

510   **"Our relations are very bad":** Shuckburgh.

511   **Chou's long speech:** Shuckburgh.

511   **Molotov to Bidault:** Russian documents, *Cold War International History Project Bulletin,* Issue 16.

512   **Bidault to Paris:** Bidault.

Without Allies the Leader Is Another Genghis Khan

512   **NSC meeting, April 28:** Committee on Foreign Relations.

The Almost Pathological Rage of Dulles

513   **Dulles to Washington:** Committee on Foreign Relations.

514   **Dulles comes for lunch:** Shuckburgh.

514   **Lunch at Molotov's:** Russian documents, *Cold War International History Project Bulletin,* Issue 16.

516   **Bidault opens lines of communication:** Bidault, and Joyaux.

516   **Wounded:** Ely.

516   **Cutler to Ike:** Committee on Foreign Relations.

I Was in the Toilet Bowl up to My Neck

517   **French intelligence:** Rocolle.

517   **Langlais:** Langlais.

518   **Langlais before commission:** Langlais.

518   **Brothel girls as nurses:** Grauwin.

518   **Bastiani report:** Roy, and Pellissier.

519   **Navarre to Ely:** Ely.

519   **Castries to Hanoi:** Rocolle.

519   **Camerone:** Windrow.

520   **Last flight of Hellcats:** Renaud.

520   **Navarre to Jacquet:** Rocolle.

520   **"rightist tendencies":** Giap, *Dien Bien Phu.*

520   **Agrarian reform:** Greg Lockhart, *Nation in Arms.*

521   **Giap's plan:** Giap, *Dien Bien Phu.*

We Were Consuming a Hundred Men a Day

522   **Verdaguer:** Journoud.

522   **Tourret:** Galabru.

522   **Castries:** Pellissier.

522   **Langlais before commission:** Bruge.

523   **Cordier:** Bruge.

523   **Leguère:** Bruge.

523   **Périou:** Journoud.

524   **Perret and Filaudeau:** Bruge.

525   **Jauze:** Bruge.

526   **Castries reports:** Pellissier.

526   **Pouget at lunch:** Jean Pouget, *Nous étions à Dien Bien Phu.*

The United States and Britain Are in Complete Disarray

527   **Weather in Geneva lovely:** Shuckburgh.

527   **Eden glad to see Smith:** Eden.

528   **Chou's report to Mao:** Chinese Archives, *Cold War International History Project Bulletin,* Issue 16.

529   **Farewell dinner for Dulles:** Shuckburgh, and Eden.

530   **Chauvel asks Smith about Marines:** Chauvel.

531   **Conditions of Vietnamese army:** Guillain.

Why the Fuck Did They Send Us Here?

531 **Edmé:** Journoud.

532 **Pouget:** Pouget.

532 **Loudspeaker in Langlais' office:** Pouget.

533 **Castries' message:** Rocolle.

533 **Dechaux before commission:** Renaud.

534 **Castries' visit to hospital:** Grauwin.

536 **"Why the fuck did they send us here?":** Langlais.

536 **Trehiou:** Langlais.

536 **Coutant:** Pouget.

All of Vietnam Will Be Lost Except for Some Enclave

537 **Bidault and Chavel dine:** Shuckburgh.

537 **Russians to dinner:** Shuckburgh.

538 **Dulles in Washington:** Committee on Foreign Relations.

540 **Bidault wires Paris:** Committee on Foreign Relations.

Looks Like This Is It, Son

541 **Death of McGovern:** Leary, and Renaud.

For You the War Is Over

542 **Castries to commission:** Bruge.

543 **"if you can't hold, fall back":** Bigeard.

543 **Attack on Eliane 2:** Pouget.

544 **Edmé and Nectoux:** Bruge.

545 **Pouget taken prisoner:** Pouget.

545 **Trehiou:** Bruge.

545 **Latanne:** Bruge.

546 **Clédic:** Journoud.

546 **Botella:** Journoud.

547 **Last group to jump is sent back:** Langlais.

547 **Dr. Staub:** Grauwin.

548 **Le Boudec:** Grauwin.

548 **Moroccans and Legionnaires:** Windrow.

Has Castries Been Taken?

549   **Bigeard recalled:** Bigeard.

550   **Castries' conversations with Cogny and Bodet:** Rocolle, and Pellissier.

553   **Allaire wants order in writing:** Bigeard.

553   **Duluat and Lepinay:** Bruge.

553   **Klotz:** Journoud.

553   **Bonny:** Journoud.

554   **"Has de Castries been taken?":** Giap, *Dien Bien Phu.*

554   **Giap tours the battlefield:** Giap, *Dien Bien Phu.*

555   **Navarre before commission:** Bruge.

I Can No Longer Communicate

556   **Jean Dens:** Journoud.

557   **Rézillot:** Pierre Accoce, *Médicins à Dien Bien Phu.*

557   **Sortie from Isabelle:** Bruge.

557   **Lalande:** Journoud.

559   **Michot and Wieme captured:** Bruge.

559   **Casualty figures:** Robert Bonnafous, *Les prisonniers Français dans les camps Vietminh.*

560   **Triage:** Bonnafous.

560   **Giap on May 7:** Giap, *Dien Bien Phu.*

I Don't Blame Castries, I Blame the High Command

561   **Navarre plans to abandon part of the Delta:** Navarre, *Agonie de l'Indochine.*

561   **Laniel in Paris:** Elgey, *La République des contradictions.*

562   *Le Figaro* **editorial:** Leonetti.

562   **Turning defeat into heroism:** Leonetti.

562   **Castries lionized:** Leonetti.

563   **Duffort:** Journoud.

563   **Bigeard on Castries:** Bigeard.

563   **Navarre tone of heroism:** Rocolle.

564   **Ho Chi Minh congratulates troops:** Duiker.

The Baby Would be Rapidly Devoured

564 **Reactions in Senate:** Committee on Foreign Relations.

564 **Bidault gloomy:** Shuckburgh.

565 **"I'm getting too old for this":** Shuckburgh.

565 **Initial session at Geneva:** Shuckburgh, and Robert Randle, *Geneva 1954.*

566 **Dulles to Bonnet:** Committee on Foreign Relations.

566 **Chou report to Mao:** Chinese Archives, *Cold War International History Project Bulletin,* Issue 16.

567 **Smith on Pham's plan:** Committee on Foreign Relations.

567 **Ike agrees to send Trapnell:** Committee on Foreign Relations.

Could the Americans Use the H-Bomb?

568 **Bidault:** Elgey.

568 **Dillon to Washington:** Committee on Foreign Relations.

568 **"They would not dare to oust me":** Shuckburgh.

569 **Laniel is a dead duck:** Elgey.

569 **Eden plans to see Chou:** Eden.

569 **Chou report to Mao:** Chinese Archives, *Cold War International History Project Bulletin,* Issue 16.

570 **Shuckburgh's last day:** Shuckburgh.

571 **Eden kept out of the loop:** Eden, and James Cable, *The Geneva Conference.*

571 **Paul Reynaud wants to ask for the H-bomb:** Elgey, *La République des contradictions.*

572 **Discarding the domino theory:** Committee on Foreign Relations.

I Want to Thank You for Your Compassionate Attitude

572 **Cesarini:** Bruge.

572 **Captain Charles:** Journoud.

573 **Jeansotte:** Pellissier.

573 **Hantz performing amputations:** Meyran.

574 **Ely to Navarre on excluding the Vietnamese:** Pellissier.

574 **Huard:** Meyran.

575 **Navarre message and reply:** Pellissier.

575 **Exchange of the wounded:** Pellissier, and Meyran.

577 **Navarre alters agreement:** Pellissier.

578 **Aulong chats with wounded:** Meyran.

578 **Aulong rebuked by Colonel Khanh:** Meyran.

578 **Chou reports to Mao:** Chinese Archives, *Cold War International History Project Bulletin*, Issue 16.

579 **Geneviève message to Ho:** Galard.

I Seem to Have Been Lied To

580 **Navarre on Cogny:** Navarre, *Le temps des vérités.*

581 **Fresh divisions and meeting of committee:** Ely.

582 **Ely report leaked to the press:** Pellissier.

582 **Ely named to command:** Ely.

583 **Aulong meets Navarre:** Meyran.

583 **Ely back in Saigon:** Ely.

Bad Afternoon, Much Confusion

583 **Restricted sessions:** Cable.

584 **Eden "flabbergasted":** Eden.

584 **Smith to Washington:** Committee on Foreign Relations.

585 **Guillermaz and Wang Ping-nan:** Joyaux.

585 **"bad afternoon, much confusion":** Eden.

586 **"gave a startling":** Committee on Foreign Relations.

586 **Churchill "promoting a second Munich":** Committee on Foreign Relations.

586 **Ridgway report:** Committee on Foreign Relations.

Peace Is Like the Pyrenees

587 **Bidault meeting with Chou:** Chinese Archives, *Cold War International History Project Bulletin*, Issue 16.

589 **Letter from Gruenther:** Eisenhower.

I'll Bet the Vietminh Is Hiding in There

590 **Meeting between Vietminh and French:** Randle.

590 **"this infernal poker game":** Elgey.

591 **Bidault to Chauvel:** Chauvel.

If You Chase Two Rabbits, You Miss Both

591   **Dulles to Smith:** Committee on Foreign Relations.

591   **Smith to Dulles:** Committee on Foreign Relations.

592   **Progress made:** Randle, and Cable.

593   **"Mendès threw himself":** Bidault.

The Cease-Fire Should Come First

594   **Smith to Congress:** Committee on Foreign Relations.

594   **Churchill visit to Washington:** Lord Moran, and Eden.

595   **Chou report to Mao, June 22:** Chinese Archives, *Cold War International History Project Bulletin*, Issue 16.

595   **Chou meets Mendès:** Chinese Archives, *Cold War International History Project Bulletin*, Issue 16.

596   **Ely and Delta pullback:** Ely.

597   **Ely and Ngo Dinh Diem:** Ely.

I Can't Feel My Feet

597   **Klotz:** Journoud.

597   **Fleury:** Journoud.

598   **"Is it the smell?":** Bergot, *Convoi 42*.

598   **"You will learn to light a fire":** René Mary, *Les bagnards d'Ho Chi Minh*.

599   **Jeans Dens volunteers:** Journoud.

600   **"I can't feel my feet":** Brancion.

601   **De Sury commission:** Bonnafous.

601   **"I intentionally did not protest":** Bonnafous.

If You Were a Prisoner, Wouldn't You Try to Escape?

601   **The four hundred:** Bergot.

602   **Escape attempt:** Bergot.

603   **Death of Trehiou:** Bergot.

In Washington There Is Much Suspicion

604 **Chou En-lai visits Ho Chi Minh:** see Chinese Archives, *Cold War International History Project Bulletin,* Issue 16.

605 **Chou meets Eden:** Chinese Archives, *Cold War International History Project Bulletin,* Issue 16.

606 **Mendès sees Molotov:** Russian Documents, *Cold War International History Project Bulletin,* Issue 16.

The Line Will Be That Geneva Is a Failure

606 **Return of Dulles to Geneva:** Committee on Foreign Relations.

608 **"Mendès fought his corner brilliantly":** Eden.

608 **Dulles reports on Paris meeting:** Committee on Foreign Relations.

Nature and the Population Are Our Guards

609 **Prisoners and camps:** Bonnafous.

609 **Long march and diet:** Bonnafous.

610 **Reeducation:** Pouget, *Le manifeste du Camp no. 1.*

Laziness Is Counterrevolutionary

611 **The camp near the Claire River:** Bergot.

611 **Staggering death rate:** Bergot.

The Wedding Band Is Not a Commercial Object

611 **On the officers' camp:** Pouget, *Manifeste.*

612 **Bigeard as group leader:** Bigeard.

613 **Reeducation sessions and manifesto:** Pouget, *Manifeste.*

614 **Castries comes to lunch:** Bigeard.

We Have Ended an Eight-Year War

615 **Mendès to Chauvel:** Chauvel.

615 **Eden "in a flurry of meetings":** Eden.

615 **Ho Chi Minh to delegation:** Giap, *Dien Bien Phu.*

615   **Molotov sees Mendès:** Russian Documents, *Cold War International History Project Bulletin,* Issue 16.

616   **Molotov sees Chou and Pham:** Russian Documents, *Cold War International History Project Bulletin,* Issue 16.

617   **Chou sees Mendès:** Chinese Archives, *Cold War International History Project Bulletin,* Issue 16.

618   **Discussions over partition line:** Randle, and Cable.

619   **Discussions between Caccia and Chang Wentian:** Chinese Archives, *Cold War International History Project Bulletin,* Issue 16.

619   **Smith talks to Mendès:** Top secret document on Geneva, Vietnam Project at Texas Tech University.

619   **Mendès discusses Laos with Chou:** Chinese Archives, *Cold War International History Project Bulletin,* Issue 16.

620   **Caccia and Chang:** Chinese Archives, *Cold War International History Project Bulletin,* Issue 16.

621   **"We have done what we could":** Eden.

621   **Eden and Molotov conversation:** Eden.

621   **Chou report to Mao, July 20:** Chinese Archives, *Cold War International History Project Bulletin,* Issue 16.

622   **Smith chats with Chou:** Vietnam Project at Texas Tech.

622   **Sam Sary threatens to scuttle:** Randle.

622   **Sam Sary meeting with Bonsal and Smith:** Vietnam Project at Texas Tech.

623   **Sam Sary is appeased:** Randle.

623   **Eden's final statement:** Eden.

623   **Mendès does not attend:** Chauvel.

624   **Saigon "spitting in the soup":** Chauvel.

624   **DRV white paper:** Qiang Zhai.

624   **McNamara study:** Bird, *The Color of Truth.*

625   **Mendès deal with Molotov:** Elgey, *La République des contradictions.*

625   **Eden's final thoughts:** Eden.

That Terrible Agreement in Geneva

625   **Wilson suspends aid:** Futrell.

626   **Eisenhower press conference:** Committee on Foreign Relations.

626   **Carriers in South China Sea:** Hooper.

626   **Chou En-lai in Moscow:** Chinese Archives, *Cold War International History Project Bulletin,* Issue 16.

I Beg to Send My Gratefulness

627   PASSAGE TO FREEDOM: Hooper.

The Angel of Dien Bien Phu

628   **Geneviève de Galard:** Galard.

In Free Vietnam There Is Political Chaos

630   **NSC reports:** Committee on Foreign Relations.

631   **O'Daniel:** Committee on Foreign Relations.

631   **Dulles:** Committee on Foreign Relations.

What Was Your Attitude During Captivity?

631   **Cease-fire commission:** Bonnafous.

632   **Bastille Day early release:** Bonnafous.

632   **Release procedure:** Bonnafous.

632   **Louis Stien:** Stien, *Les soldats oubliés.*

633   **Aulong:** Meyran.

633   **Wounded in Haiphong:** Bonnafous.

634   **Langlais:** Langlais.

634   **Bigeard:** Bigeard.

634   **Dr. Martin:** Bonnafous.

635   **Pierre Bonny:** Journoud.

635   **Ducruix and Gendre:** Bonnafous.

635   **Return of survivors:** Bonnafous.

636   **Army treatment:** Bonnafous.

636   **Martin report:** Bonnafous.

637   **Mental state:** Bonnafous.

Epilogue

639   **Commission report:** Pellissier, and Elgey, *La République des contradictions.*

641   **Tourret:** Galabru.

Index

. . .

ABOUT THE AUTHOR

TED MORGAN is a Pulitzer Prize–winning journalist
and the author of biographies of FDR, Churchill, and
Maugham, the last of which was a finalist for the
National Book Award. He is also the author of
Reds, *A Shovel of Stars*, and *Wilderness at Dawn*.

ABOUT THE TYPE

This book was set in Photina, a typeface designed by
José Mendoza in 1971. It is a very elegant design with
high legibility, and its close character fit has made it a
popular choice for use in quality magazines and art
gallery publications.